Financial Markets and the Macroeconomy

The financial instability and its spillover to the real sector have become a great challenge to macro-economic theory. The book takes a Keynesian theoretical perspective, representing an attempt to revive what Keynes stressed in his *General Theory*, namely the role of the financial market in macroeconomic outcomes. Although this book is inspired and motivated by the Asian currency and financial crises in the years 1997–8 and the experiences of the currently evolving US financial disruptions, it also focuses on reviving a modeling tradition that provides a theoretical framework that throws light on recent financial market episodes and disturbances and their macroeconomic effects.

It brings to the forefront, as Keynes has suggested, the role of financial market stability for growth and macroeconomics. It criticizes theories that see economic disruptions and shocks rooted solely in the real side of the economy. It stresses the financial real interaction as the major source for macroeconomic instability and disruptions.

This important new book from a group of Keynesian but nonetheless technically oriented economists would be of most interest to specialists and graduate students in macroeconomics and financial economics, especially those with an interest in US and European financial markets, emerging market analysis, and dynamic economic modeling.

Carl Chiarella is a Professor at the University of Technology, Sydney, Australia. He is author of *Commerce, Complexity and Evolution,* 2000. **Peter Flaschel** is Professor Emeritus at Bielefeld University, Germany. He is co-author, with Carl Chiarella, of *Dynamics of Keynesian Monetary Growth,* 2001. **Reiner Franke** is a Lecturer at the University of Kiel, Germany. **Willi Semmler** is a Professor at the New School University, New York City, USA. He is the editor of *Monetary Policy and Unemployment*, published by Routledge in 2005.

Routledge International Studies in Money and Banking

Financial Markets and the Macroeconomy

A Keynesian perspective

Carl Chiarella, Peter Flaschel, Reiner Franke, and Willi Semmler

Routledge
Taylor & Francis Group

LONDON AND NEW YORK

First published 2009
by Routledge
2 Park Square, Milton Park, Abingdon, Oxon, OX14 4RN

Simultaneously published in the USA and Canada
by Routledge
270 Madison Avenue, New York, NY 10016

Routledge is an imprint of the Taylor & Francis Group, an informa business

© 2009 Willi Semmler, Peter Flaschel, Carl Chiarella and Reiner Franke

Typeset in Times New Roman by Keyword Group Ltd.
Printed and bound in Great Britain by TJI Digital, Padstow, Cornwall

British Library Cataloguing in Publication Data

Library of Congress Cataloging in Publication Data
Financial markets and the macroeconomy : a Keynesian perspective /
Willi Semmler ... [et al.].
    p. cm.
    Includes bibliographical references.
        1. Money market. 2. Macroeconomics. 3. Keynesian economics.
        4. Keynes, John Maynard, 1883–1946. General theory of
        employment, interest and money. I. Semmler, Willi.
HG226.F55 2009
332–dc22   2009008091

ISBN10: 0-415-77100-5 (hbk)
ISBN10: 0-203-88055-2 (ebk)

ISBN13: 978-0-415-77100-9 (hbk)
ISBN13: 978-0-203-88055-5 (ebk)

Contents

Figures

Foreword

This book builds to some degree on research papers written jointly with further co-authors pursuing similar lines of research. We here have to thank in particular Toichiro Asada from Chuo University, Pu Chen from the University of Melbourne, Gang Gong from Tsinghua University, Göran Kauermann, Florian Hartmann and Christian Proaño-Acosta from Bielefeld University, Ryuzo Kuroki from Rykio University, Stefan Mittnik from the University of Munich, Andreas Roethig from Darmstadt University of Technology, as well as many colleagues from our own universities for the stimulating discussions we have had with them on many occasions in the recent and more distant past. We also want to thank Miriam Rehm and Gabi Windhorst who undertook very competent and professional editing work for the final version of the manuscript. They have very much helped the book to become a better product.

Acknowledgement

Carl Chiarella wishes to acknowledge financial support from the Australian Research Council under grant DP0773776. Willi Semmler wishes to acknowledge research support from the Schwartz Center for Economic Policy Analysis (Scepa), New School, New York, and the CEM, Bielefeld University.

Introduction

This book emphasizes the role of the financial market in macroeconomics. Its theoretical perspective is of a Keynesian nature, representing an attempt to revive what Keynes (1936) has stressed in his "General Theory", namely the role of the financial market in the determination of output and employment.

The macroeconomic research perspective here is different from recent mainstream literature that uses the Dynamic Stochastic General Equilibrium (DSGE) approach as the basic modeling device. The main features of the latter are the assumptions of intertemporally optimizing agents, rational expectations, competitive markets and price-mediated market clearing through sufficiently flexible prices and wages. The New Keynesian approach to macroeconomics has, in the last decade or so, to a large extent, also adopted the DSGE framework, building on intertemporally optimizing agents and market clearing, but favoring more the concept of monopolistic competition, sticky wages and prices, and nominal as well as real rigidities. A path-breaking work of this type is the recent book by Woodford (2003).

In the DSGE tradition, a short-cut macromodel (that is in fact a linear quadratic (LQ) version of the DSGE model), relevant for policy making, shows a simplified interaction model of the main three markets: the product market captured by an IS equation with forward-looking output and interest rates, the labor market represented by a Phillips curve with a forward-looking price, and the monetary sector with a Taylor rule for inflation targeting. The latter represents the modern central bank policy approach where the interest rate is supposed to respond to an inflation and output gap, both possibly also encompassing forward-looking variables. Both the nonlinear and the linearized version of the DSGE model have recently been in widespread use in central banks. With a welfare function as the central banks' objective function, those new models give the impression that the modern central bank can undertake some fine tuning of the welfare performance of the economy by engineering interest rate changes in some direction and so steering the economy toward some steady employment, or "natural rate of unemployment", with a low inflation rate.

Yet, from early on in the development of the DSGE paradigm, some academic economists expressed the concern that there was something important missing in this monetary macro model: namely a more detailed treatment of the financial market. The fact that the financial market, and its potential instability and disruption, were missing in those models has suddenly become clear for academics and policy makers after the US subprime and credit crises that started in the middle of 2007. As the financial market disruption and credit crisis evolved, this event became a great challenge to the central banks' new monetary policy concept. Central banks were suddenly forced to intervene heavily in the financial markets. In particular the Fed and the ECB have moved away from the inflation targeting concept in an attempt to prevent disruption to the financial system. With the outbreak of the credit crisis, triggered by the subprime sector, and the threat of a financial meltdown, central banks focused very much on intervention in the credit sector. The central banks, in particular the Fed in the US, the European Central Bank, and the Central Bank of Japan undertook drastic action — and also coordinated world-wide action — to prevent the credit crisis from spreading. In the US the Fed carried out this action not only by a policy of interest rate reduction and massive liquidity provision, but also by extensive purchase of "bad" private assets.

For the interested observer, this change in direction of monetary policy from inflation targeting to heavy intervention in the financial market did not come as a surprise. Ben Bernanke, now the Fed Chair, had already written a few years ago academic papers that advocated a strong intervention by the central bank in case of a financial market meltdown. Already, in his earlier papers, Bernanke and his co-authors had put forward the view that the central bank should buy private assets if its interest rate policy was no longer effective. This not only would prevent a further fall in asset prices but in particular would keep down the long-term interest rate. In those papers, which were originally written with an eye to the Japanese long period of stagnation starting in the 1990s, when the zero inflation rate and almost zero interest rates did not leave any room for monetary policy, Bernanke and co-authors hint already at a possible US application. Recently, Bernanke and Mishkin have reiterated the dangers of financial market disruptions and their effect on the macroeconomy. They and other academic economists have strongly advocated the view that economists need macromodels that more explicitly include financial markets and a richer array of financial assets in order to understand the modern macroeconomy and the policy challenges posed (Bernanke et al., 2004). The current book makes an attempt to address this challenge.

The preliminary work on this book had already started after the Asian crisis in the years 1997–8; it thus contains references and material on the Asian currency and financial crises. Although this book is also inspired and motivated by the experiences of the currently evolving U.S. financial crisis, we do not explicitly model or empirically treat the recent financial crisis. It is too early to judge where it is going and whether the current policy reactions will suffice to prevent a pratracted period of unemployment. Rather, we here want to focus on reviving a theoretical modeling tradition which provides a theoretical framework that could help to throw some light on financial market episodes and their macro effects, which have become a major issue since financial markets have again been extensively liberalized since the 1980s and 1990s.

We would like to argue that the equilibrium intertemporal approaches of smoothly optimizing agents and fast adjustments (which are needed to establish temporal or intertemporal marginal conditions in the product, labor and capital markets) have not been very successful in integrating financial markets, with their potentials for instability, into a macro dynamic framework. The DSGE types of model have the feature that they do not yet include macroeconomic feedback effects, with their stabilizing or destabilizing impact on the macroeconomy. While one might not want to contest the view that forward-looking behavior and (the attempt at) intertemporal optimization by the economic agents might be relevant for the dynamics of the economy, in our view the exclusive focus on these issues in the present academic literature has left aside too many interesting, important and relevant issues, specifically pertaining to the financial market. For a detailed study of how, for example, asset price and credit market shocks can accelerate a downturn on the real side, see Stiglitz and Greenwald (2003).

In particular, in the interaction of all three markets there may be nonlinear feedback mechanisms at work that do not necessarily give rise to market clearing, nor necessarily to convergence to a (unique) steady-state growth path through a jump of the relevant variables to the stable path, as the DSGE class of models assumes. In our models, we will consider the working of forces of path convergence and divergence in modern macroeconomics with an extensive financial sector. Numerous feedback mechanisms, relevant for the interaction of labor, product and financial markets, have been theoretically and empirically explored since the 1930s. We want to pursue this alternative route of model building. The emphasis of the work in this book thus lies on the study of the relative strength and interaction of these feedback mechanisms as well as the transmission channels with respect to all three markets. We place an extensive emphasis on the financial market as a possible source and magnifier of macroeconomic instability. We will do this, in particular, in the context of a fully developed dynamic system approach.

Another important methodological perspective of our work is that, as recent research has shown, there is much heterogeneity of agents and beliefs present in modern economies as well as a large variety of informational and structural frictions present in the real world. Thus, with regard to the treatment of the financial market in macroeconomics, the feedback mechanisms in macroeconomics, as well the issue of heterogeneity of agents' behaviors and beliefs, we believe that the currently dominant DSGE model leaves too many open questions so that the true understanding of the economy needs to be advanced and pursued through a variety of frameworks.

We also hope that the macroeconomic constructions and empirical evidence provided in this book will show the reader alternative approaches, demonstrating that there are indeed different (and also valid) technical tools and possibilities to specify and analyze the dynamics of a financially sophisticated macroeconomy in a different way from the current standard theory. We study the financial markets and macroeconomies where the stability properties (and their analysis) are based on the relative strength of the interacting macroeconomic feedback channels. Such a type of stability analysis, despite its importance for the understanding of the dynamics of an economy, seems not to be taken into consideration by the DSGE literature. As the ongoing occurrence of herding behavior, contagion effects, and "boom-bust" scenarios in the financial markets across the world, as well as the large macroeconomic imbalances present nowadays in the global economy show, divergent paths can indeed take place and impact on growth and employment, thus setting new challenges for policy makers.

The book is organized as follows. Part I introduces our basic framework. After an introduction to the wage–price dynamics in a macroeconomic context, we first deal with the equity market and its potential for macroeconomic instability. We start here with the influential macromodel of the stock market, interest rate and output, advanced by Blanchard in 1981, which allows us to take into account a richer array of financial assets than the usual IS–LM or AS–AD models. This will be the work horse for further extensions in subsequent parts of the book. Next, we introduce the bond market and its interaction with the macroeconomy. as originally designed by Blanchard and Fischer (1989). A treatment of the foreign exchange market and exchange rates, as introduced by Dornbusch in the late 1970s, follows. Finally, in the context of a two-country model of the Mundell–Fleming tradition, the interactions of exchange rates, equity and bond markets are studied and their potential for macroeconomic instability explored. We critically examine and consequently avoid using the common jump variable technique (resulting from the rational expectations assumption) that usually leads to unique stable paths. The dynamics of our models are explored through the use of local linearization techniques and the analysis of high dimensional Jacobians, employing some techniques suggested by Turnovsky in the late 1980s.

Part II then introduces some extensions in our financial–real interaction models. Our basic financial–real interaction model of Part I of the book is extended by introducing further nonlinearities and allowing for state-dependent reactions by the economic agents. This can give rise to more intricate interaction patterns between the financial and real sectors. After introducing capital accumulation into our basic financial macro model and considering flow and stock interactions, we extend our basic model with the stock market by allowing for heterogeneous agents in the financial market who exhibit boundedly rational behavior. Here again local stability analysis is undertaken by the use of higher order Jacobians, and global stability analysis is pursued by way of simulations. In order to address the issue of higher order stability analysis in more general terms a high-dimensional model of the financial–real interaction is studied. Finally, in this part of the book, the basic variant of our financial–real interaction model is estimated and contrasted with calibrated DSGE models that include asset markets.

Part III broadens the framework further and extends and applies our analysis to open economy issues that have been brought into the academic discussion through the Asian currency and financial crisis. We analytically and empirically study the interaction of exchange rate shocks, capital flows and currency and financial crises. Here, by and large, we work with a stock and portfolio approach of the macro dynamics of an open economy. After the introduction of a stock-flow account for an open economy, and dealing with the twin deficit problem of the government budget and current account in the context of a Mundell—Fleming–Tobin model, we add chapters on the theoretical and empirical study of the Asian currency and financial crises, a type of analysis that was mainly triggered by a series of Krugman papers at the end of the 1990s. In this context, we here also add a study of the medium-run wage price dynamics and the role of hedging strategies to counter currency shocks. We try to answer the question, to what extent such currency and financial crises could be avoided by currency hedging strategies. Finally, we give an outlook and some suggestions of how flows and stocks should be properly treated in an open economy framework in the context of financial–real interaction models.

Overall, we revive models and tools that have been developed since the 1980s in a large body of literature. We hope that the modeling approaches presented here may be of some use in helping to understand and analyze the financial–real interaction as well as the financial instabilities and disruptions that affect the performance of macroeconomies and pose great challenges for macro policies in the current period.

References

BERNANKE, B., V.R. REINHARD and B.P. SACK (2004): *Monetary Policy Alternatives at the Zero Bound: An Empirical Assessment*. Washington, DC: Federal Reserve Board, No. 48.

BLANCHARD, O. and S. FISCHER (1989): *Lectures on Macroeconomics*. Cambridge, MA: MIT Press.

KEYNES, J.M. (1963): *The General Theory of Employment, Interest and Money*. London: Macmillan (reprinted 1967).

STIGLITZ, J. and B. GREENWALD (2000): *Towards a New Paradigm in Monetary Economics*, Cambridge: Cambridge University Press.

WOODFORD, M. (2003): *Interest and Prices: Foundations of a Theory of Monetary Policy*. Princenton, NJ: Princenton University Press.

Notation

Steady-state or trend values are indicated by a superscript 'o' (or sometimes superscript $*$ – in the case of closed economies) and foreign country variables are indicated by a superscript $*$ (or F in the case of foreign bonds). When no confusion arises, letters F, G, H may also define certain functional expressions in a specific context. A dot over a variable $x = x(t)$ denotes the time derivative, a caret its growth rate: $\dot{x} = dx/dt$, $\hat{x} = \dot{x}/x$. In the numerical simulations, flow variables are measured at annual rates.

As far as possible, the notation tries to follow the logic of using capital letters for level variables and lower-case letters for variables in intensive form, propensities to save or for constant (steady-state) ratios. Greek letters are most often constant coefficients in behavioral equations (with, however, the notable exceptions being π and ω, the inflation rate and the real wage, and σ the real exchange rate. Furthermore:

B	outstanding government fixed-price bonds (priced at $p_b = 1$)
C	real private consumption (demand is generally realized)
E	number of equities
F	foreign fix-price bonds
	or foreign bonds in Part II of the book
G	real government expenditure (demand is always realized)
I	real net investment of fixed capital (demand is always realized)
J	Jacobian matrix in the mathematical analysis
K	stock of fixed capital
L^d	employment, i.e., total working hours per year (labor demand is always realized)
L	labor supply, i.e., supply of total working hours per year
M	stock of money supply
S	total real saving; $S = S_h + S_f + S_g$
s_x	savings propensities (households, firms, ...): s_f, s_g, s_h
s	nominal exchange rate (σ is the real exchange rate))
T	total real tax collections
T^c, T^w	real taxes of asset holders, workers
W	real wealth of private households

Y	real output
Y^d	real aggregate demand
$\bar{Y}$	output at normal use of capacity
e	employment rate (w.r.t. hours: u_w)
s, σ	exchange rate (nominal or real: sp^*/p)
f_x	partial derivative
n_z	growth rate of trend labor productivity; $n_z = \hat{z}$
i	nominal rate of interest on government bonds;
ℓ	labor intensity (in efficiency units)
m	real balances relative to the capital stock; $m = M/pK$
p	price level
p_e	price of equities
r	rate of return on fixed capital, specified as $r = (pY - wL - \delta pK)/pK$
s_c	propensity to save out of capital income on the part of asset owners
s_h	households' propensity to save out of total income
u	rate of capacity utilization; $u = Y/Y^p = y/y^p$
v	wage share (in gross product); $v = wL/pY$
w	nominal wage rate per hour
y	output–capital ratio; $y = Y/K$;
y^d	ratio of aggregate demand to capital stock; $y^d = Y^d/K$
y^p	potential output–capital ratio (a constant)
z	labor productivity, i.e., output per working hour; $z = Y/L^d$
α_{ii}	coefficient measuring interest rate smoothing in the Taylor rule
α_{ip}	coefficient on inflation gap in the Taylor rule
α_{iu}	coefficient on output gap in the Taylor rule
β_x	generically, reaction coefficient in an equation determining x, $\dot{x}$ or $\hat{x}$
β_{π^c}	general adjustment speed in revisions of the inflation climate π^c
β_{xy}	generically, reaction coefficient related to the determination of variable x, $\dot{x}$ or $\hat{x}$ with respect to changes in the exogenous variable y
β_{pu}	reaction coefficient of u in price Phillips curve
β_{pv}	reaction coefficient of $(1+\mu)v - 1$ in price Phillips curve
β_{we}	reaction coefficient of e in wage Phillips curve
β_{wv}	reaction coefficient of $(v - v^o)/v^o$ in wage Phillips curve
γ	G/K (a constant)
δ	rate of depreciation of fixed capital (a constant)
$\eta_{m,i}$	interest elasticity of money demand (expressed as a positive number)
κ	coefficient in reduced-form wage–price equations; $\kappa = 1/(1 - \kappa_p\kappa_w)$
κ_p	parameter weighting $\hat{w}$ vs. π in price Phillips curve
κ_w	parameter weighting $\hat{p}$ vs. π in wage Phillips curve
π^c	general inflation climate
θ	tax parameter (net of interest)
τ_w	tax rate on wages
ω	real wage rate

Part I

Real–financial market interaction

Baseline approaches

1 Price dynamics and the macroeconomy

1.1 Introduction

This book stresses the inclusion of the financial market into a macroeconomic framework. We mainly focus on the AD side of the AD–AS framework to macromodeling and leave out a more elaborate treatment of the Phillips curve. The price and wage dynamics are generally kept simple, yet a brief outline of how price dynamics can be treated in the context of the different variants of macromodels we are presenting will be provided.

New Keynesian macroeconomics is usually based on forward-looking rational expectations behavior, at least in its baseline version. It has a new type of IS curve, a new type of Phillips curve, and it uses Taylor-type interest rate rules in place of LM curves. In its baseline deterministic core with only forward-looking behavior the economy is considered in equilibrium, see Gali (2008). The dynamics are only of interest when stochastic terms are added to the model. Some of the authors of this book have investigated the merits and pitfalls of this approach elsewhere.[1]

In this book we go significantly beyond the standard structure of New Keynesian macromodels, regarding not only financial assets but also stock-flow dynamics which is rarely discussed in the New Keynesian literature. In this first chapter of the book we want to give a simple introduction to the nominal–real interaction as we see it.

1.2 Keynesian AD–AS analysis

A Keynesian model of aggregate demand fluctuations should allow for under- (or over-) utilization of labor as well as of capital in order to be general enough from the descriptive point of view. As Barro (1994), for example, observes, IS–LM is (or should be) based on imperfectly flexible wages *and* prices and thus on the consideration of wage as well as price Phillips curves.

---

1 See Chiarella et al. (2005) and subsequent work. This analysis will thus not be repeated here. For a wavelet approach to treat forward looking variables, see Ramsey et al. (2009).

This is precisely what we will do, in an introductory manner, in the following analysis. We use the observation that medium-run aspects count in both wage and price adjustment as well as in investment behavior, here still expressed in simple terms using the concept of an inflation as well as an investment climate. These climate terms are based on past observation, whereas we have model-consistent expectations with respect to short-run wage and price inflation. Thus the modification of the traditional AS–AD model that we shall introduce treats expectations in a hybrid way. There is myopic perfect foresight on the current rates of wage and price inflation on the one hand and, on the other hand, an adaptive updating of economic climate expressions with an exponential weighting scheme.

In light of the foregoing discussion, we therefore assume here two Phillips curves (PCs) in the place of only one. In this way we provide wage and price dynamics separately, both based on measures of demand pressure $e - \bar{e}, u - \bar{u}$, in the market for labor and for goods, respectively. We denote by e the rate of employment on the labor market and by $\bar{e}$ the NAIRU level of this rate, and similarly by u the rate of capacity utilization of the capital stock and by $\bar{u}$ the normal rate of capacity utilization of firms. Demand pressure influences wage and price dynamics, that is, the formation of wage and price inflation, $\hat{w}\hat{p}$. They are both augmented by a weighted average of cost-pressure terms based on forward-looking, perfectly foreseen price and wage inflation rates, respectively, and a backward-looking measure of the prevailing inflationary climate, symbolized by π^c. Cost pressure perceived by workers is thus a weighted average of the currently evolving price inflation rate $\hat{p}$ and some longer-run concept of price inflation, π^c, based on past observations. Similarly, cost pressure perceived by firms is given by a weighted average of the currently evolving (perfectly foreseen) wage inflation rate $\hat{w}$ and again the measure of the inflationary climate in which the economy is operating. We thus arrive at the following two Phillips curves for wage and price inflation, here formulated in a fairly symmetric way.

Structural form of the wage–price dynamics:

$$\hat{w} = \beta_w(e - \bar{e}) + \kappa_w\hat{p} + (1 - \kappa_w)\pi^c, \tag{1.1}$$

$$\hat{p} = \beta_p(u - \bar{u}) + \kappa_p\hat{w} + (1 - \kappa_p)\pi^c. \tag{1.2}$$

Inflationary expectations over the medium run, π^c, i.e., the *inflationary climate* in which current wage and price inflation is operating, may be adaptively following the actual rate of inflation (by use of some exponential weighting scheme), may be based on a rolling sample (with hump-shaped weighting schemes), or on other possibilities for updating expectations. For simplicity of exposition we shall here make use of the conventional adaptive expectations mechanism. Besides demand pressure we thus use (as cost pressure expressions) in the two PCs weighted averages of this economic climate and the (foreseen) relevant cost pressure term for wage setting and price setting. In this way we get two PCs with very analogous building blocks, which despite their traditional outlook turn out to have interesting and novel implications.[2]

As for the real side, note that for our current version, the inflationary climate variable does not matter for the *evolution of the real wage* $\omega = w/p$, the law of motion of which is given by:

$$\hat{\omega} = \kappa[(1 - \kappa_p)\beta_w(e - \bar{e}) - (1 - \kappa_w)\beta_p(u - \bar{u})], \quad \kappa = 1/(1 - \kappa_w\kappa_p).$$

This follows easily from the obviously equivalent representation of the above two PCs:

$$\hat{w} - \pi^c = \beta_w(e - \bar{e}) + \kappa_w(\hat{p} - \pi^c),$$
$$\hat{p} - \pi^c = \beta_p(u - \bar{u}) + \kappa_p(\hat{w} - \pi^c),$$

by solving for the variables $\hat{w} - \pi^c$ and $\hat{p} - \pi^c$. It also implies that the two cross-markets or *reduced form PCs* are given by:

$$\hat{w} = \kappa[\beta_w(e - \bar{e}) + \kappa_w\beta_p(u - \bar{u})] + \pi^c, \tag{1.3}$$

$$\hat{p} = \kappa[\beta_p(u - \bar{u}) + \kappa_p\beta_w(e - \bar{e})] + \pi^c, \tag{1.4}$$

which represent *a considerable generalization* of the conventional view of a single-market price PC with only one measure of demand pressure, the one in the labor market. This traditional expectations-augmented PC formally resembles the above reduced-form $\hat{p}$-equation if Okun's law holds in the sense of a strict positive correlation between $u - \bar{u}$, $u = Y/Y^p$ and $e - \bar{e}$, $e = L^d/L$, our measures of demand pressures on the market for goods and for labor. Yet the coefficient in front of the traditional PC would even in this situation be a mixture of all of the βs and κs of our PCs and thus represents a synthesis of goods and labor market characteristics.

With respect to the investment climate, we proceed similarly and assume that this climate is adaptively following the current risk premium $\epsilon(= r - (i - \hat{p}))$, the excess of the actual profit rate over the actual real rate of interest (which is perfectly foreseen). This gives[3]

$$\dot{\epsilon}^m = \beta_{\epsilon^m}(\epsilon - \epsilon^m), \quad \epsilon = r + \hat{p} - i,$$

---

2 These two Phillips curves have been estimated for the US economy in various ways in Flaschel and Krolzig (2006), Asada et al. (2006) and Chen and Flaschel (2005) and were found to represent a significant improvement over single reduced-form price Phillips curves, with wage flexibility being greater than price flexibility with respect to demand pressure in the market for goods and for labor, respectively. Such a finding is not possible in the conventional framework of a single reduced-form Phillips curve.

3 Chiarella et al. (2003), in response to Velupillai (2003), have used a slightly different expression for the updating of the investment climate.

which is directly comparable to

$$\dot{\pi}^c = \beta_{\pi^c}(\pi - \pi^c), \quad \pi = \hat{p}.$$

We believe that it is very natural to assume that economic climate expressions evolve sluggishly towards their observed short-run counterparts. It is, however, easily possible to introduce also forward-looking components into the updating of the climate expressions, for example based on the p^* concept of central banks and related potential output calculations. The investment function of the model of this section is given simply by $i_1(\epsilon^m)$ in place of $i_1(\epsilon)$.

Our model so far incorporates sluggish price adjustment as well as sluggish wage adjustment and makes use of certain delays in the cost pressure terms of its wage and price PC and in its investment function.[4]

Next we need to discuss our concept of the rate of capacity utilization that we will be using in the presence of neoclassical smooth factor substitution, but with Keynesian over- or under-employment of the capital stock. Actual use of productive capacity is of course defined in reference to actual output Y. As a measure of potential output Y^p, we associate with actual output Y the profit-maximizing output with respect to currently given wages and prices. Capacity utilization u is therefore measured relative to the profit-maximizing output level and is thus given by[5]

$$u = Y/Y^p \quad \text{with} \quad Y^p = F(K, L^p), \quad \omega = F_L(K, L^p),$$

where Y is determined from the IS–LM equilibrium block in the usual way. In the price PC, we assumed as a normal rate of capacity utilization one that is less than one and thus assume in general that demand pressure leads to price inflation before potential output has been reached. This is symmetric to what is assumed in the wage PC and demand pressure on the labor market. The idea behind this assumption is that there is imperfect competition in the market for goods, so that firms raise prices before profits become zero at the margin.

There is complementary reasoning of the imperfect price level adjustment we are assuming. For reasons of simplicity, we here consider the case of a Cobb–Douglas production function, given by $Y = K^\alpha L^{1-\alpha}$. According to the above we have

$$p = w/F_L(K, L^p) = w/[(1-\alpha)K^\alpha(L^p)^{-\alpha}]$$

4 In the Sargent (1987) approach to Keynesian dynamics, the $\beta_{\epsilon^m}, \beta_{\pi^c}, \beta_p$ are all set equal to infinity and $\bar{U}_c$ is set equal to one, which implies that only the current inflation rate and excess profitabilities matter for the evolution of the economy and that prices are perfectly flexible, so that full capacity utilization, not only normal capacity utilization, is always achieved. This limit case has, however, little in common with the properties of the model of this section.

5 In intensive-form expressions the following gives rise to $u = y/y^p$ with $y^p = f((f')^{-1}(\omega))$.

which, for given wages and prices, defines potential employment. Similarly, we define competitive prices as the level of prices p_c such that

$$p_c = w/F_L(K, L^d) = w/[(1-\alpha)K^\alpha(L^d)^{-\alpha}].$$

From these definitions we get the relationship

$$\frac{p}{p_c} = \frac{(1-\alpha)K^\alpha(L^d)^{-\alpha}}{(1-\alpha)K^\alpha(L^p)^{-\alpha}} = (L^p/L^d)^\alpha.$$

We thus obtain from the definitions of L^d, L^p and their implication $Y/Y^p = (L^d/L^p)^{1-\alpha}$ an expression that relates the above price ratio to the rate of capacity utilization as defined in this section:

$$\frac{p}{p_c} = \left(\frac{Y}{Y^p}\right)^{\frac{-\alpha}{1-\alpha}} \quad \text{or} \quad \frac{p_c}{p} = \left(\frac{Y}{Y^p}\right)^{\frac{\alpha}{1-\alpha}} = (u)^{\frac{\alpha}{1-\alpha}}.$$

We thus get that (for $\bar{u} = 1$) upward adjustment of the rate of capacity utilization to full capacity utilization is positively correlated with downward adjustment of actual prices to their competitive value, and vice versa. In particular, in the special case $\alpha = 0.5$ we would get as reformulated price dynamics (see equation 1.4 with $\bar{u}$ being replaced by $(p_c/p)_o$):

$$\hat{p} = \beta_p(p_c/p - (p_c/p)_o) + \kappa_p\hat{w} + (1-\kappa_p)\pi^c,$$

which resembles the New Phillips curve of the New Keynesian approach as far as the reflection of demand pressure forces by means of real marginal wage costs is concerned. For the new Keynesian Philips curve with forward looking variables, see Gali 2008.

Price inflation is thus increasing when competitive prices (and thus nominal marginal wage costs) are above the actual ones and decreasing otherwise (neglecting the cost-push terms for the moment). This shows that our understanding of the rate of capacity utilization in the framework of neoclassical smooth-factor substitution is related to demand pressure terms as used in New Keynesian approaches,[6] thus further motivating its adoption. Actual prices will fall if they are above marginal wage costs to a sufficient degree. However, our approach suggests that actual prices start rising before marginal wage costs are in fact established; i.e., in particular, we have that actual prices are always higher than the competitive ones in the steady state.

---

6 See also Powell and Murphy (1997) for a closely related approach, there applied to an empirical study of the Australian economy. We would like to stress here that this property of our model represents an important further similarity with the New Keynesian approach, yet here in a form that gives substitution (with moderate elasticity of substitution) no major role to play in the overall dynamics.

We have arrived at a model type that is much more complex, but also much more convincing, than the labor market dynamics of the traditional AS–AD dynamics. We now have five in the place of only three laws of motion, which incorporate myopic perfect foresight without any significant impact on the resulting Keynesian dynamics. We can handle factor utilization problems for both labor and capital without necessarily assuming a fixed proportions technology; i.e., we can treat AS–AD growth with neoclassical smooth-factor substitution. We have sluggish wage as well as price adjustment processes with cost pressure terms that are both forward and backward looking, and that allow for the distinction between temporary and permanent inflationary shocks. We have a unique interior steady-state solution of (one must stress) supply side type, generally surrounded by business fluctuations of Keynesian short-run as well as medium-run type. Our modified AS–AD growth dynamics therefore exhibits a variety of features that are much more in line with a Keynesian understanding of the features of the trade cycle than is the case for the conventional modelling of AS–AD growth dynamics.

Taken together, our model consists of the following five laws of motion for real wages, real balances, the investment climate, labor intensity and the inflationary climate:

$$\hat{\omega} = \kappa[(1-\kappa_p)\beta_w(\ell^d/\ell - \bar{e}) - (1-\kappa_w)\beta_p(y/y^p - \bar{u})], \tag{1.5}$$

$$\hat{m} = -\hat{p} - i\epsilon^m, \tag{1.6}$$

$$\dot{\epsilon}^m = \beta_{\epsilon^m}(r + \hat{p} - i - \epsilon^m), \tag{1.7}$$

$$\hat{\ell} = -i_1\epsilon^m, \tag{1.8}$$

$$\dot{\pi}^c = \beta_{\pi^c}(\hat{p} - \pi^c), \tag{1.9}$$

with $\hat{p} = \kappa[\beta_p(y/y^p(\omega) - \bar{u}) + \kappa_p\beta_w(\ell^d/\ell - \bar{e})] + \pi^c$.

Here we already employ reduced-form expressions throughout and consider the dynamics of the real wage, ω, real balances per unit of capital, m, the investment climate ϵ^m, labor intensity, ℓ, and the inflationary climate, π^c, on the basis of the simplifying assumptions that natural growth n determines the trend growth term in the investment function as well as money supply growth. The above dynamical system is to be supplemented by the following static relationships for output, potential output and employment (all per unit of capital) and the rate of interest and the rate of profit:

$$y = \frac{1}{1-c}[i_1\epsilon^m + n + g - t] + \delta + t, \tag{1.10}$$

$$y^p = f((f')^{-1}(\omega)), \quad F(1, L^p/K) = f(\ell^p) = y^p, F_L(1, L^p/K) = f'(\ell^p) = \omega, \tag{1.11}$$

$$\ell^d = f^{-1}(y), \tag{1.12}$$

$$i = i_o + (h_1 y - m)/h_2,\tag{1.13}$$

$$r = y - \delta - \omega \ell^d,\tag{1.14}$$

which have to be inserted into the right-hand sides in order to obtain an autonomous system of five differential equations that is nonlinear in a natural or intrinsic way. We note however that there are many items that reappear in various equations, or are similar to each other, implying that stability analysis can exploit a variety of linear dependencies in the calculation of the conditions for local asymptotic stability. This dynamical system is investigated in Asada et al. (2006) in somewhat informal terms and, with slight modifications, in a rigorous way.

As the model is now formulated it exhibits firstly the well-known real rate of interest channel, giving rise to destabilizing Mundell effects that are traditionally tamed by the application of the jump variable technique. And secondly, there is another real feedback channel (see Figure 1.1), which we have called the Rose real wage effect (based on the work of Rose (1967)) in Chiarella and Flaschel (2000). Channels like this are absent from the New Keynesian approach, see Gali (2008). The Rose effect only gives rise to a clearly distinguishable and significant feedback channel, however, if wage and price flexibilities are both finite and if aggregate demand depends on the income distribution between wages and profits. In the traditional AS–AD model it only gives rise to a directly stabilizing dependence of the growth rate of real wages on their level, while in our mature form of this AS–AD analysis it works through the interaction of the law of motion (1.5) for real wages, the investment climate and the IS curve we derived on this basis. In addition, the real marginal costs effect of the New Keynesian approach is present here in the denominator of the expression we are using for the rate of capacity utilization, $u = y/y^p$. It contributes to some extent to stability should the Rose effect by itself be destabilizing. Next, we want to give an intuition of the working of the nominal and real interaction.

There are two feedback channels interacting in our extended AS–AD dynamics which, in specific ways, exhibit stabilizing as well as destabilizing features (Keynes vs. Mundell effects and normal vs. adverse Rose effects). A variety of further feedback channels of Keynesian macrodynamics is investigated in Chiarella et al. (2000). The careful analysis of these channels and the partial insights that can be related to them form the basis of a high stability analysis dimensional, to be undertaken in Chapter 9.

In Figure 1.1 we summarize the basic feedback channels of our approach to AS–AD dynamics. Top left we have the textbook Keynes effect or stabilizing nominal rate of interest rate channel and the therewith interacting destabilizing Mundell or inflationary expectations effect which, together with the Keynes effect, works through the (expected) real rate of interest channel. In addition we have Rose (1967) effects working though the real wage channel. Figure 1.1 indicates the two conditions under which the real wage channel will be stabilizing: if investment reacts more strongly than consumption to real wage changes (which is the case in our model type, since consumption does not depend at all on the

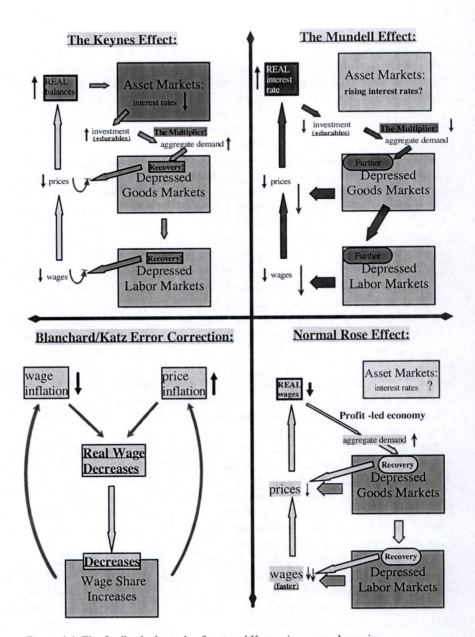

Figure 1.1 The feedback channels of matured Keynesian macrodynamics

real wage); and if this is coupled with wages being more flexible than prices. Equation (1.5) then establishes a positive link between economic activity and induced real wage changes. However, if this latter relationship does not hold, due either to a sufficient degree of price level flexibility or to higher wage rigidities, this will destabilize the economy. Shrinking economic activity caused by real wage increases will then induce further real wage increases, since the price level will be falling faster than the wage level in this state of depressed markets for goods and for labor (representing an adverse type of Rose effect). Bear in mind that the degree of forward-looking behavior in both the wage and the price level dynamics is also important, since these weights enter the crucial equation (1.5) that describes the dynamics of real wages for any changing states of economic activity. Figure 1.1 finally shows the Blanchard and Katz wage share correction mechanism (bottom left), which is discussed in detail in Asada et al. (2006).

Overall, as we have stressed above, a properly formulated Keynesian growth dynamics should – besides allowing for under- or over-employed labor – also allow for under or over- employment of the capital stock, at least in certain episodes. Thus the price level, like the wage level, should be assumed to adjust sluggishly.[7]

1.3 Conclusions

In closing this discussion of our proposed Keynesian disequilibrium AS–AD dynamics we state that the neoclassical case heavily depends on the neoclassical production function, while our general Keynesian model does not at all depend on it. Assuming fixed proportions in production simply implies that y^p, i.e., potential output per unit of capital, is a given magnitude and not dependent on the real wage as in the Neoclassical case which, however, is a difference of minor importance in the general framework.[8] The general conclusion is that real processes should be treated by gradual adjustments in a disequilibrium framework if considered in detail, or by just an advanced form of the IS-equation if financial factors are to be included. The question then remains whether financial markets can be treated in a similar way – a central topic to be discussed next.

1.4 References

ASADA, T., P. CHEN, C. CHIARELLA and P. FLASCHEL (2006): Keynesian dynamics and the wage–price spiral. A baseline disequlibrium approach. *Journal of Macroeconomics*, 28, 90–130.

BARRO, R. (1994): The aggregate supply/aggregate demand model. *Eastern Economic Journal*, 20:1, 1–6.

CHEN, P. and P. FLASCHEL (2005): Keynesian dynamics and the wage–price spiral. Identifying downward rigidities. *Computational Economics*, 25, 115–142.

---

7 See also Barro (1994) in this regard.
8 See Chiarella and Flaschel (2000, Ch. 5) for details.

CHIARELLA, C. and P. FLASCHEL (2000): *The Dynamics of Keynesian Monetary Growth: Macro Foundations.* Cambridge, UK: Cambridge University Press.

CHIARELLA, C., P. FLASCHEL, G. GROH and W. SEMMLER (2000): *Disequilibrium, Growth and Labor Market Dynamics. Macro Perspectives.* Heidelberg: Springer.

CHIARELLA, C., P. FLASCHEL, G. GROH and W. SEMMLER (2003): AS–AD, KMG growth and beyond. A reply to Velupillai. *Journal of Economics,* 78, 96–104.

CHIARELLA, C., P. FLASCHEL and R. FRANKE (2005): *Foundations for a Disequilibrium Theory of the Business Cycle. Qualitative Analysis and Quantitative Assessment.* Cambridge, UK: Cambridge University Press.

FLASCHEL, P. and H.-M. KROLZIG (2006): Wage–price Phillips curves and macroeconomic stability: Basic structural form, estimation and analysis. In: C. Chiarella, P. Flaschel, R. Franke and W. Semmler (eds.): *Quantitative and Empirical Analysis of Nonlinear Dynamic Macromodels. Contributions to Economic Analysis 277.* (Series editors: B. Baltagi, E. Sadka and D. Wildasin.) Amsterdam: Elsevier, 7–47.

FLASCHEL, P., G. KAUERMANN and W. SEMMLER (2007): Testing wage and price Phillips curves for the United States. *Metroeconomica,* 58:4, 550–581.

GALI, J. (2008): *Monetary Policy, Inflation, and the Business Cycle.* Princeton: Princeton University Press.

POWELL, A. and C. MURPHY (1997): *Inside a Modern Macroeconomic Model.* Heidelberg: Springer.

RAMSEY, J., M. GALLIGATI, M. GALLIGATI, and W. SEMMLER (2009): *Instrumental Variables, Simultaneous Equations and Wavelets.* Manuscript, New York: New York University.

ROSE, H. (1967): On the non-linear theory of the employment cycle. *Review of Economic Studies,* 34:2, 153–173.

SARGENT, T. (1987): *Dynamic Macroeconomic Theory.* Cambridge, MA: Harvard University Press.

VELUPILLAI, K. (2003): Book reviews. Chiarella, C. and Flaschel, P.: The Dynamics of Keynesian Monetary Growth: Macro Foundations/Chiarella, C., Flaschel, P., Groh, G. and Semmler, W.: Disequilibrium, Growth and Labor Market Dynamics: Macro Perspectives. *Journal of Economics,* 78, 83–95.

2 Stock market and the macroeconomy

2.1 Introduction

Next we consider an influential model advanced by Blanchard (1981), in which he extended Keynesian IS–LM analysis by taking account of a richer array of financial assets. Besides money and short-term bonds, he also included long-term bonds and equities. The significance of this generalization derives from the corresponding treatment of the real sector. Here it is assumed that investment demand I (or likewise consumption demand) varies with Tobin's average q, instead of the real rate of interest. Consequently the share price dynamics feeds back on the real sector. The short-term interest rate plays a more indirect role, as it is involved in the determination of Tobin's q on the financial markets via an arbitrage condition. Since, for simplicity, the model abstracts from inflation, the nominal rate of interest coincides with the real rate and it is determined by a textbook LM schedule of money market equilibrium. Through this channel real output Y impacts on the financial sector. Economic activity, in turn, is influenced by the level of investment through a Keynesian (dynamic) multiplier channel that describes gradual output adjustment towards Keynesian aggregate demand. For a given price level the real–financial interaction to be studied may thus be concisely summarized by the feedback loop $Y \rightarrow i \rightarrow q \rightarrow I \rightarrow Y$.

Blanchard assumes perfect substitutability between short-term bonds and financial assets and works with the hypothesis of rational expectations, as a special solution for model-consistent expectations. He applies the jump variable technique to the resulting (deterministic) dynamic system, according to which the steady state turns out to be a saddle point. The relevant price variable, Tobin's q, instantaneously jumps back onto the stable manifold of saddlepoint dynamics if the economy (or the equilibrium itself) is perturbed by an exogenous shock. Though being firmly rooted in today's mainstream economics, this treatment is not without conceptual problems.[1] We will therefore discard the rational expectations hypothesis and explore the dynamic outcomes of a different methodological approach.

---

1 See in particular Burmeister (1980) on this matter.

Traditional Keynesian Theory:
The Basic Market Hierarchy

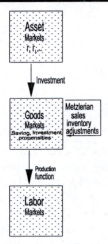

How Dominant is this Downward Causal Nexus?
What Repercussions?

Figure 2.1 The causal nexus of Chapter 18 of Keynes's General Theory.

The alternative model we put forward maintains the notion of fast adjustments of the expectational variable, but they are no longer infinitely fast. This goes along with abandoning the other assumption of perfect substitutability, mentioned above. Nevertheless, the equilibrium still exhibits saddle point instability. The explosive tendencies can then be tamed by introducing a natural nonlinearity into the excess demand function for equities. This is based on the idea that agents become more cautious when, in the presence of larger differentials in the rates of return, they expect a change in the market regime. In this way persistent but bounded fluctuations are generated, even if no shock occurs. Typically, the endogenous oscillations converge to a limit cycle, while in the limit case of myopic perfect foresight so-called relaxation oscillations come about.

Before turning to formal analysis, we may briefly discuss some elementary feedback mechanisms at an informal level. Beginning with Chapter 18 of Keynes's (1936) *General Theory*, consider the hierarchical relationship between the financial and the real sector sketched in Figure 2.1.[2] From this point of view,

---

2 The indicated Metzlerian quantity dynamics is simplified in this chapter towards a simple dynamic multiplier story, in order to have only one law of motion in the real part of the model.

financial markets are at the top of the market hierarchy. Together with the other rates of return on financial assets, they determine the rate of interest. Compared to a rate of profit, or taken in conjunction with some general state of confidence, this outcome influences fixed investment in the real sector (and possibly also durable consumption). The latter, in turn, determines aggregate output through a multiplier process that may work instantaneously or with some delay. The level of production, finally, determines the volume of employment and thus the rate of unemployment on the labor market.

Starting from a situation of high unemployment (and depressed goods markets as well), in the subsequent Chapter 19 it was already recognized by Keynes (1936) himself that there may also exist a fundamental feedback from the real markets to the financial markets. On the whole, a feedback loop comes into being that may lead to a recovery of the economy by lowering interest rates and thus improving the investment climate (and consumption demand). This favorable effect for economic stability and a return to a position of full employment has been termed the Keynes effect in the literature. (It is often combined with the so-called Pigou real balances or wealth effect, which works in the same direction.)

The argument of the Keynes effect is summarized in Figure 2.2. The diagram points out that depressed labor and goods markets diminish wages and the price level. Falling prices are tantamount to rising real money balances, which exert a downward pressure on interest rates. The direct effect is on the short-term rate of interest, but the long-term rate may be similarly affected, so that in the end demand for goods and labor is revitalized. The significance of this line of reasoning lies in the perspective on labor market problems, which are seen to arise from the interdependence of real and financial markets. Hence, unemployment might not be sufficiently cured by real wage movements (which is another debatable topic), but a recovery may (also) be initiated, or reinforced, by improving this interdependent situation through an appropriate fiscal or monetary policy. Hicks (1937) formulated on this basis the now traditional IS–LM model of the interaction of goods and financial markets, which, within a temporary equilibrium setting, concentrates on the links between output and the rate of interest.

For simplicity, in Blanchard's (1981) analysis wage and price variations in the real sector are still left aside. On the other hand, Blanchard includes a dynamic multiplier story, which says that if demand exceeds supply, production is increased until the gap is filled. Likewise, output decreases in the case of excess supply. Hence, taken on its own, the real sector is characterized by a stabilizing feedback loop (since, on the demand side, the marginal propensity to spend is less than unity).

The achievement of Blanchard's contribution lies in enriching the IS–LM framework by markets for equities and long-term bonds. Regarding the stock market, Figure 2.3[3] indicates an elementary destabilizing mechanism,

---

3 Blanchard's (1981) paper and this chapter also consider the market for long-term bonds, yet still without any real–financial interaction. This market is characterized by a figure similar to Figure 2.3, and will be briefly considered in the conclusions to this chapter.

The Keynes Effect:

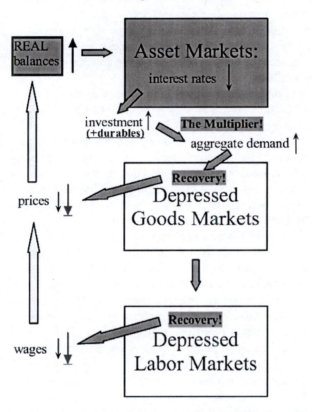

Figure 2.2 The Keynes effect as the basic stabilizing feedback from the real markets.

which explicitly involves expectations. An increasing expected rate of return on equities raises demand and so drives up the price on this market. As the rise in capital gains is expected to continue, expected capital gains are rising, too, and so does the expected rate of return. On the whole, a positive feedback loop is obtained. In Blanchard's treatment of the financial sector, this mechanism is not so clearly visible because he assumes perfect substitutability of all non-money assets as well as myopic perfect foresight of capital gains. As a consequence, there is no distinction between actual and expected capital gains, and the reaction mechanism disappears after some manipulation in a mathematical formula. Our approach, by contrast, relaxes Blanchard's assumptions in such a way that the single links of the feedback chain are recovered in Figure 2.3.

The situation in the market for long-term bonds is analogous and thus need not be discussed any further. Also, following Blanchard, real investment and

The Share or Equity Market

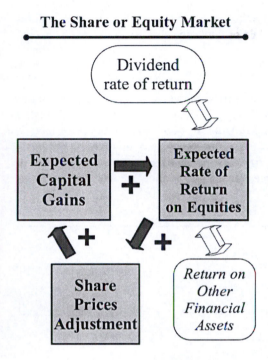

Figure 2.3 Centrifugal stock market dynamics.

consumption are supposed to be independent of the long-term rate of interest, so that this rate does not feed back on the real sector.

To sum up, both in Blanchard's and in our model version a basically unstable financial sector is coupled with a stable real sector. As mentioned above, in Blanchard's approach this interplay gives rise to saddlepoint dynamics, and the instability problem is solved by applying the jump variable technique. In our framework local stability of the equilibrium becomes possible, though instability may still be considered the normal case. So we have to turn to the global dynamics. We propose an economically meaningful concept of nonlinear price reactions on the stock market that prevent the system from exploding. It is intuitively clear that when the stabilizing forces are ruling in the outer regions of the state space, while in the vicinity of the equilibrium the destabilizing forces remain dominant, the trajectories will undergo persistent and bounded fluctuations. Whereas their main source lies in the financial sector, a complete discussion has to take the interplay of the real and financial sector into account.

The remainder of the chapter is organized as follows. We begin with a recapitulation of Blanchard's model. Section 2.2 presents the modeling equations, Section 2.3 investigates the model by means of geometric and analytical methods. This extensive discussion provides a firm background for our own approach, which is put forward in Section 2.4. The same section provides a local stability analysis.

Section 2.5 is concerned with the system's global behavior that arises if the equilibrium is unstable. It introduces the nonlinearity just alluded to and explores the resulting oscillations. Section 2.6 concludes the chapter.

2.2 The Blanchard model

All assets are treated as being given in fixed amounts; in particular, the money supply, M, the number of equities, E, and the stock of real capital, K. The latter is normalized at $K = 1$. Neglecting inflation of goods prices, the price level is also normalized at unity, $p = 1$. a_z, b_z, c_z are parameters involved in process z $(a_z, b_z > 0$, c_z may have either sign), while β_z denotes a speed of adjustment in this context. The following variables are subject to changes over time in this or the subsequent sections:

Y	total output
Y^d	aggregate demand
d	differential in rates of return
p_b	price of long-term bonds
p_e	price of equities
q	Tobin's (average) q; $q = p_e E / p K$, $E = K = p = 1$ in this chapter
i	short-term rate of interest
u	reciprocal of Tobin's q; $u = 1/q$
v	auxiliary variable; $v = -\pi_e$
π_e	expected growth rate of equity price
r	rate of return on real capital

The symbol $\dot{x}$ stands for the time derivative of a dynamic variable x, $\hat{x} = \dot{x}/x$ for its growth rate. The steady-state value of x is denoted by x^o, the expected value by x^e.

Considering what is determined within the (infinitesimally) short period, we have first aggregate demand on the goods market, Y^d, which depends positively on output as well as Tobin's (average) q,

$$Y^d = a_y Y + b_y q + c_y , \quad 0 < a_y < 1, \; c_y > 0 \tag{2.1}$$

The influence of q can be based on investment behavior (the valuation of firms on the stock market) or on consumption demand (a wealth effect).

The money market is the counterpart (the complement, so to speak) of the market for short-term bonds. Accordingly, temporary equilibrium is brought about by the short-term rate of interest, i, where it is assumed that the underlying decisions of the asset owners are not affected by the outcome on the other financial assets. In other words, money market equilibrium is represented by a textbook-like LM equation. It is furthermore linear, such that it can be solved for the interest rate as

$$i = i(Y) := a_m Y - b_m \ln M + c_m , \quad c_m = 0 \tag{2.2}$$

Given $p = 1$, the term c_m is zero in Blanchard (1981, eq. (2.2), p. 133), though it might reasonably be expected to be positive. (This issue is elaborated upon in an appendix to this chapter.) We will nevertheless follow Blanchard's specification in order to reproduce his results.

Because the real sector is reduced to a minimum, real profits vary only with capacity utilization, i.e., the level of production. Recalling the normalization of p and K, the rate of return on fixed capital, r (with denominator $pK = 1$), can be written as[4]

$$r = r(Y) := a_r Y + c_r \tag{2.3}$$

Where long-term bonds and equities are concerned, capital gains have to be taken into account. Under Blanchard's assumption of myopic perfect foresight, the (instantaneous) time rates of change of p_b (long-term bonds) and p_e (equities) are always correctly foreseen, so that there is no distinction between $\hat{p}_b^e$ and $\hat{p}_b$ or between $\hat{p}_e^e$ and $\hat{p}_e$. The yield terms of bonds and equities have to be respectively augmented by these growth rates.

The long-term bonds are consols paying one dollar per unit of time. Relating them to the corresponding financial investment, p_b, we get $1/p_b + \hat{p}_b$ as the rate of return of long-term bonds under myopic perfect foresight. On the other hand, as for equities, it is assumed that all profits, rpK, of firms are distributed to the shareholders. With $rpK/p_eE = r/q$, the rate of return of equities is $r/q + \hat{p}_e$.

The second hypothesis invoked by Blanchard is perfect substitutability of equities, long-term bonds, and short-term bonds. Arbitrage between these assets implies that the three rates of return are equal. Since there is no inflation in the model, we need not bother about real and financial rates of return.[5] Thus, the arbitrage conditions read

$$\hat{p}_b + 1/p_b = \frac{B + \dot{p}_b B}{p_b B} = i \tag{2.4}$$

$$\hat{p}_e + r/q = \frac{rK + \dot{p}_e E}{p_e E} = i \tag{2.5}$$

Equations (2.2)–(2.5) show a certain hierarchy of financial markets: the market for short-term bonds comes first and provides an anchor for the rates of return of long-term bonds and of equities. Note also that the short rate is determined in a static relationship, whereas the price formation for long-term bonds and equities involves dynamic relationships.

---

4   Since the rate of profit equals the profit share times the output–capital ratio, minus the rate of capital depreciation, the constant term c_r will be negative in equation (2.3); see the Appendix to this chapter.
5   According to Blanchard (1981, pp. 133f), $1/p_b + \hat{p}_b$ is a nominal rate of return, whereas $r/q + \hat{p}_e$ is a real rate – a statement which may require a second thought.

To complete the model, it remains to formulate the output adjustment mechanism on the goods market. The simple dynamic multiplier here assumed is given by

$$\dot{Y} = \beta_y (Y^d - Y).\tag{2.6}$$

Output of firms adjusts, as in simple textbook stories, with speed β_y towards the thereby changing level of aggregate demand currently observed by firms. Taken by itself and based on the assumption of a marginal propensity to spend of less than one, we know that this adjustment process converges to goods market equilibrium (when interest rates and stock prices are considered as given).

2.3 Analysis of the Blanchard model

2.3.1 Reduced-form dynamics

Equations (2.1)–(2.6) are easily transformed to a two-dimensional core system with output Y and Tobin's q as dynamic state variables. The differential equation for Y is obtained from (2.6) by substituting (2.1) for Y^d; the equation for q derives from $\hat{q} = \hat{p}_e$ (because p, K, E are constant and in fact set equal to one), solving (2.5) for $\hat{p}_e$, and using (2.2) and (2.3). Thus, the following system has to be studied:

$$\dot{Y} = \beta_y [-(1-a_y)Y + b_y q + c_y]\tag{2.7}$$
$$\dot{q} = i(Y)q - r(Y)\tag{2.8}$$

Apparently, long-term bonds do not feed back on these adjustments and can therefore be ignored; the dynamics of p_b are a mere appendix to equations (2.7), (2.8).[6] Note that, although the static relationships are linear specifications, equation (2.8) exhibits an intrinsic nonlinearity.

2.3.2 The IS curve: $\dot{Y} = 0$

Setting the first law of motion equal to zero and solving for q gives the locus of pairs (Y, q) that constitute temporary goods market equilibrium. It is analogous to the textbook IS curve, with the role of the short-term interest rate now being taken by Tobin's q. Hence this locus, too, may be safely called the model's IS curve. As q impacts positively on aggregate demand (while in the familiar textbook story the interest rate impacts negatively on Y^d), this IS curve is upward-sloping (rather than downward-sloping, when Y^d depends on i). In addition, if q is held constant, then all non-equilibrium points are attracted by the IS curve. These features are illustrated in Figure 2.4. Note that the IS curve must cut the horizontal

---

6 In Blanchard and Fischer (1989, ch. 10.4) and Chiarella et al. (2003), the role of equities is taken by the long-term bonds. Equities then become an appendix to the core system.

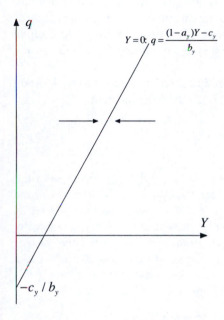

Figure 2.4 The IS curve (representing goods market equilibrium).

axis at a positive value, since the autonomous term in the aggregate demand function has been assumed as positive (representing basically the influence of fiscal policy on aggregate demand). The IS curve will shift to the right if fiscal policy is expansionary and it will be steeper with smaller a_y, the value of the marginal propensity to spend.

2.3.3 The LM Curve: $\dot{q} = 0$

In analogy to the treatment in the previous subsection, the second law of motion may be set to rest. This means that the stock market is in temporary equilibrium – in conjunction with money market equilibrium, which by (2.2) and $i(Y)$ entering (2.8) is presupposed anyway. Although $i(Y)$ was said to derive from a familiar LM condition, it will be convenient from now on to call the locus of pairs (Y, q) giving rise to $(2.8) = 0$ an LM curve. We stress that the LM curve of this chapter represents money market and stock market equilibrium and is thus more complex than the usual LM curve of the textbook literature (and in particular, not always positively sloped as in the case of the simple money market LM curve, see below).

This curve, however, is unstable. Suppose share prices and, thus, Tobin's q are so high that $i(Y)q - r(Y) > 0$, which says that the short-term interest rate i exceeds the direct returns rpK from holding equities when these are related to the value of shares (this rate of return being given by $rpK/p_eE = r/q$). In this situation share prices are driven up even higher, according to $\dot{q} > 0$ in (2.8). Likewise, adjustments take place in the other direction if the right-hand side of (2.8) is negative. This instability corresponds, in condensed form, to the positive stock market feedback mechanism mentioned in the introduction to this chapter (see Figure 2.3).

The equality $(2.8) = 0$ can be explicitly solved for q, so that the LM equilibrium value of $q = q_{LM}$ with respect to output Y is given by the function

$$q_{LM}(Y) = r(Y)/i(Y) \tag{2.9}$$

Depending on the relative (positive) slopes of $r(\cdot)$ and $i(\cdot)$, q_{LM} may rise or fall as Y increases. Blanchard calls the first case, $q'_{LM} > 0$, the *good news case*, and the second, $q'_{LM} < 0$, the *bad news case*. The following proposition assures us that either case unambiguously prevails over the entire range of economically meaningful levels of production, which are associated with a positive rate of interest $i = i(Y)$. It also establishes that in the good news case the LM curve is always convex, and is concave in the bad news case. On the basis of this information, the two cases are sketched in Figures 2.5 and 2.6.

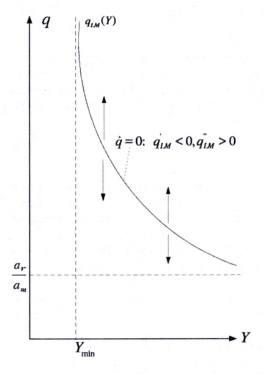

Figure 2.5 The LM curve (representing money market and equity market equilibrium): Blanchard's bad news case (BNC).

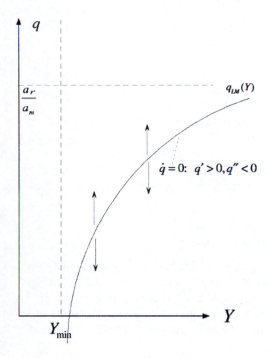

Figure 2.6 The LM curve (representing money market and equity market equilibrium): Blanchard's good news case.

Proposition 2.1:
Let $Y_{min} := (b_m \ln M)/a_m$ *be the level of output at which the short-term interest rate in (2.2) would become zero. Then, for all* $Y > Y_{min}$, *the following equivalence relationships hold true:*

$$q'_{LM}(Y) > 0 \iff q''_{LM}(Y) < 0 \iff r(Y_{min}) < 0$$

$$q'_{LM}(Y) < 0 \iff q''_{LM}(Y) > 0 \iff r(Y_{min}) > 0$$

Proof: Differentiating the function $q_{LM}(\cdot)$ yields $i^2(Y)q'_{LM}(Y) = -a_r b_m \ln M - a_m c_r = -a_m [a_r(b_m \ln M)/a_m + c_r] = -a_m r(Y_{min})$. The second derivative $q''_{LM}(Y)$ is easily seen to have the same sign as $r(Y_{min})$ if $Y > Y_{min}$. The statements of the proposition then immediately follow. □

Proof details: Making use of the definition of Y_{min}. one can easily show that

$$q_{LM}(Y) = \frac{a_r(Y - Y_{min}) + r(Y_{min})}{a_m(Y - Y_{min})}$$

holds true, since we have $a_m Y_{min} - b_m \ln M + c_m = 0$. This gives

$$q'_{LM}(Y) = \frac{a_m r(Y_{min})}{(a_m(Y - Y_{min})^2}$$

and

$$q''_{LM}(Y) = \frac{a_m r(Y_{min}) 2 a_m (Y - Y_{min}) a_m}{(a_m(Y - Y_{min}))^4}.$$

These two derivatives show that the sign of the rate of profit at Y_{min} is of decisive importance for the signs of these two derivatives, and in the way it is asserted in proposition 1.

2.3.4 Steady-state positions and local dynamics

The economy is in a state of long-run equilibrium, or, synonymously, in a steady state, if (Y, q) brings about $\dot{Y} = \dot{q} = 0$ in (2.7) and (2.8). Referring to Figures 2.7[7] and 2.8,[8] which, regarding the IS and LM curves, combine Figure 2.4 with Figures 2.5 and 2.6, respectively, Proposition 2.2 on the existence of such equilibrium points is straightforward. (The two curves rest on different parameters and are thus independent.)

Proposition 2.2:
In the bad news case, $q'_{LM} < 0$, system (7), (8) has exactly one economically meaningful steady-state position (Y^o, q^o). On the other hand, in the good news case, $q'_{LM} > 0$, there may be two, one, or no equilibrium (Y^o, q^o).

In the good news case, the equilibrium is unique if the LM curve is tangent to the IS curve. Of course, this can only happen by a fluke. It may furthermore be remarked that the problem of two or no equilibria is due to the special circumstances in the present, simplified framework. As a matter of fact, the phenomena seem to be rather spurious. Existence and uniqueness are easily re-established if the model is put in a broader (growth) perspective where, in particular, K and E vary over time. In this case, the motions of q are no longer so tightly linked to p_e, and the equilibrium value of q is formally derived in another part of the model; see Chapter 7 in this book. Table 2.1 summarizes some steady-state comparisons for the main policy variables of the model (monetary and fiscal policy) and the case of real wage increases (or productivity decreases). It shows – viewed from the common sense of textbook approaches – strange results for the bad stable equilibrium (BSE)

---

7 Note that there is a further equilibrium to the left of Y_{min} in Figure 2.7.
8 Note that the LM curve is also defined left of Y_{min} in Figure 2.8, but is economically meaningless there.

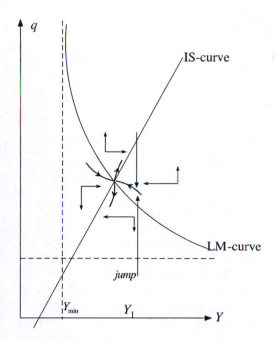

Figure 2.7 A uniquely determined steady state in Blanchard's bad news case, which, due to its economic meaninglessness, is excluded from consideration.

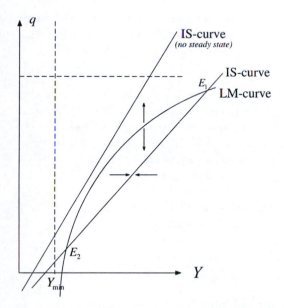

Figure 2.8 Two or no steady states in Blanchard's good news case.

Table 2.1 Comparative statics: monetary expansion, fiscal expansion and real wage increases

Cases	Variables	M	c_y	$\omega = w/p$
Bad news case	Y	+	+	−
	q	+	−	−
	i	?	+	?
Good news case	Y	+	+	−
	q	+	−	−
	i	+	+	?
Bad stable Equilibrium	Y	−	−	+
	q	−	−	+
	i	−	−	?

case and also an unusual range of stock prices with respect to fiscal expansion in the bad news case (BNC). In Blanchard's good news case (GNC), all results are as one would have expected them to be. We will come back to these results when the dynamics implied in these three cases is considered. In contrast to Blanchard, we will however not conclude that the uncommon comparative static features of the BSE case allow us to exclude this equilibrium from consideration, since unusual results will also characterize the BNC (where a booming economy is bad news for the stock market in the long run), while we will find methodological problems in the solution technique that is applied by Blanchard (1981) in the good news case.

The local dynamics around a steady state is determined by the Jacobian matrix J of the partial derivatives of (2.7), (2.8) (evaluated at this point). The properties derived from an investigation of J are summarized in the next theorem.

Proposition 2.3:
In the bad news case, $q'_{LM} < 0$, the (unique) steady state of (2.7), (2.8) is a saddle point. In the good news case $q'_{LM} > 0$, with two equilibria. The equilibrium at which the LM curve cuts the IS curve from above (point E_1 in Figure 2.9) is a saddle point. The other equilibrium, where the LM curve cuts the IS curve from below (point E_2 in Figure 2.9), is locally asymptotically stable if $i^o = i(Y^o) < \beta_y(1-a_y)$, while it is repelling if this inequality is reversed.

Proof: The Jacobian matrix evaluated at an equilibrium point (Y^o, q^o) with associated short-term interest rate $i^o = i(Y^o)$ is given by

$$J = \begin{bmatrix} j_{11} & j_{12} \\ j_{21} & j_{22} \end{bmatrix} = \begin{bmatrix} -\beta_y(1-a_y) & \beta_y b_q \\ a_m q^o - a_r & i^o \end{bmatrix} = \begin{bmatrix} - & + \\ ? & + \end{bmatrix}$$

The slopes of the IS and LM curves are obtained from the implicit function theorem (or more informally from the equations $j_{11}\, dY + j_{12}\, dq = 0$ for the IS schedule,

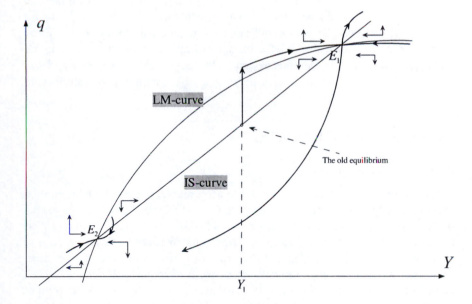

Figure 2.9 Dynamics in the good news case: saddle point and stable node or focus.

$j_{21}\,dY + j_{22}\,dq = 0$ for the LM schedule). This gives

$$
\begin{aligned}
\text{Slope IS} &= -j_{11}/j_{12} = (1-a_y)/b_y \\
\text{Slope LM} &= -j_{21}/j_{22} = -(a_m q^o - a_r)/i^o
\end{aligned}
$$

As LM is downward-sloping in the bad news case, we have $j_{21} > 0$ and thus $\det J < 0$, so that the equilibrium is a saddle point. In the good news case, slope IS > slope LM at an equilibrium is equivalent to $-\det J = -j_{11}j_{22} + j_{12}j_{21} > 0$, that is, this point is also a saddle. If slope IS < slope LM, $\det J > 0$ results, so that here local stability depends on the trace. $i^o < \beta_y(1-a_y)$ rewrites the second condition, trace $J < 0$, which is now necessary and sufficient for both eigenvalues to have negative real parts.[9]   □

The dynamic behavior is illustrated in Figure 2.7 for the bad news case. Figure 2.9[10] sketches the global dynamics that may arise in the presence of two equilibria in the good news case, assuming local stability for the lower equilibrium, which seems only natural in the light of the condition stated in the proposition.

9 Note here that the difference in the slopes of the IS and the LM curves is given by:

$$
IS' - LM' = -\frac{J_{11}}{J_{12}} + \frac{J_{21}}{J_{22}} = -\frac{\det J}{J_{12}J_{22}}.
$$

10 E_1 is the good news case (GNC) and E_2 the bad stable equilibrium (BSE).

In the good news case, Blanchard (1981, p. 134) himself concentrates on the upper equilibrium E_1 with its saddlepoint dynamics. The lower equilibrium E_2 is ruled out because of its undesirable comparative statics. It is indeed readily verified, – see Table 2.1 for further examples – that an increase in the money supply or in the coefficient c_y in (2.1), representing expansionary fiscal policy, both have a counterintuitive depressing effect on the lower equilibrium output.[11]

2.4 The jump variable technique

2.4.1 Saddle point stability

Before presenting a critical examination of asset market dynamics under rational expectations, let us here reconsider the good news and the bad news cases from the perspective of the solution procedure applied by Blanchard (1981), the so-called jump variable technique introduced by Sargent and Wallace (1973).

Figure 2.7 shows the saddlepoint dynamics as it results in the bad news case. Following the methodology originally proposed by Sargent and Wallace (1973), one of the model's state variables is classified as slow (predetermined), here output Y, the other as fast (non-predetermined), here Tobin's q or, equivalently, the share price p_e. While Y is thus predetermined at a given point in time, say when firms produce at level Y_1 in Figure 2.7, it is assumed that q adjusts infinitely fast – such that it jumps onto the stable branch of the saddlepoint dynamics, as indicated by the vertical arrow. That is to say that, though there is a definite law of motion for q, this law is temporarily switched off, at starting time $t = 0$, when a shock occurs.

Blanchard (1981) discusses a variety of applications of the jump variable technique to issues of unanticipated or anticipated fiscal or monetary policy. In the latter case, q performs a jump when the announcement of the policy action, which will change the dynamic laws, is made. The jump then takes the system to such a point in the phase space that (Y, q) reaches from there the stable branch of the new dynamics exactly at that point in time when the policy action (the shock) is implemented. The interesting point to be made is that the jump of q in the anticipated policy case is smaller than in the unanticipated case, since part of the adjustments is already smoothly carried out by the old dynamics. Such a solution of the treatment of anticipated events is, from a technical perspective, appealing. Nevertheless, the general question of the economic meaning of the jump variable procedure remains.[12]

---

11 Blanchard adds that the dynamic properties are undesirable as well. This statement is to be understood from the point of view of the jump variable technique as the obligatory method to apply. Under asymptotic stability, this technique would no longer be determinate since the jump variable may jump anywhere and the system would still converge (see below for a brief discussion).

12 Incidentally, Blanchard (1981, p. 135) calls the jump variable technique "a standard if not entirely convincing practice".

In the early contributions to the literature, as in the seminal article by Sargent and Wallace (1973), the agents are said to consider the situation from the global perspective and, being endowed with perfect foresight, decide that all trajectories up to the stable arms of the saddlepoint dynamics have undesirable properties. For example, some variables would turn negative in the long run, or policy intervention may be feared. This induces the "agents" to choose the convergent path, on which the economy lands by a sudden change in the variable(s) that is (are) not predetermined in the short run.

While this kind of reasoning is not entirely convincing (to quote from the previous footnote), more recent modeling is explicitly based on an intertemporal optimization problem over an infinite horizon. If this problem is well defined, the dynamic optimality conditions again give rise to saddlepoint dynamics around the steady state. In this context, jumping onto the stable manifold is a constituent part of the solution procedure. The modern treatment is consistent, but what is still problematic are the underlying assumptions. On the one hand, the hypothesis of perfect foresight, if taken literally, would demand a number of rather heroic capabilities from agents. On the other hand, the method rests on the representative agent, which is perhaps even more questionable in modeling decentralized economic systems than the requirement of perfect foresight (Kirman, 1992).

As an aside, it may be remarked that the good news case depicted in Figure 2.9 adds another difficulty to the application of the jump variable technique. According to Blanchard, if output is presently Y_1 and a shock occurs, agents decide to jump on the stable branch of the upper equilibrium E_1. Why should they not choose to move to a point below the IS curve, from which the economy is sent to the lower equilibrium E_2? Possibly because equilibrium E_2 is sub-optimal. Such an argument would, however, introduce an additional welfare criterion into the model, a way out that, strictly speaking, has a certain "ad-hoc" character.[13]

2.4.2 Appealing features of the jump variable technique

Before we move to a detailed presentation of such problematic features of the application of the rational expectations methodology, let us briefly summarize in graphical terms the dynamic responses of our system for the bad and good news cases, for unanticipated and for anticipated monetary as well as fiscal policy. The application to other shocks or news hitting the economy is then an easy matter and is left as an exercise to the reader here.[14]

In Figure 2.10 we consider cases of unanticipated monetary and fiscal policy shocks in Blanchard's good news case. In both cases, the jump variable technique takes us immediately to the stable arm of the new dynamics through upward jumps in the value of the stock. This is followed by further increases in this value along

---

13 In the modern parlance of mainstream economic theory, the expression *ad hoc* is reserved for unorthodox or out-of-favor approaches.

14 See also the original paper by Blanchard (1981) for various such applications.

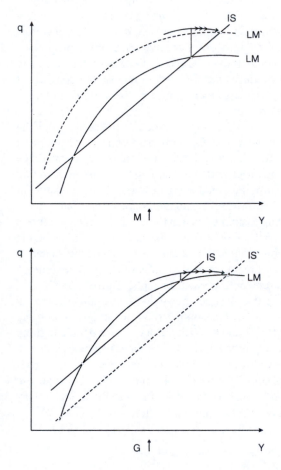

Figure 2.10 Unanticipated monetary and fiscal policy shocks in the GNC.

the stable arm, which is then accompanied by increases in real economic activity. Since the LM curve is strictly concave, a shift of this curve may have larger effects on stock prices than a shift in the IS curve, while the opposite may be true for economic activity, depending on the region where the IS curve is cutting the LM curve. Note that the dynamics does not take place along the new LM curve as in textbook IS-LM analysis, but that the jump takes the economy already above this curve, with further increases in stock prices following thereafter.

In the bad news case, shown in Figure 2.11, we now have a clear-cut difference between the working of expansionary monetary and fiscal policy, which both continue to stimulate economic activity but with contracting stock prices in the case of unanticipated fiscal policy shocks. There is thus some crowding out of investment and of the implied economic activity. This is, however, the only case for unanticipated policy shocks where crowding out effects can be observed.

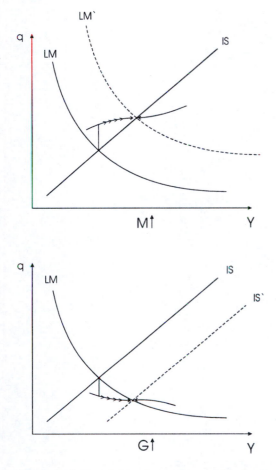

Figure 2.11 Unanticipated monetary and fiscal policy shocks in the BNC.

Fiscal expansion is in this situation a problem when viewed from the interest of stock holders and the stock market.

Next we consider the case of anticipated policy shocks. The jump variable technique provides a rigorous method for testing such issues. Imposing continuity on the path followed by the economy after the news has been provided (so that no foreseen jumps in stock prices can occur) demands that we look for that trajectory in the old dynamics since nothing has happened yet. When approached by an upward jump in stock price, the dynamics simply adjusts to these prices, and also to output, so that the economy arrives exactly on the stable arm of the new dynamics when the news that has hit the old dynamics matarializes. In the good news case Figure 2.12 this simply means smaller jumps at the moment the anticipation is formed, and then movements in the old dynamics along an accelerating (unstable) trajectory, determined by the jump in such a way that this trajectory arrives at the

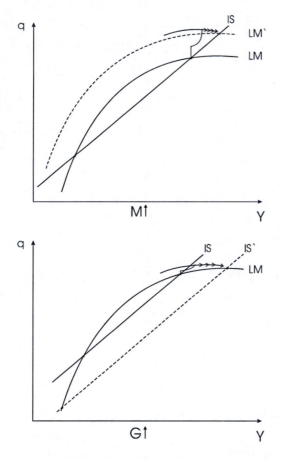

Figure 2.12 Anticipated fiscal and monetary policy shocks in the GNC.

stable arm of the new dynamics when the anticipated shock in fact occurs. The economy switches to the new dynamics at this point in time without any further jump in the value of the stock and then moves from there in a continuous fashion along the stable arm of the new dynamics towards the new steady state. There is again no crowding out; stock prices and activity can only rise along the chosen path.

This procedure of treating anticipated events is appealing to a certain degree, since it provides a seemingly general and rigorous, though somewhat mechanistic, way to solve the issue of how the economy reacts momentarily to news about future events. In the case considered, the dynamics is switched off at the moment the news hits the economy and there is a stock market rally occurring that immediately pushes the economy onto the accelerating trajectory and thus towards further stock price rallies (now with increases in activity levels). When the policy change actually takes place, the economy slows down again to a now stable adjustment to the new steady state.

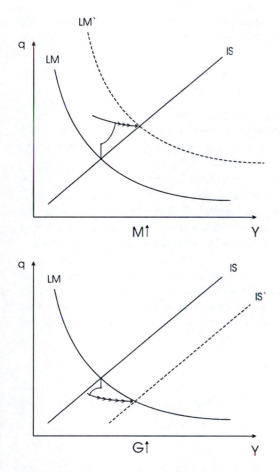

Figure 2.13 Anticipated fiscal and monetary policy shocks in the BNC.

In the bad news case Figure 2.13, the same situation also gives rise to a distinction between the effects of monetary and fiscal policy. For monetary policy there is the same type of stock price rally accompanied by increasing activity levels after the initial jump in the value of the stock. When the stable arm is reached we again get further increases in the output level, but now accompanied by some reductions in the value of the stock, until the new steady state is reached.

In the case of fiscal policy, however, in the BNC the immediate response is a contraction in the value of the stock and a subsequent recession and decline in activity levels. These go along with further falls in share prices, since the expansionary fiscal policy has not happened yet, but investment has declined due to the reduction in Tobin's *q*. We therefore have the interesting result that announced fiscal expansions cause recessions due to their immediate effects on the stock market and on investment behavior. Once the stable arm is reached again, the contraction comes to an end. Expansion sets in, even though stock prices keep falling (yet no longer in an accelerating way), due to the effects of the fiscal expansion that is taking place.

2.4.3 Strange implications of the jump variable technique

We now come to a graphical discussion of some anomalies or limitations of the rational expectations methodology. In view of what one would expect from common economic reasoning, a series of unanticipated negative demand shocks for the output of firms (which move the IS curve to the left) is not likely to increase the stock prices of firms in the form of a stock market rally. Yet this is what happens in the bad news case, as is shown in Figure 2.14. According to this Figure, we have a significant ongoing decline in the capacity utilization rate of firms, accompanied either by upward share price jumps when the contractive demand shocks are hitting the economy, or by continuous share price increases in between.

At the end of all adjustments to the negative demand shocks we have an economy where output, profits (= dividends) and interest are very low and the value of the stock held by equity owners is exceptionally high. It is to be expected that capital stock depreciation will accelerate and real investment shrink and

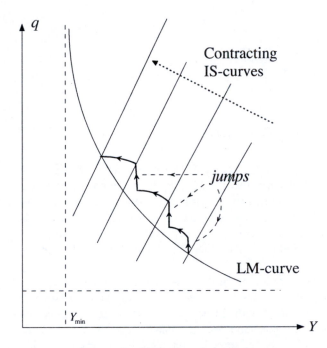

Figure 2.14 Severe economic contraction and stock price rallies.

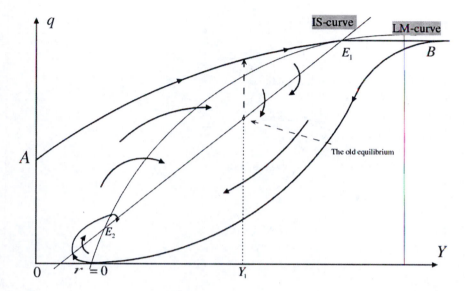

Figure 2.15 Jump variable indeterminacy.

not rise as the investment function at present employed suggests. This example implies that the model needs significant changes in order to allow for a proper treatment of such sequences of contractive demand shocks. Next, we consider the good news case and its phase portrait in more detail. We tentatively draw, in Figure 2.15, a domain $(0 - A - E_1 - B - r = 0)$ whose limit points are given by either E_1 or E_2. Only on the upper border of this domain will the system converge to E_1, while all other trajectories are attracted by E_2. The rational expectations solutions generally uses a boundedness argument to single out the trajectory to which the system will jump to after the occurrence of a shock.[15] Yet the trajectories considered here are all bounded ones and are thus all equally well-suited to be the subject of an immediate adjustment in the price of stocks. The usual criterion is therefore no longer sufficient to justify that the system will always return to $A - E_1$ (for output values below the one belonging to E_1) after the economy is hit by some shock. This is a situation of indeterminacy from the viewpoint of the jump variable technique which allows the system to behave in an arbitrary way to a certain degree. Monetary or fiscal policy is then often considered as not providing the necessary anchors for the behavior of the economy and thus as needing reformulation in order to fulfill this role. In the depicted situation not only boundedness but also the type of equilibrium one wants to converge to is used as the choice criterion, and this is combined with

---

15 See Cochrane (2007) for a recent critical view of such model variants where only a single path is allowed to be taken to approach an equilibrium.

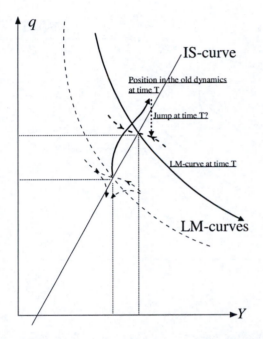

Figure 2.16 Anticipated monetary policy shock: too distant or too small to allow for the jump variable technique?

an attracting domain that is of measure zero in the domain of all convergent trajectories.

There is another problem with the jump variable technique that requires a solution. Suppose, in the case of anticipated shocks Figure 2.16, that this shock is on the one hand so far away in time and/or on the other hand so small that the time interval along the bubble in the old dynamics, before the shock occurs, in order to reach the new stable arm, starting slightly above the original steady state, is smaller than the time interval that characterizes the anticipation period. There is then no jump in the fast variable that puts the dynamics onto a point in the old phase diagram so that the stable arm of the new dynamics is exactly reached when in fact the shock occurs. Since the bubble has passed the new stable arm already, a further jump would be necessary to bring the dynamics back to convergence in the new situation.

The admittedly rigorous but mechanical treatment of anticipated events and their impact on the current state of the economy is a drawback of the rational expectations techniques applied to these anticipated events that requires either solving or abandoning this procedure on logical grounds. The use of automatic bubbles that allow for a soft landing on the new stable arm when the shock occurs is a highly stylized scenario to treat the anticipation of future events. It gives bubbles a very precise meaning and has to be augmented by situations where bubbles burst (i.e., there is no soft landing) if shocks are too small relative to the time span that elapses before they actually occur.

We finally note that in the case of an interest rate peg by the central bank (and thus endogenous money supply) the 'LM' curve reduces to

$$q = (a_r Y + c_r)/\bar{i}, \quad \bar{i} \quad \text{being the pegged rate of interest.}$$

We thus have two linear isoclines in this case and, in particular, only the BSE case when the pegged interest rate is chosen sufficiently low. In this case the RE methodology is not applicable at all, since the system is asymptotically stable and there is no further equilibrium. In this case the conclusion therefore is that monetary policy must be prepared to increase the pegged rate by a sufficient amount in order to generate saddle point dynamics and thus determinacy from the viewpoint of the jump variable technique.

2.5 Conclusions

We have reconsidered in this chapter the seminal model of a real–financial interaction put forward by Blanchard (1981), which extends the IS analysis by an output adjustment rule of the dynamic multiplier type, and, more importantly, the textbook LM analysis by stock market dynamics under the assumption of perfect substitutability and myopic perfect foresight. This system is typically characterized by saddle point dynamics. On the basis of the rational expectations methodology, Blanchard treated it by means of the jump variable technique and in this chapter we followed this treatment to a certain degree. However, we have to take some drawbacks and limitations of this rational expectations methodology into account, and will continue in this book to show that rational expectations cannot be considered the final solution to the treatment of forward-looking expectations and anticipated events. This allows, as Cochrane (2007) criticizes, only for a single path to reach an equilibrium. Mathematically speaking, rational expectations are not structurally stable with respect to minor respecifications of the dynamics and are thus exceptional in nature. Furthermore, the ideal world of rational expectations does not work universally, but is plagued by various anomalies that question its unanimous acceptance. Finally, at least in a deterministic setup, the rational expectations solution strategy is fairly mechanical in its application and excludes all heterogeneity in the behavior of economic agents.

Nevertheless, the chapter added considerable detail to Keynes's fundamental downward causal nexus that we have represented graphically in Figure 2.1. This figure can now be respecified as shown in Figure 2.17. There is a stable dynamic multiplier process on the market for goods (as a simplification of the full Metzlerian output and inventory adjustment process) and an unstable (accelerating) partial adjustment of stock prices on the financial markets. These are subject to a positive feedback chain if perfect substitution with short-term bonds and perfect

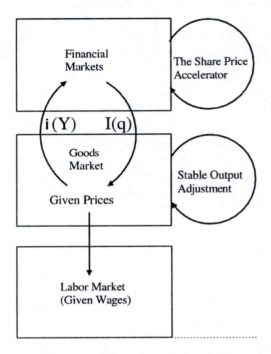

Figure 2.17 The Blanchard model of real–financial interaction.

anticipation of short-term capital gains are assumed. The link between asset and goods markets is given on the one hand by the investment function, whereby stock prices drive investment behavior, and on the other hand by the LM schedule, which in inverted form determines the short-term rate of interest as a positive function of the output level on the market for goods. We have still given wages and prices and thus not yet considered the need for monetary policy as charged with controlling inflation.

The interaction of an unstable financial accelerator with a stable output adjustment generally gives rise to saddlepoint dynamics in the model of this chapter, but we have found also a case where fully convergent dynamics was generated (yet classified as a 'bad' (stable) equilibrium state by Blanchard (1981)). The starting point of this treatment of real–financial interaction is an appealing one, since goods markets tend to be stabilizing, in this case wehe022s financial markets tend to do the opposite. However, the solution technique of the rational expectations school is, in this situation, probably a very idealized and exceptional one, as it is assumed that stock prices are always adjusting in such a way that they keep the economy on the stable branch of the generated saddlepoint situation. So output is assumed to adjust just fast enough to drive the economy towards its stationary state despite the centrifugal forces that characterize stock market dynamics when considered in isolation.

2.6 References

BLANCHARD, O. (1981): Output, the stock market, and interest rates. *American Economic Review*, 71, 132–143.

BLANCHARD, O. and S. FISCHER (1989): *Lectures on Macroeconomics*. Cambridge, MA.: MIT Press.

BURMEISTER, E. (1980): On some conceptual issues in rational expectations modelling. *Journal of Money, Credit and Banking*, 12, 217–228.

CHIARELLA, C., P. FLASCHEL and W. SEMMLER (2003): Output and the term structure of interest rates: Ways out of the jump-variable conundrum. School of Finance and Economics, UTS working paper No. 125.

COCHRANE, J. (2007): Inflation determination with Taylor rule: A critical review. Mimeo, University of Chicago.

HICKS, J. (1937): Mr. Keynes and the 'Classics': A suggested interpretation. *Econometrica*, 5, 147–159.

KEYNES, J.M. (1936): *The General Theory of Employment, Interest and Money*. New York: Macmillan.

KIRMAN, A.P. (1992): Whom or what does the representative individual represent? *Journal of Economic Perspectives*, 6:2, 117–136.

SARGENT, T. and N. WALLACE (1973): The stability of models of money and growth with perfect foresight. *Econometrica*, 41, 1043–1048.

2.7 Appendix: Some observations

2.7.1 Money market equilibrium

In order to underpin the form of the money demand function and the profit (= dividend) payment function to some extent, we briefly reconsider these functions in the following two subsections. In particular, we find that the parameters of the money demand function are based on somewhat complicated elasticity and other expressions and thus have to be interpreted with some care, especially with respect to empirical estimates.

The inverted money market equilibrium equation of Blanchard (1981) can be obtained from a standard money market equilibrium condition, as displayed in the first equation below, by converting the left-hand side into logarithms and by making a Taylor approximation of the resulting right-hand side, as shown below.[16]

$$M/p = m^d(Y, i)$$

$$\ln M - \ln p = \ln M = \ln m^d(Y, i)$$

$$\ln m^d(Y, i) \approx \ln m^d(Y_0, i_0) + \frac{m_y^d(Y_0, i_0)}{m^d(Y_0, i_0)}(Y - Y_0) + \frac{m_i^d(Y_0, i_0)}{m^d(Y_0, i_0)}(i - i_0)$$

16 Note that the point (Y_0, i_0) in the state space need not coincide with the steady state of the model to be considered later on.

$$= \ln m_0^d + (m_{y_0}^d/m_0^d)(Y - Y_0) + (m_{i_0}^d/m_0^d)(i - i_0)$$

$$= \ln m_0^d + \frac{m_{y_0}^d Y_0}{m_0^d}\left(\frac{Y}{Y_0} - 1\right) + \frac{m_{i_0}^d i_0}{m_0^d}(\frac{i}{i_0} - 1)$$

$$= \ln m_0^d + \varepsilon_{m^d,y}^0\left(\frac{Y}{Y_0} - 1\right) - \varepsilon_{m^d,i}^0\left(\frac{i}{i_0} - 1\right)$$

$$= aY - bi + c$$

By inverting the functional expressions just obtained we get the following expression for the interest rate formula employed by Blanchard (1981):

$$i = a_m Y - b_m \ln M + c_m$$

$$= \frac{\ln m_0^d - \varepsilon_{m^d,y}^0 + \varepsilon_{m^d,i}^0 - \ln M + \varepsilon_{m^d,y}^0 \frac{Y}{Y_0}}{\varepsilon_{m^d,i}^0/i_0}$$

$$= i_o + \frac{\ln m_0^d - \ln M - \varepsilon_{m^d,y}^0 + \varepsilon_{m^d,y}^0 \frac{Y}{Y_0}}{\varepsilon_{m^d,i}^0}$$

Note that the constant term in this function

$$c_m = i_o + \frac{\ln m_0^d - \varepsilon_{m^d,y}^0}{\varepsilon_{m^d,i}^0}$$

is set equal to zero in Blanchard (1981) and in the analysis of the model of this chapter. Note also that we assume that M is such that $\ln M > 0$ holds ($\ln p = 0$ by choice of dimensions).[17]

2.7.2 Fixed proportions and real profits

Assuming a standard fixed proportions technology which uses only labor as variable input and which includes capital depreciation gives rise to the following expression for real profits, where $v = \omega/x$ denotes the given wage share of the model.

$$\Pi = Y - \delta K - \bar{\omega}L^d , \quad L^d = Y/x, x = \text{const.}$$

$$= Y(1 - \bar{\omega}/x) - \delta K = Y(1 - v) - \delta K , \quad v = \bar{w}/x = \text{const.}$$

$$= a_r Y + c_r, \quad c_r \le 0 \text{ iff } (\delta \ge 0!)$$

---

17 If later analysis needs explicit representation of the price level, we only have to use $\ln(M/P) = \ln M - \ln p$ in place of $\ln M$ in all formulae.

We shall generally assume in the following that the depreciation rate is positive, i.e., that there is a negative constant in the profit function of firms (not shown in the sign preceding it). These profits are distributed to shareholders and thus fully enter the dividend rate of return component of the rate of return of shareholders. Firms thus do not have any income if one neglects that the dynamic multiplier implies unintended inventory changes of firms, which are treated only implicitly here.

3 Bond market, term structure and the macroeconomy

3.1 Introduction

Next, we reconsider a textbook model of Blanchard and Fischer (1989, 10.4) who reformulated Keynesian IS–LM analysis from the perspective of a richer array of financial assets, namely short-term and long-term bonds, and thus from the perspective of the term structure of interest rates.[1] The basic change in this extension of the IS–LM approach is that investment demand (and also consumption demand) now depends on the long-term rate of interest instead of the short-term rate. This implies that the IS curve and the LM curve are no longer situated in the same diagram, but have to be linked via the dynamics of long-term bond prices (in the approach of Blanchard and Fischer based on perfect substitutes, via perfect foresight and the jump variable technique). This creates one of the links for investigating real–financial interaction, the dynamic multiplier process and the conventional LM curve representing the other link. On the basis of this dynamic interaction of real and financial markets we will reflect the outcomes found by Blanchard and Fischer (1989) from the perspective of imperfect substitutes and imperfect forecasts of capital gains, replacing their limit case of perfect substitutes and myopic perfect foresight. On this basis, we derive two alternatives to the conventional jump variable technique and its treatment of unanticipated and anticipated monetary and fiscal policy. Our results are global in nature and do not depend on the essentially local[2] analysis of saddlepoint stability as is the case for the jump variable technique.

By understanding perfect substitutes and perfect foresight as special cases of imperfect substitutes and imperfect foresight, we will reformulate the Blanchard and Fischer (1989, 10.4) analysis of monetary and fiscal policy. There is then no need to apply the jump variable technique to the local saddlepoint situation that results from their set-up, where only the limit case but not the environment in

---

1 See Blanchard (1981) for a closely related approach which, however, focuses on the stock market instead of the market for long-term bonds.
2 Since the stable manifolds of saddlepoint situations are rarely considered from the global perspective in the case of nonlinear dynamical systems, as for example the still very simple case of the present chapter.

which this limit case may be embedded is considered. With imperfect substitutes the local saddlepoint stability of the Blanchard and Fischer approach is also given, but it can be tamed either by a nonlinearity in the excess demand function for long-term bonds or by a nonlinearity in the adjustment speed of bond market prices. Both of these alternative approaches to rational or near rational expectations thereby provide viable dynamics without further reference to the local saddlepoint situation. We thereby get, in the first alternative case, endogenous fluctuations in a uniquely determined phase diagram which, moreover, give rise to so-called relaxation oscillations (or limit limit cycles) when expectations become perfect. In the other case we combine tranquil phase diagram situations with excited ones in order to obtain regime switches between convergent long-term bond price dynamics and accelerating ones, which in sum also provide viable financial dynamics and their interaction with the output dynamics. The aim of the chapter is therefore to provide two basic alternatives to the conventional jump variable technique which exploit the idea that the really fast variable is given by the expectations mechanism. The speed of adjustment of long-term bond prices may be fast or toggle between fast and slow, but will not be infinitely fast due to institutional reasons, in particular if markets become cautious when they expect changes in the regime that governs them.

We will replace the mechanistic, purely forward-looking jump variable proce-dure, which is an exceptional case from a mathematical point of view, with an alternative method for deterministic differential and difference equations systems. In the basic case, our approach will be equally mechanistic, but not an exceptional solution to the local instability that may plague IS–LM equilibria of models where short-term and long-term bonds and their rates of return interact with each other. Our reformulation of the Blanchard and Fischer (1989) approach to the term structure of interest rates and their interaction with the output dynamics aims at understanding this interaction from the perspective of the feedback chains or mechanisms that are involved (or not yet involved) in the formulated dynamical model. In the present situation we basically have as such a mechanism the dynamic multiplier process, the Keynes effect (here as a specific relationship between interest rates, investment and output changes) and, as the important new element, a financial accelerator process on the market for long-term bonds.[3]

Starting from Keynes (1936, Ch.18), one may first of all postulate as real–financial structure the following one-sided hierarchical relationship between the real and the financial sector, in order to illustrate and motivate the changes in this structure that will be made in this chapter. In Figure 3.1, asset markets bring forth a rate of interest and returns structure by themselves without any interference from the market for goods and labor. The markets for financial assets are thus at the top of the market hierarchy of macroeconomic theorizing and are conceived as being largely independent of what happens in the real markets. Their outcome, however,

---

3 The so-called Mundell effect (of inflationary expectations and the real rate of interest) is not yet present here, due to the neglect of inflation in this short-term approach to real–financial interaction.

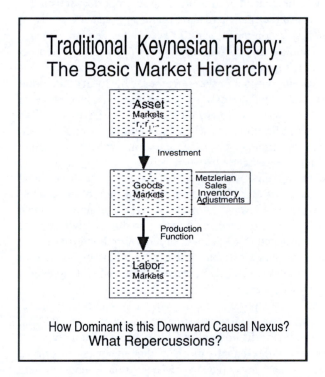

Figure 3.1 The causal nexus of Chapter 18 of Keynes's *General Theory*.

determines real investment behavior based on the structure of financial returns, in comparison with the rate of profit or the state of confidence that characterizes the sector of firms. This investment in turn determines the outcome on the market for goods and thus the production level that firms will realize via the multiplier process, which may be formulated in static, in dynamic or even in Metzlerian terms[4]. Depending on the type of production function that is assumed, this will finally determine employment and thus the rate of unemployment on the labor market.

Starting from a situation of high unemployment (and depressed goods markets as well), it was already conceded by Keynes (1936, Ch.19) himself that there may exist a fundamental feedback from the real markets to the financial markets that may improve the situation on the real markets by lowering interest rates and subsequently improving the investment climate (and also the demand for durable consumption goods in particular). This favorable effect for economic stability and the return to a position of full employment has been named the Keynes effect in the

---

4 We shall use a simple dynamic multiplier approach in the following modeling approach to the real
   dynamics; see Figure 3.4.

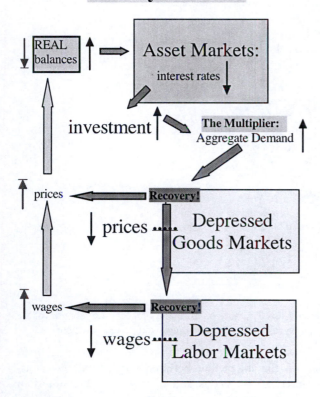

Figure 3.2 The Keynes effect, the core stabilizing feedback chain between real and financial markets.

literature (and is often also combined with the Pigou real balances or wealth effect, which works in the same direction). The working of this well-known Keynes effect is summarized in Figure 3.2.

We can see from this figure that the feedback chain from falling wages and prices via rising real liquidity to falling interest rates in the financial markets via rising investment activity and from there to increasing goods demand and output of firms as well as higher employment is a long (and maybe also uncertain) one. It does not support the argument that labor market problems can be remedied by a policy that concentrates solely on the labor market. Unemployment is here due to the interdependence of real and financial markets and can thus be cured only by improving this interdependent situation through an appropriate wage income, fiscal or monetary policy, the latter maybe in conjunction with appropriate labor market and wage management policies. Hicks (1937) formulated on this basis the standard IS–LM model of the interaction of goods and financial

The Market for Long-Term Bonds

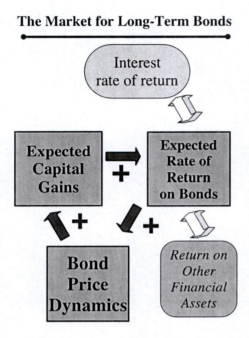

Figure 3.3 Accelerating capital gains dynamics on the market for long-term bonds (of the type $\hat{i}_l = i_l - i_o$ in the case of perfect substitutes and perfect foresight).

markets by concentrating on the interaction between output and the short-term rate of interest as described by goods and money market equilibrium curves.

On this basis, Blanchard and Fischer (1989, 10.4) add the dynamics of long-term bond prices or the long-term rate of interest as described above, coupled with a simple and stable dynamic multiplier description of the output dynamics on the market for goods. This minimal change of the conventional IS–LM equilibrium model thus allows for one real and one financial dynamic law that interact via the LM relationship between output and the short-term rate of interest. Figure 3.3 describes the bond market dynamics – and the financial accelerator they suggest – in isolation, by showing that there is a positive feedback mechanism between expected capital gains, bond price dynamics and actual capital gains, feeding back again on expected capital gains. This mechanism will be at the heart of our formulation of an alternative to the conventional jump variable technique which, in a very direct or immediate way, rests on a positive feedback of bond prices on their rate of change due to the joint assumption of perfect substitutability and myopic perfect foresight.

Rising capital gains expectations on long-term bonds drive up bond prices and thus actual capital gains which in turn lead to further increases of expected capital gains, and so on, until something in this mechanism changes to overcome this cumulative instability of bond price adjustments. In Blanchard and Fischer (1989, 10.4) we have myopic perfect foresight and thus no distinction between expected and actual capital gains. Furthermore, rates of return, i.e., in the case of long-term bonds the interest rate of return plus capital gains, and the short-term rate of interest (for fixed-price bonds), are equalized in their approach by way of the assumption that all interest-bearing assets are perfect substitutes. In our view this makes the above feedback mechanism even more forceful, by creating a law of motion that – in contrast to the dynamic multiplier – is characterized by centrifugal (instead of centripetal) forces around the asset markets equilibrium curve. Coupling this law of motion with a stable dynamic multiplier process, however, implies that there exists a one-dimensional stable manifold in the output–bond price phase space which leads output and bond prices back to their steady-state values when asset markets overcome the financial accelerator surrounding this stable manifold and always place bond prices on this stable manifold by way of discontinuous bond price adjustments. This method, the so-called jump variable technique, will be considered in Section 3.3, while alternatives to this methodology are investigated in Section 3.4.

We summarize in Figure 3.4 the considered enlargement of the Keynesian basic market hierarchy of Figure 3.1 by means of the Keynes effect of changing output $\dot{Y}$ on the short-term interest rate i (equal to the real rate, r, since the price level is constant) and the financial markets, the financial accelerator process on the market for long-term bonds and the new view on investment behavior employed in Blanchard and Fischer (1989, 10.4).[5] Note with respect to this figure that it makes use of the dynamic multiplier process, and not of a full Metzlerian inventory adjustment process. This implies monotonic convergence in the real part of the economy instead of the possibility of Metzlerian inventory cycles, and thus simplifies or trivializes the real part of the economy considerably. This may be an adequate approximation in the first investigation of the role and treatment of the (local) financial accelerator mechanism and of the question of how such mechanisms are prevented from totally destabilizing the economy. The model of this chapter provides in this respect the simplest conceivable situation that allows the study of the financial accelerator mechanism while nevertheless allowing for economic viability in various ways from the local or global perspective.

We conclude this introductory presentation of the macrodynamics of financial markets characterized by an accelerating interaction between expectations and actual outcomes with a distinction between the results obtained by applying the jump variable technique to a stable and an unstable steady-state position. The method typically applied in models of the type considered is the coupling of a stable dynamic multiplier process with an unstable bond price adjustment rule and the treatment of the resulting saddlepoint situation by way of a globally

---

5 Note in comparison to Figure 3.1 that we are now using the simpler dynamic multiplier mechanism in place of a fully-fledged Metzlerian sales–inventory adjustment process as a model of gradual output adjustment on the market for goods.

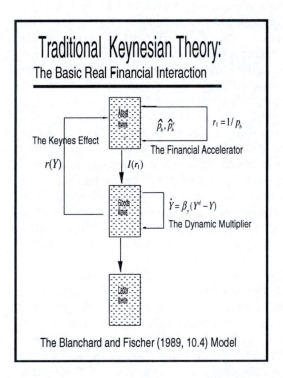

Figure 3.4 Real–financial interaction: destabilizing long-term bond price dynamics and stabilizing dynamic multiplier adjustments?

motivated jump variable technique. However, there may exist situations which are locally of this type, but which lead to different behavior when the economy departs significantly from its unstable steady-state position. It is therefore the intent of this chapter to provide at least some first steps towards alternative solutions on the same level of modelling, i.e., in a deterministic setup with laws of motion that are represented by differential equations.

3.2 The model

Let us start the presentation of the model by introducing the notation we employ.[6]

---

6 The discussion that follows parallels the one we have conducted in the case of the stock market in Chapter 2. It is – with respect to the application of the jump variable technique – considerably simpler than the one where the IS and LM curves were derived with respect to Tobin's q instead of the long-term rate of interest of the present chapter.

3.2.1 Notation

The following subsections provide the variables, the parameters and the mathematical notation we shall use in our reformulation of the Blanchard and Fischer (1989, 10.4) model of real–financial interaction, which includes the market for goods and three asset markets (money, short-term bonds and long-term bonds).

Variables

The variables of the model are as follows:

Y	Output
Y^d	Aggregate demand
i	Short-term interest rate
p_b	Price of long-term bonds (consols)
$i_l = 1/p_b$	Long-term interest rate

Parameters

The parameters of the model are as follows:[7]

B_l	Number of long-term bonds (consols)
M	Money supply
a_x, b_x, c_x	Parameters of process x
β_x	Adjustment speeds of process x
$p = 1$	Price level
$\pi^e = 0$	Inflationary expectations

Mathematical notation

We shall make use of the following mathematical notation:

$\dot{x}$	time derivative of x
$\hat{x} = \dot{x}/x$	growth rate of x
f_x, f_1	partial derivatives of f
$\varepsilon_{f,x}$	elasticity of f w.r.t. x (always positive by convention)

3.2.2 The equations of the model

The equations of the model are subdivided into algebraic (static) ones and dynamic ones, determining the statically and dynamically endogenous variables of the model.

---

7 c_x are constants that can be signed arbitrarily. All other constants are always assumed as positive.

Static equations

This block of the model exhibits a simple aggregate demand function Y^d which assumes that this demand depends positively on output Y (with a marginal propensity to spend of less than one) and negatively on the long-term rate of interest.[8] The influence of i_l on Y^d can be based on investment (as well as consumption) behavior, since it impacts on the borrowing costs of firms (who mostly borrow long). In addition, we make use of an inverted linear equation for money market equilibrium, as in Blanchard (1981), but here without the partial use of logarithms $\ln M$ and $\ln p$ ($p = 1$ in this chapter). Note that this money demand function can easily be replaced by that of Blanchard (1981) or by a loglinear Cagan-type demand function without much change in the implied results.

$$Y^d = a_y Y - b_y i_l + c_y, \ a_y \in (0, 1), c_y > 0$$

$$i = a_m Y - b_m M + c_m$$

All parameters are assumed to be positive which, in the case of the parameter c_m, can be justified by means of a simple linear form of the money demand equation. This latter assumption is made for simplicity and is not really needed in the following.

Dynamic equations

The dynamic variables are output and long-term bond prices. Output adjustment is based on the simple textbook dynamic multiplier story as simplification of the Metzlerian inventory adjustment process briefly considered in the introduction. In addition, short-term and long-term bonds are assumed to be perfect substitutes with perfect foresight on capital gains, i.e., the interest rate of return on short-term bonds and the interest rate of return on long-term bonds, augmented by actual capital gains on such bonds, must be equal.[9]

$$\dot{Y} = \beta_y \left(Y^d - Y \right)$$

$$\frac{1}{p_b} + \hat{p}_b = \frac{B_l + \dot{p}_b B_l}{p_b B_l} = i \quad \text{or} \quad i_l - \hat{i}_l = i \quad [i_l = 1/p_b]$$

These equations define a two-dimensional system of autonomous differential equations in the state variables Y, i_l which is by and large of the same type as the one considered in Blanchard and Fischer (1989, 10.4).

---

8 Note that c_y can be seen as being composed of autonomous investment including capital stock replacement, autonomous consumption and government expenditure diminished by taxation effects resulting from the definition of disposable income. Assuming $c_y > 0$ can therefore be justified from the empirical perspective.

9 Note that Blanchard and Fischer (1989, 10.4) express these formulae in a different way. in particular in terms of real magnitudes.

3.3 Instability and the jump variable technique

3.3.1 Reduced-form dynamics

The model of this section can be easily expressed as a 2D autonomous differential equations system in the variables output Y and long-term interest i_l as follows.[10] We choose the interest rate to represent bond market and bond price dynamics in order to stay close to the presentation of Blanchard and Fischer (1989, 10.4) of the interaction of output and bond market dynamics.

$$\dot{Y} = \beta_y((a_y - 1)Y - b_y i_l + c_y), \quad a_y - 1 < 0 \tag{3.1}$$

$$\hat{i}_l = i_l - (a_m Y - b_m M + c_m) \quad \text{or:} \quad \dot{i}_l = (i_l - (a_m Y - b_m M + c_m))i_l \tag{3.2}$$

The second law of motion is nonlinear solely because it makes use of a growth rate in place of a time derivative on its left-hand side which, however, will imply the existence of a second-steady-state solution to be considered later on. There is thus a natural or intrinsic nonlinearity involved in the interaction of real and financial markets of the simplest type possible.[11] The economically meaningful part of the phase space of these dynamics is the positive orthant of IR^2.

3.3.2 The IS curve: $\dot{Y} = 0$

Setting the first law of motion equal to zero and solving for Y gives the goods market equilibrium representation or $\dot{Y} = 0$ isocline of the model represented in Figure 3.5. This IS curve is attracting with regard to output levels, since the marginal propensity to spend has been assumed to be less than one. All output positions off the IS curve are therefore attracted by this curve (long-term interest being given), as indicated by the horizontal arrows in Figure 3.5. Note again that the IS curve is no longer situated in the (Y, i) phase space, as in the textbook approaches to IS–LM analysis, but depends on the relation between Y and the interest rate for long-term bonds. This curve will shift or rotate in the usual way when its parameters – representing fiscal policy, propensities to spend and to invest – are increased or decreased.

---

10 We stress that the financial part of the present model – and its modification later on – is only superficially simpler than the related share price dynamics treated in Blanchard (1981). Indeed, it can be shown that the delayed adjustment of capital gains and expectations about them, to be considered below, is formally equivalent to the one on the market for stocks if appropriately transformed; see Chiarella et al. (2003b) in this regard. Note, however, that the two approaches differ in their complexity when coupled with real output dynamics.

11 Other macro factors than the above mentioned (output and money supply) may also have an impact on the yield on long-term bonds; see Diebold et al. (2004).

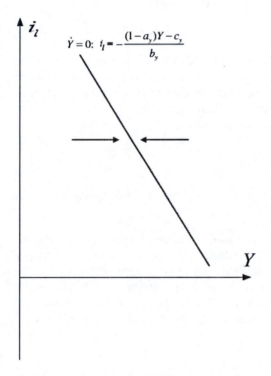

Figure 3.5 An attracting IS curve (representing goods market equilibrium).

3.3.3 An extended LM curve: $\dot{i}_l = 0$

Similarly, setting the second law of motion to rest ($= 0$) gives us the extended LM curve or stationary asset markets equilibrium curve of the model. Along this curve we have that the money market is in equilibrium, as are both of the considered bond markets. This holds everywhere in the phase plane shown. Moreover, the long-term bonds is in its long-run equilibrium, in the sense that there are no more changing bond prices p_b along this curve.[12] A static equality then holds between the interest rate of return on long-term bonds and the rate of interest on short-term bonds. Note that positions off the LM curve tend away from this curve, as indicated by the vertical arrows in Figure 3.6; i.e., long-term bond prices and the interest rate they represent are subject to centrifugal, accelerating or decelerating forces off the $\dot{i}_l = 0$ isocline. The composite dynamics will therefore be characterized by saddlepoint dynamics, as will be shown below. The present asset market characterization in its integration with the real dynamics on the market for goods is

---

12 Due to the assumption of perfect substitution there is short-run asset market equilibrium everywhere in the economically meaningful part of the phase plane.

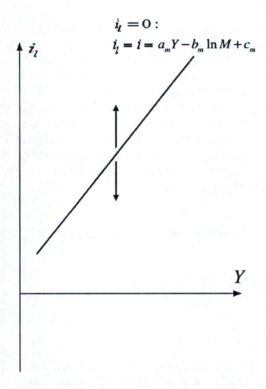

$\dot{i_l} = 0:$

$i_l = i = a_m Y - b_m \ln M + c_m$

$\dot{i_l}$

Y

Figure 3.6 A repelling LM curve (representing money market and stationary long-term bond market equilibrium).

much simpler in its structure than the one considered in Blanchard (1981), where the stock market plays the role of the long-term bonds considered here and where there are two opposing (yet both positive) influences of output changes on the returns on short- and long-term bonds.

We stress again that the LM curve represents two types of equilibria, the usual one for the short-term rate of interest and an additional one where the long-term rate has become stationary and equal to the short-term rate. It therefore describes money market equilibrium from the conventional cash management perspective (the Baumol approach to money versus short-term bond holdings) and the isocline for the perfect substitute dynamics (3.2) between long-term and short-term bonds. The conventional IS and LM curves, are in the present approach, no longer in the same diagram, since the first relies on the long-term rate and the second on the short-term rate, which however are linked together by the law of motion (3.2). Viewed as isoclines, they are therefore in the same diagram as shown in Figures 3.5 and 3.6, yet with bond price p_b and interest rate i_l dynamics off the isoclines that are always combined with a conventional short-term LM curve. These dynamics will be investigated in their details below.

3.3.4 Steady states and local stability analysis

We now investigate the steady-state positions of the dynamics (3.1) and (3.2) by means of what is shown in Figures 3.5 and 3.6. We shall find here a situation of multiple steady states, with one on the boundary of the phase plane where the long-term rate of interest, but not the short-term rate, has become zero. Note here already with respect to Figure 3.7, however, this steady state cannot be reached in finite time and that returns on both types of bonds remain equal to each other along any trajectory that approaches the boundary steady state. This second steady state, having an attracting position, therefore cannot easily be dismissed as irrelevant from the discussion of the global dynamics. Yet the jump variable technique, to be introduced below, assumes this without arguing convincingly why the attracting boundary steady state can be excluded from consideration.

Proposition 3.1:

There are exactly two steady-state solutions for the dynamics (3.1) and (3.2) which are given by:

1. $Y_o = \dfrac{b_y b_m M + c_y - b_y c_m}{b_y a_m + 1 - a_y} > 0, \quad i_{lo} = i_o = a_m Y_o - b_m M + c_m$

2. $Y_{oo} = \dfrac{c_y}{1 - a_y} > Y_o, \quad i_{loo} = 0 < i_o$

We assume that parameters are such that the first steady-state solution lies in the positive orthant of IR^2. Note that the second steady state only exists from a mathematical perspective,[13] since the long-term rate of interest is zero there (and thus also its time rate of change) but is not equal to the short-term rate of interest. Such equality is restricted to positions along the LM curve while positions below (above) it are characterized by $i_l < i$ ($i_l > i$). Note also that the dynamics must be restricted to the domain where $Y > \max\{0, (b_m M - c_m)/a_m\}$ holds true, since the short-term rate of interest can be negative for smaller values of Y. The dynamics therefore are only economically meaningful for positive output levels to the right of the intersection of the LM curve with the horizontal axis. This restriction is not operative in Figure 3.7.

Proof: Straightforward.

Remark: This multiple steady-state situation and the corresponding basins of attraction differ considerably from the case where equity financing takes the place

---

13 This need not apply to trajectories that are attracted by this steady state, which are characterized by bond price hyperinflation that just equalizes the return on long-term bonds with the short-term rate of interest. Indeed, politicians might tolerate this hyperinflation, since investment and output levels are increased thereby without imbalances in the asset markets.

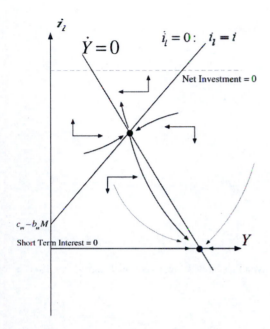

Figure 3.7 Phase portrait of the dynamics (3.1) and (3.2).

of bond financing in the investment behavior of firms. First, there may then be two interior steady-state solutions, one being a saddlepoint and the other one asymptotically stable and thus economically meaningful, with a basin of attraction that is not easy to determine. Second, in the case of equity financing there is a significant intrinsic nonlinearity present in its augmented type of LM curve. This is due to the comparison between the dividend rate of return as part of the expected total rate of return on equities with the rate of interest, both of which depend on output (see Chiarella et al. (2001) and Chiarella et al. (2003b) for details).

The Jacobian J of the dynamics reads at their economically meaningful steady state:

$$ J = \begin{pmatrix} J_{11} & J_{12} \\ J_{21} & J_{22} \end{pmatrix} = \begin{pmatrix} -(1-a_y)\beta_y & -b_y\beta_y \\ -a_m i_{lo} & i_{lo} \end{pmatrix} = \begin{pmatrix} - & - \\ - & + \end{pmatrix} $$

The dynamics are therefore of saddlepoint type, sufficiently close to this steady state (see again Figure 3.7).

At the border steady state we find instead:

$$ J = \begin{pmatrix} J_{11} & J_{12} \\ J_{21} & J_{22} \end{pmatrix} = \begin{pmatrix} -(1-a_y)\beta_y & -b_y\beta_y \\ 0 & -i_o \end{pmatrix} = \begin{pmatrix} - & - \\ 0 & - \end{pmatrix} $$

where i_{oo} denotes the short-term rate of interest vertically above (and on the LM curve) at the border steady-state value Y_{oo}. The border steady-state is therefore a stable node, as is indicated in Figure 3.7.

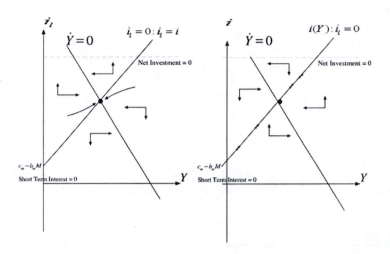

Figure 3.8 Blanchard–Fischer-type dynamics and the conventional short-term IS–LM dynamics.

3.3.5 The jump variable technique

We now proceed to the solution technique that has been established in the literature, since Sargent and Wallace's (1973) seminal contribution, for solving the instability problem (if the dynamics evolve according to predetermined initial conditions) caused by saddlepoint situations as shown in Figure 3.7. This solution technique assumes – often without any economic motivation on the descriptive macroeconomic level – that asset markets (in the situation presented) work such that the economy is always situated on the stable arms of the saddle shown in Figure 3.7. Should the economy be thrown out of that position by an unanticipated or announced policy shock, it will converge back to the interior steady state along these arms.[14] The difference between conventional IS–LM analysis and the one that is enriched by means of long-term bond price dynamics and the jump variable solution technique for overcoming the resulting instability of bond price adjustments is shown in Figure 3.8.

In order to allow for a straightforward comparison of conventional and new IS–LM wisdom we assume in the conventional dynamics (shown right) that the then attracting IS and LM curves attract with very different strengths, i.e., in the limit the conventional LM curve is often assumed to attract with infinite speed.

---

14 We stress that all our considerations apply only to descriptive approaches to macrodynamics, such as the present one, and not to model types where optimizing behavior puts the actions of economic agents onto a certain point in the phase space considered. Yet in this latter type of approach the very nature of the optimizing procedure reduces the relevant phase space to a submanifold of the full phase space and thus does not really allow the consideration of neighboring explosive dynamics as is usually the practice in macrodynamics of this type.

This means that we always have money and short-term bond market equilibrium and that adjustment towards IS–LM equilibrium is always occurring along the LM curve as shown. On the left-hand side, with long-term bonds added and dynamics of the jump variable type, we have mathematically similar convergence towards stationary IS–LM and long-term bond market equilibrium. However, this does not take place along the LM curve, but along the knife-edge curves given by the stable arms or separatrices of the new dynamics. Furthermore, the dimensionality is the Y, i_l phase space instead of the Y, i space. Nevertheless, there seems to be some similarity between the two situations. We have now included intertemporal aspects, rational model-consistent expectations and market adjustments that avoid the centrifugal, accelerating or decelerating forces off the stable arms by removing such situations from sight. The stabilizing dynamics of the multiplier process are thus coupled with the destabilizing dynamics of bond prices in such a special way that their instability is just rapid enough to allow convergence upwards or downwards towards the steady state. This is surely a very exceptional and very balanced combination of movements toward the IS curve and away from the LM curve.

Note also that conventional IS–LM analysis makes use of the short-term interest rate solely. If we modify this situation by assuming that investment depends on the long-term rate and not on the short-term rate, in line with Blanchard and Fischer (1989, 10.4), we get a situation in which the IS curve is not in the same diagram as the LM curve as far as the vertical axis is concerned. The perfect foresight or perfect substitute assumption bridges this gap and then allows us to draw the IS and LM curves in the same diagram, as shown on the left-hand side of Figure 3.8. Conventional IS–LM analysis – with i on the vertical axis – would imply convergence along the LM curve in the left-hand side figure and would delay such convergence in the right-hand side figure until the fiscal shock really occurs. This latter result is surely questionable in the case of anticipated fiscal shocks of significant size.

In situation A (Figure 3.9), an increase in the parameter c_y, i.e., an expansionary fiscal policy shock, hits the economy at time $t = 0$ and is only noticed after its execution. The jump variable technique then assumes that the dynamics considered is switched off at this moment and that unexplained, instantaneous processes move the economy vertically onto the stable arm of the new phase diagram. Through an adjustment of the variable i_l, the economy moves from the old steady state onto the new stable path after the fiscal shock has occurred. Thereafter, the dynamics of (3.1) and (3.2) sets in again and moves the economy to the new steady state. The economic consequence of such a policy shock is thus an instantaneous increase in the long-term rate of interest, without an accompanying simultaneous change in output and the short-term rate of interest Y, i. After $t = 0$, however, output and short-term interest start to move in an upward direction, since the instantaneous increase in the long-term rate has been such that a situation of excess demand is established by the fiscal expansion despite the partial crowding out of investment demand. This induces an increase in output and subsequent increases in the short-term rate until excess demand on the market for goods disappears again due to

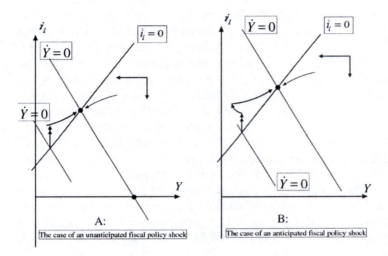

Figure 3.9 Unanticipated and anticipated expansionary fiscal policies (the latter with accelerating transitional dynamics).

a marginal propensity to spend that is assumed to be less than one and due to a further crowding out of investment demand. Note that rates of return on bonds are always equalized during this adjustment process. This also holds in the situation immediately following the shock, since the long-term rate of interest is increased up to the point where its resulting further growth rate exactly fulfills the perfect substitution condition $i_l = i + \hat{i}_l$.

In situation B (Figure 3.9), the public anticipates at time $t = 0$ that there will be an expansionary fiscal policy at some point in time $t > 0$. The dynamics and the phase diagram of the system are thus changed only at time t and remain the same from 0 to t. The assumption however is that, at the point in time where the policy actually occurs, the economy must have arrived on the stable arms of the after-shock dynamical system. This is reasoned to be due to agents' perceiving future jumps of the long-term rate of interest if they are caused by anticipated policy actions (and because they react to such a situation with arbitrarily large capital losses on long-term bonds). Despite the fact that our model assumes only myopic perfect foresight, they still anticipate the whole course of the dynamics and thus know that they will be at the new stable arm at time t. All other possibilities would create arbitrarily large future capital losses and thus unequal rates of return on long-term and short-term bonds. The problem then reduces to the determination of an increase in the long-term rate (or vertical displacement in the phase diagram) that takes the economy to a point such that it reaches exactly the stable arm of the new dynamics in the old dynamics at time t. In the situation considered presently, it is not difficult to see that the size of the vertical displacement is inversely related to the time that is needed to go from there to the stable arm of the new dynamics. Starting from size zero, we can thus find a uniquely determined jump size such that the remaining traverse just suffices to bring the economy in the old dynamics to the stable arm of the new dynamics at point t where the fiscal shock occurs.[15] The accelerating bubbles of the old phase diagram are thus used in such a way that they take the economy to the stable arm of the new dynamics exactly at that point in time where the anticipated fiscal policy actually occurs.

In the case of anticipated fiscal policy we therefore have less pronounced jumps in the not predetermined variable i_l, but on the other hand increases in this rate before the increase in aggregate demand of the expansionary fiscal policy occurs. This implies, as shown in Figure 3.9, that output will decrease due to the decrease in investment (aggregate demand) and that short-term interest rates will decrease as well until the fiscal policy comes into action. Thereafter the effects are the same as in the unanticipated case, but now starting from a lower output level. This is an interesting consequence of the application of the jump variable technique: expansionary fiscal policy – if foreseen – will be contractionary for some time due to the anticipation of increasing rates of interest. Note, finally, that there is no overshooting in the present model type (as in the Dornbusch overshooting exchange rates model, for example) due to the slope of the stable arms. For further discussions of these jump variable techniques we refer the reader to Section 10.4 in Blanchard and Fischer (1989), to Blanchard (1981) and to Turnovsky (1995).[16]

Figures 3.10 presents the monetary policy analogously to the fiscal experiments just considered. There will be no detailed explanation since the depicted adjustment processes are parallel to the ones discussed above for fiscal policy. Note that the interest rate effect in the anticipated case occurs once again at the point in time where the change in monetary policy is announced and is believed to occur. Note, furthermore, that we now also consider the occurrence of (monetary) shocks outside steady-state situations.

We conclude this discussion of the jump variable technique by the observation that the present model looks much more interesting than the conventional version of IS–LM analysis, but that it is built on dynamic assumptions which are very exceptional in nature and which are hard to justify from neighboring less perfect

---

15 This however holds only if t is small enough that even a jump size close to zero would cross the stable arm before the new policy comes into action. Otherwise there would indeed be anticipated jumps in i_l back to the stable arm at the time when the policy comes into effect. This appears to be another deficiency of the jump variable technique.

16 Blanchard (1981, p.135) himself expresses some doubts about how convincing this jump variable assumption really can be. Indeed, the current literature no longer gives any rationalization of its meaningfulness, in contrast to early contributions like the one by Sargent and Wallace (1973). There, agents considered the situation from the global perspective and then decided that all trajectories up to the stable arms had very undesirable (non-sustainability) properties, inducing them to choose this convergent path by a change in the variable of the dynamics that can be considered as non-predetermined, in this case bond prices p_b (for any given output level).

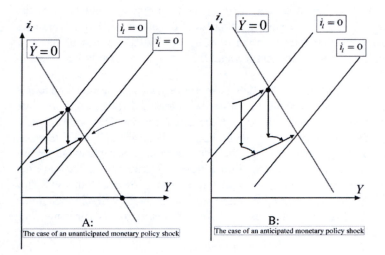

Figure 3.10 Unanticipated and anticipated expansionary monetary policies.

situations. Perfect substitution and myopic perfect foresight are just limit cases to very perfect, but not completely perfect, situations. It should therefore be possible to design adjustment and learning processes that are close to perfection and give the results obtained from the jump variable technique as a limit case of such situations. This however has not yet been proved for the type of model under investigation here.

3.3.6 Jump variable conundrums

In this subsection we briefly look into situations which question on the one hand the compellingness and on the other hand the soundness of the jump variable technique. We first investigate whether the bounded trajectory that leads the economy towards the border equilibrium Y_{oo} (see Figure 3.11) is less desirable as a law of motion of the economy than the movement along the stable arms that lead the economy to the interior steady state Y_o. The movements of the variable of our model towards the stable node Y_{oo} in time are shown in Figure 3.11.

We see in Figure 3.11 that – after a small positive money supply shock which moves the LM curve in an upward direction – the resulting dynamics without the jump variable technique would lead the economy towards the stable node, by and large just like the trajectory that is shown in Figure 3.7. We thus have increasing output, starting from the attracting output of the jump variable solution, increasing short-term and decreasing long-term interest rates, and thus an inverted yield curve type relationship. Furthermore, due to the assumed perfect substitutes and myopic perfect foresight, the difference between the two rates must be equal to the growth rate of bond prices. From the viewpoint of asset holders we thus have a bond price

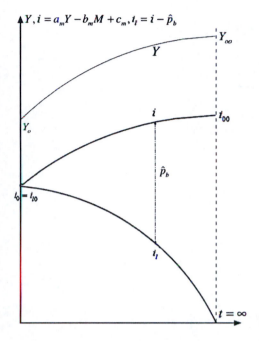

Figure 3.11 Corporate bond price rally towards border equilibrium.

rally where capital gains become more and more important and thus, finally, the sole focus of interest. In the situation considered, consumers gain from increases in their income, investors gain from cheaper credits and asset holders experience increasing wealth.

It appears as if the movement towards border equilibrium is highly desirable for the economy. This – at least to some extent – introduces some sort of indeterminacy into the considered dynamics that puts the dominance of the jump variable solution in the considered situation into doubt.

We next come to a case where such bond price rallies occur in an economy that is subject to a number of (unanticipated) contractive shocks, for example in the consumption behavior of households, which lead the economy to a very low output level. Firms are assumed to finance their investment via retained profits and long-term bonds (see the Appendix to this chapter) and thus should be considered with suspicion as the crisis deepens. Due to the jump variable solution, however, we get the situation that external financing of firms becomes cheaper as the depression deepens and asset holders become wealthier along its course, while the capital stock becomes more and more underutilized. Again, we do not see this situation – shown in Figure 3.12 – as a convincing analysis of what would actually happen in the case of several contractive shocks on the goods market.

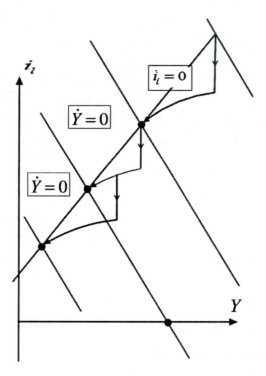

Figure 3.12 Corporate bond price rally into a deep depression.

3.4 Alternatives to the jump variable technique

In this section we extend the Blanchard bond market dynamics in order to allow, first, for (fast) adaptive expectations in the place of myopic perfect foresight and, second, for a more or less sluggish adjustment of the rate of interest and the price of long-term bonds instead of perfect asset substitutability. We show local asymptotic stability of the extended dynamics for sufficiently sluggish long-term bond prices and instability if their adjustment speeds are high. In the subsequent analysis we then concentrate on the subdynamics of the financial market and introduce two situations (relaxation oscillations and phase diagram switching) where there are meaningful limits to these subdynamics when adjustment speeds of adaptively formed expectations become infinite and thus give rise to myopic perfect foresight. Assuming myopic perfect foresight therefore need not give rise to saddlepoint dynamics if financial markets exhibit mechanisms that reduce adjustment speeds when the situation departs too much from the dynamics' fundamentals.[17]

17 Note here, however, that we do not treat the case of anticipated shocks in this section, a case where the jump variable technique remains superior to the presented alternatives, at least from the viewpoint of a rigorous mathematical treatment.

3.4.1 Reformulating the bond market dynamics

In order to obtain a starting point for alternative approaches to the treatment of myopic perfect foresight and for results that use jump variable techniques from quite different perspectives, we start here from a situation that is as simple as possible, while still allowing for behavior that can be near perfect as far as expectations are concerned. In particular, we consider fast, adaptively formed expectations and a fast adjustment of bond prices to the situation of perfect substitutes close to the steady state (plus a conventional accelerator term in this latter adjustment equation). However, far from the steady state, and for large discrepancies in rates of returns, we shall assume later that markets or agents react more cautiously or become aware of such extreme positions and thus only sluggishly continue to adjust into a direction that they believe cannot go on for much longer. This may reduce volumes of transactions and thus the speed of adjustment on the stock market, though maybe not that of capital gains expectations which indeed can remain close to perfect foresight.

To introduce these new aspects of bond market behavior that will lead us away from local instability of the saddlepoint type, we consider the following two simple revisions of the assumption of perfect substitutes and myopic perfect foresight.

$$\hat{p}_b = \beta_{p_b} \left(\frac{1}{p_b} + z - i \right) + \kappa_{p_b} z + (1 - \kappa_{p_b}) z_o, \quad i = a_m Y - b_m M + c_m \quad (3.3)$$

$$\dot{z} = \beta_z (\hat{p}_b - z), \quad z = \hat{p}_b^e, z_o = 0 \quad (3.4)$$

We thus allow for a differential in the rates of return of long-term and short-term bonds, including expected capital gains $z = \hat{p}_b^e$ on the long-term bonds, which can now differ from the actual realization of capital gains.[18] This differential drives asset demands and with them bond prices (all other things kept fixed) into the direction of a reduction of this return differential, as long as expectations remain fixed. Thus, for instance, asset demand and bond prices rise and the interest rate of return on long-term bonds decreases if the short-term rate of interest falls short of the expected rate of return $1/p_b + z$ on such bonds. Subsequently, however, expected capital gains are revised on the basis of the actual increase in bond prices, which gives further momentum to the process of increasing capital gains and so forth (see also the introduction to this chapter). Note that this process has been augmented in the usual way by additional accelerator terms based on short-term capital gain expectations (and long-term ones), giving rise to additional instability in the full interaction of actual and expected magnitudes. This term will, however, still be neglected (for reasons of simplicity) in the analysis that follows. Note finally that we have so far only analyzed the situation where

---

18 Empirically, it may be appropriate to add a risk premium to the return on long-term bonds (as a markup on the nominal rate of interest) which is, however, left aside here for simplicity.

both β_{p_b} and β_z are set equal to infinity, resulting in algebraic conditions on rates of return and expectation formation in the place of the above two laws of motion for them (of the perfect type we have discussed in Section 3 of this chapter).

With respect to the dynamics of long-term bond prices we will employ the following specification in subsequent analysis:

$$\hat{p}_b = \beta_{p_b} X \left(\frac{1}{p_b} + z - i \right)$$

where we have removed the accelerating terms as stated. We have added however – in order to be more explicit about the disequilibrium that is going to be considered – the symbol X that is supposed to represent the flow demand in or out of long-term bonds. In order to motivate this addition in more detail, consider first the following Walras Law of Stocks for the reallocation of given stocks according to changing market conditions and the flow of long-term bond demand deriving from it:

$$M + B + p_b B_l = M^d + B^d + p_b B^{ld}; \quad \dot{B}_l = \alpha \left(B^{ld} - B_l \right) = -\dot{B}$$

Depending on the return differential $\epsilon = i_l + z - i$ we here assume new stock demands $M^d, B^d; B^{ld}$ for money, short- and long-term bonds in comparison to what is given on these three markets (M, B, B_l). Actually intended changes of the stock of long-term bonds $\dot{B}_l$ are assumed to be proportional to stock excess demand $B^{ld} - B_l$ with proportionality constant α. They are of course to be balanced by corresponding changes in money and short-term bond holdings. Since stock money market equilibrium has been assumed to hold at all times, we have reduced this balancing item to short-term bonds only. This is the cash management part of portfolio consideration,s which we do reformulate here.

However, flows in and out of short-term vs. long-term bonds are assumed to be intended by the household sector, depending on the return differential that exists between these two financial assets at each moment in time (with $p_b \dot{B}_l = -\dot{B}$). The flow intended with respect to long-term bonds has been denoted by X in the above law of motion and is assumed to give rise to bond price changes $\hat{p}_b$, depending on this flow and a constant speed of adjustment β_{p_b} of these prices with respect to the imbalance X. As a whole, the household sector cannot change its holdings of bonds instantaneously, which implies that the aggregated realized flow in or out of long-term bonds must always be zero. Nevertheless, the intended flows have consequences for the asset price dynamics just described. We thus have found the law of motion for long-term bond prices though delayed adjustments – based on a portfolio view of asset markets – that will also be of use later on when nonlinearities are needed to bound the dynamics considered.

Reformulating in terms of interest rates ($i_l = 1/p_b, \hat{i}_l = -\hat{p}_b$) and adding the output dynamics of Section 3, the above dynamical extension of the model (3.1),

(3.2) gives rise now to a 3D dynamical system which reads:

$$\dot{Y} = \beta_y((a_y - 1)Y - b_y i_l + c_y), \quad a_y - 1 < 0 \tag{3.5}$$

$$\hat{i}_l = -\beta_{p_b} X(i_l - z - i) = \beta_{p_b} X(i + z - i_l), \quad i = a_m Y - b_m M + c_m \tag{3.6}$$

$$\dot{z} = \beta_z \left(\hat{i}_l - z \right), \quad z = \hat{i}_l^e = -\hat{p}_b^e \tag{3.7}$$

Note that the variable z now has a different meaning, but is not represented by a different symbol. It now expresses the expected change in the long-term rate of interest and not in the price of bonds, and is thus just the negative of the expectational variable z, that we used beforehand. Note also that we assumed the function X to be linear and thus symmetric with respect to sign changes. We refer the reader back to the introductory section for a discussion of the effects that are present in the extended dynamics (3.6) and (3.7), namely the dynamic multiplier process, the Keynes effect and a financial accelerator mechanism. The last may be tranquil in certain periods and activated or excited in others. For notational simplicity we will represent the expression $\beta_p X$ simply by β_p in the following investigation of the 3D dynamics.

The interior steady state and the one on the boundary of the positive orthant of $\mathbb{R}^3$ of this system are the same as the ones of its limit limit case $\beta_{p_b}, \beta_z = \infty$ (see proposition 1). The only difference is that the results here are augmented by $z_o = 0$ at the interior and $z_o = \beta_{p_b} r_o / (1 - \beta_{p_b})$ at the boundary steady state (where $i_l = 0$). The Jacobian J of the dynamical system at the interior and at the boundary steady state are respectively.

$$J = \begin{pmatrix} - & - & 0 \\ + & - & + \\ + & - & \beta_z(\beta_{p_b} - 1) \end{pmatrix}, \quad J = \begin{pmatrix} - & - & 0 \\ 0 & \dfrac{i_o}{1 - \beta_{p_b}} & 0 \\ + & - & \beta_z(\beta_{p_b} - 1) \end{pmatrix}$$

The determinant of the Jacobian J at the interior steady state is given by

$$|J| = \beta_{p_b} \begin{vmatrix} J_{11} & J_{12} & 0 \\ J_{21} & J_{22} & + \\ 0 & 0 & -\beta_z \end{vmatrix}$$

where the upper principal minor J_3 reads

$$J_3 = \begin{vmatrix} J_{11} & J_{12} \\ J_{21} & J_{22} \end{vmatrix} = \begin{vmatrix} - & - \\ + & - \end{vmatrix}$$

This differs from the corresponding Jacobian of the dynamics (3.1), (3.2) in that its second row is the negative of the second row of the latter Jacobian. This follows from the fact that $\hat{p}_b$ now responds negatively to $i_l - i$, whereas it was responding positively to $i_l - i$ in the Blanchard and Fischer case of perfect substitutes. In the latter situation we had $J_3 < 0$. In the present situation we consequently have $J_3 > 0$ and thus a negative value for $|J|$.

It is easy to show that the two other principal minors of J are:

$$J_1 = \begin{vmatrix} J_{22} & J_{23} \\ J_{32} & J_{33} \end{vmatrix} = \begin{vmatrix} - & + \\ 0 & - \end{vmatrix}, \quad J_2 = \begin{vmatrix} J_{11} & J_{13} \\ J_{31} & J_{33} \end{vmatrix} = \begin{vmatrix} - & 0 \\ 0 & ? \end{vmatrix}$$

respectively, both of which can be made positive (just as J_3 now). The latter, however, is positive for all adjustment speeds β_z if and only if $\beta_{p_b} < 1$ holds true. In this case the trace is also unambiguously negative.

To find whether the interior solution is asymptotically stable, we look at the Routh–Hurwitz conditions, which state that this will be the case when the coefficients $a_o = 1, a_1, a_2, a_3$[19] of the characteristic polynomial of the matrix A of partial derivatives of the above three differential equations are all positive and when, in addition, $a_1 a_2 - a_3 > 0$ holds (see Brock and Malliaris (1989, p. 75) or Gantmacher (1959) for details). We thus get *local asymptotic stability*, since $a_3 = -|J|$ is part of all positive expressions in $a_1 a_2 = (-\text{ trace } J)(J_1 + J_2 + J_3)$, implying that $b = a_1 a_2 - a_3 = (-\text{ trace } J)(J_1 + J_2 + J_3) + |J|$ must be positive, too.

Proposition 3.2:

Assume $\kappa_{p_b} = 0$ for reasons of simplicity. For the dynamics (3.5) – (3.7) the following hold:

1.   *The interior steady state of the dynamics (3.5) – (3.7) is locally asymptotically stable for all β_z if $\beta_{p_b} < 1$ holds true. This also holds for $\beta_z = \infty$, i.e., for $\hat{i}_l = z$, in which case the dynamics are only of dimension 2.*
2.   *In the case $\beta_{p_b} > 1$ (where there is a positive feedback of capital gain expectations onto themselves) local asymptotic stability gets lost at*

$$\beta_z^H < \frac{\beta_y(1 - a_y) + \beta_{p_b} i_0}{\beta_{p_b} - 1}$$

   in a cyclical fashion by way of a Hopf bifurcation.
3.   *After the loss of stability we will have one negative real eigenvalue and two with positive real parts for all $\beta_z > \beta_z^H$, i.e., there is no reswitching possible from instability back to stability.*

Proof: Assertion 3.2.1: For the trace of J we have (under the assumption $\kappa_{p_b} = 0$) the expression

$$\text{trace } J = \beta_y(a_y - 1) - \beta_{p_b} i_0 + \beta_z(\beta_{p_b} - 1)$$

which implies this assertion on the basis of what has been shown above.

---

19 $a_1 = \text{trace } A, a_2$ is the sum of principal minors of order two, $a_3 = \det A$.

Assertion 3.2.2: Note here that the Hopf bifurcation occurs exactly when $b = a_1 a_2 - a_3$ becomes zero as a function of β_z, and that this happens only once for positive values of β_z, since $b(\beta_z)$ is positive at $\beta_z = 0$ and a quadratic function of β_z with a negative parameter in front of the quadratic term in the case $\beta_{p_b} > 1$. Note furthermore that a_1 or a_2 can become zero only after b has passed through its larger root and then become negative as well. Note finally that the speed condition of the Hopf bifurcation theorem can be checked by showing that $b'\left(\beta_z^H\right) < 0$ holds, since

$$b'\left(\beta_z^H\right) = -2a'\left(\beta_z^H\right)\left[\left(\lambda_1\left(\beta_z^H\right)\right)^2 + c\left(\beta_z^H\right)^2\right]$$

holds for the three roots $\lambda_1, \lambda_{2,3} = a \pm ci$ of the characteristic polynomial of the Jacobian close to the Hopf bifurcation point $b'\left(\beta_z^H\right)$, due to Orlando's formula (see Gantmacher (1959) and Benhabib and Miyao (1981) for further details on such arguments).

Assertion 3.2.3: In the situation considered, where $\det J < 0$ always holds, we have that one eigenvalue must remain negative, since only pairs of eigenvalues can cross the imaginary axis of the complex plain (they cannot cross through zero). Once eigenvalues have crossed this axis (at $\beta_z = \beta_z^H$) they must stay to its right, since we have already shown that b remains negative for all larger β_z.

The Blanchard and Fischer type steady state is thus now attracting for adaptive expectations that adjust sufficiently slowly and, more importantly, for all such adjustment speeds if the adjustment speed on the market for long-term bonds is less than one.[20] Note here, however, that the dynamics are nearly linear, with only one linear growth law of motion as the sole nonlinearity (concerning the evolution of i_l). We therefore expect that the considered Hopf bifurcation will be of degenerate or center type, where no isolated limit cycles can be obtained. Furthermore, the locally asymptotically stable situation should also be (neglecting the possibility of negative output levels) globally asymptotically stable in the part of $\mathbb{R}^3$ where $i_l > 0$ holds, due to the nature of the involved weak nonlinearity. On the other hand, the dynamics should have no economically meaningful attractor in the locally divergent case. A switch in the adjustment speed on the market for long-term bonds from below one to above one (and back to below one) should therefore imply a switch from global convergence to global divergence (and back to global convergence). Such situations will be investigated and proved in Subsection 3.4.3 for the subdynamics of the market for long-term bonds, where the values of Y, i are frozen at their steady-state values. This suggests that the globally stable subdynamics of the real

---

20 Note that global statements in the convergent case demand the investigation of conditions that can guarantee $Y > 0$ along the trajectories of the dynamics.

part of the economy in its shaping of the overall dynamics are still of a very secondary nature and should be replaced by a real theory of the business cycle in order to provide a more interesting approach to the real–financial interaction studied in Blanchard (1981), Blanchard and Fischer (1989) and in the present chapter.

So far we could only make local statements due to the 3D dimensionality of the considered dynamics. Let us therefore briefly consider the case $\beta_z = \infty$ in the case where $\beta_{p_b} < 1$ holds. We now get the dynamics

$$\dot{Y} = \beta_y((a_y - 1)Y - b_y i_l + c_y), \quad a_y - 1 < 0 \tag{3.8}$$

$$\hat{i}_l = \frac{\beta_{p_b}}{1 - \beta_{p_b}}(a_m Y - b_m M + c_m - i_l) \tag{3.9}$$

These dynamics differ from the Blanchard and Fischer dynamics (3.1) and (3.2) by the factor $\beta_{p_b}(1 - \beta_{p_b})$ and a sign reversal in the second law of motion, while there is no change in the steady-state positions. Depending on adjustment speeds on the market for long-term bonds, we thus can have convergent dynamics for $1 - \beta_{p_b} > 0$, but will get saddlepoint dynamics of the Blanchard and Fischer type for the opposite case $1 - \beta_{p_b} < 0$. This confirms what has already been asserted above (in proposition 2.2). Note that the above statements hold globally for the economical part of the 2D Y, i_l phase space, which is easily depicted in the two situations considered.

3.4.2 Towards a global analysis of bond market dynamics

We now apply the situation of relaxation oscillation, laid out in the Appendix of Chapter 3 for the foreign exchange market, to the market for long-term bonds and its type of capital gains expectations. We will obtain similar conclusions and also look into their integration with the real dynamics, before we come to an alternative situation that allows us to tame the locally centrifugal dynamics of long-term bond prices.

In order to investigate the case $1 < \beta_{p_b}$ and the divergent situation it gives rise to in closer detail, we now disregard output adjustment and thus study the possibly destabilizing financial accelerator on the market for long-term bonds in isolation, i.e., the following 2D dynamical system:[21]

$$\hat{i}_l = \beta_{p_b}(i + z - i_l), \quad i = a_m Y_o - b_m M + c_m \tag{3.10}$$

$$\dot{z} = \beta_z\left(\hat{i}_l - z\right), \quad z = \hat{i}_l^e \tag{3.11}$$

---

21 The short-term rate of interest now acts as a fixed anchor for the long-term bonds dynamics.

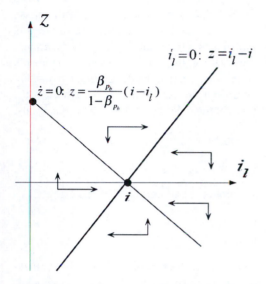

Figure 3.13 A tamed financial accelerator due to tranquil bond market adjustment.

keeping Y fixed at its steady-state value (or any other value).[22] In the convergent case, $\beta_{p_b} < 1$, we have the phase diagram for these reduced dynamics that is shown in Figure 3.13. In this situation we always have convergence to the interior steady state, which may be cyclical or monotone. There is a further steady state on the vertical axis (also indicated by a dark circle) which is of the saddlepoint type and attracting along the vertical axis. If β_z is made very large for β_{p_b} significantly below 1 (and in the limit infinitely large), we will have movement that rapidly approaches the $\dot{z} = 0$ isocline (always proceeding along this line towards the interior steady state) and thus cannot have cycles. Convergent cyclical behavior will occur, however, if the adjustment speed of the long-term interest rate approaches (or is equal to) 1 and the parameter β_z is chosen sufficiently large. In addition, the following proposition shows that the considered dynamics are always convergent in the right half-plane of $\mathbb{R}^2$.

Proposition 3.3:
Assume $\beta_{p_b} < 1$. The interior steady state $(i, 0)$ of the dynamics (3.10)–(3.11) is globally asymptotically stable in $\mathbb{R}^2_+$, i.e., all trajectories which start at a positive long-term rate of interest will converge to this steady state.

---

22 In their original notation these dynamics would read:
$$\hat{p}_b = \beta_{p_b}(i_l + z - i), \quad i = a_m Y_o - b_m M + c_m$$
$$\dot{z} = \beta_z(\hat{p}_b - z), \quad z = \hat{p}_b^e.$$

Note again that the variable z has a different meaning in this representation of the dynamics.

Proof: We show the assertion of the proposition by means of the variable transformation $i_l = \ln x, \dot{x} = \hat{i}_l$, which redefines the economic part of the phase space (the right plane of $\mathbb{R}^2$) as $\mathbb{R}^2$ and allows for the application of Olech's theorem, which is a theorem on the global asymptotic stability of a 2D dynamical system defined on the whole $\mathbb{R}^2$. In order to get this stability result from Olech's theorem one has to show that the trace is negative, that the determinant is positive and that one of its defining products is always unequal to zero in the whole phase space.[23] In the present situation we have for the redefined dynamics the equations:

$$\dot{x} = \beta_{p_b}(i + z - \ln x), \quad i = a_m Y_o - b_m M + c_m \tag{3.12}$$

$$\dot{z} = \beta_z(\beta_{p_b}(i + z - \ln x) - z) \tag{3.13}$$

These differential equations imply as Jacobian at all points of R^2 the expression:

$$J = \begin{pmatrix} -\beta_{p_b}/x & \beta_{p_b} \\ -\beta_z\beta_{p_b}/x & \beta_z(\beta_{p_b} - 1) \end{pmatrix}$$

This expression shows that trace J is always negative (for $\beta_{p_b} < 1$), the determinant of this matrix is always positive and there is no switch of sign in the diagonal or off-diagonal product in the assumed situation. □

Tranquil bond markets ($\beta_{p_b} < 1$) thus allow for the strong assertion of global convergence of the dynamics to the interior steady state for all initial situations of z and all positive long-term rates of interest i_l. This proposition is important since it implies that all movements away from the steady state can be tamed and again made convergent towards the steady state without violating boundary conditions if the adjustment speed of bonds prices p_b returns to a value below one that is far off the steady state.

Let us now investigate the opposite case where $\beta_{p_b} > 1$ is assumed to hold. In this case we will still have convergence to the interior steady state if capital gains expectations are sufficiently sluggish. This is again due to the Hopf bifurcation theorem according to which we find here, as a special case of the preceding subsection, that local stability must prevail if

$$\beta_z < \beta_z^H = \frac{\beta_{p_b}}{\beta_{p_b} - 1}$$

holds true. We stress that Olech's theorem can no longer be used to prove global stability in such a situation since the trace of the Jacobian shown in the above proof

---

23 See Flaschel (1984) for further details. Note again that the variable i_l has to be replaced by $\ln i_l$ first in order to give rise to a dynamical system defined on $\mathbb{R}^2$ to which Olech's theorem in its original formulation can be applied. After this variable transformation one basically has to check the conditions trace < 0, det > 0 and that no change in sign in the Jacobian under consideration takes place for all locations in $\mathbb{R}^2$.

will change its sign if x or i_l becomes sufficiently large. Furthermore, the boundary steady state exhibits now a negative $z_o = \frac{\beta_{pb}}{\beta_{pb}-1}i$ and a negative determinant, since

$$J = \begin{pmatrix} \beta_{pb}(i+z_o) & 0 \\ -\beta_z\beta_{pb} & \beta_z(\beta_{pb}-1) \end{pmatrix}$$

and since $i + z_o = 1/(\beta_{pb}-1)i < 0$ holds. This steady state is thus again of saddlepoint type, but now repelling along the vertical axis. It therefore exhibits a trajectory in the right half plane of the phase space that is converging to it and which therefore removes global asymptotic stability from the dynamics. In fact, all trajectories below the stable separatrix in the economic part of the phase space must go to minus infinity as far as the variable z is concerned.

In the case where the adjustment speed of capital gains expectations is sufficiently large (above β_z^H), the phase diagram shown in Figure 3.14 will be governed by explosive dynamics that may be cyclical or even monotonically explosive. Note however that the same phase diagram applies also in those situations where capital gains expectations are still allowing for convergence, without any qualitative change concerning the slopes of the curves shown in this diagram. In the locally divergent case, we conjecture that there will be

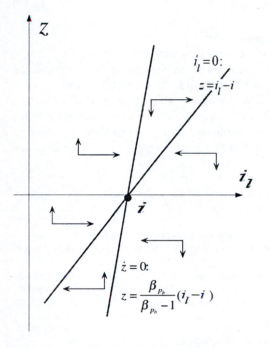

Figure 3.14 An activated financial accelerator in an excited bond market.

global divergence from the interior steady state and thus pure explosiveness of the financial accelerator mechanism investigated in this subsection.[24]

The results achieved in this subsection have prepared the ground for the discussion of two alternatives to the jump variable technique, first by means of so-called relaxation oscillations and secondly by means of switches between tranquil and accelerating financial market dynamical processes. The issue in both cases is to show how the local explosiveness of an active financial accelerator can be tamed and turned into global boundedness or economical viability of such financial adjustment mechanisms.

3.4.3 Relaxation oscillations in the financial sector

The question now is how the cases of $\beta_z > \beta_z^H$,[25] where the dynamics are explosive, can be made sense of. In order to approach this task we concentrate our investigations on the law of motion (3.6) for the moment. We thus consider now in more detail the adjustment behavior

$$\hat{i}_l = \beta_{p_b}(i + z - i_l), \quad i = a_m Y_o - b_m M + c_m \tag{3.14}$$

again by fixing i at its steady-state values i_o. Let us now reformulate the adjustment equation (3.14) in the following nonlinear form[26]

$$\hat{i}_l = \beta_{p_b}[c_0 \tanh (c_1 \varepsilon)], \quad \varepsilon = i_o + z - i_l = i_o - (i_l - z) \tag{3.15}$$

the graph of which is shown in Figure 3.15.[27]

We interpret $c_0 \tanh (c_1 \varepsilon)$ as the excess flow demand function $X(\varepsilon)$ on the market for long-term bonds (as discussed at the beginning of the preceding section[28]), with $\hat{i}_l = \beta_{p_b} X(\varepsilon)$. It is rising in the rate of excess return ε, but is nearly horizontal for large positive or negative ε while its slope at 0 is assumed to be larger than 1 (in order to have local instability of the steady state of the dynamics).[29] The nonlinearity now assumed with respect to flows in or out of long-term bonds may be due to the fact that markets expect a turn for large $\pm \varepsilon$

---

24 Note that saddlepoint dynamics come about here only when the real dynamics are integrated with the financial dynamics, i.e., in the full 3D situation.

25 $\beta_{p_b} c_0 c_1 > 1$ in the following.

26 The *tanh* specification of the nonlinearity to be considered is in fact needed only when numerical investigations of the dynamics are intended. Any function with the shape shown in Figure 3.15 would of course allow for the same derivations of global stability, etc., as well.

27 Such a diagrammatic representation can be used as in Kaldor (1940), here with multiple myopic perfect foresight equilibria and with the interest rate $i_l = 1/p_b$ as shift term, in order to get the qualitatively same type of cycle as is considered by Kaldor for the dynamic multiplier on the market for goods.

28 Representing wealth constraints, liquidity constraints or other types of constraints that reduce excess demand far off the steady state to a sufficient degree.

29 This instability holds if $\beta_{p_b} c_0 c_1 > 1$ holds true.

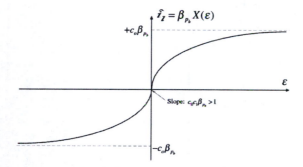

Figure 3.15 Nonlinear adjustments on the market for long-term bonds.

and thus become more and more cautious in their adjustment behavior. There may also be wealth or liquidity constraints acting on this flow excess demand that keep it bounded for large $\pm\varepsilon$ (or make it increase sufficiently slowly).

In order to study the implications of the dynamics (3.15), let us solve them in the following way by assuming perfect foresight for the time being. We then get from (3.15) the equation

$$\tanh^{-1}\left[\hat{i}_l/(\beta_{p_b}c_0)\right]/c_1 = i_0 + \hat{i}_l - i_l$$

This finally gives

$$i_l = \hat{i}_l - \tanh^{-1}\left[\hat{i}_l/(\beta_{p_b}c_0)\right]/c_1 + i_0$$

as the dynamic relationship between i_l and its rate of change $\hat{i}_l$.

The Figure 3.16[30] shows the qualitative features of this functional relationship, based on the form of $-\tanh^{-1}\left[\hat{i}_l/(\beta_{p_b}c_0)\right]/c_1$. The figure shows on the right-hand side that i_l is rising in (most of) its right-hand part and falling to the left, as indicated by the arrows. When the local maximum on the right-hand side is reached, we postulate that $\hat{i}_l$ switches to the left-hand side of the diagram at this value of i_l and thus starts falling until the local minimum is reached, where the above jump is reversed and where the dynamics thus returns to the right-hand side of the figure (as indicated by the horizontal arrows).

We thus assume that the dynamics is always capable of realizing perfect foresight situations, if necessary by a jump to a branch of the perfect foresight manifold that allows the process to be continued. This methodology of a jump variable technique based on relaxation oscillations is rationalized in Chiarella (1986) and in Flaschel and Sethi (1998).

---

30 We have drawn Figure 3.16 such that the border steady state is of no importance for the realized dynamics.

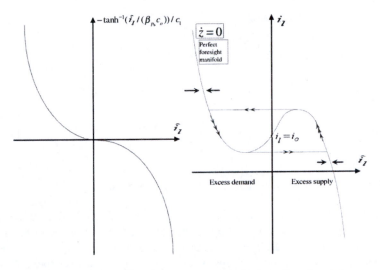

Figure 3.16 The i_l dynamics for the case of myopic perfect foresight.

To motivate these dynamics further, let us depart from the perfect foresight case and add again the law of motion for the z variable:

$$\dot{z} = \beta_z \left(\hat{i}_l - z \right)$$

The right-hand side of the Figure 3.16 then describes the $\dot{z} = 0$ isocline of this equation along which myopic perfect foresight prevails. In addition we have the $\dot{i}_l = 0$ isocline (see eq. (3.14)), which simply reads

$$i_l = i_0 + z$$

and gives a 45-degree line through the steady state of the dynamics. This gives, as phase diagram, Figure 3.17.

In Figure 3.17 we show an invariant domain of the dynamics, whose box shape is based on the form of the two isoclines of the somewhat delayed dynamics. The dynamics is trapped inside this set. Note that this statement also holds true if the $\dot{i}_l = 0$ isocline cuts the horizontal axis inside the box, since it cannot approach the horizontal line – up to the position where the boundary steady state is located. Due to the Poincaré–Bendixson theorem[31] we thus obtain that any limit set of a trajectory (to which it converges) must be a closed orbit or a persistent fluctuation, since such limit sets must be non-empty, compact (bounded and closed) and cannot contain the steady state of the dynamics (since this steady state

31 See Hirsch and Smale (1974).

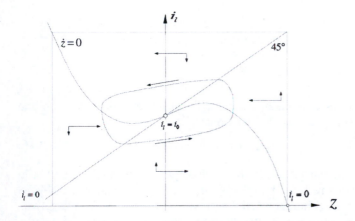

Figure 3.17 The phase portrait for fast but delayed adjustments of expectations.

was assumed to be repelling). The faster the adjustment of adaptive expectations becomes, the stronger the horizontal movement in the phase diagram shown. The closed orbit will therefore approach the limit situation of myopic perfect foresight shown in Figure 3.16, which also indicates that this closed orbit will be uniquely determined.

There is thus no longer a discontinuity involved when going from adaptive expectations to myopic perfect foresight, as is the case for the jump variable technique which is not comparable to any backward-looking learning process. In our analysis, myopic perfect foresight can be learned through adaptive behavior, which also explains the jumps needed in Figure 3.16 in order to stay on the perfect foresight manifold. The 1D dynamics constrained to the perfect foresight manifold is therefore now embedded into 2D dynamics in such a way that the jumps that occur in it can be explained economically.

It is thus easy to see that the adaptive expectations dynamics produce the dynamics of Figure 3.16 if $\beta_z \to \infty$ is assumed, since the horizontal adjustments become ever more pronounced. Letting β_z go to infinity gives rise to changes in expectations z that are always very close to actual changes $\hat{i}_l$, up to the two points where the local maxima and minima of the $\dot{z} = 0$ isocline have been reached. We conclude that the subdynamics (3.10)–(3.11) of (3.5)–(3.7) is characterized by limit (and limit limit) cycle behavior (for $\beta_z = \infty$) if the real dynamics are still fixed at their steady-state values, if $\beta_{p_b} c_0 c_1 > 1$ holds and if $\beta_z > \beta_z^H$ (sufficiently large).[32]

---

32 The proof of the existence of the attracting limit cycle shown in Figure 3.17 for all $\beta_z > \beta_z^H$ demands the application of the Poincaré–Bendixson theorem as in Chang and Smyth (1971).

3.4.4 Adding the real dynamics

Let us now integrate the real part (3.5) of the dynamics (3.5)–(3.7). We first do this by assuming goods market or IS equilibrium, i.e:

$$Y = \frac{1}{1-a_y}[-b_y i_l + c_y], \quad \beta_y = \infty$$

In this case we have as an extended definition for the excess rate of return ε, and thus for bond market dynamics, the equations:

$$\hat{i}_l = \beta_{p_b}(X(\varepsilon)), \quad \varepsilon = i + z - i_l, \quad i = a_m Y - b_m M + c_m \tag{3.16}$$

i.e., this return differential now also varies with output and the implied short-term rate of interest i. For any given $Y \in (0, \infty)$, the limit cycle dynamics considered above of course remains the same. But since $Y = [1/(1-a_y)][-b_y i_l + c_y]$, the output of firms now varies with i_l. We thus now get as the *interest rate of return* differential a function that solely depends on i_l as before, but is more complicated than the one previously considered.

$$\tilde{\varepsilon} = -(a_m Y(i_l) - b_m M + c_m - i_l)$$

We had $\tilde{\varepsilon} > 0$ in the previously considered simple situation and have this here too, since Y depends negatively on i_l. In place of the $\dot{z} = 0$ isocline of the previously considered case we thus now get $\hat{i}_l - \tanh^{-1}[\hat{i}_l/(\beta_q c_0)]/c_1 = \tilde{\varepsilon}(i_l)$ and thus $i_l = \tilde{\varepsilon}^{-1}(\hat{i}_l - \tanh^{-1}[\hat{i}_l/(\beta_q c_0)]/c_1)$. This function is of the same type as the one depicted in Figure 3.16 and thus gives rise to the same conclusions on limit and limit limit cycles that we have derived on the basis of this figure. The case of a real–financial interaction based on goods market equilibrium and myopic perfect foresight is thus of the same type as the pure financial dynamics we have considered before.

Let us now approach the general case, the dynamics (3.5)–(3.7), still for the limit case of myopic perfect foresight and also basically still from the geometrical perspective. The equations to be investigated then read

$$\dot{Y} = \beta_y((a_y - 1)Y - b_y i_l + c_y) \tag{3.17}$$

$$\hat{i}_l = \beta_{p_b}\left(a_m Y - b_m M + c_m + \hat{i}_l - i_l\right) \tag{3.18}$$

where β_{p_b} now denotes, for brevity, the function composed of tanh and the constants c_0, c_1.[33] When the second equation is solved again for the variable i_l we get:

$$\dot{Y} = \beta_y((a_y - 1)Y - b_y i_l + c_y) \tag{3.19}$$

$$i_l = \hat{i}_l - \beta_{p_b}^{-1}\left(\hat{i}_l\right) + (a_m Y - b_m M + c_m) \tag{3.20}$$

---

33 Note that this function is symmetric and fulfills $\beta_{p_b}(0) = 0$.

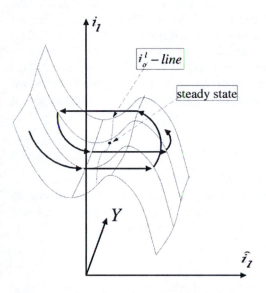

Figure 3.18 Relaxation oscillations for the 2D perfect foresight case.

Equation (3.20), for each given Y, has the shape considered in Figures 3.16 (right) and 3.17. As a function of $\hat{i}_l$, Y it implies a 3D graph as shown in Figure 3.18 which, in a straightforward way, generalizes the 2D fold of Figures 3.16 and 3.17. For any given Y we have in particular as the stationary point of eq. (3.20) the value $i_{lo} = i(Y)$, and we also know that the slope of (3.20) with respect to $\hat{i}_l$ must be positive at such points $(\hat{i}_l = 0, i_{lo})$.

Note that the full dynamics (3.5)–(3.7) should be close to the dynamics shown in Figure 3.18 for fast, but finite, adjustment speeds of adaptively formed capital gains expectations. With respect to the limit case of Figure 3.18 we can furthermore claim that the state variable Y must be rising for all $Y > 0$, $Y \approx 0$, if i_l is bounded from above by the depicted dynamics such that $-b_y i_l + c_y$ remains positive. Similarly, Y must be falling for all $Y > 0$, $Y \approx \infty$, since $(a_y - 1)Y$ then dominates the adjustment direction of the state variable Y, since the state variable i_l must remain between the local minima and maxima of the fold shown in Figure 3.18. The dynamics of output and the long-term interest rate are therefore bounded from below and from above by positive numbers. It is however not possible at present to say whether limit cycles and limit limit cycles will be implied by the relaxation oscillations dynamics shown or whether more complex behavior can result from the above 2D implicit form dynamics (3.19), (3.20). The only conjecture we thus can make at present is that the dynamics are viable and in particular bounded and qualitatively of the same type as the 1D relaxation oscillations considered earlier in this section, though possibly much more complicated now.

We conclude that systematically varying adjustment speeds on the market for long-term bonds can make the financial accelerator process on this market bounded and thus economically viable. The procedure used for bounding the dynamics, however, has the unwanted or at least problematic feature that the interior steady state is always surrounded by centrifugal forces that are limited far off the steady state in a still fairly mechanical way. The implied cyclical behavior will thus be much too regular, even if stochastic disturbances are added to it. This observation suggests that the derivation of alternative bounding mechanisms that treat adjustment speeds on the market for long-term bonds in a less mechanical way may be desirable.

3.4.5 Phase diagram switching

Let us now consider a second alternative to the jump variable technique: the method of switching asset market regimes or phase diagram switches. In order to present this methodology in the most simple and stylized terms possible we will assume that there holds for the adjustment speed of bond price dynamics:[34]

$$\beta_{p_b} = \beta_1 < 1, |\varepsilon| < c,$$
$$\beta_{p_b} = \beta_1 > 1, |\varepsilon| \geq c$$

where $c > 0$ is a given real number. This functional dependence of the adjustment speed of bond prices on rate of return differential is illustrated in Figure 3.19, firstly as a step function characterizing the adjustment speed parameter and secondly as a discontinuous law of motion for the long-term rate of interest i_l.

We thus assume in the following that there are only two states on the market for long-term bonds. First, a tranquil situation for large discrepancies ε in rates of return $i_l + z, i$ where cautiousness prevails (in the expectation of turning points in market behavior) and where we have convergence of returns back to their steady-state value. Second, an activated state for low discrepancies ε in rates of return where feedbacks are accelerating and where there is thus divergence away from the steady state, due to an adjustment speed of bond prices that is larger than one. There are of course many further possibilities to describe switches between convergent and divergent financial accelerator dynamics. For example, the domain of instability may not be connected to the interest rate differential ϵ, but a neighborhood of $\epsilon = 0$ may be excluded from it so that excited states happen only at a certain distance from the steady state of the dynamics.

The above assumption on the adjustment speed of long-term bond prices implies the phase diagram shown in Figure 3.20 for the resulting dynamics. This phase diagram actually consists of two separate phase diagrams, one for trajectories inside the shown strip and one for the trajectories outside it. Note with respect to the construction of the strip that it is based on 45-degree lines to the right and left, parallel to the interior 45-degree line that represents the $\dot{i}_l = 0$ isocline $z = i_l - i_o$.

---

34 A similar approach may also be applied to the speed of adjustment of capital gains expectations, which are still formed here in a much too regular way.

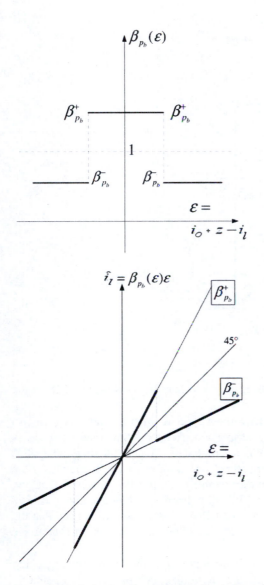

Figure 3.19 A simple adjustment speed switching mechanism.

The vertical distance to the parallel lines is given by c and $-c$, which implies that the two parallels to the considered isocline just enclose those states where the rate of return differential is smaller than c in absolute value. This follows, for example, from the fact that the upper parallel is given by the equation $z = i_l - i_o + c$. The horizontal lines closing the box from above and below are drawn such that the $\dot{z} = 0$ isocline of the divergent situation just cuts the parallels at the horizontal lines. With respect to the interior of this box Figure 3.14 is thus applicable, which

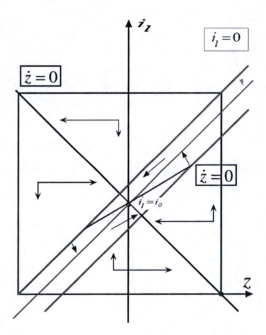

Figure 3.20 Phase diagram switching: the basic situation.

implies the depicted adjustment directions, and that the dynamics will leave the strip sooner or later.

Outside the strip, however, the convergent dynamics applies and thus gives rise to trajectories which must enter the strip again after some time interval. There is thus a switch between PD1 situations where the divergent phase diagram applies and PD2 situations where the convergent one is operative. Depending on the parameters of the model, there can thus be fairly complicated movements in and out of the illustrated strip which are difficult to handle analytically and thus have to be studied numerically.[35] Thus we only claim, but do not prove here, that the patched dynamics shown in Figure 3.20 will give rise to attracting limit cycle behavior within the invariant box, as shown.

In order to get a more precise understanding of this phase diagram switching methodology we simplify these patched phase diagrams further. We assume in particular that there is near to perfect expectations of capital gains in the convergent situation, i.e., the adjustment parameter β_z is close to infinity in the PD2 portion of the diagram. This gives rise to the situation shown in Figure 3.21. In this special case there is (nearly) vertical adjustment towards the PD2 $\dot{z} = 0$ isocline on which the dynamics are converging back to the interior steady state, by way

---

35 See Chiarella et al. (2003b) for a continuous and Chiarella et al. (2003c) for a stochastic representation of such dynamics.

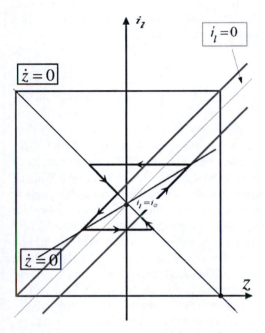

Figure 3.21 Phase diagram switching with perfect foresight in the tranquil situation.

of an upward or downward movement of the rate of interest, until the dynamics points inside the strip. When this point is reached we have convergent forces from the outside and diverging ones inside, which force the dynamics to move along the boundaries of the strip until the point is reached where these boundaries cut the $\dot{i}_l = 0$ isocline. Then, there is – as shown – another a horizontal jump back to the $\dot{z} = 0$ isocline on which convergence towards the steady state can again occur. The dynamics therefore has here generated a closed orbit – including the (nearly) infinitely horizontal movements – where phases of convergence and phases of divergence follow each other as shown in Figure 3.21.

As Figure 3.21 is drawn, we see that there are jumps to the PD2 isocline in certain situations, but not to stable separatrices as in the case of the jump variable technique, and it is not bond prices that vary, but capital gains expectations. We thus have jumps and subsequent convergence back to the steady state of quite a different type, compared to the phase diagram presentation of the jump variable methodology. In addition to this difference, convergence in this case cannot be complete, since the trajectories must enter the domain where the dynamics are explosive and where they are modified in such a way that they will leave this domain again sooner or later. Things can of course become much more complicated when the step function characterizing the adjustment speed parameter of the bond dynamics is made a continuous function with many portions above or below the critical value 1, and they become even more complicated when the real dynamics are added to the financial one and when, therefore, real–financial interaction is again considered. At present we believe that such a situation can only be studied numerically, which must however be left for future research.

3.5 Conclusions

We have reconsidered in this chapter the model of a real–financial interaction formulated by Blanchard and Fischer (1989), which extends the conventional IS–LM analysis by long-term bond market dynamics of the perfect substitute/perfect foresight type and by an output adjustment rule of the dynamic multiplier type. Blanchard and Fischer (1989) investigated these dynamics (which are basically of saddlepoint type) by means of the jump variable technique of Sargent and Wallace (1973). We have shown in this chapter, however, that there is no compelling reason that this technique must be used in order to overcome the instability of saddlepoint dynamics (by means of the assumption of saddlepoint stability). There are indeed two meaningful alternatives available when one takes into account that, on the one hand, there may be constraints on excess demand in the market for bonds that limit bond price adjustment when rate of return differentials become too large. Applying this technique to the 2D dynamics of bond prices and output, where perfect foresight but not perfect substitutes is assumed, then gives rise to bounded and economically meaningful real–financial interactions that exhibit jumps in actual (= expected) capital gains when certain boundary situations are approached.[36] On the other hand, and secondly, there may be two distinct states for asset market dynamics, periods of tranquillity and periods of hectic trading which – when coupled appropriately – also give rise to bounded dynamics with regime switches between divergence and convergence, possibly after fairly irregular intervals of time.

The alternative approaches considered are still preliminary in their analytical foundations and exhibit some problematic features that we shall attempt to overcome in future modifications of the dynamics. Relaxation oscillations, for example, imply that the trajectories of the dynamics are always (up to the jumps that occur) far, and moving away, from the steady state. Furthermore, one possible critique of the considered dynamics (for both alternatives) is that they remain much too regular and mechanistic to represent a convincing alternative to the conventional jump variable technique of the literature (with its own mechanistic features). Chiarella et al. (2003c) show how the trajectories of the model can display more realistic features when stochastic elements are added.

Summing up, in this chapter we have shown

- that adjustments in financial markets need not be plagued by local instability and an explosive accelerator under all circumstances, and

---

36 See Chiarella (1986) and Flaschel and Sethi (1998) for a detailed treatment of this approach to local saddlepoint instability and the latter reference also for the treatment of anticipated policy actions and the like.

- that there exist meaningful ways to bound the dynamics in case there is an explosive financial accelerator mechanism at work locally.

One possible avenue for future work is to look for further improvements of the alternative approaches proposed here that will allow for more irregularity in the development of bond prices than is shown in Figures 3.18, 3.20 and 3.21. Other macro factors, such as for example those in Diebold et al. (2004), may be added. The conclusion, however, is that the jump variable technique is largely hypothetical and should be abandoned as an economically meaningful solution method to saddlepoint dynamics in descriptively oriented macrodynamics with (nearly) rational expectations. This holds even more if the full range of Keynesian dynamics is allowed for, as shown in Figure 3.22, of which the present chapter has only treated the subdynamics where dynamic multiplier stability interacts with interest rate instability due to a simple financial accelerator approach.

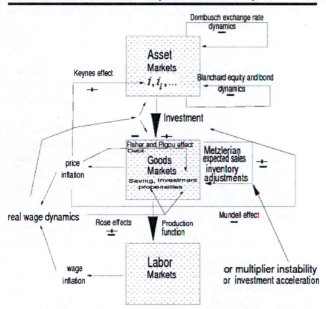

Figure 3.22 The feedback chains of Keynesian macrodynamics.

3.6 References

BENHABIB, J. and T. MIYAO (1981): Some new results on the dynamics of the generalized Tobin model. *International Economic Review*, 22, 589–596.

BLANCHARD, O. (1981): Output, the stock market, and interest rates. *American Economic Review*, 71, 132–143.

BLANCHARD, O. and S. FISCHER (1989): *Lectures on Macroeconomics*. Cambridge, MA: MIT Press.

BROCK, W.A. and A.G. MALLIARIS (1989): *Differential Equations, Stability and Chaos in Dynamic Economics*. Amsterdam: North Holland.

CHANG, W.W. and D.J. SMYTH (1971): The existence and persistence of cycles in a non-linear model: Kaldor's 1940 model re-examined. *Review of Economic Studies*, 38, 37–46.

CHIARELLA, C. (1986): Perfect foresight models and the dynamic instability problem from a higher viewpoint, *Economic Modeling*, 3, 283–292.

CHIARELLA, C., P. FLASCHEL, R. FRANKE and W. SEMMLER (2001): Output, interest and the stock market, an alternative to the jump-variable technique. *Bulletin of the Czech Econometric Society*, 13, 1–30.

CHIARELLA, C., P. FLASCHEL, R. FRANKE and W. SEMMLER (2003a): Real–financial interaction: Implications of budget equations and capital accumulation. School of Finance and Economics, UTS working paper No. 127.

CHIARELLA, C., P. FLASCHEL, and W. SEMMLER (2003b): Real–financial interaction. A reconsideration of the Blanchard model with a state-of-market dependent reaction coefficient. In: W. Barnett, C. Deissenberg and G. Feichtinger (Eds): *Economic Complexity: Nonlinear Dynamics, Multi-Agents Economies, and Learning*. ISETE Series 14. Amsterdam: Elsevier.

CHIARELLA, C., P. FLASCHEL, W. SEMMLER and P. ZHU (2003c): A stochastic Blanchard model with a state-of-market dependent reaction coefficient. *Proceedings of the IFAC Symposium on Modeling and Control of Economic Systems*, Klagenfurt. Pergamon Press.

DIEBOLD, F., G. RUDEBUSCH and S. ARUOBA (2004): The macroeconomy and the yield curve: A dynamic latent factor approach. Manuscript: University of Pennsylvania.

FLASCHEL, P. (1984): Some stability properties of Goodwin's growth cycle model. *Zeitschrift für Nationalökonomie*, 44, 63–69.

FLASCHEL, P. and R. SETHI (1999): Stability in models of money and perfect foresight: Implications of nonlinearity. *Economic Modeling*, 16, 221–233.

GANTMACHER, F.R. (1959): *Applications of the Theory of Matrices*. New York: Interscience Publishers.

HICKS, J. (1937): Mr. Keynes and the 'Classics': A suggested interpretation. *Econometrica*, 5, 147–159.

HIRSCH, M.W. and S. SMALE (1974): *Differential Equations, Dynamical Systems, and Linear Algebra*. New York: Academic Press.

KALDOR, N. (1940): A model of the trade cycle. *Economic Journal*, 50, 78–92.

KEYNES, J.M. (1936): *The General Theory of Employment, Interest and Money*. New York: Macmillan.

SARGENT, T. and N. WALLACE (1973): The stability of models of money and growth with perfect foresight. *Econometrica*, 41, 1043–1048.

TURNOVSKY, S.J. (1995): *Methods of Macroeconomic Dynamics*. Cambridge, MA: MIT Press.

3.7 Appendix: Budget equations

We have considered in this chapter a model consisting of three sectors and four markets: one real and three financial ones (money and short- as well as long-term bonds). We have three markets for the stocks in financial assets traded within the household sector. Intended flows in and out of these stocks have implicitly been the basis for the adjustment process concerning long-term bond prices, whereas money has been treated by way of the usual LM curve analysis. The treatment of financial markets in this chapter is thus to some extent an asymmetric one that may give way to a full portfolio approach to financial assets and markets in later studies. Here, however, we have followed the usual approach which is composed of a mixture of stock balance and (delayed) interest rate parity conditions.

The budget equations underlying the three sectors of the model can be assumed to be the following:

$$pS_p = wL^d + iB^s + B_l - pT_p - pC = \dot{M} + \dot{B}^s + p_b\dot{B}_l$$

$$pS_f = -pI = -p\dot{K} = p(Y - \delta K) - wL^d - B_l + p_b\dot{B}_l$$

$$pS_g = p(T_p - G) - iB^s = -\left(\dot{M} + \dot{B}^s\right)$$

where the S terms denote private savings, savings of firms and of the government. The latter two terms are assumed to be negative, due to investment financing and an assumed government deficit. In this chapter we distinguished between short-term and long-term bonds and we postulated in addition that only firms use long-term bonds (to finance their long-term investment decisions). The government's deficit is financed exclusively by short-term bonds and, to the extent that there are open-market operations by the central bank that increase money supply through the purchase of government bonds, there will also be money financing in the model.

Since we do not consider equities in the present model, firms will be left with retained earnings amounting to $p(Y - \delta K) - wL^d - B_l$ after deducting wages and interest payments to households from their net product. By assumption, firms do not pay taxes and finance their net investment I from retained earnings and from issuing new long-term bonds. All taxes are paid by households as deduction from their wage and interest income on short- and long-term bonds. Of course, other assumptions on and formulations of the budget equations of the three sectors are perfectly possible. The above only serves to show that the budgetary issues can already be quite detailed in the still very simple model of this chapter. Aggregating the three equations gives, of course:

$$S = S_p + S_f + S_g = Y - \delta K - C - G = I.$$

Note here, however, that we have implicit inventory changes in the model (due to the dynamic multiplier approach employed) which are neglected in the budget equations. These equations nevertheless show that there are important stock–flow relationships in the background of the investigated dynamics that should be integrated in future reconsideration of this approach to real–financial interaction on the macro level. Finally, we have so far also neglected the dynamics of prices on the real markets and thus the working of nominal rigidities concerning wage–price dynamics (delayed adjustments, NAIRU levels of full capacity utilization on both the labor and the goods market, cost-push accelerators). In the case of a stock market approach to real–financial interaction, we integrated such aspects in Chiarella et al. (2001, 2003a), a task that remains to be tackled in the context of the present chapter. Moreover, a complete model of the Blanchard (1981) and Blanchard and Fischer (1989) type should consider both equity and long-term bond financing of firms (and possibly also loans) in order to provide an elaborate dynamic model of real–financial interaction that stresses adjustment speeds on financial and real markets as the crucial elements that shape the working of such interaction.

4 Exchange rate and the macroeconomy

4.1 Introduction

Next, we introduce the basic framework for the investigation of the role of financial markets in open economies. We first study the basic version of the Dornbusch (1976) overshooting model. Then we explore the role of capital mobility and different expectations mechanisms in the context of the Dornbusch model.

4.2 Exchange rate dynamics in the IS–LM–PC model: level-form formulation

In this section we provide the basic results of the Dornbusch (1976) analysis of overshooting exchange rate dynamics and its medium- and long-run implications in the general framework of a nonlinear Keynesian IS–LM–PC model with international bond market equilibrium, represented by uncovered interest parity (UIP), and with regressive expectations of de- or appreciation of the domestic currency. The model presented is a direct generalization of the Mundell–Fleming model in the case of a flexible exchange rate regime and perfect international capital mobility. This section therefore also serves to demonstrate the close links and the distinguishing elements between one important regime of the Mundell–Fleming framework and the Dornbusch model (in an advanced form) with its sticky prices and its treatment of exchange rate expectations.

The following model is built on the Dornbusch (1976) model of overshooting exchange rates, but makes use of a standard type of Phillips curve, based on Keynesian effective demand and the resulting output gap. This replaces the law of demand used originally by Dornbusch (1976) and others to describe the sluggish adjustment of the price level that characterizes this approach to the short- and medium–run dynamics and stationary equilibrium of small open economies. Modified in this way, the model is thus of the Keynesian IS–LM–PC variety, though one with certain classical properties in its long–run behavior. The variables that this model seeks to explain are:

- the equilibrium level of output Y (and indirectly and implicitly employment L^d);
- the equilibrium nominal rate of interest i;
- the nominal exchange rate s;
- the expected rate of depreciation ϵ;
- the price level p (and again, indirectly and implicitly, that of money wages w).

These variables are determined via IS–LM equilibrium, the uncovered interest rate parity condition, regressive (or other types of) expectations on exchange rate dynamics, and a money-wage Phillips curve that can be identified with a price-level Phillips curve via markup pricing (with a constant markup and a constant labor productivity). These assumptions give rise to the following equations:

$$Y = C(Y - \delta\bar{K} - \bar{T}) + I(i) + \delta\bar{K} + \bar{G} + NX(Y, \bar{Y}^*, \sigma), \qquad (IS), \qquad (4.1)$$

$$\bar{M} = pm^d(Y, i), \qquad\qquad\qquad\qquad\qquad\qquad\qquad\quad (LM), \qquad (4.2)$$

$$\hat{p} = (\hat{w} =)\beta_w(Y/\bar{Y}), \quad \beta_w' > 0, \quad \beta_w(\bar{e}) = 0, \quad \bar{e} \in (0, 1), \qquad (PC), \qquad (4.3)$$

$$1 + i = (1 + \bar{i}^*) \cdot \frac{s^e}{s} = (1 + \bar{i}^*)(1 + \frac{s^e - s}{s}) = (1 + \bar{i}^*)(1 + \epsilon), \quad (UIP) \quad (4.4)$$

$$\epsilon = \frac{s^e - s}{s} = \beta_\epsilon(s_0/s), \quad \beta_\epsilon' > 0, \beta_\epsilon(1) = 0, \qquad\qquad (RE). \qquad (4.5)$$

For the consumption function C we assume as usual, with respect to the marginal propensity to consume, that $C' \in (0, 1)$ and for investment I that $I' < 0$ holds. Net exports NX depend negatively on the output Y of domestic firms, positively on foreign output $\bar{Y}^*$ and also positively – by way of the Marshall–Lerner conditions – on the real exchange rate $\sigma = s\bar{p}^*/p$ which gives the amount of domestic goods that have to be exchanged for one unit of the foreign commodity. With respect to the demand for real balances, it is assumed that $m_Y^d > 0, m_i^d < 0$ holds.

Equation (4.1) represents IS or goods market equilibrium,[1] equation (4.2) gives the money market equilibrium (LM) condition, whilst equation (4.3) is the money-wage Phillips curve (PC) coupled with constant markup pricing of the type

$$p = (1 + a)\frac{wL^d}{Y} = (1 + a)w/y,$$

where the markup a and labor productivity $y = Y/L^d$ are given exogenously (L^d = labor demand = actual employment). This provides the so-called PC part

---

1 Here $Y - \delta\bar{K} - \bar{T}$ is the disposable income of households ($\bar{T}$ are lump sum taxes, $\delta\bar{K}$ is depreciation).

of the model.[2] Full employment is represented by $\bar{Y} = y\bar{L}$, where $\bar{L}$ is the given labor supply. The ratio $Y/\bar{Y}$, the output gap expressed in logarithms, therefore represents the rate of employment $e = L^d/\bar{L} = Y/\bar{Y}$ and $\bar{e}$ is the NAIRU rate of employment, the non-accelerating–inflation rate of utilization (of the labor force), which satisfies $\bar{e} \in (0, 1)$.

The uncovered interest rate parity condition (UIP), equation (4.4), states that expected gross rates of return are equalized throughout the world, with the foreign discount rate $1 + \bar{i}^*$ (of the rest of the world) having a given magnitude that has to be augmented by expected currency depreciation in order to obtain the expected return on one unit of foreign financial investment (s^e being the expected exchange rate for the next point in time). Equation (4.5), finally, defines regressive expectations in the usual way since it assumes that the expected rate of change of the exchange rate is positive if the actual exchange rate s is below the steady-state exchange rate s_0 (and vice versa). For the purposes of this chapter, all the functions C, I, NX, m^d, β_w and β_ϵ can be as nonlinear as desired (however, with the sign restrictions we have assumed above).

The stationary state of model (4.1)–(4.5) is given by $\hat{p} = 0, \epsilon = 0$, which leads to steady-state values for the variables Y, i, p, s and ϵ given by:

$$Y_0 = \bar{Y}\bar{e}, i_0 = \bar{i}^*, p_0 = \bar{M}/m^d(Y_0, i_0), s = s_0, \epsilon_0 = 0.$$

Note here that the system (4.1)–(4.5) assumes that the economic agents are always informed on the actual steady-state value s_0 of the exchange rate, which is to be determined from the goods–market equation according to

$$Y_0 = C(Y_0 - \delta\bar{K} - \bar{T}) + I(i_0) + \delta\bar{K} + \bar{G} + NX(Y_0, \bar{Y}^*, \sigma_0), \quad \sigma_0 = s_0\bar{p}^*/p_0.$$

We assume that there is a unique positive solution to this equation. On the basis of the assumptions made, we therefore obtain that there is a uniquely determined and strictly positive steady-state solution for the dynamical model (4.1)–(4.5). Consider now an exogenous change in the money supply of size $d\bar{M}$. As a comparative static result, we find for this money supply shock with respect to the long-run behavior of the economy that

$$\frac{d\bar{M}}{\bar{M}} = \frac{dp_0}{p_0} = \frac{ds_0}{s_0}, \quad dY_0 = di_0 = d\epsilon_0 = 0.$$

In the situation considered we thus also get

$$d\sigma_0/\sigma_0 = ds_0/s_0 - dp_0/p_0 = 0,$$

i.e., not only is there the long-run neutrality of money, but we also get the PPP theorem in its relative form; namely that $\sigma_0 = $ const. with respect to changes

---

2 See Asada et al. (2009) for a more detailed discussion of this IS–LM–PC model of a closed economy.

in the money supply.[3] By contrast, for fiscal policy we obtain the result

$$d\bar{G} + NX_\sigma \cdot d\sigma_0 = 0 \Rightarrow \frac{d\sigma_0}{dG} = -NX_\sigma < 0,$$

i.e., expansionary fiscal policy implies reductions in the steady-state values of both σ and s, and leaves all other steady-state values unchanged.

4.3 Exchange rate dynamics in the IS–LM–PC model: loglinear analysis

In this section, we choose for simplicity an approach that is linear in logarithms. We thus base the analysis of the Dornbusch overshooting dynamics on the variables

$$\ln Y, \quad \ln p, \quad \ln s, \quad i \quad \text{and} \quad \epsilon,$$

and use a loglinear approximation of equations (4.1)–(4.5) in order to obtain explicit formulae for the two curves we used in the preceding section for the presentation of exchange rate and price level dynamics. In order to conform with the notation used in the literature, we use lower-case letters for logarithms and thus make use of y, p, s, i and ϵ in the following representation of the model (where p, s and of course y now represent the logarithms of the variables used in the preceding subsection).

4.3.1 Loglinear representation and analysis

Let us introduce loglinear representations of equations (4.1)–(4.5), in reverse order. First, equation (4.5) now assumes the form (here s is expressed as a logarithm)

$$\epsilon = \beta_\epsilon(\exp(s_0 - s)),$$

and it will be approximated by the derivative of this function at "zero" for the purposes of the following analysis, which thus leads to

$$\epsilon = \beta'_\epsilon(1)(s_0 - s) = \beta_\epsilon(s_0 - s), \tag{4.6}$$

where, for notational simplicity, we write β_ϵ to represent $\beta'_\epsilon(1)$.

Next, equation (4.4) immediately gives rise to

$$\bar{i}^* + \epsilon \approx i, \tag{4.7}$$

since $\ln(1 + x) \approx x$ for sufficiently small x (which we thus assume to hold for $\bar{i}^*, \epsilon$ and i). We will treat the relationship (4.7) as an equality in the following, and have

---

3 However, σ_0 is not equal to 1, as in the absolute form of the PPP theorem.

thus chosen another loglinear *approximation* for the subsequent reconsideration of the dynamics investigated in the preceding subsection.

With respect to equation (4.3), let us assume (through appropriate renormalization) that $\bar{e} = 1$ is the measure for non-accelerating inflation. Then we can rewrite this equation, as in the case of ϵ, as[4]

$$\dot{p} = \beta_w(\exp(y - \bar{y})) \approx \beta_w'(1)(y - \bar{y}) = \beta_w(y - \bar{y}), \tag{4.8}$$

with p and y denoting logarithms.

Again, we shall treat the approximate equation (4.8) as the valid equation for the dynamics of p in the following. Next, with respect to equation (4.2), we use the special Cagan-type money demand function

$$m^d(Y, i) = Y^\phi \exp(-\alpha_i i),$$

which in logarithmic variables leads to

$$\bar{m} - p = \phi y - \alpha_i i, \tag{4.9}$$

where $\bar{m}, p$ and y are now logarithms of the original variables. No approximation is therefore involved in this reformulation of equation (4.3). One may however argue, from the viewpoint of dimensional analysis, that only $\phi = 1$ gives a reasonable money demand equation. Since this does not limit the generality of the conclusions obtained in the following, we shall assume here $\phi = 1$ for notational simplicity.

Equation (4.1) remains to be considered. For the treatment of this equation we abstract for simplicity from tax policy ($\bar{T} = 0$), ignore depreciation ($\bar{\delta} = 0$) and normalize $\bar{Y}^*$ and $\bar{p}^*$ such that they are both equal to "one". Transformed to logarithms, equation (4.1) thus reads

$$y = \ln[C(\exp(y)) + I(i) + \exp(\bar{g}) + NX(\exp(y), \exp(s - p))],$$

where s, p, y and $\bar{g}(= \ln \bar{G})$ are now logarithms. The linear approximation to this equation is denoted by

$$y = \gamma y - \psi i + \delta(s - p) + \bar{u},$$

with $\gamma, \psi, \delta > 0$. Note here that all approximations are Taylor expansions (up to degree 1) around the steady state of equations (4.1)–(4.5), and that γ summarizes the effect of the marginal propensities to consume and to import, with $\gamma \in (0, 1)$ by assumption.

---

4 Note, that corresponding to the notation for β_ϵ, we write β_w to denote $\beta_w'(1)$.

In sum, the following loglinear approximation of the system (4.1)–(4.5), to be analyzed in the present subsection,[5] assumes the form

$$0 = (1 - \gamma)y + \psi i - \delta(s - p) - \bar{u}, \tag{4.10}$$

$$0 = \bar{m} - p - y + \alpha_i i, \tag{4.11}$$

$$\dot{p} = \beta_w(y - \bar{y}), \tag{4.12}$$

$$i = \bar{i}^* + \epsilon, \tag{4.13}$$

$$\epsilon = \beta_\epsilon(s_0 - s). \tag{4.14}$$

The system (4.10)–(4.14) is the IS–LM equilibrium, Phillips curve specification of the loglinear Dornbusch model of the literature. The steady-state position of this dynamical system is given by $s = s_0$, $\epsilon = 0$, $i_0 = \bar{i}^*$, $y_0 = \bar{y}$, $p_0 = \bar{m} - \bar{y} + \alpha_i \bar{i}^*$, where the level of s_0 is to be calculated from $(1 - \gamma)\bar{y} + \psi \bar{i}^* - \delta(s_0 - p_0) - \bar{u} = 0$, which gives $s_0 = p_0 + \frac{[(1-\gamma)\bar{y} + \psi \bar{i}^* - \bar{u}]}{\delta} = p_0 + \tilde{u}$. The proposition of the preceding section on the long-run effects of monetary supply shocks now reads $d\bar{m} = dp_0 = ds_0[dy_0, di_0, d\epsilon_0 = 0]$, which again refers to growth rates of the money supply, the price level and the nominal exchange rates, due to the logarithmic formulation that is now involved. We thus recover the neutrality of monetary shocks with respect to the price level and the level of the nominal exchange rate.

Let us again calculate the IS–LM–FE equilibrium curve EE and the $\dot{p} = 0$ curve (which includes IS–LM equilibrium). The simultaneous fulfillment of equations (4.10), (4.11), (4.13) and (4.14) implies first of all that the deviations of the variables y, i and $s(\epsilon)$ from their steady-state values are given by

$$i - i_0 = \beta_\epsilon(s_0 - s),$$

$$i - i_0 = [(p - p_0) + (y - y_0)]/\alpha_i,$$

$$y - y_0 = [-\psi(i - i_0) + \delta(s - s_0) - \delta(p - p_0)]/(1 - \gamma).$$

These last equations in turn give

$$\beta_\epsilon(s_0 - s) = (p - p_0)/\alpha_i - \psi \beta_\epsilon(s_0 - s)/[\alpha_i(1 - \gamma)]$$
$$+ \delta(s - s_0)/[\alpha_i(1 - \gamma)] - \delta(p - p_0)/[\alpha_i(1 - \gamma)],$$

which can be re-expressed as

$$\alpha_i(1 - \gamma)\beta_\epsilon(s_0 - s) + \delta(s_0 - s) + \psi \beta_\epsilon(s_0 - s) = (p - p_0)(1 - \gamma) - \delta(p - p_0),$$

---

5 One has to assume again that the reaction of net exports to real exchange rate changes is sufficiently small in order to obtain the usual positive reaction of the nominal rate of interest with respect to price level changes, since aggregate demand now depends positively on the price level p.

so that finally

$$s_0 - s = \frac{1 - \gamma - \delta}{\alpha_i(1 - \gamma)\beta_\epsilon + \delta + \psi\beta_\epsilon}(p - p_0) := \lambda(p - p_0). \tag{4.15}$$

As in the preceding subsection, we have to assume that δ (or NX_σ) is chosen sufficiently small in order to get a downward-sloping EE curve. In the original Dornbusch (1976) model this difficulty is avoided by the assumption that money demand (for transaction purposes) is based on $\bar{y}$ in place of y, which makes the above equation for $y - y_0$ (and goods market equilibrium) irrelevant for the determination of the EE curve. In this case (4.15) would simply become

$$s_0 - s = \frac{1}{\beta_\epsilon\alpha_i}(p - p_0). \tag{4.16}$$

Obviously, this is not a sensible procedure in the context of our IS–LM analysis augmented by price and exchange rate dynamics, which therefore will depend on the assumption $1 - \gamma > \delta$, in order to guarantee $\lambda > 0$ in (4.15).[6]

Let us next determine the $\dot{p} = 0$ curve (based on IS–LM equilibrium (4.10) and (4.11)). We again calculate everything as deviations from the steady state, and obtain

$$\text{LM} : i - i_0 = [(p - p_0) + (y - y_0)]/\alpha_i, \tag{4.17}$$

$$\text{IS} : y - y_0 = [-\psi(i - i_0) + \delta(s - s_0) - \delta(p - p_0)]/(1 - \gamma), \tag{4.18}$$

$$\dot{p} = 0 : y = y_0 = \bar{y}, \tag{4.19}$$

from which we calculate

$$0 = [-\psi(p - p_0)/\alpha_r + \delta(s - s_0) - \delta(p - p_0)]/(1 - \gamma),$$

i.e.,

$$s - s_0 = \left(1 + \frac{\psi}{\delta\alpha_r}\right)(p - p_0) = \frac{\delta\alpha_i + \psi}{\delta\alpha_i}(p - p_0)$$

as the positively sloped $\dot{p} = 0$ curve in the (s, p) plane, with slope less than one when viewed from the s axis (the horizontal axis).

The situation considered in the preceding section can now be represented as shown in Figure 4.1 (recall that s and p are logarithms). Figure 4.1 gives rise to the same dynamic story as was discussed in the preceding section in the general nonlinear case. This story will therefore not be repeated here. The simplified (linear) model, however, allows for various further analyses that we present next.

---

6 That is if a downward-sloping *EE* curve is desirable. Of course, this need not be the case, in particular if the model is reformulated from the global perspective of Section 5.2 and with extrinsic nonlinearities if necessary; see also the Appendix in this regard.

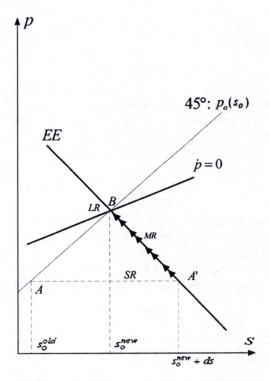

Figure 4.1 The Dornbusch diagram of overshooting exchange rates.

Let us first of all determine the extent of overshooting ds (see Figure 4.1) from equations (4.10)–(4.14). From these equations it follows for $dp = 0$ that[7]

$$0 = (1 - \gamma)dy + \psi di - \delta ds,$$
$$0 = d\bar{m} - dy + \alpha_i di,$$
$$di = -\beta_\epsilon ds,$$

which gives

$$dy = (\psi \beta_\epsilon + \delta)ds/(1 - \gamma)$$

and thus

$$d\bar{m} = [(\psi \beta_\epsilon + \gamma)/(1 - \gamma) + \alpha_i \beta_\epsilon]ds.$$

7 Note that the jump in s_0 is neglected in this calculation.

Therefore we finally calculate

$$\frac{ds}{d\bar{m}} = \frac{1-\gamma}{\beta_\epsilon(\psi + \alpha_i(1-\gamma)) + \delta}.$$ (4.20)

The overshooting of the exchange rate in the short run (over its new long-run value) is therefore the larger the lower the speed of adjustment β_ϵ of exchange rate expectations, the interest rate sensitivity of investment ψ, and the interest rate sensitivity of money demand α_i. Next, we transform the differential equation (4.12) for the dynamic variable p into a single differential equation in terms of itself. From equations (4.17) and (4.18) we obtain

$$y - y_0 = [-\psi\beta_\epsilon(s_0 - s) - \delta(s_0 - s) - \delta(p - p_0)]/(1 - \gamma)$$
$$= -\frac{\delta + \lambda(\delta + \psi\beta_\epsilon)}{1 - \gamma}(p - p_0).$$

Substitution of this last equation into the right-hand side of (4.12) yields

$$\dot{p} = \frac{\beta_w(\delta + \lambda(\delta + \psi\beta_\epsilon))}{1 - \gamma}(p_0 - p) := v(p_0 - p),$$ (4.21)

which shows that p_0 is a global attractor for the price level dynamics.

Since $s_0 - s = \lambda(p - p_0)$ and thus $\dot{s} = -\lambda\dot{p}$, we obtain the corresponding dynamics for s, namely

$$\dot{s} = v(s_0 - s).$$

We have thus demonstrated that our structural model (4.10)–(4.14) gives rise to a simple one-dimensional growth dynamics, both for price level changes and for exchange rate changes. They adjust with the same speed to the new stationary state if the system leaves the old one, for instance due to a monetary expansion.

4.3.2 Myopic perfect foresight and learning

We have shown in the preceding subsection that the growth law of motion for the exchange rate s is qualitatively of the same type as the law of motion (4.14) for the expected rate of change $\epsilon = (\dot{s}^e)$ of this rate. These laws of motion are expressed in terms of deviations from the stationary state, are both linear and, moreover, are characterized by a single adjustment parameter.

The calculations below show that the actual adjustment speed v of the exchange rate to its stationary level in fact depends nonlinearly on the adjustment speed β_ϵ of expected depreciation or appreciation. From the definition of v at equation (4.21) we calculate

$$v = \frac{\beta_w(\delta + \lambda(\delta + \psi\beta_\epsilon))}{1-\gamma}$$

$$= \frac{\beta_w}{1-\gamma}\left[\delta + \frac{\delta + \psi\beta_\epsilon)(1-\gamma-\delta)}{\alpha_i(1-\gamma)\beta_\epsilon + \delta + \psi\beta_\epsilon}\right]$$

$$= \frac{\beta_w}{1-\gamma}\left[\delta + \frac{(1-\gamma-\delta)}{\alpha_i(1-\gamma)/(\delta/\beta_\epsilon + \psi)+1}\right] = v(\beta_\epsilon),$$

where $1-\gamma-\delta$ is assumed to be positive. It is easy to see that $v(\beta_\epsilon)$ is negatively sloped and that

$$v(0) = \frac{\beta_w}{1-\gamma}[\delta + (1-\gamma-\delta)] =: \beta_w^0,$$

and

$$v(\infty) = \frac{\beta_w}{1-\gamma}\left[\delta + \frac{\psi(1-\gamma-\delta)}{\alpha_i(1-\gamma)+\psi}\right] = \beta_w^\infty$$

$$< \frac{\beta_w}{1-\gamma}[\delta + (1-\gamma-\delta)] = \beta_w.$$

The function $v(\beta_\epsilon)$ can thus be depicted as in Figure 4.2.

Figure 4.2 shows that there is exactly one positive value of the adjustment speed β_ϵ of depreciation expectations,[8] where the actual speed of adjustment v coincides with those of exchange rate expectations. Therefore, in this case perfect foresight prevails with respect to exchange rate dynamics (after a shock in the money supply, for example), i.e.,

$$\dot{s} = v(s_0 - s) = \beta_\epsilon^{MPF}(s_0 - s) = \epsilon = \dot{s}^e.$$

This is just a special value of all possible β_ϵ for which the overshooting of the short-run reaction of the exchange rate s to unanticipated money supply expansion is as determined from equation (4.20), so that

$$\frac{ds}{d\bar{m}} = \frac{1-\gamma}{\beta_\epsilon^{MPF}(\psi + \alpha_i(1-\gamma))+\delta}.$$

The result for overshooting exchange rates therefore also holds in the case of myopic perfect foresight (MPF) regarding the future evolution of the exchange rate (after the shock in the money supply has occurred).

---

8 $\beta_\epsilon^{MPF} = \beta_p(\psi + \delta\alpha_i)/2 + \sqrt{(\beta_p(\psi + \delta\alpha_i)/2)^2 + \beta_p\delta}.$

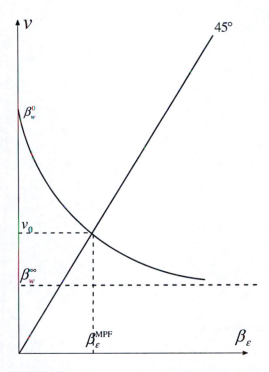

Figure 4.2 The parameter υ as a function of the adjustment speed of exchange rate expectations.

An important further property of the present model is that myopic perfect foresight need not simply be imposed on it from the outside by the economic modeler, but can in fact be learned from the dynamics it implies, as Figure 4.3 shows. It is reasonable to assume that economic agents will reduce the adjustment speed of expectations when they observe that actual adjustment is slower than expected (and vice versa). As Figure 4.3 shows, this will cause the parameter β_ϵ to converge towards β_ϵ^{MPF} and will thus lead to MPF, as considered above.

We stress that all of the calculations can be simplified considerably when Dornbusch's (1976) original money market characterization

$$\bar{m} - p = \phi\bar{y} - \alpha_i i$$

is used, where the impact of output changes on money demand is suppressed. This gives (see equation 4.20)

$$s_0 - s = \frac{1}{\beta_\epsilon \alpha_i}(p - p_0),$$

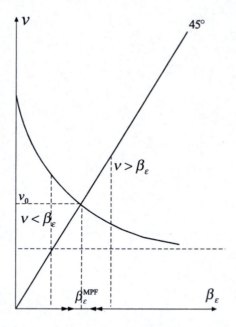

Figure 4.3 Learning the MPF parameter value of v.

which leads to

$$
\begin{aligned}
y - y_0 &= [-\psi(i - i_0) + \delta(s - s_0) - \delta(p - p_0)]/(1 - \gamma) \\
&= [-\psi\beta_\epsilon(s_0 - s) - \delta(s_0 - s) - \delta(p - p_0)]/(1 - \gamma) \\
&= -\left[(\psi\beta_\epsilon \frac{1}{\beta_\epsilon\alpha_i} + \frac{\delta}{\beta_\epsilon\alpha_i} + \delta)(p - p_0)\right]/(1 - \gamma) \\
&= -\frac{\psi\beta_\epsilon + \delta + \delta\beta\epsilon\alpha_i}{\beta_\epsilon\alpha_i(1 - \gamma)}(p - p_0) := \kappa(p_0 - p).
\end{aligned}
$$

This leaves us again with the stable dynamics

$$
\dot{p} = \beta_w\kappa(p_0 - p),
$$

with a new parameter κ as defined above, and also

$$
\begin{aligned}
\dot{s} &= \beta_w\kappa(s_0 - s) \\
&= \beta_w\frac{\psi + \delta/\beta_\epsilon + \delta\alpha_i}{\alpha_i(1 - \gamma)}(s_0 - s) = v(\beta_\epsilon)(s_0 - s).
\end{aligned}
$$

The function $v(\beta_\epsilon)$ here allows for the same considerations as in the previous case, though in a much simpler way than before.

4.3.3 Imperfect capital mobility

Let us finally consider the case of imperfect capital mobility, which may be modeled in a very simple way by writing

$$\dot{s} = \beta_s(\bar{i}^* + \epsilon - i).$$

We thus allow (expected) interest rate differentials in the world economy to play a role and assume – in the first phase of a full portfolio approach – that implicit capital flows act on the foreign exchange market in such a way that there is currency depreciation when $\bar{i}^* + \epsilon > i$ and appreciation in the opposite situation.

The dynamics are now given by two laws of motion:

$$\dot{p} = \beta_w(y - y_0),$$

$$\dot{s} = \beta_s(\bar{i}^* + \beta_\epsilon(s_0 - s) - i),$$

where y and i have to be determined from IS–LM equilibrium (4.10) and (4.1), represented in reduced form by

$$i - i_0 = [(p - p_0) + (y - y_0)]/\alpha_i,$$

$$y - y_0 = [-\psi(i - i_0) + \delta(s - s_0) - \delta(p - p_0)]/(1 - \gamma).$$

Inserting the first into the second equation gives

$$(1 + \psi/\alpha_i)(y - y_0) = [-\psi(p - p_0)/\alpha_i + \delta(s - s_0) - \delta(p - p_0)]/(1 - \gamma),$$

or

$$y - y_0 = -\frac{1}{(1 - \gamma)(1 + \psi/\alpha_i)} \cdot [(\delta + \psi/\alpha_i)(p - p_0) - \delta(s - s_0)].$$

Introducing the auxiliary variables (which transfer the steady state of the dynamics to the origin),

$$q = p - p_0, \quad f = s - s_0,$$

allows us to express the dynamics as the system of linear differential equations

$$\dot{q} = -\frac{\beta_w}{a}((\delta + \psi/\alpha_i)q - \delta f), \tag{4.22}$$

$$\dot{f} = -\beta_s\alpha_i q - \beta_s\beta_\epsilon f + \beta_s \left[\frac{\delta + \psi/\alpha_i}{a\alpha_i} q - \frac{\delta}{a\alpha_i} f \right], \quad a = \frac{1}{(1 - \gamma)(1 + \psi/\alpha_i)} \tag{4.23}$$

or in vector notation

$$\begin{pmatrix} \dot{q} \\ \dot{f} \end{pmatrix} = A \begin{pmatrix} q \\ f \end{pmatrix}, \tag{4.24}$$

with

$$\begin{pmatrix} q_0 \\ f_0 \end{pmatrix} = \begin{pmatrix} 0 \\ 0 \end{pmatrix}.$$

From equation (4.24) we calculate

$$\text{trace } A = -\frac{\beta_w}{a}(\delta + \psi/\alpha_i) - \beta_s\beta_\epsilon - \beta_s\frac{\delta}{a\alpha_i} < 0,$$

$$\det A = \frac{\beta_w}{a}(\delta + \psi/\alpha_i)\beta_s\beta_\epsilon + \frac{\beta_w}{a}\delta\beta_s\alpha_i > 0,$$

and thus have that the origin $(0,0)$ is a globally asymptotically stable point of rest of the dynamics (and as such is uniquely determined). This, of course, also implies that (s_0, p_0) is a global sink of the original $\dot{s}, \dot{p}$ dynamics.

The phase diagram of these dynamics is easily obtained from Figure 4.1 since the $\dot{p} = 0$ curve already gives one of them and the EE curve the other one ($\dot{s} = 0$). Thus from Figure 4.1 we can obtain Figure 4.4, which confirms the stability result just obtained.

Assuming now a high degree of capital mobility ($\beta_s \to \infty$) but not perfect capital mobility ($\beta_\epsilon = \infty$) gives the special case of Figure 4.4 shown in Figure 4.5.

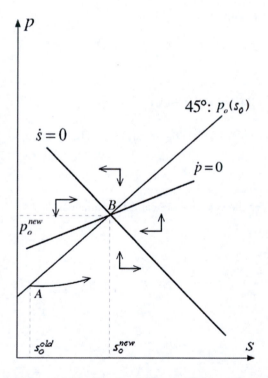

Figure 4.4 The Dornbusch diagram for imperfect capital mobility.

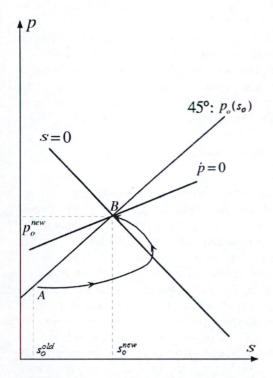

Figure 4.5 The case of high but finite capital mobility.

The obtained trajectory (after an expansionary shock $d\bar{m}$ in the money supply) is therefore close to the kinked trajectory shown in Figure 4.1 and it will approach this trajectory if β_s approaches infinity. This finding contributes to the interpretation of what occurs in Figure 4.1 since it explains the overshooting process as a dynamic adjustment process that gives rise to a rapid and monotonic appreciation of the domestic currency once the $\dot{s} = 0$ line has been crossed by the fast devaluation of s that precedes this fall in s.

There is, however, one problem with the present generalization of the IS–LM–PC–FE model. As is obvious from equation (4.23), the law of motion for $\dot{s} = \dot{f}$ is no longer of the simple form $\dot{s} = v(s_0 - s)$, but now includes the dynamic variable $q = p - p_0$ in addition to $f = s - s_0$. It is therefore no longer rational that economic agents use the forecasting rule $\epsilon = \dot{s}^e = \beta_\epsilon(s_0 - s)$, since this type of rule does not represent the law of motion of the exchange rate s that is implicitly defined by the structure of the model. Economic agents should instead use a rule of the type

$$\epsilon = \dot{s}^e = \beta_{\epsilon_1}(s_0 - s) \pm \beta_{\epsilon_2}(p - p_0), \tag{4.25}$$

and try to learn about the parameters β_{ϵ_1} and β_{ϵ_2} from the actual working of the economy. Assuming only (4.25) means that agents understand the qualitative nature of the model, but that there is still parameter uncertainty as far as quantitative exchange rate reactions are concerned.

Of course, if the way of forming expectations is revised the laws of motion (4.22), (4.23) of the model will change and will thus have to be recalculated. This will not be done in the present fairly complicated framework but will be a task for later chapters, where we investigate at length a suitable simplification of the original formulation of the Dornbusch (1976) model which allows us to summarize all the propositions of the preceding sections in a very compact form.

4.4 Rational expectations in open economy IS–LM–PC dynamics

Summarizing the results of the preceding section, we can state that the basic message of the Dornbusch model is also preserved in the case of model-consistent expectations, which were represented by myopic perfect foresight, due to the chosen deterministic framework. They were also preserved in the case of imperfect capital mobility. Excessive exchange rate volatility does not depend on the assumption that agents make systematic errors in forming their expectations, but is even present in the case when the continuous changes in the exchange rate are perfectly foreseen. Moreover, myopic perfect foresight is not just an ad hoc assumption in the present model type, but can in fact be learned by agents, for example when they employ a regressive expectations scheme and adjust the adjustment speed of this scheme in light of their observation of the current actual adjustment speed of exchange rate depreciation or appreciation towards the (known) stationary state. Such a speed of adjustment with respect to the expectational mechanism will in turn alter the actual speed of adjustment of the exchange rate, but will do this in a way that narrows the gap between them until they coincide and perfect formation of regressive expectations has been established.

We therefore find that model-consistent expectations can be established through the learning behavior of economic agents, while preserving the result that the exchange rate may exhibit an asset market-driven volatility that can be considered as posing a problem for the smooth development of international trade. This result will also hold in the investigations below which are, however, not only based on the assumption of model-consistent expectations formation as rationalized in the preceding section, but in fact on some sort of hyper-perfect foresight which not only encompasses the whole future of the economy but also makes a singular choice with respect to the perfectly foreseen time path that is actually chosen by the economic agents from the whole set of perfect foresight trajectories.

The Dornbusch loglinear IS–LM–PC exchange rate dynamics, set up from the outset with myopic perfect foresight, is represented by the following four equations:

$$y = \gamma y - \psi i + \delta(s-p) + \bar{u}, \quad \gamma < 1, \tag{4.26}$$

$$\bar{m} = p + y - \alpha_i i, \tag{4.27}$$

$$\dot{p} = \beta_w(y - \bar{y}), \tag{4.28}$$

$$\dot{s} = i - \bar{i}^*. \tag{4.29}$$

We have again the well-known IS and LM equilibrium equations (4.26) and (4.27), the Phillips curve mechanism (4.28), based on the usual output gap (but not yet expectations augmented), and finally the interest rate parity condition (4.29), here solved with respect to perfectly foreseen gains from future depreciation (or losses from future appreciation) of the domestic currency, which augment (reduce) the interest return on foreign bonds. The dynamics of the exchange rate are therefore now added to the dynamics of the price level in an independent way and driven by the interest rate differential between the domestic and the world rate of interest.

As before, the steady state of these dynamics is given by

$$y_o = \bar{y}, \quad i_o = \bar{i}^*, \quad p_o = \bar{m} + \alpha_i \bar{i} - \bar{y}, \quad s_o = p_o + (1 - \gamma)\bar{y} + \psi \bar{i}^* - \bar{u},$$

and thus uniquely determined. We will consider only deviations from these state values in the initially given dynamics (before the occurrence of any shocks) and will, for notational simplicity, continue to use the same symbols for these deviations; i.e., we apply the following variable transformation:

$$y - y_o \rightarrow y, \quad i - i_o \rightarrow i, \quad s - s_o \rightarrow s, \quad p - p_o \rightarrow p.$$

In terms of deviations from the steady state, the considered model reads (since all constants are thereby removed from the considered equations[9] and since time derivatives are the same before and after the transformation):

$$y = \gamma y - \psi i + \delta s - \delta p, \quad \gamma < 1, \tag{4.30}$$

$$0 = p + y - \alpha_i i, \tag{4.31}$$

$$\dot{p} = \beta_w y, \tag{4.32}$$

$$\dot{s} = i. \tag{4.33}$$

We consequently have to solve for the statically endogenous variables y and i as functions of the statically exogenous variables in order to get two autonomous and linear laws of motion of the dynamically endogenous variables s and p when the reduced-form equations for y and i are inserted into them. The solution to IS–LM equations is obtained by rearranging (4.30) and (4.31) to read

$$(1 - \gamma)y + \psi i = \delta s - \delta p, \tag{4.34}$$

$$-y + \alpha_i i = p, \tag{4.35}$$

---

9 By subtracting from the IS or LM equation the expressions

$$y_o = \gamma y_o - \psi i_o + \delta(s_o - p_o) + \bar{u} \text{ and } \bar{m} = p_o + y_o - \alpha_i i_o.$$

which in matrix notation becomes

$$\begin{pmatrix} 1-\gamma & \psi \\ -1 & \alpha_i \end{pmatrix} \begin{pmatrix} y \\ i \end{pmatrix} = \begin{pmatrix} \delta & -\delta \\ 0 & 1 \end{pmatrix} \begin{pmatrix} s \\ p \end{pmatrix}.$$

The solution to this last equation is given by

$$\begin{pmatrix} y \\ i \end{pmatrix} = d \begin{pmatrix} \alpha_i & -\psi \\ 1 & 1-\gamma \end{pmatrix} \begin{pmatrix} \delta & -\delta \\ 0 & 1 \end{pmatrix} \begin{pmatrix} s \\ p \end{pmatrix}, \qquad d = \frac{1}{\alpha_i(1-\gamma)+\psi}.$$

Simple matrix multiplication finally yields

$$y = d(\alpha_i\delta s - (\alpha_i\delta + \psi)p), \tag{4.36}$$

$$i = d(\delta s + (1-\gamma-\delta)p). \tag{4.37}$$

Again, as in the case of the extensive-form analysis, we have to make an assumption, namely that $1-\gamma > \delta$ holds, in order to get the same comparative static results as in the preceding section, namely $di/dp > 0$, i.e., that the Keynes effect on interest rates still dominates the interest rate lowering the negative goods-market effect of rising price levels (falling real exchange rates). The latter, of course, is not present in the case of a closed economy, where interest depends positively and unambiguously on the price level. We have therefore shown again – if the assumption just mentioned is made – that output y depends positively on the exchange rate s and negatively on the price level p, while these two state variables both act positively on the nominal rate of interest i.

Inserting these results into the two laws of motion (4.32) and (4.33) for the dynamically endogenous variables s, p finally gives

$$\dot{s} = d(\delta s + (1-\gamma-\delta)p), \tag{4.38}$$

$$\dot{p} = \beta_w d(\alpha_i\delta s - (\alpha_i\delta + \psi)p), \tag{4.39}$$

or, in matrix notation (recall that $\delta < 1-\gamma$),

$$\begin{pmatrix} \dot{s} \\ \dot{p} \end{pmatrix} = \begin{pmatrix} d\delta & d(1-\gamma-\delta) \\ \beta_w d\alpha_i\delta & -\beta_w d(\alpha_i\delta + \psi) \end{pmatrix} \begin{pmatrix} s \\ p \end{pmatrix} = \begin{pmatrix} + & + \\ + & - \end{pmatrix} \begin{pmatrix} s \\ p \end{pmatrix}.$$

Under the assumptions made, the dynamics around the steady state of the model are therefore obviously of saddlepoint type since[10]

$$\det \begin{pmatrix} + & + \\ + & - \end{pmatrix} < 0.$$

---

10 To be precise, $\det = d^2\delta\beta_w[-(\alpha_i\delta + \psi) + \alpha_i(\delta - (1-\gamma))]$.

Comparative statics may be ambiguous with respect to the nominal rate of interest, but the following analysis can also be conducted without the assumption $1 - \gamma > \delta$, since det < 0 will hold in any case.

It is easy to see (if we continue to make the assumption that $1 - \gamma > \delta$, for reasons of simplicity) that the positive root of this matrix is associated with an eigenvector x that is positively sloped in the s, p phase space. Otherwise it could be assumed to be of type $(-,+)'$ which would also imply a contradiction in the eigenvalue equation[11]

$$ Ax = \lambda x, \quad A = \begin{pmatrix} + & + \\ + & - \end{pmatrix}, \quad \lambda > 0. $$

Similarly, the negative root of this matrix is associated with an eigenvector x that is negatively sloped in the s, p phase space. Otherwise it could be assumed to be of type $(+, +)'$ which would imply a contradiction in the eigenvalue equation

$$ Ax = \lambda x, \quad A = \begin{pmatrix} + & + \\ + & - \end{pmatrix}, \quad \lambda < 0. $$

The separatrix or stable and unstable arms of the dynamics investigated are therefore of the type shown in Figure 4.6, which also implies that the $\dot{s} = 0$ and $\dot{p} = 0$ isoclines are positioned as shown in this figure (the negative slope of the $\dot{s} = 0$ isocline, for example, is obvious from the defining condition $Ax = 0$ and the sign structure of the matrix A). Furthermore, the $\dot{p} = 0$ isocline must be the same as the one shown in Figure 4.1, where this figure should be interpreted as belonging to the model-consistent parameter β_ϵ^{MPF} determined in the preceding section, since the present model consists of the same equations as the one in Section 4.3 in the case of this special parameter value. Moreover, by the same reasoning, the stable arm of the dynamics shown in Figure 4.6 must be identical to the EE curve shown in Figure 4.1. As we know from the analysis of Section 4.3, this EE curve is the decisive one for the results of the model and we will show below that this is also true for the stable arm shown in Figure 4.6. The argument will follow quite a different reasoning, however, since we now have a 2D dynamical system in place of the 1D one underlying Figure 4.1, in combination with the asset-market equilibrium curve EE.

When a shock hits the economy, its steady position (which was assumed to be zero initially by way of the above normalization of the dynamics) is displaced along the 45° line, as is obvious from the steady-state analysis at the beginning of this subsection (since $s_o = p_o + (1 - \gamma)\bar{y} + \psi\bar{i}^* - \bar{u}$ initially, before the variable transformation). After an expansionary money supply shock, for example, the

---

11 Since on the left-hand side the second element would be negative but on the right-hand side it would be positive.

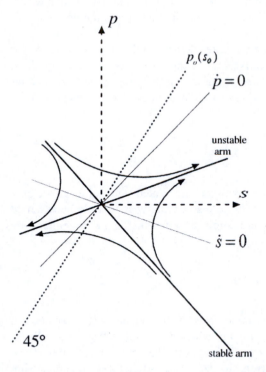

Figure 4.6 The 2D perfect foresight exchange rate dynamics.

economy is therefore in the deflationary region shown in Figure 4.7, which implies that both s and p will diverge to $-\infty$; i.e., the levels of the exchange rate and of prices will converge to zero if there is no policy intervention.

With respect to a simpler monetary model, Turnovsky (1995, p. 69) comments on such dynamic behavior:

> This rather bizarre behavior in the economy is simply a manifestation of the instability (in the traditional sense) of the economy as described by … [its laws of motion and their traditional solution, the authors].

Since Sargent and Wallace's (1973) paper and its new analysis of the dynamics of the Cagan monetary model under myopic perfect foresight it has become customary to respond to this bizarre situation in the following way. In a first step, one can surely argue that the evolution of the exchange rate – which is a very fast variable indeed – need not be constrained to move continuously in time as do so-called sluggish variables. The exchange rate may therefore be free to move discontinuously when shocks hit the economy and thus may become a variable that jumps to a new level in such a case. Such variables have been called jump variables or not predetermined variables in the literature.

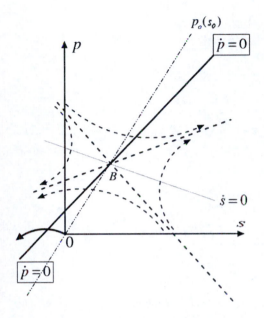

Figure 4.7 Accelerating deflation and appreciation after a positive money supply shock.

Therefore, in view of the situation shown in Figure 4.7, we are not really sure what will happen when the monetary shocks displace the phase diagram as shown.

In a second step, it is then suggested by the advocates of the so-called jump variable technique (from a pragmatic or an optimizing perspective; see Turnovsky (1995, p. 70)) that the only relevant trajectories of the dynamics are those that fulfill the side condition that neither infinite inflation nor infinite deflation will happen along them. That is, one assumes that the considered jump variable (the choice being made by the model builder) goes neither to zero nor to infinity, but remains in a compact domain that, in addition, does not include the origin. From time to time this rationalization of the jump variable is still presented in the literature, usually by some researchers who still feel a little uncomfortable with the jump variable technique and its lack of any economic underpinning; see, for example, Turnovsky (1995, pp. 75–76). The general attitude of researchers, however, is to choose the variable that is to be considered as predetermined without any justification and to assume that only solution paths that stay away from zero and infinity are the rational ones. With respect to Figure 4.7, this means that the economy is always on the stable arm immediately after the occurrence of unanticipated shocks, monetary, fiscal or otherwise.

This situation is depicted in Figure 4.8, which shows the jump from 0 to *A* and then the sluggish convergence to the new steady state *B*. The variable that makes this possible is, of course, given by the nominal exchange rate *s*, since the

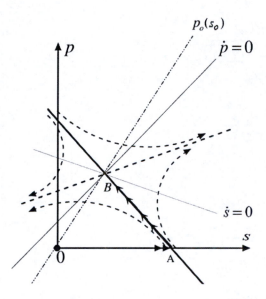

Figure 4.8 Stable adjustment to the steady state according to the jump variable
technique.

price level is a sluggish variable according to the philosophy of the Dornbusch-
type model under consideration here. Along the stable arm we have – as well
as along all other trajectories of the dynamics considered – myopic perfect
foresight as assumed by the present model. When the shock occurs, however,
the perception of the agents (and indeed the whole model) is switched off for
this very moment, since the depreciation of the domestic currency that then
occurs due to a monetary expansion does not enter the subsequent behavior
of the agents. Their only concern is that all the perfect foresight orbits of the
dynamics established after the shock – which do not stay away from zero or
infinity with respect to the not predetermined variable – must be excluded from
consideration.

The reaction of the economy to the expansionary shock is therefore as shown in
Figure 4.8 and is thus formally of the same type as the one we have discussed in
Section 4.3 in reference to Figure 4.1. The overshooting exchange rate mechanism
is now also found to apply in a world where model-consistent expectations are
assumed right from the start and are then restricted in a very strict way by choosing
from the global perspective of the whole phase diagram the one solution (if it exists
and is uniquely determined, as is here the case) where boundedness is ensured.
This approach of the so-called rational expectations school is therefore a very
special one, characterized by purely forward-looking behavior that concerns all
states in the phase diagram of the being economy investigated and that eliminates
all but one model-consistent solution from these states from further consideration.
If this approach is universally applicable, it would imply that only stable manifolds

govern the long-run evolution of actual economies and that instability is excluded by definition.

The working of the economy is therefore of shock-absorber type as far as its responses to disturbances are concerned. Persistent business fluctuations are therefore only possible if the impulses (shocks) that generate these damped responses persist over time. This approach has been called the Frisch paradigm in the literature. We note already, however, that boundedness of orbits in the above sense need not imply that they must in fact converge to the steady state of the economy. Typically, however, models of the rational expectations school are such that their deterministic part is characterized by either convergence or divergence. This is generally simply due to the fact that linear models are considered to have stable manifolds that allow for the application of the jump variable technique.[12]

One big advantage, however, of the rational expectations approach to the modeling of model-consistent expectations is the possibility it provides to discuss also the impacts of anticipated events before and after these events take place. Assume, with respect to Figures 4.7 and 4.8, that the monetary shock shown there is expected to happen in T years ($t = T$) at the current moment in time ($t = 0$). The new phase diagram therefore only applies to the situation in T years and thereafter, whereas the situation up to then is governed by the old phase diagram (see Figure 4.9).

Since agents, according to the rational expectations methodology, have perfect knowledge of the whole phase diagram before and after the shock, they enforce continuity of the time path of the state variables for all moments of time after their initial perception of the occurrence of the intended expansion in monetary policy. Otherwise, it is argued, extra capital gains would become possible if there were a foreseen jump in the exchange rate at some future point in time. Calvo (1977) discusses the possibility of the non-uniqueness of the rational expectations solution with reference to the Sargent and Wallace (1973) approach. In this respect, Turnovsky (1995, p. 75) simply states:

> The solution that resolves this difficulty is to allow the jumps to occur only at points where new information hits the economy. Jumps in the price level (here the exchange rate, P.F.) in response to such "news" are not foreseen, so that agents are unable to plan their portfolios in response to them. ... Thus the solution proposed by Sargent and Wallace of allowing the price level to jump at time zero, but requiring it to evolve continuously thereafter, is a natural one.

---

12 It is entirely possible to have nonlinear models where stable manifolds could contain limit cycles or more complex fluctuating attractors as the attracting set. In this case the rational expectations/jump variable approach could generate ongoing fluctuations without the need for persistent outside shocks.

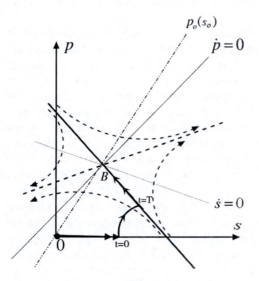

Figure 4.9 Anticipated monetary shocks, reduced depreciation, financial acceleration, and the switch back to convergence.

If we follow this solution procedure in the dynamics under present consideration, we get a jump of exchange rate at time zero (as shown in Figure 4.9) and then movement along an accelerating orbit in the old dynamics until time T, when the economy must then be on the stable arm of the new phase diagram. As is shown, there is exactly one jump and one such accelerating orbit that needs exactly T years to reach the stable arm in the new dynamics established at $t = T$. Larger jumps would imply that the accelerator process will take the economy beyond the stable arm, whereas smaller initial jumps would imply that the accelerating old dynamics will not yet have reached a position on this stable separatrix. We therefore get, from this version of rational expectations, that at the point in time when the news concerning monetary policy arrives (and is believed to be true) there occurs a jump in the exchange rate for a given price level that takes the economy into a position where the unstable forces in the old dynamics accelerate its state variables to the extent that they reach the new stable arm at exactly time T. In the case of anticipated events we therefore have to rely indeed on an unstable financial accelerator in order to bring the economy back to converge to the new steady-state position. There need not be overshooting of the exchange rate at $t = 0$, but maybe only during the time when the financial accelerator is at work.

We see again that rational expectations impose a much stricter requirement on the working of the economy than just model-consistent expectations. They in fact represent some sort of hyper-perfect foresight which makes the course of the economy heavily – if not exclusively – dependent on the beliefs of the economic agents acting on international financial markets.

There are many aspects of the application of the jump variable technique which in our view look somewhat bizarre, to say the least. Turnovsky (1995, Ch. 3) discusses basic issues of the rational expectations methodology, provides interesting examples and points to the fact that it is indeed the combination of rational expectations and continuous market clearing that creates the needed unstable roots, while stability in the traditional sense may be restored by coupling myopic perfect foresight – not rational expectations in the above purely forward-looking sense – with sluggish adjustment, for example in the money market (in the case of the Cagan inflation model).

There is a variety of further problems concerning the local (loglinear) nature of the models often used, the fact that new information will hit the economy at each moment in time, the situation that the evolution of the non-predetermined variables becomes a pure matter of beliefs (about the future evolution of the policy variable in particular), the possibility that very large T, in the case of anticipated shocks combined with small shock sizes, may create problems for the application of the jump variable technique, and so on. Some of these and further problems for the economic meaningfulness of the assumption of rational expectations (not just model-consistent expectations) are discussed in Flaschel (1993, Chs 6, 7), Flaschel et al. (1997, Chs 8, 9) and Chiarella and Flaschel (2000, Ch. 1); see also Oxley and George (1994). We want to concentrate here, however, on only one aspect, namely the usual justification for the application of the jump variable technique, that the variable under consideration should stay in a compact interval $[a, b]$ that does not contain the origin of $\Re$. This assumption, though not always sufficient, often suffices to obtain a single myopic perfect foresight path from the whole set of orbits of the dynamics which can be reached by the non-predetermined variable through a uniquely determined jump in its level (leaving all predetermined variables in place).[13] We believe that this assumption is in general insufficient to fulfill its task when loglinear approximations of macrodynamic models are replaced by their original nonlinear counterparts.

Macrodynamic models are nonlinear for a variety of reasons, from the global perspective:

- behavior may change far away from the steady state;
- behavior must change when certain floors or ceilings are reached (e.g., money demand at $i = 0$);
- there are growth rates involved in macrodynamic model building;
- some state variables will be multiplied or divided by each other by definition (example: $\sigma p = s$ for the relationship between real and nominal exchange rates, but also quantity expressions like the rate of employment);
- value expressions are the product of price terms and quantity terms (for example: interest payments of the government, the product of the number of bonds times the rate of interest);

---

13 We do not consider here the situation where there are several non-predetermined jump variables.

- certain typical functional shapes such as a production function of Cobb–
  Douglas and CES type.

We stress here once again that using logarithms of variables allows the removal of some of these nonlinearities from sight, but then at the cost that aggregate demand $Y^d = C + I + G + NX$ must be approximated as a loglinear function at the steady state of the model and can thus be applied only in the loglinear form in a certain neighborhood of the steady state (which may not be large).

In order to show that boundedness of those components of trajectories that represent non-predetermined variables is not sufficient in nonlinear situations to determine their jump position in a unique way, we consider again the situation shown in Figure 4.8, but now assume that nonlinearities in behavior are such that the dynamics exhibit a bounded invariant domain from which no trajectory can escape. Such domains are not difficult to construct in nonlinear macrodynamics, but are simply assumed to exist in order to indicate the failure of the jump variable technique to work in such an environment (the example shown is at the same time a counterexample of the application of the Poincaré–Bendixson theorem, since limit sets of trajectories do contain equilibria in this example.

In order to illustrate that the local existence of a saddlepoint does not necessarily imply unbounded global dynamics, consider the 2D phase diagram shown in Figure 4.10. There we have three steady-state positions of the dynamics, two unstable ones and one of saddlepoint type (the one in the middle). Yet, unstable arms of this saddlepoint and the stable ones coincide here, since the unstable ones bend back and approach the saddle again (surrounding one of the unstable equilibria on their way). Application of the jump variable technique in this situation

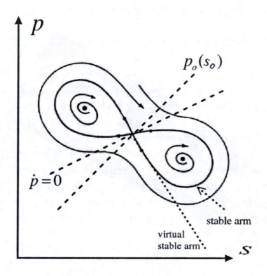

Figure 4.10 Bounded saddlepoint dynamics.

would therefore be applicable only in a certain neighborhood of the equilibrium point. Furthermore, the justification for applying the jump variable technique is now no longer compelling, since other trajectories have a future that is bounded in the above sense as well. Economically bounded dynamics with a saddlepoint steady state of the type shown in Figure 4.10 would therefore create problems for the applicability, as well as for the justification, of the jump variable technique that are not easily overcome.

Further problems for the applicability arise when the considered example is generalized to dimension three. Consider, for example, the following simple dynamic system (all parameters shown are positive):

$$\dot{x} = ay - ax, \tag{4.40}$$

$$\dot{y} = bx - y, \tag{4.41}$$

$$\dot{z} = -cz. \tag{4.42}$$

The first two laws of motion are independent of the third one and exhibit a unique steady-state position $(0, 0)$, which for parameter values $b > 1$ is a saddlepoint. The third law of motion obviously exhibits linear stable dynamics. We therefore have independent explosive and implosive trajectories in these 3D dynamics. Now assume that the saddle under consideration is linked with the third law of motion by simple multiplicative expressions (of the type present in macrodynamic model building, as we have pointed out above) as shown in the following equations:

$$\dot{x} = ay - ax, \tag{4.43}$$

$$\dot{y} = bx - y - xz, \tag{4.44}$$

$$\dot{z} = -cz + xy. \tag{4.45}$$

The dynamic equations thereby become the famous Lorenz equations with their strange attractor, shown in Figure 4.11.

The Lorenz equations are discussed in great detail in Sparrow (1982) and Strogatz (1994, Ch. 9). They exhibit (for $b > 1$) a steady state which is a saddlepoint, in fact the origin $(0, 0, 0)$ and a symmetric pair of two further steady states

$$(\sqrt{c(b-1)}, \sqrt{c(b-1)}, b-1), \quad \text{and} \quad (-\sqrt{c(b-1)}, -\sqrt{c(b-1)}, b-1),$$

which represent left- or right-turning convection rolls. The situation is therefore similar to the previously considered 2D one, but it is now one where there can be a strange attractor along which the motion is said to be chaotic. For

$$1 < b < b^H = \frac{a(a+c+3)}{a-c-1}, \quad a-c-1 > 0,$$

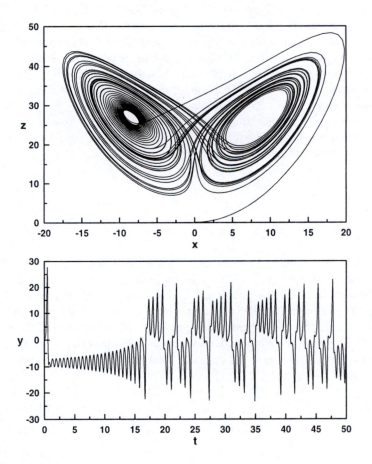

Figure 4.11 The 3D Lorenz dynamics.

the pair of symmetric equilibria represents stable equilibria which, however, lose their stability in a subcritical Hopf bifurcation at $b = b^H$. In the words of Strogatz (1994, p. 317):

> So the trajectories must have a bizarre type of long-term behavior. Like balls in a pin-ball machine, they are repelled from one unstable object after another. At the same time they are confined to a bounded set of zero volume, yet they manage to move on this set forever without intersecting themselves or others.

After an initial transient, the orbit settles into an irregular fluctuation that persists as $t \to \infty$. Viewed in dimension three it appears to settle onto an exquisitely thin set that looks like a pair of butterfly wings. The motion is aperiodic and the number of circuits made on each wing varies unpredictably from one cycle to the next. Moreover, the motion on the attractor exhibits sensitive dependence on initial conditions. This means that two orbits starting very close to each other will rapidly diverge and thereafter have totally different futures.

> The practical implication is that long-term prediction becomes impossible in a system like this, where small uncertainties are amplified enormously fast.
>
> (Strogatz (1994, p. 320)

Finally, there is indeed a time horizon (in the case of a positive Liapunov exponent λ), beyond which prediction breaks down.

> No matter how hard we work or reduce the initial measurement error, we can't predict longer than a few multiples of $1/\lambda$.
>
> (Strogatz (1994, p. 320)

The linearization of the Lorenz equations at the origin $(0,0,0)$ is given by the system (4.40)–(4.42) from which we started. We thus have a very trivial saddlepoint situation in this 3D linear system which is of not much use for the study of the nonlinear system. We do not question here the mathematical possibility of assuming, for example, that z is a non-predetermined variable and to calculate an orbit that will lead the system to the origin in certain situations; see, for example, Boucekkine (1995) for mathematical procedures that can be applied to nonlinear systems for solving nonlinear rational expectations models. What we do question, however, is the economic meaningfulness of applying the rational expectations methodology in such situations. There remains a need in economics to develop other – less mechanical – methods as sensible representations of the forward-looking behavior of economic agents in such situations, always to be based on information deduced from past data.

From the descriptive perspective, combinations of backward- and forward-looking-based methods (time series methods and projections based on structural models) may be a good alternative to the hyper-perfect scenario established by the rational expectations school. Adaptive-type expectations (the backward-looking part) may still have some advantage over such rational ones (see Section 7.2 in Flaschel et al. (1997)) and adaptive expectations schemes may perform as well as rational expectations in empirical analysis as, for example (based on the Dornbusch model), is shown in Papell (1992).[14] Backward-looking expectations may not necessarily be inconsistent with rational behavior, as is shown by Hommes (1994) and Goeree and Hommes (2000) in a simple cobweb-type model with chaotic behavior.

Despite its simple structure, it is not straightforward to construct a convincing macrodynamic model that exhibits the form of equations (4.43)–(4.45), in particular with one variable that can be considered as non-predetermined, in order

---

14 See Hey (1994) for an experimental investigation of this topic with, broadly speaking, similar conclusions.

to deal with the saddlepoint structure in the first two equations. The basic difficulty here is that the saddlepoint lies in the origin of the phase space, which means that variables are to be interpreted in terms of deviations from some steady state. The product terms would therefore represent products of deviations from the economic steady state which might be hard to justify.[15]

Soliman (1996) makes use of a discrete time model of a Phillips curve system of monetarist baseline type. He introduces into this model type two special types of nonlinear PC similar to the one used in Asada et al (2009). With respect to the parameter that characterizes the speed with which adaptively formed expectations are adjusted, he then obtains numerically period-doubling routes to chaos for this model type (which is globally asymptotically stable in its continuous time formulation) and also complicated scenarios for basins of attraction which show that long-term behavior of the system depends crucially on initial conditions. This economic example of chaotic attractors, however, is due to the discretization of the dynamics and therefore due to the fact that the economic system gets coordinated only at discrete points in time $t = 1, 2, 3, \ldots$ (whereby it may tend to overshooting as a result of parameter size and crude discretization, as in the discrete time logistic equation dynamics).

In this book, however, we want to allow for smooth adjustments only and to obtain on this basis strange attractors that generate fluctuations that roughly mirror empirical observations on business fluctuations with respect to shape, period length and amplitude, though each cycle is different because of the aperiodic behavior that is present. Our argument for the construction of such, broadly speaking, economically plausible fluctuations in prices and quantities will be – in Part II – the dimension of the economic structures to be investigated in integrated macrodynamics sooner or later. We show in Chapter 7 that such a model (of a closed economy) with full disequilibrium in its real part must at least be of dimension six. In the case of two interacting economies we thus get dimension 12 plus the two dynamics linkages between the two countries that describe the exchange rate dynamics. It is therefore quite natural to investigate 14D systems in integrated macrodynamics, then, without compromise with respect to growth rate formulations, meaningful products of state variables that properly separate

---

15 A basic formulation of an economic model that, at least to some extent, reflects the structure of the Lorenz equations can be given by

$$\dot{p} = a_1(Y_1^d - \bar{Y}) - a_2 p = a_1(a_3\sigma - \bar{Y}) - a_2 p, \quad Y_1^d = a_3\sigma$$

$$\dot{\sigma} = b_1 p(\bar{Y} - Y) - b_1\sigma, \quad \sigma = s\bar{p}^*/p, \bar{p}^* = 1$$

$$\dot{Y} = c_1(Y_2^d - Y) = c_1 c_2 p\sigma - c_1 Y, \quad Y_2^d = c_2 s$$

Here we consider prices p, real and nominal exchange rates σ, s and output levels Y. The first equation can be considered as a special type of Phillips curve, the second as an exchange rate policy and the third as an output adjustment equation. Yet, as this example indicates, growth rate formulations are neglected here and nominal and real magnitudes appear somewhat confused in this example in order to obtain the multiplicative structure of the Lorenz equations.

between nominal and real decisions and the like. We then hope to demonstrate to the reader that complex dynamics and strange attractors can arise in such systems that share features with the orbits of the Lorenz equations considered above, but are nevertheless not so erratic or strange in behavior that their connection to empirically observed types of fluctuations of important macro variables can hardly be seen.

We suggest that it can be reasonably argued that the rational expectations approach is not a universally applicable one, and furthermore that too much equilibrium behavior is arbitrarily imposed.[16] Note also once again that the jump variable technique is not even always applicable in the model types it was generally applied to in the theoretical literature, as we have shown in Section 4.3.1 for the loglinear Dornbusch model of IS–LM–PC type (if net exports are sufficiently sensitive with respect to the real exchange rate and money demand very sensitive with respect to the nominal rate of interest). Model-consistent expectations should indeed be allowed for, to some extent, in order to test their relevance for macroeconomic dynamics, but should not immediately be taken to their extreme by the assumption of rational expectations, based on hyper-perfect foresight and the consideration of globally explosive saddlepoint dynamics, then coupled with the assumption that all economically meaningful non-predetermined magnitudes can solely be found to lie within a strictly positive and compact domain in each and every phase diagram. To be really applicable, the number of non-predetermined variables must also, in particular coincide with the number of unstable roots. There are basically too many ad hoc assumptions or constructions or exclusions involved concerning the working of market economies in order to provide an approach to macrodynamics that we should all believe in. Rational expectations thus only represent an extreme case of model-consistent expectations, restricted to market-clearing approaches as far as the non-predetermined variables are concerned, and are only applicable to a restricted set of macromodels, as we have seen in particular in this section of the book.

4.5 References

ASADA, T., C. CHIARELLA, P. FLASCHEL and R. FRANKE (2009). *Lectures on Monetary Macrodynamics*. London: Routledge (forthcoming).

BOUCEKKINE, R. (1995): An alternative methodology for solving nonlinear forward-looking models. *Journal of Economic Dynamics and Control*, 19:4, 711–734.

CALVO, G. (1977): The stability of models of money and perfect foresight: A comment. *Econometrica*, 45:7, 1737–1739.

CHIARELLA, C. and P. FLASCHEL (2000): *The Dynamics of Keynesian Monetary Growth: Macro Foundations*. Cambridge, UK: Cambridge University Press.

DORNBUSCH, R. (1976): Expectations and exchange rate dynamics. *Journal of Political Economy*, 84:6, 1161–1176.

---

16 Indeed, in too mechanical a way as far as the selection of the forward-looking stable arm of the obtained saddlepoint is concerned.

FLASCHEL (1993): *Macrodynamics. Income Distribution, Effective Demand and Cyclical Growth*. Bern: Peter Lang.

FLASCHEL, P., R. FRANKE and W. SEMMLER (1997): *Dynamic Macroeconomics: Instability, Fluctuations, and Growth in Monetary Economies*. Cambridge, MA: MIT Press.

GOEREE, J. and C. HOMMES (2000): Heterogenous beliefs and the non-linear cobweb model. *Journal of Economic Dynamics and Control*, 24:5, 761–798.

HEY, J. (1994): Expectations formation: Rational or adaptive or ...? *Journal of Economic Behavior and Organization*, 25:3, 329–349.

HOMMES, C. (1994): Dynamics of the cobweb model with adaptive expectations and nonlinear supply and demand. *Journal of Economic Behavior and Organization*, 24:3, 315–335.

OXLEY, L. and D. GEORGE (1994): Linear saddlepoint dynamics 'on their head'. The scientific content of the new orthodoxy in macrodynamics. *European Journal of Political Economy*, 10, 389–400.

PAPELL, D. (1992): Exchange rate and price dynamics under adaptive and rational expectations: An empirical analysis. *Journal of International Money and Finance*, 11:4, 382–396.

SARGENT, T. and N. WALLACE (1973): The stability of models of money and growth with perfect foresight. *Econometrica*, 41, 1043–1048.

SOLIMAN, A.S. (1996): Transitions from stable equilibrium points to periodic cycles to chaos in a Phillips curve system. *Journal of Macroeconomics*, 18:1, 139–153.

SPARROW, C. (1982): *The Lorenz Equations: Bifurcations, Chaos, and Strange Attractors*. Berlin: Springer Verlag.

STROGATZ, S. (1994): *Nonlinear Dynamics and Chaos*. Reading, MA: Addison-Wesley.

TURNOVSKY, S.J. (1995): *Methods of Macroeconomic Dynamics*. Cambridge, MA: MIT Press.

4.6 Notation

The following list of symbols contains only domestic variables and parameters. Magnitudes referring to foreign quantities are defined analogously and are indicated in the text by an asterisk (*). Superscript d characterizes demand expressions (or differences), while the corresponding supply expressions do not have any index (in order to save notation). We use lowercase letters to denote logarithms of considered variables and thus the same symbol in the case of those variables that are already represented by lowercase letters in the non-loglinear setup of the considered model (the variable i is here an exception since it is always used in non-logarithmic form).

A. Statically or dynamically endogenous variables

Y	Output and income
Y^d	Aggregate demand (y^d also used for country differences)
$e = L^d/\bar{L} = Y/\bar{Y}$	Rate of employment
C, S_p	Private consumption and savings (S = total savings)
β_w	Adjustment speed of wages
I	Investment (exogenous)

NX	Real net exports in terms of the domestic currency
s	Exchange rate (units of domestic currency per unit of foreign currency: AUD, €)
ϵ	Expectation of exchange rate depreciation (percentage)
i	Nominal rate of interest
w	Level of nominal wages
p	Level of nominal prices
$\sigma = sp^*/p$	Real exchange rate
y^a	Averages
y^d	Differences

B. *Parameters of the model*

$G = \bar{G}$	Government expenditure (exogenous)
$T = \bar{T}$	Real taxes (lump-sum and exogenous)
M	Money supply
δ	Depreciation rate
$\bar{K}$	Capital stock
$\bar{Y}$	Full employment output
$\bar{L}$	Labor supply
$\bar{e}$	NAIRU employment rate
$\bar{y}$	Labor productivity
β_w	Adjustment speed of wages
β_p	Adjustment speed of prices
β_ϵ	Adjustment speed of exchange rate expectations

5 Exchange rate, the stock market and the macroeconomy
A baseline two-country model

5.1 Introduction

In this chapter we integrate the macroeconomic real–financial market interactions studied in Chapters 2 and 4, the Blanchard output and stock market dynamics, and the Dornbusch price level and exchange rate dynamics. We will investigate whether their interaction gives rise to new results for the rational expectations approaches as they were analyzed above in the two preceding chapters. We can do this here in a two-country framework with domestic and foreign money, bonds, equities and a foreign exchange market with a flexible exchange rate.[1] The model uses at first solely conventional multiplier dynamics in its real part, as in Blanchard (1981),[2] augmented by either a simple LM curve or, later on, by a simple Taylor interest rate policy rule. This is enriched throughout by a broad spectrum of domestic and foreign financial assets, based on their dynamic interaction under the assumptions of perfect substitute and perfect foresight. The implied 5D dynamics (with bond dynamics in the background of the model) is, like the one studied in Chapter 2, intrinsically nonlinear and difficult to analyze even from a local perspective,[3] since it exhibits three forward-looking variables and two predetermined ones. Thus the stable manifold must again be of dimension 2 for the jump variable technique to be applicable.

Contrary to Chapters 2 and 4 on stock market and exchange rate dynamics, we propose in this chapter to formulate and solve a revised form of the model, not only in order to avoid the assumptions of the jump variable technique (JVT) of the rational expectations school, but also because we think that the interest rate policy rule of the central bank should reflect the structure of the private sector in which it is supposed to work. The model will first be considered in its conventional form, starting from the Dornbusch (1976) overshooting exchange rate model, and will then be integrated with the Blanchard (1981) stock market approach in a two-country setup, as in Turnovsky (1986). This implies a dynamic model with five laws of motion and a variety of interacting feedback chains and their (in-)stability

---

1 This chapter is based on Flaschel and Hartmann (2007) and on Hartmann (2007).
2 The integration of price level dynamics is the subject of a later section of this chapter.
3 It can again exhibit two steady-state solutions as in the original Blanchard model.

implications for a conventional type of LM curve as well as a conventional type of interest rate policy rule. However, as already indicated, we do not show that the resulting unstable dynamics with their three non-predetermined and two predetermined variables required by the rational expectations methodology allows for a proper application of the JVT by proving the existence of three unstable and two stable roots of the Jacobian at their steady state, and by handling therewith the cases of unanticipated as well as anticipated shocks. Instead, we suggest the principle that Taylor interest rate policy rules should be designed (independently from what is happening in actual monetary policy considerations) to correspond with the feedback structure of the dynamics that are assumed to represent the behavior of the private sector.

This principle leads us to a Taylor rule that concentrates on the uncovered interest parity (UIP) condition of the Dornbusch model.[4] We assume a behavior of the central bank (CB) that is opposed to what policymakers would expect the CB to do in the case of an unwanted depreciation of their currency; i.e., we assume as Taylor rule that the nominal rate of interest is lowered in such a case (normally viewed as implying capital outflows and therefore giving further momentum to the ongoing depreciation of the exchange rate). In the present ideal modeling of financial markets (where we have perfect substitution and myopic perfect foresight everywhere), this inverted policy reaction is indeed helpful as it implies conventional asymptotic stability towards a now uniquely determined steady state (a second implication of our choice of the interest rate policy rule). We thus have that all five state variables can be considered as predetermined (but not their rates of growth) and that they are not subject to any explosive tendency. This result no longer enforces the need to apply the JVT, as would be the case in the model with a conventional Taylor rule with which we started. Such a modification of a conventional rational expectations model thus shows that it can overcome the conundrums that surround the application of the jump variable technique. We achieve this just by searching for Taylor rules that do their job of delivering stability in the assumed dynamic environment in a conventionally stabilizing way, with all variables being predetermined (so that only their time rates of change are subject to unanticipated shocks).[5]

From the methodological point of view we proceed as in Turnovsky (1986) from a general two-country approach and its uniquely determined interior steady-state position to a (partial) linearization of this model around its steady-state position and to the assumption of symmetry between the two countries, i.e., to assuming identical parameter values for them. This allows us to decompose the dynamics in to 2D average dynamics and 3D difference dynamics, both of which can be shown to be convergent under standard assumptions on the

---

4 As noted, the consideration of price level dynamics is the subject of a later section.
5 This goes together with a treatment of anticipated shocks that should be event-specific and not just subject to the mechanical use of explosive bubbles that lead us steadily in time towards a state where the stable manifold of the new dynamics comes into being.

private sector of the economy if the reaction of the interest rate is oriented to the exchange rate in a specific way, as described above. Moreover, since Turnovsky (1986) also allows for price dynamics as in Dornbusch (1976), we extend the model in a final section towards an integration of Phillips curves and can again show convergence if the Taylor rule is adjusted to this extended situation in an appropriate way.

The results of this chapter therefore question in a different way how rational expectations are exercised in forward-looking models, but also show the policy that is needed to overcome the saddlepoint instability of perfect-foresight models. This chapter therefore suggests that realistic models of financial–real interaction should consider situations of imperfect substitution between financial assets, take account of heterogeneous expectations formation and admit that adjustment processes may be fast, but not infinitely fast, in particular when the limiting situation of rational expectations is a structurally unstable one (i.e., subject to severe discontinuities in the limit).

A side product of this chapter, moreover, is that it shows that one can investigate theoretically situations in continuous time that are out of reach for the neo-Wicksellian period models used, for example, in Woodford (2003). We consider the use of continuous-time models a necessity in macromodels of real–financial markets interaction (see Chapter 1 in Flaschel et al. (2008) for the details of such an argument). It can also be used, if extended appropriately by wage–price dynamics and long-term bonds, for a structural comparison with and a theoretical investigation of empirical DSGE studies, as they are now the fashion in studies of the working of monetary policy rules (see the paper by Smets and Wouters (2003) for an example).

In the next section we briefly recapitulate the Dornbusch exchange rate dynamics for the small open economy. We then reconsider in detail, in Section 5.3, the Turnovsky two-country version of this model type and its rational expectations solutions. Section 5.4 provides a brief summary of Blanchard's stock market dynamics for the closed economy. In Section 5.5 we provide an integration of the Dornbusch and Blanchard models on a level that is similar to the Turnovsky approach. We briefly discuss there problems of saddlepoint instability, and then reformulate in Section 5.6 the Taylor rule in order to allow for stability in the conventional sense in this model type. A 5D stability analysis is carried out in Section 5.7 under the assumption of symmetry, where it can be shown then that both averages over and differences between the two economies converge to their steady-state values. In Section 5.8 we show that inflation dynamics can be added to the model without significantly altering its implications. Section 5.9 concludes this chapter.

5.2   Overshooting exchange rate dynamics

The Dornbusch (1976) exchange rate dynamics reads, in the case of the uncovered interest parity condition (UIP) and with myopic perfect foresight on the exchange rate dynamic in its simplest form, as follows (with s the logarithm of the exchange rate and p the logarithm of the price level, the foreign price level being normalized to 1):

$$\dot{p} = \beta_p(Y^d(s-p) - \bar{Y}),$$

$$\dot{s} = i(p) - \bar{i}^*.$$

We assume that the economy is at its full employment level $\bar{Y}$, but that deviations of aggregate demand Y^d (which depend only on the real exchange rate here) from this level determine the rate of inflation with adjustment speed β_p. The second law of motion is the UIP condition solved for the dynamic of the exchange rate it implies when myopic perfect foresight is assumed. The relationship $i(p)$ is a standard inverted LM curve; i.e., it describes a positive relationship between the price level and the domestic nominal rate of interest. Clearly the steady state is of saddlepoint type (the determinant of the Jacobian is negative) and the implied phase diagram is shown in figure 5.1.

The rational expectations school solves such a dynamical system in the following way. It assumes that, in the absence of anticipated shocks, the economy is always on the stable manifold of the given saddlepoint, horizontally to the right of the old steady state 0. If an unanticipated shock occurs that moves the steady state to point B, however, the economy lies in the intersection of the stable manifold

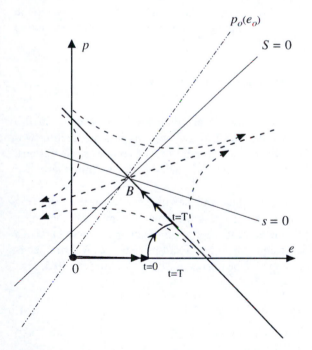

Figure 5.1 The Dornbusch exchange rate dynamics under myopic perfect foresight.

(a straight line in this simple model) with the horizontal axis, since the price level can only adjust gradually in this model. We therefore get an overshooting exchange rate (with respect to its new steady-state value) and thus an increase in goods demand which increases gradually the price level and the nominal interest rate, which in turn appreciates the exchange rate from its excessively high level until all variables reach the new steady state.

In the case of anticipated shocks the situation that is assumed by the rational expectations school becomes more complicated, since at the time of the announcement of the policy we are still in the old phase diagram around the point 0. In this case, the exchange rate jumps at $t = 0$ to the right, to a uniquely determined level from where it uses the unstable saddlepoint bubble in the old dynamics that starts at this point and from where it then reaches the stable manifold of the new dynamics exactly at time T when the announced policy shock actually takes place. We thus have – depending on T – a jump in the exchange rate that may still overshoot its new steady-state position and that then switches immediately towards a bubble of length T with both rising prices and exchange rates, from which it departs through a soft landing on the new stable manifold at time T.

This is – when appropriately extended – the rational expectations approach to exchange rate dynamics in the framework of a Dornbusch IS–LM model with a price Phillips curve. Its solution technique looks attractive, since it provides – in addition to the usual treatment of shocks – a well-defined answer in the case of anticipated events (within certain bounds, depending on the size of the anticipated shock). But it may also be viewed as a rather heroical solution to the treatment of (un)anticipated demand, supply and policy shocks from a descriptive point of view.

5.3 Symmetric two-country macrodynamics: A baseline model

In this section we introduce and make use of a technique that Turnovsky (1986) has employed to analyze Dornbusch-type IS–LM–PC analysis in a symmetric two-country setup by means of (mathematical) average and difference considerations. The analysis is then used to recover the original dynamics from these two hierarchically ordered subdynamics.

Following Turnovsky (1986), we thus consider in this section the following two-country macroeconomic model. It describes two symmetric economies, characterized by the same parameters, with each specializing in the production of a distinct good and international trading of distinct fixed-price bonds. All parameters in the following model are assumed to be positive (with $a_1 < 1$ and $\alpha \in (0.5, 1)$ in addition).

$$y = a_1 y^* - a_2(i - \dot{z}) + a_3(p^* + s - p) + \bar{u}, \tag{5.1}$$

$$y^* = a_1 y - a_2(i^* - \dot{z}^*) - a_3(p^* + s - p) + \bar{u}^*, \tag{5.2}$$

$$\bar{m} - z = b_1 y - b_2 i, \tag{5.3}$$

$$\bar{m}^* - z^* = b_1 y^* - b_2 i^*, \tag{5.4}$$

$$i = i^* + \dot{s}, \tag{5.5}$$

$$z = \alpha p + (1-\alpha)(p^* + s) = p + (1-\alpha)(p^* + s - p), \tag{5.6}$$

$$z^* = \alpha p^* + (1-\alpha)(p - s) = p^* - (1-\alpha)(p^* + s - p), \tag{5.7}$$

$$\dot{p} = \beta_w y, \tag{5.8}$$

$$\dot{p}^* = \beta_w y^*. \tag{5.9}$$

In these equations we make use of the following notation:

$y =$ deviation of real output Y (in logarithms) from its natural rate level,
$p =$ price of output, expressed in logarithms,
$z =$ consumer price index, expressed in logarithms,
$s =$ exchange rate (of the domestic economy), measured in logarithms,
$i =$ nominal interest rate,
$\bar{m} =$ nominal money supply, expressed in logarithms,
$\bar{u} =$ real government expenditure, expressed in logarithms.

Domestic variables as usual are unstarred; foreign variables are shown with an asterisk. Equations (5.1) and (5.2) describe goods market equilibrium, or the IS curves, in the two economies. Private goods demand depends upon output in the other country, upon the real rate of interest, measured in terms of consumer price inflation, and the real exchange rate. Because of the assumed symmetry, the corresponding effects across the two economies are identical, with the real exchange rate influencing demand in exactly offsetting ways. The money market equilibrium in the economies is of standard textbook type. It is described by eqs (5.3) and (5.4). These four equations thus provide a straightforward extension of the conventional IS–LM block to the case of two symmetric interacting economies.

The perfect substitutability of domestic and foreign bonds is described by the uncovered interest parity condition described by eq (5.5). Eqs (5.6) and (5.7) define the consumer price index (CPI) at home and abroad. The assumption is made that the proportion of consumption α spent on the respective home good is the same in the two economies. We assume $\alpha > \frac{1}{2}$, so that residents in both countries have a preference for their own good. Finally, eqs, (5.8) and (5.9) define the price adjustment in the two economies in terms of simple Phillips curves (which are not expectations augmented). We note that y is already measured as deviation of output from its steady-state level, which is not true for the other variables of the model. Because of the two-country approach here adopted, the world interest rate is not a given magnitude but will be determined by the equations of the model.

The two-country world described by eqs (5.1)–(5.9) represents a linear 3D dynamical system in the domestic and foreign price levels p, p^*, and the exchange rate, s. Following the methodology developed in the preceding section, we assume that the prices p, p^* can only adjust continuously, while the exchange rate is free to jump in response to new information and will always jump in such a way that the dynamic responses generated remain bounded away from zero and infinity. The jump variable technique therefore now applies to a 3D phase space and can no longer be depicted graphically in the easy way considered in the preceding section.

Fortunately, however, due to the symmetry assumption and the linearity of the considered model, the analysis can be simplified considerably by defining the averages and differences for all variables involved, say x for example, as

$$x^a \equiv \frac{1}{2}(x + x^*),$$

$$x^d \equiv x - x^*.$$

Through elimination of the variables z and z^*, the dynamics can be rewritten in terms of a decoupled system for averages and differences as described below.

5.3.1 The behavior of the "average economy"

Equations (5.10)–(5.12) describe the aggregate world economy. The aggregate IS and LM curves (5.12) and (5.13) determine the average output level and average nominal interest rate in terms of the average price level, the evolution of which is described by the Phillips curve (5.12). Thus

$$(1 - a_1 - a_2\beta_w)y^a = -a_2 i^a + \bar{u}^a, \tag{5.10}$$

$$\bar{m}^a - p^a = b_1 y^a - b_2 i^a, \tag{5.11}$$

$$\dot{p}^a = \beta_w y^a. \tag{5.12}$$

The behavior of this virtual average economy is therefore characterized by virtual IS–LM equilibrium and a virtual Phillips curve, which is not expectations augmented. Note here however that inflation is reflected in aggregate demand in both countries, which depends on the actual real rate of interest in both countries where inflation is substituted out by means of the PCs of the model. We assume in this regard

$$b = 1 - a_1 - \beta_w a_2 > 0,$$

i.e., that wages adjust sufficiently sluggishly so that the resulting IS curve in y^a, i^a space is downward sloping. We have the stabilizing Keynes effect present in this formally conventional IS–LM model and no destabilizing Mundell effect. This does not happen, however, by reducing the real rate of interest to a nominal one, but because of the assumption that the Phillips curves are not yet expectations augmented (i.e., they exhibit stationary expectations). It can therefore indeed be expected that the linear dynamical model for the averages will converge to its steady-state solution. Note that this decoupled part of the original model behaves just like a closed economy.

5.3.2 The dynamics of differences

The differences in the two economies, together with the exchange rate, are described by

$$(1+a_1)y^d = a_2(1-2\alpha)(\dot{s}-\dot{p}^d) + 2a_3(s-p^d) + \bar{u}^d, \tag{5.13}$$

$$\bar{m}^d - 2(1-\alpha)s + (1-2\alpha)p^d = b_1 y^d - b_2 \dot{s}, \tag{5.14}$$

$$\dot{p}^d = \beta_w y^d. \tag{5.15}$$

It is shown below that the virtual dynamics of the state variable s and p^d are of the saddlepoint type that we considered in the preceding section for the case of a small open economy.

It is convenient to begin with a characterization of the *steady-state* equilibrium. Characterizing steady-state values by indexation with zeros, we calculate the equilibrium from the conditions $\dot{p} = \dot{p}^* = \dot{s} = 0$, and first of all get $y_o = 0$ and $i_o = i_o^*$. Thus the steady-state equilibrium in the goods and money markets of the two economies is given by

$$a_2 i_o - a_3(p_o^* + s_o - p_o) = \bar{u},$$

$$a_2 i_o + a_3(p_o^* + s_o - p_o) = \bar{u}^*,$$

$$\bar{m} - p_o - (1-\alpha)(p_o^* + s_o - p_o) = -b_2 i_o,$$

$$\bar{m}^* - p_o^* + (1-\alpha)(p_o^* + s_o - p_o) = -b_2 i_o.$$

The solutions to these equations are

$$i_o = \frac{1}{2a_2}(\bar{u} + \bar{u}^*) = \bar{u}/a_2 = i_o^*, \tag{5.16}$$

$$\sigma_o \equiv p_o^* + s_o - p_o = \frac{1}{2a_3}(\bar{u} - \bar{u}^*) = \bar{u}^d/(2a_3), \tag{5.17}$$

$$p_o = \bar{m} + \left\{\frac{b_2}{2a_2} + \frac{(1-\alpha)}{2a_3}\right\}\bar{u} + \left\{\frac{b_2}{2a_2} - \frac{(1-\alpha)}{2a_3}\right\}\bar{u}^*, \tag{5.18}$$

$$p_o^* = \bar{m}^* + \left\{\frac{b_2}{2a_2} - \frac{(1-\alpha)}{2a_3}\right\}\bar{u} + \left\{\frac{b_2}{2a_2} + \frac{(1-\alpha)}{2a_3}\right\}\bar{u}^*, \tag{5.19}$$

$$s_o = \bar{m} - \bar{m}^* + \left\{\frac{1-2\alpha}{2a_3}\right\}(\bar{u} - \bar{u}^*). \tag{5.20}$$

We obtain that the steady world rate of interest is independent of monetary policy as well as the real exchange rate. With respect to monetary policy we thus have neutrality results as well as constant real exchange rates, as in the Dornbusch (1976) model.

We investigate the *stability properties of the average economy* first. For its steady-state position we get, from the above, that

$$i_o^a = \frac{1}{a_2} \bar{u}^a,$$

$$p_o^a = \bar{m}^a + \frac{b_2}{a_2} \bar{u}^a,$$

$$y_o^a = 0.$$

We can see that the steady-state world interest rate $i_o = i_o^* = i_o^a$ depends only on fiscal policy in the two countries and the interest rate elasticity of the aggregate demand function (of the aggregate investment demand function in particular). For the steady-state average price level we get the additional influences of the interest rate elasticity of the money demand functions as well as the average world money supply. The steady-state of the average economy is therefore of a very simple type.

In order to discuss its stability, we have to solve the IS–LM equations of the average economy for y^a and i^a first. Making use of the abbreviation $b = 1 - a_1 - \beta_w a_2$ we get from the IS and LM equation for the average economy the linear system

$$\begin{pmatrix} b & a_2 \\ b_1 & b_2 \end{pmatrix} \begin{pmatrix} y^a \\ i^a \end{pmatrix} = \begin{pmatrix} \bar{u}^a \\ \bar{m}^a - p^a \end{pmatrix}.$$

This in turn gives

$$\begin{pmatrix} y^a \\ i^a \end{pmatrix} = \frac{1}{zb_2 + a_2 b_1} \begin{pmatrix} b_2 & a_2 \\ b_1 & -b \end{pmatrix} \begin{pmatrix} \bar{u}^a \\ \bar{m}^a - p^a \end{pmatrix}.$$

Setting $d = 1/(zb_2 + a_2 b_1)$, we therefore get

$$\begin{pmatrix} y^a \\ i^a \end{pmatrix} = d \begin{pmatrix} b_2 \bar{u}^a + a_2(\bar{m}^a - p^a) \\ b_1 \bar{u}^a - b(\bar{m}^a - p^a) \end{pmatrix},$$

which has the expected signs in front of the coefficients that characterize fiscal and monetary policy. Inserting the expression obtained for the output gap y^a into the average PC then leads us to the linear differential equation in the average price level p^a,

$$\dot{p}^a = \beta_w d(b_2 \bar{u}^a + a_2 \bar{m}^a - a_2 p^a),$$

which shows that the steady-state level $p_o^a = \bar{m}^a + b_2/a_2\bar{u}^a$ is obviously a global attractor for the average price level. The average world economy is therefore globally asymptotically stable in a very straightforward way.

Remark: However, the PC that is employed in Turnovsky (1986) is *not expectations augmented* and may still allow for stability results in contrast to what is known about destabilizing Mundell inflationary expectations effects. We therefore briefly discuss the case when expectations-augmented PCs are used in the two-country approach under consideration here. Expectations of workers concern the consumer price indices z and z^* in the present context. Due to the definition of the consumer price index (by way of functions of the Cobb–Douglas type) we get for the derivative of its logarithm (and thus for the growth rate of the consumer price index),

$$\dot{z} = \alpha\dot{p} + (1 - \alpha)(\dot{p}^* + \dot{s}), \quad \dot{z}^* = \alpha\dot{p}^* + (1 - \alpha)(\dot{p} - \dot{s}).$$

As expectations-augmented Phillips curves we now define[6]

$$\dot{p} = \beta_w y + \pi, \quad \dot{p}^* = \beta_w y^* + \pi^*,$$

where π and π^* denote the expected growth rates for the consumer price indices of the two countries. For these expected rates we now assume an adaptive expectations mechanism, which in the present context and for the two countries considered must be of the form

$$\dot{\pi} = \beta_\pi(\dot{z} - \pi), \quad \dot{\pi}^* = \beta_\pi(\dot{z}^* - \pi^*),$$

derived by employing again the symmetry assumption for the two-country model considered.

Note that Turnovsky (1986) and our above presentation of his approach both make use of myopic perfect foresight with respect to price inflation (in the aggregate demand function), but disregard the fact that this might fix the output level at its NAIRU level. The PC of the above model can therefore be positively sloped, since it has not been augmented by inflationary expectations in the usual way. We now depart from this procedure by inserting expected consumer price inflation into the aggregate demand function in the place of actual consumer price inflation in order to be in line with the conventional IS–LM–PC model. We therefore now consider a mixed situation with respect to expectations formation: rational expectations in the financial markets and adaptive ones with respect to goods markets, labor markets and wage and price inflation. We justify the choice of such a mixed situation with reference to applied models such as the one of McKibbin and Sachs (1991) (see also the IMF Multimod Mark III model)

---

6 These equations are based on level representations of the type $\hat{p} = \beta_w \ln(Y/\bar{Y}) + \pi$.

where, however, a more complicated situation is considered, since inflationary expectations are there based on forward- and backward-looking elements and not included directly in the investment or consumption demand function.

In terms of averages, the equations just discussed give rise to

$$\dot{\pi}^a = \beta_\pi(\dot{z}^a - \pi^a) = \beta_\pi(\dot{p}^a - \pi^a),$$
$$\dot{p}^a = \beta_w y^a + \pi^a.$$

There is thus an immediate extension of the model by adaptive inflationary expectations such that an IS–LM–PC analysis is established for the average economy that is of the type considered in Chiarella et al. (2000, 2.2) for the case of a closed economy. Note here, however, that the IS–LM part of the model is now given by

$$(1 - a_1)y^a = -a_2(i^a - \pi^a) + \bar{u}^a,$$
$$\bar{m}^a - p^a = b_1 y^a - b_2 i^a,$$

the solution of which for the variable y^a, r^a now gives [with $d = 1/((1 - a_1)b_2 + a_2 b_1)$]

$$\begin{pmatrix} y^a \\ i^a \end{pmatrix} = d \begin{pmatrix} b_2 a_2 \pi^a + b_2 \bar{u}^a + a_2(\bar{m}^a - p^a) \\ b_1 a_2 \pi^a + b_1 \bar{u}^a - (1 - a_1)(\bar{m}^a - p^a) \end{pmatrix},$$

again with the expected signs in front of the coefficients that characterize fiscal and monetary policy (and now the role of inflationary expectations). Inserting the expression for output y^a into the revised dynamical system finally gives

$$\dot{p}^a = \beta_w y^a + \pi^a = \beta_w d(b_2 a_2 \pi^a + b_2 \bar{u}^a + a_2(\bar{m}^a - p^a)) + \pi^a,$$
$$\dot{\pi}^a = \beta_\pi \beta_w y^a = d(b_2 a_2 \pi^a + b_2 \bar{u}^a + a_2(\bar{m}^a - p^a)).$$

These IS–LM–PC dynamics are of the same qualitative type as the ones investigated in Chiarella et al. (2000, 2.2). They therefore now contain the destabilizing Mundell effect (represented by the coefficient $db_2 a_2$) in addition to the stabilizing Keynes effect (represented by the coefficient $-da_2$) and thus will not be locally asymptotically stable if the Mundell effect works with sufficient strength. However, the present analysis is strictly local in nature, since aggregate demand $Y^d = C + I + G$ has been approximated by a loglinear expression of the type $a_1 y^a - a_2(i^a - \pi^a) + \bar{u}^a$. The completion of the analysis by means of a kinked PC and the proof of global stability of these average dynamics is therefore not possible here, but demands a level-form representation of the whole model which is necessarily nonlinear in nature – to which the averaging method of this section can then no longer be applied. The analysis of this section therefore becomes considerably more complicated when a global IS–LM–PC approach is attempted that generalizes Chiarella et al. (2000, 2.2) to the case of two (symmetric) interacting open economies.

For the loglinear approximation of this section and the use of positively sloped PCs (static expectations of wage earners) and myopic perfect foresight with respect to price inflation by investors, we have however shown that the average economy is (locally) monotonically and asymptotically stable and thus behaves much more simply than even the traditional monetarist base model and its extension to IS–LM–PC analysis.

Let us now consider *the dynamics of differences* which, when slightly reformulated, are given by:[7]

$$(1+a_1)\dot{p}^d/\beta_w = a_2(1-2\alpha)(\dot{s}-\dot{p}^d)+2a_3(s-p^d)+\bar{u}^d,$$

$$\bar{m}^d - 2(1-\alpha)(s-p^d) - p^d = b_1\dot{p}^d/\beta_w - b_2\dot{s}.$$

Rearranging these equations appropriately and using the auxiliary variable $k = s - p^d$ then gives

$$2a_3k + \bar{u}^d = (1+a_1)/\beta_w\dot{p}^d - a_2(1-2\alpha)\dot{k},$$

$$2(1-\alpha)k + p^d - \bar{m}^d = (b_2 - b_1/\beta_w)\dot{p}^d + b_2\dot{k}.$$

In matrix notation this in turn gives, with respect to the signs involved in these two equations,[8]

$$\begin{pmatrix} + & + \\ - & + \end{pmatrix} \begin{pmatrix} \dot{p}^d \\ \dot{k} \end{pmatrix} = \begin{pmatrix} 0 & + \\ + & + \end{pmatrix} \begin{pmatrix} p^d \\ k \end{pmatrix}.$$

Since the determinant of the matrix on the left-hand side of this matrix equation is positive (and thus also the determinant of the inverse of this matrix) and the determinant of the matrix on the right-hand side is negative, we find that this implicit differential equation system gives rise to a negative system determinant when solved explicitly (by multiplying the right-hand side by the inverse of the matrix on the left-hand side). Not surprisingly, we therefore get (for adjustment speeds of wages chosen sufficiently small) that the difference dynamics are of saddlepoint type with respect to their unique steady-state solution, which is given by

$$p_o^d = \bar{m}^d + (1-\alpha)/a_3\bar{u}^d, \quad s_o = s_o - p_o^d = -\bar{u}^d/(2a_3) \quad \text{(and } y_o^d = 0).$$

Of course, reformulating the dynamics in terms of p^d and s provides us with the same result (see Turnovsky (1986, p. 143) in this regard). We thus have now the situation that the jump variable technique of the rational expectations school must be applied to the differences between the two countries and be translated back to the individual countries thereafter in order to discuss the consequences of monetary or fiscal shocks in such a two-country framework.

---

7 Note that the third equation is solved for y^d and inserted into the first two equations of the difference dynamics.

8 If β_w is again assumed to be sufficiently small and considering that $\alpha \in (0.5, 1)$.

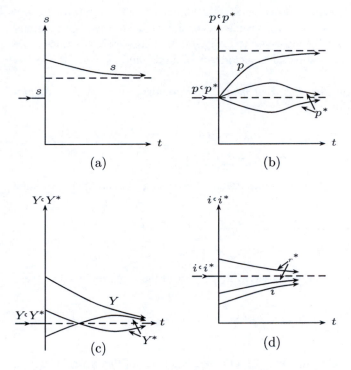

Figure 5.2 Unanticipated monetary expansion: (a) exchange rate; (b) prices; (c) outputs; (d) interest rates. (adapted from Turnovsky, 1986).

In this way Turnovsky (1986) obtains, for example, the following two results on unanticipated and anticipated monetary shocks, specifically an increase in the domestic money supply by one unit with foreign money supply held constant, which raises the steady-state values of p and s by one unit and leaves the steady-state value of p^* unaltered. For both situations we quote directly from Turnovsky (1986) in order to describe the results of this analysis in the spirit of the presentation and explanation that were originally chosen.[9]

5.3.3 Unanticipated monetary expansion

The formal solution to the model in the case of an unanticipated monetary disturbance is illustrated in [Figure 5.2]. In this case, the exchange rate overshoots its long-run response, on impact, thereafter appreciating toward

---

9 Note that we have changed references to figures and their notation to conform with the numbering and notation of this chapter.

its new steady-state level. The price of domestic output gradually increases, while domestic output initially increases, thereafter falling monotonically towards its natural rate level. The monetary expansion causes an immediate fall in the domestic interest rate, which thereafter rises monotonically toward its equilibrium. All these effects are familiar from the Dornbusch model or its immediate variants. The effects of the domestic monetary expansion on the foreign economy are less clear cut. The rate of inflation p^* of foreign goods and the level of output abroad will rise or fall on impact, depending on an eigenvalue relationship.

5.3.4 *Announced monetary expansion*

Consider now the behavior of the economy in response to a monetary expansion which the authorities announce at time zero to take place at some future time $T > 0$. The time paths for the relevant domestic and foreign variables are illustrated in figure [5.3].

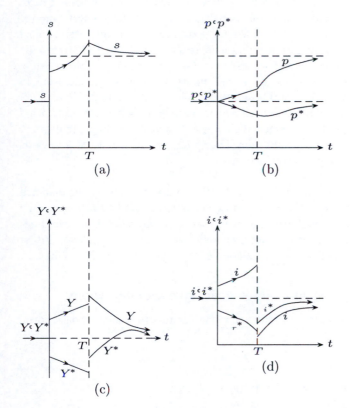

Figure 5.3 Announced monetary expansion: (a) exchange rate; (b) prices;(c) outputs; (d) interest rates. (adapted from Turnovsky, 1986).

At the time of announcement ($t = 0$) the domestic currency immediately depreciates in anticipation of the future monetary expansion. Whether the initial jump involves overshooting of the exchange rate depends upon the lead time T. Following the announcement, the domestic currency continues to depreciate until time T, when it reaches a point above the new long-run equilibrium. Thereafter, it appreciates steadily until the new steady-state equilibrium is reached. This behavior is identical with that in the Gray and Turnovsky (1979) model. The anticipation of the future monetary expansion causes the domestic price level to begin rising at time zero. The inflation rate increases during the period 0 to T, when the monetary expansion occurs. This expansion causes a further increase in the inflation rate, which thereafter begins to slow down as the new equilibrium price level is approached. The behavior of the inflation rate is mirrored in the level of output. The positive inflation rate generated by the announcement is accompanied by an immediate increase in output, which increases continuously until the monetary expansion occurs at time T. At that time a further discrete increase in output occurs. [...] At the same time, the initial increase in domestic real output, stimulated by the depreciation of the domestic currency as a result of the announcement, increases the demand for real money balances. In order for domestic money market equilibrium to be maintained, the domestic nominal interest rate must rise. As the price of domestic output increases during the period prior to the monetary expansion, the real domestic money supply contracts further, while the increasing real income causes the real money demand to continue rising. In order for money market equilibrium to be maintained, the domestic nominal interest must therefore continue to rise. At time T, when the anticipated monetary expansion takes place, the domestic interest rate drops, falling to a level below its long-run equilibrium. Thereafter, it rises steadily back towards its (unchanged) long-run equilibrium.

This only partial discussion of the very detailed and numerous results obtained in Turnovsky (1986) shows that interesting conclusions can be drawn from the application of the jump variable technique to unanticipated and even more to anticipated policy shocks. The reader is referred to this very rigorous article for further details on the formal and verbal explanation of these and other policy studies.

5.4 Blanchard-type stock-market–goods-market interactions

The Blanchard (1981) output and stock market dynamics read, in their basic form, as follows:

$$\dot{Y} = \beta_y(Y^d(Y, q) - Y) \tag{5.21}$$

$$i(Y) = r(Y)/q + \hat{q} : \quad \Rightarrow \quad \dot{q} = i(Y)q - r(Y) \tag{5.22}$$

We here combine a standard dynamic multiplier story for the dynamics of the output level Y (where, however, aggregate demand Y^d depends positively on

Tobin's q in place of a negative dependence on the real rate of interest) with the situation that bonds and equities are perfect substitutes, including myopic perfect foresight concerning the capital gains on equities. We here identify Tobin's average $q = p_e E / pK$ with the share price p_e by assuming that the number of equities E to the value of the capital stock pK is constant and set equal to 1. We denote by $i(Y)$ the inverted LM curve and by $r(Y)$ the profit rate function of the economy (profits per unit of capital), with all profits paid out as dividends to equity owners. The ratio $r(Y)/q$ is then the dividend rate of return on equities (since pK cancels) and $\hat{q} = \dot{q}/q$ are the capital gains per unit of equity, i.e., $r(Y)/q + \hat{q}$ is the (total) rate of return on equities, set equal to the interest rate here because of the perfect substitute assumption.

The two laws of motion of the Blanchard output and stock-market dynamics give rise to two isoclines, an example of which was considered in Chapter 2 (see Figure 2.14). Moreover, they typically imply saddlepoint dynamics for their intersections (for the exceptions, see below). Their phase diagram and the stable arm that is directed towards the saddlepoint steady-state can therefore be used as usually applying the jump variable technique (JVT) of the rational expectations school. This is extensively done in Blanchard's (1981) original paper and need not be repeated here.

There are, however, some problems with this approach to a real–financial market interaction. Even in the case where all behavior is assumed as linear, we have obtained here a 2D non-linear dynamical system as indicated in Figure 2.7 for Blanchard's bad news case, (with a decreasing LM curve). In Blanchard's good news case, where the interest rate is more sensitive to output changes than the profit rate, the LM curve of Figure 2.8 is positively sloped and it allows for situations of 2, 1 or no steady-state, with one steady-state being a stable node or focus in the first case. The JVT of the rational expectations school is therefore not always applicable, which again shows one of its limitations.

We concentrate here, however, on the case shown in Figure 5.4 where the relevant stable manifold of the then uniquely determined steady-state of saddlepoint type is an upward sloping curve. We assume that the economy is hit by three severe and unanticipated contractive demand shocks which shift the IS curve of this model significantly to the left, as shown in Figure 2.14. Equity-financed firms thus experience severe underutilization problems with respect to their productive capacity, but the stock market shows a strong stock-price rally until the final steady-state is reached, with low rates of capacity utilization of firms, low dividend payments, but high stock prices. This is a situation which surely needs some explanation from the proponents of the RE approach in their justification of the economic meaningfulness of the JVT.

5.5 Synthesizing Blanchard stock-market with Dornbusch exchange rate dynamics in a two-country framework

Since the preceding model types are well documented in the literature on real–financial markets interaction, we do not pursue a further investigation of the

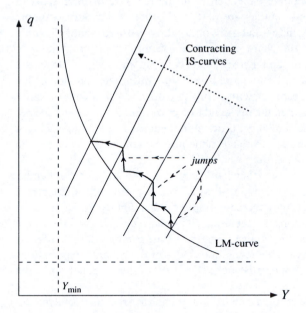

Figure 5.4 Contracting IS curve.

Blanchard and Dornbusch model here; see Chapters 2 and 4 in this respect. Instead, we ask the question what the outcome will be if we synthesize the Dornbusch and Blanchard model into a two-country model of the world economy. This is a big step forward in the dynamics to be considered and is therefore simplified here somewhat by considering, for the time being, prices (and wages) as given, and normalized to 1. Phillips-curve-driven price dynamics is however the next step that has to be considered (see Section 5.8).

As Keynesian aggregate demand functions we postulate now the relationship (all prices $= 1$, but the nominal exchange rate $s[EUR/US]$ is perfectly flexible):

$$Y^d = C(Y,s) + I(q,s) + G(s) + X(Y^*,s)$$

$$Y^{d*} = C^*(Y^*,-s) + I^*(q^*,-s) + G^*(-s) + X^*(Y,-s)$$

concerning the two goods markets that exist in this two-country, two-commodity world.[10] These functions represent the demand side of the two economies considered and they are to be inserted again into the dynamic multiplier process

---

10 C = consumption, I = investment, G = government expenditure and X = exports.

of the Blanchard model:

$$\dot{Y} = \beta_y(Y^d(Y, Y^*, q, s) - Y) \tag{5.23}$$

$$\dot{Y}^* = \beta_{y^*}(Y^{d*}(Y^*, Y, q^*, s) - Y^*) \tag{5.24}$$

in order to provide a full description of the dynamics of the real part of the economy. We note that domestic demands, as well as exports, depend of course on the exchange rate s (positively in the domestic economy and negatively in the foreign one). We have made this latter negative dependency an explicit one, since we can then simply say that the case of symmetric economies is characterized by identical demand functions and adjustment speeds in the two economies. In the local stability analysis we shall later on work with their linearizations and thus with identical corresponding parameter values in order to allow to us calculate average as well as difference economies from the model of this section.

In addition to these two laws of motion we have now six financial assets in our world economy (two types of money, two types of bonds and two types of equities) which, under the assumptions of perfect substitution and myopic perfect foresight, now give rise to three independent laws of motion:[11]

$$i(Y) = r(Y)/q + \hat{q}: \quad \Rightarrow \quad \hat{q} = i(Y) - r(Y)/q \tag{5.25}$$

$$i^*(Y^*) = r^*/q^* + \hat{q}^*: \quad \Rightarrow \quad \hat{q}^* = i^*(Y^*) - r^*(Y^*)/q^* \tag{5.26}$$

$$i(Y) = i^*(Y^*) + \hat{s}: \quad \Rightarrow \quad \hat{s} = i(Y) - i^*(Y^*) \tag{5.27}$$

We now interpret the inverted LM functions $i(Y), i^*(Y^*)$ as interest rate policy rules which here only exhibit the output gap as an argument, since inflation is still excluded from the dynamics under considerations.

Concerning steady-state calculations, we here refer to the discussion below of the situation of symmetric countries, which implies that averages behave exactly as in the closed economy case considered in Blanchard (1981). All difficulties of the original Blanchard model with respect to its steady-state determination are therefore also present in the two-country case. The Jacobian of the considered 5D dynamical system in the state variables Y, Y^*, q, q^*, s reads, in its sign structure, as follows:

$$J_0 = \begin{pmatrix} - & + & + & 0 & + \\ + & - & 0 & + & - \\ \pm & 0 & + & 0 & 0 \\ 0 & \pm & 0 & + & 0 \\ + & - & 0 & 0 & 0 \end{pmatrix}$$

---

11 The following equations imply that all rates of return on the internationally traded asset must be the same (and therefore also equal to $r^*(Y^*) + \hat{q}^* + \hat{s} = r(Y) + \hat{q} - \hat{s}$).

The Dornbusch and Blanchard type feedback chains (between Y, s and Y, q) are clearly visible, but this does not easily imply that this matrix will have three unstable and two stable roots as would be needed for a successful application of the JVT. Since the model has, in correspondence to the characteristics of its eigenvalues, three forward-looking, non-predetermined variables q, q^*, s and two predetermined ones Y, Y^* that are only gradually adjusting, the task for the rational expectations school is to determine a 2D stable manifold (and a 3D unstable manifold) in the 5D phase space such that the non-predetermined variables can always jump to a unique point of the stable manifold with predetermined (temporarily given) output levels of the two countries. This must hold in the case of unanticipated shocks, while in the case of anticipated shocks, one has to find in addition the single bubble of length T in the old 5D dynamics through a jump to a position in the 5D phase space such that this bubble has a soft landing on the new stable manifold exactly at time T (where the anticipated shock would occur).[12]

The solution to these problems (with significant calculation costs for the theorist as well as for the assumed type of economic agent) assumes calculation capabilities that are far beyond anything that can be characterized as "rational expectations". We view such a procedure as a wrong axiomatization of what is actually happening in the real world, with an inherent tendency to use more and more complicated constructions or eventually purely mathematical iteration mechanisms in order to get, by assumption, the result that the economic dynamics of such models – in their deterministic core – are always of the shock absorber type (or occupied with finding the correct bubble that leads them safely to the new shock absorber, which comes into existence at time T). It is obvious that we do not regard this as a promising route for further macrodynamic investigation. We therefore will now reconsider the structure of the private sector in order to find an interest rate policy rule that can stabilize it, in the conventional sense of this word.

5.6 A model-adequate reformulation of the Taylor interest rate rule

Instead of pursuing the JVT methodology any further, we now raise the question whether the central banks, in view of their interest rate policy rule, should not consider the given structure of the economy first before deciding on the economic signals that should guide their choice of an interest rate in such a world. We thus stress that the Taylor rule should be modified in view of the structure of the economy in which it is supposed to work. Since output dynamics are of the stable multiplier type, and since repelling forces only concern the financial

---

12 In the situation considered here it is in fact easy to show that the determinant of the Jacobian matrix J is negative for all interest rates i_o chosen sufficiently low. It is therefore not possible in such a case that the dynamics exhibit two stable and three unstable roots.

sector of the economy (tamed by assumption through the JVT of the RE school), it appears plausible to look at the evolution of either Tobin's q or the UIP exchange rate dynamics to find the variables that should steer the interest rate setting strategy of the CBs. After some experimentation with these possibilities, we propose here to use and test the rules:

$$i = i_o + a_i(s_o - s) \tag{5.28}$$

$$i^* = i_o^* - a_i^*(s_o - s) \tag{5.29}$$

When these rules are applied to the UIP condition of the private sector

$$i \overset{UIP}{=} i^* + \hat{s}$$

they deliver the astonishingly simple result:

$$\hat{s} = i_o + a_i(s_o - s) - (i_o^* - a_i^*(s_o - s)) = g(s)$$

with

$$g(s_o) = i_o - i_o^*, \ g'(s) < 0$$

We thus get that the exchange rate dynamics become independent of the rest of the economy under these choices of policy rules in the two countries and give rise to monotonic convergence to the steady-state value s_o jointly set by the two CBs if policy coordination implements the condition $i_o = i_o^*$.

Policy formulation of the kind described, which exhibits awareness of the private sector structure, therefore removes all repelling forces from the exchange rate dynamic as considered in Figure 5.1. The only troubling aspect here may be that the above implies that the CBs should do just the opposite of what they might be induced to do in the real world, since – for example the ECB – should lower the interest rate in the case of an exogenous upward jump in the nominal exchange rate s, being a depreciation of the Euro. Leaning against a depreciation in actual economies may, however, mean that one should attract capital inflows and thus raise the domestic rate of interest, but in the model we are considering this would imply instability and not convergence to the steady-state value s_o.

In order to investigate the full dynamics of the model one also has to consider, of course, the remaining four laws of motion. These laws of motion are fully interacting and thus, from the perspective of the Routh–Hurwitz stability conditions, somewhat demanding. In the next section we will therefore consider the case of symmetric economies, as in Turnovsky (1986), and will linearize the model around its (indeed now uniquely determined) steady-state position to prove the local asymptotic stability of the steady-state of such a two-country interaction between real and financial markets.

The chosen modified form of the Taylor rule does not only simplify the dynamics that are implied by the model, but also implies that there is in general a unique steady-state solution, in contrast to the Blanchard model type considered beforehand. We here use, as in Blanchard (1981), linear aggregate demand functions and ignore the already given steady-state position s_o in their formulation.[13] Against this background they read:

$$Y^d = a_y Y + b_y q + G + c_y Y^* + \text{const.}$$

$$Y^{d*} = a_{y*} Y^* + b_{y*} q^* + G^* + c_{y*} Y + \text{const.}$$

with the propensities to consume, invest and export all given parameters. For Tobin's q we similarly get (assuming a linear profit rate function as in Blanchard (1981)):

$$q = (a_r Y + b_r)/i_o, \qquad q^* = (a_{r*} Y^* + b_{r*})/i_o^* \quad (i_o = i_o^*).$$

Inserting these two equations, which are now linear, into the two goods-market equilibrium conditions provides us with two linear equations for the state variables Y, Y^* which in general have a uniquely determined solution. Of course, in addition, the parameters of the model have to be chosen such that the steady-state levels of the outputs of the two countries are positive and imply positive profit rates for both of them. We therefore, in sum, conclude that coordinated monetary policy provides us with the steady-state values of both i and s via the UIP condition, while stationary financial market equilibrium allows us to remove Tobin's q from the goods market equilibrium conditions which then imply steady-state values for both Y and Y^*, on the basis of which the steady-state values of the q_s can then be determined.

Linearizing also the above 5D dynamics (with the exception of the intrinsically nonlinear q dynamics) in this way (around the steady-state position which has just been determined) gives the dynamical system

$$\dot{Y} = \beta_y[-(1-a_y)Y + b_y q + c_y Y^* + d_y s + e_y]$$

$$\dot{Y}^* = \beta_{y*}[-(1-a_{y*})Y^* + b_{y*} q^* + c_{y*} Y - d_{y*} s + e_{y*}]$$

$$\dot{q} = (i_o + a_i(s_o - s))q - r, \quad r = a_r Y + b_r$$

$$\dot{q}^* = (i_o^* - a_i^*(s_o - s))q^* - r^*, \quad r^* = a_r^* Y^* + b_r^*$$

$$\hat{s} = i_o + a_i(s_o - s) - (i_o^* - a_i^*(s_o - s))$$

---

13 Note however that we will apply this linearity assumption in the next section also (where s is a variable). This means that we will have to linearize the goods market demand function (with respect to the s influence) and thus will get local results only.

The Jacobian matrix of these linearized dynamics exhibits the following sign structure:

$$J_0 = \begin{pmatrix} - & + & + & 0 & + \\ + & - & 0 & + & - \\ - & 0 & i_o & 0 & - \\ 0 & - & 0 & i_o & + \\ 0 & 0 & 0 & 0 & - \end{pmatrix}$$

The stability of this unique steady-state solution will be investigated in the following section by means of an important simplifying device that can be applied to study the interaction of large economies that are sufficiently similar to each other in their real as well as their financial parts.

5.7 Symmetric countries: Stability analysis

We consider now the artificial variables $Y^a = (Y + Y^*)/2$, $q^a = (q + q^*)/2$, the averages of the GDPs and Tobins qs as well as $Y^\delta = Y - Y^*$, $q^\delta = q - q^*$, the differences of the GDPs and Tobin's qs and will use in the following the above (partial) linear representation, which includes the export functions $X(Y^*, s), X^*(Y, -s)$. Moreover we now use the pair of Taylor rules $i = i_o + a_i(s_o - s)$, $i^* = i_o - a_i(s_o - s)$ for our stability investigations of the symmetric two-country case. It is obvious from the preceding section that the steady values of the case of a difference economy are zero as far as outputs and Tobin's qs are concerned; i.e., the steady-state average values share symmetry with the parameters of the model and are given just by the unique values Y_o, q_o of the case of the average economy.

5.7.1 The average economy

In order to show the stability of the full 5D dynamics we assume the case of two symmetric large open economies, in which case all corresponding parameters of the two countries are of the same size, with opposite signs if the exchange rate is involved (this applies also to the policy rules). Taking averages $Y^a = (Y + Y^*)/2$, $q^a = (q + q^*)/2$ therefore allows us to combine the goods market equilibrium conditions into a single world market equation, where the exchange rate effect has been canceled. The stock market dynamics can in the same way be aggregated into a single equation. This, in sum, gives a two-dimensional dynamical system as shown below. This average economy represents a hypothetical economy that is of the Blanchard (1981) closed economy type (without the intrinsic nonlinearities in the equity dynamic that have complicated the Blanchard stock market model, since the product iq is now simply given by $i_o q$).

$$\dot{Y}^a = \beta_y[(a_y + c_y - 1)Y^a + b_y q^a + const.]$$

$$\dot{q}^a = i_o q^a - a_r Y^a + const.$$

For the Jacobian matrix of this economy we immediately get the result:

$$J = \begin{pmatrix} \beta_y(a_y + c_y - 1) & \beta_y b_y \\ -a_r & i_o \end{pmatrix} = \begin{pmatrix} - & + \\ - & i_o \end{pmatrix}$$

if we have multiplier stability $(a_y + c_y < 1)$ and if the output adjustment speed is sufficiently large $(\beta_y[1 - (a_y + c_y)] > i_o$ is solely needed). These conditions are of conventional type in the first case and not at all restrictive in the second case, implying that the average economy is generally asymptotically stable and thus always convergent to its steady-state position. Since the interest rate i_o is indeed a small number, setting it to 0 exemplifies, in addition, that adjustment to the steady-state is cyclical for an intermediate range of the output adjustment speed.

5.7.2 The difference economy

Taking differences $Y^\delta = Y - Y^*, q^\delta = q - q^*$ implies a three-dimensional dynamics with these state variables and the exchange rate s. This dynamics is, as formally seen, of the type of small open economy considered in Dornbusch (1976). Note that we now have a $d_y s$ term in the aggregate demand equation and that the domestic Taylor rule is given by $i = a_i(s_o - s) + i_o$, whereas the equation of the foreign economy has a negative sign in front of the adjustment speed a_i.

$$\dot{Y}^\delta = \beta_y[(a_y - c_y - 1)Y^\delta + b_y q^\delta + 2d_y s]$$

$$\dot{q}^\delta = [-2a_i(s - s_o) + i_o]q^\delta - a_r Y^\delta$$

$$\hat{s} = -2a_i(s - s_o)$$

$$J_0 = \begin{pmatrix} \beta_y[(a_y - c_y - 1) & \beta_y b_y & \beta_y 2d_y \\ -a_r & i_o & -2a_i q_o^\delta \\ 0 & 0 & -2a_i s_o \end{pmatrix} = \begin{pmatrix} - & + & + \\ - & i_o & - \\ 0 & 0 & - \end{pmatrix}$$

It is obvious from the structure of this Jacobian that asymptotic stability and convergence hold here under the same (and even weaker) conditions as in the case of averages.

5.7.3 Summary

Summing up, we have that differences must converge to 0 (and s to s_o) and that averages must converge to their common steady-state values, implying that the full 5D dynamics are also characterized by convergence towards their steady-state position. This is a convenient short-cut to the analysis of the full 5D system when the parameters of the two countries differ from each other. We thus now have an economy that is stable in the conventional sense of this word. These results should be of interest to policy makers if they could accept that leaning against the wind means, in this set-up, just the opposite of what they might be inclined to do intuitively.

5.8 Adding inflation dynamics

As in Turnovsky (1986), we now add inflation dynamics in the two countries in the form of the following two Phillips curves (again assuming symmetry between the two countries):

$$\hat{p} = \beta_w(Y - \bar{Y}), \quad \hat{p}^* = \beta_w(Y^* - \bar{Y})$$

We thus assume that the current output gaps drive the current inflation rate, but we do not yet consider acceleration terms in these two Phillips curves.

Linearizing these equations around the steady-state position (for local stability analysis) gives rise to[14]

$$\dot{p} = \beta_w p_o(Y - \bar{Y}), \quad \dot{p}^* = \beta_w p_o^*(Y^* - \bar{Y}).$$

Since the price levels in the two countries are now moving in time we now have to use the real exchange rate $\sigma = sp^*/p$ in the goods markets dynamics behind the parameter d_y, which when linearized by first-order Taylor approximation gives rise to the following modification of the model considered in Section 5.6 (with symmetry now assumed, in addition):

$$\dot{Y} = \beta_y \left[-(1 - a_y)Y + b_y q + c_y Y^* + d_y \sigma_o \left(\frac{s}{s_o} + \frac{p^*}{p_o^*} - \frac{p}{p_o} \right) + e_y \right]$$

$$\dot{Y}^* = \beta_y \left[-(1 - a_y)Y^* + b_y q^* + c_y Y - d_y \sigma_o \left(\frac{s}{s_o} + \frac{p^*}{p_o^*} - \frac{p}{p_o} \right) + e_y \right]$$

$$\dot{q} = (i_o + a_i(s_o - s))q - r, \quad r = a_r Y + b_r$$

$$\dot{q}^* = (i_o - a_i(s_o - s))q^* - r^*, \quad r^* = a_r Y^* + b_r$$

$$\hat{s} = 2a_i(s_o - s)$$

$$\dot{p} = \beta_w p_o(Y - \bar{Y})$$

$$\dot{p}^* = \beta_w p_o^*(Y^* - \bar{Y})$$

Considering the averages of this 7D dynamical system gives rise to the same 2D dynamics as already investigated in Section 5.7. Convergence to the steady-state averages is therefore ensured in this extension of the model of Section 5.6. With respect to differences, we now, however, get the following 4D dynamics

14 Note here and in the following that we do not use logarithms, but only use first-order Taylor approximations for the terms we want to linearize.

(under the assumption that $p_o = p_o^*$ holds, see below):

$$\dot{Y}^\delta = \beta_y[-(1 - a_y - c_y)Y^\delta + b_y q^\delta + 2d_y \sigma_o \frac{s}{s_o} - 2d_y \sigma_o/p_o \cdot p^\delta]$$

$$\dot{q}^\delta = [-2a_i(s - s_o) + i_o]q^\delta - a_r Y^\delta$$

$$\hat{s} = -2a_i(s - s_o)$$

$$\dot{p}^\delta = \beta_w p_o Y^\delta$$

We assume again that the autonomous dynamics of the nominal exchange rate has already settled down at its steady-state position s_o. We need therefore only investigate the stability of the remaining 3D dynamics in the state variables $Y^\delta, q^\delta, p^\delta$. The Jacobian matrix of this reduced dynamics exhibits the following sign structure:

$$J_0 = \begin{pmatrix} - & + & - \\ - & i_o & 0 \\ + & 0 & 0 \end{pmatrix}$$

It is easy to show that the Routh–Hurwitz stability conditions are all fulfilled (since i_o is small) with the exception of the determinant of J_o which is positive in this case (but small, due to its multiplicative dependence on i_o). The system is therefore slightly explosive and needs further stabilizing effort from the side of monetary policy in order to allow full convergence to its steady-state position.

Moreover, this steady-state position needs some further discussion, since output values are now equal to the NAIRU value $\bar{Y}$ in the steady-state and are therefore no longer determined through goods market equilibrium but through labor market equilibrium instead. From the (nonlinearized) equations of the model we can first of all conclude that s must be equal to the value s_o (not yet determined) via the UIP condition. This in turn implies, by means of the postulated Taylor rules, that $i = i^* = i_o$, i.e., interest rate equality with the steady-state rate of interest rate set by the central banks. We then obtain for the values of Tobin's q given expressions of the type $r(\bar{Y})/i_o$ which, when inserted into the goods market equilibrium equations (which are identical for the two countries), determine the steady-state value of the real exchange rate σ, since output must be equal to its natural level. We now assume that the central banks know this natural level of σ and base their interest rate policy on the (so far undetermined) condition $s_o = \sigma_o$. This then finally implies that $p_o = p_o^*$ must hold true in the steady-state, a condition that is needed for the application of the symmetric country assumption and the mathematical methodology based on it (concerning $\dot{p}^\delta$ here).

In order to get full convergence in the above two-country model with Dornbusch inflation dynamics we now augment the coordinated Taylor rules of the two countries as follows:

$$i = i_o + a_i(s_o - s) + b_i\hat{p} \tag{5.30}$$

$$i^* = i_o - a_i(s_o - s) + b_i\hat{p}^* \tag{5.31}$$

This now gives for the law of motion for s the equation:

$$\hat{s} = i - i^* = 2a_i(s_o - s) + b_i\hat{p} - b_i\hat{p}^* = 2a_i(s_o - s) + b_i\hat{p}^\delta$$

$$= 2a_i(s_o - s) + b_i\beta_w p_o Y^\delta$$

This extended Taylor rule modifies the Jacobian of the difference economy for the now four interacting state variables Y^δ, q^δ, s, p^δ as follows:

$$J_0 = \begin{pmatrix} - & + & + & - \\ - & i_o & 0 & 0 \\ 0 & 0 & - & + \\ + & 0 & 0 & 0 \end{pmatrix}$$

Since i_o is small, the trace of the matrix J_o is surely negative. Using the same argument again, the sum of principal minors of order two is easily shown to be positive. It is also easily shown that the determinant of the 4D Jacobian is positive (and small). For the sum of principal minors of order three we finally get a negative value if the value of the new parameter b_i in the Taylor rule is chosen sufficiently small. We thus find that the coefficients a_i of the characteristic polynomial of the matrix J_o are all positive, as is required by the Routh–Hurwitz stability conditions. According to Asada et al. (2003, Theorem A.6) we have, however, to show in addition for the validity of asymptotic stability that the following holds: $a_1 a_2 a_3 - a_1^2 a_4 - a_3^2 > 0$. Since the determinant of J_o is small, we have that a_4 is close to zero. There thus remains to be shown that $a_1 a_2 - a_3 > 0$ holds true for the trace and the principal minors of order 2 and 3. Using again the condition that i_o is small and if b_i is chosen with care, then this result is also implied, since the expressions in $a_1 a_2$ are then dominating the principal minors of order three of the Jacobian matrix J_o.

We thus conclude that a cautious anti-inflationary interest policy rule can stabilize the economy where Phillips curve dynamics has been added to the goods and asset markets dynamics that we have considered in the preceding sections. This makes our model comparable to the Turnovsky (1986) IS–LM two-country model, but now with Tobin's q in the aggregate demand function in place of the real rate of interest of conventional textbook analysis. We here, however, arrive at the result that the central banks should use conventional gaps as well as an unconventionally signed nominal exchange rate gap in order to stabilize the economy in the presence of perfect substitution between bonds and equities and perfect foresight on capital gains through stock price and exchange rate dynamics.

5.9 Outlook: Imperfect capital markets

This chapter has shown – if one accepts the perfectness assumptions made with respect to asset substitution and expected capital gains – that a better solution to the instability problems considered (the centrifugal exchange rate as well as stock price dynamics) may be to choose the Taylor interest rate policy rule appropriately in the light of the structure of the private sector, rather than to try to enforce three unstable roots and two stable ones on the dynamics by a more or less conventional type of Taylor rule in order to allow for the application of the JVT of the RE school. Yet, even if one can generate stability in this way, this solution procedure nevertheless shows that the extremely perfect structure of the financial sector implies the need for a – from an applied point of view – rather strange interest rate reaction function as far as financial markets are concerned, where it has to be assumed that a monetary policy intended to counteract the country's exchange rate depreciation should lower the interest in this country, not increase it as conventional wisdom might suggest.

The reason for this strange result can be easily detected if exchange rate dynamics are formulated with some sluggishness in their reaction to interest rate differentials. A simple illustration is provided by the following example, where we assume given exchange rate expectations $\hat{s}^e$ for the time being:

$$\hat{s} = \beta_s(i^*(s) + \hat{s}^e - i(s)).$$

Clearly, a positive reaction of the domestic interest rate and a negative reaction of the foreign interest rate to the exchange rate, the opposite of what we have used in the preceding section, would contribute now to exchange rate stability, if it is (of course) assumed that exchange rates are increasing if expected returns on foreign bonds are higher than the returns on domestic bonds. This postulated exchange rate reaction is compatible with the direction of capital flows behind the assumed adjustment equation. Yet, going from such fast to infinitely fast exchange rate reactions implies $i(s) = i^*(s) + \hat{s}^e$, which, together with the assumption of myopic perfect foresight, gives

$$\hat{s} = \hat{s}^e = i(s) - i^*(s),$$

i.e., a sign reversal with respect to the role played by the interest rate differential. This is the reason why policy must also accept a sign reversal in its orientation in order to be successful in this limit case. It also suggests that approaching the limit case is producing a discontinuity in the behavior of the economy. More generally speaking, we claim here that the limit case is structurally unstable with respect to any model that allows for imperfect substitution and imperfect foresight; i.e., it cannot be approached by considering degrees of imperfection that are shrinking to zero. But if the limit is only of strictly isolated importance, it may be questioned whether it is useful for policy advice. This also holds for the models of Sections 5.3 and 5.5 which are close in spirit to the nowadays popular DSGE approach, which is in fact used for applied policy analysis and policy recommendations (see Smets and Wouters (2003) for an example).

The conclusion we draw from this is that models of portfolio choice with only imperfect asset substitution augmented by heterogeneous (necessarily imperfect) expectation formation and somewhat delayed adjustment processes are the better choice if one wants to model the world in a way that is seen to be mathematically robust and descriptively relevant, in place of the extremely idealized stock market (long-term bond markets) and exchange rate dynamics of today's DSGE models, where determinacy and convergence are enforced but not proved. Such modifications of the perfectness assumptions of the present chapter will be the topics investigated in the later chapters of the book.

5.10 References

ASADA, T., C. CHIARELLA, P. FLASCHEL and R. FRANKE (2003): *Open Economy Macrodynamics: An Integrated Disequilibrium Approach.* Heidelberg: Springer.

BLANCHARD, O. (1981): Output, the stock market, and interest rates. *American Economic Review*, 71, 132–143.

CHIARELLA, C., P. FLASCHEL, G. GROH and W. SEMMLER (2000): *Disequilibrium, Growth and Labor Market Dynamics.* Heidelberg: Springer.

DORNBUSCH, R. (1976): Expectations and exchange rate dynamics. *Journal of Political Economy*, 84, 1161–1175.

FLASCHEL, P. and F. HARTMANN (2007): Perfect finance-led world capitalism in a nutshell. *CEM Working Paper* 145, Bielefeld University, Germany.

FLASCHEL, P., G. GROH, C. PROAÑO and W. SEMMLER (2008): *Topics in Applied Macrodynamic Theory.* Heidelberg: Springer.

GRAY, M. and S. TURNOVSKY (1979): The stability of exchange rate dynamics under myopic perfect foresight. *International Economic Review*, 20, 641–660.

HARTMANN, F. (2007): Perfect finance-led world capitalism in a nutshell. Blanchard stock-market and Dornbusch exchange-rate dynamics, a synthesis. Diploma thesis, Bielefeld University, Germany.

MCKIBBIN, W. and J. SACHS (1991): *Global Linkages. Macroeconomic Interdependence and Cooperation in the World Economy.* Washington, DC: The Brookings Institution.

SMETS, F. and R. WOUTERS (2003): An estimated stochastic dynamic general equilibrium model of the Euro area. *Journal of the Economic Association*, 5, 1123–1175.

TURNOVSKY, S.J. (1986): Monetary and fiscal policy under perfect foresight: a symmetric two country analysis. *Economica*, 53, 139–157.

WOODFORD, M. (2003): *Interest and Prices. Foundations of a Theory of Monetary Policy.* Princeton, NJ: Princeton University Press.

Part II

Stock market dynamics and the macroeconomy

Some extensions

6 Output and stock market dynamics with state-dependent financial market reactions

6.1 Introduction

The Blanchard (1981) model of real–financial interaction provides one of the paradigm models of interaction between real and financial markets. As already discussed the model reformulates Keynesian IS–LM analysis from the perspective of a richer array of financial assets, namely long-term bonds and equities besides the usual presence of money and short-term bonds of (or textbook presentations of) the IS–LM model.[1] The basic change in Blanchard's extension of the IS–LM approach is that investment demand (and consumption demand) now depend on Tobin's average q in the place of the real rate of interest. As a consequence, share price dynamics (but not yet long-term bond price dynamics)[2] feed back into the real sector, thereby creating one of the links for real–financial interaction. The conventional LM schedule or money market equilibrium of this approach, which as usual is dependent on real output and income, in turn provides the channel back from real to financial markets. The share price dynamics is determined by assuming a situation of perfect substitution and perfect foresight with respect to the interest-bearing assets.

In this chapter we reconsider and generalize Blanchard's description of real–financial interaction with two objectives in mind. Our first objective concerns the formulation of the model. We seek to make the role of Tobin's q in the investment demand more transparent. We give a more consistent formulation that avoids some variables being expressed in their naturally occurring units (e.g. output) and others being expressed as logarithms of their naturally occurring units (e.g. money and price). Our formulation is also made consistent with the broader macroeconomic framework developed in Chiarella and Flaschel (2000) as a preliminary step to the development of consistent financial market dynamics in a broader framework. Our second and more significant objective (which is also important for our first objective) is to reconsider the dynamics of real–financial

---

1 Or long-term bonds in the place of short-term ones if the Baumol–Tobin inventory approach to money holdings is replaced by a Keynesian approach to speculative money holdings as in the Tobin portfolio choice model (see Crouch (1972) for details).
2 See Blanchard and Fischer (1989) for incorporation of interest rate dynamics.

interactions in a way that does not rely on the poorly motivated jump variable technique to resolve the dilemma of unstable saddle-path dynamics around the steady state. The achievement of these two objectives constitutes an essential preliminary step in the construction of more detailed, consistently formulated models of real–financial interaction that will allow the inclusion of, for example, capital accumulation, flexible prices, stabilization policies and other important features of the macroeconomy.

In Section 6.2 we outline the model of real–financial interaction, focusing on the role of Tobin's average q in the investment function and on the role of the differential between expected equity returns and the short-term rate of interest in driving the stock market dynamics. Our framework is also more general than that of Blanchard in that we assume less than infinite speed of adjustment to this return differential, and we also assume less than perfect foresight of expectations of the change in Tobin's q. In Section 6.3 we analyze the dynamics of the model along the lines of Blanchard, in particular assuming infinite adjustment of the share market to the return differential and myopic perfect foresight expectations. We also discuss how the jump variable technique is used to "close" the dynamics of the variant of the model analyzed in this section and what we perceive as some of the shortcomings of this approach. In Section 6.4 we consider the more general version of the model with less than infinite adjustment speed to return differentials in the stock market and less than perfect foresight expectations. We also introduce a mechanism by which the speed of adjustment of the stock market to the return differential changes according to the state of the market. We show how to analyze the qualitative dynamic behavior of this model by the technique of phase-diagram patching, which makes clear how the dynamics can alternate between periods of stock market upswings and downswings having both tranquil and activated phases. In Section 6.5 we present an alternative way to avoid the use of the jump variable technique which gives prominence to inflationary expectations and a non-linear price adjustment mechanism. The dynamics of the resulting system collapses to a three-dimensional relaxation cycle in the perfect of foresight limit. In Section 6.6 we draw some conclusions.

6.2 The model

In this section we introduce the notation and set out the static and dynamic economic relationships that define the macroeconomy with real–financial interaction that will be the object of our study. Since these issues have already been treated extensively in Chapter 2, we shall be brief here as far as the treatment of the dynamics of the model under rational expectations is concerned.

6.2.1 Notation

The following subsections provide the variables, the parameters and the mathematical notation we shall use in our reformulation of the Blanchard (1981) model of real–financial interaction, exhibiting the market for goods and the four asset markets (money, short-term bonds, long-term bonds and equities). Note that we use extensive-form variables (and thus not logarithms of money and price level as in Blanchard (1981)) throughout and that the money demand function, though here completely linear, represents a generalization of the form that was used by Blanchard (1981) in his equation (6.2). For simplicity, Tobin's q is only used (in average form) in the investment function, which is based on the assumption of fixed proportions in production. Adding a dependence of consumption to Tobin's q would not alter the conclusions obtained in this chapter. We focus on the case of fixed proportions in production in order to make more transparent the dynamic structure of the economic processes under study. This follows the same style of treatment as in Chiarella and Flaschel (2000), who show that the case of smooth substitution in production does not alter the basic qualitative dynamic features of the type of dynamic macroeconomic models under study here.

Variables

The variables of the model are:

Y	Output
Y^d	Aggregate demand
p_e	Share price
$q = p_e E/(pK)$	Tobin's average q
m^d	Demand for real balances
i	Short-term interest rate
p_b	Bond price
Π	Real profits
$r = \Pi/K$	Rate of profit
L^d	Labor demand
$p_e^e(\hat{p}_e^e)$	Expected value of (rate of change in) the price of equities
$q^e(\hat{q}^e)$	Expected value of (rate of change in) Tobin's q
$\varepsilon = (\Pi/K)/q + \hat{p}_e^e - i$	Expected return differential between equities and the short-term interest rate

Parameters

The parameters of the model are:[3]

$c \; (0 < c < 1)$	Marginal propensity to consume
ψ	Marginal propensity to invest
T	Real taxes
G	Real government consumption
M	Money supply

---

3 All parameters are assumed to be positive unless otherwise stated.

$p (=1!)$	Price level
w	Nominal wages
k, h_1, h_2	Money demand parameters
m	Real balances
B	Number of long-term bonds
E	Number of equities
K	Real capital stock
δ	Depreciation rate of the capital stock
$x = Y/L^d$	Labor productivity
$v = wL^d/(pY) = w/(px)$	Wage share
I	Autonomous component of investment
C	Autonomous component of consumption
β_x	Adjustment speed of variable x

6.2.2 The equations of the model

The equations of the model are subdivided into algebraic (= instantaneous) ones and dynamic ones, which together determine the statically and dynamically endogenous variables of the model.

Algebraic equations

This block of the model describes a simple aggregate demand function Y^d (equation 6.1) depending on output (via consumption) and Tobin's average q (via investment). The demand for real balances (equation 6.2) is a traditional one depending positively on output and negatively on the short-term interest rate. Equation 6.3 is a standard equation for money market equilibrium. Finally, we have an obvious equation for real profits (equation 6.4), which depend solely on economic activity Y. Thus we have:

$$Y^d = C + c(Y - \delta K - T) + I + \psi(q - 1) + \delta K + G, c \in (0,1), \tag{6.1}$$

$$m^d = M^d/p = kY + h_1 - h_2 i, \tag{6.2}$$

$$m = m^d, \tag{6.3}$$

$$\Pi = (1 - v)Y - \delta K. \tag{6.4}$$

Dynamic equations

The dynamic variables are output, share price and bond price. Output adjustment is based on the simple textbook dynamic multiplier story as indicated in equation (6.5). Blanchard assumes that short-term bonds, long-term bonds and shares are perfect substitutes and there is myopic perfect foresight on capital gains. Thus equations (6.6) and (6.7) indicate that the dividend rate of return on equities and the interest rate of return on long-term bonds have both to be augmented by a corresponding expression for capital gains when their full return is compared with the return on short-term fixed price bonds. Thus we write[4]

$$\dot{Y} = \beta_y(Y^d - Y), \tag{6.5}$$

$$i = \frac{p\Pi + \dot{p}_e E}{p_e E} = \frac{p\Pi}{p_e E} + \hat{p}_e = \frac{\Pi/K}{q} + \hat{q} \quad (K, E, p = \text{const!}), \tag{6.6}$$

$$i = \frac{B + \dot{p}_b B}{p_b B} = \hat{p}_b + \frac{1}{p_b}. \tag{6.7}$$

Note also that the bond price dynamics do not feed back into the rest of the system, since there are neither wealth effects nor interest rate effects in the aggregate demand function on the market for goods.

We shall generalize Blanchard's treatment of share price dynamics in the following way:

$$\hat{q} = \beta_q \left(\frac{\Pi/K}{q} + z - i \right) = \beta_q \varepsilon, \tag{6.8}$$

$$\dot{z} = \beta_z(\hat{q} - z), z \equiv \hat{p}_e^e = \hat{q}^e. \tag{6.9}$$

This extension assumes (equation (6.8)) that there is imperfect substitution between shares and short-term bonds and that share prices p^e (as reflected by Tobin's q) react with less than infinite speed to ε, the differential between expected equity returns (dividend return plus expected capital gains) and the short-term rate of interest. Equation (6.9) states that expectations of capital gains adjust, with some lag, to share price changes. The original Blanchard model is recovered by setting $\beta_q = \infty$ in equation (6.8), which then collapses to the arbitrage condition

$$\frac{\Pi/K}{q} = i - z, \tag{6.10}$$

and $\beta_z = \infty$ in equation (6.9), which becomes the myopic perfect foresight rule

$$\hat{q} = z. \tag{6.11}$$

Note that we use the term myopic perfect foresight to indicate that agents form expectations according to (6.11). We use the term entirely perfect foresight when it is assumed, in addition, that agents have full knowledge of the model and its dynamics, so, that they are in a position to carry out all the calculations required by the jump variable technique, to be discussed below.

Note that we are assuming a background of a stationary economy in which the capital stock is not growing and no new shares are issued. Furthermore, the assumption of constant nominal and real money stock will result in no inflation and so, in steady state, there is no increase in equity price.

---

4 For a dynamic variable x we write $\hat{x} = \dot{x}/x$.

6.3 Analysis of the model

In this section we analyze the dynamics of the model in a similar fashion to Blanchard (1981) in that we consider the limit case of β_q and β_z equal to infinity in equations (6.8) and (6.9). In other words, we assume instantaneous adjustment of share prices to the expected return differential, perfect substitutability and myopic perfect foresight of expected share price changes.

6.3.1 Reduced-form dynamics

The inverted money market equilibrium, from equations (6.2) and (6.3), reads[5]

$$i = \frac{kY + h_1 - m}{h_2}, \quad m = M/p. \tag{6.12}$$

The use of this equation and the assumption that β_q and β_z are infinite reduces equations (6.5)–(6.9) to the following nonlinear autonomous differential equation system of dimension 2:

$$\dot{Y} = \beta_y(C + c(Y - \delta K - T) + I + \psi(q - 1) + \delta K + G - Y)$$

$$= \beta_y(-(1 - c)Y + \psi(q - 1) + A), \ A \equiv C + I + \delta K + G - c(T + \delta K), \tag{6.13}$$

$$\dot{q} = \frac{kY + h_1 - m}{h_2} q - ((1 - v)Y/K - \delta) = iq - r. \tag{6.14}$$

The laws of motion for Y and q are interdependent and thus interact solely with each other, since there are no interest or wealth effects in aggregate demand as far as the holding of long-term bonds is concerned. The law of motion for p_b given by equation (6.7) is thus an appended one.[6]

Note that the second law of motion, equation (6.14), is nonlinear due to the multiplicative Yq term and similarly for the third appended law of motion because of the Yp_b term. There are thus natural or intrinsic nonlinearities in the interaction of real and financial markets (if fully interdependent) that give the dynamics a structure with some similarities to the famous Lorenz equations (see Strogatz (1994, p. 301)). However, in the present situation these intrinsic nonlinearities are not sufficient to bound the dynamics in situations of instability of the steady state.

---

5 This should be contrasted with Blanchard's equation (6.2) which uses the logarithm of m in place of our m.

6 The dynamics of long-term bond prices should, however, be allowed to feed back into the rest of the dynamics in future extensions of the model.

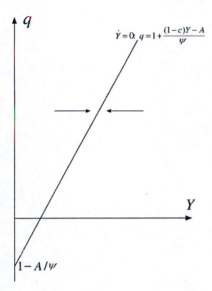

$\dot{Y}=0, \ q=1+\dfrac{(1-c)Y-A}{\psi}$

$1-A/\psi$

Figure 6.1 The IS–curve (representing goods market equilibrium).

6.3.2 The IS curve: $\dot{Y}=0$

Setting the first law of motion equal to zero and solving for Y gives the goods market equilibrium representation ($\dot{Y}=0$ isocline) of the model. This IS curve,

$$\dot{Y}=0: \quad Y=\frac{1}{1-c}[A+\psi(q-1)], \tag{6.15}$$

is attracting, since the marginal propensity to spend has been assumed to be less than one. All positions off the IS curve are therefore attracted by this curve, as indicated by the horizontal arrows in Figure 6.1.

6.3.3 The LM curve: $\dot{q}=0$

Similarly, setting the second law of motion to rest ($\dot{q}=0$) gives us the LM curve or asset markets equilibrium curve of the model:

$$\dot{q}=0: \quad q(Y)=\frac{((1-v)Y/K-\delta)h_2}{kY+h_1-m}\equiv\frac{h_2[(1-v)Y/K-\delta]}{D(Y)}. \tag{6.16}$$

We point out that this isocline is a hyperbola with two branches. Furthermore, it is important to distinguish two cases:[7] the first, $q'(Y)<0, q''(Y)>0$, that

---

7 We note that

$$q'(Y)=h_2\frac{(1-v)(h_1-m)/K+\delta k}{D(Y)^2}.$$

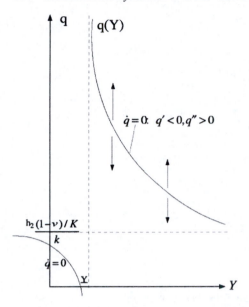

Figure 6.2 The LM curve (representing money market and equity market equilibrium): Blanchard's bad news case.

corresponds to Blanchard's bad news case (when the stock market and output move in opposite directions); the second, $q'(Y) > 0, q''(Y) < 0$, that corresponds to Blanchard's good news case (when the stock market and output move in the same direction). These two cases are displayed in Figures 6.2 and 6.3.

We have denoted by $\underline{Y}$ in Figure 6.2 the solution of $D(Y) \equiv kY + h_1 - m = 0$, i.e., the unique value of Y where money market equilibrium displays a zero rate of interest. To the left (right) of $\underline{Y}$ interest is negative (positive), so only the output levels to the right of $\underline{Y}$ are economically meaningful (see Figure 6.3 for a further restriction on the economic phase space).

Along the $\dot{q} = 0$ isocline we have that the money market is (as always) in equilibrium and so is the stock market, in the sense that share prices are no longer changing and there is a static equality between the dividend rate of return and the rate of interest on short-term bonds. Note that positions off the LM curve tend away from this curve, as indicated by the vertical arrows in Figures 6.2 and 6.3, i.e., share prices are subject to centrifugal forces off the $\dot{q} = 0$ isocline. Depending on the slope of the LM curve, the dynamics may therefore be characterized by saddlepoint dynamics, as will be shown below.

The properties of the IS and LM curves have already been extensively discussed in Chapter 2 and will thus be summarized here only graphically. We also consider only briefly the steady-state positions of the dynamics of equations (6.13) and (6.14) and the dynamics surrounding them by means of Figures 6.4 and 6.5.

Note that Blanchard (1981) only investigates the situation where the IS curve is steeper than the LM curve, i.e., only the steady states E_1 of Figures 6.4 and 6.5,

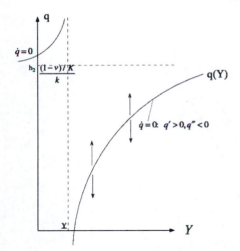

Figure 6.3 The LM curve (representing money market and equity market equilibrium): Blanchard's good news case.

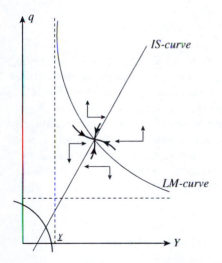

Figure 6.4 A uniquely determined steady state in Blanchard's bad news case.

while he states in a footnote that E_2 has undesirable comparative static and stability properties. This however is not so obvious since the instability of the adjustment rule for share prices q would be overcome there by a strongly stabilizing multiplier effect that would indeed make the dynamics converge to E_2. In such a situation one of the unstable saddle arms of E_1 converges to E_2, as shown in Figure 6.5.

In this section we have reviewed, within the context of the framework laid out in Section 6.2, the dynamics of real–financial interaction when there is perfect myopic

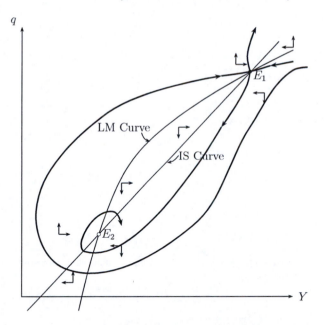

Figure 6.5 The good news case: saddle (E_1) and stable node (E_2).

foresight ($\beta_z = \infty$) and perfect substitution ($\beta_q = \infty$). The typical equilibrium, E_1, is saddlepoint in nature and we shall henceforth focus on the dynamics around this equilibrium. For the sake of completeness of the discussion we have shown the dynamics around the equilibrium E_2 in Figure 6.5. However, it turns out that when the mechanism of real–financial interaction is embedded into more completely specified models, as in Chiarella et al. (2000a, b and 2003), the equilibrium is unique and of type E_1. We now proceed to discuss the solution technique that has been established in the literature for solving the instability problems that are caused by the saddlepoint nature of E_1-type equilibria if the dynamics evolve from predetermined initial conditions.

6.3.4 The dynamics according to the jump variable technique

We now discuss the dynamics of the good news and the bad news cases from the perspective of the jump variable technique solution procedures applied by Blanchard (1981) (see also Blanchard and Fischer (1989) for a closely related approach to real–financial interaction).

   Figure 6.4 shows for the bad news case the locally unstable saddlepath situation that always results in this case from an attracting IS and a repelling LM curve. This instability is overcome (following the methodology proposed by Sargent and Wallace (1973)) by assuming that the fast variable q (or better p_e) is considered as infinitely fast in its adjustment and that this adjustment always puts this variable onto one of the stable arms shown in Figure 6.4 in the case of unanticipated shocks, in particular fiscal and monetary shocks. Thus, although there is a well specified law of motion for the variable q, this law is temporarily switched off at the moment when the shock occurs and q undergoes infinitely fast vertical motion onto the only path that is capable of bringing this variable back to the steady-state position that is relevant in the after-shock situation.

Blanchard (1981, p. 135) himself seems to imply some doubt about how convincing the jump variable assumption really can be.[8] Burmeister (1980) stresses many of the conceptual issues that such saddlepoint instability raises and Oxley and George (1994) also give a cogent critique of the jump variable methodology. But by and large the literature has uncritically accepted the jump variable technique methodology and indeed no longer bothers to give any rationalization of its meaningfulness and use. If a dynamic economic model is properly specified, then equilibrium selection should be an outcome of the operation of the dynamics engendered by its laws of motion. If the equilibrium selection is the result of an arbitrary assumption on the placement of a certain dynamic variable onto a particular point in the phase space of the dynamics, then, in our view, the dynamics of the model has not been properly or fully specified.[9]

From our perspective, the jump variable technique has shortcomings on a number of fronts. First, it gives to the agents complete knowledge of the model and its dynamics as well as unlimited computational ability to calculate the precise magnitude and nature of the jump required to arrive precisely on the stable manifold of the saddlepoint.[10] Of course, none of this may seem a problem if one accepts uncritically all the tenets of the rational expectations paradigm. Second, there is an assumption of infinite speed of adjustment to asset return differentials coupled with an assumption of perfect substitutability of assets. Whilst we agree that agents adjust very rapidly to return differentials, this adjustment may not be infinite and may vary according to market conditions. Also, some imperfect substitutability between assets may exist for a variety of motives. Third is the assumption of entirely perfect foresight of expectations. This assumption came to be uncritically accepted because the jump variable methodology developed in the era when only the totally rational and omniscient economic agent inhabited

8 To quote Blanchard's exact words on p. 135 at the end of section II; "Following a standard if not entirely convincing practice, I shall assume that q always adjusts so as to leave the economy on the stable path to equilibrium".

9 We stress here that all of our comments apply only to descriptive approaches to macrodynamics, such as the present one, and not to model types where optimizing behavior puts the actions of economic agents onto a certain point in the considered phase space. In this latter type of approach the very nature of the optimizing procedure reduces the relevant phase space to a stable submanifold of the full phase space.

10 This computational burden may not seem too onerous in the simple model discussed in this paper, but we suggest it would become massive in a higher-order model involving any degree of nonlinearity. These computations are manageable in a linearized framework and there is a developed methodology (see, e.g., Buiter (1984)), but we would suggest the agents would face considerable computational difficulties in determining the stable manifold of the underlying nonlinear model.

the world of macroeconomic theorizing. In an era when some place is also being found for boundedly rational agents, it would seem appropriate to consider the impact of less than perfect foresight of expectations.

6.4 State-of-market dependent reaction speed – an alternative to the JVT

As we pointed out in the previous section, the jump variable solution technique relies on perfect asset substitutability and on agents adjusting infinitely rapidly to asset return differentials. Entirely perfect foresight expectations are also assumed. A relaxation of all of these assumptions is the basis of the alternative to the jump variable technique (JVT) in Chiarella (1986) and Flaschel and Sethi (1999) in relation to a monetary dynamics model, and in Chiarella (1990a) for the Dornbusch (1976) model of exchange rate dynamics. This approach essentially relies on the imperfect substitutability between alternative assets and in particular on portfolio constraint considerations that must become binding as the economy moves further and further from steady state. However, the eventual operation of portfolio constraints may take a long time to become binding. Furthermore, this solution leaves economic agents no scope to react to changing market conditions. The solution to the saddlepoint instability problem that we develop in this section seeks to address these two shortcomings, and leaves far more scope for agents to react to expected asset return differentials.

We shall assume that our economic agents are less perfect than those who inhabit the world of rational expectations. Recall that in the present context perfection means the agents have full knowledge of the model and its dynamics and display speed-of-reaction coefficients $\beta_z = \infty$ and $\beta_q = \infty$. However, we do assume that they are not too far removed from this (economists') ideal perfect state, in that their value of β_z is still very high so that they are operating with close to myopic perfect foresight expectations. We remove from the agents full knowledge of the model (i.e., they do not know the laws of motion) but do allow them to have some reasonable knowledge of its steady state. Our most radical departure from the world of rational expectations is our assumption about the reaction coefficient β_q, which is allowed to change as a function of market conditions, in particular as a function of the expected return differential ε between equity and the short-term rate of interest. When market conditions are such that ε is close to its steady state ε_0, the reaction coefficient β_q is rather high so that agents are reacting strongly to the expected return differential. However, the high β_q (coupled with the high β_z) causes the steady state to be locally unstable and leads to a rise (or fall) in the stock market and hence a rise or fall in the expected return differential. Agents initially follow this general movement in the stock market; however, as it proceeds further and further they are conscious that the economy is moving ever further from its steady state (of which they are assumed to have some reasonable idea) and they start to react more cautiously to the expected return differential. This cautiousness is reflected in an eventual lowering of the value of the coefficient β_q, to a value sufficiently low to cause a turn-around in the dynamics that once again becomes

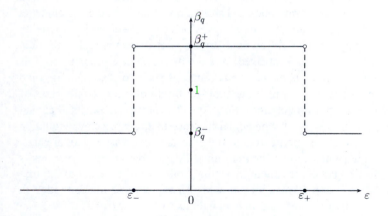

Figure 6.6 The behavior of the reaction coefficient β_q.

stable towards the steady state. Eventually β_q returns to its former high levels and the possibility of another upward (or downward) stock market movement is established.

The behavior of β_q as a function of the difference in ε from its steady-state value ε_0 is illustrated in Figure 6.6. We have drawn this function somewhat skewed to the right to indicate greater (less) caution when the share market is below (above) its steady-state value. We have taken a highly stylized form for β_q which can only assume two values: $\beta_q^+ (> 1)$ close to steady state; $\beta_q^- (< 1)$ far from steady state. This stylized form makes very transparent the dynamic behavior of the model. The analysis could later be extended to allow for a continuous function β_q.[11] We now seek to analyze the qualitative nature of the dynamics that this state-of-market dependent reaction coefficient brings about.

6.4.1 Local stability analysis

Referring to equations (6.5), (6.8) and (6.9), we now consider the following 3D dynamical system:

$$\dot{Y} = \beta_y(-(1-c)Y + \psi(q-1) + A), \tag{6.17}$$

$$\hat{q} = \beta_q\left(\frac{(1-v)Y/K - \delta}{q} + z - i\right), \quad i = (kY + h_1 - m)/h_2, \tag{6.18}$$

$$\dot{z} = \beta_z(\hat{q} - z), \quad z = \hat{q}^e. \tag{6.19}$$

---

11 A similar continuous type of reaction function has been introduced into a model of monetary dynamics by Chiarella and Khomin (2000).

We thus now allow, via equation (6.18), for an expected rate-of-return differential between short-term bonds and shares, resulting from the current level of Tobin's q and expected capital gains $z = \hat{q}^e$, which can now differ from actually realized capital gains.[12] This differential drives asset demands and with them share prices (all other things kept fixed) into the direction of a reduction of this return differential (as long as expectations remain fixed); for example, up (and the dividend rate of return down) if the short-term rate of interest falls short of the expected rate of return on equities. Subsequently, however, expected capital gains are revised on the basis of the actual increase in share prices via equation (6.19), which gives further momentum to the process of increasing capital gains, and so forth. As we noted earlier, the traditional JVT analysis of the dynamics as discussed in Section 6.2 comes about by setting both β_q and β_z equal to infinity, resulting in algebraic conditions on rates of return and expectation formation in place of the above two laws of motion in equations (6.18) and (6.19).

The steady state Y_0, q_0 and z_0 of the dynamical system (6.17) – (6.19) is given by $z_0 = 0$ and the simultaneous solution of (6.15) and (6.16) for Y_0 and q_0. It is important to realize that this system represents two dynamical systems: one for the dynamic motion close to the steady state when $\beta_q = \beta_q^+$; the other for dynamic motion far from the steady state when $\beta_q = \beta_q^-$. The steady states of both of these systems are the same as those of the limit case $\beta_q = \beta_z = \infty$. The Jacobian of the dynamical system (6.17)–(6.19), calculated at a steady state, turns out to be

$$
J^{3D} = \begin{bmatrix} J_{11} & J_{12} & 0 \\ -\beta_q J_{21} & -\beta_q J_{22} & \beta_q q_0 \\ -\dfrac{\beta_z \beta_q}{q_0} J_{21} & -\dfrac{\beta_z \beta_q}{q_0} J_{22} & \beta_z(\beta_q - 1) \end{bmatrix}, \tag{6.20}
$$

where the elements J_{11}, J_{12}, J_{21} and J_{22} are the elements of the Jacobian matrix J^{2D} of equations (6.13) and (6.14) and are given by

$$ J_{11} = -(1-c)\beta_y, \quad J_{12} = \psi\beta_y, \quad J_{21} = kq_0/h_2 - (1-v)/K, \quad J_{22} = i_0. $$

By setting β_q equal to $\beta_q^+(\beta_q^-)$ in (6.20) we obtain the Jacobian $J_+^{3D}(J_-^{3D})$ for the dynamical system close to (far from) steady state. Routine calculations yield

$$ \det J^{3D} = \beta_q \beta_z \det J^{2D}, \tag{6.21} $$

and that the principal minors of J^{3D} satisfy

$$ J_1^{3D} = \beta_z \beta_q J_{22} > 0, \quad J_2^{3D} = \beta_z(\beta_q - 1)J_{11} \quad \text{and} \quad J_3^{3D} = -\beta_q \det J^{2D}. \tag{6.22} $$

---

12 From an empirical perspective, it may be appropriate to add a risk premium to the return of shares (as a markup on the nominal rate of interest), but for simplicity this is left aside here.

We recall the Routh–Hurwitz necessary and sufficient conditions for the local asymptotic stability of a steady state of the 3D dynamical system (6.17)–(6.19),[13] namely

$$\text{trace}\,(J^{3D}) < 0, \quad \Theta \equiv J_1^{3D} + J_2^{3D} + J_3^{3D} > 0, \quad \det J^{3D} < 0, \qquad (6.23)$$

and

$$\Delta \equiv -\text{trace}\,(J^{3D})(J_1^{3D} + J_2^{3D} + J_3^{3D}) + \det J^{3D} > 0. \qquad (6.24)$$

At the steady state E_1 considered by Blanchard (where the IS curve is steeper than the LM curve) we can easily check that $\det J^{2D} < 0$. Hence by equations (6.21) and (6.22), we must have at such a steady state that $\det J^{3D} < 0$, $J_1^{3D} > 0$ and $J_3^{3D} > 0$, independently of whether β_q equals β_q^+ or β_q^-.

Consider the dynamics close to the steady state where $\beta_q = \beta_q^+ > 1$. In this case it is clear that by choosing β_z sufficiently large we can always obtain trace $(J_+^{3D}) > 0$, thus overturning the first of the conditions (6.23) for local asymptotic stability. Hence we can assert that for β_z sufficiently large, the dynamics close to the steady state is locally unstable.

Consider the dynamics far from the steady state where $\beta_q = \beta_q^- < 1$. In this case $J_2^{3D} > 0$ and so all of the conditions (6.23) for local asymptotic stability are fulfilled. The only problematic condition for local asymptotic stability of this dynamics is (6.24).

The quantity Δ may be expressed in the form

$$\Delta = \alpha_0 + \alpha_1 \beta_z + \alpha_2 \beta_z^2,$$

where

$$\alpha_0 \equiv -(\beta_y(1-c) + \beta_q i_0)\beta_q \det J^{2D},$$

$$\alpha_1 \equiv \beta_q^2 \det J^{2D} + (\beta_y(1-c) + \beta_q i_0)(|J_{11}| + \beta_q(J_{22} - |J_{11}|)),$$

$$\alpha_2 \equiv (1 - \beta_q)(|J_{11}| + \beta_q(J_{22} - |J_{11}|)).$$

We note that $\alpha_0 > 0$ but it is not possible to give a definite sign to α_1 and α_2, both of whose signs depend on the sign of $(J_{22} - |J_{11}|)$. Unfortunately it is not possible to make any definite assertion about the sign of the quantity $|J_{11}| - J_{22}$ $(= (1-c)\beta_y - i_0)$; either $+$ or $-$ is plausible, depending on the relation between the speed of adjustment in the output market, the propensity to consume and the steady-state interest rate. We now assert

---

13 See Brock and Malliaris (1989, p. 75) or Gantmacher (1959).

Proposition 6.1:

We consider steady states of Blanchard type solely. The steady states of type E_1 of the dynamics (6.17)–(6.19) are locally asymptotically stable for sufficiently large β_z if $\beta_q < 1$.

Proof: The crucial quantity is α_2, which can also be written

$$\alpha_2 = (1 - \beta_q)(\beta_q^* - \beta_q)(|J_{11}| - J_{22})$$

where

$$\beta_q^* \equiv |J_{11}|/(|J_{11}| - J_{22}).$$

We need to consider the two cases, (a) $|J_{11}| < J_{22}$ and (b) $|J_{11}| > J_{22}$:

(a) Suppose $J_{22} > |J_{11}|(\Rightarrow \beta_q^* < 0)$, then $\alpha_2 > 0$ and α_1 is of indefinite sign. Hence the relationship between Δ and β_z must be one of the situations shown in Figure 6.7. Whichever situation prevails we can assert that for β_z sufficiently large $\Delta > 0$ and all Routh–Hurwitz conditions for local asymptotic stability are satisfied.

(b) Suppose $J_{22} < |J_{11}|(\Rightarrow \beta_q^* > 1)$; again $\alpha_2 > 0$ and α_1 is of indefinite sign. The same argument as in (a) applies.

Thus under both cases (a) and (b) the proposition holds. ☐

Thus, with expectations adjusting very rapidly (though not necessarily infinitely fast), we have established that Blanchard-type steady states are attracting (repelling) in states of the market in which speed of adjustment on the market for equities is relatively low (high). This analysis suggests that the overall dynamics must stay in some bounded region of the phase space and is converging to some sort of attractor. However, for three-dimensional systems it is difficult to prove any of these assertions about global behavior. We shall present the results of some simulations below. We also note that the steady-state position E_2 in Figure 6.5 is now always unstable since $\det J^{3D} > 0$ there. Its counterintuitive comparative static properties are thus no longer of any relevance.

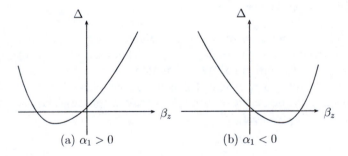

Figure 6.7 The Routh–Hurwitz quantity Δ; $\beta_q < 1$.

6.4.2 *The qualitative behavior of the financial dynamics – phase diagram switching*

In order to focus on the financial market dynamics we make the observation that it will typically be much faster than the real market dynamics, particularly during periods of upswings and downswings. Thus we can obtain an understanding of the qualitative features of the dynamics of (6.17)–(6.19) by setting the initial value of Y at its steady-state value Y_0 and holding it steady at this value by choosing $\beta_y = 0$. We are then able to use the perspective of a two-dimensional phase space to obtain a more transparent description of the dynamics.

We therefore now consider the dynamics of the financial sector from the perspective of the two laws of motion[14] and use the fact that $r_0 = i_0 q_0$. Thus

$$\widehat{q} = \beta_q \left(\frac{i_0 q_0}{q} + z - i_0 \right), \tag{6.25}$$

$$\dot{z} = \beta_z (\widehat{q} - z). \tag{6.26}$$

The Jacobian of the dynamics (6.25), (6.26) at the steady state $q_0, z_0 = 0$ reads:

$$J = \begin{pmatrix} -\beta_q i_0 & \beta_q q_0 \\ -\beta_z \beta_q i_0/q_0 & \beta_z(\beta_q - 1) \end{pmatrix},$$

and we readily calculate $\det J = \beta_q \beta_z i_0 > 0$, irrespective of the value of β_q. Thus, for all adjustment speeds β_z that are sufficiently large, the dynamics has two regimes:

Regime 1: $\det J > 0$, trace $J < 0$ for $\beta_q = \beta_q^-(< 1)$: stable nodes or foci.

Regime 2: $\det J > 0$, trace $J > 0$ for $\beta_q = \beta_q^+(> 1)$: unstable nodes or foci.

We now construct the phase diagram for the dynamical system (6.25)–(6.26) which is in fact a piecewise (or patched) system. The full description of the dynamics is

$$\hat{q} = \beta_q^+ (\frac{i_0 q_0}{q} + z - i_0), \tag{6.27}$$

$$\dot{z} = \beta_z(\hat{q} - z), \tag{6.28}$$

for

$$\varepsilon_- < \frac{i_0 q_0}{q} + z - i_0 < \varepsilon_+, \tag{6.29}$$

---

14 Since the real part of the model is deactivated, we have a uniquely determined steady-state solution q_0 (calculated as described earlier), $z_0 = 0$, for this two-dimensional subsystem.

and

$$\hat{q} = \beta_q^- (\frac{i_0 q_0}{q} + z - i_0),$$
(6.30)

$$\dot{z} = \beta_z(\hat{q} - z),$$
(6.31)

for

$$\frac{i_0 q_0}{q} + z - i_0 < \varepsilon_-, \quad \varepsilon_+ < \frac{i_0 q_0}{q} + z - i_0.$$
(6.32)

It turns out to be much easier to analyze the phase plane by making the transformation

$$\upsilon = \frac{q_0}{q} \quad \text{and} \quad y = \hat{\upsilon}^e,$$
(6.33)

which essentially converts curved isoclines to linear isoclines. With this change of variable the system equations become

$$\hat{\upsilon} = \beta_q(y - i_0 \upsilon + i_0),$$
(6.34)

$$\dot{y} = \beta_z(\hat{\upsilon} - y),$$
(6.35)

with $\beta_q = \beta_q^+$ in the strip

$$-i_0 - \varepsilon_+ + i_0 \upsilon < y < -i_0 - \varepsilon_- + i_0 \upsilon,$$
(6.36)

and $\beta_q = \beta_q^-$ outside the strip defined by (6.36). The strip is indicated by the dotted lines in Figure 6.8.

The isocline of equation (6.34) is the straight line

$$y = -i_0 + i_0 \upsilon,$$
(6.37)

which runs along the middle of the strip as shown in Figure 6.8.

The isocline of equation (6.35) is more complicated as it involves the piecewise function β_q. Substituting (6.34) into (6.35), we see that in general the isocline of (6.35) is given by

$$y = \frac{\beta_q}{(1 - \beta_q)} i_0 (1 - \upsilon).$$
(6.38)

Inside the strip, equation (6.38) becomes

$$y = \frac{\beta_q^+}{(\beta_q^+ - 1)} i_0 (\upsilon - 1),$$
(6.39)

whilst outside the strip

$$y = \frac{\beta_q^-}{(1 - \beta_q^-)} i_0 (1 - \upsilon).$$
(6.40)

The segments (6.39) and (6.40) of the $\dot{y} = 0$ isocline are indicated in Figure 6.8.

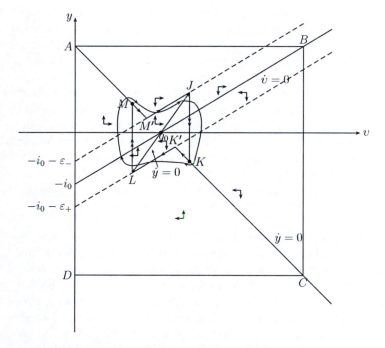

Figure 6.8 The patched phase plane for the financial dynamics.

Once the isoclines have been determined we are able to fill in the directions of motion, which are also indicated in Figure 6.8. The opposing directions of motion of y on either side of the upper right and lower left boundaries of the strip may seem a little strange since the boundaries of the strip are not isoclines. But what in fact happens is that as the boundaries of the strip are crossed the time derivative of y undergoes a discontinuous change.

As we saw from the Jacobian analysis, the directions of motion show movement away from the steady state inside the strip and towards the steady state outside the strip. We can demonstrate that, as a result of these opposing directions of motion, trajectories must remain within a bounded region of the (y, v) plane. The patched phase plane situation depicted in Figure 6.8 shows a typical situation. Motion towards the cycle shown in Figure 6.8 is suggested by the directions of motion and the local linear analysis. It is clear that the region *ABCD* is a trapping region of the phase space as motion is always pointing inwards from the boundaries of this region. The other situations that need to be taken into account are those in which the intersection of the line *LJ* with boundaries of the strip places *J* above (or *L* below) the line *AB* (*CD*) shown in Figure 6.8. But in these cases a trapping region can still be constructed by taking an enlarged box with a new point *A* (*D*) sufficiently high (low) on the vertical axis. Normally in such situations with continuously defined planar systems we could appeal to Poincaré–Bendixson theory to prove the existence of a limit cycle. But we are unable to do so here because of the piece-wise nature of the dynamical system; we can only argue that trajectories converge to some attractor within the trapping region. The simple limit cycle shown in Figure 6.8 represents just one possibility that remains strongly suggested by our analysis and is backed up by some of the numerical simulations reported later.

When translated to motion in the $q-z$ phase space, the limit cycle has the qualitative shape shown in Figure 6.9. The qualitative nature of the time series pattern for q is indicated by Figure 6.10, and is also confirmed by the simulations in Figure 6.11 discussed in Section 6.4.3. Initially q is in the depressed phase $D_0 D_1$, then there is the phase of euphoria $D_1 \rightarrow D_4$; this is followed by the pessimistic phase $D_4 \rightarrow D_6$ and then the decline ($D_6 \rightarrow D_7$) into the depressed phase $D_7 \rightarrow D_1$ again, and so forth. The periods spent in the pessimistic and depressed phases are to a large extent dependent on the speed of expectations coefficient β_z. As this increases in value the time spent between the boom phase and the decline phase reduces.

In principle, as $\beta_z \rightarrow \infty$ we should arrive at the limiting perfect foresight dynamics. It is difficult to give a formal discussion of the perfect foresight limit for dynamical systems defined via the patched dynamics. However, we know from Chiarella (1986) that a rigorous discussion of the perfect foresight limit is possible when the dynamics is defined continuously. Such a continuous system could be obtained by making the β_q schedule in Figure 6.6 continuous; however, we leave analysis of this situation to future research. For the patched phase plane situation under consideration in this chapter, Figure 6.8 suggests that as β_z approaches infinity the cycle shown there seems to converge to the limiting limit cycle $MM'JKK'LM$. Close to the branches JK and LM, motion is very rapid for large β_z (indicating a rapid change in expectations). Close to the branches $MM'J$ and $KK'L$, the motion represents the slower boom and decline phases. Numerical simulations (reported in the next section) for large β_z suggest that the

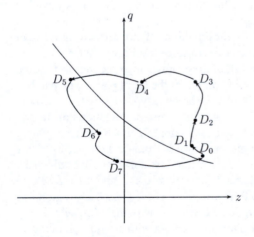

Figure 6.9 The $q-z$ phase plane.

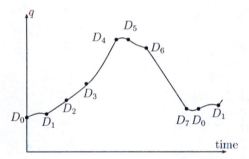

Figure 6.10 The time series pattern for q (including later stochastic variation around these trends).

Table 6.1 Parameter set for simulations.

h_1	3	h_2	55
m	5.5	k	0.25
c	0.7	ψ	10
A	10	δ	0
v	0.7	K	94.2857
β_y	0.9	β_z	5
β_q^+	1.4	β_q^-	0.7
ε^+	0.12	ε^-	-0.08

cycle of the system (6.34)–(6.35) is close to a cycle such as $MM'JKK'LM$ and converges to it as $\beta_z \to \infty$.

6.4.3 Some simulations

We simulate directly the 3D dynamical system (6.17)–(6.19). We have used the numerical values displayed in Table 6.1. Some of these (C, i, β_y, β_z, h_2) have been chosen in line with estimated values obtained in Chiarella et al. (2002), the others have been obtained by numerical experimentation. These parameter values yield the steady state $q_0 = 1$, $Y_0 = 33.3$ and $z_0 = 0$.

Figure 6.11(a) shows the long-run cycle in 3D phase space and Figure 6.11(b) shows the projection onto the $q - Y$ phase plane; the economy converges to this cycle after about $t = 100$. The rapid changes in expectations of capital gains (z) that accompany the end of an upswing or downswing of the stock market (q) are clearly evident. This is of course a consequence of our choice of a relatively large value of β_z (the expectations adjustment coefficient). Lower values of β_z would smooth out this effect and ultimately lead to stability.

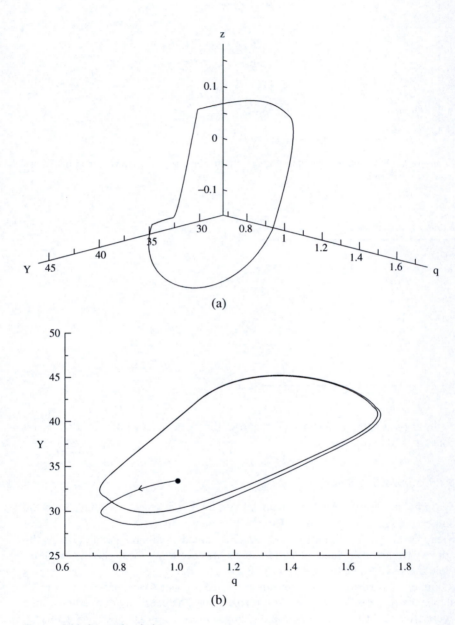

Figure 6.11 Some simulations.

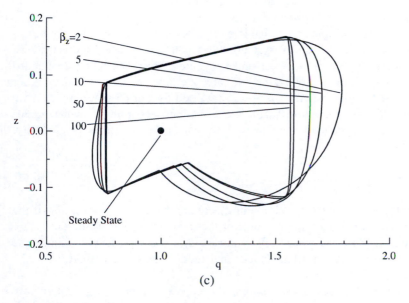

Figure 6.11 Continued

To better appreciate the role of β_z in the dynamics we display, in Figure 6.11(c), the effect on the cycle in the $q-z$ phase space of increasing β_z. By about $\beta_z = 100$ the cycle is settling onto a limiting limit cycle as discussed in relation to Figure 6.8.

Our theoretical and simulation analyses both indicate upswings and downswings in the stock market accompanied by rapid changes in expectations from time to time. All we have been able to do here is to sketch out the dynamic implications of one important basic mechanism that is at work in real–financial interaction. Obviously the cycles generated by the simple model developed here are too regular to realistically describe the type of fluctuation we observe in stock markets. To move in the direction of more descriptive realism the framework adopted here needs a number of additional features, some of which are discussed in the concluding section.

6.5 Relaxing perfection

Apart from rational expectations (perfect foresight) in choosing the stable saddle-point path, the financial sector set up by Blanchard (1931) relies on perfect asset substitutability, such that the rates of return on bonds and equities are always equalized, and additionally on myopic perfect foresight regarding capital gains. In our alternative approach to the jump variable technique, which we now present, rational expectations are, of course, abandoned altogether. The other two assumptions are relaxed in a continuous way. This means they would be re-established as a limit case if the corresponding reaction coefficients, which are finite in our treatment, became infinitely large.

Let us begin with the capital gains of equities (long-term bonds continue to be appended to the dynamical system) and denote the expected growth rate of equity prices $(\hat{p}_e^e)$ by π_e. Whereas under myopic perfect foresight π_e coincided with the actual growth rate $\hat{p}_e$, the two rates are now generally distinct. As for revisions of the forecast errors $\hat{p}_e - \pi_e$, it will do for our present purpose if we work with the assumption of adaptive expectations, according to which agents try to avoid overpredictions and so seek to reduce the forecast error gradually. Formally,

$$\dot{\pi}_e = \beta_\pi \left(\hat{p}_e - \pi_e\right) \tag{6.41}$$

The coefficient β_π is the speed of adjustment at which π_e approaches $\hat{p}_e$; if the latter remained constant in the course of these adjustments it would take $1/\beta_\pi$ time units until π_e had reached $\hat{p}_e$. The case $\beta_\pi = \infty$ represents the limit case where the revisions are infinitely fast and myopic perfect foresight, $\pi_e = \hat{p}_e$, prevails.

Turning to the second assumption, the concept of perfect substitutability between short-term bonds and equities conveys the notion that any difference in the rates of return between the two assets would immediately be eliminated by arbitrage sales or purchases and the corresponding price changes. Imperfect substitutability says that these price adjustments take place at a finite speed. In concrete terms, consider the rate of return of equities, which is given by $rpK/p_eE + \pi_e = r/q + \pi_e$. If it exceeds i, which is the rate of return of the alternative asset, equities become relatively more attractive and the demand for them will drive up the price of shares.[15] This process may be further accelerated if p_e is expected to rise, i.e., if π_e is positive. Likewise, the equity price falls if short-term bonds are more attractive, when $r/q + \pi_e < i$, unless this is compensated by sufficiently optimistic expectations about the capital gains. In sum, price formation on the stock market is formalized as

$$\hat{p}_e = \beta_e(r/q + \pi_e - i) + \kappa_e\pi_e \tag{6.42}$$

The parameter κ_e indicates the strength of what, for short, may be called a financial accelerator. The coefficient β_e stands for a general responsiveness to the pressure of demand. Conceptually more important, it can also be viewed as measuring the degree of substitutability of short-term bonds and equities. A low value of β_e indicates that equities, because of the risk associated with them, are only a weak alternative to the almost risk-free government bonds. Hence, even if equities offer a markedly higher rate of return, the pressure of demand on the stock market

---

15 More precisely, the differential between the two rates of return should also include a risk premium for holding equities. It is here set equal to zero as a matter of notational convenience.

and the price increases resulting from it are only limited. With respect to a given (positive) differential in the two rates of return, a higher value of β_e signifies a greater pressure of demand on the share price, since agents are more easily willing to switch from short-term bonds to equities, or to invest their current savings in equities rather than bonds. The coefficient β_e is currently treated as a constant, but will be variable in a global analysis of the dynamics later on.

Going to the limit, $\beta_e \to \infty$, leads us back to the case of perfect substitutability: p_e immediately jumps to the level at which $r/q + \pi_e - i = rpK/p_e E + \pi_e - i = 0$. In the other cases with a finite β_e and thus a finite rate of change of p_e, the differential, under a *ceteris paribus* perspective, is reduced more gently. If, however, by virtue of (6.41) the simultaneous changes of π_e in the same direction are stronger than those of the share prices, the differential, in absolute terms, may even increase. We then have a destabilizing effect, as discussed in the introduction. Under what conditions this may happen, and may even destabilize the entire economy, has to be investigated by a mathematical stability analysis.

6.5.1 Local stability analysis of the alternative system

Dropping the assumption of myopic perfect foresight adds expected capital gains as another variable to the original system. Reiterating equation (6.13) for the output adjustments, which remain unaffected, and using $\hat{p}_e = \hat{q}$ together with (6.2), (6.4) in (6.41) and (6.42), the following three-dimensional differential equations system in (Y, q, π_e) is obtained:

$$\dot{Y} = \beta_y \left[-(1-c)Y + \psi q + A - \psi \right] \tag{6.43}$$

$$\dot{q} = -\beta_e \left[i(Y)q - r(Y) \right] + (\beta_e + \kappa_e) q \pi_e \tag{6.44}$$

$$\dot{\pi}_e = -\beta_\pi \beta_e \left[i(Y)q - r(Y) \right]/q - \beta_\pi (1 - \beta_e - \kappa_e) \pi_e \tag{6.45}$$

The steady-state positions are, of course, exactly the same as in the Blanchard model. Their local stability properties, however, can be quite different. A first key to understanding the change in results is a comparison of eqs (6.14) and (6.44). In (6.14), Tobin's q depends positively on the term $iq - r$; in (6.44) it is just the other way round. For the lower equilibrium in the economy with two equilibria, point E_2 in Figure 6.5, this almost reverses the stability proposition. This type of equilibrium could reasonably be supposed to be stable in Blanchard's setting, whereas it is always unstable now.

Proposition 6.2:
   In the good news case, $q'_{LM} > 0$, with two equilibria, the low-output equilibrium of system (6.43)–(6.45) is unstable.

Proof: Let A be the Jacobian matrix of (6.43)–(6.45), evaluated at an equilibrium point. Referring to $J_{11}, J_{12}, J_{21}, J_{22}$, the elements of the matrix J^{2D} defined in the line below equation (6.20), A is given by

$$A = \begin{bmatrix} J_{11} & J_{12} & 0 \\ -\beta_e J_{21} & -\beta_e J_{22} & (\beta_e+\kappa_e)q^o \\ -\beta_e\beta_\pi J_{21}/q^o & -\beta_e\beta_\pi J_{22}/q^o & -\beta_\pi(1-\beta_e-\kappa_e) \end{bmatrix}$$

Straightforward calculation shows that the determinants of the two matrices are related by

$$\det A = \beta_e \,\beta_\pi \,\det J^{2D}$$

$\det J^{2D}$ was observed to be positive if slope iS < slope LM, i.e., at the lower equilibrium. Hence $\det A > 0$, too, which violates one of the necessary conditions for the eigenvalues of A to have non-positive real parts.   □

Stability becomes possible for Blanchard's saddlepoint equilibria. The key parameters for this are the responsiveness on the stock market (β_e), the speed of adjustment of adaptive expectations for capital gains (β_π) and the financial accelerator (κ_e). The most important statements are collected in Proposition 6.3.

Proposition 6.3:
Consider a steady state where the LM curve cuts the IS curve from above. Then, with respect to system (6.43)–(6.45), the following statements hold true:

1 *The equilibrium is locally asymptotically stable for all β_π sufficiently small.*
2 *If $\beta_e + \kappa_e < 1$, the equilibrium is also locally stable if β_π is large enough.*
3 *If $\beta_e + \kappa_e < 1$, there exists a positive number β_π^H such that the equilibrium is locally stable if $\beta_\pi < \beta_\pi^H$, and it is unstable if $\beta_\pi > \beta_\pi^H$.*
4 *At least if the adjustment speed β_π is close to β_π^H, the local dynamics is of a cyclical nature.*

In short, it may therefore be said that expectations are destabilizing, either in the form of fast adaptive expectations or in the form of the financial accelerator, and that strong reactions on the stock market have a similar effect. The main significance of the proposition lies in this characterization. On the other hand, the stability results for $\beta_e + \kappa_e < 1$ are certainly of theoretical interest, but the reverse inequality, $\beta_e + \kappa_e > 1$, may be considered the normal case.[16]

The last item of the proposition indicates also that the type of dynamics may be different from the adjustment paths studied by Blanchard, where convergence toward the steady state was always monotonic. The point could be further sharpened, as it is easily inferred from the proof that the critical parameter value

16 A closer inspection of the Routh–Hurwitz terms in the proof of the proposition could reveal further conditions that ensure stability in point 2, not only for small and large β_π but for all values of β_π. In the light of the limited relevance of the condition $\beta_e + \kappa_e < 1$, we do not dwell on this issue.

β_π^H, at which the system changes from being locally stable to being locally divergent, gives rise to a Hopf bifurcation (this phenomenon motivated the superscript "H"). Hence, over a certain range of parameter values β_π there even exist strictly periodic trajectories (which may, or may not, be attracting).

The cyclical behavior originates in the financial sector itself. This can be seen by fixing Y in the real sector and investigating eqs (6.44), (6.45) on their own. A standard argument establishes that points 3 and 4 of the proposition apply to this subsystem for the motions of (q, π_e) as well.[17]

Proof: The proof is based on the Routh–Hurwitz stability conditions for the matrix A set up in the proof of Proposition 6.2. Accordingly, a necessary and sufficient condition for all eigenvalues to have negative real parts is that the expressions b_1, b_2, b_3, b_4 below are all positive. As slope IS > Slope LM and thus $\det J^{2D} < 0$ by hypothesis (cf. the proof in Section 6.4.1), they are given by

$$b_1 = -\operatorname{trace}A \quad\quad = |J_{11}| + \beta_e J_{22} + \beta_\pi (1 - \beta_e - \kappa_e)$$

$$b_2 = A_1 + A_2 + A_3 = \beta_e \beta_\pi J_{22} + \beta_\pi |J_{11}|(1 - \beta_e - \kappa_e) + \beta_e |\det J^{2D}|$$

$$b_3 = -\det A \quad\quad = \beta_e \beta_\pi |\det J^{2D}|$$

$$b_4 = b_1 b_2 - b_3 \quad = (|J_{11}| + \beta_e J_{22})\beta_e |\det J^{2D}| + \alpha_1 \beta_\pi + \alpha_2 \beta_\pi^2$$

where the A_is are the principal minors of A (the determinants of the 2×2 matrices resulting from deleting the ith row and the ith column of A), and b_4 is written as a function of the parameter β_π.

Point 1 of the proposition follows from the observation that b_1, b_2, b_4 are strictly positive for $\beta_\pi = 0$, while $b_3 = 0$ in that case. Hence $b_1, b_2, b_3, b_4 > 0$ if β_π is close to zero. As for point 2, $\beta_e + \kappa_e < 1$ implies that b_1 and b_2 are linearly increasing functions of β_π, so that $b_1, b_2, b_3 > 0$ for all β_π. Moreover, the coefficient α_2 in b_4 is positive, too. Hence $b_4 > 0$, at least if β_π is sufficiently large.[18]

To demonstrate point 3, note that b_1 is now decreasing in β_π. Regarding b_2, distinguish by case and consider first $db_2/d\pi > 0$, which implies $\alpha_2 < 0$ and $b_4 < 0$ for large β_π. Since $b_4 > 0$ at $\beta_\pi = 0$, the function $b_4 = b_4(\pi)$ has an odd number of roots, and since it is quadratic there is exactly one number $\beta_\pi = \beta_\pi^H$ at which b_4 vanishes. Since $b_3 > 0$ anyway, b_1, b_2, b_3 and b_4 are all greater than 0 and thus ensure stability for all $\beta_\pi < \beta_\pi^H$ and instability to the right of β_π^H since $b_4 < 0$ from then on.

---

17 The corresponding Jacobian is the 2×2 lower diagonal submatrix of the matrix A specified in the proof of Proposition 6.2, whose determinant is $\beta_e \beta_\pi J_{22} > 0$. With $\beta_e + \kappa_e < 1$, this matrix is stable for low values of β_π (since the trace is negative then), and unstable beyond that value of β_π at which the trace becomes zero (and positive afterwards).

18 If one is interested to check whether b_4 is positive throughout, the coefficient α_1 would have to be investigated.

On the other hand, consider $db_2/d\pi < 0$, which implies $\alpha_2 > 0$ and $b_4 > 0$ for large β_π. When, with β_π increasing, one or more eigenvalues cross the imaginary axis in the complex plane (from the left), there must be a pair of purely imaginary eigenvalues since $\det A \neq 0$ for all β_π (a real eigen-value $\lambda = 0$ would entail $\det A = 0$). It is well known that this situation is associated with $b_4 = 0$. Then, let β_1 and β_2 be the two values of β_π where $b_1(\cdot)$ and $b_2(\cdot)$ intersect the β_π-axis. At these points, $b_1 b_2 = 0$, and between β_1 and β_2 we have $b_4 < b_1 b_2 < 0$. On the whole, the function $b_4 = b_4(\pi)$ has two roots β_3 and β_4, such that $\beta_3 < \beta_1, \beta_2 < \beta_4$. The terms b_1, b_2, b_3, b_4 are all positive for $\beta_\pi < \beta_3$, whereas at least one of them is negative for $\beta_\pi > \beta_3$. We can therefore conclude $\beta_\pi^H = \beta_3$.

Point 4 of the proposition follows immediately from the fact just pointed out that, at $\beta_\pi = \beta_\pi^H$, the eigenvalues with the largest real part are a pair of complex eigenvalues. □

It will be expected that the statements in Propositions 6.2 and 6.3 for large values of the adjustment speed β_π of adaptive expectations equally hold true in the limit case $\beta_\pi = \infty$, when myopic perfect foresight of capital gains is reintroduced. In this case the dynamics is again reduced to a two-dimensional system in Y and q. Substituting $\pi_e = \hat{p}_e = \hat{q} = \dot{q}/q$ in eq. (6.44) and solving for $\dot{q}$ yields the differential equation

$$\dot{q} = \frac{\beta_e}{\beta_e + \kappa_e - 1}\,[i(Y)q - r(Y)].\tag{6.46}$$

Comparing this type of economy, which is constituted by eqs (6.13) and (6.46), with Blanchard's system (6.13), (6.14), it is seen that the two systems are practically equivalent if only the stock market is moderately responsive, such that $\beta_e + \kappa_e > 1$. The decisive feature is the sign of the coefficient in front of the right-hand side of (6.46) and (6.14), respectively, which is positive in both cases. In particular, there is no more scope for cyclical dynamics around the Blanchard equilibria; they again turn out to be saddle points.[19]

6.5.2 Nonlinear price reactions on the stock market

On the basis of the analysis of our system's local dynamics we had to conclude that the equilibria are typically locally unstable. Since there are only mild intrinsic nonlinearities in the system (6.43)–(6.45), the local behavior carries over to the global trajectories. Hence, as the equations underlying (6.43)–(6.45) are specified, they only make sense in the vicinity of the steady states (unless we want to return to the jump variable technique).

Rather than introduce additional feedback mechanisms, which would increase the model's dimension, let us have a closer look at the price adjustments on the

---

19 With $\beta_e + \kappa_e > 1$, the determinant of the Jacobian of system (6.13), (6.46) has the same sign as $\det J$ for system (6.13), (6.14).

stock market. To ease the exposition, we neglect the financial accelerator and suppose $\kappa_e = 0$ from now on. According to eq. (6.42), the growth rate of the share price increases in proportion to the differential

$$d := r/q + \pi_e - i \tag{6.47}$$

of the two rates of return of equities and short-term bonds. These linear price adjustments are a reasonable formulation if the differential d is small, but this may be modified if the deviations of $r/q + \pi_e$ from i become large.

In extending our model to the global case, we assume that in such a phase of the financial market dynamics the agents become more cautious in their (excess) demands for equities. Regarding $d > 0$, they may perceive a greater risk in equities because π_e is already quite high, so that in the near future a reduction of $\hat{p}_e$ will be expected, perhaps even an about-turn. Another reason may be a high profitability $r = r(Y)$ in the real sector, which similarly will not be expected to continue to prevail at this level for too long. Thus, the positive excess demand for equities will rise less than proportionately with d if the latter further increases. Similar arguments in the opposite direction may apply for $d < 0$, so that the excess supply of equities rises less than proportionately with d if d further declines.

The gist of this reasoning is that the growth rate $\hat{p}_e$ also changes less than proportionately with d as d gets large in absolute value. Referring to the remarks concerning eq. (6.42), it may likewise be said that the degree of substitutability, as it is perceived by the agents, decreases, which would result in less rapid price reactions on the stock market. That is, the coefficient β_e is no longer a constant parameter but varies with the differential d. A convenient device to capture this idea is to model the right-hand side of eq. (6.42) as a sigmoid function like the hyperbolic tangent. In detail, we maintain β_e as a fixed parameter and introduce m_e as the maximal value $\hat{p}_e$ can possibly attain. Equation (6.42) is then respecified as

$$\hat{p}_e = f_e(d) := m_e \tanh[(\beta_e/m_e)d] \tag{6.48}$$

As the derivative of $\tanh(x)$ is 1 at $x = 0$, the slope of the function $f_e(\cdot)$ at an equilibrium point where $d = 0$ is given by β_e. Its upper and lower bounds are $\pm m_e$. The shape of this function is illustrated in Figure 6.12.

With (6.48), eq. (6.44) for the motions of Tobin's q is replaced with

$$\dot{q} = q f_e[r(Y)/q + \pi_e - i(Y)] \tag{6.49}$$

Clearly, the local stability analysis of system (6.42), (6.49), (6.44) is exactly the same as for (6.42)–(6.44).

In the remainder of this section we sketch the global dynamics generated by (6.49), given $\beta_e > 1$ in (6.48) so that the steady states are unstable. For a better understanding of the nonlinearity effects it is helpful to consider a number of special cases. Thus, in the following two sections real output is fixed at its equilibrium value in order to focus on the financial sector. Here we first employ the

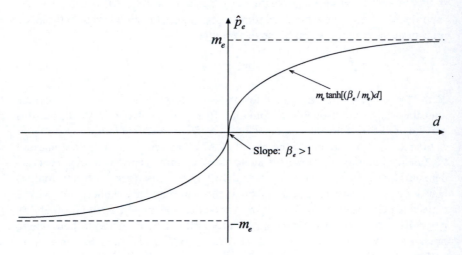

Figure 6.12 Nonlinear adjustment function on the stock market.

myopic perfect foresight hypothesis, $\beta_\pi = \infty$ (case 1 below), and subsequently the adaptive expectations of capital gains, $\beta_\pi < \infty$ (case 2). With respect to variable output Y, we next consider the special case $\beta_y = \infty$ in (6.43), i.e., the goods market is always supposed to be in an IS equilibrium (case 3). Finally, when dealing with a finite adjustment speed β_y, it is convenient to use myopic perfect foresight once again (case 4). The nature of the general dynamics when also $\beta_\pi < \infty$ (but large) is then easily derived from this investigation.

Case 1: $Y = Y^o$, $\beta_\pi = \infty$

To simplify notation, we adopt the symbol $u := 1/q$ for the reciprocal of Tobin's q. Also, suppose $r^o = r(Y^o) = i^o$, which gives $q^o = 1$ in an equilibrium. With $\hat{u} = -\hat{q} = -\hat{p}_e = -\pi_e$, and writing $\tilde{\beta}_e = \beta_e/m_e$, (6.48) and (6.49) then become $\hat{u} = -m_e \tanh[\tilde{\beta}_e(i^o u - \hat{u} - i^o)]$. Inverting $\tanh(\cdot)$ allows us to express u as a function of its growth rate $\hat{u}$,

$$u = F(\hat{u}) := \frac{1}{i^o}[\hat{u} - \tanh^{-1}(\hat{u}/m_e)/\tilde{\beta}_e + i^o] \tag{6.50}$$

This equation is a complete one-dimensional dynamical system of the stock market, though being written in implicit form. While an analytical treatment of (6.50) would be technically involved, the geometric procedure is very intuitive and poses no further problems.

Figure 6.13(a) depicts the inverse hyperbolic tan function, i.e., the relationship $\hat{u} \mapsto -\tanh^{-1}(\hat{u}/m_e)/\tilde{\beta}_e$. Figure 6.13(b) draws the graph of the function $F(\cdot)$.

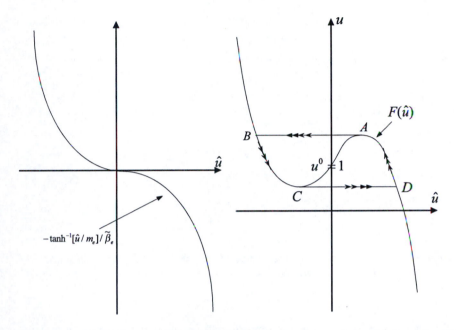

Figure 6.13 (a) The inverse tanh function. (b) The relaxation cycle for the dynamics of $u = 1/q$ generated by (6.50).

In the right half-plane of Figure 6.13(b) where $\hat{u} > 0$, u increases on this locus; in the left half-plane u decreases on it. When $\hat{u}$ reaches the local maximum at point A in the right half-plane (which it can be shown to do in finite time), the only possibility for the dynamics to continue is that there be a jump to the other leaf of the graph of $F(\cdot)$, to point B. Similarly the reverse jump, from point C to point D. In this way the stock market undergoes persistent and, moreover, strictly periodic fluctuations, which are marked by the loop A $\rightarrow$ B $\rightarrow$ C $\rightarrow$ D $\rightarrow$ A. Such a phenomenon is known as relaxation oscillations.[20]

It should be pointed out that, although in Blanchard's treatment as well as in eq. (6.50) the asset price dynamics is characterized by discontinuous changes of a state variable, these jumps are of a rather different kind. In Blanchard's model, the jump onto the stable saddle path is achieved by a sudden change in Tobin's q. By contrast, in (6.50) it is the growth rate of q ($\hat{u} = -\hat{q}$) that performs the jump; the time path of Tobin's q itself maintains a continuous motion.

---

20 See Minorsky (1962, Part IV) for a detailed discussion of this concept. In an economic context, a similar diagram was obtained as early as 1951 in Goodwin's seminal paper on the nonlinear accelerator (Goodwin, 1951, p. 5). Since then relaxation oscillations have been studied in a variety of economic applications; see in particular Chiarella (1986, 1990b) and Flaschel and Sethi (1999).

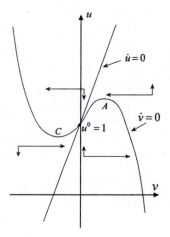

Figure 6.14 Phase portrait of the system (6.51), (6.52) with fast adjustments of expectations. Note that $u = 1/q$ and $v = -\pi_e$.

Case 2: $Y = Y^o$, $\beta_\pi < \infty$

Departing from myopic perfect foresight, $\beta_\pi < \infty$, it is useful in the present context to refer to the variable $v := -\pi_e$. Thus the system to be studied is given by

$$\hat{u} = -f_e[i^o u - v - i^o]$$ (6.51)

$$\dot{v} = \beta_\pi (\hat{u} - v)$$ (6.52)

Figure 6.14 is the phase diagram of (6.51), (6.52). The isocline $\hat{u} = 0$ is easily checked to be the straight line $u = 1 + v/i^o$. The isocline $\dot{v} = 0$ can be taken over from Figure 6.13(b); it is just the graph of the function $v \mapsto F(v)$. The diagram clearly shows the system's cyclical behavior. The oscillations are undamped since the equilibrium point $(v^o, u^o) = (0, 1)$ is repelling. By way of a standard geometric argument it can furthermore be demonstrated that they are uniformly bounded as well (being finally confined to a compact set in the phase plane). On this basis, the Poincaré–Bendixson theorem ensures that each trajectory of (6.51), (6.52) converges to a limit cycle.[21]

The long horizontal arrows in Figure 6.14 indicate fast adjustments in the adaptive expectations mechanism. It is obvious that this type of dynamics is similar to the relaxation oscillations in Figure 6.13(b). For large β_π, the changes in expectations v are always very close to the actual changes $\hat{u}$, so that (v, u) move in a close neighborhood of the $\dot{v} = 0$ isocline. The only exception is when (v, u) come near the local extrema of the isocline, at points A or C. At that stage of the

21 A first important economic paper in this respect is Chang and Smyth (1971).

process, the changes in v become much more pronounced than the changes in u. Here the horizontal dynamics may be said to take over; the motions of (v, u) will then resemble the jump from A to B, or from C to D, in Figure 6.13(b).

The discussion of Figure 6.13(b) may have been followed with a certain uneasiness, since eq. (6.50) fails to specify the change in u at the points A and C. Strictly speaking, the jumps A $\rightarrow$ B and C $\rightarrow$ D were imposed from outside this formal representation. By contrast, system (6.51), (6.52) is everywhere well defined, however large β_π may be. In this way, the loop A $\rightarrow$ B $\rightarrow$ C $\rightarrow$ D $\rightarrow$ A in Figure 6.13(b) with its discontinuous changes in $\hat{u}$ can be understood as the limit, for $\beta_\pi \rightarrow \infty$, of the limit cycles in Figure 6.14.[22]

Case 3: $\beta_y = \infty$, $\beta_\pi \leq \infty$

To include the real sector with variable production levels Y in a simple and convenient way, assume that the goods market is always in an IS equilibrium, which will be shifting over time. This supposition corresponds to the shorthand notation $\beta_y = \infty$ with respect to eq. (6.43). Setting the right-hand side of (6.43) equal to zero and solving for Y gives the IS equilibrium output as a function of q, or $u = 1/q$ for our present purpose,

$$Y = Y_{IS}(u) := (A - \psi + \psi/u)/(1 - c).$$

Consider $\beta_\pi < \infty$. Equation (6.52) remains the same, whereas i^o in (6.51) has to be replaced with $i(Y) = i[Y_{IS}(u)]$, and $r^o u$ with $r(Y) = r[Y_{IS}(u)]u$. Abbreviating

$$e(u) := r[Y_{IS}(u)]u - i[Y_{IS}(u)],$$

eq. (6.51) becomes $\hat{u} = -f_e[e(u) - v]$ or, taking (6.48) into account,

$$\hat{u} = -m_e \tanh\{\tilde{\beta}_e[e(u) - v]\}. \tag{6.53}$$

Thus we are concerned with the (v, u) dynamics described by eqs (6.52) and (6.53). Of course, $(v^o, u^o) = (0, 1)$ is maintained as the system's equilibrium point.

Before going on, let us note that both functions $r = r[Y_{IS}(u)]$ and $i = i[Y_{IS}(u)]$ are decreasing in u. Let us here assume that the coefficient a_r in the specification of the profit rate in (2.3) is sufficiently small, such that $e'(u) > 0$ throughout.

The key to the analysis of (6.53), (6.52) is once more the $\dot{v} = 0$ isocline, where $v = \hat{u}$. By the same procedure as in case 1, (6.53) is then seen to be equivalent to the equation $e(u) = \hat{u} - \tanh^{-1}(\hat{u}/m_e)/\tilde{\beta}_e$. Since the function $e(\cdot)$ is strictly increasing everywhere, it too can be inverted. We thus arrive at the relationship

$$u = G(\hat{u}) := e^{-1}[\hat{u} - \tanh^{-1}(\hat{u}/m_e)/\tilde{\beta}_e] \tag{6.54}$$

22 Experience with formally similar systems shows that, at least for large β_π, the limit cycles are indeed unique. Otherwise, one may concentrate on the outermost limit cycles of (6.51), (6.52).

The analogy of (6.54) with (6.50) is obvious. Since also e^{-1} is strictly increasing in its argument, $G(\cdot)$ can be viewed as a monotonic transformation of the function $F(\cdot)$ in (6.50). Accordingly, the graph of $G(\cdot)$ will have the same qualitative features as the function $F(\cdot)$ in Figure 6.13(b). Hence, given the assumption on the composite function $e = e(u)$, the conclusions that have been made for system (6.51), (6.52) with its fixed output $Y = Y^o$ carry over to the system (6.53), (6.52), where the output is endogenously determined by the IS equilibrium concept. The same holds true for the limit case, $\beta_\pi = \infty$.

Case 4: $\beta_y < \infty$, $\beta_\pi = \infty$

Also under goods market disequilibrium, $\beta_y < \infty$ in (6.43), it is instructive to approach the dynamics from a geometrical perspective. To reduce the dimensions, expectations $v = -\pi_e$ are neglected. Concentrating on the myopic perfect foresight case, $\beta_\pi = \infty$, the system to be investigated is

$$\dot{Y} = \beta_y [-(1-a_y)Y + b_y/u + c_y] \tag{6.55}$$

$$\hat{u} = -m_e \tanh\{\tilde{\beta}_e [r(Y)u - \hat{u} - i(Y)]\} \tag{6.56}$$

The procedure for the treatment of (6.56) is analogous to case 1. By inverting the tanh, u can be expressed as a function of $\hat{u}$ and, in addition, Y:

$$u = H(\hat{u}, Y) := \frac{1}{r(Y)} [\hat{u} - \tanh^{-1}(\hat{u}/m_e)/\tilde{\beta}_e + i(Y)] \tag{6.57}$$

This relationship generalizes (6.50) in an obvious way. For each given value of Y, the function $\hat{u} \mapsto H(\hat{u}, Y)$ has the same shape as the graph of $F(\cdot)$ in Figure 6.13(b). The corresponding equilibrium value of u, a stationary point of (6.56), is then $u^o(Y) = i(Y)/r(Y)$. If $Y = Y^o$ and so $i(Y^o) = r(Y^o)$ (according to the above-mentioned convention), then $u^o(Y^o) = 1$. That is, with a slight slip in notation, $(Y^o, u^o) = (A/(1-c), 1)$ is the equilibrium point of the full system (6.55), (6.56).

As Y varies, the function $\hat{u} \mapsto H(\hat{u}, Y)$ shifts in the $(\hat{u}, u)$ plane. In a three-dimensional diagram, the graph of $H(\cdot, \cdot)$ may look like the surface in Figure 6.15. The diagram also sketches the relaxation oscillations to which it gives rise. Certainly, the jump mechanism is the same as that discussed in case 1.

The trajectories that are generated by high, though finite, speeds of adjustment in the adaptive capital gains expectations, $\beta_\pi < \infty$, should resemble the oscillations in Figure 6.15. Again, the driving force is the price adjustment process on the stock market, i.e., the interaction between p_e and π_e, where the latter is close to $\hat{p}_e$ most of the time. Referring to the variables u and v, the main argument has been given in case 3. However, while in Figure 6.14 the existence of at least one limit cycle for the (v, u) trajectories can be firmly established by means of the Poincaré–Bendixson theorem, this is no longer possible for the three-dimensional dynamics in (v, u, Y). Verifying a global boundedness condition is more complicated, and

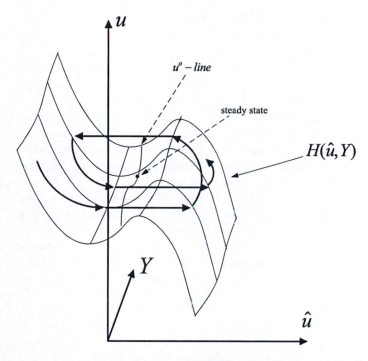

Figure 6.15 The three-dimensional relaxation oscillation generated by the system (6.55), (6.56) with variable output under myopic perfect foresight.

even then the dynamics could be more complex than the limit cycle behavior in the plane. Nevertheless, the simplified cases studied before can guide us in what we can reasonably expect: feasible, bounded and persistent oscillations. How regular, i.e. periodic, quasi-periodic or erratic, they may turn out, or the conditions favoring one of these outcomes, would be a matter of systematic computer simulations and their evaluation.

6.6 Conclusion

We have reconsidered in this chapter the seminal model of real–financial interaction put forward by Blanchard (1981), which extends the IS analysis by an output adjustment rule of the dynamic multiplier type, and, more importantly, the textbook LM analysis by stock market dynamics under the assumption of perfect substitutability and myopic perfect foresight. This system is typically characterized by saddlepoint dynamics. On the basis of the rational expectations methodology, Blanchard treated it by means of the jump variable technique à la Sargent and Wallace (1973).

We have developed an extension to Blanchard's analysis, the key features of which are imperfect substitution between alternative assets, less than perfect foresight expectations and (most importantly) a state-of-market dependent coefficient of reaction to the expected return differential between different assets. The original Blanchard model can be recovered as the limiting case when there is perfect substitution and perfect foresight. Because the reaction coefficient is relatively high close to the steady state, the extended Blanchard model also exhibits local instability. However, as there is movement away from the steady state, the state-of-market dependent reaction coefficient operates in such a way that motion eventually is back towards the steady state, where the reaction coefficient rises again. In this way the alternance between stock market upswing and downswing phases is established. Also, an economically plausible alternative method to the poorly motivated jump-variable technique to "close" the dynamics of an otherwise unstable economic process has been established.

In Section 6.5 we have shown another plausible and economically meaningful alternative to the jump variable procedure, which can also overcome the local instability problems. This approach starts out by relaxing the assumption of perfect substitution between the financial assets, equities and short-term bonds, such that the adjustments of the equity price and the corresponding returns to the short-term interest rate are no longer instantaneous. There may nevertheless be strong forces of instability locally around the steady state(s), but these are tamed in the outer regions of the state space, when large differentials in the rates of return and their nonlinear effects on the excess demand for equities are properly taken into account. These economically meaningful mechanisms are strong enough to limit the otherwise explosive tendencies in the evolution of share prices.

We do not conceal the fact that the procedures proposed in this chapter still exhibit some problematic features. For instance, the sudden changes, or even jumps, in the expected growth rate of capital gains may be considered unsatisfactory. In any case, owing to the stylized nature of the behavioral equations, the dynamics are too regular and mechanistic to represent an already superior alternative to the conventional jump variable technique, which however also looks fairly mechanistic in the deterministic setup considered here. But these shortcomings may be improved in some of the future research directions suggested below. The important point is that our approach, together with similar work in this vein, lays the foundation for a descriptively oriented macrodynamic theory that does not need to rely on the poorly motivated jump variable technique to handle situations of local instability caused by accelerating stock price dynamics.

A number of generalizations and extensions of the framework developed here are possible. First, it could be incorporated into the broader and consistently formulated framework of disequilibrium macroeconomic dynamics of Chiarella and Flaschel (2000), in particular to develop a consistent financial market dynamics in that broader framework. Additional elements such as capital accumulation, inventories and flexible wages and prices could be added. The resulting framework of real–financial interaction would be sufficiently rich to allow a study of various anticipated and unanticipated monetary and fiscal shocks as well as stabilization policies. Initial steps in this direction have been taken in Chiarella et al. (2001a, b).

Second, the proper inclusion of the bond price dynamics needs to be considered. As we pointed out in Section 6.2, there is no feedback of the bond price dynamics into the rest of the economy. This could be done, for example by allowing interest rate effects in the aggregate demand function.

Third, the shape of the reaction coefficient β_q could be modeled in a more sophisticated way than that displayed in Figure 6.6. Empirically, we observe that stock markets remain close to steady state more frequently than Figure 6.10 suggests. It is more likely that the schedule for the coefficient β_q is subject to market perceptions (which can change from time to time for a variety of reasons) and to large news events. These features could be captured by allowing the whole schedule to move up and down randomly from time to time (perhaps using a Poisson jump process to model the changes in perception and large new events). Under "normal" market conditions the β_q schedule could be in a position such that $\beta_q^+ < 1$. In this way the alternance between upswing and downswing regimes would not be so regular, depending rather on the timing of shocks and their sign. It would also be important to capture the steady arrival of regular news events in the stock market by rewriting the dynamic equation for the dynamics of q as a stochastic differential equation perturbed by Wiener increments. A preliminary study of the interaction of nonlinear and stochastic elements in the model treated here is given in Chiarella et al. (2006).

Fourth, heterogeneous agents (fundamentalists and chartists) could be introduced into the model and so give more rationale to the story of a variable reaction coefficient. Fundamentalists would presumably be dominant during tranquil phases, whilst chartists would become more dominant during activated phases. The ideas introduced by Brock and Hommes (1997) could be used to model the changing role of fundamentalists and chartists during the various phases of the cycle. A model of this type is studies in Chapter 8.

Fifth, here we have relied on a variable reaction coefficient (β_q) to expected return differentials as a means to "close" the dynamics of an otherwise unstable system. An alternative approach would involve leaving β_q constant and instead allowing the speed of adjustment of expectations (β_z) to vary according to market conditions.[23]

6.7 References

BLANCHARD, O. (1981): Output, the stock market, and interest rates. *American Economic Review*, 71, 132–143.

BLANCHARD, O. and S. FISCHER (1989): *Lectures on Macroeconomics*. Cambridge, MA: MIT Press.

BROCK, W.A. and C.H. HOMMES (1997): A rational route to randomness. *Econometrica*, 65(5), 1059–1095.

---

23 Attempts in this direction are made in Chiarella et al. (2000a, b and 2003).

BROCK, W.A. and A.G. MALLIARIS (1989): *Differential Equations, Stability and Chaos in Dynamic Economics*. Amsterdam: North-Holland.

BUITER, W. (1984): Saddlepoint problems in continuous time rational expectations models: A general method and some macrodynamic examples. *Econometrica*, 52, 665–680.

BURMEISTER, E. (1980): On some conceptual issues in rational expectations modelling. *Journal of Money, Credit and Banking*, 12, 217–228.

CHANG, W.W. and D.J. SMYTH (1971): The existence and persistence of cycles in a non-linear model: Kaldor's 1940 model re-examined. *Review of Economic Studies*, 38, 37–46.

CHIARELLA, C. (1986): Perfect foresight models and the dynamic instability problem from a higher viewpoint. *Economic Modelling*, 3, 283–292.

CHIARELLA, C. (1990a): Excessive exchange rate variability: A possible explanation using nonlinear economic dynamics. *European Journal of Political Economy*, 6, 315–352.

CHIARELLA, C. (1990b): *The Elements of a Nonlinear Theory of Economic Dynamics*. Berlin: Springer.

CHIARELLA, C. and A. KHOMIN (2000): The dynamic interaction of rational fundamentalists and trend chasing chartists in a monetary economy. In: Delli Gatti, D., Gallegati, M. and A. Kirman (eds.): *Market Structure, Aggregation and Heterogeneity. Lecture Notes in Economics*. New York: Springer.

CHIARELLA, C. and P. FLASCHEL (2000): *The Dynamics of Keynesian Monetary Growth: Macrofoundations*. Cambridge, UK: Cambridge University Press.

CHIARELLA, C., P. FLASCHEL, R. FRANKE and W. SEMMLER (2000a): Output, financial markets and growth. An extension of the Blanchard stock market approach. School of Finance and Economics, *UTS Working Paper No. 108*. Electronic copy available at: http://WWW.business.uts.edu.au/finance/research/wpapers/wp108.pdf

CHIARELLA, C., P. FLASCHEL and W. SEMMLER (2000b): Real–financial interaction. A reconsideration of the Blanchard model with a state-of-market dependent reaction coefficient. School of Finance and Economics, *UTS Working Paper* No. 111. Electronic copy available at: http://www.business.uts.edu.au/finance/research/wpapers/wp111.pdf

CHIARELLA, C., P. FLASCHEL and W. SEMMLER (2003): Output and the term structure of interest rates: The dynamics of switching phase diagrams. Mimeo, University of Bielefeld.

CHIARELLA, C., P. FLASCHEL, R. FRANKE and W. SEMMLER (2001a): Output, financial markets and growth. An extension of the Blanchard stock-market approach. In: R. Friedmann, L. Knüppel and H. Lütkepohl (eds.): *Econometric Studies: A Festschrift in Honour of Joachim Frohn*. Münster: Lit Verlag, 159–184.

CHIARELLA, C., P. FLASCHEL, R. FRANKE and W. SEMMLER (2001b): Real–financial interaction: Integrating supply side wage–price dynamics and the stock market. School of Finance and Economics, *UTS Working Paper* No. 112. Electronic copy available at: http://www.business.uts.edu.au/finance/research/wpapers/wp112.pdf

CHIARELLA, C., P. FLASCHEL, X. HE and H. HUNG (2006): 'A stochastic model of real–financial interaction with boundedly rational heterogeneous agents', In: C. Chiarella, R. Franke, P. Flaschel, and W. Semmler, (eds): *Quantitative and Empirical Analysis of Nonlinear Dynamic Macromodels*. UK: Elsevier.

CHIARELLA, C., S. MITTNIK, W. SEMMLER and P. ZHU (2002): Stock market, interest rate and output: a model and estimation for US time series data. *Studies in Nonlinear Dynamics and Econometrics*, 6:1, Article 2.

CROUCH, R. (1972): *Macroeconomics*. New York: Harcourt Brace Jovanovich.

DORNBUSCH, R. (1976): Expectations and exchange rate dynamics. *Journal of Political Economy*, 84, 1161–1176.

FLASCHEL, P. and R. SETHI (1999): The stability in models of money and perfect foresight: Implications of nonlinearity. *Economic Modelling*, 16:2, 221–233.

GANTMACHER, F.R. (1959): *Applications of the Theory of Matrices*. New York: Interscience.

GOODWIN, R.M. (1951): The nonlinear accelerator and the persistence of business cycle. *Econometrica*, 19, 1–17.

MINORSKY, N. (1962): *Nonlinear Oscillations*. New York: Van Nostrand.

OXLEY, L. and D.A.R. GEORGE (1994): Linear saddlepoint dynamics "On their head": The scientific content of the new orthodoxy in macrodynamics. *European Journal of Political Economy*, 10, 389–400.

SARGENT, T. and N. WALLACE (1973): The stability of models of money and growth with perfect foresight. *Econometrica*, 41, 1043–1046.

STROGATZ, S.H. (1994): *Nonlinear Dynamics and Chaos*. New York: Addison-Wesley.

7 Real–financial market interaction

Implications of budget equations and capital accumulation

7.1 Introduction

In this chapter, we investigate the real–financial interaction of an approach of Blanchard to stock market and multiplier dynamics from the stock-flow consistency perspective by including in the model the capacity and financing effect of the decisions of firms to invest. We thus add budget equations as well as the growth law for capital stock to the Blanchard dynamics and investigate the implications of these additions for steady-state locations and their stability. We show that the steady-state solutions of the Blanchard approach are no longer of relevance here, but are replaced by a unique interior long-run solution. We demonstrate asymptotic stability with respect to this steady state when stock market adjustment is sufficiently sluggish, even in the case of myopic perfect foresight. In the opposite situation, if the stock market adjusts sufficiently fast, the system loses stability by way of a Hopf bifurcation for increasing adjustment speeds of capital gains expectations and will generate purely explosive behavior shortly thereafter.

We indicate for this case how a regime (or phase diagram) switching methodology between activated and tranquil stock market behavior may nevertheless ensure global viability of the dynamics, despite the occurrence of shorter or longer episodes of explosive financial acceleration. This result follows from the assumption that stock markets must return to tranquillity after certain thresholds are surpassed, where financial acceleration due to high adjustment speeds in the market for equities disappears. The chapter thereby contributes to macrodynamic modeling methodology by providing alternatives to the jump variable technique of models with myopic perfect foresight. This methodology allows stability of (near) perfect foresight dynamics to be obtained without the arbitrary imposition of terminal positions on the trajectories that are considered relevant from an economic perspective.

In Section 7.2 we provide the extensive form of the model, including the budget constraints of the three sectors considered and the feedbacks that derive from them. Furthermore, besides equity accumulation we also allow for the capacity effect of investment and thus for capital stock growth. In Section 7.3 we present and discuss the intensive form of the model. The resulting dynamical system is of dimension 4 and is based on sluggish adjustment of output and capital stock as well as a somewhat sluggish adjustment of Tobin's q and capital gains expectations. The limit case of myopic perfect foresight is derived as well as the limit limit case of perfect foresight plus perfect substitutes, i.e., the case that is considered by Blanchard (1981) for given stocks of capital, equities and bonds.

Section 7.4 investigates the unique[1] interior steady state of these 4D dynamics and its local asymptotic stability. It is shown that the dynamics are generally convergent when expectations are stationary, or adjusting with a speed that is sufficiently low. Increasing this speed of adjustment, however, implies the occurrence of so-called Hopf bifurcations where the system loses stability in a cyclical fashion, giving rise to explosiveness of the dynamics if the considered adjustment speed is increased even further. The dynamics are thus not yet well defined from the economic perspective in such situations.

Section 7.5 therefore shows that the dynamics are convergent for all adjustment speeds of expectations if stock markets are sufficiently tranquil, i.e., if the adjustment speed on these markets is sufficiently low and if the downward link from financial to real markets is sufficiently weak.[2] For a low dependence of investment decisions of firms on Tobin's q we therefore can show, as in Chiarella et al. (2001, 2003b), that a financial accelerator based on high adjustment speeds of share prices and capital gains expectations will be tamed if such periods of explosive upward or downward movements in share price and Tobin's q are overcome by returns or switches to low adjustment speeds of share prices. The latter may be caused by a switch to cautiousness of behavior in the stock markets and thus to tranquillity and a return to convergent dynamics, until this process is disrupted again through increases in the speed of adjustment of equity prices. This switch between different phases of stock market behavior and between explosive and convergent financial feedback mechanisms can be accompanied by any strength of the adjustment speed of adaptive capital gains expectations and thus also holds if the limit case of perfect foresight is assumed. We consider this outcome as more convincing than the one that would be obtained by applying the jump variable technique (in the cases where it is applicable), which gives rise to very erratic outcomes once intrinsic changes in the dimension of the considered dynamics are taken into account, as Section 7.5 will show.

The chapter thus focuses on the stock market, firms' investment decisions and the rates of return on short-term bonds and equities as the crucial elements in the interaction of real and financial markets. The budget equation of firms plays an important role, but not yet those of households and the government, the former

---

1 The short-run version of the dynamics exhibits, as in Blanchard (1981), the possibility of no or two interior steady-state solutions of the system's dynamics, a difficulty that is here overcome by the fact that these steady states are not really stationary.

2 The latter condition may not really be necessary, as a brief investigation of the Routh–Hurwitz conditions indicates. Yet, due to the complexity of these conditions, a proof of this conjecture is currently not available and can therefore only be demonstrated here by means of numerical simulations of the dynamics.

since the effects of wealth and interest rates on consumption are still excluded and the latter since we assume a particular type of tax collection rule. What still remain to be considered are long-term bonds (see Blanchard (1981), Blanchard and Fischer (1989) and Chiarella et al. (2003a) in this regard). Finally, we do not yet allow for an adjustment of wages and prices; see, however, Chiarella et al. (2002) for such an integration. We therefore investigate here growth and fluctuations without their implications for capacity utilization of labor and capital and their implications on wage and price changes.[3] Real growth equals money supply growth ($\mu = n$) and there is thus no inflation in the steady state.

7.2 The Blanchard model with intrinsic stock-flow dynamics

We first provide the notation used in the presentation of our extended model of the real–financial interaction shown below, where all budget equations are now specified and where also the capacity effect of the investment to be undertaken is included.

7.2.1 Notation

Endogenous variables

Y^d	Aggregate demand
Y^D	Disposable income
Y^p	Potential output
Y	Output
K	Capital stock
i	Nominal rate of interest
B	Number of bonds (short-term only)
T	Real taxes
G	Government expenditure
L^d	Employment
Π	Real profits
S_p	Private savings
$S_f = 0$	Firms' savings
S_g	Government savings
E	Number of equities
p_e	Share or equity price
I	Net investment $I/K = i(q-1)+n$
q	Tobin's average q
r	Rate of profit $(1-u)y - \delta$
$z = \hat{p}_e^e$	Expected growth rate of share prices

---

3 Wages and prices are set equal to 1 for notational simplicity in the following; see again Chiarella et al. (2002) for the integration of their dynamics.

Exogenous variables

$\overline{w}(=1)$	Nominal wages
$\overline{p}(=1)$	Price level
$\overline{\mu} = \widehat{M} = n$	Growth rate of the money supply
$n = \widehat{L}$	Natural growth
c	Marginal propensity to consume
ψ	Investment parameter
δ	Depreciation rate
g	Fiscal policy parameter
t	Fiscal policy parameter
$\beta's$	Adjustment speeds
v	Wage share
$\kappa's$	Weights in capital gain expectations $[\in (0, 1)]$
k, h_1	Money demand parameters
i_0	Steady-state rate of interest
$x = Y/L^d$	Labor productivity
$y^p = Y^p/K$	Potential output–capital ratio

Mathematical notation

$\dot{x}$	Time derivative of x
$\widehat{x} = \dot{x}/x$	Growth rate of x
$\ln x$	Logarithm of x
f_x, f_1	Partial derivatives of f
$\varepsilon_{f,x}$	Elasticity of f w.r.t. x (always positive by convention)
$m = M/K$	Intensive form variables

7.2.2 The equations of the model

We now provide the equations of the model where, however, we no longer distinguish explicitly the algebraic equations from the dynamical equations. Note also that we still use assumptions that suppress the effects of interest income and wealth on the dynamic evolution of the model. Note finally that the model no longer exhibits expressions for autonomous consumption and investment (up to the trend growth term in the investment function). The following equations describe aggregate demand, disposable income, various saving items, fiscal policy rules, the laws of motion of output and share prices, money market equilibrium, including the definition of the steady-state rate of interest, capital gains expectations, capital accumulation, the new issue of equities, Tobin's average q, and given labor and capital productivity indices:

$$Y^d = cY^D + (\psi(q-1) + \delta + n)K + G, \tag{7.1}$$

$$Y^D = Y - \delta K + iB - T = \omega L^d + \Pi + iB - T, \quad \Pi = (1-v)Y - \delta K, \tag{7.2}$$

$$S_p = (1-c)Y^D = \dot{M} + \dot{B} + p_e\dot{E}, \quad \dot{M} = \bar{\mu}M, \tag{7.3}$$

$$-S_g = G + iB - T = \dot{M} + \dot{B}, \quad \dot{M} = \bar{\mu}M, \tag{7.4}$$

$$S_f = 0, \tag{7.5}$$

$$S = S_p + S_q + S_g = p_e\dot{E} = I, \tag{7.6}$$

$$G/K = \text{const.} = g, \tag{7.7}$$

$$(T - iB)/K = \text{const.} = t, \tag{7.8}$$

$$\dot{Y} = \beta_y(Y^d - Y) + nY, \tag{7.9}$$

$$\widehat{p}_e = \beta_{p_e}\left(\frac{(1-v)Y - \delta K}{p_eE} + z - i\right) + \kappa_{p_e}z + (1 - \kappa_{p_e})z_o, \quad z_o = 0, \tag{7.10}$$

$$M = kY + h_1(i_0 - i)K, i_0 = (1-v)\left(\frac{Y}{K}\right)_0 - \delta, \tag{7.11}$$

$$\dot{z} = \beta_z(\widehat{p}_e - z), \tag{7.12}$$

$$\widehat{K} = I/K = \psi(q-1) + n, \tag{7.13}$$

$$\dot{E} = I/p_e, \tag{7.14}$$

$$q = p_eE/K, \tag{7.15}$$

$$x = Y/L^d = \text{const} : e = L^d/L \text{ not needed yet}, \tag{7.16}$$

$$y^p = Y^p/K = \text{const} : u = Y/Y^p \text{ not needed yet}. \tag{7.17}$$

As the model is formulated, it is only the budget constraints for firms that influence the evolution of Tobin's q, whereas the government budget constraint and those of households are not yet of real importance. Furthermore, the evolution of inventories is disregarded in the quantity adjustment process of the model. Incorporation of these various factors will be the subject of future extensions of the model of this chapter.

7.3 Intensive form of the model

In order to derive the intensive-form laws of motion and their point of rest we first have to define the state variables that we shall use in the following analysis of the dynamics.

7.3.1 The state variables

In the present formulation of real–financial interaction we do not yet consider growth, apart from exogenous labor force growth with rate n. It turns out to be convenient to express everything in per unit of capital form in order to analyze the dynamics implied by the model. Thus we set

$$y = Y/K, \tag{7.18}$$

$$m = M/K, \tag{7.19}$$

$$q = p_e E/K, \tag{7.20}$$

$$z = \hat{p}_e^e. \tag{7.21}$$

Note that we now have to make use of the term $\hat{E} - \hat{K} = [(1-q)/q]\hat{K}$ in order to obtain the law of motion of Tobin's q from the law of motion of share prices p_e.[4]

7.3.2 The laws of motion

Differentiating (7.18) to (7.21) and making use of appropriate expressions from equations (7.1) to (7.17), we obtain

$$\dot{y} = \beta_y(c(y - \delta - t) + \psi(q - 1) + \delta + n + g - y) - \psi(q - 1)y, \tag{7.22}$$

$$\widehat{m} = -\psi(q - 1), \tag{7.23}$$

$$\widehat{q} = \beta_{p_e}\left(\frac{(1-v)y - \delta}{q} + z - (i_0 + \frac{ky - m}{h_1})\right) + \kappa_{p_e}z + \frac{1-q}{q}(\psi(q-1) + n), \tag{7.24}$$

$$\dot{z} = \beta_z(\beta_{p_e}\left(\frac{(1-v)y - \delta}{q} + z - (i_0 + \frac{ky - m}{h_1})\right) - (1 - \kappa_{p_e})z). \tag{7.25}$$

From the viewpoint of real–financial interaction we can deduce from these dynamic equations that the link from the financial to the real markets is given solely by Tobin's q, whereas the link back to the financial markets is based on output and resulting dividend changes which determine the dividend rate of return, and on changing money balances per unit of capital which determine the short-term rate of interest. The comparison of these two rates (including capital gains expectations) basically determines the movement of share prices and Tobin's q and thus, in turn, the change in investment behavior and so forth.

We stress that the limit case considered on a less complete level in Blanchard (1981), since the law of motion for real balances is disregarded, is recovered by assuming $\beta_q = \beta_z = \infty$, i.e., by assuming perfect substitutes and perfect foresight. The special case of *myopic perfect foresight* considered in Blanchard (1981) gives

---

4 There holds $\hat{E} = \dot{K}/(p_e E) = \hat{K} \cdot K/(p_e E) = \hat{K}/q$ $(p = 1)$.

rise in the present model to the dynamics

$$\dot{y} = \beta_y(c(y - \delta - t) + \psi(q - 1) + \delta + n + g - y) - \psi(q - 1)y, \qquad (7.26)$$

$$\widehat{m} = -\psi(q - 1), \qquad (7.27)$$

$$\widehat{q} = \frac{1}{1 - \beta_{pe} - \kappa_{pe}} \beta_{pe} \left(\frac{(1 - v)y - \delta}{q} - (i_0 + \frac{ky - m}{h_1}) \right)$$

$$+ \frac{1 - q}{q}(\psi(q - 1) + n). \qquad (7.28)$$

Note that the steady-state solution of these dynamics is identical to the one of the 4D system if the variable z is now disregarded.

Furthermore, assuming that bonds and equities are *perfect substitutes* (by assuming $\beta_{pe} = \infty$) implies the following special case of the above 3D dynamics:

$$\dot{y} = \beta_y(c(y - \delta - t) + \psi(q - 1) + \delta + n + g - y) - \psi(q - 1)y, \qquad (7.29)$$

$$\widehat{m} = -\psi(q - 1), \qquad (7.30)$$

$$\widehat{q} = i_0 + \frac{ky - m}{h_1} - \frac{(1 - v)y - \delta}{q} + \frac{1 - q}{q}(\psi(q - 1) + n). \qquad (7.31)$$

This is the 3D analog to the 2D system considered in Blanchard (1981), with new growth-dependent terms in the output and q dynamics and with a new law of motion for real balances per unit of capital. Note that the steady-state solution of these dynamics is identical to the one of the 4D system (if the variable z is disregarded for the moment).

7.4 Analysis

7.4.1 Steady-state determination

With regard to steady-state analysis we have the following proposition.[5]

Proposition 7.1:
The interior steady-state ($m \neq 0, q \neq 0$) of the above laws of motion is uniquely determined and given by:

$$q_0 = 1,$$

$$m_0 = ky_0,$$

$$z_0 = 0,$$

---

5 Note that the steady-state value for i was used in the formulation of the laws of motion that surround it.

$$y_0 = \frac{1}{1-c}(\delta + n + g - c(\delta + t)) \quad [= \delta + g + \frac{n}{1-c} \; if \, g = t],$$

$$i_0 = (1-v)y_0 - \delta.$$

In contrast to the model without budget equations and capital accumulation or decumulation, we thus no longer have the possibility of no or two steady-state solutions as in the approach of Blanchard (1981), or even in the generalized Blanchard case, eqs (7.26) to (7.28). This is due to the fact that q can now become stationary only at the value $q = 1$ and not at the steady-state values of q that belong to the short-run system considered in Chiarella et al. (2001), which extended Blanchard (1981) by allowing for imperfect substitutes and less than perfect foresight. There are thus no algebraic equations established in the limit that can imply two roots for the solution of Tobin's q. Note also that income distribution is still kept fixed and that supply-side considerations on the market for labor and for goods are still excluded (see Chiarella et al. (2002) for an inclusion of wage–price dynamics and the investigation of the role of income distribution in the current approach to real–financial interaction).

One can of course again calculate IS–LM curve equilibria, as in Blanchard (1981), by setting $\dot{y}$ and $\dot{q}$ equal to zero and by freezing capital stock movements (and by fixing M). These IS–LM equilibria are, however, now in fact moving in time and even though they may be relevant as partial attractors they are no longer of real importance, since the movement of the system can be analyzed independently of them. These shadow equilibria furthermore are not really helpful in understanding the equilibrium and the stability properties of the full dynamics. Note also that the stationary values for y and q are determined here by simpler expressions than the ones of the short-run dynamics where M and K were still stationary.

7.4.2 Dynamics

We investigate for the dynamics (7.22)–(7.25) the case $\beta_z = 0$ first. In this case the Jacobian J at the steady-state reads:

$$J = \begin{pmatrix} -(1-c)\beta_y & 0 & (\beta_y - y)\psi \\ 0 & 0 & -\psi m_o \\ \left((1-v) - \frac{k}{h_1}\right)\beta_{pe} & \beta_{pe}/h_1 & -i_0\beta_{pe} - n \end{pmatrix}$$

$$= \begin{pmatrix} - & 0 & \pm \\ 0 & 0 & - \\ \pm & + & - \end{pmatrix} \overset{\beta_y \uparrow}{\underset{=}{}} \begin{pmatrix} - & 0 & + \\ 0 & 0 & - \\ \pm & + & - \end{pmatrix}.$$

For $\beta_y > y$ we get for the coefficients of the Routh–Hurwitz polynomial of the matrix J (with J_i denoting the principal minors of J of order two):

$$a_1 = -\operatorname{trace} J > 0,$$

$$a_2 = J_1 + J_2 + J_3 > 0 \text{ if } h_1 \text{ is sufficiently small, since we have}$$

$$J_1 = \begin{vmatrix} J_{22} & J_{23} \\ J_{31} & J_{33} \end{vmatrix} = \operatorname{sign} \begin{vmatrix} 0 & - \\ + & - \end{vmatrix} > 0, \quad J_3 = \begin{vmatrix} J_{11} & J_{12} \\ J_{21} & J_{22} \end{vmatrix} = 0 \quad \text{and}$$

$$J_2 = \begin{vmatrix} J_{11} & J_{13} \\ J_{31} & J_{33} \end{vmatrix} = \begin{vmatrix} -(1-c) & \psi - (y/\beta_y)\psi \\ (1-v) - k/h_1 & -i_0 - n/\beta_{p_e} \end{vmatrix} \beta_y \beta_{p_e} > 0,$$

the latter, since the off-diagonal can then be considered the dominant element in the determinant J_2 if the parameter h_1 is sufficiently small. For the determinant of J we furthermore find that

$$a_3 = -\det J = -\begin{vmatrix} - & 0 & + \\ 0 & 0 & - \\ - & + & - \end{vmatrix} = J_{32} J_{11} J_{23} > 0.$$

Finally, we have for the composite coefficient of the Routh–Hurwitz conditions for local asymptotic stability:

$$b = a_1 a_2 - a_3 = -(J_{11} + J_{33})(J_{32} J_{23} + \ldots) - J_{11} J_{23} J_{32} > 0,$$

i.e., the positive terms in the $a_1 a_2$ expression include the negative of the determinant of J and thus dominate the negative term $-J_{32} J_{11} J_{23}$. We therefore get, in sum:

Proposition 7.2 ($z = 0$ still):
   *Assume $\beta_y > y$ and $h_1 < k/(1-v)$. Then: The interior steady-state of the dynamics (7.22)–(7.24) is **locally asymptotically stable**.*

Proof: See the above and Brock and Malliaris (1989) or Gantmacher (1959) for the formulation of the Routh–Hurwitz condition for local asymptotic stability. □

Remark: The above proof of Proposition 7.2 shows that stability problems can only arise due to the term J_2, or even more specifically due to $-(1-v)\psi(\beta_y - y)\psi < 0$, in the condition that $a_2 > 0$ if $\beta_y > y$ holds true. This term can, for example, be made the dominant one in a_2 by choosing h_1 and β_y sufficiently large and the parameter c sufficiently close to 1. Another channel for overthrowing the stability of the dynamics is considered in the following proposition.

Proposition 7.3 (3D dynamics):
   *Assume $(1-v)(\beta_y - y) > \psi m_0/h_1 + (1-c)\beta_y i_0 + (\beta_y - y)\psi k/h_1$ by appropriate choices of the parameters h_1 and c. The local **stability** found in the preceding*

*proposition **gets lost** by way of a Hopf bifurcation (i.e., in a cyclical fashion) if the parameter β_{p_e} is made sufficiently large.*

Proof: The assumption made implies that the coefficient a_2 depends negatively on β_{p_e}. Since this functional dependence is linear, we thus get that a_2 must become negative for β_{p_e} chosen sufficiently large. We note that the Hopf bifurcation must occur before $a_2 = 0$ has been reached, since b must change sign before this situation occurs. The speed condition of the Hopf bifurcation theorem at the Hopf bifurcation point finally follows from Orlando's formula (see Gantmacher (1959))[6]

$$b = -(\lambda_1 + \lambda_2)(\lambda_1 + \lambda_3)(\lambda_2 + \lambda_3),$$

for the three eigenvalues λ_i of the Jacobian J. At the Hopf bifurcation we find (by choosing eigenvalues in an appropriate order) that λ_1 is negative and $\lambda_2 + \lambda_3 = 0$. Orlando's formula thus applies at the Hopf bifurcation point $b'(\beta_{p_e}) = 2|\lambda_1 + \lambda_2|^2(\beta_{p_e})(Re\lambda_2)'(\beta_{p_e})$, where $|\cdot|$ denotes distance measurement in the complex plane and Re the real part of the eigenvalues. Eigenvalues thus cross the imaginary axis with positive speed $(Re\lambda_2)'(\beta_{p_e}) > 0$ if and only if $b'(\beta_{p_e}) < 0$ holds true. The latter condition is, however, obvious, since the parameters in front of β_{p^e} in the expressions forming b have to be negative due to the assumption made and the fact that the trace and determinant of J are also linear functions of β_{p_e} with only negative parameter values. See Benhabib and Miyao (1981) for a related consideration of Orlando's formula and Wiggins (1990) and Strogatz (1994) for presentations of the Hopf bifurcation theorem. □

Remark: In the case $\beta_y < y$ we can always get a Hopf bifurcation as considered in Proposition 7.3 by simply choosing h_1 sufficiently small.

Remark: As in the original approach of Blanchard (1981), we have the $\dot{y} = 0$ and $\dot{q} = 0$ isoclines and now in addition an $\dot{m} = 0$ isocline, which are determined as follows:

$$\dot{y} = 0: \quad q = 1 + \frac{(1-c)y + c(\delta + t) - (\delta + n + g)}{(1 - y/\beta_y)\psi} = q_1(y),$$

$$\dot{q} = 0: \quad q = \frac{r}{i} = \frac{(1-v)y - \delta}{i_o + (ky - m)/h_1} = q_2(y, m),$$

$$\dot{m} = 0: \quad q \equiv 1.$$

The first isocline is the IS curve, while the second one represents the LM curve of Blanchard's approach. Such isoclines, however, no longer matter in the following

6 note that the b used here is not denoting bonds as usual.

stability analysis of the present dynamics, which means that we do not need to care about the slope of the IS and LM curves and so the distinction between good news and bad news cases no longer arises as it did in Blanchard (1981).

Proposition 7.4:

Assume the situation considered in Proposition 7.2. The same proposition on **local asymptotic stability** *then holds also for the 4D dynamics (7.22)–(7.25) for all parameters β_z sufficiently small.*

Proof: The determinant of the 4D Jacobian J can be reduced to

$$|J| = \begin{vmatrix} J_{11} & J_{12} & J_{13} & J_{14} \\ J_{21} & J_{22} & J_{23} & J_{24} \\ J_{31} & J_{32} & J_{33} & J_{34} \\ 0 & 0 & 0 & J_{44} \end{vmatrix},$$

with $J_{44} = \beta_z(\beta_{p_e} - \kappa_{p_e}) < 0$ by assumption, by adding appropriate multiples of its second and third rows to its fourth row. There follows:

$$\text{sign} \, |J| = - \begin{vmatrix} J_{11} & J_{12} & J_{13} \\ J_{21} & J_{22} & J_{23} \\ J_{31} & J_{32} & J_{33} \end{vmatrix} > 0.$$

For small β_z we thus have three eigenvalues close to those of the Jacobian J of the first proposition which thus must all have negative real parts. See Sontag (1990) for the theorem that eigenvalues depend continuously on the parameters of the dynamics. Since $|J| > 0$ for the 4D case the fourth eigenvalue of J must then be negative in addition, since the determinant is given by the product of all eigenvalues. ☐

Proposition 7.5:

The local **stability** *found in the preceding Proposition 7.4* **gets lost** *by way of a Hopf bifurcation if $\beta_{p_e} > 1 - \kappa_{p_e}$ holds and if β_z is made sufficiently large.*

We conjecture from numerical experience with such dynamics that the limit cycles implied by the Hopf bifurcation only exist locally and give way to purely explosive dynamics fairly soon after the Hopf bifurcation point has been passed. The situation considered in Proposition 7.5 will therefore basically be one of financial acceleration with (rapid) departure from a situation of return parities towards more and more increasing return differentials. Sooner or later such an accelerating process must come to an end, since agents expect it to turn and thus become more and more cautious in their market transactions, thereby reducing the speed of adjustment in the stock market. This may create the type of situation considered in the proposition, possibly with basins of attraction that are sufficiently large.

Proof: Same as in Proposition 7.3 if one notes that $J_{44} = \beta_z(\beta_{p_e} - (1 - \kappa_{p_e})) > 0$ holds true in the assumed situation.   □

Remark: Demonstrating the Routh–Hurwitz conditions for the characteristic polynomial of the Jacobian J at the steady state of the full 4D dynamics is generally not at all an easy task, since these conditions on the coefficients a_j of this polynomial $\lambda^4 + a_1\lambda^3 + a_2\lambda^2 + a_3\lambda + a_4$ then read:

$$a_j > 0 \quad (j = 1, 2, 3), \quad b_o = a_1a_2 - a_3 > 0, \quad b_1 = a_3b_o - a_1^2a_4 > 0,$$

and since the principal minors to be calculated for the determination of the coefficients a_2 and a_3 are now 6 and 4 in number, respectively. It is however not difficult to show for the dynamics considered here that all a_j must be positive (in fact all principal minors of order two and three are nonnegative in the situation considered) if $\beta_y > y, h_1 < k/(1 - v), \beta_{p_e} < 1 - \kappa_{p_e}$. This is because its sign structure in this situation is given by

$$|J| = \begin{vmatrix} - & 0 & + & 0 \\ 0 & 0 & - & 0 \\ - & + & - & + \\ - & + & - & - \end{vmatrix}.$$

We furthermore note that in this case the positivity of b_o is implied by the positivity of b_1. Looking at the expression $b_1 = a_3(a_1a_2 - a_3) - a_1^2a_4$ for large β_z, we thus get the following proposition:

Proposition 7.6:
*Assume $\beta_y > y, h_1 < k/(1 - v), \beta_{p_e} < 1 - \kappa_{p_e}$. The steady-state of the 4D dynamics (7.22)–(7.25) is **locally asymptotically stable** for all parameters β_z sufficiently large.*

We claim, but cannot prove here, that the proven stability is in fact generally not restricted to be close to the steady-state. Basins of attraction may indeed be quite large, and at least sufficiently large such that a convergent process is established if the accelerator situations considered in the preceding proposition come to rest. This would take place through a decline in the speed of adjustment of the stock market that allows for the application of Proposition 7.5.

Proof: We have to show that $b_1 = a_3(a_1a_2 - a_3) - a_1^2a_4 > 0$ holds true in such a situation. We first note in this respect that a_4 is given by $a_3^{3D}(-J_{44})$, where a_3^{3D} denotes the corresponding Routh–Hurwitz coefficient of the 3D dynamics (see the proof of Proposition 7.4), i.e.,

$$a_3^{3D} = - \begin{vmatrix} J_{11} & J_{12} & J_{13} \\ J_{21} & J_{22} & J_{23} \\ J_{31} & J_{32} & J_{33} \end{vmatrix}.$$

There follows that

$$\begin{vmatrix} J_{11} & J_{12} & J_{13} \\ J_{21} & J_{22} & J_{23} \\ J_{31} & J_{32} & J_{33} \end{vmatrix} (J_{44})^3$$

gives the dominant term for the β_z influence in $a_1^2 a_4$ when this parameter is made sufficiently large ($J_{44} = \beta_z(\beta_{p_e} - (1 - \kappa_{p_e})) < 0$). This term is however included among the product terms to be found in $a_3 a_1 a_2$ and can thus be removed from consideration. There are, however, further expressions of the form const. $(\beta_z)^3$ in the products that form $a_3 a_1 a_2$ and none of this type in $-(a_3)^2$. This implies that b_1 is a polynomial in β_z of degree three with a positive coefficient in front of $(\beta_z)^3$ which implies the assertion. $\qquad\square$

Remark: It is also easy to show (at least for n equal to zero) that the Routh–Hurwitz condition $b_o > 0$ holds for the 4D dynamics without any restriction on the parameter β_z, but of course with $\beta_y > y, h_1 < k/(1-v), \beta_{p_e} < 1 - \kappa_{p_e}$. To demonstrate this it suffices to note that three of the four minors of order 3 of the Jacobian J (the fourth is zero) reappear with opposite sign in the products that form the expression $a_1 a_2$ due to Proposition 7.2 and its proof and due to the partial linear dependency that exists between the entries in the second plus third and the fourth row of J. This allows us to express these minors as products of second-order and first-order minors (as they reappear in a_1 and a_2). Only the condition $b_1 > 0$ may thus cause problems for local asymptotic stability and this only for values of β_z that are bounded away from zero and infinity. It can therefore be expected that the situation where

$$\beta_y > y, h_1 < k/(1-v), \beta_{p_e} < 1 - \kappa_{p_e}$$

holds is, by and large, one of (not only) local asymptotic stability for all speeds of adjustment of capital gains expectations. Stability for all β_z under the assumptions of Proposition 7.6 can be easily proved, for example, when the link from financial markets to real markets is made sufficiently weak, as the following proposition shows. We therefore indeed conjecture that the conditions $\beta_y > y, h_1 < k/(1 - v), \beta_{p_e} < 1 - \kappa_{p_e}$ are, by and large, sufficient to imply local asymptotic stability for all speeds of adjustment β_z. A dynamic multiplier that is sufficiently fast, a Keynes effect that is sufficiently strong and a stock market adjustment that is sufficiently tranquil can therefore be expected to represent sufficient conditions for the convergence of our four state variables y, m, q, z back to the steady state in case of shocks that throw the dynamics out of the steady state (and that are not too large). Of course, the admissible sizes of the shocks and thus the basin of attraction of the interior steady-state solution can only be determined numerically for these 4D dynamics.

Proposition 7.7:
*Assume $h_1 < k/(1-v)$, $\beta_{p_e} < 1 - \kappa_{p_e}$. The steady-state of the 4D dynamics (7.22)–(7.25) is **locally asymptotically stable** for all parameters β_z if the investment parameter ψ is sufficiently small.*

Proof: Assuming $\psi = 0$ implies, for the characteristic polynomial of the Jacobian J at the steady-state, the form (here I is the identity matrix):

$$|\lambda I - J| = \begin{vmatrix} \lambda - J_{11} & -J_{12} & 0 & 0 \\ -J_{21} & \lambda - J_{22} & 0 & 0 \\ -J_{31} & -J_{32} & \lambda - J_{33} & -J_{34} \\ -J_{41} & -J_{42} & -J_{43} & \lambda - J_{44} \end{vmatrix}$$

$$= \begin{vmatrix} \lambda - J_{11} & -J_{12} \\ -J_{21} & \lambda - J_{22} \end{vmatrix} \cdot \begin{vmatrix} \lambda - J_{33} & -J_{34} \\ -J_{43} & \lambda - J_{44} \end{vmatrix}.$$

This implies that the zeros of this polynomial are given by the zeros of the characteristic polynomial of the real and financial part of the economy considered in isolation. Under the assumptions made we thus get that three roots of the characteristic polynomial must be negative and one zero, since the Jacobians of the real and the financial part of the economy are given by

$$J_{real} = \begin{pmatrix} -0 \\ -0 \end{pmatrix} \quad \text{and} \quad J_{financial} = \begin{pmatrix} -+ \\ -- \end{pmatrix}.$$

Continuity of the eigenvalues with respect to the parameters of the dynamics and the fact that $|J| > 0$ for the full 4D system then imply that small changes in ψ must leave the three negative real parts negative. The zero eigenvalue must become negative as well, in order to give rise to a positive determinant of the Jacobian of the full dynamics at the steady state. $\square$

What has been shown above for large β_z is reflected in the following Proposition 7.8 on the limit case of myopic perfect foresight:

Proposition 7.8:
Assume $\beta_y > y$. In the special case of perfect foresight, i.e., system (7.26)–(7.28):

$$\dot{y} = \beta_y(c(y-\delta-t)+\psi(q-1)+\delta+n+g-y)-\psi(q-1)y,$$

$$\widehat{m} = -\psi(q-1),$$

$$\widehat{q} = \frac{1}{1-\beta_{p_e}-\kappa_{p_e}}\beta_{p_e}\left(\frac{(1-v)y-\delta}{q} - \left(i_0 + \frac{ky-m}{h_1}\right)\right) + \frac{1-q}{q}(\psi(q-1)+n),$$

*we have **local asymptotic stability** at the interior steady-state of these dynamics if h_1 is sufficiently small and if $\beta_{p_e} < 1 - \kappa_{p_e}$ holds true.*

Proof: For the Jacobian of these dynamics at the steady state we have

$$\begin{pmatrix} - & 0 & + \\ 0 & 0 & - \\ - & + & - \end{pmatrix}$$

where the only difference to the Jacobian in Proposition 7.2 is given by the fact that the third row in this Jacobian is now multiplied by $1/(1 - \beta_{p_e} - \kappa_{p_e})$.[7] This implies the assertion of the proposition. $\qquad\square$

Note that the isoclines of (7.26)–(7.28) are the same as the ones discussed above and that again they are of not much importance in discussing the stability properties of these dynamics. Perfect foresight is not crucial for these properties either. Instead, as long as there is a sufficiently sluggish adjustment of share prices (a cautious stock market, combined with a fast dynamic multiplier and a strong Keynes effect), there will be asymptotic stability and thus not the saddlepoint dynamics of the Blanchard (1981) paper. The question therefore has become whether markets in disequilibrium may react in this way or not. We suggest that they may not always react in this way, but may indeed be forced to adopt this type of behavior when disequilibria become too large.

Remark: The situation of explosive dynamics can be integrated with the situation of convergent dynamics by way of a regime-switching methodology as considered in Chiarella et al. (2003b). The system can thereby be made viable even in the case of myopic perfect foresight by allowing it to run through certain sequences of bull and bear markets which are sometimes tranquil, producing convergence, and sometimes activated with diverging dynamics.

Let us discuss finally the extreme limit case where both adjustment speeds β_{p_e} and β_z are set equal to infinity, i.e., where we have perfect foresight and perfect substitutes at the same time. This applies to the system (7.29)–(7.31) introduced above, namely

$$\widehat{m} = -\psi(q-1), \tag{7.32}$$

$$\dot{y} = \beta_y(c(y-\delta-t)+\psi(q-1)+\delta+n+g-y)-\psi(q-1)y, \tag{7.33}$$

$$\widehat{q} = i_0 + \frac{ky-m}{h_1} - \frac{(1-v)y-\delta}{q} + \frac{1-q}{q}(\psi(q-1)+n). \tag{7.34}$$

In this case we get as Jacobian

$$J = \begin{pmatrix} 0 & 0 & -\psi m_o \\ 0 & \beta_y(c-1) & (\psi - y/\beta_y)\beta_y \\ -1/h_1 & k/h_1 - (1-v) & -i_o - n \end{pmatrix}.$$

---

7 Up to the term $-n$ in the entry J_{32}.

It is easily shown that $\det J < 0$ and trace $J < 0$ must be true if β_y is sufficiently large. Furthermore, $J_3 = 0, J_2 > 0$ is always true whereas the sign of $J_1 = \beta_y(c-1)(i_o - n) - (\psi - y/\beta_y)\beta_y(k/h_1 - (1-v))$ is ambiguous. We assume in the following that this determinant has a positive sign. This implies that all Routh–Hurwitz conditions on local asymptotic stability hold, since $\det J$ is part of the term trace $J \cdot (J_1 + J_2 + J_3)$. We thus get in sum the proposition:

Proposition 7.9:
> *The limit case $\beta_{p_e} = \beta_z = \infty$ exhibits a unique steady-state equilibrium which is **locally asymptotically stable** if the dynamic multiplier is sufficiently fast and if h_1 is sufficiently large. We therefore have indeterminacy from the viewpoint of the jump variable technique in this situation.*

The limiting dynamics investigated in Blanchard (1981) thus need not exhibit a problematic steady-state situation (none or two steady states) and saddlepoint dynamics if the parameters of the dynamics are chosen in the above way. The dynamics of the capital stock may be slow relative to the other adjustment processes, but this framework avoids the need for a discussion of short-run equilibria (good news and bad news cases), as in Blanchard (1981), that may be surrounded by saddlepoint dynamics. Note however that the Keynes effect must be weak in the present case instead of being large as before, since that the case of perfect substitutes reverses the sign of the entry where the sign is ambiguous. Otherwise, the saddlepoint dynamics considered in Blanchard (1981) for the state variables y and q reappears in this extended dynamical system.

7.5 Jump variable conundrums

In this section we briefly reconsider the 3D case of myopic perfect foresight and perfect substitutes considered in Proposition 7.8 in the case where saddlepoint dynamics found to be surrounding the steady state (where therefore Proposition 7.8 does not apply and where there is a single unstable root). In this case conventional wisdom would apply the rational expectations solution procedure to find the actual dynamics of the model, i.e., would apply the jump variable technique in order to place the economy always onto the 2D submanifold where convergence back to the steady state is ensured again after a shock.

However, we assume for the moment that the private agents of the economy do not take the fact that the stocks of real capital and equities are changing over time into account; i.e., they apply Figure 7.1 in order to see what will happen in the economy. Yet this figure is but one slice in the full phase space, as is shown in Figure 7.2.

If agents disregard that K, E are changing in time, the dynamics underlying the situation preceding Proposition 7.8 simplifies to the following two laws of motion:

$$\dot{y} = \beta_y(c(y - \delta - t) + \psi(q - 1) + \delta + n + g - y), \tag{7.35}$$

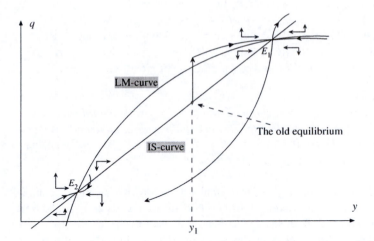

Figure 7.1 The 2D dynamics of Blanchard's good news case: saddle point and stable node or focus.

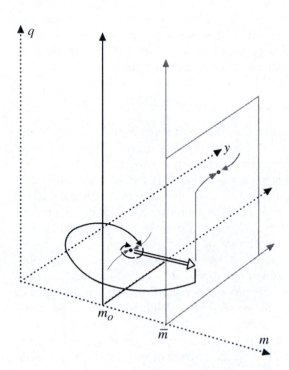

Figure 7.2 The stock-flow-augmented 3D dynamics of the Blanchard model.

$$\hat{q} = i_0 + \frac{ky - m}{h_1} - \frac{(1 - v)y - \delta}{q}. \tag{7.36}$$

Though still written in intensive form they thus become identical in mathematical form to the one considered in Chapter 2 ($\bar{m}$ fixed at m_o for the time being). The figures of Chapter 2 are therefore applicable. We choose the one that shows Blanchard's good news case here:

In Chapter 2, we discussed in detail the 2D Blanchard (1981) model of real–financial interaction from its short-run perspective (excluding capital and equity stock changes). We obtained, in one of its typical scenarios, the type of phase diagram shown in Figure 7.1, which exhibits two interior steady states, one a saddle and one a stable node or focus. This phase diagram allows the application of the jump variable technique only from a local perspective. It furthermore ignores the fact that there is one unstable arm in the upper equilibrium that leads the economy to the lower one, which would also permit the application of the jump variable technique on the basis of its assumption that agents choose converging paths only when they adjust the share price p_e or Tobin's q after a shock has thrown the economy out of its steady state. The short-run analysis of Chapter 2 therefore implies in this situation that the jumps imposed by the jump variable technique do not necessarily lead the economy towards E_1, nor are they really needed if the trajectories are already situated in the basin of attraction of E_2. In the following we shall, however, disregard this problem for the application of the jump variable technique and assume that the good news case of Blanchard (1981) holds, i.e., that the upper stable arms are the only relevant attracting trajectories.

The jump variable technique faces a variety of other problems (see for example Asada et al. (2003) for a recent summary and also for references on further arguments concerning this issue). The present chapter allows us to add an additional aspect to our critique of the arbitrariness of this rational expectations solution to myopic perfect foresight dynamics, and of the saddlepoint behavior it may imply. If capital accumulation is taken into account in the short-run Blanchard good news case, then the depicted steady-state situation is no longer stationary but starts moving more or less rapidly, depending on the strength of the investment behavior of the original Blanchard (1981) model.

How would rational expectations agents behave in this extended situation? Would they ignore capital accumulation and attempt to jump onto one of the stable arms of the equilibrium E_1? This is now much more difficult, since this equilibrium and its stable arms are now moving in time. This imposes higher demands on agents' intellectual capabilities. They now have to be in complete control of the situation for any given value of m. Furthermore, they need to know perfectly the movements to which this plane is subject to and recalculate the dislocation of their stable arm during the movements in the 3D space. But which path are they then following, and where will this path finally lead them to? Being on a stable arm – that is, however, shifting – at every point in time does not directly imply anything for the path they are following.

We conclude from this situation that the jump variable technique should be applied to the full 3D dynamics and to the stable arms it may exhibit. But this would imply that the original analysis of Blanchard (1981) is completely spurious, since the stable arms in the 3D case need not have anything in common with the ones of the original 2D dynamics. The jump variable solution therefore depends critically on the choice of the dynamics that agents take into consideration and on what they leave out of their conception of the world. Simple changes concerning the agents' view of the dimension of the world in which they live – here from 2D to 3D or vice versa, just by adding or subtracting the role of capital accumulation that is intrinsic to the model – change the dynamics in a radical way and thus make the modeling of the economic world in which agents live very erratic or even futile. It is needless to say that such radical overhauls of the dynamics of the real world are not to be expected to be supported by the facts. The situation just discussed is shown in Figure 7.2.

From the comparative static analysis of Chapter 2 we easily get the following proposition for the comparison of Blanchard's short-run equilibrium values (*sr*) and the uniquely determined equilibria of our stock-flow augmented dynamics.

Proposition 7.10:
As a comparative static exercise there holds, on the basis of Chapter 2:

$$\bar{m} \gtrless m_o \Leftrightarrow q_{sr} \gtrless q_o \Leftrightarrow y_{sr} \gtrless y_o \quad [\Leftrightarrow r_{sr} \gtrless r_o]$$

Disturbing the steady-state situation of the model of this chapter by an (unanticipated) expansionary monetary shock thus increases both output and stock prices above their given steady-state position. In Figure 7.2 this means that the plane in which the restricted 2D dynamics of Blanchard (1981) takes place shifts to the right and the short-run GNC equilibrium shifts to a higher position (as shown). If Blanchard's jump variable solution could be applied, the economy would move immediately to a higher stock price such that it places the dynamics on the stable arm that is shown in Figure 7.2. However, the steady state of the dynamics restricted to this plane in the full 3D space is a purely hypothetical one, since the true steady-state is not changed by the shock applied to one of the state variables of the full model. It is easily conceivable that the 2D stable submanifold (assumed to exist) of the full dynamics is situated such that in these dynamics stock prices must decrease in order to be placed onto this stable manifold (see Figure 7.2). Of course, the trajectory that is chosen in this way then converges to the uniquely determined steady state in the full dynamics, as exemplified in the figure.

Increasing the model by seemingly secondary additions (stock-flow relationships with unchanged economic behavior) thus not only implies a uniquely determined steady-state position, but also that the restricted 2D dynamics is not at all nested in the larger system. It is in fact completely different from the behavior of this larger system, augmented solely by implied stock-flow relationships. Despite indeterminacy, we therefore find that model uncertainty is a crucial problem for the rational expectations school. Can we consider the present model as the correct one for application, or should we enlarge these dynamics even further (see Chapter 9) in order to arrive again at a situation that is not at all comparable to what is happening in the lower dimensional case? The conclusion is that what we learn on economic behavior from one particular type of model may not at all be preserved when we move on to even slight generalizations of this model. This is due to the solution procedure of the rational expectations school which is structurally unstable in a significant way, as shown in this section.

We thus believe that the model of the present chapter, when applied to the case of myopic perfect foresight in a situation where saddlepoint dynamics can still be proved to exist locally, should not be forced into a framework that relies on the jump variable technique. They should instead be analyzed with one of the alternatives we introduced in Chiarella et al. (2003a) and Chiarella et al. (2003b), in order to obtain globally bounded and economically meaningful dynamics in the case of local saddlepoint situations as well. We thus end this chapter with a brief description of the phase diagram switching methodology first introduced in the two papers just cited.

Let us assume $\kappa_{p_e} = 0$ for reasons of simplicity. On the basis of Propositions 7.6 and 7.7 and the observations accompanying them, we expect that a sufficiently strong dynamic multiplier and a sufficiently strong Keynes effect (and possibly also a small parameter ψ) will imply convergence back to the steady-state if $\beta_{p_e} < 1$ holds true. That is, stability is given when the stock market exhibits cautious share price adjustment (due to the expectation of a turning point in stock price movements and a low trading volume in the stock market). Tobin's q and share prices p_e are then indeed slowly moving back to their steady state values, accompanied by nearly perfect foresight with respect to capital gains if adaptive expectations are adjusted with sufficient speed. Such a situation of tranquillity may, however, slowly increase the trading volume in the stock market, as agents become less cautious. Due to fast adaptive expectations, this will imply an explosive movement accelerating away from the steady state as soon as the parameter β_{p_e} has become larger than 1. Though explosive, the dynamics are cyclical in nature and thus may produce turning points that induce economic agents to become cautious again, which reestablishes the stability of the dynamics. We stress that this scenario is not subject to arbitrary changes when the dimension of the considered dynamics is changed, but it is of course subject to considerable change should the mood in the financial markets change in the way just described.

In this way we may expect the dynamics to switch back and forth between periods of tranquillity and convergence and periods of accelerating activity and divergence in an unpredictable manner by way of phase diagram switches, as were analyzed in detail for the isolated q, z dynamics in the papers just quoted. Because of the higher dimension of the dynamics considered in the present chapter, it is however not directly possible to repeat this analysis in its details here. Instead we may have to rely on numerical demonstrations of the phase diagram switching methodology, to be applied on the basis of Propositions 7.5, 7.6 and 7.7 above.

7.6 Conclusions

In the current chapter, we have investigated the real–financial interaction of an approach of Blanchard to stock market and multiplier dynamics from the stock-flow perspective by taking the capacity and the financing effect of the investment decision of firms into account. We added budget equations as well as the growth law for the capital stock to the Blanchard dynamics and investigated the implications of these additions for steady-state locations and their stability. We showed that the steady-state solutions of the Blanchard approach are no longer relevant here, but are replaced by a unique interior long-run solution. We demonstrated asymptotic stability with respect to this steady state when stock market adjustment is sufficiently sluggish, even in the case of myopic perfect foresight. In the opposite situation, if stock market adjustment is made sufficiently fast, the system loses stability by way of a Hopf bifurcation for increasing adjustment speeds of capital gains expectations and will generate purely explosive behavior shortly thereafter.

We indicated for this case how a regime (or phase diagram) switching methodology between activated and tranquil stock market behavior may nevertheless ensure global viability of the dynamics, despite the occurrence of shorter or longer episodes of explosive financial acceleration. This comes about from the assumption that stock markets must return to tranquillity after certain thresholds are surpassed, where financial acceleration due to high adjustment speeds in the market for equities disappears. The chapter thereby contributes to macrodynamic modeling methodology by providing alternatives to the jump variable technique of models with myopic perfect foresight. This methodology allows stability of (near) perfect foresight dynamics to be obtained without the arbitrary imposition of terminal positions on the trajectories that are considered as relevant from an economic perspective.

Overall, in this chapter we have focused on the stock market, firms' investment decisions and the rates of return on short-term bonds and equities as the crucial elements in the interaction of real and financial markets. The budget equation of firms plays an important role, but not yet those of households and the government, the former since the effects of wealth and interest rates on consumption are still excluded and the latter since we assume a particular type of tax collection rule. What still remains to be considered is long-term bonds (see Blanchard (1981), Blanchard and Fischer (1989) and Chiarella et al. (2003a) in this regard). Finally, we note that we do not yet allow for an adjustment of wages and prices; see, however, Chiarella et al. (2002) and Chapter 14 for such an integration.

7.7 References

ASADA, T., C. CHIARELLA, P. FLASCHEL and R. FRANKE (2003): *Open Eco nomy Macrodynamics. An integrated disequilibrium approach.* Heidelberg: Springer.

BENHABIB, J. and T. MIYAO (1981): Some new results on the dynamics of the generalized Tobin model. *International Economic Review*, 22, 589–596.

BLANCHARD, O. (1981): Output, the stock market, and interest rates. *American Economic Review*, 71, 132–143.

BLANCHARD, O. and S. FISCHER (1989): *Lectures on Macroeconomics*. Cambridge, MA: MIT Press.

BROCK, W.A. and A.G. MALLIARIS (1989): *Differential Equations, Stability and Chaos in Dynamic Economics*. Amsterdam: North Holland.

CHIARELLA, C., P. FLASCHEL, R. FRANKE, and W. SEMMLER (2001): Output, interest and the stock market, An alternative to the jump-variable technique. *Bulletin of the Czech Econometric Society*, 13, 1–30.

CHIARELLA, C., P. FLASCHEL, R. FRANKE and W. SEMMLER (2002): Stability analysis of a high-dimensional macrodynamic model of the real–financial interaction: a cascade of matrices approach. School of Finance and Economics, UTS working paper No. 123.

CHIARELLA, C., P. FLASCHEL, R. FRANKE and W. SEMMLER (2003a): Output and the term structure of interest rates: Ways out of the jump-variable conundrum. School of Finance and Economics, UTS working paper No. 125.

CHIARELLA, C., P. FLASCHEL and W. SEMMLER (2003b): Real–financial interaction. A reconsideration of the Blanchard model with a state-of-market dependent reaction coefficient. In: W. Barnett, C. Deissenberg and G. Feichtinger (eds,): *Economic Complexity: Nonlinear Dynamics, Multi-Agent Economies, and Learning*. ISETE Series, 14, Amsterdam: Elsevier.

GANTMACHER, F.R. (1959): *Applications of the Theory of Matrices*. New York: Interscience.

SONTAG, E.D. (1990): *Mathematical Control Theory: Deterministic Finite Dimensional Systems*. New York: Springer.

STROGATZ, S. H. (1994): *Nonlinear Dynamics and Chaos*. New York: Addison-Wesley.

WIGGINS, S. (1990): *Introduction to Applied Nonlinear Dynamical Systems and Chaos*. Heidelberg: Springer.

7.8 Appendix: Adding the dynamics of the government budget constraint

We have so far assumed that taxes net of interest payments of the government are constant per unit of capital. This is a convenient assumption as long as fiscal policy and the dynamics of the GBR are considered a secondary issue and analysis is thus concentrated on the private sector of the economy. However, this distorts asset returns after taxes in a specific way that must be assumed to be unobserved by private agents, in particular in the case where perfect asset substitution is assumed. Sooner or later such an assumption on tax collection which suppresses interest payments in the budget constraints of households and the government must be removed. The aim here is therefore to investigate the consequences of a full integration of all budget constraints, in particular that of the government, into a stock-market-augmented real–financial interaction of the IS–LM type.

In this appendix we only show the two changes that are implied for the dynamics of the body of the paper, and leave the analysis of the resulting 5D dynamics for future research. Instead of $(T - iB)/K = $ const., we now assume in close correspondence to the assumption made on government expenditures that only $T/K = $ const. holds. Fiscal policy is thus again treated by means of simple parameters in the intensive form of the dynamics, but no longer by parameters that suppress interest payments of the government in the resulting laws of motion.

7.8.1 Intensive form of the model

In order to derive the intensive-form laws of motion and their point of rest we first have to define the state variables that we shall make use of in the following.

The state variables

As in the body of the paper, we do not yet consider growth apart from that of the exogenous labor force with rate n in the present formulation of real–financial interaction. We express everything in per unit of capital form in order to derive the laws of motion of the dynamics, extended by an explicit treatment of the interest payments of the government. The state variables are thus

$$y = Y/K,$$
$$m = M/K,$$
$$q = p_e E/K,$$
$$z = \hat{p}_e^e,$$
$$b = B/K.$$

Note that we have to make use again of the term $\hat{E} - \hat{K} = [(1-q)/q]\hat{K}$ in order to obtain the law of motion of Tobin's q from the law of motion of the share price p_e.

The revised laws of motion

The laws of motion of the extended dynamics are as follows:

$$\dot{y} = \beta_y(c(y - \delta + ib - t) + \psi(q - 1) + \delta + n + g - y) - \psi(q - 1)y, \quad (7.37)$$

$$\hat{m} = -\psi(q - 1), \quad (7.38)$$

$$\hat{q} = \beta_{p_e}\left(\frac{(1-v)y - \delta}{q} + z - (i_0 + \frac{ky - m}{h_1})\right) + \kappa_{p_e}z + \frac{1-q}{q}(\psi(q - 1) + n), \quad (7.39)$$

$$\dot{z} = \beta_z(\beta_{p_e}\left(\frac{(1-v)y - \delta}{q} + z - (i_0 + \frac{ky - m}{h_1})\right) - (1 - \kappa_{p_e})z), \quad (7.40)$$

$$\dot{b} = g + ib - t - \bar{\mu}m - [\psi(q - 1) + n]b. \quad (7.41)$$

We now have interest income per unit of capital ib in the definition of disposable income used to determine consumption expenditures of households. This simple change in the consumption function employed in equation (7.37) demands that the dynamics of government debt now feed back into the rest of the dynamics and can therefore no longer be ignored in their investigation. The dynamics of the GBR are shown in equation (7.41) which, up to the explicit representation of the interest payments of the government, is still of a fairly simple type, since g, t and $\bar{\mu}$ are given parameters of the model.

The GBR in intensive form is to be derived from equation (7.4) in the body of the paper by making use of the relationship $\hat{b} = (\dot{B}/K)(1/b) - \hat{K}$ or $\dot{b} = \dot{B}/K - \hat{K}b$. Note with respect to this form of the GBR that $\bar{\mu}m = \dot{M}/K$ stands for that part of the government deficit $g + ib - t$ that is financed by money (through open market operations of the monetary authority which issues money in view of real growth $n = \bar{\mu}$ by buying government bonds). Note furthermore that the last item in this GBR is solely due to the fact that everything is expressed in per unit of capital form. It implies that the dependence of $\dot{b}$ on b is given by $i_o - n$ at the steady-state and is thus an explosive one if the steady-state rate of interest exceeds the natural rate of growth. This tendency towards accelerating government debt may, however, be checked by stabilizing forces deriving from the rest of the dynamics.

We stress again that the limit case considered on a less complete level (disregarding the law of motion for real balances) in Blanchard (1981) is recovered by assuming $\beta_q = \beta_z = \infty$, i.e., by assuming perfect substitutes and perfect foresight. The special case of perfect foresight considered in Blanchard (1981) reads, for the present model:

$$\dot{y} = \beta_y(c(y - \delta + ib - t) + \psi(q - 1) + \delta + n + g - y) - \psi(q - 1)y, \tag{7.42}$$

$$\widehat{m} = -\psi(q - 1), \tag{7.43}$$

$$\widehat{q} = \frac{1}{1 - \beta_{pe} - \kappa_{pe}} \beta_{pe}\left(\frac{(1 - v)y - \delta}{q} - (i_0 + \frac{ky - m}{h_1})\right) + \frac{1 - q}{q}(\psi(q - 1) + n), \tag{7.44}$$

$$\dot{b} = g - t - \bar{\mu}m - [\psi(q - 1) + (n - i)]b. \tag{7.45}$$

Note that the steady-state solution of this dynamics is identical to the one of the 5D system (the variable z is disregarded now).

Furthermore, assuming bonds and equities to be perfect substitutes (i.e. $\beta_{pe} = \infty$) implies, in addition, the following special case of the above 4D dynamics:

$$\dot{y} = \beta_y(c(y - \delta + ib - t) + \psi(q - 1) + \delta + n + g - y) - \psi(q - 1)y, \tag{7.46}$$

$$\widehat{m} = -\psi(q - 1), \tag{7.47}$$

$$\widehat{q} = i_0 + \frac{ky - m}{h_1} - \frac{(1 - v)y - \delta}{q} + \frac{1 - q}{q}(\psi(q - 1) + n), \tag{7.48}$$

$$\dot{b} = g - t - \bar{\mu}m - [\psi(q - 1) + (n - i)]b. \tag{7.49}$$

7.8.2 Steady-state determination

With regard to the steady-states of the 5D dynamics (7.37)–(7.41) we have the following proposition:

Proposition 7.11:

The interior steady-state(s) of the laws of motion (7.37) – (7.41) is determined by the following set of equations:

$$q_0 = 1,$$

$$z_0 = 0,$$

$$m_0 = k y_0,$$

$$b_o = \frac{g - t - n m_o}{n - i_o},$$

$$i_0 = (1 - v) y_0 - \delta,$$

$$y_0 = \frac{1}{1 - c}(\delta + n + g + c(i_o b_o - \delta - t)).$$

Note that the last four equations of these steady-state conditions are fully interdependent and not easily solved. They already indicate that an analysis of the dynamics with GBR feedback into the private sector of the economy is not an easy matter, even on the level of steady-state analysis. This difficulty becomes more pronounced once the issue of the stability of the resulting steady-state is approached.

8 Bounded rationality and the real-financial interaction: A stochastic analysis

8.1 Introduction

> History can be thought of as society's memory. If it is fuzzy or inaccurate we may be condemned to relive it. There does seem to be a danger that the application of some recent developments in economics, such as extreme versions of the rational expectations approach, are in danger of depriving us of manias, panics, crashes, and even modest booms and slumps. This may not be helpful in terms of society's memory. But perhaps a certain amount of this is a matter of semantics or of emphasis. Those who argue that it is rational to buy when prices are rising if the expectation is that prices will keep rising sound entirely reasonable. Those who say it is folly are surely simply shifting the emphasis to the fact that we do not know when the terminal condition, that is the change in fashion or whatever, will come. To describe all of these episodes as rational surely stretches the definition of rationality to an unhelpful extent.
>
> F. Capie, *Early Asset Bubbles*, in White (1990)

The above quotation is taken from an article by one of the discussants in White (1990) on two essays giving a current perspective on contemporary accounts of two of the most famous examples of financial mania, panic and subsequent crash – the tulip mania of the 17th century and the South Sea bubble of the 18th century. It serves to emphasize the point that standard macroeconomic models leave little place for extreme market movements, except as the result of some exogenous stochastic process.

As recent events have reminded us, moods of extreme optimism and then pessimism, long periods of deviation by even supposedly well-informed agents from anything remotely resembling valuation of expected return on securities based on economic fundamentals seem to be a permanent feature of financial markets, at least from a perspective of almost four centuries. Yet one would search in vain in modern finance and economics texts for any discussion of the effect of such factors on the financial sector of the economy. Rather, modern theory assumes an economy populated with rational agents who seem to have full knowledge (at least in the sense of probability distributions) of the laws driving the economic system they inhabit and who perform a very precise decision calculus to optimally trade-off risk and return. The perturbations that one observes in such markets are supposedly due solely to exogenous semi-martingale processes. The agents are too rational to allow themselves to experience bouts of optimism or pessimism, or to be influenced by what they perceive other agents to be doing. There is usually an implied assumption that if (somehow) all external noise impacts were to cease, the economy would be stable to its steady state.

Perhaps the only economist to write seriously about such "irrational" behavior is Kindleberger (1978). The concept of boundedly rational agents was developed by Simon (1997) over a number of years, but it is really only in the last decade or so that researchers have started to look seriously at stock market models involving heterogenous agents, positive feedback (leading to self-reinforcement of trends up and down), herding behavior and critical points (when extreme optimism changes to pessimism or vice versa).

For empirical evidence of these phenomena we can cite Sornette and Zhou (2002), and there is certainly no shortage of theoretical models: Day and Huang (1990), Chiarella (1992), Lux (1995, 1997), Lux and Marchesi (1999), Brock and Hommes (1997) and Andresen (1998).

This chapter is motivated by the observation that almost no work has been done to incorporate features such as heterogeneity, positive feedback and switching from optimism to pessimism into standard macroeconomic models. Following the tradition established in earlier chapters we take the well-known Blanchard (1981) model of real–financial interaction and incorporate into its structure fundamentalists and chartists as well as a mechanism that allows infact optimism and pessimism. We allow for extrinsic background in fact (Wiener process) noise in the stock market that may be interpreted either as noise-trading or as the incessant arrival of market news.

Here we modify the original Blanchard model in a number of ways. We change Blanchard's investment demand to depend on Tobin's average q in place of the real rate of interest order to give a more prominent role to the impact of the share market on the real sector of the economy. This change causes the share price dynamics feed back into the real sector, thereby creating one of the key links of the real–financial interaction. The conventional LM schedule or money market equilibrium of this approach continues to provide the channel back from real to financial markets. The Blanchard model is also enriched by allowing for imperfect asset substitution and less-than-perfect foresight. A further important change is the introduction of a state-of-market dependent reaction function in the way agents react to disequilibria in the stock market. We know from the work of Chiarella et al. (2003) that these extensions to the Blanchard model can generate regimes of stock market upswings and downswings. The main change to that earlier work is that we allow for heterogeneity of agents by introducing two groups – rational fundamentalists and trend-chasing chartists. Initially we hold the proportion of these groups fixed; and subsequently allow them to evolve as a function of the evolution of the stock-market dynamics à la Brock and Hommes (1997). We show that in a deterministic setting these mechanisms can generate a locally unstable equilibrium that is stable to some fluctuating attractor. We go on to add noise to the model and consider, by use of simulation analysis, how the model in its locally unstable regime can generate more stock market booms and crashes than in the stable regime. We study in particular how the severity of the booms and crashes is affected by various reaction parameters of the two groups.

This chapter is structured as follows: After introducing the notation, in Section 8.3 we outline the real and financial sector of the model, in particular the imperfect substitutability between stocks and bonds. In Section 8.4 we discuss the role of the two groups of agents, rational fundamentalists and trend-chasing chartists, how they form their expectations and how their optimism or pessimism about the short-run evolution of the stock market feed into the stock market dynamics. Section 8.5 studies the deterministic skeleton of the model when all external noise sources are absent. We analyze the steady state and determine how local stability turns to instability as certain key parameters affecting expectations and the mood of optimism or pessimism are varied. We also study in this section the global dynamics in situations when the steady state becomes locally unstable. Section 8.6 studies the stochastic version of the model. We use Monte-Carlo simulation to obtain the distributions of booms and busts and see how these are affected by the expectation and mood parameters. Section 8.7 concludes.

8.2 Notation

The variables of the model are:[1]

Y	Output
Y^d	Aggregate demand
p_e	Share price
$q = p_e E/(pK)$	Tobin's average q
m^d	Demand for real balances
i	Short-term interest rate
p_b	Bond price
Π	Real profits
$r = \Pi/K$	Rate of profit
L^d	Labor demand
$p_e^e(\hat{p}_e^e)$	Expected value of (rate of change in) the price of equities
q^e	Expected value of Tobin's q
z	Expected value of rate of change in Tobin's q
$\varepsilon = [(\Pi/K)/q] + \hat{p}_e^e - i$	Expected return differential between equities and the short-term interest rate
n	The measure of the balance of fundamentalists and chartists

---

1 Note $t =$ time, $PG =$ physical good (e.g. steel).

The parameters of the model are the following:[2]

$c(0 < c < 1)$	Marginal propensity to consume
$\psi(> 0)$	Marginal propensity to invest
T	Real taxes
G	Real government consumption
M	Money supply
$p(= 1!)$	Price level
w	Nominal wages
$k(> 0)$	Money demand parameter
$h_1(> 0)$	Money demand parameter
$h_2(> 0)$	Money demand parameter
m	Real balances
B	Number of long-term bonds
E	Number of equities
K	Real capital stock
$\delta(> 0)$	Depreciation rate of the capital stock
$x = Y/L^d$	Labor productivity
$v = wL^d/(pY)$	
$\quad = w/(px)$	Wage share
I	Autonomous component of investment
C	Autonomous component of consumption
$\beta_x(> 0)$	Adjustment speed of a variable x
f	fundamentalists (superscripts)
c	chartists (superscripts)

8.3 The model

In this section we set out the static and dynamic economic relationships that define the macroeconomy with real–financial interaction that will be the object of our study. Note that we use extensive-form variables[3] (and thus not logarithms of money and the price level as in Blanchard (1981)) throughout and that the money demand function, though here completely linear, represents a generalization of the form that was used by Blanchard (1981). For simplicity, Tobin's q is only used (in average form) in the investment function, which is based on the assumption of fixed proportions in production. This assumption allows us to make more transparent the dynamic structure of the model by simplifying some of the algebraic relationships between the endogenous variables and also reducing by one the number of laws of motion. In subsequent developments of the model one would need to gauge the impact of smooth factor substitution.

---

2 All parameters are assumed to be positive unless otherwise stated.
3 The variables and parameters of the model are listed above.

First, consider the static relations that describe a simple aggregate demand function Y^d (equation (8.1)) depending on output (via consumption) and Tobin's average q (via investment). The demand for real balances (equation (8.2)) is a traditional one depending positively on output and negatively on the short-term interest rate. Equation (8.3) is a standard equation for money market equilibrium. Finally, we have an obvious equation for real profits (equation (8.4)), which depend solely on economic activity Y. Thus we have:

$$Y^d = C + c(Y - \delta K - T) + I + \psi(q - 1)$$
$$+ \delta K + G, \quad c \in (0, 1), \tag{8.1}$$

$$m^d = M^d / p = kY + h_1 - h_2 i, \tag{8.2}$$

$$m = m^d, \tag{8.3}$$

$$\Pi = (1 - v)Y - \delta K. \tag{8.4}$$

The dynamic variables are output, share and bond prices. Output adjustment is based on the simple textbook dynamic multiplier story as indicated in equation (8.5). Blanchard assumes that short-term bonds, long-term bonds and shares are perfect substitutes and there is myopic perfect foresight on capital gains. Thus equations (8.6) and (8.7) indicate that the dividend rate of return on equities and the interest rate of return on long-term bonds have both to be augmented by a corresponding expression for capital gains when we compare their full return with the return on short-term fixed price bonds. Thus we write

$$\dot{Y} = \beta_y(Y^d - Y), \tag{8.5}$$

$$i = \frac{p\Pi + \dot{p}_e E}{p_e E} = \frac{p\Pi}{p_e E} + \hat{p}_e = \frac{\Pi/K}{q} + \hat{q}$$
$$(K, E, p = \text{const!}), \tag{8.6}$$

$$i = \frac{B + \dot{p}_b B}{p_b B} = \widehat{p_b} + \frac{1}{p_b}. \tag{8.7}$$

The stock market reacts to the expected return differential $((\pi/K)/q + z - i)$ where z is the market's expectation of the capital gain $\hat{q}(= \hat{p}_e)$. For share price dynamics we consider the stochastic differential equation

$$dq = \beta_q(\frac{\Pi/K}{q} + z - i)qdt + \sigma_q qdW$$
$$= \beta_q \varepsilon qdt + \sigma_q qdW, \tag{8.8}$$

with

$$\varepsilon = \frac{\Pi/K}{q} + z - i. \tag{8.9}$$

Here $W(t)$ is a Wiener process and σ_q is the standard deviation of the stock market return. This extension assumes (equation (8.8)) that there is imperfect substitution between shares and short-term bonds, and that share prices p^e (as reflected by Tobin's q) react with less than infinite speed (β_q) to ε, the differential between expected equity returns (dividend return plus expected capital gains) and the short-term rate of interest. The Wiener increments dW can be interpreted as noise trading (Black (1986)) or as random fluctuations in the stock market brought about by the incessant arrival of "news".

Our assumption of a standard fixed proportions technology with only labor as variable input, and with capital depreciation, gives for real profits (Π) and rate of profit (r) the expressions

$$\Pi = Y - \delta K - (w/p)L^d \, , \ (L^d = Y/x, x = \text{ const.}),$$

$$= Y(1 - w/(px)) - \delta K$$

$$= Y(1 - v) - \delta K, \quad (v = w/(px) = \text{ const.}), \tag{8.10}$$

$$r = \Pi/K = (1 - v)Y/K - \delta, \tag{8.11}$$

where v denotes the (given) wage share. Thus, substituting (8.10) into (8.9), we have

$$\varepsilon = \frac{(1 - v)Y/K - \delta}{q} + z - i. \tag{8.12}$$

The inverted money market equilibrium, from equations (8.2) and (8.3), reads[4]

$$i = \frac{kY + h_1 - m}{h_2}, \quad m = M/p, \tag{8.13}$$

and we use this relation to determine i in equation (8.12).

Note that we are assuming a background of a stationary economy in which the capital stock is not growing and no new shares are issued. Furthermore, the assumption of constant nominal and real money stock will result in no inflation and so, in steady state, there is no increase in the equity price.

In discrete time equations (8.5) and (8.8) may be written

$$Y_{t+\Delta t} = Y_t + \beta_y \Delta t(-(1 - c)Y_t + \psi(q_t - 1) + A), \tag{8.14}$$

$$q_{t+\Delta t} = q_t + \beta_q \varepsilon_t q_t \Delta t + \sigma_q q_t \sqrt{\Delta t} \tilde{\xi}_t, \tag{8.15}$$

where Δt is the length of the "trading day". Let N be trading frequency per year, then $\Delta t = 1/N$. Typically, $N = 1, 12, 52, 250$ for a trading frequency of

---

4 This should be contrasted with Blanchard's equation (8.2) which uses the logarithm of m in place of our m.

a year, month, week, and day respectively. Note also that $\tilde{\xi}_t \approx N(0, 1)$ and that $A = C + I + G - cT + (1 - c)\delta K$. We interpret z_t as the expected share market capital gain/loss over the next time interval, i.e.

$$z_t = \mathbb{E}_t \left[\frac{q_{t+\Delta t} - q_t}{\Delta t q_t} \right];$$

where $\mathbb{E}_t$ denotes expectations formed at time t for quantities at $t + \Delta t$.

In order to close the model we need to specify how z_t is formed. This we do in the next section.

8.4 Heterogenous expectations

We assume that there are two groups of agents in the market: rational fundamentalists who are able to form model-consistent expectations, and trend-chasing chartists. The market's expectation is a combination of fundamentalist (z_t^f) and chartist (z_t^c) expectations, where n_t^f and n_t^c respectively denote the fraction of fundamentalists and chartists in the economy. Each group of agents uses its expectation of $\hat{q}_t$ to form an estimate of the expected return differential between stocks and bonds; i.e. they form

$$\varepsilon_t^c = \frac{(1 - v)Y_t/K - \delta}{q_t} + z_t^c - i_t \tag{8.16}$$

and

$$\varepsilon_t^f = \frac{(1 - v)Y_t/K - \delta}{q_t} + z_t^f - i_t. \tag{8.17}$$

If we assume that each group reacts to its expected return differential with its own speed of adjustment (β_q^f and β_q^c respectively), then equation (8.15) will be modified to read

$$q_{t+\Delta t} = q_t + (n_t^f \beta_q^f \varepsilon_t^f + n_t^c \beta_q^c \varepsilon_t^c)q_t \Delta t + \sigma_q q_t \sqrt{\Delta t} \tilde{\xi}_t. \tag{8.18}$$

Consider first the chartists, who are of the classical trend-chasing kind, and so form expectations according to[5]

$$z_t^c = (1 - \beta_{z_c})z_{t-\Delta t}^c + \beta_{z_c}\left(\frac{q_t - q_{t-\Delta t}}{\Delta t q_{t-\Delta t}}\right), \quad (0 \leq \beta_{z_c} \leq 1/\Delta t). \tag{8.19}$$

---

5 Note that β_{z_c} may be interpreted as a speed of adjustment, and hence $1/\beta_{z_c}$ as the mean time delay in adjusting expectations. We thus must impose the restriction $1/\beta_{z_c} \geq \Delta t$, otherwise the chartists would be revising expectations more frequently than they are receiving information on the evolution of the quantity about which they form expectations.

The fundamentalists are assumed to form expectations using traditional rational expectations (it is also assumed that they know the chartists react according to equation (8.19)); thus from (8.18) they form

$$z_t^f = \mathbb{E}_t^f \left[\frac{q_{t+\Delta t} - q_t}{\Delta t q_t} \right] = n_t^f \beta_q^f \varepsilon_t^f + n_t^c \beta_q^c \varepsilon_t^c, \tag{8.20}$$

which may be solved for z_t^f to yield

$$z_t^f = \frac{(n_t^f \beta_q^f + n_t^c \beta_q^c) \left(\frac{(1-v)Y_t/K - \delta}{q_t} - i_t \right) + n_t^c \beta_q^c z_t^c}{1 - n_t^f \beta_q^f}, \tag{8.21}$$

provided $1 - n_t^f \beta_q^f \neq 0$.[6] We further assume that both groups view their reaction coefficients β_q and β_q^s as depending on the state of the market, in particular as a function of the most recently observed return differential $\varepsilon_{t-\Delta t}$ between equity and the short-term rate of interest. When market conditions are such that ε is close to its steady state ε_0, the reaction coefficients are rather high, so that the agents react strongly to the expected return differential. However, the high reaction coefficients (coupled with a high β_{z_c} on the part of chartists) cause the steady state to be locally unstable and lead to a rise (or fall) in the stock market and hence a rise or fall in the expected return differential. Both groups will initially follow this general movement in the stock market; however, as it proceeds further and further they are conscious that the economy is moving ever further from its perceived steady state and they start to react more cautiously to the return differential. This cautiousness is reflected in an eventual lowering of the value of the reaction coefficients β_q, to a value sufficiently low as to cause a turn-around in the dynamics that once again becomes stable towards the steady-state. Eventually the β_q return to former high levels and the possibility of another upward (or downward) stock market movement is established. The behavior of β_q as a function of the difference in ε from its steady state value ε_0 is as illustrated in Figure 6.6. We have drawn this function somewhat skewed to the right to indicate greater (less) caution when the share market is below (above) its steady-state value. Each group would have its own particular values of β_q^+, β_q^-, ε^- and ε^+, so allowing for differing degrees of optimism or pessimism between each group.

So far we have not discussed how the proportions n_t^f and n_t^c are formed. In this study we shall make two assumptions. First, we shall assume the proportions are constant and analyze the dynamic properties of the model as these proportions are changed. Second, we shall assume that they change as a function of realized returns of each group (assumed known to all market participants) according to the

---

6 Note that during the simulations reported below it does occasionally happen that $1 - n_t^f \beta_q^f = 0$. Such points have been removed from the bifurcation diagrams.

Brock and Hommes (1997) mechanism. Under this assumption we would have

$$n_t^i = N_t^i/Z_t \quad (i \in \{c,f\}), \tag{8.22}$$

where

$$N_t^i = \exp\{-\lambda[(\varepsilon_{t-1} - \varepsilon_{t-1}^i)^2 + \kappa^i]\} \quad (\lambda > 0), \tag{8.23}$$

and

$$Z_t = N_t^c + N_t^f. \tag{8.24}$$

The quantities κ^c and κ^f represent the costs incurred by each group in forming expectations. Typically we would expect $\kappa^f > \kappa^c$, reflecting the fact that fundamentalists incur greater costs in learning about the fundamentals driving the economy.

It turns out to be convenient to keep track of the proportions of fundamentalists and chartists in terms of the single quantity n_t, defined via

$$n_t^f = (1+n_t)/2 \quad \text{and} \quad n_t^c = (1-n_t)/2,$$

where $-1 \le n_t \le 1$.

The laws of motion of the economy are given by equations (8.14), (8.18), (8.19) and (8.21) in the case of fixed proportions of agents, or, in the case of variable proportions, the laws for n_t^c and n_t^f, equations (8.22)–(8.24), also need to be appended.

The original Blanchard model is recovered by taking $\sigma_q = 0$ in equation (8.8) and setting $\beta_q^f = \beta_q^c = \infty$ in equation (8.18), which then collapses to the arbitrage condition $(\pi/K)/q = i - z$, and setting $n_t^c = 0$, $n_t^f = 1$ in equation (8.20) so that only rational fundamentalists are present in the market.

8.5 Analysis of the deterministic skeleton

In this section we analyze the dynamics of the underlying deterministic model, i.e. when $\sigma_q = 0$. In section 8.5.1 we discuss the steady state, in Section 8.5.2 we analyze the local stability of the steady state, in Section 8.5.3 we consider the special case when only rational fundamentalists exist in the market and, in Section 8.5.4, we gain some impressions of the global dynamics via numerical simulations.

8.5.1 The steady state

Proposition 8.1:
Assume

$$\frac{1+n}{2}\beta_q^f \ne 1, \quad \frac{1+n}{2}\beta_q^f + \frac{1-n}{2}\beta_q^c \ne 0, 1.$$

The steady state of the dynamical system (8.14), (8.18), (8.19) and (8.21) (the case of fixed proportions) is characterized by

$$\bar{Y} = \frac{A + \psi(\bar{q} - 1)}{1 - c}, \quad \text{(IS curve)} \tag{8.25}$$

$$(1 - v)\frac{\bar{Y}}{K} = \delta + \bar{q}\frac{k\bar{Y} + h_1 - m}{h_2}, \quad \text{(LM curve)} \tag{8.26}$$

$$\bar{z}^c = 0. \tag{8.27}$$

The steady-state value of the interest rate is given by

$$\bar{i} = \frac{k\bar{Y} + h_1 - m}{h_2}.$$

In the case of variable proportions (when equations (8.22)–(8.24) are appended to the dynamics), the steady-state values of $\bar{Y}$, $\bar{q}$ and $\bar{z}_c$ remain the same. In addition, the steady-state values of the population proportions are given by

$$\bar{n}_i = \frac{e^{\kappa_i}}{e^{\kappa_c} + e^{\kappa_f}} \quad i \in (c, f). \tag{8.28}$$

Proof: For convenience write (8.14), (8.18) and (8.19) as

$$Y_{t+\Delta t} \equiv F_1(Y_t, q_t, z_t^c),$$

$$q_{t+\Delta t} \equiv F_2(Y_t, q_t, z_t^c),$$

$$z_t^c \equiv F_3(Y_t, q_t, z_t^c),$$

where

$$F_1(Y, q, z^c) = Y + \beta_y \Delta t[-(1 - c)Y - \psi(q - 1) + A],$$

$$F_2(Y, q, z^c) = q + q\Delta t \, G(Y, q, z^c),$$

$$F_3(Y, q, z^c) = (1 - \Delta t \beta_{z_c})z^c + \Delta t \beta_{z_c} G(Y, q, z^c),$$

with

$$G(Y, q, z^c) = \frac{1}{1 - n_t^f \beta_q^f} \left\{ n_t^c \beta_q^c z_t^c + (n_t^f \beta_q^f + n_t^c \beta_q^c)\left(\frac{(1 - v)Y_t/K - \delta}{q_t} - i_t\right) \right\},$$

and we recall that

$$i_t = \frac{kY_t + h_1 - m}{h_2}. \tag{8.29}$$

Let $E(\bar{Y}, \bar{q}, \bar{z}^c)$ denote the steady state. Then it follows from $\bar{Y} = F_1(\bar{Y}, \bar{q}, \bar{z}^c)$ that

$$\bar{Y} = \frac{\psi(\bar{q} - 1) + A}{1 - c},$$

which is the IS curve. From $\bar{q} = F_2(\bar{Y}, \bar{q}, \bar{z}^c)$, we have

$$G(\bar{Y}, \bar{q}, \bar{z}^c) = 0, \tag{8.30}$$

from which

$$\frac{1}{1 - \frac{1+n}{2}\beta_q^f} \left\{ \frac{1-n}{2}\beta_q^c \bar{z}^c + \frac{(1+n)\beta_q^f + (1-n)\beta_q^c}{2} \right.$$

$$\left. \times \left(\frac{(1-v)\bar{Y}/K - \delta}{\bar{q}} - \frac{k\bar{Y} + h_1 - m}{h_2} \right) \right\} = 0. \tag{8.31}$$

It follows from $\bar{z}^c = F_3(\bar{Y}, \bar{q}, \bar{z}^c)$ and (8.30) and (8.31) that

$$G(\bar{Y}, \bar{q}, \bar{z}^c) = \bar{z}^c = 0. \tag{8.32}$$

It then follows from (8.31) and (8.32) that

$$\frac{(1-v)\bar{Y}}{K} - \delta - \bar{q}\frac{k\bar{Y} + h_1 - m}{h_2} = 0, \tag{8.33}$$

from which the LM curve (8.26) follows. The steady-state value for r follows directly from (8.29). Equations (8.21), (8.32) and (8.33) imply that

$$\bar{z}^f = 0. \tag{8.34}$$

Next we note that (8.16), (8.17), (8.26), (8.32) and (8.34) imply that

$$\bar{\varepsilon}^c = \bar{\varepsilon}^f = 0. \tag{8.35}$$

Substituting (8.35) into (8.23) yields (8.28).

We refer the reader to Chiarella et al. (2003) for a detailed discussion of the characterization of the steady states in the real sector.[7] For reasons discussed there we follow Blanchard and consider the steady state at which the slope (as measured by $d\bar{q}/d\bar{y}$) of the IS curve is steeper than the slope of the LM curve.

---

7 These authors consider a model without fundamentalists and chartists. However, the steady state of the real sector is the same as that here.

8.5.2 Local stability analysis

Defining

$$B^f = \frac{1+n}{2}\beta_q^f, \quad B^c = \frac{1-n}{2}\beta_q^c, \quad B = B^f + B^c$$

the Jacobian of the dynamical system (8.14), (8.18), (8.19) and (8.21) at the steady state may be written

$$J = \begin{pmatrix} 1-(1-c)\Delta t\beta_y & \psi\,\Delta t\beta_y & 0 \\ \frac{B}{1-B^f}\left(\frac{1-v}{K}-\frac{k\bar{q}}{h_2}\right)\Delta t & 1-\frac{B\bar{i}}{1-B^f}\Delta t & \frac{B^c\bar{q}}{1-B^f}\Delta t \\ \frac{B}{1-B^f}\left(\frac{1-v}{K}-\frac{k\bar{q}}{h_2}\right)\Delta t\beta_{z_c}\bar{q} & -\frac{B\bar{i}}{1-B^f}\frac{\beta_{z_c}}{\bar{q}}\Delta t & 1-\left(\frac{1-B}{1-B^f}\right)\beta_{z_c}\Delta t \end{pmatrix}$$

so that the characteristic equation may be written

$$\Gamma(\lambda) \equiv \lambda^3 + p_1\lambda^2 + p_2\lambda + p_3 = 0, \tag{8.36}$$

where

$$p_1 = \text{trace}(J),$$

$$p_2 = \text{sum of the principal minors of } J,$$

$$p_3 = \det(J).$$

Proposition 8.2:

The roots of the characteristic equation (8.36) lie within the unit circle (and hence the dynamical system (8.14), (8.18), (8.19) and (8.21) is locally asymptotically stable) if and only if $\Delta_i > 0$ ($i = 1, 2, 3$) and $p_2 < 3$, where

$$\Delta_1 = 1 + p_1 + p_2 + p_3,$$

$$\Delta_2 = 1 - p_1 + p_2 - p_3,$$

$$\Delta_3 = 1 - p_2 + p_3(p_1 - p_3).$$

Furthermore

(i)   *If $\Delta_1 = 0$, two eigenvalues lie in the unit circle and the third satisfies $\lambda = 1$; this case corresponds to a saddle-node bifurcation.*
(ii) *If $\Delta_2 = 0$, two eigenvalues lie in the unit circle and the third satisfies $\lambda = -1$; this case corresponds to a flip bifurcation.*
(iii) *If $\Delta_3 = 0$, one eigenvalue lies in the unit circle and the other two satisfy $\lambda_{2,3} = e^{\pm 2\pi\psi\theta}$; this case corresponds to a Hopf bifurcation.*

The conditions for local stability may be difficult to analyze in general. However, Proposition 8.2 indicates that loss of local stability is accompanied by a rich bifurcation structure, depending on which bifurcation boundary ($\Delta_1 = 0$, $\Delta_2 = 0$ or $\Delta_3 = 0$) is crossed.

8.5.3   The model with rational fundamentalists only

It is of interest to consider the limiting case in which there are only rational fundamentalists in the market. Thus, setting $n_t^c = 0$, $n_t^f = 1$ and writing z_t instead of z_t^f, the deterministic difference equations for q and Y become

$$q_{t+\Delta t} = q_t + \Delta t \beta_q \left[\frac{(1-v)Y_t/K - \delta}{q_t} + z_t^f - i_t \right] q_t, \tag{8.37}$$

$$Y_{t+\Delta t} = Y_t + \Delta t \beta_y [-(1-c)Y_t + \psi(q_t - 1) + A]. \tag{8.38}$$

In the notation of this subsection equation (8.20) reduces to

$$z_t^f = \beta_q^f \varepsilon_t^f = \beta_q \left[\frac{(1-v)Y_t/K - \delta}{q_t} + z_t^f - i_t \right],$$

from which

$$z_t^f = \frac{\beta_q}{1 - \beta_q} \left[\frac{(1-v)Y_t/K - \delta}{q_t} - i_t \right]. \tag{8.39}$$

Hence, the dynamics of q are governed by

$$q_{t+\Delta t} = q_t + \Delta t \frac{\beta_q}{1 - \beta_q} \left[\frac{(1-v)Y_t}{K} - \delta - i_t q_t \right].$$

Setting

$$\bar{\beta}_q = \frac{\beta_q}{1 - \beta_q},$$

we may then write the dynamics in the case of rational fundamentalists only as

$$q_{t+\Delta t} = q_t + \Delta t \bar{\beta}_q \left[\frac{(1-v)Y_t}{K} - \delta - i_t q_t \right],$$

$$Y_{t+\Delta t} = Y_t + \Delta t \beta_y [-(1-c)Y_t - \psi(q_t - 1) + A]. \tag{8.40}$$

The steady state of the system (8.40) is still given by Proposition 8.1.

Proposition 8.3:

The steady state E of the system (8.40) is locally stable if and only if

   (i) $\beta_y \bar{\beta}_q [\bar{i}(1-c) - \psi B] > 0,$

  (ii) $2[2 - (\bar{\beta}_q \bar{i} + \beta_y(1-c))\Delta t] + \beta_y \bar{\beta}_q [\bar{i}(1-c) - \psi B](\Delta t)^2 > 0,$

 (iii) $\beta_y \bar{\beta}_q [\bar{i}(1-c) - \psi B](\Delta t) < \beta_y(1-c) + \bar{\beta}_q \bar{i},$

where

$$B = \frac{1-n}{K} - \frac{k}{h_2} \bar{q}.$$

In addition,

  (i)   *the eigenvalue $\lambda = 1$ occurs if*

$$\bar{i}(1-c) - \psi A = 0,$$

 (ii)   *the eigenvalue $\lambda = -1$ occurs if*

$$2[2 - (\bar{\beta}_q \bar{i} + \beta_y(1-c))\Delta t] + \beta_y \bar{\beta}_q [\bar{i}(1-c) - \psi B](\Delta t)^2 = 0,$$

(iii)   *a Hopf bifurcation occurs if*

$$\beta_y \bar{\beta}_q [\bar{i}(1-c) - \psi B](\Delta t)^2 = 2 - r,$$

where $r = 2\cos(2\pi\theta)$, and the corresponding eigenvalues are given by $\lambda_{\pm} = e^{\pm\psi 2\pi\theta}$.

Proof: Set

$$F_1(q, Y) = q + \Delta t \bar{\beta}_q \left[\frac{1-n}{K} Y - \delta - \frac{kY + h_1 - m}{h_2} q \right],$$

$$F_2(q, Y) = Y + \Delta t \beta_y [-(1-c)Y - \psi(q-1) + A].$$

Then, at the steady state E, we calculate the partial derivatives

$$\frac{\partial F_1}{\partial q} = 1 - \Delta t \bar{\beta}_q \bar{i},$$

$$\frac{\partial F_1}{\partial Y} = \bar{\beta}_q B \Delta t$$

$$\frac{\partial F_2}{\partial q} = \psi \beta_y \Delta t,$$

$$\frac{\partial F_2}{\partial Y} = 1 - \beta_y(1-c)\Delta t,$$

so that the Jacobian at steady state is given by

$$J = \begin{pmatrix} 1 - \Delta t \bar{\beta}_q \bar{i} & \bar{\beta}_q B \Delta t \\ \psi \beta_y \Delta t & 1 - \beta_y (1-c) \Delta t \end{pmatrix}.$$

The characteristic equation is given by

$$\Gamma(\lambda) = |\lambda I - J| = \lambda^2 + p_1 \lambda + p_2 = 0,$$

where

$$p_1 = -2 + [\bar{\beta}_q \bar{i} + \beta_y (1-c)] \Delta t,$$
$$p_2 = 1 - [\beta_y (1-c) + \bar{\beta}_q \bar{i}] \Delta t + \beta_y \bar{\beta}_q [\bar{i}(1-c) - \psi B](\Delta t)^2.$$

The steady state E is stable if and only if

    (i) $\Gamma(1) \equiv 1 + p_1 + p_2 > 0,$
   (ii) $(-1)^2 \Gamma(-1) = 1 - p_1 + p_2 > 0,$
  (iii) $|p_2| < 1.$

Note that

$$\Gamma(1) = 1 + p_1 + p_2 = \beta_y \bar{\beta}_q [\bar{i}(1-c) - \psi B],$$
$$\Gamma(-1) = 1 - p_1 + p_2$$
$$= 2[2 - (\bar{\beta}_q \bar{i} + \beta_y (1-c)) \Delta t] + \bar{\beta}_q \beta_y [\bar{i}(1-c) - \psi B],$$

and $|p_2| < 1$ is equivalent to (using $\Gamma(-1) > 0$)

$$\beta_y \bar{\beta}_q [\bar{i}(1-c) - \psi B](\Delta t) < \beta_y (1-c) + \bar{\beta}_q \bar{i}.$$

□

8.5.4 Simulating the global dynamics

In this section we seek to gain some insight into the global dynamics of the deterministic skeleton of the model.

First we consider the case of fixed proportions of agents and simulate directly the 3D dynamical system (8.14),(8.18),(8.19) and (8.21). We have used the numerical values displayed in Table 8.1. Some of these (in particular C, ψ, β_y, β_z, h_2) have been chosen in line with estimated values obtained in Chiarella et al. (2002); the others have been obtained by numerical experimentation. These parameter values yield the steady state $q_0 = 1$, $Y_0 = 33.3$ and $z_0 = 0$. Note also that unless otherwise stated we assume that both groups have common values for the set of parameters β_q^+, β_q^-, ε^+ and ε^-.

Table 8.1 Parameter set for simulations
of the deterministic skeleton.

h_1	3	h_2	55
m	5.5	k	0.25
c	0.7	ψ	10
A	10	δ	0
v	0.7	K	94.2857
β_y	0.9	β_{z_c}	5
β_q^+	1.4	β_q^-	0.7
ε^+	0.12	ε^-	-0.08

Figure 8.1 shows the long-run cycle in the 3-D phase space (a) and the projection onto the q–Y phase plane (b) for the case of equal proportions of fundamentalists and chartists, i.e. $n = 0$; the economy converges to this cycle after about $t = 100$. The rapid changes in expectations of capital gains (z_c) on the part of the chartists that accompany the end of an upswing or downswing of the stock market (q) are clearly evident. This is of course a consequence of our choice of a relatively large value of β_{z_c} (the chartist expectations adjustment coefficient). Lower values of β_{z_c} tend to smooth out this effect and ultimately lead to stability. The values of q range from about 0.8 in the depression phase to about 1.6 in the boom phase. Generally, the three-dimensional phase plots are similar to the one in Figure 8.1, so we do not reproduce them for the subsequent simulations.

Figure 8.2 gives a bifurcation diagram for q as a function of n. By and large the fluctuations in q do not vary greatly across the range of n values. The amplitude of the fluctuations is somewhat larger when the chartists dominate the market, as we might expect.

In Figure 8.3 we see the influence of changing β_{z_c} on the bifurcation diagrams for q when $n = -0.5$, so that the market consists of 75% chartists. We see that once the steady state becomes locally unstable at around $\beta_{z_c} = 0.5$, the amplitudes of the fluctuations remain similar for a wide range of β_{z_c}.

Figure 8.4 studies the influence of the optimism/pessimism variables (β_q^+, β_q^-), with the chartists adjusting expectations fairly rapidly ($\beta_{z_c} = 5$). We maintain a constant difference $\beta_q^+ - \beta_q^- = 0.7$ and obtain a bifurcation diagram for q as a function of β_q^-. Once local instability occurs, the fluctuations seem to display some sensitivity to the optimism/pessimism variables, with fluctuations increasing as the base level β_q^- increases.

Figures 8.5 and 8.6 give an impression of the dynamics behavior when the proportion of agents is allowed to switch according to equations (8.22)–(8.24). Figure 8.5 gives a bifurcation diagram for q as a function of β_{z_c}. Interestingly, as in Figure 8.3, there seem to be two basic phases – the steady state is stable or there is a cyclical pattern of booms and recessions that remains much the same for a large range of β_{z_c}. Figure 8.6 shows that, as in the case of fixed proportions, changes in the optimism/pessimism parameters (β_q^-, β_q^+) have a significant impact

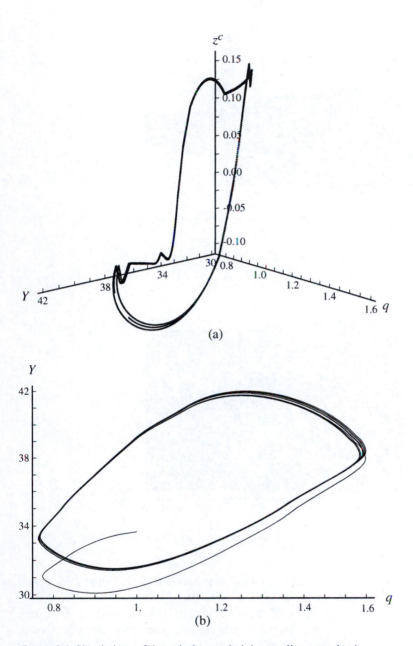

(a)

(b)

Figure 8.1 Simulations of the noiseless underlying nonlinear mechanism.

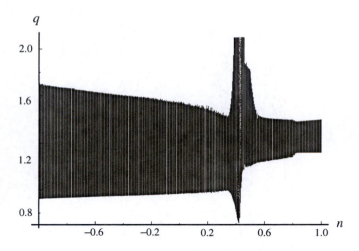

Figure 8.2 Bifurcation diagram of q as a function of n.

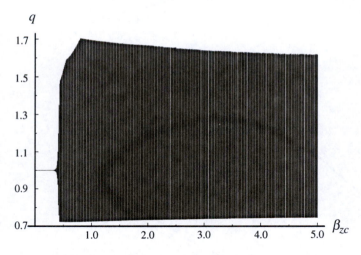

Figure 8.3 Bifurcation diagram of q as a function of β_{z_c}. Here $n = -0.5$ and $\beta_q^- = 0.7$.

on the gap between the boom and recession phases. Figure 8.7 shows the typical evolution of $q(t)$ and $n(t)$ in the case $\beta_q^- = 0.7$ and $\beta_q^+ = 1.4$.

The main impressions gained from these simulations are as follows. First, once the chartists' speed of adjustment of expectations goes past the critical value leading to local instability the fluctuations remain qualitatively similar with respect to further increases in β_{z_c}. Second, in the case of fixed proportions, variation in n does not greatly change the qualitative features of the fluctuations in the locally unstable situation. Third, the optimism/pessimism variables (β_q^+, β_q^-) seem to have the largest influence on the qualitative features of the fluctuations. Fourth,

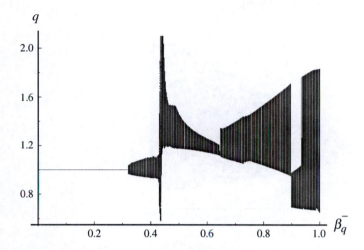

Figure 8.4 The effect of increasing levels of optimism with $\beta_{z_c} = 5$ and $n = 0.76$ ($\beta_q^+ - \beta_q^- = 0.7$).

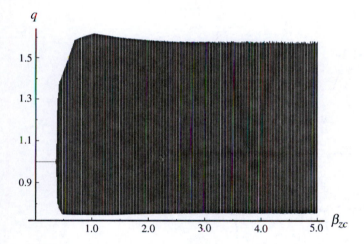

Figure 8.5 Bifurcation diagram of q as a function of β_{z_c}. The case of fluctuating proportions. Here $\beta_q^- = 0.7$, $\beta_q^+ = 1.4$, $\lambda = 40$, $\kappa^c = 0.01$, $\kappa^f = 0.02$.

the observations on the qualitative behavior with regard to β_{z_c} and (β_q^+, β_q^-) also hold for the case of fluctuating proportions of fundamentalists and chartists.

8.6 Analysis of the nonlinear stochastic model

In this section we simulate the model with Wiener process noise (in (8.18) we set $\sigma_q = 0.1$) over a 120-year period using a weekly time interval.

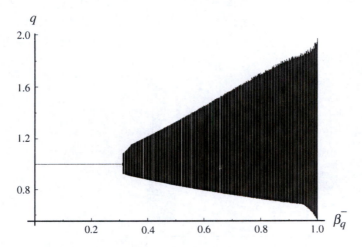

Figure 8.6 Bifurcation diagram of q as a function of β_q^-. The case of fluctuating proportions. Here $\beta_{z_c} = 5$, $\lambda = 40$, $\kappa^c = 0.01$, $\kappa^f = 0.02$.

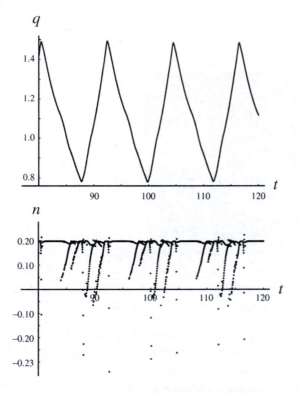

Figure 8.7 Calculating the time series of q and n over phases of booms and recessions. Same parameters as in Figure 8.6 with $\beta_a^- = 0.7$.

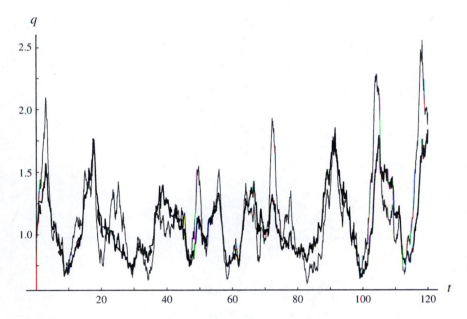

Figure 8.8 A stochastic simulation of q. The darker (lighter) curve is for the case when the noiseless model is locally stable (unstable).

We have compared the time path of q when the underlying deterministic model is stable ($\beta_q^+ = 1.0, \beta_q^- = 0.3$) with that when the underlying deterministic model is unstable ($\beta_q^+ = 1.4, \beta_q^- = 0.7$), using the same sequence of Wiener increments. Figure 8.8 shows the result of such a simulation and, at least for this simulation, the unstable deterministic case generates more stock market booms and crashes than the stable case. A similar pattern has been observed in a number of simulations. Of course, this could be a statistical aberration, so we have run 50,000 such simulations and for each simulated path have recorded the max and min of q in both the stable and unstable cases. Figures 8.9 and 8.10 shows the distributions of the max (i.e. the distribution of the highpoint of booms) and the min (i.e. the distribution of the lowpoint of busts) for a range of pairs (β_q^-, β_q^+). Here we took $n^c = 0.12$ and $n^f = 0.88$ so that fundamentalists dominate the market, as well as $n^c = 0.88$, $n^f = 0.12$ so that chartists are more dominant. These distributions indicate that the unstable model generates bigger booms and crashes and this effect is somewhat more pronounced when chartists dominate the market.

Figure 8.11 displays the distribution of booms and busts for the same situation as Figure 8.10 but with the proportions of fundamentalists and chartists evolving according to (8.22)–(8.24). Again we see that the locally unstable model generates bigger booms and crashes.

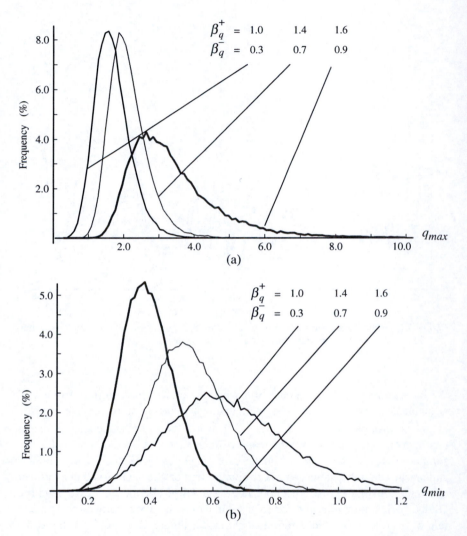

Figure 8.9 Distribution of "booms" and "crashes" for various β_q and $n^c = 0.12$, $n^f = 0.88$, $\beta_{z_c} = 5.0$.

8.7 Conclusions

We have extended the Blanchard (1981) model of stock market–real market interaction developed in earlier chapters. The key features of this extension are imperfect substitution between alternative assets, less than perfect foresight expectations and (most importantly) a state-of-market dependent coefficient of reaction to the expected return differential between different assets. The stock market of the model contains two groups: rational fundamentalists and

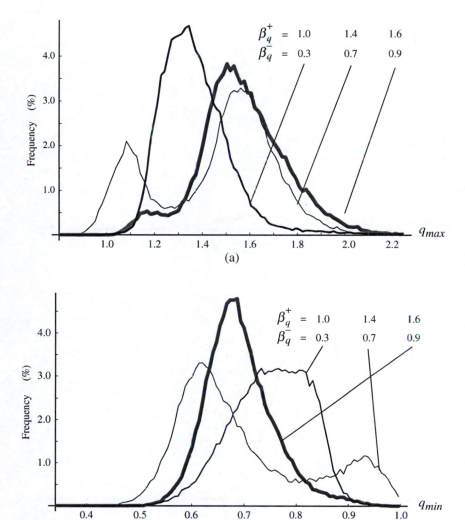

Figure 8.10 Distribution of booms (a) and busts (b) for various β_q and $n^c = 0.88$, $n^f = 0.12$, $\beta_z = 5.0$.

trend-chasing chartists. The original Blanchard model reappears as the limiting case when there is perfect substitution and the rational fundamentalists become the only agents.

Because the reaction coefficient is relatively high, the model exhibits local instability close to the steady state. The trend-chasing chartists also play a role in bringing about local instability if they react sufficiently quickly to their expected capital gain. When there is movement away from the steady state, the

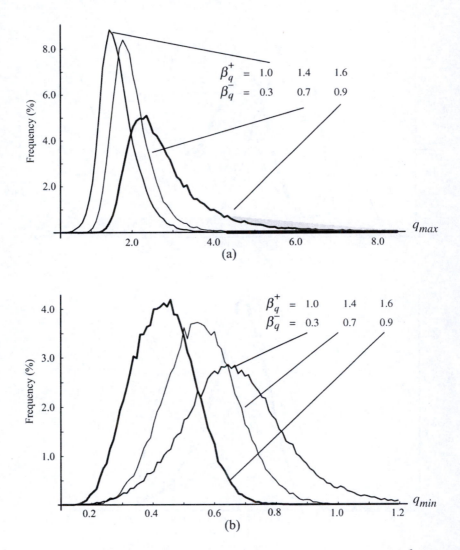

Figure 8.11   Distribution of booms (a) and busts (b) for various β_q. Here n^c and n^f fluctuate according to the expected returns, and $\beta_{z_c} = 5.0$.

state-of-market dependent reaction coefficient of both groups of agents operates in such a way that motion eventually swings back towards the steady state, where the reaction coefficient rises again. In this way the alternance between stock market upswing and downswing phases is established for the underlying deterministic driving mechanism of the model. We then added some background (steady news arrival) noise process to the dynamics for the stock market, using the increments of a Wiener process.

We have used numerical simulations to demonstrate that the interaction of these noise processes with the unstable underlying nonlinear mechanisms generates the booms and crashes characteristic of the stock market. The simulations suggest that the distributions of peaks of booms and lows of recessions are affected by the local stability/instability of the underlying nonlinear deterministic mechanism. In particular, local instability is associated with higher booms and deeper recessions.

8.8 References

ANDRESEN, T. (1998): A model of short- and long-term stock market behavior. *Complexity International*, 6. www.csu.edu.au/ci/vol06/andresen/andresen.html.

BLACK, F. (1986): Noise. *Journal of Finance*, 41:3, 529–544.

BLANCHARD, O. (1981): Output, the stock market, and interest rates. *American Economic Review*, 71, 132–143.

BROCK, W. and C. HOMMES (1997): A rational route to randomness. *Econometrica*, 65:5, 1059–1095.

CHIARELLA, C. (1992): The dynamics of speculative behavior. *Annals of Operations Research*, 37, 101–123.

CHIARELLA, C., S. MITTNIK, W. SEMMLER and P. ZHU (2002): Stock market, interest rate and output: A model and estimation for US time series data. *Studies in Nonlinear Dynamics and Econometrics*, 6:1, Article 2.

CHIARELLA, C., P. FLASCHEL and W. SEMMLER (2003): Real–financial interaction: A reconsideration of the Blanchard model with a state-of-market dependent reaction coefficient. In: W. Barnett, C. Deissenberg and G. Feichtinger (eds): *Economic Complexity*. ISETE Series, Vol. 14, Amsterdam: Elsevier.

DAY, R. and W. HUANG (1990): Bulls, bears and market sheep. *Journal of Economic Behavior and Organization*, 14, 299–329.

KINDLEBERGER, C. (1978): *Manias, Panics and Crashes: A History of Financial Crises*. London: Macmillan.

LUX, T. (1995): Herd behavior, bubbles and crashes. *Economic Journal*, 105, 881–896.

LUX, T. (1997): Time variation of second moments from a noise trader/infection model. *Journal of Economic Dynamics and Control*, 22, 1–38.

LUX, T. and M. MARCHESI (1999): Scaling and criticality in a stochastic multi-agent model of financial markets. *Nature*, 397:11, 498–500.

SIMON, H. (1997): *Models of Bounded Rationality*. Vol. 3., New Haven, CT: MIT Press.

SORNETTE, D. and W. ZHOU (2002): The US 2000–2002 market descent: How much longer and deeper? *Quantitative Finance*, 2, 468–481.

WHITE, E.N. (1990): *Crashes and Panics: The Lessons from History*. New York: Dow Jones–Irwin.

9 A high-dimensional model of real–financial market interaction

9.1 Introduction

This chapter synthesizes and generalizes some results of the previous chapters regarding wage–price dynamics. We also refer here to some basic modeling approaches used in Chiarella and Flaschel (2000) and Chiarella et al. (2000). As in the previous chapters and as in Blanchard (1981) and Blanchard and Fischer (1989, Ch. 10.4), we here also reconsider real–financial interaction. As in previous chapters, Blanchard's treatment is modified by relaxing his hypothesis of rational expectations and perfect substitutability of non-money financial assets. This chapter thus develops a model of real–financial interaction that merges in a consistent way these two approaches from the literature. The subsequent analysis seeks to uncover its basic dynamic properties and feedback mechanisms.[1]

The development of this type of model stresses the role of Tobin's average q in the investment function.[2] The real–financial interaction is built around it by modeling carefully the feedback loop from capacity utilization to profits and nominal interest rates, from there to Tobin's q through to investment and back to utilization again. As a consequence, the role of the wage–price dynamics involved here goes beyond what is traditionally investigated in low-order macrodynamics of two or three dimensions.

The main methodological contribution of the chapter arises from the fact that the dynamic system at which we finally arrive is of dimension 7. We present a systematic approach that allows us to derive a set of meaningful conditions on

---

1 We presume the above-mentioned Keynesian macro approach here, because of the extreme difficulty that the intertemporal optimizing procedures of microfounded approaches have in delineating in a clear-cut fashion the type of dynamic feedback mechanisms that we want to study here.

2 While economic theory focuses almost exclusively on marginal q as determining investment, the validity of this approach rests on very stringent assumptions concerning markets and adjustment costs. The use of Tobin's average q, by contrast, as *one* of the main explanatory variables of investment remains valid under a wide variety of scenarios. This point is emphasized by Caballero and Leahy (1996).

the behavioral parameters that ensure local stability of the long-run equilibrium position. It proceeds by considering dynamical subsystems of successively higher dimension for which stability can be established, in such a way that basically only the (well-behaved) determinants of the higher-order systems have to be computed. We use in this proof strategy a cascade of stable matrices, and we believe that this approach may also be of more general applicability to the analysis of high-dimensional dynamic economic models beyond the specific model of this paper.

The material is organized as follows. Section 9.2 presents the building blocks of the model. Section 9.3 translates these equations into intensive form, which yields a 7th-order differential equation system. Section 9.4 studies two-dimensional subdynamics in the real and financial sector, respectively, thus highlighting the main positive and negative feedback loops. Section 9.5 returns to the full seven-dimensional dynamics and develops the techniques for examining the stability and instability conditions of the system's Jacobian matrix. Section 9.6 concludes.

9.2 Formulation of the model

The core of real–financial interaction is constituted by Tobin's q. It is here assumed that investment I varies, not with the real rate of interest, but with Tobin's average q. Regarding the financial sector, it is similar to the set-up in our previous chapters in Part I of the book. It is the stock price dynamics that feeds back into the real sector. The influence of the (nominal) interest rate, i, is in this respect more indirect; it is only used by investors on the stock market, who compare the (inflation-augmented) equity rate of return to it. This difference then drives equity prices and ultimately Tobin's q, whereby a risk premium can be considered. Regarding the real sector, output Y impacts on the interest rate through the usual transaction motive of money demand. In addition, Y, i.e. capacity utilization, affects the equity rate of return via the rate of profit, r, and the corresponding dividend payments of firms. The real–financial interaction to be studied may thus be concisely summarized by the feedback loop $Y \rightarrow (r, i) \rightarrow q \rightarrow I \rightarrow Y$.

Yet this picture still leaves out the role of inflation and the wage–price dynamics. We here assume that the relative adjustments of wages and prices, into which inflationary expectations also enter, determine income distribution in the form of the wage share and, partly, the rate of return on capital. Because of differential savings of workers and asset owners, the wage share has an impact on aggregate demand via consumption expenditures. Its impact on investment is channeled through Tobin's q, since the rate of return on capital is not a direct argument in the investment function but only co-determines the equity rate of return, which in turn has a bearing on the movements of equity prices and Tobin's q.

In the following the model is set up in extensive form, which still refers to the level variables.

9.2.1 Constant growth rates

We begin by postulating constant growth rates for labor productivity $z = Y/L$, labor supply L^s, and money M:

$$\hat{z} = g_z = \text{const.} \tag{9.1}$$

$$\hat{L}^s = g_\ell = \text{const.} \tag{9.2}$$

$$\hat{M} = g_m = \text{const.} \tag{9.3}$$

$$g^o = g_z + g_\ell \tag{9.4}$$

$$\pi^o = g_m - g^o \tag{9.5}$$

g^o is the real growth rate that must prevail in a long-run equilibrium position; π^o is the rate of inflation supporting this growth path.

The model can be employed to study business cycle mechanisms. The technological assumption on the labor inputs can be augmented by allowing for procyclical variations of labor productivity (relative to some trend), such as was proposed in Franke (2001). The local stability analysis, however, would not be seriously impaired by this feature, so we may now proceed with eq. (9.1) as it stands.

9.2.2 The goods market

The following equations specify the components of final demand Y^d: consumption C, net investment I, replacement investment δK (δ being the constant rate of depreciation) and government spending G. They are complemented by a simple tax rule and the laws of motions for capital and output.

$$Y^d = C + I + \delta K + G \tag{9.6}$$

$$pC = wL + (1-s_c)(pY - wL - \delta pK + iB - T_c) \tag{9.7}$$

$$I = [g^o + \beta_I(q-1)]K \tag{9.8}$$

$$G = \gamma K \tag{9.9}$$

$$T_c = \theta pK + iB \tag{9.10}$$

$$\dot{K} = I \tag{9.11}$$

$$\dot{Y} = g^o(Y - g^o\beta_n y^n K) + \beta_y[Y^d - (Y - g^o\beta_n y^n K)] + g^o\beta_n y^n I \tag{9.12}$$

Equation (9.7) states that wage income wL is fully spent on consumption, whereas asset owners save a constant fraction s_c of their non-wage income ($0 < s_c \leq 1$). The latter is made up of firms' profits, which are in their entirety distributed to shareholders, and interest payments at interest rate i for the presently outstanding fixed-price bonds B (the bond price being normalized at unity), minus (nominal) taxes T_c. As mentioned in the Introduction, the investment function (9.8) focuses on the influence of Tobin's (average) q, which is defined as $q = p_e E / pK$ (E being the number of shares and p_e their price). As it is formulated, (9.8) implicitly presupposes that $q = 1$ is indeed supported as the economy's long-run equilibrium value of Tobin's q. This will have to be confirmed later on.[3] Equation (9.9) may be seen as a variant of neutral fiscal policy; γ is a constant. The tax rule (9.10) is conveniently aimed at making the term $iB - T_c$ in the expression for disposable income in (9.7) likewise proportional to the capital stock.

While the change in fixed capital in (9.11) is just the capacity effect of investment, eq. (9.12) for the change in output is a behavioral equation that requires some additional explanation. It arises from the implications of allowing for goods market disequilibrium. This means that a positive excess demand is served from the existing stock of inventories, and production in excess of demand fills up inventories. To keep the model simple we neglect here possible dynamic feedback effects from these inventories. Nevertheless, since the economy is growing over time, inventories, even if remaining in the background, must be growing, too. Accordingly, besides producing Y^{md} to meet final demand, firms produce an additional amount to increase a stock of desired inventories N^d. Adopting the equilibrium growth rate g^o for this purpose, we have $Y = Y^{md} + g^o N^d$.

The output component Y^{md} is adjusted to reduce the current gap between final demand Y^d and Y^{md}. Letting β_y be the corresponding adjustment speed and taking (trend) growth into account, Y^{md} evolves like $\dot{Y}^{md} = g^o Y^{md} + \beta_y (Y^d - Y^{md})$. On the other hand, desired inventories N^d may be proportional with factor β_n to productive capacity Y^n, which in turn is linked to the capital stock K by what may be called a "normal" output–capital ratio y^n. Hence, $N^d = \beta_n Y^n = \beta_n y^n K$, where y^n itself is treated as an exogenous and constant technological coefficient. Differentiating the thus-determined output Y with respect to time, then, yields eq. (9.12).

9.2.3 Wage–price dynamics

The adjustment of wages brings the employment rate e into play; this is defined in (9.13). Labor demand and supply, L and L^s, are measured in hours, and L^s is thought to refer to normal working hours. Hence e may well exceed unity, if workers work overtime or firms organize extra shifts. $e = 1$ corresponds to normal employment.

$$e = L/L^s \tag{9.13}$$

$$\hat{p} = \kappa_p(\hat{w} - g_z) + (1 - \kappa_p)\pi + \beta_p(y - y^n) \tag{9.14}$$

---

3 The stability analysis would not be affected if also a (limited) capacity utilization effect on I is considered in (9.8), which could be easily represented by the output–capital ratio.

$$\hat{w} = g_z + \kappa_w \hat{p} + (1-\kappa_w)\pi + \beta_w(e-1) \tag{9.15}$$

$$\dot{\pi} = \beta_{\pi p}(\hat{p} - \pi) \tag{9.16}$$

The subsequent two equations (9.14) and (9.15) put the determination of prices and wages on an equal footing by positing a price as well as a wage Phillips curve, augmented by inflationary expectations π. In their core, both price and wage inflation respond to the pressure of demand on the respective markets. These are the deviations of capacity utilization from normal on the one hand (as they are captured by the difference between the output–capital ratio $y = Y/K$ and the normal ratio y^n) and the deviations of the employment rate from normal on the other hand. For price inflation, the cost-push term is a weighted average of expected inflation, π, and current wage inflation (corrected for labor productivity growth); in parallel, the cost-push term for wage inflation is a weighted average of the same rate of expected inflation and current price inflation. It goes without saying that the two weighting coefficients κ_p and κ_w are between zero and one.[4]

In eq. (9.16), the rate of expected inflation is supposed to be governed by adaptive expectations with adjustment speed $\beta_{\pi p}$. As π refers not to the next (infinitesimally) short period, but to a longer time horizon of about a year, say, this rate may perhaps be better called a general inflation climate. With this interpretation, it also makes more sense that, as implied by (9.16), π systematically lags behind $\hat{p}$. In further support of such a mechanism it should be pointed out that a similar pattern is found in the survey forecasts made in the real world (see, e.g., Evans and Wachtel, 1993, Fig. 1 on p. 477, and pp. 481ff).

9.2.4 The money market

The bond rate of interest i is determined by an ordinary LM schedule. With parameters $\beta_{mo}, \beta_{mi} > 0$, it is formulated as

$$M = pY(\beta_{mo} - \beta_{mi}\,i) \tag{9.17}$$

9.2.5 The stock market dynamics

The third financial asset, besides money and government bonds, is equities. In eq. (9.18) it is explicitly stated that they are issued by firms to finance investment (and there is no other source of internal or external finance). The next two equations put forward an elementary speculative dynamics on the stock market in two variables: the equity price p_e and expected capital gains π_e, i.e., the expected

---

4 Franke (2001) points out that, in their combination, the Phillips curves (9.14) and (9.15) have undesirable cyclical implications. It is shown there that the cyclical features can be improved upon by adding further adjustment mechanisms in the two equations, which are both channeled through the wage share. This idea may be taken up in a later version of the model.

rate of stock price inflation. Equation (9.21) defines the real rate of return, r, in the real sector.

$$pI = p_e \dot{E} \tag{9.18}$$

$$\hat{p}_e = \beta_e (rpK/p_eE + \pi_e - \xi - i) + \kappa_e\pi_e + (1-\kappa_e)\pi^o \tag{9.19}$$

$$\dot{\pi}_e = \beta_{\pi e}(\hat{p}_e - \pi_e) \tag{9.20}$$

$$r = (pY - wL - \delta pK)/pK \tag{9.21}$$

The adjustment equation (9.19) rests on the supposition that, unlike in the usual LM treatment, bonds and equities are imperfect substitutes. While perfect substitutability between bonds and equities conveys the notion that any difference in the rates of return of the two assets would immediately be eliminated by arbitrage sales or purchases and the corresponding price changes, imperfect substitutability implies that these price adjustments take place at a finite speed. The (nominal) rate of return on equities is given by the dividends which, as has already been mentioned above, are fully paid out to the shareholders. In addition, the expected capital gains π_e have to be considered, and a risk premium ξ may be deducted. Thus $r_e := rpK/p_eE + \pi_e - \xi$ is compared to the bond rate i. If $r_e > i$, then equities have become more attractive than the alternative asset, the consequence being that the demand for equities increases and bids up the equity price; corresponding downward adjustments of p_e take place if $r_e < i$.

Equation (9.19) expresses this mechanism in growth rate form. The equation furthermore takes into account that the changes in stock prices have to be related to a general growth trend of p_e. This is specified as a weighted average of currently expected stock price inflation π_e and inflation of stock prices in a long-run equilibrium, which, as shown below, must be equal to the long-run equilibrium rate of price inflation π^o.

A low value of β_e in (9.19) would indicate that equities, because of the risk associated with them, are only a weak alternative to the almost risk-free government bonds. Hence, even if equities offer a markedly higher rate of return, the pressure of demand on the stock market and the price increases resulting from it are only limited. With respect to a given (positive) differential in the two rates of return, a higher value of β_e would signify a greater pressure of demand on the share price, since agents are more easily willing to switch from bonds to equities, or to invest their current savings in equities rather than bonds. The limit at which $\beta_e = \infty$ would correspond to the situation of perfect substitutability.

Equation (9.20) invokes adaptive expectations for the expected capital gains, which are therefore treated analogously to the general inflation climate in (9.16). The speed of adjustment $\beta_{\pi e}$, however, would typically be faster than $\beta_{\pi p}$.

It is not very hard to set up versions of speculative stock market dynamics that specify some of the relevant features in finer detail. They may, in particular, explicitly distinguish fundamentalists and chartists as the two prototype trading groups on this market (see, for example, Franke and Sethi, 1998), or the speeds of adjustments in eqs (9.19) or (9.20) could be dependent on the recent history of returns (*ibid.*) or the economic climate in general (as in Chiarella et al., 2002). The basic stabilizing and destabilizing feedback mechanisms, however, would be very similar, at least as far as the local dynamics is concerned. For this reason the elementary adjustment equations (9.19) and (9.20) may, for the present, suffice.

9.3 The model in intensive form

In order to analyze the dynamics generated by eqs (1)–(21), the model has to be translated into intensive form. In this way a seven-dimensional differential equation system comes about, with state variables:

$$
\begin{array}{ll}
y = Y/K & \text{Output–capital ratio} \\
v = wL/pY & \text{Wage share} \\
q = p_e E/pK & \text{Tobin's } q \\
\pi_e & \text{Expected capital gains} \\
m = M/pK & \text{Real balances ratio} \\
k = K/zL^s & \text{Capital per head} \\
\pi & \text{Expected price inflation}
\end{array}
$$

Capital per head is a shorthand expression for capital per hour of labor supplied, measured in efficiency units (recall z is labor productivity).

9.3.1 The differential equations

We first sketch the way in which the differential equations for the state variables are obtained, including the composite expressions of some of the variables entering them. For a better overview, the complete equations are subsequently collected.

The time rate of change of the output–capital ratio is obtained from $\dot{y} = \hat{Y} - \hat{K}y$ and, in particular, eq. (9.12). Making use of (9.7)–(9.11), the aggregate demand term $y^d = Y^d/K$ in (9.22) is easily computed as stated in eq. (9.29) below. In order to determine the rate of inflation in (9.16) and also the changes in the wage share, the mutual dependence of $\hat{p}$ and $\hat{w}$ in the two Phillips curves has to be eliminated. Defining $\kappa := 1/(1 - \kappa_p \kappa_w)$, the reduced-form equations read

$$
\hat{p} = \pi + \kappa[\beta_p(y - y^n) + \kappa_p \beta_w(e - 1)]
$$

$$
\hat{w} = \pi + g_z + \kappa[\kappa_w \beta_p(y - y^n) + \beta_w(e - 1)]
$$

On this basis, the changes in the wage share $v = wL/pY = w/pz$ derive from $\hat{v} = \hat{w} - \hat{p} - g_z$; see (9.23), with κ given in (9.34). Obviously, the two weights κ_p and κ_w must not both be unity simultaneously. Eq. (9.30) makes explicit how the employment rate entering (9.23) can be expressed in terms of the state variables y and k. This formula is the simple decomposition $e = (Y/K)(L/Y)(K/L^s) = (Y/K)(K/zL^s)$. The equation for the rate of inflation will also be referred to in the next steps and so is reiterated in (9.31). To get the law of motion for Tobin's q, observe first that, with (9.18), the growth rate of the number of equities is $\hat{E} = p_e \dot{E}/p_e E = (pI/pK)(pK/p_e E) = \hat{K}/q$. Thus, $\hat{q} = \hat{p}_e + \hat{E} - \hat{p} - \hat{K} = \hat{p}_e - \hat{p} + [(1-q)/q]\hat{K}$. Eq. (9.24) follows from substituting (9.19) for $\hat{p}_e$. As (9.32) shows, the rate of return on capital entering here is dependent on y and v. Furthermore, the bond rate i in (9.24) depends on y and m. It is the solution of the LM equation (9.17) in intensive form, $m = y(\beta_{mo} - \beta_{mi} i)$, given in eq. (9.33).

The adjustments of the expected capital gains in (9.25) combine eq. (9.20) with (9.19). The motions of the remaining three variables are less involved. Logarithmic differentiation of $m = M/pK$ and $k = K/zL^s$, together with the growth rate specifications (9.1)–(9.5), yields the differential equations (9.26) and (9.27) for these two variables. Lastly, (9.28), for the adaptive expectations of the inflation climate π, is a restatement of (9.16).

$$\dot{y} = \beta_y [y^d - (y - g^o \beta_n y^n)] - (y - g^o \beta_n y^n)\beta_I (q-1) \tag{9.22}$$

$$\dot{v} = v\kappa [\beta_w (1-\kappa_p)(e-1) - \beta_p (1-\kappa_w)(y - y^n)] \tag{9.23}$$

$$\dot{q} = q \left\{ \beta_e \left[\frac{r}{q} + \pi_e - \xi - i \right] + \kappa_e \pi_e + (1-\kappa_e)\pi^o - \hat{p} \right.$$

$$\left. + \quad [(1-q)/q][g^o + \beta_I (q-1)] \right\} \tag{9.24}$$

$$\dot{\pi}_e = \beta_{\pi e} \left\{ \beta_e \left[\frac{r}{q} + \pi_e - \xi - i \right] - (1-\kappa_e)(\pi_e - \pi^o) \right\} \tag{9.25}$$

$$\dot{m} = m[\pi^o - \hat{p} - \beta_I (q-1)] \tag{9.26}$$

$$\dot{k} = k \beta_I (q-1) \tag{9.27}$$

$$\dot{\pi} = \beta_{\pi p} (\hat{p} - \pi) \tag{9.28}$$

$$y^d = y^d(y, v, q) = (1-s_c)y + s_c vy + \beta_I(q-1) + g^o + s_c\delta + \gamma - (1-s_c)\theta \tag{9.29}$$

$$e = e(y, k) = yk \tag{9.30}$$

$$\hat{p} = \hat{p}(y, k, \pi) = \pi + \kappa [\beta_p(y - y^n) + \kappa_p \beta_w(e-1)] \tag{9.31}$$

$$r = r(y, v) = (1-v)y - \delta \tag{9.32}$$

$$i = i(y, m) = \beta_{mo}/\beta_{mi} - m/(\beta_{mi} y) \tag{9.33}$$

$$\kappa = 1/(1 - \kappa_p \kappa_w) \tag{9.34}$$

9.3.2 Long-run equilibrium

A steady-state position of the economy is constituted by a rest point of system (9.22)–(9.28). Proposition 9.1 ensures that it exists and that, at least if the system is not degenerate, it is unique. The steady-state values of the variables are denoted by a superscript 'o'. Note that expected inflation π in the steady state is indeed equal to π^o as defined in (9.5), which justifies the slight abuse of the notation for equilibrium inflation.

Proposition 9.1:

System (9.22)–(9.28) has a stationary point given by

$$y^o = y^n, \qquad v^o = 1 - [g^o(1 + \beta_n y^n) + s_c \delta + \gamma - (1-s_c)\theta]/s_c y^n$$
$$q^o = 1, \qquad (\hat{p})^o = (\pi)^o = (\pi_e)^o = \pi^o$$
$$k^o = 1/y^n, \quad m^o = [\beta_{mo} - \beta_{mi}((1 - v^o)y^n - \delta + \pi^o - \xi)]y^n$$

Provided that the parameters $\beta_I, \beta_p, \beta_w, \beta_{\pi p}, \beta_e, \beta_{\pi e}$ are all strictly positive, this position is uniquely determined.

Proof: We proceed in a number of successive steps. Setting $\dot{k} = 0$ gives $q = q^o = 1$; setting $\dot{m} = 0$ gives $\hat{p}^o = \pi^o$; setting $\dot{\pi} = 0$ gives $(\pi)^o = \hat{p}^o = \pi^o$ for the inflation climate. Then, consider $\dot{q} = 0$ and $\dot{\pi}_e = 0$ (the terms in parentheses only). Subtracting the second equation from the first gives $[\kappa_e + (1-\kappa_e)](\pi_e - \pi^o) = 0$, hence $(\pi_e)^o = \pi^o$.

From $\dot{v} = 0$ we get $\beta_w(1 - \kappa_p)(e - 1) - \beta_p(1 - \kappa_w)(y - y^n) = 0$, while from $\hat{p} = \pi$ in (9.31) we have $\beta_w \kappa_p (e - 1) + \beta_p(y - y^n) = 0$. This can be viewed as two equations in the two unknowns $(e - 1)$ and $(y - y^n)$. An obvious solution is $(e - 1) = 0$, $(y - y^n) = 0$, and it is easily seen to be the only one if κ_p and κ_w are not both unity simultaneously. $e = 1$ implies $k = k^o = 1/y^n$, by eq. (9.30).

Putting $\dot{y} = 0$ and solving the resulting equation $y^n - g^o \beta_n y^n = (y^d)^o$ for v yields v^o, as stated in the proposition. Returning to $\dot{q} = 0$ and setting $r^o = (1 - v^o)y^n - \delta$ in (9.32), this equation now amounts to $r^o + \pi^o - \xi - i = 0$, or $r^o + \pi^o - \xi = i(y^n, m) = \beta_{mo}/\beta_{mi} - m/(\beta_{mi}y^n)$ with (9.33). Solving this for m gives the proposition's expression for the equilibrium real balances. $\qquad\square$

9.4 Subdynamics in the real and financial sector

To get an impression of the basic stabilizing and destabilizing forces in the economy, it is instructive to study the dynamics of its underlying subsystems. One of them represents the stock market, the other the goods and labor market in the real sector.

9.4.1 Stock market subdynamics

Let us first consider the dynamics on the stock market in isolation from the rest of the economy. Two variables are determined here: Tobin's q reflecting the adjustments of equity prices, and expected capital gains π_e.

There is only one channel through which the stock market impacts the real sector. This is Tobin's q in the investment function of the firms. Hence the real sector may continue to grow in its steady-state proportions if the investment coefficient β_I in (9.8) is set equal to zero. Freezing the five state variables

y, v, m, k, π (that characterize the behavior of the real sector) at their equilibrium values and denoting $r^o = r(y^o, v^o)$, $i^o = i(y^o, m^o)$, the differential equations (9.24), (9.25) become

$$\dot{q} = q \left\{ \beta_e \left[\frac{r^o}{q} + \pi_e - \xi - i^o \right] + \kappa_e(\pi_e - \pi^o) + \frac{(1-q)g^o}{q} \right\} \tag{9.35}$$

$$\dot{\pi}_e = \beta_{\pi e} \left\{ \beta_e \left[\frac{r^o}{q} + \pi_e - \xi - i^o \right] - (1-\kappa_e)(\pi_e - \pi^o) \right\} \tag{9.36}$$

An obvious destabilization mechanism is the positive feedback loop of expected capital gains. A rise in π_e increases the demand for equities and thus drives up share prices. If p_e rises sufficiently fast relative to general inflation, the gap between $\hat{p}_e$ and π_e in eq. (9.20) widens, so that π_e increases further. On the other hand, the resulting increase in Tobin's q lowers the rate of return on equities (the expression r^o/q), which tends to reduce equity demand. Whether the positive or negative feedback dominates depends on the speed at which expectations of capital gains are adjusted upward: instability (stability) should prevail if $\beta_{\pi e}$ is sufficiently high (low). Proposition 9.2 makes more precise the conditions under which this happens.

Proposition 9.2:
Suppose the equilibrium rate of profit exceeds the real growth rate, $r^o > g^o$. Then the equilibrium q^o, π^o of system (9.35), (9.36) for the stock market subdynamics is locally asymptotically stable if either $\beta_e \leq 1 - \kappa_e$, or (with $\beta_e > 1 - \kappa_e$) if

$$\beta_{\pi e} < (g^o + \beta_e r^o)/(\beta_e + \kappa_e - 1).$$

The equilibrium is unstable if in the latter case ($\beta_e > 1 - \kappa_e$) the inequality for $\beta_{\pi e}$ is reversed.

The supposition of the relative size of the profit rate r^o can be safely taken for granted.[5] Furthermore, overly sluggish reactions of equity prices, as represented by low values of β_e, do not really seem plausible. The proposition's inequality for the adjustment speed of expected capital gains, $\beta_{\pi e}$, is therefore the central stability condition for the stock market.

Proof: The Jacobian of (9.35), (9.36) is given by

$$J = \begin{bmatrix} -(\beta_e r^o + g^o) & \beta_e + \kappa_e \\ -\beta_{\pi e}\beta_e r^o & \beta_{\pi e}(\beta_e + \kappa_e - 1) \end{bmatrix}$$

---

5 Indeed, taxes must be extraordinarily (unless inconsistently) high for the inequality $r^o > g^o$ to be violated. This can be seen from substituting the expression for v^o from Proposition 9.1 in $r(y^o, v^o)$, which yields $r^o = [g^o(1 + \beta_n y^n) + \gamma - (1 - s_c)(\delta + \theta)]$.

$r^o > g^o$ is sufficient for the determinant to be positive, since $\det J = \beta_{\pi e}[\beta_e(r^o - g^o) + g^o(1 - \kappa_e)]$. The statements in the proposition then derive from the second stability condition that the trace be negative.   □

9.4.2 The income distribution subdynamics

Neglecting variations in fixed investment by putting $\beta_I = 0$ not only decouples the real sector from the stock market, but there is also no feedback of money balances m on the goods market, since we do not have to consider the impact of the bond rate $i = i(y, m)$ on Tobin's q. Furthermore, capital per head k remains constant at the employment rate $e = e(y, k)$. For simplicity, let us here also ignore the inflationary climate and its influence on current inflation $\hat{p}$ in eq. (9.31) by fixing π at π^o. In this way we concentrate on a two-dimensional subdynamics in output y and the wage share v, which reads:[6]

$$\dot{y} = \beta_y[y^d(y, v, q^o) - y + g^o \beta_n y^n]$$ (9.37)

$$\dot{v} = v\kappa\{\beta_w(1 - \kappa_p)[e(y, k^o) - 1] - \beta_p(1 - \kappa_w)(y - y^n)\}$$ (9.38)

The stability of this reduced system crucially depends on the relative speeds at which wages and prices respond to the disequilibrium on the labor and goods market. To see this, suppose a positive shock on the wage side has raised the wage share above its steady-state level. The immediate effect is an increase in consumption demand on the part of workers. Since there are no possibly counterbalancing effects in investment, aggregate demand y^d and then total output y both increase. The corresponding overutilization of the capital stock raises inflation in the price Phillips curve (9.14), while the correspondingly higher employment rate e raises wage inflation in (9.15). If the price level rises faster than the nominal wage rate (discounting for the productivity growth rate g_z in the wage Phillips curve), the wage share falls back towards normal. In this way we identify a negative, stabilizing feedback loop. Otherwise the wage share increases and moves the economy further away from equilibrium.

This short chain of effects may be called the real wage effect, or the Rose effect, whereby we pay tribute to a seminal contribution on the stability implications of wage and price adjustments by Rose (1967) or, more comprehensively later on, by Rose (1990). Normally this effect may be expected to be stabilizing, so we may speak of an adverse Rose effect in the destabilizing case. Schematically, the two cases may be summarized as follows, where ↑↑ indicates a faster

---

6 Adopting the (useful otherwise) notation $y^d = y^d(\cdot, \cdot, \cdot)$ for aggregate demand, the supposition $\beta_I = 0$ is expressed by plugging in q^o. This nevertheless does not rule out that q may be actually moving on the stock market.

rate of change than ↑:

Normal Rose effect: $v \uparrow \longrightarrow y^d \uparrow \longrightarrow \begin{cases} y \uparrow \longrightarrow \hat{p} \uparrow\uparrow \\ e \uparrow \longrightarrow \hat{w} \uparrow \end{cases} \longrightarrow v \downarrow$

Adverse Rose effect: $v \uparrow \longrightarrow y^d \uparrow \longrightarrow \begin{cases} y \uparrow \longrightarrow \hat{p} \uparrow \\ e \uparrow \longrightarrow \hat{w} \uparrow\uparrow \end{cases} \longrightarrow v \uparrow$

Proposition 9.3 shows that in the real sector subsystem the sign of the Rose effect is the decisive stability argument. The key expression for stability is α_{wp}, which contrasts the adjustment speeds β_w and β_p in the two Phillips curves,

$$\alpha_{wp} = \beta_w(1-\kappa_p)/y^n - \beta_p(1-\kappa_w) \tag{9.39}$$

Note, however, that α_{wp} not only involves β_w and β_p, but also the weighting parameters κ_w and κ_p in (9.14), (9.15).

Proposition 9.3:
   The equilibrium point y^o, v^o of the real sector subsystem (9.37), (9.38) is locally asymptotically stable if $\alpha_{wp} < 0$. It is unstable if the inequality is reversed.

Proof: The Jacobian is

$$J = \begin{bmatrix} -s_c\beta_y(1-v^o) & s_c\beta_y y^o \\ v^o\kappa\,\alpha_{wp} & 0 \end{bmatrix}$$

Its trace is always negative, and $\det J = -s_c\beta_y y^o v^o \kappa\,\alpha_{wp}$. Hence stability is given if and only if $\det J > 0$, that is, if and only if α_{wp} is negative.

In evaluating the Rose effect, the proposition warns against exclusively looking at the direct wage and price adjustment speeds. Though conceptually the weights κ_w and κ_p are of secondary importance, their dynamic implications for the real wage, or the wage share, are by no means innocent.[7] In particular, if price adjustments are independent of the inflation climate, i.e. if $\kappa_p = 1$, the Rose effect will always be normal, even if β_w itself might be excessively high.[8] A converse reasoning applies for $\kappa_w = 1$. The distorting effect of κ_w and κ_p is more directly expressed if (assuming $\kappa_p < 1$) the stability condition is rewritten as

$$\beta_w < \frac{(1-\kappa_w)y^n}{1-\kappa_p}\beta_p \tag{9.40}$$

It may finally be remarked that, though it is tempting to relax the assumption $\beta_l = 0$ and merge the stock market dynamics (9.35), (9.36) with the real sector

---

7 Empirical estimations of Phillips curves, however, do not seem to pay much attention to coefficients like κ_w and κ_p. They are possibly fairly sensitive to the specific proxy adopted for inflationary expectations.

8 We recall that, for κ in (9.34) to be well defined, κ_w cannot also be unity, in this case.

subdynamics (9.37), (9.38), the resulting four-dimensional system would not be consistent, even if π were still kept at π^o. On the one hand, k is now being changed in (9.27) by the variations of Tobin's q, which feeds back into $e = e(y, k)$ in (9.38). On the other hand, the variable real balances m from (9.26) make themselves felt in the interest rate $i = i(y, m)$ in (9.35). In addition, such a combined system would not be easily tractable, either. Results going beyond what can also be obtained for the general system would be hard to come by. We therefore proceed directly to the stability analysis of the full 7th-order dynamics, which integrates consistently the stock market and real sector dynamics.

9.5 Local stability analysis of the full 7D dynamics

9.5.1 Immediate instability results

The local stability analysis of the full seven-dimensional differential equations system (9.22)–(9.28) is based on the Jacobian matrix J, evaluated at the steady-state values. It is useful in this respect to change the order of the differential equations. Maintaining the first three for y, v, q and rearranging the remaining four in the order m, k, π, π_e, the Jacobian is computed as

$$J = \begin{bmatrix} -s_c\beta_y(1-v) & s_c\beta_y y & \beta_I\alpha_{yn} & 0 & 0 & 0 & 0 \\ \nu\kappa\alpha_{wp} & 0 & 0 & 0 & \nu\kappa\alpha_{wk} & 0 & 0 \\ \beta_e\alpha_{vi}-\hat{p}_y & -\beta_e y & -(\beta_e r + g) & -\beta_e i_m & -\hat{p}_k & -1 & \beta_e+\kappa_e \\ -m\hat{p}_y & 0 & m\beta_I & 0 & -m\hat{p}_k & -m & 0 \\ 0 & 0 & k\beta_I & 0 & 0 & 0 & 0 \\ \beta_{\pi p}\hat{p}_y & 0 & 0 & 0 & \beta_{\pi p}\hat{p}_k & 0 & 0 \\ \beta_{\pi e}\beta_e\alpha_{vi} & -\beta_{\pi e}\beta_e y & -\beta_{\pi e}\beta_e r & -\beta_{\pi e}\beta_e i_m & 0 & 0 & \beta_{\pi e}(\beta_e+\kappa_e-1) \end{bmatrix}$$

Here the superscript 'o' is omitted and, besides α_{wp}, which has already been defined in (9.39), the following abbreviations are used:

$$\begin{aligned} \alpha_{yn} &= \beta_y - (1 - g\beta_n)y & \hat{p}_y &= \partial\hat{p}/\partial y = \kappa\,[\beta_p + \beta_w\kappa_p k] \\ \alpha_{vi} &= (1-v) - \partial i/\partial y & \hat{p}_k &= \partial\hat{p}/\partial k = \kappa\,\beta_w\kappa_p y \\ \alpha_{wk} &= \beta_w\,(1-\kappa_p)y & i_m &= \partial i/\partial m = -1/\beta_{mi}\,y \end{aligned}$$

One of the necessary conditions for local stability is a negative trace. With $\beta_e > 1 - \kappa_e$, this condition is obviously violated whenever $\beta_{\pi e}$ in the diagonal entry j_{77} of matrix J is large enough. We can thus immediately recognize that the stock market dynamics can always destabilize the whole economy if the expected capital gains adjust sufficiently fast to the previously observed changes in the equity price.

Proposition 9.4:
   Given that $\beta_e > 1 - \kappa_e$, the steady state of system (9.22)–(9.28) is unstable if $\beta_{\pi e}$ is sufficiently large.

In many monetary growth models with adaptive expectations of an expected rate of inflation, the same type of result obtains if the speed of adjustment of inflationary expectations is sufficiently fast. In the present framework this would mean that $\beta_{\pi p}$, too, could destabilize the economy. However, $\beta_{\pi p}$ does not show up in the diagonal entry j_{66}, so that the straightforward argument involving the trace of J is no longer available. As a matter of fact, it can be shown (see below) that low values of $\beta_{\pi p}$ are stabilizing, whereas we have so far not been able to prove that high values of $\beta_{\pi p}$ are (largely) sufficient for instability.

Another mechanism that, at least at a theoretical level, is likewise capable of destabilizing the whole economy is an adverse Rose effect. The mathematical argument refers to the principal minor of order 2 which is constituted by the determinant of the 2×2 submatrix in the upper-left corner. Denoting it by $D^{(2)}$, we have, as in the proof of Proposition 3, $D^{(2)} = -s_c \beta_y y^o v^o \kappa \alpha_{wp}$. One of the more involved Routh–Hurwitz conditions necessary for stability says that the sum of all second-order principal minors must be positive. Since α_{wp} enters no other of these principal minors, a negative $D^{(2)}$ can dominate the sum if α_{wp} is large enough. We thus obtain

Proposition 9.5:
Given that $\kappa_p < 1$, the steady state of system (9.22)–(9.28) is unstable if β_w is sufficiently large.

After these negative results we should now inquire into the conditions for the long-run equilibrium growth path to be attracting.

9.5.2 *The proof strategy: a cascade of stable matrices*

Stability conditions for system (9.22)–(9.28) can be derived in a number of successive steps, where we proceed from lower- to higher-order matrices. Our method rests on the following lemma.

Lemma:
Let $J^{(n)}(\beta)$ be $n \times n$ matrices, $h(\beta) \in \mathbb{R}^n$ row vectors, and $h_{n+1}(\beta)$ real numbers, all three varying continuously with β over some interval $[0, \varepsilon]$. Put

$$J^{(n+1)}(\beta) = \begin{bmatrix} J^{(n)}(\beta) & z \\ h(\beta) & h_{n+1}(\beta) \end{bmatrix} \in \mathbb{R}^{(n+1)\times(n+1)},$$

where z is an arbitrary column vector, $z \in \mathbb{R}^n$. Assume $h(0) = 0$, $\det J^{(n)}(0) \neq 0$, and let $\lambda_1, \ldots, \lambda_n$ be the eigenvalues of $J^{(n)}(0)$. Furthermore, for $0 < \beta \leq \varepsilon$, $\det J^{(n+1)}(\beta) \neq 0$ and of opposite sign of $\det J^{(n)}(\beta)$. Then, for all positive β sufficiently small, n eigenvalues of $J^{(n+1)}(\beta)$ are close to $\lambda_1, \ldots, \lambda_n$, while the

$n+1$st eigenvalue is a negative real number. In particular, if matrix $J^{(n)}(0)$ is asymptotically stable, so are these matrices $J^{(n+1)}(\beta)$.

Proof: With respect to $\beta = 0$, it is easily seen that $J^{(n+1)}(0)$ has eigenvalues $\lambda_1, \ldots, \lambda_n, \lambda_{n+1}(0)$. In fact, if λ is an eigenvalue of $J^{(n)}$ with right-hand eigenvector $x \in \mathbb{R}^n$, the column vector $(x, 0) \in \mathbb{R}^{n+1}$ satisfies $J^{(n+1)}(x, 0) = \lambda \cdot (x, 0)$. (We omit reference to the argument β for the moment.) This shows that λ is an eigenvalue of $J^{(n+1)}$, too. It is furthermore well known that the product of the eigenvalues of a matrix equals its determinant, which gives us $\det J^{(n)} = \lambda_1 \cdot \ldots \cdot \lambda_n$ and $\det J^{(n+1)} = \lambda_1 \cdot \ldots \cdot \lambda_n \cdot \lambda_{n+1}$. On the other hand, expanding $\det J^{(n+1)}$ by the last row yields $\det J^{(n+1)} = h_{n+1}(0) \cdot \det J^{(n)} \neq 0$. Hence $\lambda_{n+1} = h_{n+1}(0)$.

Then consider the situation in the lemma and denote the $n+1$ eigenvalues of $J^{(n+1)}(\beta)$ by $\lambda_i(\beta)$. It has just been shown that $\lambda_i(0) = \lambda_i$ for $i = 1, \ldots, n$, while $\lambda_{n+1}(0)$ is a real number. Eigenvalues vary continuously with the entries of the matrix.[9] As $\det J^{(n)}(0) \neq 0$, this implies that $\mathrm{sign}[\lambda_1(\beta) \cdot \ldots \cdot \lambda_n(\beta)] = \mathrm{sign}[\lambda_1 \cdot \ldots \cdot \lambda_n] = \mathrm{sign}[\det J^{(n)}(0)]$ also for small positive β. The relationship $\det J^{(n+1)}(\beta) = \lambda_1(\beta) \cdot \ldots \cdot \lambda_n(\beta) \cdot \lambda_{n+1}(\beta)$ entails $\mathrm{sign}[\det J^{(n+1)}(\beta)] = \mathrm{sign}[\det J^{(n)}(0)] \cdot \mathrm{sign}[\lambda_{n+1}(\beta)] \neq 0$. Since $\det J^{(n+1)}(\beta)$ and $\det J^{(n)}(0)$ have opposite signs, $\lambda_{n+1}(\beta)$ is a negative real number for all β sufficiently small (but, of course, β still positive, should $h_{n+1}(0)$ happen to be zero).

The final statement about the stability of $\det J^{(n+1)}(\beta)$ follows from the fact that, by hypothesis, the n eigenvalues of $\det J^{(n)}(0)$ have all strictly negative real parts. So, for small β, the same holds true for the $\lambda_i(\beta)$.   □

We thus proceed with the above Jacobian matrix in the following manner. Suppose in the nth step, so to speak, a submatrix $J^{(n)}$ made up of the first n rows and columns of J, $n < 7$, has been established to be stable. Suppose, moreover, that there exists a parameter β such that all entries of the $n+1$st row, except perhaps for the diagonal entry $j_{n+1, n+1}$, converge to zero as $\beta \to 0$. If we are able to verify that the determinant of the augmented matrix $J^{(n+1)} = J^{(n+1)}(\beta)$ has the opposite sign of $\det J^{(n)}(\beta)$, the lemma applies and we conclude that $J^{(n+1)}(\beta)$ is stable as well if only β is chosen sufficiently small.

In this way a collection of parameter values are found that render the submatrix consisting of the first $n+1$ rows and columns of J stable. This result completes the $n+1$st step and we can go over to consider matrix $J^{(n+2)}$, etc. On the whole, we therefore strive to obtain a cascade of stable matrices $J^{(n)}, J^{(n+1)}, J^{(n+2)}, \ldots,$ until at $n = 7$ stability of the full system has been proved.

The argument, of course, equally applies if it is the $n+1$st column that exhibits the property just indicated. Likewise, if β does not enter matrix $J^{(n)}$, the $n+1$st column or row may also converge to zero as β itself tends to infinity.

---

9 This proposition is so intuitive that it is usually taken for granted. Somewhat surprisingly, a rigorous proof, which indeed is non-trivial, is not so easy to find in the literature. One reference is Sontag (1990, pp. 328ff).

9.5.3 Local stability of the full system

We are now ready to consider the full dynamical system (9.22)–(9.28) and put forward conditions on the behavioral parameters that ensure local stability of its long-run equilibrium.[10]

Proposition 9.6:

Consider the non-degenerate system (9.22)–(9.28) (in particular, $\beta_p > 0$, $\beta_l > 0$). Suppose that $\kappa_w < 1$, $\beta_l < s_c r^o$, and $\beta_y > (1 - g^o \beta_n) y^o$. Then the steady-state position is locally asymptotically stable if β_w, $\beta_{\pi p}$, $\beta_{\pi e}$ are sufficiently small while β_{mi} is sufficiently large.

Proof: Our starting point is the submatrix $J^{(3)}$ given by the first three rows and columns of J. For the time being, we assume that $\beta_w = 0$ (so that $\alpha_{wp} = -\beta_p(1 - \kappa_w) < 0$) and $\beta_{mi} = \infty$ (so that $\partial i / \partial y = 0$ and $\alpha_{vi} = 1 - v$). Given that $\beta_l < s_c r^o$, it has to be shown that $J^{(3)}$ satisfies the Routh–Hurwitz conditions. This demonstration may be summarized as 'steps 1–3'.

Steps 1–3:   The Routh–Hurwitz conditions require that the following terms a_1, a_2, a_3, b are all positive. Again, here and in the rest of the proof, superscripts "o" are omitted.

$$
\begin{aligned}
a_1 &= -\,\text{trace}\,J &&= |j_{11}| + |j_{33}| = s_c \beta_y (1-v) + (\beta_e r + g) \\
a_2 &= J_1^{(3)} + J_2^{(3)} &&= 0 + [\,\beta_y \beta_e (1-v)(s_c r - \beta_l) + \kappa \beta_p \alpha_{yn} + a_{21}\,] \\
&\quad + J_3^{(3)} &&\quad + v\kappa y s_c \beta_y\, |\alpha_{wp}| \\
a_3 &= -\,\det J^{(3)} &&= |\alpha_{wp}|\, v\kappa y\,[\,\beta_y \beta_e (s_c r - \beta_l) + s_c \beta_y + \beta_e \beta_l (1 - g\beta_n) y\,] \\
&&&= |\alpha_{wp}|\, v\kappa y\, \beta_y s_c\,(\beta_e r + g) - |\alpha_{wp}|\, v\kappa y\, \beta_e \beta_l\, \alpha_{yn} \\
&&&=: a_{31} \;-\; a_{32} \\
b &= a_1 a_2 - a_3 &&= (|j_{11}| + |j_{33}|)(J_2^{(3)} + J_3^{(3)}) - a_{31} + a_{32}
\end{aligned}
$$

Positivity of a_1 is obvious. a_{21} in the determination of $J_2^{(3)}$ is a positive residual term, while $\alpha_{yn} > 0$ by the assumption on β_y. Hence $a_2 > 0$ by virtue of $s_c r - \beta_l > 0$. The latter inequality also ensures $a_3 > 0$, as is seen in the first line of the computation of a_3. Decomposing a_3 as indicated in the second line allows us to infer $b > 0$. It suffices to note here that $-a_{31}$ cancels against $|j_{33}| \cdot J_3^{(3)}$, so that only positive terms remain.

Step 4:   Regarding $J^{(4)}$, consider its 4th column and take $i_m = \partial i / \partial m = -1/\beta_{mi} y$ as the relevant parameter when referring to the lemma. Since $i_m \to 0$ as $\beta_{mi} \to \infty$, and $\det J^{(3)} < 0$, we have to show that $\det J^{(4)} > 0$ for $i_m \neq 0$ (i.e., $\beta_{mi} < \infty$). In fact, expanding $\det J^{(4)}$ by the 4th column and the remaining determinant by

---

10 Regarding the variations of the reaction coefficient β_{mi} in the money demand function (9.17), it is understood that they are accompanied by appropriate changes of the intercept β_{mo} that leave the equilibrium rate of interest i^o unaffected. Concretely, β_{mo} is assumed to be given by $\beta_{mo} = (M/pY)^o + \beta_{mi} i^o$.

the 2nd column, it is easily seen that $\det J^{(4)} = \beta_e i_m (-s_c \beta_l) v\kappa \, \alpha_{wp} (-m\beta_l) > 0$ (recall $i_m < 0$, $\alpha_{wp} < 0$).

Step 5:   Realize that in the 5th column of $J^{(5)}$, α_{wk} and $\hat{p}_k$ tend to zero as $\beta_w \to 0$. It therefore remains to verify that the determinant of $J^{(5)}$ is negative as $\beta_w > 0$. This can be seen by expanding $\det J^{(5)}$ by the 4th column, the newly arising determinant by the 4th row, and the next one by the 2nd column, which yields $\det J^{(5)} = \beta_e i_m (-k\beta_l)(-s_c\beta_y y) v\kappa m \cdot \det \tilde{J}^{(2)}$, where

$$\det \tilde{J}^{(2)} = \det \begin{bmatrix} \alpha_{wp} & \alpha_{wk} \\ -\hat{p}_y & -\hat{p}_k \end{bmatrix} = y\kappa \, \beta_p \, \beta_w \, (1 - \kappa_p \kappa_w) > 0$$

Step 6:   For $J^{(6)}$, the lemma applies with respect to the 6th row and $\beta_{\pi p} \to 0$, so only $\det J^{(6)} > 0$ has to be shown. While the previous determinants could be computed directly, it is here useful to carry out certain row operations that leave the value of the determinant unaffected but lead to a convenient structure of zero entries in the matrix. Apart from that, a couple of multiplicative terms are factorized (they do not involve a sign change since they are all positive). To ease the presentation, we do all this directly for the final matrix $J^{(7)} = J$, the result being the determinant $D^{(7)}$ below. Observe, however, that none of the first six rows is modified by adding or subtracting the 7th row. Hence the determinant of the first six rows and columns in $D^{(7)}$ exhibits the same sign as $\det J^{(6)}$. In detail, $D^{(7)}$ is obtained as follows.

1. Factorize $v\kappa$, m, k, $\beta_{\pi p}$, $\beta_{\pi e}$ in rows 2, 4, 5, 6, 7, respectively.
2. Add the 5th row to the 4th row, to let entry j_{43} vanish.
3. Add the (new) 4th row to the 6th row, which makes entries j_{61} and j_{65} vanish while j_{66} becomes -1.
4. Subtract the (new) 4th row from the 3rd row, so that $\hat{p}_y$ disappears from j_{31}, and j_{35}, j_{36} both become zero.
5. Subtract the (new) 3rd row from the 7th row, resulting in that $j_{71} = j_{72} = j_{74} = j_{75} = j_{76} = 0$, $j_{77} = -1$, and $j_{73} = g^o$.
6. Subtract g^o/β_l times the 5th row from the 7th row, which renders j_{73} zero and leaves the other entries in that row unaffected.

$$D^{(7)} = \det \begin{bmatrix} -s_c\beta_y(1-v) & s_c\beta_y y & \beta_l \, \alpha_{yn} & 0 & 0 & 0 & 0 \\ \alpha_{wp} & 0 & 0 & 0 & \alpha_{wk} & 0 & 0 \\ \beta_e \alpha_{vi} & -\beta_e y & -(\beta_e r^o + g^o) & -\beta_e i_m & 0 & 0 & \beta_e + \kappa_e \\ -\hat{p}_y & 0 & 0 & 0 & -\hat{p}_k & -1 & 0 \\ 0 & 0 & \beta_l & 0 & 0 & 0 & 0 \\ 0 & 0 & 0 & 0 & 0 & -1 & 0 \\ 0 & 0 & 0 & 0 & 0 & 0 & -1 \end{bmatrix}$$

Regarding $D^{(6)}$, the determinant of the first six rows and columns in $D^{(7)}$, it is easily checked that

$$D^{(6)} = (-1)(\beta_e i_m)(-s_c \beta_y y)(-\beta_I) v \kappa m \cdot \det \tilde{J}^{(2)}$$

$$= \beta_e |i_m| s_c \beta_y y \beta_I \, v \kappa m y \kappa \, \beta_p \beta_w (1 - \kappa_p \kappa_w)$$

and therefore $\det J^{(6)} > 0$.

Step 7: As for $J^{(7)} = J$, the lemma applies with respect to the 7th row and $\beta_{\pi e} \to 0$. Since $D^{(7)} = (-1) \cdot D^{(6)}$, $\det J^{(7)}$ if of opposite sign to $\det J^{(6)}$. Summarizing that β_{mi} is sufficiently large in step 4 and $\beta_w, \beta_{\pi p}, \beta_{\pi e}$ are sufficiently small in steps 5, 6, 7, respectively, this completes the proof. $\qquad\square$

The condition $\beta_I < s_c r$ in Proposition 9.6 is reminiscent of similar formulations in many Keynesian-oriented macro models with explicit reference to a rate of return on capital and a propensity to save out of profit (or rental) income. There, for example, such an inequality ensures a negative slope of an IS curve. The analogy is somewhat surprising since not only is the present model more complex, but also the investment reaction coefficient β_I refers to a variable, Tobin's q, which is usually not considered in these lower-order macro models. On the other hand, a closer look at the Routh–Hurwitz terms a_2 and a_3 in the proposition's proof shows that the condition $\beta_I < s_c r$ is not a necessary one and, depending on the relative size of various other parameters, there is some room for relaxing it.

The main result of the stability analysis can be succinctly summarized by saying that slow reactions or adjustments of the following kind are favorable for stability: sluggish reactions of the bond rate of interest, as brought about by a high interest elasticity of money demand (captured by the parameter β_{mi}); sticky adjustments of nominal wages (low parameter β_w); slow revisions of the inflationary climate variable (low adjustment speed $\beta_{\pi p}$); and slow adjustments of expected capital gains (low adjustment speed $\beta_{\pi e}$).

9.5.4 A note on cyclical dynamics

As concerns the parameters whose stabilizing effects have just been discussed, it may be conjectured that values of them lying in the other extreme are conducive to instability. Propositions 9.4 and 9.5 have confirmed this with respect to high values of β_w and $\beta_{\pi e}$, but it has been indicated that similar statements for other coefficients would be much harder to obtain. We nevertheless know what happens if the system loses its stability. As a side result of the stability proof, it is easily inferred that the transition from the stable to the unstable case occurs by way of a Hopf bifurcation.

Proposition 9.7:

Let the steady state of the (non-degenerate) system (9.22)–(9.28) be locally asymptotically stable. Consider a parameter, generically denoted by α, *and suppose that under continuous ceteris paribus changes of α the steady state becomes unstable at some critical value α_H. Then, at α_H, the system undergoes a Hopf bifurcation.*

Proof: Step 7 in the proof of Proposition 9.6 has established that the Jacobian J is non-singular for all admissible (non-zero) values of the parameters. This implies that if the eigenvalue $\lambda = \lambda(\alpha)$ with largest real part crosses the imaginary axis in the complex plane, at $\alpha = \alpha_H$, we have a pair of purely imaginary eigenvalues, $\lambda(\alpha_H) = \pm i b$ in the usual notation. This is the key condition for a Hopf bifurcation to occur. The (very) technical details connected with the Hopf theorem are largely avoided (in particular, the velocity condition) if one uses the version of "theorem A" presented in Alexander and Yorke (1978, pp. 263–266).   □

A Hopf bifurcation asserts that, for some interval of parameter values close to α_H, strictly periodic orbits of the dynamical system exist (which may be attracting or repelling). While we do not wish to overstate this phenomenon as such, we emphasize the more general feature associated with this result, namely, that the dynamics is determined by complex eigenvalues. We can therefore conclude that there is broad scope for the economy to exhibit cyclical behavior, which at the present state of the investigation may be damped or undamped.

9.6 Conclusions

The economic contribution of this chapter is a model that combines a financial sector, with special emphasis on the stock market, and a real sector that allows for disequilibrium on the goods as well as the labor market. It thus includes a Phillips curve-like wage dynamics. The model is a Keynesian-oriented one that gives a greater role to income distribution, as it is determined by adjustments Phillips curves for both price and wage inflation, and it also drops the usual assumption that bonds and equities are perfect substitutes. The feedback mechanisms here involved are so rich that the dynamics are described by a 7th-order system of differential equations. The methodological contribution of the chapter is to work out a systematic way of performing a stability analysis of such a high-order dimensional system. It was thus possible to derive economically meaningful conditions for the local stability of the long-run equilibrium position. The technique of the cascade of stable matrices developed here for that purpose could be applicable to a wide range of high-dimensional dynamic economic models.

On the whole, the model that we discussed provides a consistent framework for subsequent theoretical and empirical studies of real–financial interaction. One aspect we should recall is that goods market disequilibrium, as we have perceived it, implies the presence of inventories as buffers for excess demand or supply. It has been assumed that deviations of inventories from some target level do not feed back on the production decisions of firms. This restriction is legitimate in simplifying the model, but it should be improved upon if it is desired to study the medium-run and long-run evolution of the economy, especially if we are to turn to an analysis of the global dynamics.[11]

Another important topic for further work on the model concerns the market for equities. It may be noted that a generalization of the standard Keynesian LM sector can go in two directions. One option is to use Tobin's portfolio approach that formulates the demand for the additional assets (besides money and bonds) as stock magnitudes. Here, Tobin's q as the variable that represents the stock market would be determined as a statically endogenous variable, within the temporary equilibrium solution of the financial sector.[12] On the basis of our chapters in Part I of the book, we followed in this chapter the second direction where equities are treated somewhat differently from money and bonds, such that Tobin's q becomes a dynamic variable. The advantage of this approach is that the structure of the model would not be essentially affected if the present equity price adjustments were extended to a more clearly conceived speculative asset price dynamics. Thus, as indicated at the end of Section 9.2 of this chapter, the two prototype trading groups of fundamentalists and chartists and their formulation of demand could be explicitly incorporated into the present setting.

If a high responsiveness of expectations to capital gains is viewed as the main destabilizing force for the whole model in line with Propositions 9.2 and 9.4, then suitable and economically well-motivated nonlinearities that prevent the stock market dynamics from diverging become particularly critical. An additional point is that already very elementary mechanisms working to that effect are also capable of generating complex ("chaotic") dynamics.[13] It would be interesting to see how this kind of speculative dynamics interacts with the ("normal") rest of the model. Clearly, these themes call for a global analysis, which has to be left for future research.

9.7 References

ALEXANDER, J.C. and J.A. YORKE (1978): Global bifurcations of periodic orbits. *American Journal of Mathematics*, 100, 263–292.

BLANCHARD, O.J. (1981): Output, the stock market and interest rates. *American Economic Review*, 71, 132–143.

BLANCHARD, O. and S. FISCHER (1989): *Lectures in Macroeconomics*. Cambridge, MA: MIT Press.

11 A proven model building block in this respect is a Metzlerian inventory mechanism along the lines of Franke (1996), Chiarella and Flaschel (2000, Ch. 6.3) and, most extensively, Chiarella et al. (2005, Chs 4 and 6).

12 For the integration of such a financial sector into the real sector of the economy with, in particular, the aforementioned Metzlerian inventory mechanism, see Köper and Flaschel (2000). A separate study of a similar (but more extensive) financial sector and its adjustments over the business cycle is conducted by Franke and Semmler (1999).

13 Various approaches to tackle the issue of boundedness can be found in Sethi (1996), Franke and Sethi (1998), Chiarella and Khomin (2000) and Chiarella et al. (2001, 2002). Complex dynamics may be easily brought about by the mechanisms studied in the first two papers.

CABALLERO, R.J. and J.V. LEAHY (1996): Fixed costs: The demise of marginal *q*. *NBER Working Paper* 5508.

CHIARELLA, C. and P. FLASCHEL (2000): *The Dynamics of Keynesian Monetary Growth: Macrofoundations.* Cambridge, UK: Cambridge University Press.

CHIARELLA, C. and A. KHOMIN (2000): The dynamic interaction of rational fundamentalists and trend chasing chartists in a monetary economy. In: Delli Gatti, D., M. Gallegati and A. Kirman (eds), *Interaction and Market Structure: Essays on Heterogeneity in Economics.* New-York: Springer, 151–165.

CHIARELLA, C., P. FLASCHEL, G. GROH and W. SEMMLER (2000): *Disequilibrium, Growth and Labor Market Dynamics: Macro Perspectives.* Berlin: Springer.

CHIARELLA, C., P. FLASCHEL, W. SEMMLER and P. ZHU (2001): A stochastic Blanchard model with a state-of-market dependent reaction coefficient. *Proceedings of the IFAC Symposium on Modeling and Control of Economic Systems*, Klagenfurth, Austria.

CHIARELLA, C., P. FLASCHEL and W. SEMMLER (2002): Real–financial interaction: A reconsideration of the Blanchard model with a state-of-market dependent reaction coefficient. Discussion paper, University of Technology, Sydney.

CHIARELLA, C., P. FLASCHEL and R. FRANKE (2005): *Foundations for a Disequilibrium Theory of the Business Cycle: Qualitative Assessment and Quantitative Analysis.* Cambridge, UK: Cambridge University Press.

EVANS, M. and P. WACHTEL (1993): Inflation regimes and the sources of inflation uncertainty. *Journal of Money, Credit, and Banking*, 25, 475–511.

FRANKE, R. (1996): A Metzlerian model of inventory growth cycles. *Structural Change and Economic Dynamics*, 7, 243–262.

FRANKE, R. (2001): Three wage–price macro models and their calibration. University of Bielefeld Center for Empirical Macroeconomics, http://www.wiwi.uni-bielefeld.de/~semmler/cem/wp.htm#2001.

FRANKE, R. and R. SETHI (1998): Cautious trend-seeking and complex asset price dynamics. *Research in Economics (Ricerche Economiche)*, 52, 61–79.

FRANKE, R. and W. SEMMLER (1999): Bond rate, loan rate and Tobin's *q* in a temporary equilibrium model of the financial sector. *Metroeconomica*, 50, 351–385.

KÖPER, C. and P. FLASCHEL (2000): Real–financial interaction: A Keynes–Metzler–Goodwin portfolio approach. *University of Bielefeld Department of Economics Discussion paper*, 442.

ROSE, H. (1967): On the non-linear theory of the employment cycle. *Review of Economic Studies*, 34, 153–173.

ROSE, H. (1990): *Macroeconomic Dynamics: A Marshallian Synthesis.* Cambridge, MA: Basil Blackwell.

SETHI, R. (1996): Endogenous regime switching in speculative markets. *Structural Change and Economic Dynamics*, 7, 99–118.

SONTAG, E.D. (1990): *Mathematical Control Theory: Deterministic Finite Dimensional Systems.* New-York: Springer.

10 Stock market, interest rate and output

A model and estimation for US time series data

10.1 Introduction

The interaction of the asset market and output has recently become an important topic in macroeconomic research. A large number of papers have studied the relationship between the asset market and real activity. In this new line of research a considerable body of economic and financial literature has attempted to explain asset price changes, using proxies for the changes in macroeconomic fundamentals. Taking contemporaneous or leads of macroeconomic variables as proxies for news on expected returns, future cash flows or as proxy for the discount rate, such studies have only been partially successful in explaining asset price movements.

At the same time there are also a large number of papers that study the impact of financial variables on real activity. Recently, in many studies, the impact of asset prices or Tobin's q, interest rate spread and the term structure of the interest rates on real activity have in particular been studied. This is a new and important area of research in empirical macroeconomics since, beside real variables, financial variables appear to be good explanatory variables and predictors of variations in output (Lettau and Ludvigson 2000, 2001, 2002, Stock and Watson 1989, Estrella and Hardouvilis 1991, Estrella and Mishkin 1997).

Researchers nowadays often employ stochastic optimal growth models of RBC (real business cycle) type for studying the relationship of asset market and real activity. Intertemporal decisions are at the heart of the RBC methodology and it is thus natural to study the asset market–output interaction in the context of those models. Some advances have been made by using stochastic growth models to predict asset prices and returns. The asset market implications of the RBC models are, for example, studied in Rouwenhorst (1995), Danthine et al. (1992), Lettau (1997), Lettau and Uhlig (1997), Lettau et al. (2001) and Boldrin et al. (2001). The RBC model with technology shocks as the driving force for macroeconomic fluctuations attempts to replicate basic stylized facts of the stock market such as the excess volatility of asset prices and returns, the spread between asset returns (for example, between equity and risk-free assets)[1] and the Sharpe ratio as a measure of returns relative to risk.

In this paper we pursue an alternative macroeconomic modeling approach to explain the relationship of stock price, interest rate and aggregate activity. As in former chapters, the starting point of our analysis is a macrodynamic model whose origin is Blanchard (1981) and which was further developed by Blanchard (1997). This alternative class of models has also been employed as a baseline model for the study of monetary policy shocks by McMillan and Laumas (1988). The Blanchard variant is, however, a perfect foresight model that exhibits saddle path stability, and only the imposition of a jump to the stable branch makes the trajectories stable. Again, we replace the perfect foresight jump variable technique by gradual adjustments, in particular gradual expectations adjustments based on adaptive expectations. The limiting behavior of our model, which admits (amongst other properties) cyclical paths, yields the Blanchard perfect foresight model as a limiting case[2] when the expectations adjust infinitely fast. The model is solved through discrete time approximation and empirically estimated for US time series data.

The remainder of the chapter is organized as follows. Section 10.2 gives a more detailed overview of macroeconomic literature on the stock market and discusses basic stylized facts. Section 10.3 reviews and presents our generalized variant of the Blanchard model. The implied dynamics are studied in Section 10.4. Section 10.5 sets out the discretization of the model that is employed and explains the estimation methodology. Section 10.6 sets out some econometric results, employing US time series data by employing nonlinear least-squares methodology.[3] Section 10.7 discusses some stochastic simulations and impulse response analysis of the estimated model. Section 10.8 provides some conclusions. The mathematical proofs are collected in the appendices.

10.2 Stylized facts and macromodels

A large number of macroeconometric studies on the stock market and output are based on the consumption-based capital asset pricing (CCAP) model. Econometric literature has shown that good predictors of stock prices and returns have proved to be dividends, earnings and growth rate of real output (Fama and French 1988, 1989, Fama 1990), and to some extent inflation rates (Schwert 1990). Moreover, financial variables such as interest rate spread and term structure of interest rates have also been significant in predicting stock prices and stock returns (Fama 1990, Schwert 1990). Other balance sheet variables, such as firms' leverage ratio, net worth and liquidity, have been successful to a lesser extent (Schwert 1990).

---

1 For the latter, see Mehra and Prescott (1985).
2 Further discussion of this type of treatment of saddlepoint stability can be found in Flaschel et al. (1997).
3 Additional estimation results using smooth transition regression (STR) methodology are reported in Chiarella et al. (1997).

There is another group of macroeconometric studies that departs from the market efficiency hypothesis and adopts the overreaction hypothesis when employing macro variables as predictors for stock prices and stock returns (Schiller 1991, Summers 1986, Poterba and Summers 1988). Moreover, in this tradition the role of shocks – monetary, fiscal and external – is seen to be relevant (Cutler, et al. 1989). Although in the long run stock prices may revert to their mean determined by macroeconomic proxies of fundamentals, in the short run speculative forces may be more relevant than prospective yields. This view was, with some success, tested in the mean reversion hypothesis of Poterba and Summers (1988).[4]

For the reverse relation, the impact of financial variables on real activity, there is also a considerable number of recent econometric studies. The early work by Burns and Mitchell (1943) initiated studies on leading indicators to predict changes in real activity. In the more recent business cycle literature the emphasis has been on financial variables. Recent contributions by Stock and Watson (1989), Jaeger (1991) and Plosser and Rouwenhorst (1994) show that financial variables, in particular interest rates (interest rate spread and the term structure of interest rates) as well as stock returns, lead turning points in aggregate activity and are able to capture future development of real activity.[5]

There is also econometric work on the interaction between stock market and output in the tradition of Hamilton's regime switching models. The idea of Hamilton (1989) that output follows two different autoregressions, depending on whether the economy is in an expanding or contracting regime, is extended to a study of the stock market (Hamilton and Lin 1996). Connecting to the above work by Schwert it is presumed that time periods of high volatility may interchange with periods of low volatility of stock returns, depending on whether the economy is in a recession or an expansion. On the other hand, an important factor for the output at business cycle frequency appears to be the state of the stock market. In their version, Hamilton and Lin (1996) show some predictive power of the stock market for output and, using a regime change model, the state of the economy as predictor for the volatility of stock returns.

In general, however, it is well recognized that the studies of the interaction of financial and real variables have difficulties in fully capturing the lead and lag patterns in financial and real variables when tested econometrically. To overcome this deficiency, the use of the VAR framework to test for lead and lag patterns has been appealing but the VARs, as the regime change models, do not reveal important structural relations. Dynamic macromodels are needed to provide some

---

4 The overreaction of equity prices in relation to news on fundamentals originates, in this view, in positive feedback mechanisms operating in financial markets. Important contributions have been made that study the social interaction of heterogeneous equity traders, for example the interaction of fundamentalists and chartists (Day and Huang 1990, Chiarella 1992, Aoki 1996) or arbitrageurs and noise traders (DeLong et al. 1990). These are, however, models with short-run asset price dynamics which are not yet well connected to changes in long-run macro variables.

5 See, in particular, Estrella and Mishkin (1997).

rationale for structural relationships and to highlight relevant restrictions on empirical tests.

In contrasting stylized facts and macro models we will focus on the above two types of dynamic macro models which imply some predictions for the asset market–output interaction. We elaborate on stochastic growth models of RBC type and on a variant of an IS–LM version with money market and stock market. Both variants imply some predictions for the interaction of asset market and real activity.

It has been a tradition for the RBC methodology to contrast the historical with the model's time series and to demonstrate to what extent the model's time series can mimic historical data. Models are required to match statistical regularities of actual time series in terms of the first and second moments, cross-correlation with output or in terms of impulse–response functions. We thus want to review some stylized facts on macroeconomic fluctuations and asset market against which models can be measured.

In Table 10.1 we present summary statistics of US time series on GNP, consumption, investment, employment treasury bill rate, equity return and the Sharpe ratio. The latter measure of financial market performance has recently become quite a convenient measure to match theory and facts, since, as a measure of the risk–return trade-off, the Sharpe ratio captures both excess returns and excess volatility.[6] We employ quarterly data.

Table 10.1 Stylized facts on real variables and asset markets: US data.[7]

Variable	Std. dev.	Mean
GNP	0.97	
Consumption	0.77	
Investment	2.88	
Employment	0.46	
T-bill	0.86	0.18
Stock return	7.53	2.17
Equity premium	7.42	1.99
Sharpe ratio		0.27

The hierarchy of volatility measured by the standard deviation is the usual one for US data. As is known from the excess volatility debate (Shiller 1991), the stock

6   See Lettau (1997), Lettau and Uhlig (1997) and Lettau et al. (2001), where the Sharpe ratio is employed as a measure to match theory and facts in the financial market.

7   The real variables are measured in growth rates, 1970.1–1993.3. Data are taken from Canova and Nicola (1995) (the exact time series can be found in Citibase (1995); the notations are GNP82, GC82, GIN82, Lhours (man hours employed per week)). Asset market data represent real returns and are from Lettau et al. (2001) and represent 1947.1-1993.3. All data are at quarterly frequency. Asset market units are per cent per quarter. The T-bill rate is the 3 months T-bill rate. The Sharpe-ratio is the mean of the equity premium divided by it's standard deviation.

return exhibits the strongest volatility. The second strongest volatility is exhibited by investment, followed by consumption. In addition, the equity return carries an equity premium as compared to the risk free interest rate. This excess return was first stated by Mehra and Prescott (1985) as the equity premium puzzle. As can be observed, the market return exceeds by far the return from the risk-free rate. As shown in a variety of recent papers,[8] the RBC modeling approach insufficiently explains the equity premium and the excess volatility of equity return and thus the Sharpe ratio. The standard RBC asset market models employ the Solow residual as technology shocks – as impulse dynamics. For given variance of the technology shock, however, the standard utility functions and no adjustment costs asset market facts are hard to match (for details see Lettau et al. 2001).

In summary, for the actual time series compared to the data from the standard RBC model we observe a larger equity return and stronger volatility of equity prices in contrast to the risk free rate. These two facts are measured by the Sharpe ratio which basically cannot be matched by standard RBC models.[9] Moreover, it is worth noting that in stochastic growth models there is only a one-sided relationship. Real shocks affect stock prices and returns but shocks to asset prices – or overreaction of asset prices relative to changes in fundamentals – have no effects on real activity. The asset market is always cleared and there are no feedback mechanisms to propagate financial shocks to the real side.

In this chapter, we thus employ an alternative framework, a modified macro-model by Blanchard (1981) for studying the stock market–output interaction. Here, there are, in principle, cross effects between asset prices and real activity. Along the line of Tobin (1969) it is presumed that output, through consumption and investment functions, is driven by real activity as well as by stock prices. As many studies have recently shown, there appears to be some correlation of output and stock prices through consumption and investment behaviors, although a contemporaneous relation of output and the stock price may be weak. When lags are introduced and Tobin's q is measured as marginal q, as some studies do (Abel and Blanchard 1984), the relationship appears to improve.

On the other hand, since the Blanchard macromodel is a rational expectations model, shocks to macroeconomic variables cause the stock price to jump whilst keeping the output fixed (rather than allowing it to adjust gradually). Thus, because the stock price jumps, there is no feedback effect on output. Once the stock price is on the stable branch, output also gradually adjusts.[10] The stock

---

8 See, for example, Rouwenhorst (1995), Danthine et al. (1992), Boldrin et al. (2001), Lettau (1997), Lettau and Uhlig (1997) and Lettau et al. (2001).

9 Danthine et al. (1992), who study the equity return, also state:"To the equity premium and risk free rate puzzles, we add an excess volatility puzzle: the essential inability of the (RBC) models to replicate the observation that the market rate of return is fundamentally more volatile than the national product" (p. 531).

10 Blanchard states: "Following a standard if not entirely convincing practice, I shall assume that q always adjusts so as to leave the economy on the stable path to the equilibrium" (Blanchard 1981:135); see also p. 136 where Blanchard discusses the response of the stock price to shocks,

price overshoots its steady-state value during its jump and decreases thereafter. Blanchard's macromodel thus predicts that unless unanticipated shocks occur, the stock price moves monotonically toward a point of rest or, if it is there, it will stay there. Thus, in fact, only exogenous shocks will move stock prices. This line of research has been econometrically pursued in papers by Summers (1986), Cutler et al. (1989) and McMillan and Laumas (1988). As in other rational expectations models, in its basic version no feedback mechanisms exist that can lead to an endogenous propagation of shocks and fluctuations.

Based on the Blanchard variant, this chapter pursues a modeling strategy for the relationship of asset market and real activity in order to overcome shortcomings of both the RBC model and the rational expectations version of a macromodel. In our model, unlike in the RBC-type stochastic growth model, the financial market will impact the real activity and, differently from the Blanchard model, stock price jumps to their stable path are avoided by positing gradual adjustments of stock prices and output. This, in turn, will give rise to strong endogenous propagation mechanisms and fluctuations of both stock prices and output.

10.3 A generalized Blanchard model

We follow more or less the notation of Blanchard (1981). Also, we focus in this study only on the case in which output prices are fixed.[11] Thus q is the value of the stock market, y is income, g the index of fiscal expenditure so that aggregate expenditure d[12] is given by

$$d = aq + \beta y + g \quad (a > 0, \quad 0 \le \beta < 1). \tag{10.1}$$

Output adjusts to changes in aggregate expenditure with a delay according to

$$\dot{y} = \kappa_y(d - y) = \kappa_y(aq - by + g), \tag{10.2}$$

where $b \equiv 1 - \beta$ so that $0 < b \le 1$ and the speed of output adjustment $\kappa_y > 0$.

From the standard assumption of LM equilibrium in the asset market we can write

$$i = cy - h(m - p) \quad (c > 0, h > 0), \tag{10.3}$$

where i denotes the short-term rate of interest, m and p the logarithms of nominal money and prices respectively.

---

for example, unanticipated monetary and fiscal shocks. For a detailed discussion on policy shocks in the context of the Blanchard model, see McMillan and Laumas (1988).

11 The inclusion of a slowly varying output price, by assuming some sluggish price adjustment as in Rotemberg and Woodford (1997), would presumably not change the results significantly.

12 The impact of the stock market on consumption as well as investment spending has been thoroughly studied in recent papers by Lettau and Ludvigson (2000, 2002).

Real profit is given by

$$\pi = \alpha_0 + \alpha_1 y \quad (\alpha_1 \geq 0), \tag{10.4}$$

so that $(x + \alpha_0 + \alpha_1 y)/q$ is the instantaneous expected real rate of return from holding shares, where we use x to denote the instantaneous expected change in the value of the stock market. Hence the instantaneous differential between returns on shares and returns on short-term bonds (i.e., the instantaneously maturing bond) is given by

$$\epsilon = \frac{x + \alpha_0 + \alpha_1 y}{q} - i. \tag{10.5}$$

A key assumption of Blanchard's approach is that this differential is always zero.[13] This is tantamount to assuming that the two financial assets are regarded as perfect substitutes and that any differential between them is arbitraged away instantaneously. However, again following former chapters, in our more general treatment we allow for a degree of imperfect substitutability between the two assets and posit that the excess demand for stocks (q^d) is a monotonically increasing function of the instantaneous differential between ϵ and the long-run constant equity premium $\bar{\epsilon}$.[14] We further assume that the stock market adjusts to the excess demand with a speed of adjustment that also depends on the differential ($\epsilon - \bar{\epsilon}$). All of these effects can be captured by writing adjustment in the stock market as

$$\dot{q} = \kappa_q(\epsilon - \bar{\epsilon}) \cdot (\epsilon - \bar{\epsilon}), \tag{10.6}$$

where $\kappa_q(> 0)$ is the speed of adjustment of the stock market to excess demand for stocks and is itself assumed to be a function of the excess demand. Blanchard assumes that $\kappa_q = \infty$ so that, from equations (10.5) and (10.6), we recover

$$\frac{x + \alpha_0 + \alpha_1 y}{q} = i + \bar{\epsilon} \tag{10.7}$$

for all time, one of the key assumptions of Blanchard's original analysis.[15] However, Beja and Goldman (1980) and Damodaran (1993) advance arguments as to why κ_q should not be set to ∞ and we shall focus here on the implications of this assumption.

---

13 Note that ϵ may be defined as net of a constant risk premium on equity. Since we want to focus on the equity price and equity premium we subsequently do not consider the term structure of interest rates.

14 The existence of such a long-run constant equity premium is another assumption of our model.

15 Note that Blanchard's analysis has $\bar{\epsilon} = 0$.

The final building block of the model is the same rule for the formation of expectations about the expected change in the value of the stock market. Here we assume the adaptive expectations scheme

$$\dot{x} = \kappa_x(\dot{q} - x),\tag{10.8}$$

where $\kappa_x(> 0)$ is the speed of revision of expectations. The inverse κ_x^{-1} may be interpreted as the time lag in adjustment of expectations. By assuming this time lag to be zero (i.e., $\kappa_x = \infty$), equation (10.8) reduces to the perfect foresight case

$$x = \dot{q},\tag{10.9}$$

which is also a key assumption in Blanchard's model.

Our most radical departure from the original Blanchard framework is our assumption about the reaction coefficient κ_q, which changes as a function of market conditions. When market conditions are such that q is close to its steady state q_0 (i.e., ϵ is close to $\bar{\epsilon}$), the reaction coefficient κ_q is rather high, so that agents are reacting strongly to the return differential. However, the high κ_q (coupled with the high κ_x) causes the steady state to be locally unstable and hence leads to a rise (or fall) in the stock market. Agents initially are prepared to go with this general movement in the stock market; however, as it proceeds further and further they are conscious that the economy is moving ever further from its steady state (of which they are assumed to have some reasonable idea) and they start to react more cautiously to the return differential. This cautiousness is reflected in a gradual lowering of the value of the coefficient κ_q, which eventually becomes sufficiently low to cause a turn-around in the dynamics that once again become stable towards the steady-state. Eventually κ_q returns to its former high levels and the possibility of another upward (or downward) stock market movement is established. The behavior of κ_q as a function of the difference in ϵ from its steady-state value $\bar{\epsilon}$ is illustrated in Figure 10.1. We have drawn this function somewhat skewed to the right to indicate greater (less) caution when the share market is below (above) its steady-state value. This relation may also exhibit both euphoric (the higher graph) and depressed (the lower graph) states, depending on particular news events arriving in the market.

We thus have fast, adaptively formed expectations and a fast adjustment of share prices to the return differential *close to the steady state*. However, *far from the steady state* we assume that agents are aware that the economy is approaching some sort of extreme situation and become increasingly cautious, and thus only more and more sluggishly continue to adjust into a direction that they believe cannot continue for much longer.

Consider more closely the functional form $\kappa_q(\epsilon - \bar{\epsilon}) \cdot (\epsilon - \bar{\epsilon})$ with κ_q having the functional form shown in Figure 10.1. Effectively the monotonically increasing function $(\epsilon - \bar{\epsilon})$ is being multiplied by a high value for $(\epsilon \simeq \bar{\epsilon})$ and low values for ϵ far from $\bar{\epsilon}$. Hence the combined functional form has the general shape shown in Figure 10.2. It will be convenient to express the combined functional form

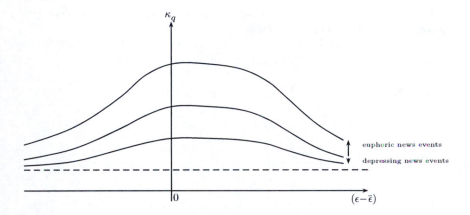

Figure 10.1 The behavior of the reaction coefficient κ_q.

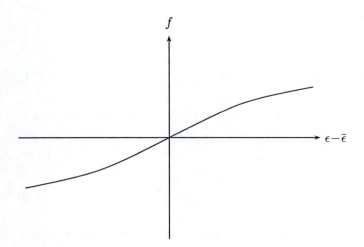

Figure 10.2 The function f.

in terms of just one function f, which with slight abuse of notation, we define according to

$$\kappa_q(\epsilon - \bar{\epsilon}) \cdot (\epsilon - \bar{\epsilon}) = \kappa_q f(\epsilon - \bar{\epsilon}). \qquad (10.10)$$

We stress that κ_q on the right-hand side is a constant which we have "pulled out" of the function f in order to make transparent the speed of adjustment at the steady state. The essential features of f are its lower slope far from steady state compared to its slope at steady state. It is also possible, depending on the function κ_q, for f to have some turning points and these could lead to a richer dynamic behavior. However, in this study we shall concentrate only on the case where f ends up having the slope shown in Figure 10.2.

Our generalized Blanchard model consists of equations (10.2), (10.6) and (10.8) which we rewrite here as the three-dimensional dynamical system

$$\dot{y} = \kappa_y(aq - by + g), \tag{10.11}$$

$$\dot{q} = \kappa_q f(\frac{x + \alpha_0 + \alpha_1 y}{q} - cy + \delta'), \tag{10.12}$$

$$\dot{x} = \kappa_x(\kappa_q f(\frac{x + \alpha_0 + \alpha_1 y}{q} - cy + \delta') - x), \tag{10.13}$$

where we write $\delta \equiv h(m - p)$ and $\delta' = \delta - \bar{\epsilon}$. The equilibrium of the system (10.11)–(10.13) is given by

$$\bar{x} = 0 \tag{10.14}$$

and the values $(\bar{y}, \bar{q})$ that solve

$$aq - by + g = 0, \tag{10.15}$$

$$\frac{\alpha_0 + \alpha_1 y}{q} = cy - \delta'. \tag{10.16}$$

For the equilibrium of (10.11)–(10.13), two sets $(\bar{y}, \bar{q})$ are possible and are given by

$$\bar{y} = \frac{\psi \pm \sqrt{\psi^2 - 4bc(g\delta' - a\alpha_0)}}{2bc}, \tag{10.17}$$

$$\bar{q} = \frac{b\bar{y} - g}{a}, \tag{10.18}$$

where $\psi \equiv gc + b\delta' + a\alpha_1$. Provided we assume $\delta > 0$, there will always be at least one positive pair $(\bar{y}, \bar{q})$ which is the equilibrium considered by Blanchard.

The determination of $(\bar{y}, \bar{q})$ is illustrated in Figure 10.2. Quite a number of subcases are possible, depending upon what we assume about the sign of α_0, the relationship of $h(m - p)/c$ ($\equiv y_i$) to $-\alpha_0/\alpha_1$ ($\equiv y_\pi$), the relationship of b/g to $-\alpha_0/\alpha_1$ and the relationship of g/a to $\alpha_0/h\delta'$. We assume $m - p > 0$ as it seems reasonable that the price level would be less than the nominal stock of money. Note that this assumption also implies that y will be the positive level of output at which the nominal interest rate falls to zero. Blanchard's famous "bad news" and "good news" scenarios revolve around the relationship between y_π and y_i, as discussed in detail in Chapter. 2. In Figure 10.3 we illustrate the two cases (a) $y_i > y_\pi$ (the "bad news" case) and (b) $y_i < y_\pi$ (the "good news" case) there is also (c) $y_i = y_\pi$ (the "neutral" case). In cases (a) and (b) we show

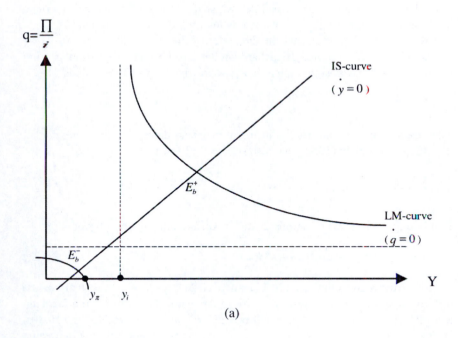

(a)

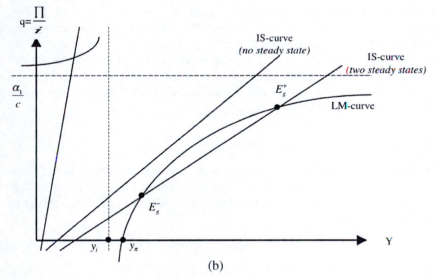

(b)

Figure 10.3 (a) A uniquely determined steady state in Blanchard's bad news case; (b) Two or no steady states in Blanchard's good news case.

the second, lower, equilibrium point as being in the positive quadrant, though this need not necessarily be the case. In case (b) we have assumed that g is sufficiently large that the two equilibria exist. Here we shall focus on the dynamics around the positive equilibria E_g^+, E_b^+ obtained by taking the positive root in (10.17).

Before proceeding to discuss the dynamics of the system (10.11)–(10.13) we first show how the original Blanchard model can be recovered from it. First we assume perfect foresight by letting $\kappa_x \to \infty$ which, by (10.13), yields

$$\dot{q} = x. \tag{10.19}$$

Then we assume instantaneous adjustment to excess demand in the stock market by letting $\kappa_q \to \infty$ in (10.12) and also set $\bar{\epsilon} = 0$. Hence

$$\frac{x + \alpha_0 + \alpha_1 y}{q} = cy - h(m - p). \tag{10.20}$$

Combining the last two equations yields the differential equation for q, viz

$$\dot{q} = q[cy - h(m - p)] - \alpha_0 - \alpha_1 y. \tag{10.21}$$

The differential equations (10.11) and (10.21) for y and q constitute the dynamical system studied by Blanchard. In Appendix 1 we outline the Jacobian analysis which indicates that the equilibria E_b^+, E_g^+ in Figures 10.3(a) and 10.3(b) are saddle points in this perfect foresight case. It may be worth noting in passing that if the jump variable procedure that is used by Blanchard is not adopted then the global dynamics need to be considered. This means taking into account the second equilibrium points E_b^-, E_g^- which can become attractors under certain circumstances, as discussed in Chiarella et al. (2001). However, we do not undertake this more detailed analysis here as our main purpose is to understand and estimate the three-dimensional generalized Blanchard model given by the differential system (10.11)–(10.13).

10.4 The dynamics of the model

The differential system (10.11)–(10.13) is nonlinear because of the assumed shape of the function f and also because of the quotient $(x + \alpha_0 + \alpha_1 y)/q$. To understand its dynamics we first calculate its Jacobian at an equilibrium point, and this turns out to be

$$J_3 = \begin{bmatrix} -\kappa_y b & \kappa_y a & 0 \\ \lambda\kappa_q\left(\frac{\alpha_1}{q} - c\right) & -\lambda\kappa_q(cy - \delta')/q & \lambda\kappa_q/q \\ \lambda\kappa_x\kappa_q\left(\frac{\alpha_1}{q} - c\right) & -\lambda\kappa_x\kappa_q(cy - \delta')/q & \kappa_x(\lambda\kappa_q/q - 1) \end{bmatrix}. \tag{10.22}$$

Here we have set $\lambda \equiv f'(0)$ and, for notational convenience, have omitted the bars indicating equilibrium values. Note also that we have made use of the relation (10.20) to simplify the expression for the elements J_{22} and J_{32}. The characteristic equation of J_3 turns out to be

$$\gamma^3 + A_1 \gamma^2 + A_2 \gamma + A_3 = 0, \qquad (10.23)$$

where

$$A_1 = \kappa_y b + \frac{\lambda \kappa_q}{\bar{q}}(c\bar{y} - \delta') - \kappa_y \left(\frac{\lambda \kappa_q}{\bar{q}} - 1 \right),$$

$$A_2 = -\frac{\lambda \kappa_y \kappa_q}{\bar{q}} + \kappa_x \left[\frac{\lambda \kappa_q}{\bar{q}}(c\bar{y} - \delta') - \kappa_y b \left(\frac{\lambda \kappa_q}{\bar{q}} - 1 \right) \right],$$

$$A_3 = \frac{\lambda \kappa_y \kappa_q}{q} [b(c\bar{y} - \delta') + a(c\bar{q} - \alpha_1)].$$

At the equilibrium E_g^+, E_b^+ it turns out that $A_3 > 0$, which indicates that at these equilibrium points the real parts of the eigenvalues of J_3 have the sign distribution $(-,-,-)$ or $(-,+,+)$. Chiarella et al. (2001) show that the parameter κ_x can act as a bifurcation parameter and there exists a value κ_x^* such that the sign distribution is $(-,-,-)$ for $\kappa_x < \kappa_x^*$ and $(-,+,+)$ for $\kappa_x > \kappa_x^*$. Furthermore, the conditions of the Hopf bifurcation theorem are satisfied at κ_x^*. Thus the qualitative behavior around the equilibrium will be as shown in Figure 10.4 under the assumption that the limit cycle born at κ_x^* is stable. For κ_x sufficiently large, the dynamics consists locally of a stable and one unstable manifold as shown in Figure 10.3(b). For a wide range of parameter values the nonlinearity of the function f acts to turn the locally unstable motion on the unstable manifold into motion stable to a limit cycle as shown in Figure 10.3(b). Chiarella et al. (2001) demonstrate this result for a stylized form of the function $\kappa_q(\epsilon - \bar{\epsilon})$.

The traditional analysis of perfect foresight models as undertaken by Blanchard (1981) (and many other authors) collapses the two differential equations (10.12) and (10.13) into the one differential equation (10.21) and therefore, from the outset, loses sight of the fact that the two-dimensional perfect foresight system is in fact

(a)   (b)

Figure 10.4 (a) $\kappa_x < \kappa_x^*$;   (b) $\kappa_x > \kappa_x^*$.

the limiting case of a three-dimensional adaptive expectations system. A detailed analysis of how this limiting process works in the case of models of monetary dynamics is given in Chiarella (1992) and in Flaschel et al. (1997). The limiting process is of the same qualitative nature in our generalized Blanchard model, as is demonstrated in Chiarella et al. (2001). It is also worth noting that the adoption of the three-dimensional viewpoint obviates the need to impose the arbitrary jump variable technique to ensure that the economy arrives on a stable path from any arbitrary initial conditions. We have cited earlier Blanchard's own comment on the inadequacy of that procedure.

10.5 Discrete time form for observable variables

In order to estimate the system (10.11)–(10.13) we need to express it as a dynamical system solely in terms of the observable variables y and q. It is possible to derive both a bivariate dynamical system in y and q and a univariate dynamical system in either y or q. We will derive here the discrete time form for a bivariate system in q and y as this will allow us to use observations on both output and the stock market in our estimation procedures.

By eliminating the expectational variable x from the system (10.11)–(10.13) we obtain the bivariate dynamical system in y and q

$$\dot{y} = \kappa_y(aq - by + g), \tag{10.24}$$

$$\ddot{q} = -\frac{\phi_1}{\phi_3}\dot{y} + \frac{(\kappa_x - \phi_2)}{\phi_3}\dot{q} - \frac{\kappa_x}{\phi_3}\phi(y, q, \dot{q}). \tag{10.25}$$

After some straightforward manipulations we find that the two-dimensional dynamical system (10.24)–(10.25) may be reduced to the third-order differential equation representing a univariate process,

$$\dddot{y} = -\kappa_y\left[b + a\frac{H^{(1)}}{H^{(3)}}\right]\dot{y} + \frac{(\kappa_x - H^{(2)})}{H^{(3)}}[\kappa_y by + \ddot{y}] - \frac{a\kappa_y\kappa_x}{H^{(3)}}G(y, \dot{y}, \ddot{y}). \tag{10.26}$$

The functions ϕ, G, $H^{(i)}$ are defined as

$$\phi(y, q, \dot{q}) = -\alpha_0 - \alpha_1 y + q[cy - \delta' + f^{-1}(\dot{q}/\kappa_q)], \tag{10.27}$$

$$G(y, \dot{y}, \ddot{y}) = \phi\left(y, \frac{b}{a}y + \frac{1}{a\kappa_y}\dot{y} - \frac{g}{a}, \frac{b}{a}\dot{y} + \frac{1}{a\kappa_y}\ddot{y}\right), \tag{10.28}$$

$$H^{(i)}(y, \dot{y}, \ddot{y}) = \phi_i\left(y, \frac{b}{a}y + \frac{1}{a\kappa_y}\dot{y} - \frac{g}{a}, \frac{b}{a}\dot{y} + \frac{1}{a\kappa_y}\ddot{y}\right), \quad (i = 1, 2, 3) \tag{10.29}$$

where ϕ_i denotes the partial derivative of ϕ with respect to its ith argument.

In our empirical study and in our numerical simulations we take

$$f(x) = \bar{f}\tanh(\lambda x), \quad (\lambda > 0, \bar{f} > 0). \tag{10.30}$$

The expressions for ϕ, G and H^i implied by equation (10.30) are given below.

For an empirical estimation we can discretize (10.24)–(10.25) and (10.27)–(10.29) by using the standard discretizations[16]

$$\dot{z}(t) = \frac{z(t) - z(t - \Delta t)}{\Delta t}, \tag{10.31}$$

$$\ddot{z}(t) = \frac{z(t) - 2z(t - \Delta t) + z(t - 2\Delta t)}{(\Delta t)^2}, \tag{10.32}$$

$$\dddot{z}(t) = \frac{z(t) - 3z(t - \Delta t) + 3z(t - 2\Delta t) - z(t - 3\Delta t)}{(\Delta t)^3}. \tag{10.33}$$

Employing (10.31), the discrete time form of (10.24) can be written as

$$y_t = y_{t-h} + h\kappa_y(aq_{t-h} - by_{t-h} + g), \tag{10.34}$$

where the step size $h = \Delta t$.

The discrete time form of (10.25) can be derived by using the discretization (10.32), thus

$$q_t = 2q_{t-h} - q_{t-2h} - h^2\frac{\phi_1}{\phi_3}\dot{y} + h^2\frac{\kappa_x - \phi_2}{\phi_3}\dot{q} - \frac{\kappa_x h^2\phi(y_{t-h}, q_{t-h}, \dot{q})}{\phi_3}, \tag{10.35}$$

where again $\dot{y}, \dot{q}$ can be approximated by (10.31). Thus we set

$$\dot{y} = \frac{y_{t-h} - y_{t-2h}}{h} \tag{10.36}$$

and

$$\dot{q} = \frac{q_{t-h} - q_{t-2h}}{h}. \tag{10.37}$$

Using the form (10.30) for f, it turns out that

$$\phi(y, q, \dot{q}) = -\alpha_0 - \alpha_1 y + q\left[cy - \delta' + \frac{1}{2\lambda}\ln\left(\frac{\kappa_q\bar{f} + \dot{q}}{\kappa_q\bar{f} - \dot{q}}\right)\right], \tag{10.38}$$

16 Since the differential equations (10.25), (10.26) will be estimated with the addition of noise terms we are in fact dealing with the discretization of stochastic differential equations (see Kloeden and Platen 1995).The discretization used here corresponds to the simple Euler–Maruyama scheme. In a separate study we have used the higher-order Milstein scheme, but this does not appear to alter substantially the results; see Chiarella et al. (2002).

and

$$\phi_1(y, q, \dot{q}) = -\alpha_1 + cq, \tag{10.39}$$

$$\phi_2(y, q, \dot{q}) = cy - \delta' + \frac{1}{2\lambda} \ln\left(\frac{\kappa_q \bar{f} + \dot{q}}{\kappa_q \bar{f} - \dot{q}}\right), \tag{10.40}$$

$$\phi_3(y, q, \dot{q}) = \frac{q}{\lambda} \frac{\kappa_q \bar{f}}{(\kappa_q \bar{f} - \dot{q})(\kappa_q \bar{f} + \dot{q})}. \tag{10.41}$$

Use of (10.36)–(10.41) in (10.35) gives us the discrete time form of the stock price equation. Note that in the bivariate model (10.34), (10.35) the output equation (10.34) is linear with one lag whereas the stock price equation (10.35) is nonlinear with two lags. The univariate model (10.26) can be discretized in a similar way using (10.31)–(10.33), giving then rise to a nonlinear difference equation in y with three lags. A related nonlinear difference equation for the stock price, q, is more tedious to derive and will here be left aside.

Since in a univariate representation of our model, as in (10.26), or in a dynamic equation for stock price, q, some information will be lost, we rather prefer to pursue an estimation of the bivariate system (10.34)–(10.35) for the observable variables y and q.

10.6 Empirical results for US time series data

We estimate the parameters of the nonlinear bivariate system (10.34)–(10.35) by again employing NLLS estimation. For the US data discussed in Section 10.2, estimation results are reported below.[17] We employ for our estimations monthly data on real stock price and real output.

We directly estimate the parameters of the discrete time nonlinear bivariate system (10.34)–(10.35) with the number of lags constrained to what arises from using the Euler–Maruyama scheme. The estimated parameters, obtained from the BP-filtered[18] data, are reported in Table 10.2. As can be seen from this table, all parameters have the predicted sign, except δ. Note, however, that this may be due to the fact that δ is taken as a constant. Also, the estimates of the speeds of adjustment have the expected positive sign. One can observe the hierarchy in

---

17 The above model (10.34)–(10.35), however, constrains the lag structure. There are many frameworks within which nonlinearities in economic time series can be tested with longer lag structure. Threshold models may be useful for this purpose; see Tong (1990) and Granger and Teräsvirta (1993). We therefore have also used a more data-based methodology and let the data determine the type of nonlinearities and the lag structure. In Chiarella et al. (1997) we report for US data the results of a regime change model of smooth transition regression type with an unconstrained lag structure. Moreover, there are also estimation results reported for the above model (10.34)–(10.35) for a European data set.

18 The band-pass filter developed and applied by Baxter and King (1995) has been employed in order to detrend the data.

Table 10.2 Parameter estimates, US: 1960.01–1993.10, detrended data.[19]

Economic structure	Speeds of adjustment	Government policy
$a = 0.122$	$\kappa_y = 0.185$	$g = 0.000$
$b = 0.370$	$\kappa_q = 0.240$	$\delta = -6.670$
$\alpha_0 = 0.065$	$\kappa_x = 1.120$	
$\alpha_1 = 6.620$		
$c = 1.568$		
$\lambda = 0.036$		
$\bar{f} = 0.205$		

Table 10.3 Parameter estimates, US: 1960.01–1993.10, detrended data.*

Economic structure	Speeds of adjustment	Government policy
$a = 0.122$	$\kappa_y = 0.285$	$g = 0.000$
$b = 0.370$	$\kappa_q = 1.998$	
$\alpha_0 = 0.397$	$\kappa_x = 1.798$	
$\alpha_1 = 0.05$		
$c = 0.400$		
$h = 0.100$		
$\bar{f} = 0.025$		
$\bar{\epsilon} = 0.035$		

* In this variant the estimation is undertaken with real balances as a time series and a term for the equity premium.

the speeds of adjustment that other studies would also suggest. In particular, the slowness of output adjustment compared to the speed of stock price adjustment seems to match empirical facts.

In model (10.34)–(10.35) the term $\delta = h(m - p)$ is fixed. Since historically real balances might substantially vary, we also undertake, for the BP-filtered data, estimations including real balances as the exogenous variable. We use the time series of real balances to form $\delta_t = h(m_t - p_t)$ as an exogenous sequence.[20] In addition, we can account for the long-run equity premium $\bar{\epsilon}$. The results with real balances and equity premium are presented in Table 10.3. In this variant, the effect of the equity premium is picked up in the parameter $\bar{\epsilon} = 0.035$. The terms for the real balances, h, and the equity premium now have the correct signs. Note that the

---

19 We employ monthly data taken from the Hamilton and Lin (1996) data set. As real stock price we take the Standard & Poor's composite index deflated by the consumer price. For the output variable we take the monthly production index. All variables here are detrended by the BP filter. The standard errors for the parameters could not be computed since the Hessian matrix was not positive definite.

20 The data for the time series of $m_t - p_t$ are obtained from Citibase (1995).

Table 10.4 MSPE for the two variants.

	Variant 1	Variant 2
MSPE for stock price	17.455	15.4
MSPE for output	0.545	0.545

parameters (a and b) for the output equation do not change for the variants of Tables 10.2 and 10.3.

In terms of the mean square prediction error (MSPE) for the model reported in Tables 10.2 and 10.3 we obtain the results of Table 10.4. The MSPE improves for the stock price as one moves from variant 1 to variant 2, in which a time series for the real balances is employed and a term for the risk premium is implicitly estimated. We want to note, however, that we cannot measure the size of the risk premium directly from our coefficient $\bar{\epsilon}$, since we are using detrended data.[21] Note that the MSPE for output does not change since the estimated parameters for the output equation are independent of the specification of the stock price equation.

10.7 Stochastic simulations and impulse response functions

In order to evaluate further the model's match with the data we first perform some simulation experiments with the estimated nonlinear model and, second, estimate a VAR and compare the impulse response functions obtained from the data with those from the model. The main aim of the simulations is to see how well the estimated model can reproduce the stylized facts on real and financial times series data as presented in Section 10.2 . We use the estimated parameters reported in Table 10.3 for the variant 2 referred to in Section 10.6, namely the estimation that used the historical time series for real balances. In Section 10.7.1 we use the estimated parameters in a stochastic version of the original set of differential equations (10.11)–(10.13) for y, q and x. Here we focus on the correlation and autocorrelation features and the financial statistics such as the volatility of asset prices and returns, equity premium and the Sharpe ratio of the model. In Section 10.7.2 we study the impulse–response functions from a VAR estimation of the data and compare these with the responses of the model to similar shocks.

10.7.1 Stochastic simulations

We suppose that external noise processes are impinging on both the output market and the stock market. We capture the resulting nonlinear stochastic dynamics by

21 We also undertook estimations for first-differenced data but when we performed the estimations by including the real balances as the exogenous variable the estimations always became unstable, so we abandoned this approach. The instability of the estimates is presumably due to the fact that first differencing of the time series, particularly for the stock price, makes the time series very volatile.

writing stochastic differential equation versions of (10.11)–(10.13) as

$$dy = \kappa_y(aq - by + g)dt + s_y dw_y, \tag{10.42}$$

$$dq = \kappa_q f(\xi)dt + s_q dw_q, \tag{10.43}$$

$$dx = \kappa_x(\kappa_q f(\xi) - x)dt + \kappa_x s_q dw_q, \tag{10.44}$$

where we set $\xi \equiv (x + \alpha_0 + \alpha_1 y)/q - cy + \delta'$; dw_y, dw_q are assumed to be increments of independent Wiener processes and s_y, s_q denote the standard deviations per unit time (here annualized) of the direct changes in y and changes in q over dt due to the external noise processes.

We have used the estimates in Table 10.3, together with the historical time series for real balances, and generated 1,000,000 paths for dw_y and dw_q over a period of 35 years, taking $dt =$ one month. Along each path we also calculated the interest rate and equity premium according to equations (10.3) and (10.5) respectively. In our simulations we have taken the standard deviations of the extenal noise processes to be

$$s_y = 0.022 \quad \text{and} \quad s_q = 0.154. \tag{10.45}$$

We stress that s_y and s_q do not correspond to the standard deviation of the y and q distributions since the external noises feed through equations (10.42)–(10.44) which are interlinked, here, in a nonlinear manner. In fact, from the simulation, we obtained different values of standard deviation from the q and y distributions, with the corresponding annualized values being $\sigma_y = 0.0473$ and $\sigma_q = 0.150$. They are of the same order and with a similar ratio to the annualized values calculated from the historical time series of y and q respectively, namely $\sigma_y = 0.051$ and $\sigma_q = 0.20$.

From the 1,000,000 simulations we calculated a number of statistics. In Figure 10.5(a) and (b) we plot the final distribution of y, q, i and ϵ. The distribution of y, q and ϵ seem to be centered around reasonable values, but the nominal interest rate seems to be centered around rather high values, perhaps reflecting the high interest rates experienced during the 1980s.

Figure 10.6 displays the distribution of the q–y correlation as well as the y autocorrelation and the q autocorrelation, calculated along the 1,000,000 simulated paths. Figure 10.7 displays the correlation between the changes in q and y, and the autocorrelation of changes in q and changes in y.

Table 10.5 gives some comparative statistics on the performance of our estimated nonlinear model, the baseline RBC model and a modified RBC model as reported by Boldrin et al. (2001). In the Data column of this table, σ_y and σ_q as well as $\rho(x)$ and $\rho(\Delta x)$ are computed from monthly data, using the Hamilton and Lin (1996) data set; *EP* and *SR* are taken from Boldrin et al. (2001);[22] $\rho(\Delta x)$ means autocorrelation of first differences of the detrended data.

---

22 To what extent the Sharpe ratio *SR* may be time varying, i.e., varying over the business cycle, is explored in Wöhrmann et al. (2001). For our purpose it suffices to presume a constant Sharpe ratio.

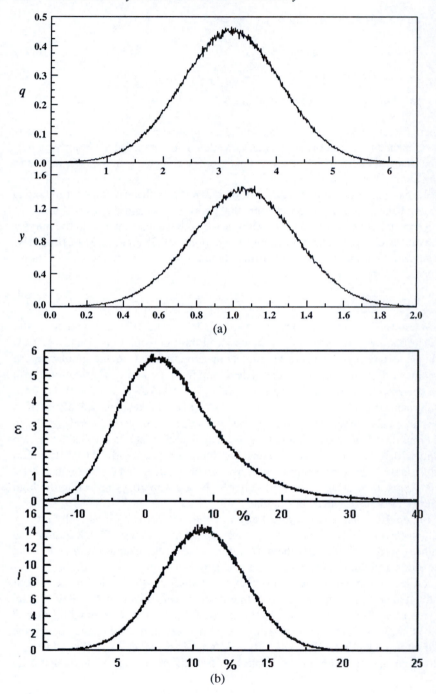

Figure 10.5 (a) Final distribution of *q* and *y*;
(b) Final distribution of the premium and interest rate.

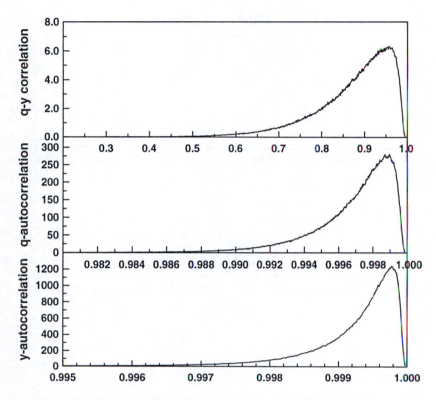

Figure 10.6 Distribution of q–y correlation, q autocorrelation and y autocorrelation.

The column SSMM represents results from the stochastic simulations of the macro model (10.42)–(10.44). The simulated results are obtained from 1,000,000 replications of an Euler–Maruyama discretization of (10.42)–(10.44). For the simulations a ratio of s_y/s_q was chosen as input such that the resulting output of the ratio σ_y/σ_q corresponded roughly to the σ_y/σ_q as obtained for the actual time series, reported in column 2. Based on the σ_q as obtained from the simulated series, the quarterly σ_q is roughly 0.075 or 7.5 percent. This was used for computing the Sharpe ratio, *SR*, of our simulations. The computed *SR* turns out to be 0.45 and seems a bit too high when compared to that for the data. Yet we note that $SR = 0.45$ can only be used as an indicator of the Sharpe ratio, since our indicator of the equity premium of 3.5 percent is not an actual equity premium from non-stationary actual time series, but rather is obtained from the estimated and simulated time series which were both detrended. Since, however, the standard deviation $\sigma_q = 15$ percent and the $EP = 3.5$ percent are obtained from the 1,000,000 simulations, the value of *SR* obtained can be interpreted as a reasonably good indicator of the *SR*.

The column BLRBC represents results for the baseline RBC model. We use here the statistics for the baseline RBC model as reported by Boldrin et al. (2001).

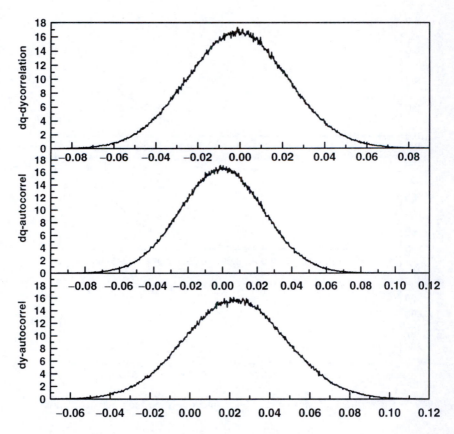

Figure 10.7 Distribution of correlation between the changes in q and y, and the autocorrelation for changes in q and changes in y.

As can be observed, the basic statistics for the asset price – the standard deviation of the equity price is only $\sigma_q = 0.40$ percent in column 4 – cannot be matched at all even if a technology shock with a standard deviation of $\sigma_y = 2.11$ percent is used as input in the computation of asset prices in the context of the baseline RBC model. Thus the *EP* and the *SR* come out much too small.

The column BCFRBC reports the statistics from a modified RBC model which takes into account habit formation in the utility function, adjustment cost of capital and a two sector model. The statistics are also annualized and in percentages. The modified model is more successful as far as the financial statistics, *EP* and the *SR*, are concerned, but, as the results in Boldrin et al. (2001) show, the simulated improved model fails along some real dimensions. Note that their $\rho(\Delta y)$ are computations from growth rates and therefore have an interpretation different from those in the SSMM column. Note also that their results on the standard deviations of the actual time series σ_y and σ_q are different from those for SSMM,

Table 10.5 Financial statistics of the different models.*

Statistic	Data	SSMM	BLRBC	BCFRBC
σ_y(%p.a.)	5.20	4.73	2.11	1.97
σ_q(%p.a.)	20.04	15.0	0.40	18.40
EP(%p.a.)	6.63	3.50	0.001	6.63
SR	0.34	0.45	0.002	0.36
$\rho(y,q)$	0.002	0.95	–	0.16
$\rho(y)$	0.834	0.99	–	–
$\rho(q)$	0.877	0.99	–	–
$\rho(\Delta y, \Delta q)$	−0.019	0.00	–	–
$\rho(\Delta y)$	0.182	0.02	0.02	0.36
$\rho(\Delta q)$	0.208	0.00	–	–

*σ_x denotes the standard deviation of the variable x, annualized, in percent; EP the equity premium; SR the Sharpe ratio, in percent; $\rho(x,y)$ the correlation between x and y (both variables detrended) and $\rho(x)$ and $\rho(\Delta x)$ denote autocorrelations. The sign "– " means not available or inapplicable.

since they employ a different time period and use growth rates. Their simulated results are obtained from 500 replications, whereas, as stated above, we have used 1,000,000 replications.

10.7.2 VAR and impulse–response functions

Another way to study how the model matches the data is to compare impulse–response functions from historical data and from our nonlinear model. First, we undertake the VAR estimation with first-differenced data and then study the impulse–response functions for the impact effect of shocks as well as the cumulative impulse–response functions, which give us the level effects.

In our model the interest rate is determined implicitly when the money supply – in our case real balance – is given. In the subsequent VAR we will, however, directly employ the interest rate.[23] Thus, the variables included in the VAR model are monthly industrial production (PR), monthly T-bills (TB) and stock prices (ST), with PR and ST entering in first differences (DPR and DST).[24] For the sample period from 1961:01 to 1993:06 the Akaike information criterion suggests a lag length of two. We employ Cholesky decomposition to orthogonalize the residuals, with the order of the variables being as listed above. By doing so, we assume that stock prices respond immediately to all shocks to the system; T-bills respond immediately to own shocks and shocks to production, but only

23 It appears to us a better procedure to employ the interest rate instead of the money supply, since the latter may, as has been shown in many papers, empirically exhibit a very unstable relationship to the interest rate.

24 The source of the data is the same as that employed for the estimations reported in Tables 10.2 and 10.3. The monthly T-bill rate is also from the Hamilton and Lin (1996) data set.

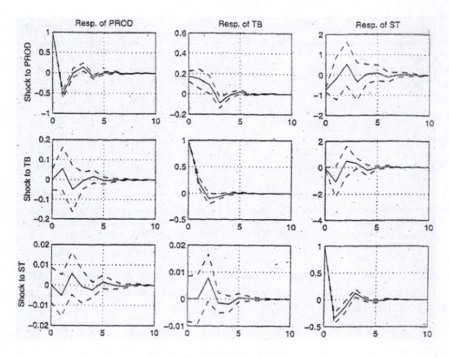

Figure 10.8 Impulse–response for first differences.

with delay to shock in stock prices; and only own shocks have simultaneous effects on production.

Figure 10.8 shows the nine unit-impulse–response functions (solid lines) implied by the estimated VAR model. To judge the significance of these responses we computed asymptotic two-standard-deviation confidence bands (dashed lines), following Mittnik and Zadrozny (1993). The estimated impulse responses are as follows. A positive shock to DPR has only short-run effects on DPR, which become significantly negative after two periods and then die out; the short-run reaction of TB is significantly positive but vanishes after three periods; the simultaneous response to DST is negative, while lagged responses are insignificant. A shock to TB affects TB itself positively for one lag, but the effect disappears beyond the second period. The initial response of DST to the interest rate shock is, as one would expect, negative. It is (marginally) significant, but then practically disappears after lag one. There are responses of DPR to the interest rate shock but they appear as not significant.[25] Finally, a positive shock to the stock returns (DST) is followed by a significantly negative return in the following period which

---

25 It is well known in the empirical literature on the impact of the interest rate on output that the output reacts to interest rate changes only with a delay. Therefore, the number of lags underlying

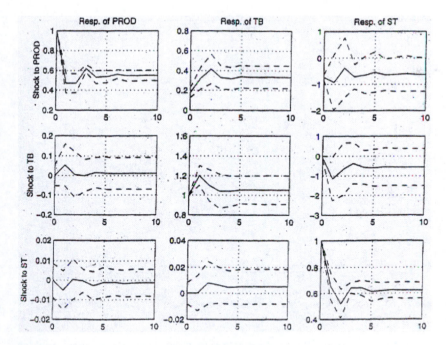

Figure 10.9 Cumulative impulse–responses.

is about one-quarter of the size of the shock, whereas higher-order responses are practically zero. The responses of DPR and DTB to DST are also not significant.

Figure 10.9 displays the cumulative impulse–responses or so-called step responses. For the differenced variables DPR and DST the step responses indicate the effects in terms of their levels, PR and ST. The results suggest that a one-time shock to production has a significant positive long-run effect on production, which is about 55 percent of the original shock. The response in stock prices is negative, but only marginally significant. A shock to TB does not appear to affect production significantly. The stock prices, again, as one would expect, react negatively to the shock in the TB. For lags zero and one we have (marginal) significance. A positive shock to stock prices has lasting positive and significant effects on stock prices, with about 60 percent of the original shock persisting in the long run; the responses of production are insignificant.

Altogether, we see that shocks in differences and levels exhibit strong autoregressive effects. Although the cross-effects from output to the other variables as well as a cross-effect of the interest rate to stock price and output

our VAR model may not sufficiently represent a lag structure that is needed to see an impact of the interest rate on output.

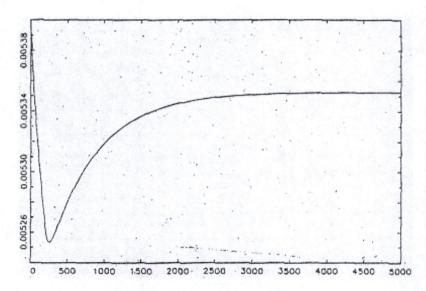

Figure 10.10 Stock price response to interest rate shocks, nonlinear model, US data.

appears to be observable, the cross-effects from stock price to the other variables are weak or insignificant. As other empirical studies have shown, the shocks to stock price do not appear to affect output significantly.[26] A similar result of no lasting effect of asset price volatility on output is also shown in Lettau and Ludvigson (2000).[27]

An impulse–response study can also be undertaken by employing our dynamic model (10.11)–(10.13). We report results from the model's impulse–responses when the estimated parameters of Table 10.3 are employed.

In Figures 10.10 and 10.11 the response of the stock price and output are depicted for shocks to the equity market. In the context of our model, the shock to the equity price is set up in such a way that it reflects a shock to the interest rate which, in our set-up, gradually affects the equity price. In the model simulation

---

26 Note, however, that in the context of linear impulse–response functions we cannot distinguish between the possibly different effects of large and small shocks, for example, of the stock price on output. To study such effects properly, nonlinear impulse–response functions would have to be employed. In our context we think of the above-employed impulse–response functions as tools to study the linearized behavior of our model around equilibrium. There may exist a transmission mechanism, for example, exerted through the credit market, as suggested by the work on the financial accelerator, that may generate a strong effect of asset price shocks on output if the asset price shocks are large, but which cannot be captured in linear impulse–response studies.

27 Lettau and Ludvigson (2000) use a VECM to estimate the stock price effect on consumption and find no lasting effect of stock prices on consumption but only a transitional effect.

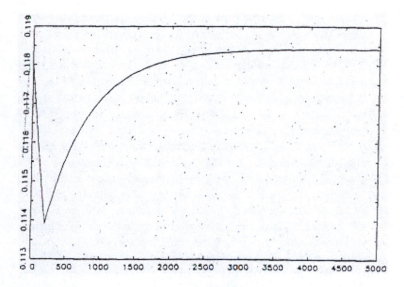

Figure 10.11 Output response to interest rate shocks, nonlinear model.

we employ persistent shocks for a number of periods.[28] As can be observed the features of the impulse–response functions obtained from the above VAR for first differences, Figure 10.8, and, in particular, the cumulative impulse–response functions representing level effects, Figure 10.9, are matched by the system simulation employing estimated parameters in our nonlinear model. In particular, the positive interest rate shock moves the stock price down but output also falls.

10.8 Conclusions

In this chapter we have further generalized the well-known model of real and stock market interaction originating in the work by Blanchard (1981). In contrast to the perfect foresight–jump variable model of Blanchard, we continued to allow for imperfect asset substitution between stocks and bonds in the asset market and for gradual portfolio adjustment. We modeled expectations as adaptive, with perfect foresight being a limiting case, and analyzed the type of dynamics that can arise in the full three-dimensional system, contrasting that with the Blanchard (1981) limit case of perfect foresight. The model we studied can also be viewed as an alternative to RBC models including an asset market. In order to empirically apply our continuous time model we used the Euler–Maruyama

---

28 Given our small step size, we have chosen persistent shocks of 100 periods' duration in order to make the effect on the stock price visible.

scheme to obtain a discrete time approximation of the solution path as well as to estimate the discretized continuous time model. A discretization in terms of observable variables is proposed and an estimation procedure for a nonlinear bivariate system in stock price and output is suggested. A direct estimation of our proposed bivariate model is undertaken, using nonlinear least squares. The results of the latter procedure suggest the existence of nonlinearities in the real and stock market interaction. In the context of our model we can also make some inference on the equity premium and the Sharpe ratio. We have performed some simulation experiments on a stochastic version of our estimated nonlinear model and compared the resulting statistics with those obtained from the RBC model. In addition, following Mittnik and Zadrozny (1993), a VAR with confidence bands for historical data was estimated and cumulative impulse–response functions were compared to the model's impulse response functions. Overall, the stochastic version of our estimated nonlinear model performs reasonably well on most of the measures we discussed. Finally, we note that our approach could be further developed to study the effects of shocks, for example, monetary policy or exchange rate shocks on the interest rate, stock price and output in the context of the more fully developed nonlinear dynamic macromodels of the type discussed in Chiarella and Flaschel (2000) and Chiarella et al. (2000).

10.9 References

ABEL, B. and O. BLANCHARD (1984): The peresent value of profits and the cyclical movements in investment. *Econometrics*, 54:2, 249–273.

AOKI, M. (1996): *New Approaches to Macroeconomic Modeling – Evolutionary Stochastic Dynamics, Multiple Equilibria, and Externalities as Field Effects*. Cambridge, UK: Cambridge University Press.

BAXTER, M. and R. KING (1995): Measuring business cycles' approximate band-pass filters for economic time series. *NBER Working Paper*, No. 50220.

BEJA, A. and M.B. GOLDMAN (1980): On the dynamic behavior of prices in disequilibrium. *Journal of Finance*, 35, 235–248.

BLANCHARD, O. (1981): Output, the stock market, and interest rate. *American Economic Review*, 71:1, 132–143.

BLANCHARD, O. (1997): *Macroeconomics*. New York: Prentice Hall.

BOLDRIN, M., L. CHRISTIANO and J. FISHER (2001): Habit persistence, asset returns, and business cycle. *American Economic Review*, 91:1, 149–167.

BURNS, A. and W. MITCHELL (1943): *Measuring Business Cycles*. Cambridge, MA: NBER Press.

CANOVA, F. and G. DE NICOLA (1995): Stock returns and real activity: A structural approach. *European Economic Review*, 39, 981–1015.

CHIARELLA, C. (1992): The dynamics of speculative behavior. *Annals of Operations Research*, 37, 101–123.

CHIARELLA, C. and P. FLASCHEL (2000): *The Dynamics of Keynesian Monetary Growth – Macrofoundations*. Cambridge, UK: Cambridge University Press.

CHIARELLA, C., W. SEMMLER and S. MITTNIK (1997): Stock market, interest rate and output: A model and estimations for U.S. and European time series data. *New School for Social Research*, New York, mimeo.

CHIARELLA, C., P. FLASCHEL, G. GROH, and W. SEMMLER (2000): *Disequilibrium, Growth and Labor Market Dynamics – Macro Perspectives.* Heidelberg: Springer.

CHIARELLA, C., P. FLASCHEL and W. SEMMLER (2001): Real–Financial interaction: A reconsideration of the Blanchard model with state-of-market dependent reaction coefficient. *Working Paper, School of Finance and Economics*, UTS.

CHIARELLA, C., W. SEMMLER and P. ZHU (2002): Some methodological issues in discretizing and estimating a class of stochastic nonlinear macrodynamic models. *Working Paper, School of Finance and Economics*, UTS.

CITIBASE (1995): Data set.

CUTLER, D., J. POTERBA and L. SUMMERS (1989): What moves stock prices? *NBER Working Paper,* No. W2538.

DAMODARAN, A. (1993): A simple measure of price adjustment coefficients. *Journal of Finance*, 48:1, 378–400.

DANTHINE, J., J. DONALDSON and R. MEHRA (1992): The equity premium and the allocation of income risk. *Journal of Economic Dynamics and Control*, 16:3/4, 509–532.

DAY, R. and W. HUANG (1990): Bulls, bears and market sheeps. *Journal of Economic Behavior and Organization*, 14:3, 299–329.

DELONG, B., A. SHLEIFER, L. SUMMERS, and K. WALDMANN (1990): Positive feedback investment strategies and destabilizing rational speculation. *Journal of Finance*, 45, 379–395.

ESTRELLA, A. and G. HARDOUVELIS (1991): The term structure as a predictor of real economic activity. *Journal of Finance*, 46, 555–576.

ESTRELLA, A. and F. MISHKIN (1997): The predictive power of the term structure of interest rates in Europe and the United States: Implications for the European Central Bank. *European Economic Review*, 41:7, 1375–1401.

FAMA, E. (1990): Returns and real activity. *Journal of Finance*, 45:4, 1089–1107.

FAMA, E. and K.R. FRENCH (1988): Dividend yields and expected stock returns. *Journal of Financial Economics*, 22, 3–25.

FAMA, E. and K.R. FRENCH (1989): Business conditions and expected returns on stocks and bonds. *Journal of Financial Economics*, 25, 23–49.

FLASCHEL, P., R. FRANKE, and W. SEMMLER (1997): *Dynamic Macroeconomic: Instability, Fluctuation, and Growth in Monetary Economies.* Cambridge, MA: MIT Press.

GRANGER, C.W.J. and T. TERÄSVIRTA (1993): *Modelling Nonlinear Economic Relationships.* Oxford: Oxford University Press.

HAMILTON, J. (1989): A new approach to the economic analysis of nonstationary time series data and the business cycle. *Econometrica*, 57, 357–384.

HAMILTON, J. and G. LIN (1996): Stock market volatility and the business cycle. *Journal of Applied Econometrics*, 11, 573–593.

JAEGER, A. (1991): The slope of the yield curve as predictor of business cycle fluctuations. *WIFO Working Paper*, 46, Vienna.

KLOEDEN, P.E. and E. PLATEN (1995): *Numerical Solution of Stochastic Differential Equations.* Heidelberg: Springer.

LETTAU, M. (1997): Asset prices and business cycles: A diagnostic view. Center of Economic Research, Tilburg, mimeo.

LETTAU, M. and H. UHLIG (1997): Preferences, consumption smoothing and risk premia. Center of Economic Research, Tilburg, mimeo.

LETTAU, M. and S.C. LUDVIGSON (2000): Understanding trend and cycle in asset values: bulls, bears and the wealth effect. Department of Finance, New York University, mimeo.

LETTAU, M. and S.C. LUDVIGSON (2001): Consumption, aggregate wealth and stock returns. *Journal of Finance*, 56:3, 815–845.

LETTAU, M. and S.C. LUDVIGSON (2002): Time-varying risk premia and the cost of capital: an alternative implication of the Q theory of investment. *Journal of Monetary Economics*, 49, 31–66.

LETTAU, M., G. GONG and W. SEMMLER (2001): Statistical estimation and moment evaluation of a stochastic growth model with asset market. *Journal of Economic Behavior and Organization*, 44, 85–103.

MCMILLAN, W.D. and G.S. LAUMAS (1988): The impact of anticipated and unanticipated policy actions on the stock market. *Applied Economics*, 20, 377–384.

MEHRA, R. and E. C. PRESCOTT (1985): The equity premium puzzle. *Journal of Monetary Economics*, 15, 145–161.

MITTNIK, S. and P.A. ZADROZNY (1993): Asymptotic distributions of impulse responses, step responses, and variance decompositions of estimated linear dynamic models. *Econometrica*, 61:4, 857–870.

PLOSSER, C. and G. ROWENHORST (1994): International term structure and real economic growth. *Journal of Monetary Economics*, 33, 133–155.

POTERBA, J. and L. SUMMERS (1988): Mean reversion in stock prices. *Journal of Financial Economics*, 22, 27–59.

ROTEMBERG, J. and M. WOODFORD (1997): An optimization based framework for the evaluation of monetary policy. Princeton University, mimeo.

ROUWENHORST, G.K. (1995): Asset pricing implications of equilibrium business cycle models. In: T.F. Cooley (Ed.): *Frontiers of Business Cycle Research*. Princeton, NJ: Princeton University Press.

SCHWERT, G. W. (1990): Stock returns and real activity: A century of evidence. *Journal of Finance*, 45:4, 1237–1257.

SHILLER, R. (1991): *Market Volatility*. Cambridge, MA: MIT Press.

STOCK, J. and J. WATSON (1989): New indexes of coincident and leading economic indicators. (ed,): In: O. Blanchard and S. Fischer *NBER Macroeconomic Annual*. Chicago: University of Chicago Press.

SUMMERS, L. (1986): Does the stock market rationally reflect fundamental values? *Journal of Finance*, 41:3, 591–602.

TOBIN, J. (1969): General equilibrium approach to monetary theory. *Journal of Money, Credit, and Banking*, 1, 15–29.

TONG, H. (1990): *Nonlinear Time Series. A Dynamical System Approach*. Oxford: Oxford University Press.

WÖHRMANN, P, W. SEMMLER and M. LETTAU (2001): Nonparametric estimation of time-varying characteristics of intertemporal asset pricing models. Department of Economics, Bielefeld University, mimeo.

10.10 Appendix 1: Stability analysis of the Blanchard model

The Jacobian of the differential equation system (10.11) and (10.12) at an equilibrium point $(\bar{y}, \bar{q})$ is easily calculated to be

$$J_2 = \begin{pmatrix} -\kappa_y b & \kappa_y a \\ c\bar{q} - \alpha_1 & c\bar{y} - h\delta' \end{pmatrix}.$$

Thus the determinant of the Jacobian is given by

$$|J_2| = -\kappa_y[b(c\bar{y} - h\delta') + a(c\bar{q} - \alpha_1)].$$

In the cases considered in Figure 10.3 it is always the case that $c\bar{y} - h\delta > 0$. At the equilibrium E_b^+ in Figure 10.3(a) we have $c\bar{q} - \alpha_1 > 0$, hence $|J_2| < 0$ at this equilibrium, which is thus a saddle point.

At the equilibrium E_g^+ in Figure 10.3(b) the fact that the slope of $\dot{y} = 0$ is less than the slope of $\dot{q} = 0$ can be expressed algebraically as

$$\frac{b}{a} > \frac{\alpha_1 - c\bar{q}}{c\bar{y} - h\delta}.$$

This latter condition implies that $|J_2| < 0$ at the equilibrium E_g^+, which is also a saddle point.

10.11 Appendix 2: The characteristic equation of the generalized Blanchard model

Consider first of all the calculation of $|J_3|$, where J_3 is defined in equation (10.20) of the main text. By an elementary row operation we find that

$$|J_3| = \begin{vmatrix} -\kappa_y b & \kappa_y a & 0 \\ \lambda\kappa_q\left(\frac{\alpha_1}{q} - c\right) & -\lambda\kappa_q(cy - \delta')/q & \lambda\kappa_q/q \\ 0 & 0 & -\kappa_x \end{vmatrix}$$

$$= -\kappa_x[\lambda\kappa_y\kappa_q b(cy - \delta')/q - \lambda\kappa_y\kappa_q a(\alpha_1/q - c)]$$

$$= -\lambda\kappa_y\kappa_q\kappa_x[b(cy - \delta')/q - a(\alpha_1/q - c)]$$

$$= \frac{-\lambda}{q}\kappa_q\kappa_x\kappa_y[b(cy - \delta') + a(cq - \alpha_1)]$$

$$= -\lambda\kappa_q\kappa_q|J_2|/q,$$

where $|J_2|$ is given in Appendix 1.

Using the analysis of the equilibrium points E_g^+, E_b^+ given in Appendix 1, we can assert that at these equilibrium points

$$|J_3| > 0,$$

which indicates that the real parts of the eigenvalues of J_3 have the sign distribution $(-,-,-)$ or $(-,+,+)$.

Part III

Exchange rate dynamics, capital flows and currency crises

11 Capital account and government budget dynamics in perfect open economies

11.1 Introduction

In Part III of this book, beginning with this chapter, we return to the modeling of open economy dynamics. We begin with a study of the capital account and the budget dynamics in an open economy. We thus, among others, deal with the twin deficit. Many modeling aspects are pursued under the assumption of a perfectly open economy. We also touch upon fiscal and monetary policy in the perfect open economy. Since we now use a number of new notations it is worth summarizing those notations in the separate section below.

11.2 Notation

The following list of symbols contains only domestic variables and parameters. Magnitudes referring to the foreign country are defined analogously and are indicated by an asterisk ($*$), while domestic and foreign commodities are distinguished by the indices 1 and 2 respectively (in the two-commodity case where consumer price levels have to be formed). Real magnitudes are generally expressed in terms of the domestic good when composite commodities are considered. Superscript d characterizes demand expressions, while the corresponding supply expressions do not have any index (in order to save notation). A 'dot' is used to characterize time derivatives and a 'hat' for corresponding rates of growth (but sometimes also for comparative static exercises that concern growth rate expressions); see footnote 5 for statements on basic growth rate rules. We furthermore use an index o to denote steady-state expressions and sometimes add-ons like 'new', 'old' to distinguish pre- and after- shock situations (and 'SR' for short-run effects). Finally, we characterize exogenous variables by means of a bar over the variable in question.

A. *Statically or dynamically endogenous variables*:

Y	Output
Y^d	Aggregate demand
C	Private consumption
C_1	Consumption of the domestic good (index 1: good originates from country 1 = domestic economy)

C_2	Consumption of the foreign good (index 2: good originates from country 2 = foreign economy)
w	Nominal wages
p	Price level
π	Expected rate of inflation
s	Exchange rate (units of domestic currency per unit of foreign currency: €/\$)
M	Money supply (index d: demand, growth rate μ_0)
R	Stock of foreign exchange
X	Exports in terms of the foreign good
J	Imports in terms of the domestic good
$NX^n = pX - ep^*J$	Nominal net exports in terms of the domestic currency
$\sigma = sp^*/p$	The real exchange rate (goods/goods*)

B. *Parameters of the model*:

$\bar{v}$	Income velocity of money
$\bar{Y}$	Full employment output level
δ	Consumption proportion with respect to the home country
$\bar{\mu}$	Growth rate of the money supply
β_w	Wage adjustment parameter
β_p	Price adjustment parameter
β_π	Inflationary expectations adjustment
p_G	Price of gold

11.3 The basic one-good monetary model of international commodity trade

We consider a world with two countries (the Euro area and the USA, for the sake of concreteness and in order to have expressions for the currency units of the two countries: € and \$) producing one and the same commodity at full employment levels (established by perfectly flexible wages) and assume also perfectly flexible prices that clear the world market for goods. We relate the model to the period of the gold standard (1870–1914), the quantity theory of money and the neglect of underemployed factors of production. According to the rules of the gold standard the nominal exchange rate is considered as given and the strict form of the quantity theory of money is used to determine aggregate goods demand in each of the two countries, each with a given aggregate supply of the same commodity. This extremely simple approach to the study of international trade in goods, price formation and specie-flows already allows for interesting dynamic analyzes that proceed from short-run considerations to medium-run adjustment processes and end with stable long-run stationary state solutions. The *exogenously given data* of the model are thus:

$\bar{Y}$,   the full employment output level in the domestic economy,

$\bar{Y}^*$,   the full employment output level in the foreign economy,

$\bar{v}$,   the expenditure velocity of money in the domestic economy,
$\bar{v}^*$,   the expenditure velocity in the foreign economy,
$\bar{s}$,   the nominal exchange rate measured by the € price of the US dollar.

The *six endogenous variables* of the model are:

Y^d, Y^{d*}, the goods demands in both countries for the one commodity produced in the world economy, to be equated to aggregate supply on the world market,

p, p^*, the price levels in both countries, together with the goods demands forming the four statically endogenous variables of the model,[1]

M, M^*, the quantity of money in both countries, the two dynamically endogenous variables of the model.

The model consequently consists of *six equations* (two behavioral or demand equations, two equilibrium conditions with respect to international trade and two laws of motion for the domestic money supplies) which read as follows:

$$Y^d = \bar{v}M/p, \quad Y^{d*} = \bar{v}^*M^*/p^*, \tag{11.1}$$

$$p(\bar{Y} + \bar{Y}^*) = p(Y^d + Y^{d*}) = pY^d + \bar{s}p^*Y^{d*} = \bar{v}M + \bar{s}\bar{v}^*M^*, \tag{11.2}$$

$$p = \bar{s}p^*, \tag{11.3}$$

$$p\bar{Y} = pY^d + \dot{M}, \quad p^*\bar{Y}^* = p^*Y^{d*} + \dot{M}^*. \tag{11.4}$$

Equations (11.1) state that nominal (real) spending is proportional to nominal (real) money holdings, where the proportionality factor is given by the expenditure velocity of money. Equation (11.2) is the equilibrium condition for the world commodity market, which equates aggregate nominal supply of commodities with aggregate nominal demand for goods, both expressed in €, the domestic currency. Equation (11.3) is the law of one price or the absolute form of the purchasing power parity condition (PPP), which states that there are no arbitrage possibilities in international trade. Equations (11.4), finally, are the budget equations of the two countries under consideration, which state that excess supply $p(\bar{Y} - Y^d) > 0$, equal to the exports of the domestic economy, leads to an increase of domestic money (via gold imports, exchanged into domestic money), while excess demand does the opposite.

The above model (11.1) – (11.4) is identical to the model considered in Dornbusch (1980, Ch.7.I) where the reader also finds an alternative presentation of the analysis that now follows. Note that the model does not consider the adjustment

---

1 We use p to denote the historically given price level, and dp its immediate change after the occurrence of a shock, leading to a new short-run price level to be denoted by p_{SR} if it is compared with the price level before the shock. Similarly, we use p_{LR} (and also p_o) for the long-run (stationary) price level and will denote the change in the long-run level, leading from p_o^{old} to p_o^{new}, by dp_o.

processes that might lead to equations (11.2) and (11.3), i.e., to world market equilibrium and the absolute form of the PPP.

As the model is formulated it exhibits four statically endogenous variables (p, Y^d, p^*, Y^{d*}) that will adjust immediately to their new equilibrium levels when there is a change in the data of the model. There are, in addition, two dynamically endogenous variables (M, M^*) that will change sluggishly when a shock displaces the statically endogenous variables into new equilibrium positions. We will show below that only one of these laws of motion needs to be treated, since the other one simply represents a complementary law of motion which does not add any new insight. The temporary (or static) equilibrium conditions (11.4) are easily solved for the domestic equilibrium price level, and give rise to the formula

$$p = \frac{\bar{v}M + \bar{s}\bar{v}^*M^*}{\bar{Y} + \bar{Y}^*}, \qquad (p^* = p/\bar{s}), \tag{11.5}$$

for each state of the distribution of money supply in the world. The price level for the foreign country is then simply given by the PPP equilibrium condition $p^* = p/\bar{s}$, possibly implying demand functions at home and abroad that need not be equal to domestic supply and the foreign supply, respectively. As stated earlier, in this situation, the budget equations (11.4) would imply for the exporting country the influx of gold and thus an increase in domestic money supply and, for the importing country, just the opposite.

A further important implication of the model is that the dynamic relationship

$$\dot{M} + \bar{s}\dot{M}^* = 0, \quad \text{i.e.,} \quad M + \bar{s}M^* = M^w = \text{const.},$$

must hold at all times when the economy is not subject to monetary shocks (which at present are of the type of 'helicopter' money[3] solely). Up to exogenous increases or decreases in the money supply at home or abroad, the world quantity of money $M^w = M + \bar{s}M^*$ is thus invariant in the short, the medium and the long-run. Note that the above invariance assertion is implied by equations (11.2), (11.3) and (11.4) by means of the aggregated quantity $p\bar{Y} + \bar{s}p^*\bar{Y}^*$. It can also be represented in the following form

$$NX^n = p(Y - Y^d) = \dot{M} = -\bar{s}\dot{M}^* = -\bar{s}p^*(\bar{Y}^* - Y^{d*}) = -\bar{s}NX^{n*},$$

which states that nominal domestic net exports of goods (net imports of gold) are the negative of nominal foreign net exports of goods (net imports of gold), everything being measured in domestic currency. Note that there is no possibility for two-way trade in the present model, which means that NX^n is either equal to

---

2 With respect to the official settlement accounts (the balance of official reserve transactions) in the two countries we, of course, have for the flow of gold reserves $\bar{p}_G \dot{R} = -\bar{s}\bar{p}_G^* \dot{R}^*$, which is a positive quantity in the case of Euro area exports and a negative one in the case of Euro area imports.

3 Or pure government transfers or taxes.

exports or to imports (the opposite holding for the foreign economy). Note also that the change in gold reserves R of the domestic central bank is given by

$$\bar{s}\dot{R} = \dot{M}$$

if the price of one unit of gold is given by $1\,[\$/\text{Gold}]$, since $\dot{M}^*$ then represents the gold export (or import) of the USA corresponding to their import or export of commodities. The balance of payments is thus very simple in the situation under consideration and is given by one of the two possibilities shown in Table 11.1. There is no international investment and thus also no investment income account, and there is also no other services account. The trade account is thus equal to the current account and is reflected in size in the change of the gold reserves at home and abroad.

The above model, reduced to a single closed economy, is completely trivial, as its graphical representation in Figure 11.1 shows and as is obvious also from its algebraic form, which then consists of only one equation for the determination of the price level that corresponds to the assumed full employment position of the economy. The sole use of Figure 11.1 thus lies in the determination of the equilibrium price level of the considered economy, by obvious quantity theoretic considerations. Since there is no international trade, there are no induced changes in the money supply M which then is completely under the control of the monetary authority. Furthermore, by converting the quantity theory $p = \bar{v}M/\bar{Y}$ to rates of growth, we get:

$$\frac{dp}{p} = \frac{dM}{M} + \frac{d\bar{v}}{\bar{v}} - \frac{d\bar{Y}}{\bar{Y}} = \frac{dM}{M}.$$

There is thus strict neutrality of money, even in the short run, this being the central implication of this simple monetary model of fully flexible wages and prices.

Table 11.1 Trade account and domestic balance of payments representations (R = the gold reserves of the central bank)[2]

Balance of payments (with domestic real exports $X = \bar{Y} - Y^d > 0$):

Uses	Resources
—	$pX(= \bar{s}p^*X)$
$\bar{s}p_G^*\dot{R}(= p_G\dot{R}) > 0$	—

Balance of payments (with domestic real imports $J = Y^d - \bar{Y} > 0$):

Uses	Resources
$\bar{s}p^*J(= pJ)$	—
$p_G\dot{R}(= \bar{s}p_G^*\dot{R}) < 0$	—

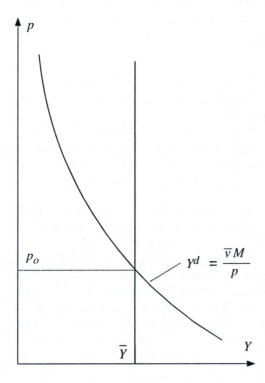

Figure 11.1 The closed economy case.

The question now is how much will change if two interacting economies of this type are considered, as in model (11.1)–(11.4), in place of the trivial situation in the case of the closed economy.

In Figure 11.2 we show, in preparation for the analysis of the following section, the case of two open economies of equal size, where the prices of the foreign economy have been recalculated in terms of the domestic currency. The initial situation is given by long-run autarky in the two countries, which is established at the price level $p_o = \bar{s}p_o^*$.

After the shock in the money supply in the domestic economy shown in Figure 11.2 there is, at given prices, excess demand in the domestic economy and still goods market equilibrium on the autarky level in the foreign one. Equilibrium in the world market for goods now requires that domestic as well as foreign prices increase up to the point where the remaining domestic excess demand becomes equal to the excess supply caused in the foreign economy by the rising dollar price level. This situation is shown by the bold curve and line in Figure 11.2. It represents the immediate shock effect from which the analysis of the following section will start and from which we will derive the medium-run and long-run consequences of the international trade that now takes place.

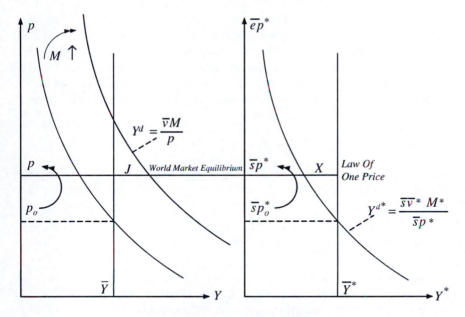

Figure 11.2 Two symmetric open economies and the impact effect of a domestic money supply shock.

11.4 The monetary adjustment process

11.4.1 The law of motion for the domestic money supply

As already shown in the last section, in the two-country case considered, the domestic price level is determined by equation (11.5), viz.

$$p = \frac{\bar{v}M + \bar{s}\bar{v}^*M^*}{\bar{Y} + \bar{Y}^*}$$

through the world commodity market at each moment in time, while the foreign one is given by $p^* = p/\bar{s}$; see again equations (11.1), (11.2) and (11.3).

The change in domestic money supply (in the case where exports or imports are occurring) can therefore be represented as follows:

$$\dot{M} = p(\bar{Y} - Y^d) = p\bar{Y} - \bar{v}M$$

$$= \frac{\bar{Y}}{\bar{Y} + \bar{Y}^*}(\bar{v}M + \bar{s}\bar{v}^*M^*) - \bar{v}M$$

$$= \Theta(\bar{v}M + \bar{v}^*(M^w - M)) - \bar{v}M$$

$$= \Theta\bar{v}^*M^w - [\Theta\bar{v}^* + (1 - \Theta)\bar{v}]M$$

$$= \Theta\bar{v}^*M^w - \phi M, \quad \phi = \Theta\bar{v}^* + (1 - \Theta)\bar{v},$$

where $\Theta = \bar{Y}/(\bar{Y} + \bar{Y}^*)$ represents the share of the domestic economy in world production and ϕ is a weighted (cross-over) average of the expenditure velocities in the two countries. M^w is the world quantity of money as defined in the preceding section. Since Θ, ϕ and M^w are given magnitudes, we thus have derived a single law of motion concerning the domestic money supply, induced through the one-sided trade occurring in this simple world economy and represented by a simple linear inhomogeneous differential equation with constant coefficients. The solution to this equation is given by

$$M(t) = M_0 + (M(0) - M_0)exp(-\phi t),$$

where $M = M(0)$ denotes the initial money supply (at time $t = 0$) and M_0 the point of rest of this dynamic equation (the steady-state value of the money supply). This steady-state value is given by[4]

$$M_0 = \frac{\Theta \bar{v}^* M^w}{(1 - \Theta)\bar{v} + \Theta \bar{v}^*} = \frac{\Theta \bar{v}^*}{\phi} M^w = \lambda M^w, \quad \lambda = \frac{\Theta \bar{v}^*}{\phi}.$$

The corresponding steady-state value for the domestic price level is given by $p_o = \bar{v}M_o/\bar{Y}$. This equation is in fact an equation in initially two unknowns M_o, p_o which needs the input of the stationary value of the above law of motion in order to allow for a uniquely determined solution for the steady-state values of the model. Note that the determination of price level is based on the quantity theory of money, as for the case of a closed economy, since the establishment of $\dot{M} = 0$ implies that the domestic economy has returned to autarky. There is no international trade in the steady-state. A redistribution of money throughout the world has occurred such that demand for goods equals supply in each country. In graphical terms, the above dynamic is represented as shown in Figure 11.3. This figure shows that the steady-state M_0, and thus the monetary adjustment mechanism, is globally asymptotically stable. On the basis of this result, let us describe this monetary adjustment process or price specie[5]-flow mechanism in more detail.

11.4.2 Monetary policy shocks: Short-, medium- and long-run implications

Assume that the economy is initially in a steady-state position M_o, p_o, M_o^*, p_o^*, but is then hit by an *expansionary monetary shock* dM/M (a money transfer) of, for example, 10 percent of the money supply already existing in the economy.[6]

---

4 These equations immediately also imply $\bar{s}M_0^* = (1 - \lambda)M^w$ for the steady-state value of the foreign money supply and $(M^w - M(t))/\bar{s}$ as its law of motion.

5 Or gold, see Krugman and Obstfeld (2003, Ch.19) for details on this phrase. Specie-flows, caused by monetary or other shocks to one of the countries or to both of them, thus redistribute demand for goods throughout the world such that autarky of both countries is established in the course of time.

6 Which is not expansionary in the usual sense of the word, since the economy is operating at the full employment ceiling.

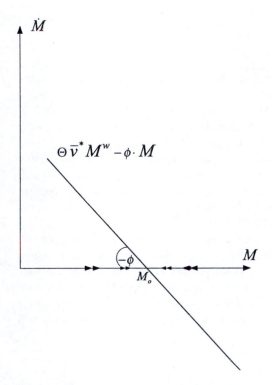

Figure 11.3 The monetary adjustment mechanism.

This shock immediately increases the world quantity of money $M^w = M + \bar{s}M^*$ by an amount

$$\frac{dM^w}{M^w} = \frac{dM}{M + \bar{s}M^*} = \frac{dM}{M} \cdot \frac{M}{M + \bar{s}M^*} < \frac{dM}{M} = 0.1$$

that is determined by the proportion of domestic money M in the world money supply M^w, which gives also the increase of the steady-state value of domestic money, since

$$\frac{dM_0}{M_0} = \frac{d\lambda}{\lambda} + \frac{dM^w}{M^w} = \frac{dM^w}{M^w}.$$

We note that world money supply M^w is only changed once (at the time where the domestic money supply shock occurs) and stays constant thereafter, due to the equality between $\dot{M}$ and $-\bar{s}\dot{M}^*$.

We obtain, from $p = (\bar{v}M + \bar{s}\bar{v}^*M^*)/(\bar{Y} + \bar{Y}^*)$, for the immediate response of the price level to the domestic increase in money supply, the expression

$$0 < \frac{dp}{p} = \frac{\bar{v}M}{\bar{v}M + \bar{s}\bar{v}^*M^*} \frac{dM}{M} < \frac{dM}{M},$$

and thus, by the PPP assumption, also

$$0 < \frac{dp^*}{p^*} = \frac{\bar{v}M}{\bar{v}M + \bar{s}\bar{v}^*M^*} \frac{dM}{M} < \frac{dM}{M}.$$

Both price levels are therefore increased by the domestic monetary shock by the same percentage less than the percentage increase in this money supply. On the side of quantities we find $dY^d/Y^d = dM/M - dp/p > 0$ and $dY^{d*}/Y^{d*} = -dp/p < 0$, which on the one hand states that goods demand is indeed increased in the domestic economy through the assumed money transfer (due to the insufficient increase in the domestic price level). On the other hand, goods demand in the foreign economy is decreased, due to the increased foreign price level which is there confronted with an unchanged money supply. This must be so, since world supply and demand for goods must stay the same by reason of the full employment assumption and the assumption of world goods market equilibrium.

The initial response is therefore an increase in both price levels by a certain fraction of dM/M and an increase in domestic goods demand and a decrease in the foreign one, the former because domestic prices rise less than domestic money creation (in percent) and the latter because foreign prices rise without any increase in the foreign quantity of money. The domestic economy therefore now exhibits excess demand for goods and the foreign economy excess supply of the same real or nominal amount, since

$$\frac{d(Y^d + Y^{d*})}{Y^d + Y^{d*}} = \frac{d(\bar{Y} + \bar{Y}^*)}{\bar{Y} + \bar{Y}^*} = 0.$$

The monetary shock therefore redistributes world commodity demand by inducing foreign exports that match domestic imports. The consequence is that domestic money supply starts falling again (from its now higher level), because of

$$p(\bar{Y} - Y^d) = \dot{M} < 0.$$

Symmetrically, $p^*(\bar{Y}^* - Y^{d*}) = \dot{M}^* > 0, p^* = p/\bar{s}$, and money (gold) thereby gets redistributed in the world economy (to the foreign economy) such that domestic goods demand now is decreasing (from its initially higher level) while foreign demand starts to recover. This adjustment process continues until the new stationary levels

$$M_0^{new} = \lambda M_{new}^w > \lambda M_{old}^w = M_0^{old},$$

$$M_0^{*new} = (1 - \lambda)M_{new}^w/\bar{s} > (1 - \lambda)M_{old}^w/\bar{s} = M_0^{*old},$$

are reached, which reestablishes that goods demand has again become equal to domestic goods supply in each of the two countries considered.

Note that we also have

$$M + dM + \bar{s}M^* = M_0^{new} + \bar{s}M_0^{*new} > M_0^{old} + \bar{s}M_0^{*old}$$

but $M + dM > M_0^{new}$. The initial increase in the domestic money supply therefore gets redistributed throughout the world, such that

$$p_0 \bar{Y} = \bar{v} M_0, \quad p_0^* \bar{Y}^* = \bar{v} M_0^*,$$

is reestablished (via continuously changing p *and* M), to the point where there is again no international trade of commodities.

We have

$$\frac{dM_0}{M_0}(=\frac{dp_0}{p_0}) = \frac{dM_0^*}{M_0^*}(=\frac{dp_0^*}{p_0^*}) = \frac{dM^w}{M^w} = \frac{dM}{M} \cdot \frac{M}{M + \bar{s}M^*} < \frac{dM}{M},$$

i.e., in the long-run both money stocks are changed in the same proportion, which is less than the initial growth rate of the domestic stock of money, since

$$p_0 = \frac{\bar{v} M_0}{\bar{Y}} = \frac{\bar{v} \Theta \bar{v}^*}{\phi \bar{Y}} M^w, \text{ i.e., } \frac{dp_0}{p_0} = \frac{dM^w}{M^w}.$$

This means that all nominal magnitudes are raised by the initial percentage change in world money supply which the increase dM in M implies. Indeed, there holds

$$p_0 = \frac{\bar{v} \bar{v}^*}{(1 - \Theta)\bar{v} + \Theta\bar{v}^*} \cdot \frac{M^w}{Y^w}, \quad Y^w = \bar{Y} + \bar{Y}^*,$$

which is a much more complicated expression than we had in the case of the closed economy which now relates world production and world money by a kind of average $\bar{v}^w = \bar{v}\bar{v}^*/((1 - \Theta)\bar{v} + \Theta\bar{v}^*)$ of the expenditure velocities in the two countries. This is some sort of world quantity theory of money, however with the side condition that long-run percentage effects are less in amount than the initial percentage increase in domestic money supply.

Finally, comparing short-run and long-run price level effects, we get, for the changes in p, and p_0, the relationship

$$\frac{dp}{p} = \frac{\bar{v}M}{\bar{v}M + \bar{s}\bar{v}^*M^*} \frac{dM}{M} \gtreqqless \frac{dp_0}{p_0} = \frac{M}{M + \bar{s}M^*} \frac{dM}{M}$$

if and only if $\bar{v} \gtreqqless \bar{v}^*$. And for the medium-run evolution of the price level

$$p = \frac{\bar{v}M + \bar{s}\bar{v}M^* + \bar{s}(\bar{v}^* - \bar{v})M^*}{\bar{Y} + \bar{Y}^*}$$

$$= \frac{\bar{v}M^w + \bar{s}(\bar{v}^* - \bar{v})M^*}{\bar{Y} + \bar{Y}^*}$$

which implies rising (falling) prices p if $\bar{v}^* > \bar{v}$ ($\bar{v}^* < \bar{v}$) holds, since M^* is rising in the situation considered. In sum, we therefore get for $\bar{v} > \bar{v}^*$ that short-run price level changes overshoot the new long-run price level and that, in the medium run, a falling price level will lead us back to the new long-run level in this case, (the opposite occurs for $\bar{v} < \bar{v}^*$). In the border case, $\bar{v} = \bar{v}^*$, we have that the short-run reaction of the price level is already equal to its long-run level, though of course we still have trade and specie-flows between the short and the long-run until autarky is regained.

We summarize the above discussion of short-, medium- and long-run effects of expansionary domestic money supply changes by means of the graph shown in Figure 11.4. In the situation considered in this figure we have assumed $\bar{v}^* > \bar{v}$, i.e., short-run equilibrium prices p will further increase over the medium run until they reach their final long-run level p_o^{new}. The monetary shock $dM > 0$ at first moves the $\dot{M} = p\bar{Y} - \bar{v}M$ schedule to the left (from the old position shown), giving rise to increased world market prices p. These prices induce (as we have seen) subsequent decreases in M and increases in M^* which move both curves shown to the right now, with the $\dot{M}^*$-schedule shifting "faster" than the $\dot{M}$-schedule (since $\bar{v}^* > \bar{v}$).

All medium-run intersections of the two curves therefore lie above the initially changed p and are monotonically increasing until the new steady-state position $\dot{M} = -s\dot{M}^* = 0$ is reached (p_o^{new}). In this state, world trade in the unique commodity ceases again and each country is then just producing what is domestically demanded. The price specie-flow mechanism therefore redistributes money across countries in such a way that trade decreases until the position of autarky is again reached simultaneously.

We thus have that the country with the higher expenditure velocity, if it exercises the monetary shock, is subject to overshooting price level adjustment. This is plausible, since the demand shock is proportional to this expenditure velocity.

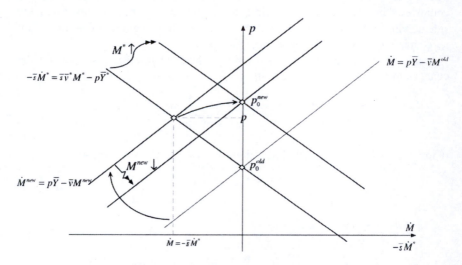

Figure 11.4 The adjustment process towards the new long-run equilibrium following an expansionary shock in domestic money supply.

Note also that, in the case of a small domestic economy, both $\bar{Y}$ and M_o must be small relative to the other country, which implies that short- as well as long-run price reactions to shocks in the domestic money supply will be small.

11.4.3 Currency devaluation: Short-, medium- and long-run effects

Let us close this section with a brief consideration of the effects of a domestic currency devaluation.

In terms of Figure 11.4 one here (by again starting from a steady-state configuration) arrives at the situation shown in Figure 11.5 and, from the equations

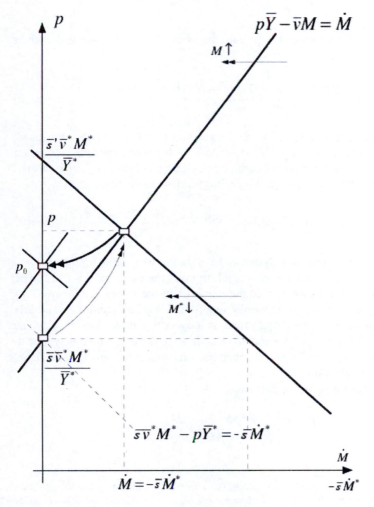

Figure 11.5 Short-run, medium-run and long-run effects of a devaluation (for $\bar{v}^* > \bar{v}$).

of the model, the following comparative static results.[7] The rise in the exchange rate (to the level $\bar{s}' = \bar{s} + d\bar{s}$) in the ultra-short-run decreases foreign prices p^* for given domestic prices $p = \bar{s}'p^*$ and thus first of all increases nominal foreign and therefore world demand above nominal world supply in this assumed situation of a fixed domestic price level p:

$$p(\bar{Y} + \bar{Y}^*) = p\bar{Y} + \bar{s}'p^*\bar{Y}^* < pY^d + \bar{s}'p^*Y^{d*} = \bar{v}M + \bar{s}'\bar{v}^*M^*.$$

The immediate response is an increase in p to a short-run equilibrium level p that restores world market equilibrium, as shown in Figure 11.5. At this price level we have $p(\bar{Y} + \bar{Y}^*) = \bar{s}'p^*(\bar{Y} + \bar{Y}^*) = \bar{v}M + \bar{s}'\bar{v}^*M^*$, which shows that

$$p > p_o^{old}, \quad p^* < p_o^{*old}$$

must hold at the new short-run equilibrium, where M and M^* are still at their initially given levels:

$$p_{SR} = \frac{\bar{v}M + \bar{s}'\bar{v}^*M^*}{\bar{Y} + \bar{Y}^*}, \quad p_{SR}^* = \frac{\bar{v}M/\bar{s}' + \bar{v}^*M^*}{\bar{Y} + \bar{Y}^*}. \tag{11.6}$$

Domestic prices are increased by the devaluation and foreign ones decreased, which also implies that domestic goods demand is decreased and foreign demand increased, leading to the export of commodities and the import of gold as desired by the mercantilistic trade policy. There thus follows, in the real economy:

$$Y^d - \bar{Y} = \frac{\bar{v}M}{p} - \bar{Y} < 0 \quad \text{(imports)}, \quad Y^{d*} - \bar{Y}^* = \frac{\bar{v}^*M^*}{p^*} - \bar{Y}^* > 0 \quad \text{(exports)}.$$

The decrease in domestic goods demand and the increase of the foreign demand are of equal size (due to the assumed equilibrium in the world market), implying a trade flow of this magnitude from the domestic to the foreign economy. This trade flow implies that domestic money supply will increase continuously while the foreign one is shrinking though time as long as this trade flow occurs. The curves shown in Figure 11.5 are therefore shifting to the left, which may lead to further increases of p – or decreases, depending on whether the new long-run level p_o is above p or below it.

As Figure 11.5 suggests, we will have

$$\frac{dp_o}{p_o} < \frac{d\bar{s}}{\bar{s}} \quad \text{(and} \quad \frac{dp}{p} = \frac{d\bar{s}}{\bar{s}} \frac{\bar{s}\bar{v}^*M^*}{\bar{v}M + \bar{s}\bar{v}^*M^*} < \frac{d\bar{s}}{\bar{s}}),$$

---

7 Note that the downward-sloping curve is shifting faster than the upward-sloping one in the situation considered in Figure 11.5. There is thus no overshooting in this figure, which could, however, easily be manipulated to give rise to overshooting situations as well.

Table 11.2 The various effects of a devaluation of the domestic currency.

	Domestic economy	Foreign economy	
Prices	$\frac{dp}{p} = \frac{\bar{s}\bar{v}^*M^*}{\bar{v}M+\bar{s}\bar{v}^*M^*}\frac{d\bar{s}}{\bar{s}} > 0$	$\frac{dp^*}{p^*} = -\frac{\bar{v}M}{\bar{v}M+\bar{s}\bar{v}^*M^*}\frac{d\bar{s}}{\bar{s}} < 0$	Short-run
Quantities	$\frac{dY^d}{Y^d} = -\frac{dp}{p} < 0$	$\frac{dY^{d*}}{Y^{d*}} = -\frac{dp^*}{p^*} > 0$	
Nominal magnitudes	$pY^d = \text{const.}$	$p^*Y^{d*} = \text{const.}$	
$v^* > v$	$p \downarrow$	$p^* \downarrow$	Medium-run evolution
$v^* < v$	$p \uparrow$	$p^* \uparrow$	
Prices and money supply	$\frac{dp_0}{p_0} = \frac{dM_0}{M_0} = (1-\lambda)\frac{d\bar{s}}{\bar{s}}$	$\frac{dp_0^*}{p_0^*} = \frac{dM_0^*}{M_0^*} = -\lambda\frac{d\bar{s}}{\bar{s}}$	Long-run
Quantities	$Y^d = \bar{Y}$	$Y^{d*} = \bar{Y}^*$	
Gold reserves	$R \uparrow$	$R^* \downarrow$	

implying that the devaluation will increase the domestic price level in the long-run *and* decrease the foreign price level p_0^*. This is the only persistent effect of the devaluation which thus cannot secure its initial motive, to stimulate exports (and to import gold) permanently, as a mercantilistic view of the "wealth of nations" might have suggested as desirable.

In sum, the monetary adjustment mechanism that follows a devaluation in the domestic currency redistributes money throughout the world in such a way that both countries become independent of each other in the long run, with inflation in the depreciating country and deflation in the other one. This is quite different from domestic expansionary monetary policy, which leads to inflation in both countries. In the limit case $\Theta = \bar{Y}/(\bar{Y}+\bar{Y}^*) \approx 0$ of a small open (domestic) economy we finally get $dp_0/p_0 = d\bar{s}/\bar{s} = dM_0/M_0$ and $dp_0^*/p_0^* \approx 0$; i.e., the small open economy will then produce inflation to the extent that it devaluates its currency with no long-run effect on the foreign economy. Table 11.2 summarizes the results we have obtained in this section.

11.4.4 Summing up and outlook

Extending the case of a closed economy and its extremely simple theory of the price level, defined in Figure 11.1, to the case of two interacting countries producing at first only one and the same commodity, gives rise to interesting basic results which are much less obvious than in the trivial case for the closed economy from which we started. Inflation in our two-country world is a purely monetary phenomenon and comes about solely through continuous increases in the money supplies of the two countries. Nevertheless, the classical theory of world inflation, the foundations of which have been laid in this chapter, is not straightforward with respect to medium-run and long-run results concerning the distribution of inflationary impulses in the world, the possibility of under- or overshooting of short-run price level behavior and the role of the parameters characterizing the two countries in their short-, medium- and long-run behavior. There is one thing, however, that applies uniformly to this classical theory of price level dynamics, namely the global asymptotic stability of the long-run positions of the two economies.

However, this still simple classical theory of international trade, and the monetary adjustment mechanism it gives rise to, is based on various assumptions that are of a very restrictive nature. In future extensions, or reconsideration of the model $(11.1)-(11.4)$, these assumptions must be replaced by more general or more appropriate hypotheses on the structure of the world economy, in particular when modern open economies like the Euro area (as interacting with the US economy) are points of reference for the two-country model considered. Such extensions would involve relaxing:

1. The oversimplified theory of aggregate demand: $Y^d = \bar{v}M/p$, which does not distinguish between the various sources of aggregate demand and does not discuss their various determinants such as income and the rate of interest.
2. The extreme form of the PPP: $\bar{s}p = p^*$, which assumes the law of one price to hold at each moment in time for each traded commodity.
3. The flexprice assumptions concerning both wage and price formation and the resulting assumption of full employment, generally based on the neoclassical theory of employment, of the real wage and of aggregate supply.
4. The one-commodity framework so far considered.
5. The assumption of fixed exchange rates $\bar{s}$, based on the rules of the gold standard.

Relaxing (or, better, modifying) assumption 1 will be the subject of Chapter 12, while a more refined treatment of assumption 2 as a long-run proposition was presented in Chapter 4. The extension of assumption 4 to the case of a two-commodity world will be the subject of the next section, while flexible exchange rates will be considered in the closing section of this chapter; i.e., these two topics will be considered from the classical perspective in the remainder of the present chapter. Moreover, the classical theory of unemployment – based on sluggish wage adjustments in the two countries–is presented in Section 11.7. This section shows that unemployment can arise in the classical world simply due to nominal wage rigidities, without deficient Keynesian goods demand considerations, a type of unemployment that is then more quickly removed (in a globally convergent fashion) the faster wages adjust in the light of the labor market imbalances existing in the two countries.

Such assumptions of rigid money wages will give rise to upward-sloping AS curves as usual and allow us to treat the case of unemployment in both countries in isolation as well as in their interaction in the usual way. The policy experiments we have discussed in this and the preceding section will then give rise to price as well as world production fluctuations and thus also to changing unemployment situations. In particular, one can then show that a monetary expansion in the domestic economy will improve the level of employment in both countries in the shorter run, while a domestic devaluation improves the position of the domestic economy and worsens the situation with respect to employment in the foreign economy. Hamada and Sakurai (1978) have already considered such a world by also adding money–wage dynamics and inflationary expectations (by assuming augmented Phillips curves of the conventional type) and have considered in more detail the adjustment processes of such a classical, in their case two-commodity, world without specialization.

11.5 The two-commodity extension

In order to allow for persistent international trade it is necessary to allow at least two different commodities to be produced and traded in the world economy. We shall consider in the following the simplest case of this type, i.e., complete specialization, with the domestic economy producing good G, say corn, and the foreign economy producing commodity G^*, for example wine, as in the Ricardian approaches to the pure theory of international trade, both producing again at their full employment levels. Both commodities may be substitutes to some extent and give rise to a new concept in our model $(11.1) - (11.4)$, the real exchange rate σ measured by $\bar{s}p^*/p$, which has the dimension

$$[\text{€}/\$] \cdot [\$/G^*]/[\text{€}/G] = [G/G^*].$$

This magnitude need no longer be equal to one (since G and G^* are not perfect substitutes) and it determines how many units of commodity G the domestic economy has to supply in exchange for one unit of the foreign commodity G^*.

The theory of goods demand can now be extended to this two-commodity case by writing:

$$pC_1 = \delta(\sigma)\bar{v}M, \quad \bar{s}p^*C_2 = (1 - \delta(\sigma))\bar{v}M, \quad \delta(\sigma) \in (0, 1),$$

$$pC_1^*/\bar{s} = \delta^*(\sigma)\bar{v}^*M^*, \quad p^*C_2^* = (1 - \delta^*(\sigma))\bar{v}^*M^*, \quad \delta^*(\sigma) \in (0, 1).$$

These equations suggest that the home country produces $\bar{Y} = \bar{Y}_1$ $(p = p_1)$ of commodity 1, which is demanded at home in amount C_1 and abroad in amount C_1^*. Similarly, $\bar{Y}^* = \bar{Y}_2^*$ $(p^* = p_2)$ denotes the foreign production, which is confronted with commodity demand C_2 from country 1 (the home country, with no asterisks added) and commodity demand C_2^* for commodity 2 from the foreign country (country 2).

Total nominal demand in each country is, as before, given by $\bar{v}M$ and $\bar{v}^*M^*$, respectively, but is now split in the proportions δ, $1 - \delta$ and δ^*, $1 - \delta^*$ into demand for commodity 1 (produced by country 1) and demand for commodity 2 (produced by country 2), respectively. Note that all nominal demands are expressed in terms of the domestic currency in the above equations. Note also that it is reasonable to assume $\delta'(\sigma) \geq 0$ and also $\delta^{*'}(\sigma) \geq 0$ as reaction to changes in the real exchange rate of the split of demand between commodity 1 and commodity 2 in both countries.

In this full generality, the model (11.1) – (11.4), extended in the above way, is already fairly difficult to analyze. It exhibits eight equations, four behavioral equations, two equilibrium conditions and the two laws of motion of the money supplies, which are sufficient to determine the six static variables C_1, C_2, C_1^*, C_2^*, p, p^* and two dynamic variables M, M^*. The complexity of the analysis, due to the increase in the number of commodities, will be offset in the following by the simplification $\bar{v} = \bar{v}^*$, i.e., by a uniform expenditure velocity across both countries. Furthermore, we assume δ and δ^* to be constant and thus independent of the real exchange rate σ, which means that we assume G and G^* to be complements rather than substitutes. We thus now neglect effects arising from the different behavior of aggregate demand and concentrate on basic aspects of persistent international trade. The new model therefore now reads:

$$p\bar{Y} = \delta\bar{v}M + \bar{s}\delta^*\bar{v}M^*, \tag{11.7}$$

$$\bar{s}p^*\bar{Y}^* = (1-\delta)\bar{v}M + \bar{s}(1-\delta^*)\bar{v}M^*, \tag{11.8}$$

$$\dot{M} = \bar{s}\delta^*\bar{v}M^* - (1-\delta)\bar{v}M, \tag{11.9}$$

$$\dot{M}^* = (1-\delta)\bar{v}M/\bar{s} - \delta^*\bar{v}M^*. \tag{11.10}$$

We now have two goods–market equilibrium conditions, (11.7) and (11.8), in place of only one, equation (11.2), and have already made use of the demand functions in their explicit form in place of equation (11.1). The PPP statement (11.3) is no longer valid and the change in the money supply $\dot{M}, \dot{M}^*$ at home and abroad is now driven by nominal net exports

$$NX^n = \bar{s}\delta^*\bar{v}M^* - (1-\delta)\bar{v}M,$$

$$NX^{n*} = (1-\delta)\bar{v}M/\bar{s} - \delta^*\bar{v}M^*,$$

via the gold flows in the world economy, which are converted into domestic currency in both countries by their central banks. In the steady-state we have $NX^n = NX^{n*} = 0$ and thus

$$\bar{s}\delta^*\bar{v}M^* = (1-\delta)\bar{v}M,$$

$$(1-\delta)\bar{v}M = \bar{s}\delta^*\bar{v}M^*.$$

These equations imply that $p\bar{Y} = \bar{v}M, p^*\bar{Y}^* = \bar{v}M^*$ holds at the steady-state; i.e., total nominal demand then equals total nominal supply in both economies, despite the fact that part of both supplies is exported due to the persistence of trade in the steady-state.

Note that $NX^n + \bar{s}NX^{n*} = \dot{M} + \bar{s}\dot{M}^* = 0$ must again hold true at all points in time so that either equation (11.9) or equation (11.10) can be considered as redundant in the following analysis. Note also that, in general, both (11.7) and (11.8) contain as statically endogenous variables the two price levels p, p^* of the two economies and thus would then constitute a nonlinear system of two equations in the two unknowns p, p^*. Following that our assumption $\delta, \delta^* = \text{const.}$, however, the equations (11.7), (11.8) can indeed be solved separately and give rise to what is shown in Figure 11.6. They can also be aggregated and then lead to (for $\bar{v} = \bar{v}^*$):

$$\bar{v}(M + \bar{s}M^*) = \bar{v}M^w = p\bar{Y} + \bar{s}p^*\bar{Y}^*, \tag{11.11}$$

thereby giving rise to the additional curve (labelled WW) shown in Figure 11.6 (for given M, M^*).

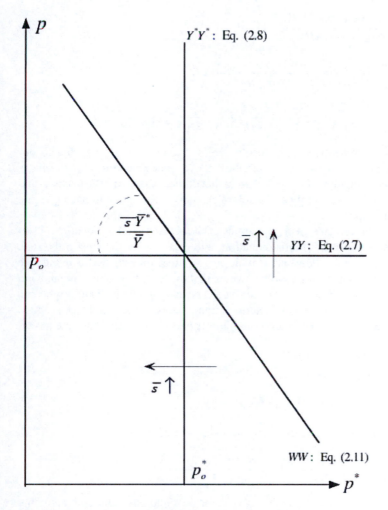

Figure 11.6 Equilibrium curves in the two-commodity case.

This is a special case of the situation shown in Dornbusch (1980, Ch.7), where δ, δ^* both depend on σ and thus lead to an upward-sloping YY curve in particular. Note that any two of the above three equations, and the curves in Figure 11.6, are sufficient to determine the price levels p and p^* that clear the two commodity markets considered. Note however that equation (11.11) is now obtained in a different way, since $\bar{v} = \bar{v}^*$ holds and since Θ is no longer defined and applicable in the present context

Note here that all three curves shown in Figure 11.6 will shift when a change in the exchange rate $\bar{s}$ occurs, which, in the case of a depreciation of the domestic currency, increases domestic prices and decreases foreign ones, with an ambiguous effect on the real exchange rate σ. In terms of rates of growth we get, for the short-run reactions of prices and the real exchange rate, the expressions:

$$\frac{dp}{p} = \frac{\bar{s}\delta^*\bar{v}M^*}{\delta\bar{v}M + \bar{s}\delta^*\bar{v}M^*}\frac{d\bar{s}}{\bar{s}} > 0, \tag{11.12}$$

$$\frac{dp^*}{p^*} = -\frac{(1-\delta)\bar{v}M}{(1-\delta)\bar{v}M + \bar{s}(1-\delta^*)\bar{v}M^*}\frac{d\bar{s}}{\bar{s}} < 0, \tag{11.13}$$

$$\frac{d\sigma}{\sigma} = [\frac{\bar{s}(1-\delta^*)\bar{v}M^*}{(1-\delta)\bar{v}M + \bar{s}(1-\delta^*)\bar{v}M^*} - \frac{\bar{s}\delta^*\bar{v}M^*}{\delta\bar{v}M + \bar{s}\delta^*\bar{v}M^*}]\frac{d\bar{s}}{\bar{s}} \gtreqless 0, \tag{11.14}$$

and thus the comparative static results claimed above. Note that, due to our assumptions on consumption behavior, the real exchange rate does not really play a role in the determination of trade flows and that domestic net exports increase (and foreign ones decrease) simply as a result of changes in foreign nominal aggregate demand and supply.

Let us now investigate the $\dot{M}$ dynamics of the revised model. Equation (11.9) again defines a linear differential equation with constant coefficients in the state variable M, as we shall show below, which is then to be investigated as in the case of a single-commodity world. Note however that this equation is now obtained in a different way, since $\bar{v} = \bar{v}^*$ holds and since Θ is no longer defined and applicable in the present context, where the determination of the domestic and foreign price levels is no longer related by purchasing power parity considerations. We have

$$\dot{M} = \bar{v}(\bar{s}\delta^*M^* - (1-\delta)M)$$

$$= \bar{v}(\delta M + \bar{s}\delta^*M^* - M)$$

$$= p\bar{Y} - \bar{v}M = p(M)\bar{Y} - \bar{v}M = H(M),$$

where the domestic price level is determined by the equation

$$p = p(M) = \frac{\delta\bar{v}M + \bar{s}\delta^*\bar{v}M^*}{\bar{Y}} = \frac{\delta^*\bar{v}M^w + (\delta - \delta^*)\bar{v}M}{\bar{Y}},$$

with $M^w = $ const. up to monetary shocks or devaluations. The corresponding equation for the foreign price level is given by substituting $1 - \delta$, $\bar{Y}^*$ in place of

δ, $\bar{Y}$ respectively, which shows that relative prices will be a fairly encompassing fraction composed of the parameters of the model.

Since $\delta^* \bar{v} M^w + (\delta - \delta^*) \bar{v} M > 0$ holds, the above relations imply for $p(M)$ the property

$$0 \geqq \frac{p'(M)M}{p} = \frac{(\delta - \delta^*)\bar{v}M}{p\bar{Y}}$$

$$= \frac{(\delta - \delta^*)\bar{v}M}{\delta^* \bar{v} M^w + (\delta - \delta^*)\bar{v}M} < 1,$$

i.e., the relative (short-run) price change dp/p caused by the change dM/M is less than this change in the money supply. Inserting, as already indicated above, the function $p(M)$ into the $\dot{M}$ equation gives

$$\dot{M} = p(M)\bar{Y} - \bar{v}M = H(M),$$

with

$$H'(M) = p'(M)\bar{Y} - \bar{v} = (\delta - \delta^*)\bar{v} - \bar{v}$$

$$= [(\delta - \delta^*) - 1]\bar{v} < 0,$$

$$M(0) = \delta^* \bar{v} M^w,$$

since both δ and δ^* are less than one. The dynamics of money supply in country 1 is therefore again given by a linear inhomogeneous differential equation of order one (with constant coefficients).

The steady-state M_0 of the linear dynamics $\dot{H} = H(M)$ is thus globally asymptotically stable, as in the model (11.1)–(11.4) of the preceding section. This steady-state value M_0 is now, however, given by

$$M_0 = \frac{\delta^*}{\delta^* + (1 - \delta)} M^w = \lambda M^w, \quad M^w = M + \bar{s}M^*,$$

since $\bar{v}(1 - \delta)M_0 = \bar{s}\bar{v}\delta^* M_0^*$ ($M^w = M + \bar{s}M^* = M_0 + \bar{s}M_0^*$). Note that the parameter λ differs significantly from the one of the preceding section, which for $\bar{v} = \bar{v}^*$ was given by Θ.

Let us now consider again the effects of a devaluation $d\bar{s} > 0$ (implying $Y^d - \bar{Y} < 0$) on p_0, M_0 (and p_0^*, M_0^*) and now also on $\sigma_0 = \bar{s}p_0^*/p_0$. As in the preceding section, we have (with respect to the initial values of money supply at home and abroad):

$$\frac{dp_0}{p_0} = \frac{dM_0}{M_0} = \frac{dM^w}{M^w} = \frac{d\bar{s}M_o^*}{M^w} = \frac{\bar{s}M_o^*}{M^w}\frac{d\bar{s}}{\bar{s}}$$

$$= (1 - \lambda)\frac{d\bar{s}}{\bar{s}}, \tag{11.15}$$

and, as stated above, we now have

$$\lambda = \frac{\delta^*}{\delta^* + (1 - \delta)}$$

in place of $\lambda = \Theta = \bar{Y}/(\bar{Y} + \bar{Y}^*)$. Similarly, because $\bar{s}M_0^* = (1 - \lambda)M^w$, we have

$$\frac{dp_0^*}{p_0^*} = \frac{dM_0^*}{M_0^*} = \frac{dM^w}{M^w} - \frac{d\bar{s}}{\bar{s}} = (1 - \lambda)\frac{d\bar{s}}{\bar{s}} - \frac{d\bar{s}}{\bar{s}} = -\lambda\frac{d\bar{s}}{\bar{s}}. \qquad (11.16)$$

We have already shown in equation (11.12) that

$$\frac{dp}{p} = \frac{\bar{s}\delta^*\bar{v}M_o^*}{\delta\bar{v}M_o + \bar{s}\delta^*\bar{v}M_o^*}\frac{d\bar{s}}{\bar{s}} = \frac{\bar{s}M_o^*}{(\delta/\delta^*)M_o + \bar{s}M_o^*}\frac{d\bar{s}}{\bar{s}} = \frac{(1 - \lambda)}{(\delta/\delta^*)\lambda + (1 - \lambda)}\frac{d\bar{s}}{\bar{s}}, \qquad (11.17)$$

where the last equality follows from use of $M_0 = \lambda M^w$ and $\bar{s}M_0^* = (1 - \lambda)M^w$. Equations (11.15) and (11.17) imply that

$$\frac{dp_0}{p_0} \gtrless \frac{dp}{p}, \quad \text{if and only if } \delta \gtrless \delta^*,$$

holds for the comparison of the long-run and short-run price effects arising from the devaluation. The short-run price effect overshoots the long-run position if and only if $\delta^* > \delta$, which is intuitively understandable from the domestic goods market equilibrium condition (11.7).

The results of the preceding section are thus confirmed in a two-commodity world, but with a different factor λ. Furthermore, unlike (11.1)–(11.4), there is now an endogenously determined real exchange rate $\sigma_0 = \bar{s}p_0^*/p_0 \neq 1$ for which (by use of 11.16 and 11.17) the relative form of the PPP theorem holds.

$$\frac{d\sigma_0}{\sigma_0} = \frac{d\bar{s}}{\bar{s}} - \lambda\frac{d\bar{s}}{\bar{s}} - (1 - \lambda)\frac{d\bar{s}}{\bar{s}} = 0$$

The long-run real exchange rate σ_0 does not depend on the size of the nominal exchange rate $\bar{s}$. This last result implies that

$$\frac{d\bar{s}}{\bar{s}} = \frac{dp_0}{p_0} - \frac{dp_0^*}{p_0^*},$$

the PPP theorem in its so-called relative form, which comes about here as an implication of the model and not as an assumption as was the case in the preceding section. Note that the relative form of the PPP theorem can hold even though there is no perfect basis for a comparison of the two goods that are produced in the world economy.

Finally, we now have persistent trade (trade in the long-run) of size

$$(1-\delta)\bar{Y} = \bar{v}(1-\delta)M_0/p_0 : \text{ imports in terms of } G,$$

$$\delta^* \bar{Y}^* = \bar{s}\bar{v}\delta^* M_0^*/(\bar{s}p_0^*) : \text{ exports in terms of } G^*,$$

with $(1-\delta)\bar{v}M_0 = \bar{s}\delta^*\bar{v}M_0^*$. Exports

$$\frac{\bar{s}\delta^*\bar{v}M_0^*}{p_0} = \frac{\bar{s}p_0^*}{p_0}\delta^*\bar{Y}^*,$$

measured in terms of commodity 1 and imports measured in terms of commodity 2,

$$\frac{\bar{v}(1-\delta)M_0/\bar{s}}{p_0^*} = \frac{p_0}{p_0^*\bar{s}}(1-\delta)\bar{Y},$$

are therefore independent of the size of the nominal exchange rate $\bar{s}$ in the long-run. Note that international trade is balanced in the steady-state, whereas there are adjusting monetary flows if the steady-state is disturbed by devaluations or monetary shocks. The model, as it is, thus supports laissez-faire and non-intervening monetary or exchange rate policies. A mercantilistic exchange rate policy can increase the amount of gold accumulated domestically by stimulating the temporary import of gold and additional export of commodities through currency devaluation, but it has no long-run effects on the real part of the economy.

The general case $\delta'(\sigma) \geq 0$, $\delta^{*'}(\sigma) \geq 0$ is treated in Dornbusch (1980, Ch.7.III) and leads to similar conclusions to the ones we have just derived for the case $\delta, \delta^* = $ const. The even more general case where both countries produce both commodities is, however, more demanding as it also requires a model of how labor is allocated to the two sectors now present in both economies. In such a situation, the law of one price may again be assumed to hold, now for the two commodities under consideration:

$$p_1 = \bar{s}p_1^*, \qquad p_2 = \bar{s}p_2^*.$$

We will not go here into a further investigation of such extensions of the classical model considered in this chapter, but will instead consider in the next section analytical simplifications of our two-country approach and its results as they are discussed in great detail in Copeland (1989, Ch. 5).

We note finally that in the case of a monetary union the model considered in this section reduces to

$$p_1\bar{Y}_1 = \delta\bar{v}M, \tag{11.18}$$

$$p_2\bar{Y}_2 = (1-\delta)\bar{v}M, \tag{11.19}$$

which determines both prices p_1, p_2 trivially via the quantity theory of money, applied now to a two-commodity world. However, we will have trade in this two-region world with only one currency that will redistribute the one given currency in a way similar to the case of the two-currency world considered beforehand.

11.6 The perfectly open economy: Basic and advanced formulations

11.6.1 The classical two-country monetary model: Flexible exchange rates

It may be asked with respect to the two preceding sections why the exchange rate is kept fixed in the simple world modeled in these sections. It can be argued and assumed that the exchange rate s should be and is perfectly flexible, which – as we shall show now – makes the monetary adjustment mechanism obsolete and guarantees that our long-run results will even hold in the short-run.

In the two-country case, the short-run would then be described by (in case of a single commodity produced throughout the world):

$$\bar{v}\bar{M} = p\bar{Y}, \quad \text{i.e.} \quad p = \bar{v}\bar{M}/\bar{Y},$$

$$\bar{v}^*\bar{M}^* = p^*\bar{Y}^*, \quad \text{i.e.} \quad p^* = \bar{v}^*\bar{M}^*/\bar{Y}^*,$$

$$p = sp^*, \quad \text{i.e.} \quad s = p/p^* = \frac{\bar{M}/\bar{M}^*}{\bar{v}^*\bar{Y}^*/\bar{v}\bar{Y}}.$$

The price levels would then be determined as in the case of a closed economy and the determination of the exchange rate would simply be given through the ratio of these two predetermined national price levels. However, there would be no trade in such a world economy and thus no role for the exchange rate s, the existence of which is therefore hard to justify (except in some very hypothetical ultra-short-run adjustment processes, for example).

A two-commodity world is therefore needed to give substance to such an approach, which is discussed in Copeland (1989) in great detail and will only be briefly summarized in this section. In the case of two commodities and a perfectly flexible exchange rate the model of the preceding section reads ($\bar{v} = \bar{v}^*$ again for reasons of simplicity):[8]

$$p\bar{Y} = \delta\bar{v}\bar{M} + s\delta^*\bar{v}\bar{M}^*,$$

$$sp^*\bar{Y}^* = (1 - \delta)\bar{v}\bar{M} + s(1 - \delta^*)\bar{v}\bar{M}^*,$$

$$\bar{v}(1 - \delta)\bar{M} = s\bar{v}\delta^*\bar{M}^*,$$

which gives

$$s = \frac{(1 - \delta)\bar{M}}{\delta^*\bar{M}^*}, \qquad (\hat{s} = \hat{\bar{M}} - \hat{\bar{M}}^*).$$

---

8 The case $\bar{v} \neq \bar{v}^*$ is, however, now much easier to treat than in the case of the fixed exchange rates that are the focus of this chapter (as well as the further extension in which both countries produce both commodities, where therefore the allocation of resources within each country also has to be considered).

We thus derive

$$p = p_o = \bar{v}(\delta \bar{M} + s \delta^* \bar{M}^*)/\bar{Y},$$

$$p^* = p_o^* = \bar{v}((1 - \delta)\bar{M}/s + (1 - \delta^*)\bar{M}^*)/\bar{Y}^*,$$

which alters the direction of "causation" compared to a one-commodity world.

In the model with a fixed exchange rate $\bar{s}$ we would instead have (in the long run):

$$p_0 \bar{Y} = \delta \bar{v} M_0 + \bar{s} \delta^* \bar{v} M_0^*,$$

$$\bar{s} p_0^* \bar{Y}^* = (1 - \delta)\bar{v} M_0 + \bar{s}(1 - \delta^*)\bar{v} M_0^*,$$

$$(1 - \delta)\bar{v} M_0 = \bar{s} \delta^* \bar{v} M_0^*,$$

$$M^w = M_0 + \bar{s} M_0^* = M(0) + \bar{s} M^*(0) = \text{ given },$$

which, as was shown, leads us to the four equations (to be solved in this order):

$$M_0 = \lambda M^w, \quad \lambda = \frac{\delta^*}{\delta^* + (1 - \delta)},$$

$$M_0^* = (1 - \lambda) M^w / \bar{s},$$

$$p_0 = \bar{v}[\delta M_0 + \bar{s} \delta^* M_0^*]/\bar{Y},$$

$$p_0^* = \bar{v}[(1 - \delta) M_0 / \bar{s} + (1 - \delta^*) M_0^*]/\bar{Y}^*,$$

concerning the determination of long-run money supplies and the price levels. The simpler case of a one-commodity world is, in the latter case (in the long run), given by:

$$\bar{v} M_0 = p_0 \bar{Y},$$

$$\bar{v}^* M_0^* = p_0^* \bar{Y}^*,$$

$$p_0 = \bar{s}_0 p_o^*,$$

$$M^w = M_0 + \bar{s} M_0^* = \text{ const.},$$

which leads to:

$$M_0 = \lambda M^w, \quad \lambda = \frac{\Theta \bar{v}^*}{(1 - \Theta)\bar{v} + \Theta \bar{v}^*}, \quad \Theta = \frac{\bar{Y}}{\bar{Y} + \bar{Y}^*},$$

$$M_0^* = (1 - \lambda) M^w / \bar{s},$$

$$p_0 = \bar{v} M_0 / \bar{Y},$$

$$p_0^* = \bar{v}^* M_0^* / \bar{Y}^*.$$

Such algebraic determinations of short-run (flexible exchange rate) and long-run (fixed exchange rate) positions of interacting monetary economies received renewed interest in the discussion of exchange rate theories of the early 1970s and are investigated at length in Copeland (1989, Ch. 5). The results obtained can be generalized to differing expenditure velocities $\bar{v} \neq \bar{v}^*$, propensities to consume δ and δ^* that depend on the real exchange rate σ, two-commodity production in both countries and nominal wage rigidity and upward-sloping AS curves. We add finally that the small open economy case can be obtained from the above by taking $\bar{p}_0^*$ as given and dropping all other equations that refer to the foreign economy.

The above pure monetary model received a brief revival at the beginning of the 1970s. However, it suffers severely from its identification of short-run and long-run aspects, which is too radical to be really convincing. This is not so in the case of fixed exchange rates, where the modeling of the short run is, however, not convincing due to its oversimplified treatment of aggregate demand and the too perfect assumptions on price and wage level flexibility.

11.6.2 Perfectly open economies: An advanced formulation

There exists an advanced formulation of this model type which integrates all ideal or perfectness assumptions within the classical framework from a modern perspective, and which may therefore be considered the modern counterpart of the classical approach of the present chapter. We follow Rødseth (2000, Ch. 5) and present a brief summary of this ideal model type, here at first for a small open economy, and its various extensions investigated in detail in Rødseth (2000). The model type obtained can be usefully contrasted with the Mundell–Fleming–Tobin approach to small open economies, which will be introduced in Chapter 12.

The model of the present chapter collects in an ideal fashion the assumptions of a perfect working of a small open economy in a classical environment, including now internationally traded interest-bearing financial assets. This model type, of an extremely or perfectly open classical economy, will be only briefly reviewed here with respect to its structural equations and their fundamental implications. We will in particular find that the introduction of interest-bearing assets and their international trade will give rise to the possibility that the specie-flow mechanism no longer works in the stable fashion so far proved to be the case in the previous sections. In addition, destabilizing elements are not only working through cumulative or accelerating capital account adjustments, but are also present in the evolution of government debt and government budget constraint. The general model to be considered below allows for the possibility that twin deficits (or surpluses or mixed combinations) show explosive or implosive tendencies to be counteracted by active policy intervention.

For simplicity, in the following we consider again a one-commodity world, but now add domestic as well as foreign bonds, B, F, to the situation so far considered. We furthermore assume that domestic bonds are perfect substitutes for foreign bonds, but do not consider the inflow and outflow of bonds explicitly, since the model of this chapter does not consider stock constraints for asset demand functions explicitly. Instead, the (balanced) exchange of domestic against foreign bonds is operating in the background of our presentation of the balance of payments and thus is explicitly present only in the uncovered interest rate parity condition to be considered below. We will make these "hidden" capital flows in the capital account visible in Chapter 15, when imperfect substitutes are allowed for by way of a Tobinian portfolio approach and the flow considerations then added to it.

Let us first consider the *flow budget equations* of the three sectors of Rødseth's extremely open economy: households, the government and the central bank. (Firms only produce output Y by means of labor N, and they do not invest and transfer all profit income to the household sector. They need not be considered from the perspective of budget equations.) These equations read, in the order of the named sectors:

$$p(Y - T) + iB_p + s\bar{i}^* F_p \equiv pC + \dot{M} + \dot{B}_p + s\dot{F}_p \qquad (11.20)$$

$$pT + s\bar{i}^* F_c + \dot{B} \equiv p\bar{G} + iB_p \qquad (11.21)$$

$$\dot{M} \equiv \dot{B}_c \qquad (11.22)$$

Equation (11.20) states that wage, profit and interest incomes (domestic and foreign) of private households after taxes, are spent on consumption and additions to money, domestic and foreign fixprice bond holdings (with prices set equal to one in the respective currency). We here denote by i and $\bar{i}^*$ the domestic and foreign rates of interest and by B_p and F_p the current stocks of domestic and foreign bonds held by the private sector. In (11.21) we state that government finances its expenditures and its interest rate payments to households through taxes, new issues of bonds and also the domestic and foreign interest proceeds of the central bank (which are transferred to the government sector). The latter uses open market operations concerning domestic bonds[9] in order to change continuously the quantity of money in the form of time derivatives (as shown). We furthermore allow for discontinuous policy changes in the financial stocks held in the domestic economy, through open market or foreign exchange market transactions of the central bank (CB) of the following form:

Central bank stock policy constraint:

$$\text{CB-PC:} -M + B_c + sF_c : \quad -dM + dB_c + sdF_c = 0$$

We therefore distinguish between rule-determined continuous changes in the money supply and isolated policy interventions in the financial markets of the economy.

In the above flow identities we assume consistency (equality) between the flow supplies $\dot{M}$ and $\dot{B} - \dot{B}_c$ provided by the government and the central

---

9 Of course, the Central Bank could also buy foreign bonds from domestic residents.

bank and the flow demands $\dot{M}$ and $\dot{B}_p$ of households. Furthermore, the central bank has some holdings of government bonds B_c, due to past open market operations (which concern both stock and flow constraints). However, since it transfers (by assumption) interest on these bonds back into the government sector, we need not consider these bond holdings explicitly in the above budget equations (11.20)–(11.22). Open market operations thus can also change stocks instantaneously and thus have to be considered as wealth reallocations of households with respect to their wealth constraint later on. Note that the resulting budget equation of the central bank is formulated in a way that allows for consistent steady-state calculations in the case of steady-state inflation.

The consistency assumption made with respect to equations (11.20)–(11.22) implies, for the aggregate of these three equations, that

$$p(Y - C - \bar{G}) + s\bar{i}^*(F_p + F_c) \equiv s\dot{F}_p, \tag{11.23}$$

that is, the balance of payments is always balanced in the assumed situation without need for central bank intervention and is independent of the exchange rate and money supply regime the economy is subject to.

We assume with respect to this identity that the considered economy produces a single commodity that it can either export (if $Y - C - \bar{G} > 0$ holds) or import ($Y - C - \bar{G} < 0$) and that there are no restrictions on the world market for doing so. This is some sort of Say's law, since there is then no demand constraint (or supply constraint) operating on the domestic goods market. Interpreting equation (11.23) in this way implies that the balance of payments of the domestic economy is always balanced, since the left-hand side represents the current account and the right-hand side (the negative of) the capital account of this economy. This also holds if the capital flows underlying the assumed perfect asset substitutability are made explicit. In fact, in the present chapter we have to go one step further by assuming that only infinitesimal capital flows are needed to ensure the UIP condition of the model considered below, so that the explicitly treated law of motion for the evolution of the foreign bond holdings of domestic residents is determined solely by the current account. This is a significant disadvantage of a model type that does not treat financial asset demands explicitly (as is finally the case in the Mundell–Fleming–Tobin model of our Chapter 15).

We define the real wealth of the economy by the following aggregate:

$$W = W_p + W_g + W_c = \frac{M + B_p + sF_p}{p} + \frac{-M - B_p}{p} + \frac{sF_c}{p}, \quad \text{i.e.:} \tag{11.24}$$

$$W = \frac{s(F_p + F_c)}{p} = \frac{sF}{p}, \tag{11.25}$$

which shows that the real wealth of all sectors in the economy (private households, government and the central bank) adds up exactly to the real value of the foreign bonds held in the domestic economy (the amount of government bonds B_c held by the central bank has already been canceled in these equations [10]).

In terms of growth rates equation (11.25) implies that

$$\hat{W} = \hat{s} + \hat{F} - \hat{p} \quad or \quad \dot{W} = \hat{s}W + s\dot{F}/p - \hat{p}W.$$

Using equation (11.23) thus yields the following balance of payments dynamics in real terms:

$$\dot{W} = (\hat{s} - \hat{p})W + [p(Y - C - \bar{G}) + s\bar{i}^*F]/p = (\bar{i}^* + \hat{s} - \hat{p})W + Y - C - \bar{G}$$
$$(11.26)$$

resulting from what was shown for the balance of payments in nominal (domestic) terms. The change in real domestic wealth, given by the real value of foreign bonds held in the domestic economy, therefore reflects the capital account in real terms if the real rate of return $\bar{r}^* = \bar{i}^* - \bar{\pi}^* = \bar{i}^* + \hat{s} - \hat{p}$ (see the assumptions of the model presented below) is applied in the interest income balance to calculate real interest flows (as shown above). Equation (11.26) thus reflects the balance of payments (11.23) in real (domestic) terms. In fact, it provides the first equation, indeed the core equation, of this model of an extremely open economy as formulated in Rødseth (2000, ch. 5), if a certain taxation policy is implemented. [11] The remaining equations of the model are (with $\bar{N}$ the full employment level on the labor market):

$$w = pf'(\bar{N}), \tag{11.27}$$

$$Y = f(\bar{N}) \tag{11.28}$$

$$p = sp^*, \quad \hat{p}^* = \bar{\pi}^* = \text{const.}, \tag{11.29}$$

$$M/p = m^d(Y, i), \quad m^d_Y > 0, \quad m^d_i < 0, \tag{11.30}$$

$$i = \bar{i}^* + \hat{s}, \tag{11.31}$$

$$C = C(Y_p, W_p, \bar{r}^*), \quad C_1 > 0, C_2 > 0, C_3 < 0 \tag{11.32}$$

$$Y_p = Y + \bar{r}^*W - \bar{G}, \quad W = W_p + \bar{W}^a_g \tag{11.33}$$

$$W_p = (M + B_p + sF_p)/p \tag{11.34}$$

$$\bar{W}^a_g = W_g + W_c = -(M + B)/p + sF_c/p = \text{const}, \tag{11.35}$$

10 Since government bonds held by central bank are irrelevant for the trajectories followed by the economy we completely ignore them from now on and thus use now, for notational simplicity the letter B in place of B_p. Note also that we always have $\dot{F} = \dot{F}_p$ by assumption.

11 The assumption that $W^a_g = $ const. holds is justified by a corresponding rule for the collection of government taxes; see Rødseth (2000, 117).

$$W = W_p + \bar{W}_g^a = sF/p \qquad (11.36)$$

$$\bar{r}^* = \bar{i}^* - \bar{\pi}^* = \bar{i}^* + \hat{s} - \hat{p} = i - \hat{p} = r = \text{const} \qquad (11.37)$$

We consider an economy that is small compared to the world market and that can satisfy all excess demand $C + \bar{G} - Y$ via imports and can export all excess supply $Y - C - \bar{G}$ in the opposite case. The world market nominal rate of interest $\bar{i}^*$ is assumed to be of a given magnitude in this case, as is the world inflation rate $\bar{\pi}^*$. We assume in the above model a standard LM curve of the Keynesian variety, the absolute form of the PPP condition, the UIP condition as characterization of international capital mobility, labor market equilibrium and, on this basis, the usual description of full employment output. We supplement this model type by a Keynesian consumption function, the Hicksian definition of disposable income and the definitions of private and government wealth.

Note that the second part of the last one of the above equations follows directly from equation (11.29) when transformed to rates of growth. Assumption (11.35) is made only for the time being (and later on discarded in Rødseth (2000, Ch. 5) as well as in this chapter). It is based on the implicit assumption of a certain taxation policy, as we shall show below, and it allows us to substitute W_p in equation (11.32) by $W - \bar{W}_g^a$ and thus reduce this term to one that governs the dynamics of the capital account in the balance of payments (minus a constant). Finally, equations (11.33) for (Hicksian) disposable income of households are also a consequence of assuming $W_g^a = (sF_c - M - B)/p$ as a constant, see again below. Making use of the government budget restriction and the budget restriction of the central bank ($W_c = sF_c/p$), we first of all get:

$$\dot{W}_g^a = \frac{s\dot{F}_c + \dot{s}F_c - \dot{M} - \dot{B}}{p} - \hat{p}\frac{sF_c - M - B}{p}$$

$$= \hat{s}W_c + \bar{i}^* W_c + T - \bar{G} - iB/p - \hat{p}W_c + \hat{p}\left(\frac{M}{p} + \frac{B}{p}\right).$$

This expression can be fixed to zero if the tax variable T is adjusted accordingly. On the basis of this assumption we get, for the corresponding taxation rule:

$$(i - \hat{p})\frac{B}{p} - \hat{p}\frac{M}{p} = T + (\bar{i}^* + \hat{s} - \hat{p})W_c - \bar{G}.$$

The Hicksian concept of household disposable income, i.e., the income which, when consumed, would keep households' real wealth on a constant level, is defined by:

$$Y_p = Y - T + (\bar{i}_* + \hat{s} - \hat{p})\frac{sF_p}{p} + (i - \hat{p})\frac{B}{p} - \hat{p}\frac{M}{p}.$$

This then implies for real disposable income the expression:

$$Y_p = Y - T + \bar{r}^*\frac{sF_p}{p} + T + \bar{r}^* W_c - \bar{G}$$

$$= Y - \bar{G} + \bar{r}^* \frac{sF}{p} = Y - \bar{G} + \bar{r}^* W.$$

The disposable income Y_p, like W_p, therefore depends only on $W = W_p + \bar{W}_g^a = sF/p$ as far as wealth effects are concerned (with a given real rate of return $\bar{r}^*$ in addition).

Let us now investigate the model (11.30)–(11.37) for an exogenously given money supply (with $\bar{\pi}^* = 0, p^* =$ const. in addition) and (as was assumed above) with endogenous taxation that keeps the value of W_g^a constant. Let us also ignore wealth effects in the consumption function for the moment. The model implies for the exchange rate s the autonomous law of motion:

$$\hat{s} = i - \bar{i}^* = \frac{\ln k + \ln Y + \ln s + \ln p^* - \ln M}{\alpha}$$

if the money market equilibrium is based on a Cagan money demand function $M^d/p = kY \exp(\alpha(\bar{i}^* - i))$.

On the basis of the rational expectations solution for price level and exchange rate adjustments, and in the case of an unanticipated shock in the money supply $(dM = -dB)$, we must then have $\hat{p} = \hat{s} = 0$, and thus know that i is given by $\bar{i}^*$. The LM curve (11.30) then determines the perfectly flexible after-shock price level p, whilst the PPP assumption (11.29) determines the after-shock level of the exchange rate s. If perfectly flexible nominal variables are thus adjusting, as is assumed to be the case since Sargent and Wallace's (1973) introduction of the jump variable technique, we thus get in the case of an unanticipated monetary shock a strict neutrality result for the economy considered, as far as the price level, the nominal exchange rate and the nominal rate of interest are concerned. (However, this is no longer true if real wealth enters the consumption function of households.) In addition, the value of $W = sF/p$ remains unchanged in such a situation; i.e., the economy just remains in the steady-state position in such an event.

In the case of $C_2 > 0$, however, we get a jump in the wealth variables W_p, W_g^a and thus a change on the right-hand side of eq. (11.38); i.e., there will be real effects of unanticipated jumps in money supply in general. This also holds true in the case of anticipated shocks in money supply where the economy jumps to an exchange rate level, such that the old unstable dynamics drives it to the new steady state position in the time that passes by until the jump in money supply occurs. According to the PPP condition, the same applies to the movement of the price level p, which is here to be considered as being non-predetermined as well (an assumption that is not easily reconciled with empirical facts on price level changes). This suggests that we should only use predetermined variables in this model type and formulate a monetary policy rule (an anchor) that makes the unstable dynamics of the private sector stable (see the section on policy rules later in this chapter).

In the case of real shocks,[12] for example an unanticipated government expenditure shock, the stock magnitudes F, W, the nominal and real holdings of foreign bonds in the considered economy, start moving continuously in time after the shock, which therefore always sets in motion the dynamics we have derived above for the real variable W:

$$\dot{W} = \bar{r}^* W + Y - C(Y + \bar{r}^* W - \bar{G}, W - \bar{W}_g^a, \bar{r}^*) - \bar{G} \qquad (11.38)$$

This real balance of payments dynamics represents a single autonomous differential equation for the evolution of the domestic holdings of foreign bonds (or domestic indebtedness to foreigners) $W = sF/p$, since $\bar{r}^* = r, Y = Y(\bar{N}), \bar{G}$ are given magnitudes. The whole model (11.30)–(11.37) therefore can then be reduced to and analyzed by an autonomous law of motion for the real value of foreign bonds held in the domestic economy, as is implied by the equilibrated balance of payments of the economy.

Yet, the perfect world assumed by equations (11.26)–(11.37) with all prices flexible, the permanent fulfillment of the PPP and the UIP, and with myopic perfect foresight in the working of the latter, then faces one significant problem, namely the possibility of an explosive evolution of the real value of foreign assets held domestically *if and only if*

$$(1 - C_{Y_p}(\cdot))\bar{i}^* - C_{W_p}(\cdot) > 0$$

holds true, i.e. when wealth effects in consumption are sufficiently weak. The steady-state level of W behind this stability condition is given by[13]

$$\bar{r}^* W_0 = C(Y - \bar{G} + \bar{r}^* W_0, W_0 - \bar{W}_g^a, \bar{r}^*) + \bar{G} - Y,$$

and is then surrounded by centrifugal forces which drive W towards $+\infty$ for $W(0) > W_0$ or to $-\infty$ for $W(0) < W_0$. The specie-flow mechanism of the classical open economy model can thus now be unstable in a global way, if interest rate effects are present in the model being considered, here due to a Keynesian consumption function. However this unstable balance of payments adjustment process with respect to the accumulation of foreign bonds or dollar-denominated debt in the domestic economy undermines the application of the jump variable technique. Then, in the considered model, there does not exist a bounded trajectory onto which the jump variables p, s can jump and that brings the economy back to its steady-state after having been thrown out of this position by a real shock. This case is therefore excluded or blocked out from consideration in Rødseth (2000, p. 121).

---

12 where $W(0)$ remains constant due to the PPP condition.
13 We assume here again that there is a single – positive or negative – solution W_0 to this equation (describing a creditor or debtor position for the private sector of the economy considered).

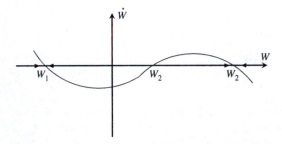

Figure 11.7 Multiple stationary points for the balance of payments adjustment process.

It is however possible to further investigate such an unstable adjustment process within the balance of payments if it is assumed that wealth effects become dominant far off the steady state, to the extent that not only the slope of the right-hand side of eq. (11.38) with respect to W becomes negative, but that also two further equilibria of the $\dot{W}$ dynamics are created, as shown in Figure 11.7.

Figure 11.7 shows two stable and, in between, one unstable stationary point for balance of payments adjustment. Flukes apart, the economy will therefore converge over time to either W_1 or W_3. Let us assume the latter situation; i.e., the economy approaches a high creditor position with respect to the rest of the world (due to its consumption behavior along this path). Assume now that government increases its expenditures in such a situation as long as there is a surplus in the current account of the economy. The $\dot{W}$ curve shown in Figure 11.7 is thereby shifted in a downward direction, accompanied by reductions in the actual as well as the stationary level of real foreign wealth held domestically. This process may reach a point where the upper equilibrium W_3 gets lost (right after the situation where $W_2 = W_3$ is established). There is then only one stable equilibrium left, W_1, to which the economy will therefore converge over time. Along this path the creditor position of the domestic economy will sooner or later change to a debtor position (in the situation shown in Figure 11.7). This process is accompanied by current account deficits until the new stationary point is reached where the current account has again become balanced. Appropriate nonlinearities in consumption behavior may therefore be used to explain long-lasting regime switches away from a strong economy towards a regime of increasing foreign debt of the domestic economy (and vice versa). This is a Kaldor (1940)-type cycle mechanism that may be used to explain long phase fluctuations in the foreign debt position of the domestic economy and in government expenditure.

Of course, the government can also pursue a growth rate rule for the money supply, $\hat{M} = $ const., or one for the exchange rate, $\hat{s} = $ const., where in the latter case the money supply must be given by $M = pm^d(Y, \bar{i}^* + \hat{s})$. Alternatively, the government may attempt an interest rate peg $i = \bar{i}$ (or a Taylor-type interest rate policy rule), then implying $\hat{s} = \bar{i} - \bar{i}^*$ for the determination of the exchange rate.

In the case $\hat{M} = \hat{p}^* = \bar{\pi}^* = $ const., we get as a law of motion for the exchange rate s (in addition to the one for W):

$$\hat{s} = i - \bar{i}^* = i(Y, M/p) - \bar{i}^* = i(Y, M/(sp^*)) - i^*$$

and thus

$$\hat{p} = \bar{\pi}^* + i(Y, M/p) - \bar{i}^*$$

where Y and $M/p*$ are given magnitudes. This gives an explosive law of motion for the nominal exchange rate, since the employed reduced-form LM-curve $i(Y, M/p)$ depends (as usual) negatively on real balances M/p and thus positively on s. The standard way out of this explosive behavior of exchange rate dynamics is again given by the so-called jump variable technique. In the case of an unanticipated shock to Y, M or $\bar{\pi}^*$, this technique would imply that s would always react such as to place the economy in the steady-state position

$$i(Y, \frac{M}{p^*} \frac{1}{s_0}) = \bar{i}^*$$

in order to overcome the centrifugal forces outside the steady-state. Exchange rate dynamics is therefore only possible in the case of anticipated shocks.[14] With respect to price level dynamics, or rather the dynamics of the domestic inflation rate, this implies similarly that p jumps in line with M to the level that again guarantees the equality $\bar{i}^* = i(Y, M/p)$. This in turn implies that the equality $\hat{p} = \bar{\pi}^*$ again determines the future evolution of the domestic price level.

The central result of our above considerations is, however, that the steady-state of the extreme monetary approach to open economies that are small relative to the world market may be unstable (if wealth effects in consumption are so small that they do not turn exports into imports as wealth is accumulated in terms of foreign bonds). This result has been shown here in a perfect flexprice environment with a Keynesian LM curve and Keynesian consumption behavior, but with no IS restriction on the economy ($I \equiv 0$ still). Rødseth (2000, Ch. 5) goes beyond this analysis by also considering imperfect capital mobility with fixed or with flexible exchange rates, government deficit and changing $\bar{W}_g^a$ and nominal (real) wage rigidity, by way of an expectations-augmented money–wage Phillips curve (with myopic perfect foresight), again with fixed or flexible exchange rates. In the present chapter we will now dispense with the assumption made on the tax rate policy and assume instead that $T = \bar{T}$ is determined exogenously. This implies that aggregate government wealth $\bar{W}_g^a$ is changing and will lead us to a situation where this magnitude is interacting dynamically with total wealth W and also with the price level p.

---

14 That is if $C_2 = 0$ is assumed again for reasons of simplicity. Note that W is given by $s(F_P + F_c)/$ $p = F/p^*$ and is thus not subject to jumps (if s does jump) unless there is a jump in p^*. Instability in the W dynamics thus cannot be remedied by the jump variable technique in this model of an extremely open economy.

11.6.3 Integrating the dynamics of the government budget constraint

We start again from the budget equations of the three relevant sectors: households, the government and the central bank. With respect to firms, we again assume that all of their income is transferred to the household sector. They do not invest in the present framework and thus are only organizing the production of the full employment output Y by means of the given labor supply $\bar{N}$. Note that the CB holds both types of government bonds and may change these holdings by way of an open market operation of foreign exchange market policies, but that this does not influence the budget equations shown, since all interest income from these bond holdings is transferred to the government sector which therefore only has to pay interest on the bonds B held by the private sector.

The relevant flow budget restrictions of the small open economy are (when government and the central bank are considered in integrated form):

$$p(Y - T) + iB + s\bar{i}^*F_p = pC + \dot{M} + \dot{B} + s\dot{F}_p$$

$$pT + s\bar{i}^*F_c + \dot{B} + \dot{M} = p\bar{G} + iB.$$

Their implications for the evolution of domestic and foreign bonds held by the domestic economy (describing – if positive – the public debt of the government and of the foreign economy) are:

$$\dot{B} = iB + p(\bar{G} - \bar{T}) - s\bar{i}^*F_c - \dot{M}s\dot{F}$$

$$s\dot{F} = p(Y - C - \bar{G}) + s\bar{i}^*F, \quad F = F_p + F_c.$$

Considering the same situation from the viewpoint of savings, we can write:

$$pS_p = p(Y - \bar{T}) + iB + s\bar{i}^*F_p - pC = \dot{M} + \dot{B} + s\dot{F}_p$$

$$pS_g = p\bar{T} + s\bar{i}^*F_c - p\bar{G} - iB = -\dot{B} - \dot{M},$$

which, as expected, gives for total savings pS :

$$pS = pY - pC - pG + s\bar{i}^*(F_p + F_c) = s\dot{F}_p = s\dot{F}.$$

This is simply a reformulation of the fact that the balance of payments must be balanced in the assumed situation without any further adjustment processes (solely based on the assumption that the issue of new money $\dot{M}$ and new government bonds $\dot{B}$ is accepted by the household sector, which is made implicitly in the above formulation of the two budget equations of our economy).

In analogy with the Hicksian definition of private disposable income we now define and rearrange this concept for the aggregate government sector (including the foreign interest income of the central bank). On this basis we can show in particular that the aggregate real wealth of this sector W_g^a is in its time rate of change – as in the case of the private sector – determined by deducting the consumption of this sector from its real disposable income. This then also provides us with a law of motion for real aggregate wealth of the government sector, besides the one we have already determined for the total wealth of the economy. These two laws describe the evolution of surpluses or deficits in the government sector and the evolution of current account surpluses or deficits, and thus, in particular, allow the joint treatment of the issue of twin deficits in an open economy with a government sector, but not yet extended towards capital accumulation and economic growth.

The following calculations concern the sources of income and consider as disposable in this regard that part of accounting income that, when consumed, just preserves the current level of wealth of the sector considered (here the government sector).

$$Y_g^a := T - \frac{iB}{p} + \frac{\bar{s}i^* F_c}{p} + \hat{p}\frac{M+B}{p} + (\hat{s}-\hat{p})\frac{sF_c}{p}$$

$$= T - (i-\hat{p})\frac{M+B}{p} + i\frac{M}{p} + (\bar{i}^* + \hat{s} - \hat{p})\frac{sF_c}{p}$$

$$= T + i\frac{M}{p} - (i - \bar{i}^* - \hat{s})\frac{M+B}{p} + (\bar{i}^* + \hat{s} - \hat{p})\frac{-(M+B)+sF_c}{p}$$

$$= T + i\frac{M}{p} + \xi\frac{M+B}{p} + \bar{r}^*\frac{-(M+B)+sF_c}{p}, \quad \xi = \bar{i}^* + \hat{s} - i, \quad \text{with}$$

$$W_g^a := \frac{-(M+B)+sF_c}{p} = -\frac{(M+B)}{p} + \frac{sF_c}{p} = W_g + W_c, \quad \text{i.e.,}$$

$$\dot{W}_g^a = \frac{-(\dot{M}+\dot{B})+\dot{s}F_c}{p} - \frac{\dot{p}}{p}\frac{-(M+B)+sF_c}{p}$$

$$= \frac{-(pG + iB - pT - \bar{i}^* sF_c) + \hat{s}sF_c}{p} - \hat{p}\frac{-(M+B)+sF_c}{p}$$

$$= T - G - i\frac{B}{p} + \hat{p}\frac{M+B}{p} + (\bar{i}^* + \hat{s} - \hat{p})\frac{sF_c}{p}$$

which finally gives

$$W_g^a = Y_g^a - G$$

$$= \bar{r}^* W_g^a + \xi\frac{M+B}{p} + i\frac{M}{p} + T - G.$$

In the perfect open economy of this chapter (where $\xi = 0$ and $\hat{s} = \hat{p} - \bar{\pi}^*$ holds) this then gives, for a Cagan-type real money demand function $m^d = kY\exp(\alpha(\bar{i}^* - i))$, i.e., for the reduced-form LM curve $i = \bar{i}^* + (\ln p + \ln Y + \ln k - \ln M)/\alpha$ as law of motion for aggregate government wealth or better debt:

$$\dot{W}_g^a = \bar{r}^* W_g^a + im^d(Y, i) + T - G, \quad i.e.,$$

$$\dot{W}_g^a = \bar{r}^* W_g^a + \left(\bar{i}^* + \frac{\ln p + \ln Y + \ln k - \ln M}{\alpha}\right)\frac{M}{p} + T - G.$$

This shows that the evolution of this debt is governed (in a destabilizing way) by its level, but that it is also dependent on the price level and its evolution, and on the budget surplus.

Since this debt position of the government is now no longer constant, we next repeat the equations for the evolution of total wealth $W = sF/p$ of the economy for this case and then consider again private disposable income Y_p and private wealth W_p in their interaction with the evolution of aggregate government debt.

$$W := W_p + W_g + W_c = \frac{sF}{p}, \quad F = F_p + F_c$$

$$\hat{W} = \hat{s} + \hat{F} - \hat{p}$$

$$\dot{W} = \hat{s}W + \frac{s\dot{F}}{p} - \hat{p}W$$

$$= \hat{s}W + \frac{p(Y - C - G) + s\bar{i}^* F}{p} - \hat{p}W$$

$$= (\hat{s} - \hat{p})W + \bar{i}^* \frac{sF}{p} + Y - C - G$$

$$= (\bar{i}^* + \hat{s} - \hat{p})W + Y - C(Y_p, W_p, \bar{r}^*) - G$$

$$\dot{W} = \bar{r}^* W + Y - C(Y_p, W - W_g^a, \bar{r}^*) - G$$

where we have, for the definition of private wealth and disposable income:

$$W_p = \frac{M + B + sF_p}{p} = W - W_g^a$$

$$Y_p = Y - T + (\bar{i}^* + \hat{s} - \hat{p})\frac{sF_p}{p} + (i - \hat{p})\frac{B}{p} - \hat{p}\frac{M}{p}$$

$$= Y - T + (\bar{i}^* + \hat{s} - \hat{p})W_p - (\bar{i}^* + \hat{s} - \hat{p})\frac{M + B}{p} + (i - \hat{p})\frac{B}{p} - \hat{p}\frac{M}{p}$$

$$= Y - T + \bar{r}^* W_p - \xi \frac{M + B}{p} i \frac{M}{p}$$

$$= Y - T + \bar{r}^*(W - W_g^a) - \xi \frac{M + B}{p} - i\frac{M}{p},$$

with $\xi = 0$ in the case of a perfect open economy.

From the results on the disposable income of households and the government we finally also get:

$$Y_p = Y - Y_g^a + \bar{r}^* W \quad \text{or} \quad Y_p + Y_g^a = Y + \bar{r}^* W$$

as the relationship between total disposable income, domestic product and real interest on domestically held foreign bonds.

In the case where the price level p, money supply M, government expenditure G and taxes T are all held constant, we get from the above that the evolution of government debt W_g^a is always explosive or implosive around its steady-state level

$$W_{go}^a = \frac{\bar{T} - \bar{G} - \left(\bar{i}^* + \frac{\ln p_0 + \ln Y + \ln k - \ln \bar{M}}{\alpha}\right) \frac{\bar{M}}{p_0}}{\bar{r}^*}.$$

There is thus the compelling demand for an active fiscal policy, and maybe an accompanying monetary policy (not necessarily supported by price-level adjustments according to a standard expectations-augmented Phillips curve), in order to stabilize the government budget. Without such a policy both the budget of the government and the behavior of the capital account will be unstable, since the government deficit feeds back into the capital account via the consumption behavior of households (but is in the present situation completely independent from the rest of the economy). Using the steady-state value of W_g^a in the law of motion for W then implies the same stability characterization for the adjustment of domestic foreign bond holdings as before. It is therefore now, in addition, driven by an unstable behavior of government debt, but otherwise behaves as it did in the case of constant government debt. We thus have to integrate an active fiscal policy rule, price level adjustments and an active monetary policy rule in order to get less one-sided results on the evolution of twin deficits and the stability of the evolution of government debt and the balance of payments adjustment process.

11.7 Twin deficits and PPP/UIP-driven price dynamics

We have assumed at the end of the preceding section that the price level is a given constant in order to study the evolution of deficits or surpluses in the GBR and in the BOP in isolation. Yet prices (and the exchange rate) are moving if the price level is shocked out of its steady-state position p_0, where the nominal rate of interest implied by the LM curve is not equal to the given world interest rate. In such a case we have that the resulting interest rate differential determines the growth rate of the nominal exchange rate (via the UIP condition) and consequently (via the PPP) also the growth rate of domestic prices. Changes in the domestic price level feed back into the laws of motion for W as well as W_g^a (but not vice versa) and thus make the dynamics of these two stock variables more complicated. In this section we study these integrated dynamics of the private sector in their still fairly recursive format before we analyze, in Section 11.8, the question of what fiscal and monetary policy can do in view of this extreme formulation of the dynamics of the private sector.

11.7.1 Price-level dynamics in the perfectly open economy

The full set of three laws of motion for the private sector in a perfectly open economy considered in this chapter, with foreign inflation set equal to zero and still with fixed policy parameters $(\bar{\pi}^* = 0, \bar{M}, \bar{T}, \bar{G})$, now coupled with the law of motion for the price level p, reads, on the basis of the Cagan money demand function of this section:

1. $\hat{p} = [\hat{s} =] \quad \dfrac{\ln p + \ln Y + \ln k - \ln M}{\alpha}$,

2. $\dot{W}_g^a = \bar{r}^* W_g^a + i\dfrac{\bar{M}}{p} + \bar{T} - \bar{G}$,

3. $\dot{W} = \bar{r}^* W + Y - C(Y + \bar{r}^* W - \bar{r}^* W_g^a - i\dfrac{M}{p} - \bar{T}, W - W_g^a, \bar{r}^*) - \bar{G}$,

based on the definitions:

$$W = \frac{sF}{p}, \quad i = \bar{i}^* + \frac{\ln p + \ln Y + \ln k - \ln M}{\alpha}, \quad W_g^a = \frac{-(M+B) + sF_c}{p}.$$

The steady-state of this dynamical system is determined by:

$$p_o = \frac{\bar{M}}{Y} \qquad [\ln p_o = \ln \bar{M} - \ln Y]$$

$$\left(i\frac{\bar{M}}{p}\right)_o = \bar{i}^* \frac{\bar{M}}{p_o} = \bar{i}^* Y$$

$$(W_g^a)_o = \frac{\bar{i}^* Y \exp(-\alpha \bar{i}^*) + \bar{T} - \bar{G}}{\bar{r}^*}$$

$$(Y_p)_o = Y - \bar{G} + \bar{r}^* W_o$$

$$(W_p)_o = W_o - (W_g^a)_o$$

$$W_o = \frac{Y - C((Y_p)_o, (W_p)_o, \bar{r}^*) - \bar{G}}{\bar{r}^*}$$

Note that the equations for private disposable income and wealth have to be inserted into the last equation in order to get a single equation in the only unknown W_o that must then be solved for this term.

The three laws of motion shown above – describing the dynamics of the private sector of our extremely open economy as a result of all the ideal assumptions made on its performance – can be structured hierarchically in the following way:

$$\hat{p} = \frac{\ln p + \ln Y + \ln k - \ln \bar{M}}{\alpha} = \hat{p}(p) \qquad\qquad (11.39)$$

$$\dot{W}_g^a = \bar{r}^* W_g^a + \left(\bar{i}^* + \frac{\ln p + \ln Y + \ln k - \ln \bar{M}}{\alpha} \right) \frac{\bar{M}}{p} + \bar{T} - \bar{G} = \dot{W}_g^a(p, W_g^a)$$

(11.40)

$$\dot{W} = \bar{r}^* W + Y - C(Y - \bar{r}^* W_g^a - \left(\bar{i}^* + \frac{\ln p + \ln Y + \ln k - \ln \bar{M}}{\alpha} \right) \frac{\bar{M}}{p}$$

$$- \bar{T} + \bar{r}^* W, W - W_g^a, \bar{r}^*)x - \bar{G} = \dot{W}(p, W_g^a, W).$$

(11.41)

Inserting the steady-state values p_o, $(W_g^a)_o$ into the law of motion for $\dot{W}$ would lead us back to the situation considered in the preceding section, since both p and W_g^a do not depend on the evolution of total domestic wealth, as a result of the hierarchy in the laws of motion of the 3D dynamics that characterize the private sector of this extremely open economy. But now the price level p and the representation of aggregate government debt W_g^a are moving in general and must be investigated for their stability properties.

The law of motion for the price level is of the type already considered in Sargent and Wallace (1973) in their formulation of the jump- variable technique of the rational expectations approach. It could in principle be treated as these authors did in their paper, but we would here be confronted with the problem of how the real magnitudes W_g^a, W have to be treated in view of such jumps in the price level. In view of the many deficiencies of the JVT discussed in former chapters, we do not follow such an approach here, but investigate the 3D dynamics from the perspective that all three of its three variables are predetermined and that an implied instability of the system must be overcome by conscious policy actions. We therefore avoid imposing appropriate jumps on a set of variables that are assumed to be non-predetermined, a situation that is hard to believe to govern the general level of prices in an applicable macromodel.

11.7.2 Stability analysis

The Jacobian of the given 3D dynamics considered at the steady-state is characterized by

$$J = \begin{pmatrix} + & 0 & 0 \\ \mp & + & 0 \\ \mp & + & \mp \end{pmatrix},$$

where the sign of J_{21}, J_{31}, is given by the slope of the function

$$f(p) = \bar{i}^* + \frac{\ln p + \ln Y + \ln k - \ln M}{\alpha} \cdot \frac{\bar{M}}{p}$$

with respect to p. The sign of J_{33} is determined in the same way as was discussed in the original one-dimensional setting of this chapter. Reformulating $f(p)$ as a function of the rate of interest i, we get

$$\tilde{f}(i) = f(p(i)) = im^d(Y, i)$$

and thus

$$\tilde{f}'(i) = im_i^d + m^d = m^d\left(\frac{m_i^d}{m^d} + 1\right)$$

i.e., the sign of this function is determined by the interest rate elasticity of the money demand function:

$$\tilde{f}'(i) \gtreqless 0 \Longleftrightarrow f'(p) \gtreqless 0 \Longleftrightarrow \frac{dm^d/m^d}{di/i} \lesseqgtr -1.$$

Since the law of motion for the price level p is independent of the two other state variables of the model, we of course immediately get the instability of the steady-state of the considered dynamics, since there is a positive eigenvalue corresponding to the first row of the Jacobian J that is equal to J_{11}. Depending on this accelerating price level dynamics, we then have again the subdynamics of the government debt and the foreign debt of the domestic economy which in itself obeys the same laws of motion as we already considered for a given price level p. We thus need even more impacts from active fiscal as well as active monetary policy rules in order to get a bounded evolution of the private sector and the government budget of the perfect classical macroeconomy, under.

11.7.3 A digression: The dynamics in nominal terms

In a world where the steady-state is inflation-free ($M = \bar{M}, \bar{\pi}^* = 0$), we can discuss the dynamics (11.39)–(11.41) also in nominal terms and get in this case for its three laws of motion:

$$\hat{p} = i - \bar{i}^* = \frac{\ln p + \ln Y + \ln k - \ln M}{\alpha} = \hat{p}(p)$$

$$\dot{B} = iB + p(\bar{G} - \bar{T}) - \bar{i}^* p \bar{W}_c = \left(\bar{i}^* + \frac{\ln p + \ln Y + \ln k - \ln M}{\alpha}\right) B + p(\bar{G} - \bar{T})$$

$$-\bar{i}^* p \bar{W}_c = \dot{B}(p, B)$$

$$\dot{W} = \bar{i}^* W + Y - \bar{G} - C\left(Y + \bar{i}^*(W - \bar{W}_c) + \bar{i}^* \frac{\bar{M} + B}{p}\right)$$

$$-\left(\bar{i}^* + \frac{\ln p + \ln Y + \ln k - \ln M}{\alpha}\right)\frac{\bar{M}}{p} - \bar{T}, W - \bar{W}_c + \frac{\bar{M} + B}{p}, \bar{i}^*\right)$$

or indeed, translated back into nominal terms:

$$\dot{F} = \bar{i}^* F + \bar{p}^*(Y - \bar{G}) - \bar{p}^* C \left(Y + \bar{i}^* \left(\frac{F}{\bar{p}^*} - \bar{W_c} \right) + \bar{i}^* \frac{\bar{M} + B}{p} \right.$$

$$\left. - \left(\bar{i}(\bar{i}^* + \frac{\ln p + \ln Y + \ln k - \ln M}{\alpha} \right) \frac{\bar{M}}{p} - \bar{T}, \frac{F}{\bar{p}^*} - \bar{W_c} + \frac{\bar{M} + B}{p}, \bar{i}^* \right)$$

where we have made use again of $W = sF/p = F/\bar{p}^*, \bar{W_c} = sF_c/p = F_c/\bar{p}^* =$ const. The stability analysis for system (11.39) – (11.41) of course also applies to this special case, now with respect to the dynamics variables p, B, F. For an application of the jump variable technique we then find that only p can be a candidate; i.e., we must construct for its application a case where there is exactly one unstable root of the Jacobian J of the dynamics at the steady-state. This can be the case if and only if the determinant of J (the product of the three eigenvalues of the matrix J) is positive, in which case these three eigenvalues must be real and positive. Thus there is no case within these dynamics where the jump variable can find application. From the perspective of current New Keynesian theory one may call such a situation an indeterminate one which should be blocked out from consideration. From this perspective, the task would then be to find policy rules that bring determinacy to the system, i.e., that establish the existence of one unstable root for the thereby extended dynamics. The very existence of these rules would bring jump-variable stability to the system, so that, for example, an unanticipated jump in the money supply would cause the price level to jump in the same proportion without any reaction of the other variables of the system (with the exception of the nominal exchange rate that also has to jump by the percentage change in the money supply). In this situation, therefore, latent rules cause the economy to return to its real steady-state immediately by purely nominal adjustments and thus provide stability without any need for policy intervention.

Our approach to such a situation, however, is to assume that, if the system is unstable, it behaves in a predetermined way according to the above three laws of motion, and is thus unstable (which is necessarily monotonic, as we have just seen) with increasing or decreasing price levels and increasing imbalances in the budget of the government and in the current and the capital account. We could then, for example, assume policy reactions (fiscal or monetary) when these imbalances pass certain thresholds, which are aimed at reducing single or twin deficits in the budget and the current account by tailored policy reactions. To consider such behavior in more detail is the objective of the following section.

11.8 Active fiscal and monetary policy in the perfect open economy

In this section we formulate some monetary and fiscal policy rules that – at least from a partial perspective – are capable of taming the cumulative forces in the price level, the budget deficit and the current account deficit (however, only separately).

We later combine these policy rules in a general set-up of the model in order to allow future research to analyze (at least numerically) their potential for stabilizing the extremely open economy either locally around the steady-state or – if policy is still inactive – globally if the economy has departed significantly from its steady-state position. This section leads to the conclusion that policy anchors in the form of given policy targets and policy rules for realizing these targets are needed for a proper working of the ideal economy considered in this chapter.

11.8.1 Stabilizing monetary policy

In view of the special type of price dynamics characterizing our perfectly open economy (where the law of motion of the price level is a direct consequence of the UIP and the PPP condition), we now assume as monetary policy the rule shown below which, in its formulation, implies an independent 2D dynamics for the state variables p, M.

$$\hat{p} = \frac{\ln p + \ln Y + \ln k - \ln M}{\alpha}$$

$$\hat{M} = \beta_{m_1}(M_o/M - 1) + \beta_{m_2}(p/p_o - 1),$$

with steady state $p_o = 1 = M_o$ by way of an appropriate choice of the measurement of output Y. Because of the isolated nature of price level changes this dynamical system is an autonomous one that can be studied in isolation from the remaining laws of motion of the considered economy.

The Jacobian of these dynamics at the steady-state is given by:

$$J = \begin{pmatrix} 1/\alpha & -1/\alpha \\ \beta_{m_2} & -\beta_{m_1} \end{pmatrix}$$

The steady-state is therefore locally asymptotically stable iff

$$1/\alpha < \beta_{m_1} < \beta_{m_2}$$

holds true. Commenting on this result, it is a bit strange to see that the ideal monetarist world of this chapter in its advanced form needs money supply increases in order to fight inflation. This is due to the destabilizing feedback channel that leads from rising prices to rising interest rates, from there to rising growth rates of the exchange rate (following the UIP assumption) and then via the PPP to rising inflation rates in the domestic economy. Increasing money supply in such a feedback chain then means that the increase in interest rates is counteracted so that under the above conditions the positive feedback mechanism between the price level and its rate of change is neutralized; thus the economy can indeed converge back to the steady-state after the occurrence of isolated shocks. We thus have a stabilizing anti-monetarist monetary policy rule in a model that is extremely monetarist in nature.

11.8.2 Stabilizing fiscal policy I

We consider next a fiscal policy rule that attempts to suppress the cumulative forces in the evolution of government debt by way of a debt to GDP target, as in the Maastricht treaty of the European Community. We formulate again an isolated 2D dynamics that only shows the interaction of this rule with the dynamics of the government budget constraint and thus ignores all influences of the dynamics of the price level (and of the money supply). We assume for this purpose that the above steady-state values $p_o, M_o = 1$ are underlying the discussion of the next policy regime (again, in addition $s_o = 1, \bar{p}^* = 1, i_o = \bar{i}^*$).

$$\dot{B} = i_o B + \bar{G} - T - \bar{i}^* \bar{W}_c$$

$$\hat{T} = \beta_{t_1}(T_o/T - 1) + \beta_{t_2}(B/Y - \bar{d}).$$

We assumed in the second law of motion that government wants to achieve a certain debt to GDP ratio $\bar{d}$ by adjusting taxes accordingly with a certain speed parameter β_{t_2}. In addition, there is lump sum tax smoothing with a speed parameter β_{t_1}. The steady-state values of these partial dynamics (where government expenditure is also held constant) are: $B_o = \bar{d}Y, T_o$, where the latter is determined such that $\dot{B} = 0$ is established. For the Jacobian at the steady-state we get in this case:

$$J = \begin{pmatrix} i_o & -1 \\ \beta_{t_2} T_o/Y & -\beta_{t_1} \end{pmatrix}.$$

The steady state is therefore locally asymptotically stable iff $\beta_{t_1} > i_o$ and $i_o \beta_{t_1} Y < \beta_{t_2} T_o$ holds true. A taxation rule with some tax smoothing and a term that attempts to steer lump sum taxes such that the debt to GDP ratio approaches a given percentage (60 percent as in the Maastricht treaty, for example) is thus successful in stabilizing the government deficit if government expenditure is held constant during this adjustment process and if the price level dynamics is fixed at its steady-state position. Note here that the limit case $\beta_{t_1} = \infty$ has already been considered earlier as the case where taxation is determined such that government debt (there, W_g^a) is kept constant.

11.8.3 Stabilizing fiscal policy II

We have just seen that a debt to GDP target of the government may stabilize the originally cumulative forces in the GBR if taxes are varied into the direction of obtaining such a debt ratio and if this variation is occurring with sufficient strength. Regarding the second possibly cumulative instability in the balance of payments adjustment process, we assume now as a further fiscal policy rule that government expenditures are varied such that current account surpluses or deficits are reduced intentionally. This is again accompanied by a second component in this fiscal policy rule that adds some expenditure smoothing. We assume now (for a partial investigation of the implications of such a policy rule) that the steady-state values p_o, M_o, B_o are underlying the discussion of this policy regime (plus again $s_o = 1, \bar{p}^* = 1, i_o = \bar{i}^*$) and that lump sum taxes are of a fixed magnitude here.

$$\dot{W} = \bar{i}^* W + Y - G - C\left(Y + \bar{i}^*(W - \bar{W}_c) + \bar{i}^* \frac{M_o + B_o}{p_o}\right.$$
$$- \left(\bar{i}^* + \frac{\ln p_o + \ln Y + \ln k - \ln M_o}{\alpha}\right)\frac{M_o}{p_o} - \bar{T}, W - \bar{W}_c + \frac{M_o + B_o}{p_o}, \bar{i}^*\right)$$
$$\dot{G} = \beta_{g_1}(G_o - G) + \beta_{g_2}\dot{W}.$$

Improvements in the current account thus lead to increases in government spending from this partial perspective. In the steady-state we have $G = G_o$, which can here be given from the outside (within certain limits). We then obtain the value of W_o by setting the first equation equal to zero. The Jacobian of this dynamics at the steady-state reads:

$$J = \begin{pmatrix} \dot{W}_W & \dot{W}_G \\ \beta_{g_2}\dot{W}_W & \beta_{g_2}\dot{W}_G - \beta_{g_1} \end{pmatrix}.$$

It implies local asymptotic stability iff

$$\dot{W}_W = i_o(1 - C_1) - C_2 < \beta_{g_1} + \beta_{g_2}, \quad \dot{W}_W \beta_{g_1} > 0$$

holds true. In the case $\dot{W}_W < 0$, i.e., for a stable balance of payments adjustment process, this demands that $\beta_{g_1} > 0$ holds, i.e., the occurrence of government expenditure smoothing. In the opposite case, however, we need $\beta_{g_1} < 0$, i.e., the government should then revert its smoothing rule into a rule with a centrifugal instead of a centripetal adjustment pattern. Stimulating government expenditure above its steady-state level, besides responding positively to current account improvements, then induces an adjustment in the current account and in the level of government expenditure that implies convergence back to the steady-state should the economy be shocked out of this steady-state position.

11.8.4 Outlook: The integrated dynamics

Looking at the system as a whole, we can state that monetary policy here works independently of fiscal policy, whereas the previous two dynamical systems depend on each other, the first through changing G and the second through changing T. They of course also depend on what is going on in the nominal part of the economy. It is therefore necessary to consider the integrated interaction of the monetary policy rule and the two fiscal rules. The resulting 6D dynamics read:

$$\hat{p} = \frac{\ln p + \ln Y + \ln k - \ln M}{\alpha}$$

$$\hat{M} = \beta_{m_1}(M_o/M - 1) + \beta_{m_2}(p/p_o - 1)$$

$$\dot{B} = \left(\bar{i}^* + \frac{\ln p + \ln Y + \ln k - \ln M}{\alpha}\right)B + pG - pT - \bar{i}^* p\bar{W}_c - \dot{M}$$

$$\hat{T} = \beta_{t_1}(T_o/T - 1) + \beta_{t_2}(B/(pY) - \bar{d})$$

$$\dot{W} = \bar{i}^* W + Y - G - C\left(Y + \bar{i}^*(W - \bar{W}_c) + \bar{i}^*\frac{M+B}{p}\right.$$

$$\left. - \left(\bar{i}^* + \frac{\ln p + \ln Y + \ln k - \ln M}{\alpha}\right)\frac{M}{p} - T, W - \bar{W}_c + \frac{M+B}{p}, \bar{i}^*\right)$$

$$\dot{G} = \beta_{g_1}(G_o - G) + \beta_{g_2}\dot{W},$$

where $W = F/\bar{p}^*$, $\bar{W}_c = F_c/\bar{p}^*$. The steady-state of these dynamics is characterized by ($G_o = \bar{G}$ again given exogenously):

$$p_o = 1, \ M_o = 1, \ B_o = \bar{d}Y, \ W_{co} = M_o/p_o = 1, \ (T - G)_o = \bar{i}_o^*(B_o - M_o),$$

$$T_o = G_o + (G - T)_o,$$

while W_o can then be determined from the $\dot{W} = 0$ equation on the basis of the steady-state values for fiscal and monetary policy.[15]

We note that the laws of motion for the price level p and the money supply M are again independent from the rest of the system, while the remaining laws of motion depend on them and are now fully independent from each other. We note that the only link from the capital account block to the block describing the budget dynamics is given by the term G in the government budget constraint, while the laws of motion for W, G depend on all state variables of the model. It is not possible here to provide a proof of local asymptotic stability, due to the complexity of the considered dynamics.

In fact, one may furthermore assume that the considered policy rules come into effect only outside a certain neighborhood of the steady-state. Numerical tools therefore have to be used for the nonlinear system under investigation in order to check whether the proposed fiscal and monetary policy rules indeed bound the dynamics to an economically meaningful domain or whether other policy rules have to be found for such an outcome. The result to be achieved would then, in sum, imply that even the ideal world of the extremely open economy under consideration here – due to its centrifugal forces – needs the visible hand of

---

15 If one uses as a government expenditure rule the law of motion $\dot{G} = \beta_{g_1}(G_o - G) + \beta_{g_2}(Y - C - G - X_o)$, which focuses on the trade account instead of the current account and which assumes a given government target X_o for exports X, one can determine the steady-state value of W by $W_o = X_o/\bar{i}^*$ and, on this basis, now a unique steady-state value for G from the $\dot{W} = 0$ equation, by making use of the given steady-state value for $G - T$. In this case we have the anchors $\bar{d}, X_o$ in place of $\bar{d}, \bar{G}$ for the long-run position of the economy.

economic policy to limit these forces to an economically feasible domain (not to speak of convergence back to the steady-state). Instability due to myopic perfect foresight and the UIP condition – transferred to price level dynamics by the PPP – and augmented by eventually cumulative processes in the accumulation of deficits or surpluses in the budget and the current account thus need policy intervention even under the ideal conditions of this advanced classical model of a small open economy.

11.9 Conclusions

As a prelude to the study of important issues of the open economy dynamics with respect to financial–real interaction, we considered in this chapter the simultaneous interaction of capital account and budget dynamics. We have also discussed here, in a preliminary way, fiscal and monetary policy, still from the perspective of a perfectly open economy. The twin deficits, as well as fiscal and monetary policies, are further studied in the next chapters in a more complex and also more realistic setting.

11.10 References

COPELAND, L.S. (1989): *Exchange Rates and International Finance*. New York: Addison-Wesley.

DORNBUSCH, R. (1980): *Open Economy Macroeconomics*. New York: Basic Books.

HAMADA, K. and M. Sakurai (1978): International transmission of stagflation under fixed and flexible exchange rates. *Journal Political Economy*, 86, 877–895.

KALDOR, N. (1940): A model of the trade cycle. *Economic Journal*, 50, 78–92.

KRUGMAN, P. and M. OBSTFELD (2003): *International Economics. Theory and Policy*. Boston, MA: Addison-Wesley.

RØDSETH, A. (2000): *Open Economy Macroeconomics*. Cambridge, UK: Cambridge University Press.

SARGENT, T. and N. WALLACE (1973): The stability of models of money and growth with perfect foresight. *Econometrica*, 41, 1043–1048.

11.11 Appendix: Two-country and other extensions of the model

We return here to the consideration of given fiscal and monetary policy parameters, but consider now the data of the rest of the world as being endogenously determined in interaction with the dynamics that has been considered so far. The situation in country 1, the domestic economy, is then described by:

$$\hat{p} = i - r = i_o + \frac{\ln p + \ln Y + \ln k - \ln M}{\alpha} - r \tag{11.42}$$

$$\dot{W}_g^a = rW_g^a + \left(i_o + \frac{\ln p + \ln Y + \ln k - \ln M}{\alpha} \right) \frac{\bar{M}}{p} + \bar{T} - \bar{G} \tag{11.43}$$

$$\dot{W} = rW + Y - C\left(Y + rW - \left(i_o + \frac{\ln p + \ln Y + \ln k - \ln M}{\alpha}\right)\frac{\bar{M}}{p} - \bar{T}\right.$$

$$\left. - rW_g^a, W - W_g^a, r\right) - \bar{G}. \tag{11.44}$$

since $i^* \neq i$ and $r = i - \hat{p} = r^* = i^* - \hat{p}^*$ are now endogenously determined variables. For the foreign economy there holds in the same way, on the basis of the assumptions for extremely open economies:

$$\hat{p}^* = i^* - r = i_o + \frac{\ln p^* + \ln Y^* + \ln k^* - \ln \bar{M}^*}{\alpha^*} - r \tag{11.45}$$

$$\dot{W}_g^{a*} = rW_g^{a*} + \left(i_o + \frac{\ln p^* + \ln Y^* + \ln k^* - \ln \bar{M}^*}{\alpha^*}\right)\frac{\bar{M}^*}{p^*} + \bar{T}^* - \bar{G}^* \tag{11.46}$$

$$-\dot{W}^* = \dot{W} = rW + Y - C\left(Y + rW - \left(i_o + \frac{\ln p + \ln Y + \ln k - \ln \bar{M}}{\alpha}\right)\frac{\bar{M}}{p}\right.$$

$$\left. - \bar{T} - rW_g^a, W - W_g^a, r\right) - \bar{G}. \tag{11.47}$$

The uniquely determined real rate of interest, the world real rate of interest r, is then to be determined as the "natural rate" from the world goods market equilibrium relationship:

$$Y + Y^* = C\left(Y + rW - \left(i_o + \frac{\ln p + \ln Y + \ln k - \ln \bar{M}}{\alpha}\right)\frac{\bar{M}}{p} - \bar{T} - rW_g^a,\right.$$

$$W - W_g^a, r) + \bar{G} + C^*\left(Y^* - rW - \left(i_o + \frac{\ln p^* + \ln Y^* + \ln k^* - \ln \bar{M}^*}{\alpha^*}\right)\right.$$

$$\frac{\bar{M}^*}{p^*} - \bar{T}^* - rW_g^{a*}, -W - W_g^{a*}, r) + \bar{G}^*. \tag{11.48}$$

The rate has to be inserted into the above five laws of motion for $p, p^*, W_g^a, W_g^{a*}, W$ in order to arrive at an autonomous system of five differential equations describing the dynamic interactions in our two-country world economy. We note that the rate r depends – according to the world goods market equilibrium – on all five state variables of the considered dynamics. Finally, the dynamics of the nominal exchange rate is obtained as an appended law of motion, via the PPP, through $\hat{s} = \hat{p} - \hat{p}^*$. Due to the form of this law of motion we see that it depends linearly on the laws of motion for p, p^*, which implies that zero root hysteresis is present in this two-country model as far as the evolution of the nominal exchange rate is concerned.

The model under consideration shows how the world real rate of interest (which has so far been considered a given magnitude) is determined in a world of two extremely open economies. On this basis the dynamics of goods prices can be obtained together with the laws of motion for aggregate government debts and the debt–creditor relationship between the two economies. The dynamics that results from these interacting two-country macrodynamics is of course fairly involved. It should, in our view, be solved on the basis of gradually adjusting price levels and, of course, gradually adjusting wealth expressions. If locally unstable, mechanisms in the private sector or fiscal and monetary policy reactions must again be found that limit the local explosiveness, at least far off the steady state, so that the world economy remains economically viable.

Further extensions may concern the assumption of a two-commodity, two-country world, the removal of the full employment condition and its replacement by a conventional type of Phillips curve, the existence of Keynesian demand restrictions on the world market for the domestic commodity, i.e., the assumption of an export demand function, the inclusion of investment behavior, imperfect asset substitution and others.

12 Twin deficits and inflation in the Mundell–Fleming–Tobin model

12.1 Introduction

In this chapter, we now introduce – in contrast to Chapter 11 – a Keynesian demand constraint on the market for goods in place of the assumption of some sort of Say's law that we used in the previous chapter (according to which the world market delivered or consumed everything not present or not needed in the domestic economy). This will be done by adding a net export function (and now also an investment function) to the description of aggregate goods demand. In addition, we now also assume imperfect substitutability of financial assets in place of the UIP condition of the previous chapter. This imperfectness is here coupled with the assumption that domestic bonds are nontradables; i.e., the amount of foreign bonds held domestically can only be changed to the extent that there is a surplus or a deficit in the current account and not via balanced exchanges of domestic bonds against foreign ones (or vice versa). International capital movements of this sort will be the subject of the Chapter 15 of this book. Finally, we will now assume regressive expectations formation in the place of rational expectations, which has two effects: on the one hand, it avoids the questionable jump variable technique of the rational expectations school (in order to get stability in an otherwise unstable saddlepoint environment) and, on the other hand, it allows for maximum stability of the dynamics in question, since only fundamentalist and, in principle, converging expectations revisions are allowed for.

We thus now allow for labor and capital being underutilized because of insufficient effective demand on the goods market.[1] They can result from Keynesian consumption and investment demand – augmented by a net export schedule in the open economy – and the goods market equilibrium condition based on these aggregate demand functions. We now also assume a Tobinian portfolio structure in the financial part of the economy. We consider on this basis a Keynesian type of business cycle dynamics in the real part of the model (based on an IS curve that equates savings to investment). Due to our use of a standard open-economy money-wage Phillips curve, this real cycle – to be considered in

---

1 Of course, this also permits overutilized labor and capital depending on the state of aggregate demand.

the second part of the chapter – is accompanied by labor-market-driven inflation or deflation dynamics which, in combination with a capital account dynamics and government budget dynamics of the type we have already considered in the preceding chapter, provides a dynamic model that goes significantly beyond standard Mundell–Fleming-type approaches. Finally, since we are considering exports and imports simultaneously we are of course now using a two-commodity (but single small country) approach, in contrast to the preceding chapter where primarily one-commodity cases were considered.

12.2 Temporary equilibrium

In this section we extend the LM representation of the financial part of the conventional Mundell–Fleming model[2] by making explicit the financial structure of the model that may be associated with its textbook theory of money and the LM curve. We do so, however, only with respect to government bonds and still leave implicit the treatment of the financial assets traded between households and firms.[3] We therefore now add the explicit treatment of domestic and foreign government bonds and their allocation in a small open economy between households and the central bank by way of a Tobinian portfolio approach to the wealth-holding of the household sector. In this approach we follow Rødseth (2000, Ch. 6) who calls this type of extension of the Mundell–Fleming framework the Mundell-Fleming-Tobin model. The advantage of this extension is that it makes explicit the financial market operations of the central bank, for example in the case of sterilization, and that it allows for a consideration of further alternatives for exchange rate regimes (six instead of the three possible regimes of the Mundell–Fleming model). We thus consider a fairly general extension of the Mundell–Fleming framework that, however, by and large preserves the spirit of this approach.

12.2.1 The IS–LM part of the model

In our formulation of the Mundell–Fleming–Tobin model of a small open economy of Rødseth (2000, 6.2) we start with the presentation of the IS–LM part of the model, which is here given in fairly general terms by:[4]

$$Y = C(Y_p, W_p, i - \bar{\pi}, \bar{i}^* + \epsilon(s) - \bar{\pi}) + I(i - \bar{\pi}, \bar{i}^* + \epsilon(s) - \bar{\pi}) + \bar{G} + NX(Y, \sigma, \bar{Y}^*)$$

$$(12.1)$$

$$\frac{M^s}{p} = m^d(Y, i),$$

$$(12.2)$$

---

2 See Asada et al. (2003, Ch. 4) for a presentation of this model type.
3 Where we basically assume that all profit income obtained by firms is transferred to households, which in turn finance their investment expenditures.
4 The goods market equilibrium equation can be rewritten in terms of domestic goods by reducing absorptions to their domestic components and by replacing $NX(Y, \sigma, \bar{Y}^*)$ $X(\sigma, \bar{Y}^*)$

where $\bar{\pi}$ is the given rate of inflation of the domestic economy in the first part of this chapter, and the symbols $\bar{\pi}$, etc. are again used to denote variables that are exogenous to the model. We here denote by σ the real exchange rate sp^*/p, by $W_p = (M + B + sF_p)/p$ current real private wealth and by Y_p private disposable income to be defined below. We shall also make use in various places of the abbreviations $r = i - \bar{\pi}, r^* = \bar{i}^* + \epsilon(s) - \bar{\pi}$, as in Rødseth (2000), for the expected rate of returns on domestic and foreign bonds. We note that consumption and investment as usual depend negatively on the real rates of interest, and in addition consumption depends positively on income and wealth. The function $\epsilon(s)$, $\epsilon'(s) < 0$, $\epsilon(s_o) = 0$ represents expectations formation with regard to expected depreciation or appreciation of the nominal exchange rate and defines a regressive scheme of depreciation expectations (where people expect the exchange rate to approach its present steady-state value over time with a certain adjustment speed ϵ'). Private consumption depends on disposable income Y_p, wealth W_p and expected real returns on domestic and foreign bonds B, F. Bonds are of the fixed price variety, denominated in Norwegian Kroner and USD for example, implying that risk is only involved in the domestic holding of foreign bonds due to unanticipated changes in the exchange rate s, the expected rate of depreciation of which depends on its current level by way of the assumption of regressive expectations (to be considered in more detail in the next chapter). Here – following Rødseth (2000, 6.2) – we have simply postulated a negatively sloped function $\epsilon(s), \epsilon'(s) < 0$, which is zero at the (correctly perceived) steady state rate of exchange s_o (see also Rodseth's Chapter 5 in this regard). This function therefore simply says that domestic agents expect depreciation of the domestic currency if the exchange rate falls below its steady-state value and vice versa. These regressive expectations of a return of the exchange rate to its steady state value is a very simple hypothesis on expectations formation in financial markets. It will be of great use in the next chapter, where instability scenarios can be created despite the simple and seemingly stabilizing role that is played by such exchange rate expectations.

The risk-free expected rate of return on domestic bonds is given by i and the risky one on foreign bonds is given by $\bar{i}^* + \epsilon - \bar{\pi}$, the expected nominal return on foreign bonds. The latter includes expected gains from currency depreciation or losses from expected currency appreciation, minus the domestic inflation rate (since $\bar{i}^* + \epsilon$ transforms the dollar rate of interest into a Kroner rate of return on these bonds). Consumption behavior depends negatively on both of these expected rates of return and positively on disposable income and the current wealth of households. The latter concept – as already stated – is defined to consist of the Kroner sum of the stock of money, domestic and foreign bonds currently held by the domestic household sector, expressed in real terms as

$$W_p = (M + B + sF_p)/p.$$

We note that real wealth can only change in the short run via exchange rate changes, since all other magnitudes are given quantities in each moment of time (the initial financial endowments of the private sector of the economy).

12.2.2 Disposable income calculations

In Rødseth (2000, 6.2), real income Y_p of the private sector is based on the Hicksian concept of disposable income, which means that factual income (based on standard national accounting procedures) and disposable income are distinguished from each other here. The latter is defined by the condition that real wealth will stay constant if all disposable income is consumed. Income is therefore disposable only when real wealth, which is shrinking in an inflationary environment, is brought back to its initial level by savings out of factual accounting income (while deflation would provide additions to actual income due to the gains in the purchasing power of the wealth of households). In the present model we define factual or accounting nominal disposable income by

$$pY^{Da} = pY + iB + s\bar{i}^* F_p - pT,$$ (12.3)

i.e., as income from production (gross wages and gross profits) and interest income from the domestic and foreign bond holdings of domestic residents diminished by the nominal tax payments of the domestic household sector. With respect to the Hicksian concept of disposable income we have to deduct from (12.3) the items that express the loss of purchasing power of money and of both types of bonds (and have to add to it the expected capital gains on foreign bonds), thereby arriving at the expression

$$pY^{Dh} = pY + (i - \bar{\pi})B + (\bar{i}^* + \epsilon - \bar{\pi})sF_p - \bar{\pi}M - pT.$$ (12.4)

Equation (12.4) can be rearranged into the form

$$pY^{Dh} = pY + (\bar{i}^* + \epsilon - \bar{\pi})pW_p - (\bar{i}^* + \epsilon - i)(M + B) - iM - pT.$$ (12.5)

In equation (12.5) we see the expected real rate of return on foreign bonds ($r^* = \bar{i}^* + \epsilon(s) - \bar{\pi}$) applied to the whole nominal wealth of the household sector, corrected by (i) an expression that subtracts the amount $\xi(M + B)$ (with $\xi = \bar{i}^* + \epsilon - i$ being the risk premium that households obtain on their foreign bond holdings) from the returns on money and domestic bond holdings, and (ii) an expression representing the interest loss on money holdings with regard to the risk-free rate obtained on domestic bonds. This representation of Y^{Dh} therefore applies the expected real rate of return on foreign bonds as a benchmark rate to all components of the wealth of domestic households. It then corrects the obtained result by means of the foreign risk premium as far as domestic wealth is concerned and by the interest-free loan from the public to the central bank, the gain the central bank has from this.[5]

---

5 Note here that our definition of the risk premium ξ is the negative of Rødseth's definition and that $r + \xi = r^*$ holds, by definition.

Real taxes T^n – considered exogenous to the model – are defined in Rødseth (2000, 6.2) in a particular way, namely net of the real return on private domestic bond and money holdings and augmented by the real return of the central bank on money and the foreign bonds held by the monetary authority.[6] This gives the expression

$$T^n = T - (i - \bar{\pi})B/p + \bar{\pi}M/p + (\bar{i}^* + \epsilon - \bar{\pi})F_p/p = \text{ const.}$$

where B_c denotes the stock of foreign bonds held by the central bank. Note that we assume here that all income of the central bank is transferred to the government sector and thus has to appear in its budget constraint to be considered later on. Domestic government bonds held by the central bank therefore do not cause interest payments for the government, and interest return on the foreign bonds held by the central bank is added to the tax income of the government. Holding taxes net of all such real returns constant now implies a simplification for the calculation of the real disposable income Y^{Dh} of households (see equation (12.4)) that also simplifies the treatment of the IS equilibrium of the model significantly, since we obtain from this assumption the expression

$$pY_p := pY^{Dh} = pY + (\bar{i}^* + \epsilon(s) - \bar{\pi})sF - pT,$$

where F is given by the sum of the private and the central bank holding of dollar-denominated assets $F_p + F_c$. Domestic wages and profits are thus now simply to be augmented by the expected real return on all foreign bonds, which after taxes then provides the expression for disposable income of the household sector to be used in the following analysis.

12.2.3 Conventional implications for IS–LM analysis (regime A1)

As regime A1 we consider the case where the domestic money supply and the nominal exchange rate are kept fixed by the central bank. In this case the excess demand (supply) of the private sector for domestic and foreign bonds must be provided (absorbed) from the stocks of these financial assets held by the central bank in order to defend the fixed levels of M and s.

Summarizing the discussion of the IS–LM block of the model, we thus find that it is of the conventional type, but now includes wealth effects and effects of the expected rate of return on dollar-denominated bonds, the latter in both the consumption and investment functions as well as with respect to consumption via both an income and a substitution effect. The signs of the partial derivatives of consumption and investment functions are the usual ones, i.e. negative with

---

6 This is justified in Rødseth (2000, 6.2) by the convenient implication that it avoids keeping account of the different flows of interest payments within the country. Yet it is obvious that this cutting off of certain feedback channels in the generation of sectoral income formation represents a very artificial assumption that must be removed from the model sooner or later.

respect to the shown rates of return. In addition, Rødseth (2000, 6.2) assumes that the income effect of the rate r^* is dominated by the substitution effect in the consumption function, i.e., that aggregate demand depends negatively on the real rate of return r^*. An interesting aspect of this modification of the IS–LM block of the Mundell–Fleming model is that exchange rate changes now influence consumption via changes in disposable income, real wealth, and the rate of return on foreign bonds in addition to the usual channel via the real exchange rate in the net export function. Again, the only ambiguity in the overall reaction to exchange rate changes now comes from the definition of disposable income that provides a negative influence of the exchange rate on aggregate demand, assumed to be dominated by the three positive influences just enumerated. We thus, in sum, get that the behavior of the IS–LM part is formally – from the mathematical point of view – identical to the one of the Mundell–Fleming approach, though richer now in the feedback channels allowed for here.

12.2.4 The determination of stock market equilibria

The next block of equations provides the core innovation of the model, i.e., the portfolio approach to financial markets, here with three financial assets, money M, domestic bonds B, B_c and foreign bonds F_p, F_c, shown in the amounts currently held by the private sector and the central bank, respectively. The real portfolio demands of the private sector are given by (with money demand shown again for reasons of completeness)

$$M^d/p = m^d(Y, i), \quad m_Y^d > 0, m_i^d < 0, \tag{12.6}$$

$$sF_p^d/p = f^d(\xi, W_p) = f^d(\bar{i}^* + \epsilon(s) - i, W_p), \quad f_\xi^d > 0, 0 < f_{W_p}^d < 1, \tag{12.7}$$

$$B^d = W_p - f^d(\bar{i}^* + \epsilon(s) - i, W_p) - m^d(Y, i). \tag{12.8}$$

These equations state that interest-bearing financial assets are demanded on the basis of the rate of return differential between them, here represented by the demand function f^d for dollar-denominated assets (in domestic real terms). Domestic bonds are demanded on the same basis, but a part of them is allocated to non-interest-bearing money holdings. This bond demand is thus the difference between real wealth currently held and the real demand for money and foreign bonds, which is just another representation of the stock constraint of the household sector of the model. The other agent on the stock markets for financial assets is the central bank whose stock constraint is represented by

$$(M^s - M)/p = (B_c^d - B_c)/p + (sF_c^d - sF_c)/p. \tag{12.9}$$

Note here that this constraint allows for the injection of new money $M^s - M$ into the private sector of the economy by way of open market operations of foreign exchange market operations. Note too that the excess demands of the central bank on the right-hand side of the equations can also be negative magnitudes, which then means that the central bank supplies domestic or foreign bonds to the private sector. Note finally that – depending on the exchange rate regimes to be introduced below – some of these demands and supplies of the central bank can be considered as exogenously given and subject to policy modeling.

A crucial assumption generally made in Rødseth (2000, ch. 6) is that the stock magnitude $F = F_p + F_c$, the total amount of dollar-denominated assets (in the Norwegian economy), is a given magnitude in the short run considered by this model. That is, dollar-denominated assets are only supplied domestically to the stock markets at each moment in time (from the initial endowments held by private sector and the central bank). This assumption of Rødseth (2000) is justified by the assumption that Kroner bonds are not traded internationally and are thus restricted by the initial endowments of the domestic economy.[7] In this case, an exchange rate fixed by the central bank can only be maintained when it holds enough stocks in USD-denominated bonds in order to always fulfill the excess demand for these bonds by the private sector. Otherwise, part of the excess demand must appear on the international markets and thus reappear as USD demand at the central bank from these markets. In the case of flexible exchange rates, excess demand on the stock market for foreign bonds will drive up the nominal exchange rate until this excess demand disappears. This conclusion is, of course, only justified if the stock demand for foreign bonds of the private sector

$$F_p^d = pf^d(\xi, W_p)/s$$

depends negatively on the nominal exchange rate. This indeed holds, since $f_{W_p}^d < 1$ has been assumed. Note here also that we will show below that the balance of payments is always balanced without intervention by the central banks if the flow of new assets from the domestic government is accepted by the household sector.

On the basis of the above, asset market equilibria in the three markets considered can be represented by

$$\frac{M^s}{p} = m^d(Y, i), \tag{12.10}$$

$$\frac{s\bar{F}}{p} = f^d(\bar{i}^* + \epsilon(s) - i, W_p) + \frac{sF_c^d}{p}, \tag{12.11}$$

$$\frac{\bar{B}}{p} = W_p - f^d(\bar{i}^* + \epsilon(s) - i, W_p) - m^d(Y, i) + \frac{B_c^d}{p}, \tag{12.12}$$

where M^s is the new stock of money as supplied by the central bank, $\bar{F}$ the given amount of dollar-denominated bonds in the domestic economy and $\bar{B}$ the given amount of government bonds in the economy. Depending on the exchange rate

---

7 See however chapter 15 for the integration of international capital flows into such a stock approach.

regime that is chosen, the quantities $M^s/p, B_c^d/p, sF_c^d/p$ may be endogenous or exogenous variables of the model. We will denote by BB the equilibrium curve for domestic bonds and by FF the one for foreign bonds, both situated in the same diagram as the LM curve already considered.

The stock constraint of the private sector and the central bank can be aggregated and then gives rise to the following Walras law of stocks:

$$0 = pm^d - M^s + B_a^d - B_a + sF^d - sF, \tag{12.13}$$

$$B_a = B + B_c, F = F_p + F_c, B_a^d = B^d + B_c^d, F^d = F_p^d + F_c^d.$$

This law implies (as usual) that only two market-clearing conditions are needed to imply full equilibrium of asset markets. Note here that M^s, B_c, F_c may be policy parameters of the central bank in the currently considered short-run analysis, but that total stocks B, F are always given magnitudes at each moment of time. Note also that the private demand for foreign bonds is assumed in this model to be never larger than the stock of foreign bonds existing in the domestic economy. Excess demand of the household sector for foreign bonds is thus either reduced to its supply of foreign bonds by a flexible exchange rate or satisfied by the central bank through the stocks of foreign bonds it holds.

12.2.5 Flow budget constraints and the balance of payments (consistency requirements)

For reasons of completeness and consistency we also present the flow constraints of the economy which, however, have no impact on the current state of the economy but only influence its behavior as time evolves. With respect to the private sector, we first of all have

$$pS_p = pY + iB + s\bar{i}^* F_p - pT - pC = \dot{M} + \dot{B} + s\dot{F}_p + pI. \tag{12.14}$$

Note here that all domestically produced income is paid out to households in the form of wages or profits augmented by the interest payment from the domestic government and from abroad. Deducting actual taxes and planned consumption then gives households' nominal savings pS_p as shown in equation (12.14). These nominal savings are then allocated to the flow demand for money, domestic and foreign bonds and finally the direct investment decision of the household sector (and of firms). Note that there is no resale market for real capital goods in this model, which implies that the capital stock of firms owned by households need not be included in their wealth constraint. Note also that actual tax payments are an endogenous magnitude of the model, due to the tax policy rule assumed by Rødseth (2000).

For the government, we similarly get

$$pS_g = pT + s\bar{i}^* F_c - iB - pG = -\dot{B} - \dot{M},$$

and for the central bank

$$\dot{M} = \dot{B}_c \quad (= \bar{\mu}M, \; \mu = \bar{\pi}).$$

We here assume that all interest income of the central bank is channeled back to the government sector and that the government issues new debt of the amount $\dot{B} + \dot{B}_c$, but that part of this new debt is purchased by the central bank through the issue of new money $\dot{M}$ which is assumed to follow a path of constant growth.

Assuming that the flow of new money and new government bonds is always accepted by the household sector as additions to their existing portfolio, we obtain by aggregating the savings of the public and the government, on the one hand, the expressions

$$pS = p(S_p + S_g) = pY + s\bar{i}^*F - pC - pG = pI + pNX + s\bar{i}^*F,$$

due to the assumed goods market equilibrium condition. This equation states the familiar accounting relationship that aggregate savings must be equal to aggregate investment plus the current account, which is the sum of the trade account and the interest payments (here only received from abroad since domestic bonds are not held internationally). On the other hand, we can write

$$pS = p(S_p + S_g) = pI + s\dot{F}_p = pI + s\dot{F},$$

which is the sum of nominal investment and the capital account. We thus have that the capital account (with respect to the notation and sign convention chosen here) is always equal to the current account or, in other terms, that the balance of payments (a flow not a stock balance) is always balanced without any intervention of the central bank. This shows that we can restrict the discussion of foreign market interventions of the central bank in the present framework to the stock markets and thus can leave the present discussions of flows in the background of the model. It also shows that changes in the holdings of foreign bonds come about here only through flows in the balance of payments. These changes may be positive or negative, depending on whether net exports are positive or negative. Furthermore, the import of new dollar-denominated bonds solely goes into the private sector, since the central bank is not actively represented in balance of payments operations in the present form of the model. Note that these considerations are also true in the case of the fixed exchange rate regimes to be considered below. Finally, we point out that the state of the current account and the trade account are of no importance in the portfolio equilibrium to be investigated below, and that this portfolio approach and the approach to flow conditions have been modeled such that the dollar reserves of the central bank indeed stay constant in time.

12.3 The six economic regimes of the model

Summarizing our discussion of the Mundell–Fleming–Tobin model for the small open economy, we can state that it consists of the following four equations, one goods market equilibrium condition and three asset markets equilibrium conditions, one of which however is redundant in the way we described above:[8]

$$Y \overset{IS}{=} Y^d = C(Y_p, W_p(s), i - \bar{\pi}, \bar{i}^* + \epsilon(s) - \bar{\pi}) \qquad (12.15)$$

$$+ \quad I(i - \bar{\pi}, \bar{i}^* + \epsilon(s) - \bar{\pi}) + G + NX(Y, \sigma, \bar{Y}^*), \quad \sigma = sp^*/p, \quad (12.16)$$

$$M^s \overset{LM}{=} pm^d(Y, i), \qquad (12.17)$$

$$B_a \overset{BB}{=} B^d + B_c^d = p[W_p(s) - m^d(\cdot, \cdot) - f^d(\cdot, \cdot)] + B_c^d, \quad B_a = B + B_c, \qquad (12.18)$$

$$F \overset{FF}{=} F^d + F_c^d = pf^d(\bar{i}^* + \epsilon(s) - i, W_p(s))/s + F_c^d, \quad F = F_p + F_c, \qquad (12.19)$$

where Y_p is defined as $Y + (\bar{i}^* + \epsilon(s) - \bar{\pi})s\bar{F}/p - \bar{T}$. In these equations goods market equilibrium is always endogenous. All other variables $i, s, M^s, B^d, B_c^d, F_p, F_c^d$, however, can be made endogenous or exogenous, depending on the exchange rate regime that is considered. We note that B^d is – in equilibrium – a given magnitude if $B_c^d = B_c$ is established by the central bank, since the total amount of domestic bonds is fixed in each moment of time. Similarly, F_p^d is a given magnitude in market equilibrium if there holds $F_c^d = F_c$ because of the policy behavior of the central bank. The set of candidates for the description of different regimes therefore reduces to $i, s, M^s, B_c^d = B_c, F_c^d = F_c$. In view of the number of equations of the model we can thus predetermine three variables of this list (one in a trivial way by accommodating policy and demand side considerations solely due to the assumed Walras law of stocks) by choosing the other two as being exogenously determined.

In the case of a fixed exchange rate regime[9] we thus can fix, in addition, the domestic rate of interest i (via a Taylor rule-type interest rate policy of the central bank), the money supply M^s (a conventional type of money supply rule, here justified and established by way of sterilizing actions of the central bank) or the amount of domestic bonds B available for the household sector of the model. In all three cases the central bank accommodates to the demand for dollar-denominated bonds of the household sector and thereby removes any pressure from the exchange rate and the foreign exchange market.

In the opposite case of the regime of a perfectly flexible exchange rate[10] we can fix, in addition, the domestic rate of interest i if an interest rate policy is pursued,

---

8 For the moment we follow Rødseth (2000, 6.2) in the formulation of the assumed consumption and investment behavior, but will reformulate these equations later on, since they are not yet consistently formulated in view of the assumed net export function.

9 Where F_c should be considered and must be made endogenous (and sufficiently large in amount) in order to allow (always) for asset market equilibrium in all three markets.

10 Where F_c can be considered as being exogenously given, since the central bank need not intervene on the foreign exchange market.

Table 12.1 The three policy regimes for a fixed exchange rate.

A1	$\bar{M}^s:$	Y endogenous	i endogenous	$B_o^d \neq B$ in general
A2	$\bar{i}:$	Y endogenous	M^s endogenous	$B_o^d \neq B$ in general
A3	$B^d = B:$	Y endogenous	M^s endogenous	i endogenous

the money supply M^s if money supply policy is implemented via sterilizing actions of the central bank, or the amount of domestic bonds B available for the household sector of the model. In all three cases the exchange rate is assumed to clear the market for dollar-denominated bonds. Here, households – if they want to increase their foreign bond holdings, for example – would exchange some of their other assets for dollars, which would create an excess demand for dollars. The result would be to drive up the exchange rate until the excess demand for dollars disappears, since the central bank does not intervene in the foreign exchange market.

Taken together we thus now have six different regimes, as compared to the three regimes (fixed exchange rates with and without sterilization, and flexible exchange rates) of the original Mundell–Fleming approach. There are even four more regimes conceivable from the purely mathematical perspective, namely given (s, F_c) in the case of a fixed exchange rate, and given (M^s, i), given (B_c, i) and given (M^s, B_c) in the case of a flexible exchange rate. However, from the economic perspective, these regimes do not seem to be of much interest, since they combine fixed exchange rates with a fixed supply of dollar denominated assets on the foreign exchange market, and flexible exchange rates with an accommodating value of F_c and thus an action of the central bank that is not needed. The regimes that are to be investigated below are therefore those shown in Tables 12.1 and 12.2.

In the case of Table 12.1 the condition $F_o^d = pf^d(\cdot, \cdot)/\bar{s}$ always holds, i.e., as already noted, excess demand for foreign bonds is always fulfilled by appropriate changes in the stock of foreign bonds held by the central bank. We have full sterilization in case A1 by means of accompanying open market operations of the central bank, which thus sells or buys domestic government bonds to an extent that keeps the money supply on the level desired by the central bank – despite the fact that the change in the holding of foreign bonds has changed the money stock held by the public initially. This sterilization is not attempted in the second regime A2 where the interest rate is kept fixed by the central bank and where money supply must therefore be adjusted to money demand. The same holds in regime A3 where households in equilibrium just hold the bonds they own (since here the central bank does not sell or purchase such bonds) and where money supply must therefore again be accommodated to money demand.

In the case of flexible exchange rates in Table 12.2, the condition $F_c^d = F_c$ holds in all three cases. At first sight it may seen astonishing that we now have one more endogenous variable than in the case of a fixed exchange rate. Yet, in the presently considered situation, the central bank is either accommodating to money demand or to domestic bond demand, which therefore is automatically satisfied and thus not a binding equilibrium condition of the model. This role was uniformly played

Table 12.2 The three policy regimes for a flexible exchange rate.

B1	$\bar{M}^s$:	Y, s endogenous	i endogenous	$B_o^d \neq B$ in general
B2	$\bar{i}$:	Y, s endogenous	M^s endogenous	$B_o^d \neq B$ in general
B3	$B^d = B$:	Y, s endogenous	i endogenous	M^s endogenous

by F_p^d in the case of the fixed exchange rate regime that in fact provides the fourth variable in this case. In the case of flexible exchange rates, the money supply is in principle controlled by the central bank, as shown in regime B1 in Table 12.2. Yet if an interest rate policy is pursued by the central bank it must of course then supply the money demanded by the public; see regime A2. The same also holds for regime A3 where the central bank does not trade domestic bonds, since money supply M^s can then not be fixed in addition, as we will see below in detail.

In the case of floating exchange rates, domestic financial markets (for domestic and foreign bonds) regulate the level of both i and s, as long as the rate of interest is determined by market forces, while the level of output is the variable that clears the market for goods. Monetary policy can now affect domestic money or bond holdings, while a given rate of interest again characterizes a Taylor-type monetary policy, without yet, however, presenting a rule for the adjustment of domestic interest rates.

12.3.1 Comparative static exercises: Foundations

As we have seen above, the Tobin extension of the Mundell–Fleming model is very rich in the possibilities it provides for the consideration of different exchange rate regimes and, within this framework, for alternative policy scenarios. These policy scenarios will now be discussed to some extent with respect to the comparative static results that they allow for.

Fixed exchange rate regimes

We investigate the regime A1 first where s, M are kept fixed. Here the model results are very familiar (despite the advanced structure assumed for consumption as well as investment demand), since the IS–LM block then determines output Y and the interest rate i in the usual way, as a domestic equilibrium, independently of what characterizes the open part of the economy. On the basis of the domestically determined IS–LM equilibrium we can then determine the demand for foreign bonds of the household sector (to which the central bank is adjusting) and then residually – from the Walras law of stocks – the demand for domestic bonds, again of the household sector (with or without adjustment behavior of the central bank). The case of sterilization thus again shows that domestic equilibrium is then of course the decisive component of the model – as long as the sterilization policy of the central bank can be maintained.

In the alternative situation of an interest rate policy pursued by the central bank, the comparative static exercises become even simpler, since the IS part of the model then determines equilibrium output Y independently of the rest of the model. Money demand then determines money supply M^s, the market for foreign bonds determines the current foreign bond holdings of domestic households, and finally the market for domestic bonds determines the domestic bond holdings of households, again in a residually determined way. Therefore asset markets here adjust to the IS-equilibrium in a simple step-by-step procedure.

Finally, in regime A3, the part of the LM curve in regime A1 is simply taken over by the BB curve of the model, which is also positively sloped. Output and the interest rate are therefore then determined by the intersection of the IS curve with the BB curve in place of the intersection of the IS curve with the LM curve. The money supply and the foreign bond supply by the central bank then adjust to household behavior and the results implied from their behavior. This is due to the fact that households must then always hold the amount of domestic bonds they already have in their portfolio, which means that the bond market assumes the role normally played by the money market. Note however that the BB curve is less steep than the LM curve (both are positively sloped). This is due to its defining equation which (in the considered case of no trade in domestic government bonds by the central bank) is given by

$$B \overset{BB}{=} p(W_p(\bar{s}) - m^d(Y, i) - pf^d(i)/\bar{s}).$$

This equation implies

$$\frac{di}{dY} = -\frac{1}{m_i^d + pf_i^d/\bar{s}} m_Y^d = -\frac{m_Y^d}{m_i^d + pf_i^d/\bar{s}} > 0,$$

which is clearly smaller than the corresponding expression obtained from the LM curve $(di/dY = m_Y^d/(-m_i^d))$, due to the fact that m_i^d, f_i^d are both negative.

We stress finally that the case of a fixed exchange rate is always based on the accommodating supply or demand of foreign bonds by the central bank and, of course, characterized by $\epsilon = 0$, since the exchange rate is fixed. In this case, private wealth is thus also always a given magnitude and the risk premium ξ varies only with the domestic rate of interest i. Either money or domestic bonds is used to buy the foreign currency if households intend to increase their foreign bond holdings, in which case the dollars bought then return to the central banks through the change in their foreign bond holdings that then flows from households' demand. Financial markets are therefore never rationed in these formulations of regimes of fixed exchange rates, with or without sterilization, or with a Taylor interest rate policy rule that implies a given rate of interest in the short run of the model. We have thus obtained very clear-cut and straightforward implications in the case of regimes with fixed rates of exchange.

Floating exchange rate regimes

Things are not so simple, however, in the flexible exchange rate regime, since a much more integrated feedback structure is then generated due to the exchange rate links between real and financial markets. The simplest case is again that of an interest rate peg through the central bank, i.e., regime B2 in Table 12.2. Since the central bank here just keeps its foreign bond holding invariant ($F_c^d = F_c$), the market for foreign bonds determines the exchange rate in a unique way, independently of what happens in the other markets. IS equilibrium can then be used to determine the equilibrium output of firms, which in turn provides the actual money demand of households that is always fulfilled by the central bank as a result of the chosen interest rate policy. Finally, the demand for domestic bonds is then fulfilled through the accommodation of the monetary authority both on the money market and on the market for foreign bonds. Note however that the causal nexus now runs from the market for dollar-denominated bonds to the goods market and from there to the reallocation of money and domestic bond holdings in the portfolio of households.

In order to see in more detail what happens on the market for goods, we solve the equilibrium condition on the foreign exchange market, viz.

$$F - F_c = F_p^d = pf^d(\bar{i}^* + \epsilon(s) - i, W_p(s))/s, \quad f_1^d > 0, f_2^d \in (0, 1)$$

for the nominal exchange rate s, which by the implicit function theorem can be expressed by the functional relation

$$s = s(i - \bar{i}^*, p, F_c, F), \quad s_1 < 0, s_2 > 0, s_3 > 0, s_4 < 0.$$

The signs of the partial derivatives follow from the fact that the function

$$H(s; i - \bar{i}^*, p, F_c, F) := pf^d(\bar{i}^* + \epsilon(s) - i, W_p(s))/s - F + F_c$$

depends positively on p and F_c and negatively on $i - \bar{i}^*$ and F, whilst the partial derivative of H with respect to the exchange rate s is given by

$$H_1(= H_s) = pf_1^d \epsilon'/s + (f_2^d F_p - \frac{p}{s} f^d)/s$$

which is negative because $f_2^d < 1$ and $pf^d/s = F_p$. We thus find that the exchange rate s depends negatively on the given domestic rate of interest i and positively on the foreign rate. Interest rate increases at home and decreases abroad thus lead to an appreciation of the domestic currency.

Rødseth (2000, 6.4) inserts the function $s = s(i - \bar{i}^*, \bar{p}, F_c, F)$ into the IS equilibrium condition and obtains from that a revised IS schedule in Y, i space, called the ISFF equilibrium schedule, where the effect of interest changes on the exchange is also taken into account. This schedule is also downward sloping, but flatter than the original one from the case of a fixed exchange rate. This last result is easily seen by applying the implicit function theorem to the equilibrium condition

$$Y^d(Y, i, s(i - \bar{i}^*, p, F_c, F) - Y = 0,$$

which results in

$$\frac{di}{dY} = -\frac{1}{Y_i^d + Y_s^d s_1}(Y_Y^d - 1) = \frac{1 - Y_Y^d}{Y_i^d + Y_s^d s_1}.$$

The last expression has a positive numerator and a negative denominator, which moreover is larger in magnitude than the one in the case of a given exchange rate s.

Indeed, we get here quite generally a negative relationship $s(i)$, defined by equilibrium on the market for foreign bonds, which can always be inserted into the IS schedule, giving rise to a single curve ISFF that represents simultaneous goods and foreign bond market equilibrium. In regime B2 of a given interest rate (still under consideration here), we then simply have to use the given interest rate and obtain the corresponding equilibrium output by inserting this rate into the ISFF schedule. The obtained result then also determines money supply and the new amount of domestic bonds held by the household sector, as has already been shown above.

In the other two cases, B1 and B3, we have to use the ISFF schedule together with the LM and BB schedules, respectively, in order to determine output and the rate of interest simultaneously by the intersection of the ISFF–LM or ISFF–BB schedules. In the case of regime B1 this is obvious, since M^s is then given exogenously and the LM curve is just another implicit relationship between the endogenous variables Y and i, just like the ISFF curve. In regime B3 we have to recall that the BB schedule is then given by

$$B \overset{BB}{=} p[W_p(s(i)) - m^d(Y, i) - sF_p/p] = p[(M + B)/p - m^d(Y, i)],$$

where B, F_p are given magnitudes (initial endowments) and where M^s is always adjusted to money demand by choice of regime. This gives, for the determination of the BB schedule, the equation

$$M/p \overset{BB}{=} m^d(Y, i),$$

and thus the same curve as in the B1 regime, as long as money supply in the current period is not changed by the central bank. Keeping money supply unchanged or keeping the endowment of domestic bonds of the central bank unchanged thus amounts to the same thing as far as the variation of other exogenous variables of the model is concerned.

12.3.2 Comparative static exercises: Applications

We now present some applications of the comparative statics just discussed, first for the case of fixed and then for the case of flexible exchange rates. The reader is referred to Rødseth (2000, Ch 6) for a more detailed discussion of these applications and further comparative static exercises.

Fixed exchange rate regimes

In the case of fixed exchange rates we have very straightforward results for fiscal as well as for monetary policy. Let us consider fiscal policy first. In the case of sterilization, M^s fixed, we have the standard results of the IS–LM analysis of closed economies, since the domestic economy and its domestic equilibrium are kept shielded from the other asset markets. In the case of an interest rate policy by the central bank, we, in addition, even avoid the partial crowding-out by investment and consumption of the closed economy case. In the case where B_c, the initial endowment of the central bank with domestic government bonds, is kept unchanged, we have to employ the BB schedule in place of the LM schedule, together with the IS schedule. Since the BB schedule – as shown – is less steep than the LM schedule we find that the interest rate effect of fiscal policy is smaller than that of monetary policy and thus there is less crowding-out than in the case of a monetary policy (in regime A1). As far as an expansionary fiscal policy is concerned, overall we have that the output effect is the largest for an interest rate policy, the second largest effect when no sterilization is made, while the sterilization regime has the smallest effect on output.

Let us next consider monetary policy in the case of a fixed exchange rate. In the case of sterilization (A1) we have the usual closed economy result with respect to expansionary monetary policy and resulting output changes. In the case of an expansionary interest rate policy (a decrease in the domestic rate of interest), we obtain of course the same effect when the decrease in the rate of interest is of the same size. A change in B_c and M^s has the same effect on output in regimes A1 and A3 as far as shifts in the LM and BB curves are concerned. Since LM curve is steeper than the BB curve it follows that the interest rate and output effect are stronger in the case of sterilization than with non-sterilization; that is, monetary policy is more effective in the former case than in the latter. We do not go into any more detail here, however, but refer the reader to Rødseth (2000, 6.3) for further comparative static analysis and also for graphical representations of the case of a fixed exchange rate regime.

Floating exchange rate regimes

Let us again consider briefly the case of floating exchange rates, in particular when there is an expansionary fiscal policy. In the case of an interest rate policy (which keeps this rate fixed) we have a given exchange rate and thus the same effect on output in both the fixed and the floating exchange rate regimes. In the other two regimes, B1 and B3, it turns out that output is increased more in the fixed exchange rate regime than in the floating one, since the increase in the domestic interest rate is accompanied by an appreciation in the case of floating exchange rates. Also, not unexpectedly, we have the result that monetary policy will be more powerful in the case of flexible exchange regimes than in the case of fixed ones, due to the depreciation it causes. Again the reader is referred to Rødseth (2000, 6.4), for more details on comparative static results in the case of flexible exchange rates.

The stress of the present section has been, however, not so much on comparative static exercises (which nevertheless confirm the intuition gained from the simple Mundell–Fleming model in many ways), but rather on the presentation of an extended framework of Mundell–Fleming–Tobin (or portfolio) type by which the lack of consistency of the basic Mundell–Fleming approach could be removed so as to allow us to gain a broader understanding of the real–financial interaction of small open economies. We have considered Keynesian goods market equilibrium in conjunction with three asset market equilibria, reflecting the given stocks in financial assets in a small open economy, and have also shown that there are no inconsistencies involved in the flow constraints of the economy as they are reflected in the balance of payments. We thereby have arrived at model type that is rich in structure and in implications and that really shows the power of the Mundell–Fleming approach for analyzing short-run adjustments in small open economies. For further applications and graphical representations of the comparative static exercises just discussed, the reader is referred to Rødseth (2000, 6.3/4) for details.

We finally stress that it can be useful to compare the model of this section with the model of an extremely open economy considered in Rødseth (2000, Ch 5), which we have briefly discussed in the preceding chapter when the pure monetary approach to open economy macroeconomics was considered.

In the following considerations that now allow stocks to change, we once again change the financing conditions of investment and now assume that all investment is performed as a direct investment decision of the household sector and is thus now integrated into its savings decision. This allows us to develop a medium-run dynamics later on that is close to the one considered in Section 6.6 in Rødseth (2000, Ch 6). With respect to notation, we return to the one used in the preceding chapter to ease comparison with the analysis of the extremely open economies considered there.

12.4 Twin deficits and price level dynamics under fixed and floating exchange rates

As in Chapter 11, we start again from the budget equations of the three relevant sectors: households, the government and the central bank. With respect to firms, which now also organize investment decisions (but are embedded into the budget restriction of the household sector), we thus assume that all of their income is transferred to the household sector and that households give them credit on this basis to finance their investment expenditures (by and large the same as a direct investment by the household sector). Note with respect to the following that the CB may change their government bond holdings by way of an open market policy $dB_c = dM$,[11] but that this does not influence the flow budget equations shown here. This results from all interest income from these bond holdings being transferred

---

11 Similarly, $dF_c = dM$ may also apply.

back to the government sector which therefore only has to pay interest on the bonds B held by the private sector. The domestic bond holdings of the CB can therefore be neglected in the following and an indexation of the bond holdings of the household sector can thus be avoided.

12.4.1 Budget restrictions: A recapitulation

Recall that

$$p(Y - \bar{T}) + iB + s\bar{i}^* F_p \equiv pC + pI + \dot{M} + \dot{B} + s\dot{F}_p \tag{12.20}$$

$$p\bar{T} + s\bar{i}^* F_c + \dot{B} + \dot{M} \equiv p\bar{G} + iB \tag{12.21}$$

$$\dot{M} \equiv \dot{B}_c, \tag{12.22}$$

and their implications for the evolution of domestic and foreign bonds held by the domestic economy:

$$\dot{B} = iB + p(\bar{G} - \bar{T}) - s\bar{i}^* F_c - \dot{M}$$

$$s\dot{F} = p(Y - C - \bar{G} - I) + s\bar{i}^* F.$$

These equations show the nominal evolution of the government debt and of the countries' foreign debt (or foreign assets) as they are implied by the balance of payments. Recall also that the latter is always balanced, independently of the exchange rate and monetary regime that is to be investigated, in accordance with the assumptions regarding the budget equations of the three sectors of our economy.

Considering the same situation from the viewpoint of savings, we can write:

$$pS_p = p(Y - \bar{T}) + iB + s\bar{i}^* F_p - pC = pI + \dot{M} + \dot{B} + s\dot{F}_p$$

$$pS_g = p\bar{T} + s\bar{i}^* F_c - iB - p\bar{G} = -\dot{B} - \dot{M}$$

which gives for the total savings pS of the economy:

$$pS = pY + s\bar{i}^* (F_p + F_c) - pC - p\bar{G} = pY + s\bar{i}^* F - pC - p\bar{G} = pI + s\dot{F}_p$$

$$= pI + s\dot{F}, \ F = F_p + F_c$$

This is again a formulation of the fact that the balance of payments must be balanced in the situation considered without any further adjustment processes; this is a solely based on the assumption that new money $\dot{M}$ and new government bonds $\dot{B}$ issued are in fact accepted by the household sector (as is implicitly made in the above formulation of the three budget equations of our economy).

12.4.2 Real disposable income and wealth accounting

In analogy with the Hicksian definition of private disposable income, we now define and rearrange this concept for the aggregate government sector (including the foreign interest income of the central bank) and show on this basis that the aggregate wealth of this sector W_g^a is in its time rate of change – as in the case of the private sector – determined by deducting from its disposable income the consumption of this sector. This then also provides us with a law of motion for real aggregate wealth of the government sector, besides the one we have already determined for the total wealth of the economy in Chapter 11 (see also below). These two laws describe on the one hand the evolution of surpluses or deficits in the government sector and on the other hand the evolution of current account surpluses or deficits, and thus allow the joint treatment of the issue of twin deficits in an open economy with a government sector. However, as above, capital accumulation and economic growth (to be determined via $\dot{K} = I$) are not yet dealt with, and will be looked into in Chapter 15.

The following calculations concern the sources of income and consider as disposable the income which, when consumed, just preserves the current level of wealth of the considered sector, here at first for the government sector and thereafter as recapitulation for the sector of private households (see also Chapter 11 in this regard). Since the rate of inflation $\hat{p}$ will become a variable in the following extension of the model, we will use this expression now in the definition of the real rates of interest to be employed (in place of a given rate $\bar{\pi}$ that we have so far employed).

$$
\begin{aligned}
Y_g^a :=&\ \bar{T} - \frac{iB}{p} + \frac{s\bar{i}^* F_c}{p} + \hat{p}\frac{M+B}{p} + (\hat{s}-\hat{p})\frac{sF_c}{p} \\
=&\ \bar{T} - (i-\hat{p})\frac{M+B}{p} + i\frac{M}{p} + (\bar{i}^* + \hat{s} - \hat{p})\frac{sF_c}{p} \\
=&\ \bar{T} + i\frac{M}{p} - (i - \bar{i}^* - \hat{s})\frac{M+B}{p} + (\bar{i}^* + \hat{s} - \hat{p})\frac{-(M+B)+sF_c}{p} \\
=&\ \bar{T} + i\frac{M}{p} + \xi\frac{M+B}{p} + r^*\frac{-(M+B)+sF_c}{p}, \quad \xi = \bar{i}^* + \hat{s} - i, \quad \text{with}
\end{aligned}
$$

$$
W_g^a := \frac{-(M+B)+sF_c}{p} = -\frac{(M+B)}{p} + \frac{sF_c}{p} = W_g + W_c, \quad \text{i.e.,}
$$

$$
\begin{aligned}
\dot{W}_g^a =&\ \frac{-(\dot{M}+\dot{B})+\dot{s}F_c}{p} - \frac{\dot{p}}{p}\frac{-(M+B)+sF_c}{p} \\
=&\ \frac{-(p\bar{G}+iB-p\bar{T}-\bar{i}^* sF_c)+\hat{s}sF_c}{p} - \hat{p}\frac{-(M+B)+sF_c}{p} \\
=&\ \bar{T} - i\frac{B}{p} + \hat{p}\frac{M+B}{p} + (\bar{i}^* + \hat{s} - \hat{p})\frac{sF_c}{p} - \bar{G}
\end{aligned}
$$

which finally gives

$$\dot{W}_g^a = Y_g^a - \bar{G} = r^* W_g^a + i\frac{M}{p} + \xi\frac{M+B}{p} + \bar{T} - \bar{G}$$

Since this debt position is now no longer constant, we repeat next the equations for the evolution of total wealth W of the economy in this case and then consider again private disposable income Y_p and private wealth W_p in its interaction with the evolution of aggregate government debt. Note that we assume goods market equilibrium $Y - C - I - G = NX$ in the following derivations.

$$W := W_p + W_g + W_c = \frac{sF}{p}, \quad F = F_p + F_c$$

$$\hat{W} = \hat{s} + \hat{F} - \hat{p}$$

$$\dot{W} = \hat{s}W + \frac{s\dot{F}}{p} - \hat{p}W$$

$$= \hat{s}W + \frac{p(Y - C - \bar{G} - I) + s\bar{i}^*F}{p} - \hat{p}W$$

$$= (\hat{s} - \hat{p})W + \bar{i}^*\frac{sF}{p} + Y - C - \bar{G} - I$$

$$\dot{W} = (\bar{i}^* + \hat{s} - \hat{p})W + Y - C - \bar{G} - I = r^*W + Y - C - \bar{G} - I$$

We have for the definition of actual private wealth and actual disposable income from our earlier analysis:

$$W_p = \frac{M + B + sF_p}{p} = W - W_g^a,$$

with W, W_g^a as determined above,

$$Y_p = Y - \bar{T} + (\bar{i}^* + \hat{s} - \hat{p})\frac{sF_p}{p} + (i - \hat{p})\frac{B}{p} - \hat{p}\frac{M}{p}$$

$$= Y - \bar{T} + (\bar{i}^* + \hat{s} - \hat{p})W_p - (\bar{i}^* + \hat{s} - \hat{p})\frac{M+B}{p} + (i - \hat{p})\frac{B}{p} - \hat{p}\frac{M}{p}$$

$$= Y - \bar{T} + r^*W_p - (\bar{i}^* + \hat{s} - i)\frac{M+B}{p} - r\frac{M}{p}$$

$$Y_p = Y - \bar{T} + r^*(W - W_g^a) - \xi\frac{M+B}{p} - i\frac{M}{p}$$

From the results on the disposable income of households and the government we finally also get:

$$Y_p = Y - Y_g^a + r^*W \quad \text{or} \quad Y_p + Y_g^a = Y + r^*W$$

as the relationship between total disposable income, domestic product and real interest on domestically held foreign bonds.

12.4.3 Laws of motion (and temporary equilibrium) of the MFT economy: A summary

In the following we set foreign inflation equal to zero ($\bar{\pi}^* = 0$), assume given policy parameters ($\bar{M}, \bar{T}, \bar{G}$), and finally assume for the domestic price level dynamics that it is determined by a standard expectations augmented Phillips curve.[12] Those then, in sum, read:[13]

1. $\dot{W} = r^*W + Y - C(Y_p, W - W_g^a, r, r^{*e}) - I(Y, r, r^{*e}) - \bar{G}$
   $= r^*W + NX(Y, \sigma, \bar{Y}^*), \quad r^* = \bar{i}^* + \hat{s} - \hat{p}$

2. $\dot{W}_g^a = r^*W_g^a + \xi\frac{M+B}{p} + i\frac{M}{p} + \bar{T} - \bar{G}, \xi = \bar{i}^* - \hat{s} - i,$

now, as stated above, to be coupled with the law of motion for the price level p:[14]

3. $\hat{p} = \beta_w(Y - \bar{Y}) + \gamma\hat{p} + (1 - \gamma)(\bar{\pi}^* + \epsilon(s)) = \beta_w(Y - \bar{Y})/(1 - \gamma) + \epsilon(s),$
   $\gamma \in (0, 1),$

and with the definitions

$$Y_p = Y + r^{*e}(W - W_g^a) - i\frac{M}{p} - \xi^e\frac{M+B}{p} - \bar{T}, r = i - \hat{p}, r^{*e} = \bar{i}^* + \epsilon(s) - \hat{p},$$

$$\sigma = s\bar{p}^*/p, \xi^e = \bar{i}^* + \epsilon(s) - i,$$

and where the temporary equilibrium description of the goods and the asset markets reads:

$$Y \overset{IS}{=} C(Y_p, W - W_g^a, r, r^{*e}) + I(Y, r, r^{*e}) + \bar{G} + NX(Y, \sigma, \bar{Y}^*)$$

$$M^s/p \overset{LM}{=} m^d(Y, i),$$

$$W \overset{FF}{=} sF/p = s(F^d + F_c^d)/p = f^d(\xi^e, W - W_g^a) + sF_c^d/p,$$

$$\text{based on} \quad F = F_p^d + F_c^d,$$

---

12 See Rødseth (2000, Ch. 6) for its motivation and note that this form of a Phillips curve derives from an expectations-augmented curve where the cost pressure item (concerning the consumer price index) is initially given by a weighted average of domestic and import price inflation of the form $\gamma\hat{p} + (1 - \gamma)(\bar{\pi}^* + \epsilon(s))$ and where myopic perfect foresight is assumed with regard to the evolution of the domestic inflation rate.

13 Note that $Y - C - I - \bar{G}$ can always be replaced by NX if this is convenient for certain calculations of the model's implications.

14 Here β_w indicates that wages are the driving force behind inflation, where the output gap measures the demand pressure on the labor market and the accelerator term in this Phillips curve measure the CPI inflation cost pressure for workers' consumption.

to be solved (by means of the implicit function theorem) and to be inserted into the laws of motion. We then obtain an autonomous system of ordinary differential equations, describing domestic price level dynamics, the dynamics of the government budget constraint, and that of the foreign position of the domestic economy. Of course, the definitions of Y_p, r, r^*, σ also have to be inserted. Finally, the variables M^s, B, i, s may become policy parameters, depending on the monetary and exchange regime under consideration.[15]

Note that the above laws of motion for W, W_g^a are actual laws of motion based on actual rates of return and actual changes in the exchange rate, while some arguments in the consumption function and the investment function are expected ones (relying on our use of a regressive expectations scheme) and thus have to be characterized by an index e for "expected". Furthermore, we assume myopic perfect foresight with respect to the inflation dynamics and thus do distinguish between expected and actual inflation rates; the former will be used in the behavioral relationships later on, while the latter apply to the actual laws of motion for the wealth variables considered. The distinction between actual and perceived rates of return will become important when exchange rate dynamics is considered later on (in our representation of the Dornbusch model in a Tobinian approach to financial markets). Note also that we have extended the consumption function of Rødseth (2000, Ch. 6) slightly, since we intend to distinguish between the consumption of the domestic and the foreign commodity later on and thus have to include the real exchange rate into the consumption function explicitly. Note also that nothing has been said yet about which of the regimes A1–A3 and B1–B3 is actually prevailing in the economy in question. Naturally, the choice of regime will determine which variables of the model have to be considered as endogenous and which ones as exogenous.

Stability analysis in the case of flexible exchange rates $(M, F_c$ are given magnitudes under the control of the central bank; i.e., $F = F_p + \bar{F}_c$ is also a given magnitude)

The way it is formulated, the above model faces one big difficulty in the case of flexible exchange rates, since we have to use the law of motion for the nominal exchange rate in order to calculate the real rate of interest on foreign bond, $r^* = \bar{i}^* + \hat{s} - \hat{p}$ from the viewpoint of domestic residents.[16] This rate enters the law of motion for both W and W_g^a and cannot be reduced any more to $\bar{i}^* - \bar{\pi}^*$ as in the case of the PPP assumption in Chapter 11. Due to this complication in the real laws of motion for foreign bonds held domestically and the real wealth of the government, it is preferable instead of obtaining the law of motion for s by differentiating and transforming the FF curve to a sufficient degree,[17] – to use the laws of motion for the considered stock magnitudes in nominal terms and to build their stability

15 In the case of a flexible exchange rate regime and a given money supply we will get jumps in s, σ, W, W_g^a when there is a shock in the money supply.
16 The same difficulty applies to the use of the risk premium ξ in the law of motion for W_g^a unless $M + B$ is assumed as zero (which is not a reasonable assumption). Note here again that such magnitudes are replaced by expected ones as far as definitions of disposable income and other parameters are concerned.
17 It is not difficult to show by means of the implicit functions theorem that the equilibrium exchange rate on the foreign exchange market is still a relatively simple function $s = s(W, W_g^a, p)$ in the special case where output in the LM curve is frozen at its steady-state level, i.e., where the theory of the nominal interest rate is independent of what happens on the goods market. In this case

analysis on such a representation. Doing this then gives rise to the following equivalent representation of the Mundell–Fleming–Tobin model in its general form:[18]

$$\dot{F}_p = \bar{i}^*(F_p + \bar{F}_c) + NX(Y, \sigma, \bar{Y}^*)/\sigma, \quad \sigma = \frac{s}{p}, \quad \bar{p}^* = 1 \tag{12.23}$$

$$\dot{B} = iB + p\bar{G} - p\bar{T} - s\bar{i}^*\bar{F}_c, \tag{12.24}$$

to be coupled again with the law of motion for the price level p:

$$\hat{p} = \beta_w(Y - \bar{Y})/(1 - \gamma) + \epsilon(s), \tag{12.25}$$

and with the description of the temporary equilibrium part now being given by

$$Y \overset{IS}{=} C(Y_p, W_p, i - \hat{p}, \bar{i}^* + \epsilon(s) - \hat{p})$$
$$+ I(Y, i - \hat{p}, \bar{i}^* + \epsilon(s) - \hat{p}) + \bar{G} + NX(Y, \sigma, \bar{Y}^*), \tag{12.26}$$

$$\bar{M} \overset{LM}{=} pm^d(Y, i), \tag{12.27}$$

$$F_p \overset{FF}{=} F_p^d = pf^d(\bar{i}^* + \epsilon(s) - i, W_p)/s, \tag{12.28}$$

to be coupled with the definitions

$$Y_p = Y - \bar{T} + (\bar{i}^* + \epsilon(s) - \hat{p})\frac{sF_p}{p} + (i - \hat{p})\frac{B}{p} - \hat{p}\frac{M}{p} \tag{12.29}$$

$$= Y + (\bar{i}^* + \epsilon(s) - \hat{p})\frac{\bar{M} + B + sF_p}{p} - i\frac{\bar{M}}{p} - (\bar{i}^* + \epsilon(s) - i)\frac{\bar{M} + B}{p} - \bar{T} \tag{12.30}$$

$$W_p = \frac{\bar{M} + B + sF_p}{p}. \tag{12.31}$$

This is the model we shall analyze in the remainder of this section with respect to its steady-state solution, its short-run comparative static features and the stability scenarios that derive from them.

12.4.4 Steady states: A simplified solution

In order to allow for a sequential determination of the steady-state values of the model, we proceed as follows. We assume for now (and will prove later on) that the steady-state value

we get

$$\hat{s} = s_W \dot{W} + s_{W_g^a} \dot{W}_g^a + s_p \hat{p}.$$

Such an expression must be used to substitute the $\hat{s}$ component in the variables r^*, ξ, giving rise to an implicit differential equation system that is very difficult to handle.

18 Such an approach is further justified by the observation that the dynamics of the nominal stock magnitude B is involved in the real dynamics considered above as long as $\xi \neq 0$ holds true, which shows that the real dynamics is then in fact a hybrid as far as the distinction between real and nominal variables is concerned.

i_o of i is given by $\bar{i}^*$; i.e., we have $\xi = 0$ in the steady state. From the Phillips curve we furthermore know that $Y_o = \bar{Y}$ must hold true. The given quantity of money $\bar{M}$ then allows to determine the steady-state value of p as $p_o = \bar{M}/m^d(\bar{Y}, \bar{i}^*)$. Setting $\dot{B} = 0$ furthermore gives a simple positive relationship between B_o and s_o. The FF curve implies on this basis:

$$F_{po} = p_o f^d(0, \frac{\bar{M} + B_o(s_o) + s_o F_{po}}{p_o}) = p_o f^d(0, \frac{\bar{M}}{p_o} + \frac{\bar{T} - \bar{G}}{\bar{i}^*} + \frac{s_o(F_{po} + \bar{F}_c)}{p_o}),$$

which defines a positive relationship between s_o and F_{po}, the FFB curve in Figure 12.1 (where we use linear curves for reasons of simplicity).

From $\dot{F} = 0$, we furthermore, get

$$\bar{i}^* F_o + p_o NX(\bar{Y}, s_o/p_o, \bar{Y}^*) = 0,$$

i.e., a negative relationship between s_o and F_{po}. If we assume that $\bar{M} + B_o$ is nonnegative (compare Figure 12.1), we have a nonnegative demand for foreign bonds at $s_o = 0$ and thus a nonnegative value of F_{po} associated with it. In the case of linearity (which need not hold in general), we will then get an intersection of the $\dot{F} = 0$ and the FFB curve in the positive half plane of the (F, s) space which gives us positive steady-state values of both F_p and s (since one can assume that there is a positive value s where $NX = 0$ holds). Under the stated conditions we thus have that the private agents of the domestic economy will hold a positive amount of foreign bonds in the steady state. Net exports must therefore be negative in the steady state, due to a value of the exchange rate that is below the one that balances the trade balance. In the general situation where both curves in Figure 12.1 are nonlinear, one must show that the $\dot{F} = 0$ curve is not too flat in view of the intersection of the FFB curve with the vertical axis and that both curves are not approaching $+\infty$ for finite values of the nominal exchange rate.

Inspecting the IS curve on the basis of what has been determined so far shows, however, that there is then no endogenous variable left that allows for IS equilibrium at the full employment level $\bar{Y}$ and the foreign interest rate $\bar{i}^*$. We therefore now adjust the values $\bar{T}, \bar{G}$ such that $\bar{T} - \bar{G}$ remains unchanged (that is, without impact on the left-hand side of the government budget constraint) until the IS curve also passes through the determined steady-state values. This holds if G, T are, on the basis of a given value for $G - T$, determined by

$$\bar{Y} = C(\bar{Y} - T + \bar{i}^* s_o F_{po}/p_o + \bar{i}^* B_o/p_o, \bar{i}^*, \bar{i}^*) + G_o + NX(\bar{Y}*, s_o/p_o, \bar{Y}^*),$$

if $I = 0$ holds in the steady state (see below).

Note here also that B_o/p_o is given by $(\bar{T} - \bar{G})/\bar{i}^* + \sigma_o \bar{F}_c$, which need not be positive and in fact must be negative in the case of a value of $\bar{T} - \bar{G}$ that is sufficiently negative. This is due to the fact that interest payments iB_o are positive in the steady state in the case of a positive value of government debt, implying that real government income $\bar{T} + s_o \bar{F}_c/p_o$ must be sufficiently high relative to $\bar{G}$ to allow for the given interest obligation of the government (since there is no issue of new government debt in the steady state). Note also that we assume the behavioral functions and parameters of the model to be such that disposable income Y_p is positive at the steady state. Note finally that our regressive expectation depreciation function for exchange rate depreciation or appreciation is always assumed to fulfill $\epsilon(s_o) = 0$ in the steady state (i.e. is assumed to be asymptotically rational) and is therefore shifting with the steady-state solution for s_o.

We have determined the steady-state values for p, i, Y, r, r^* in advance and then simultaneously the steady-state values for s, σ, F_p, B, basically from stock equilibrium conditions. So far, we have not mentioned the capital stock K, whose growth rate is to be determined by Y/K. The model's dynamics is in fact treated without any consideration of the law of motion of the capital stock. We justify this here by assuming as a further consistency condition that $I(\bar{Y}, \bar{i}^*, \bar{i}^*) = 0$ holds in the steady state. The capital stock will then converge to a certain finite value which is of no importance in the model as it has been formulated so far (since we have constant markup pricing by firms, i.e., prices do not react to demand pressure on the market for goods). Measuring this demand pressure by Y/K, for example, would suggest that this term should enter the investment function in the place of Y. The dynamics of the capital stock would then feed back into the goods market and become interdependent with the rest of the dynamics, even if prices do not react to such a demand pressure term.

Figure 12.1 shows, on the basis of the above, the determination of the steady-state values of both the nominal exchange rate and the value of foreign debt held domestically, and also indicates how these values can be influenced by fiscal and monetary policy. It shows that fiscal consolidation will make the currency stronger and increase the amount of $-denominated debt held domestically. The latter effect is also produced by a monetary expansion, whose effect on the value of s may, however, be ambiguous, depending on the competitiveness of the economy in question, i.e., on the elasticity of the net export function with respect to the real exchange rate at the steady state of the economy. Note that at this steady state we have a negative trade account and a positive interest rate account and, of course, a balanced capital account in the balance of payments.

In the policy regime under present consideration we will now derive a situation where the steady state of the model is surrounded by centrifugal forces (and is therefore repelling). This case will then be contrasted with a situation where an attracting steady state is given.

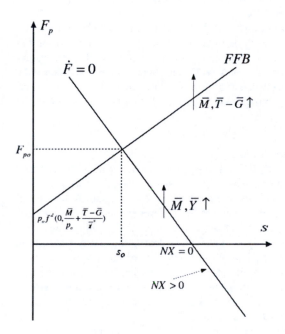

Figure 12.1 Steady-state stock equilibrium ($B_O > 0$).

The calculations needed to show these two results will show that there exists a multiplicity of situations where either stability or instability may prevail around the steady state. The conclusions will be that, first, empirical and numerical methods are needed in order to get a more complete picture of the stock-flow dynamics of the open MFT economy under consideration and that, second, it is likely that this policy must be more active than is currently assumed (in particular with respect to the government budget) in order to enforce convergent behavior around the steady state of such a small open economy.

12.4.5 Comparative statics: Output, interest and exchange rate determination

The dynamically endogenous variables are the price level p and the domestic and foreign bonds B, F_p held in the private sector. They are given at each moment of time and determine at each point in time the levels of the statically endogenous variables Y, i and s due to the monetary regime that is here considered.

In the present derivation of their comparative static properties we assume, for reasons of simplicity, that money demand is based on the full employment output level $\bar{Y}$, which immediately implies, by means of the implicit function theorem, that we get for the rate of interest in its reduced-form representation the formula

$$i = i(p, \bar{M}, \bar{Y}) \quad \text{with} \quad i_1 > 0, i_2 < 0, i_3 > 0.$$

The theory of the nominal rate of interest is thus the standard or even textbook one of Keynesian macroeconomics and is closely related to the working of the so-called Keynes effect whereby money wage changes stimulate the economy when they imply price level changes in the same direction and, on this basis, interest rate changes in the opposite direction which then work on consumption and investment via the real rate of interest. Inserting this result into the equation describing equilibrium in the market for foreign bonds gives one equation in the endogenous variables s and p and thus provides us with a theory of the nominal exchange rate in its dependence on dynamically endogenous stock variables B, F_p and the price level p.

$$sF_p - pf^d(\bar{i}^* + \epsilon(s) - i(p, \bar{M}, \bar{Y}), \frac{\bar{M} + B + sF_p}{p}) = 0.$$

We recall that $f_1^d, f_2^d > 0$ holds and that we have $\epsilon'(s) < 0$ due to our assumption of a regressive formation of expectations of exchange rate depreciation or appreciation. Making use furthermore of the portfolio choice condition $f_2^d < 1$ then gives, as partial derivatives with respect to the dynamically endogenous variables and by means of the implicit function theorem, the following expressions:

$$\frac{\partial s}{\partial F_p} = -\frac{s(1 - f_2^d)}{F_p(1 - f_2^d) - pf_1^d \epsilon'} < 0$$

$$\frac{\partial s}{\partial B} = \frac{f_2^d}{F_p(1 - f_2^d) - pf_1^d \epsilon'} > 0$$

$$\frac{\partial s}{\partial p} = \frac{f^d - pf_1^d i_1 - f_2^d W_p}{F_p(1 - f_2^d) - pf_1^d \epsilon'} = \frac{sF_p(1 - f_2^d)/p + pf_1^d i_1 - f_2^d \frac{\bar{M} + B}{p}}{F_p(1 - f_2^d) - pf_1^d \epsilon'}.$$

We note that the last partial derivative will be positive if the degree of capital mobility with respect to the risk premium is chosen sufficiently high, which is what we will do in the following. Note finally that the first two partial derivatives will approach zero if capital mobility approaches infinity and that in this case the limit of the partial derivative with respect to p is simply given by i'/ϵ'.

Turning finally to the IS equilibrium condition,

$$Y = C(Y_p, W_p, i - \hat{p}, \bar{\imath}^* + \epsilon(s) - \hat{p}, \sigma) + I(Y, i - \hat{p}, \bar{\imath}^* + \epsilon(s) - \hat{p})$$
$$+ \bar{G} + NX(Y, \sigma, \bar{Y}^*),$$

we find as comparative static results in the case where the speed of adjustment of money wages β_w is chosen sufficiently low:

$$\frac{\partial Y}{\partial F_p} > 0, \qquad \frac{\partial Y}{\partial B} > 0, \qquad \frac{\partial Y}{\partial p} < 0$$

This holds again only in the case where capital mobility is sufficiently high. We leave the lengthy calculations of the involved partial derivatives here to the reader and only state that increasing wealth of private households with respect to domestic and foreign bond holdings stimulates economic activity, while an increasing price level will reduce economic activity through various channels in the model, in particular through real wealth effects in consumption demand, but also through interest rate increases and real exchange rate decreases.

Remark: In the case where capital mobility is nearly perfect ($f_\xi^d \approx \infty$) and wages nearly rigid with respect to demand pressure ($\beta_w \approx 0$), we may summarize the comparative static properties – as far as the dynamically endogenous variables are concerned – and the laws of motion of the model approximately as follows:

$$i = i(p), i' > 0, \quad s = s(p), s' > 0, \quad Y(F_p, B, p), Y_1 > 0, Y_2 > 0, y_3 < 0.$$

Inserting these functions into the laws of motion for the variables F_p, B, p then gives rise to the following eigen-feedbacks of the considered state variables (if $\partial Y/\partial F_p$ is used in explicit form in the first partial derivative):

$$\frac{\partial \dot{F}_p}{\partial F_p} = \bar{\imath}^*(1 - C_Y)\frac{-NX_Y}{1 - C_Y - I_Y - NX_Y}) - C_{W_p}\frac{-NX_Y}{1 - C_Y - I_Y - NX_Y} < 0,$$

if $1 - C_Y - I_Y > 0$ and C_{W_p} is sufficiently large.

$$\frac{\partial \dot{B}}{\partial B} = \bar{\imath}^* > 0,$$

$$\frac{\partial \dot{p}}{\partial p} = \epsilon'(s)s'(p) < 0.$$

We thus have, in such a situation, that the trace of the Jacobian of the dynamics at the steady state is neither unambiguously positive nor negative and therefore all three state variables are subject to repelling forces as far as their steady-state position is concerned.

If one assumes, however, that the first of the above partial derivatives is positive (i.e., if the accumulation of foreign and domestic forces is not by itself subject to destabilizing forces) we get for the considered Jacobian approximately the following sign structure:

$$
J = \begin{pmatrix} + & - & \pm \\ 0 & + & \pm \\ 0 & 0 & - \end{pmatrix},
$$

due to the assumed nearly perfect capital mobility and the nearly rigid money wage dynamics as far as demand pressure is concerned. This Jacobian has a positive determinant and also exhibits a tendency towards negative principal minors of order 2. The latter observation may also hold in the case where only one minus sign is in the trace of the Jacobian where stable as well as unstable situations may be given. Only in the case where all signs in the trace are negative do we have the unambiguous situation of convergence back to the steady state. However, this requires that wages become sufficiently flexible with respect to demand pressure, and in this case the comparative static properties of the system may change significantly and may again induce instability by way of the complicated feedback channels that are then established. We conclude that the combination of sluggish wages and high capital mobility will be problematic for the stability of the balance of payments adjustment process, the evolution of the government debt and for the price level of the small open MFT-type economy under consideration.

12.5 Capital account and inflation with interest and exchange rate pegs

We are now going to consider the dynamic implications of a particular regime among the ones we have discussed in the preceding section. We here follow Rødseth (2000, Ch. 6.6) and choose a case where in fact the asset markets are left in the background of the model, a case which therefore solely studies the interactions of the IS curve with a conventional type of Phillips curve and the dynamics of the capital account. The conventional type of IS–PC analysis (without an LM curve) is therefore augmented here by the change in foreign assets from the excess of domestic savings over domestic investment. The assumptions we employ in order to derive this special case from our general framework are the following:

1. $i = \bar{i}^*$: An interest rate peg by the central bank (via an accommodating monetary policy).
2. $s = \bar{s} = 1$: A fixed exchange rate via an endogenous supply of dollar-denominated bonds by the central bank (which is never exhausted).
3. Given $\bar{Y}^*, \bar{p}^*(\bar{i}^*)$: The small country assumption.
4. $\bar{W}_g^a$: A tax policy of the government that keeps the aggregate wealth of the government fixed.
5. $G_2, I_2 = 0$: Only consumption goods are import commodities which are never rationed.
6. $\bar{\omega}$: The real wage is fixed by a conventional type of markup pricing.
7. $\bar{r}_f^n$: The normal (capacity utilization) rate of return of firms is fixed (since the real wage is a given magnitude) and set equal to $\bar{i}^*$ for simplicity.
8. $Y^p = \bar{y}^p K, N^d = Y/\bar{x}$: Fixed proportions in production.

9. $\bar{K}$: The capacity effect of investment is ignored. Potential output $\bar{Y}^p = 1$ is therefore a given magnitude.

10. $\bar{Y} = \bar{x}\bar{N} = 1$: A given level of full employment output.

On the basis of these assumptions we get that the real rates of interest are equalized for the domestic economy: $r^* = i^* + \hat{s} - \hat{p} = i - \hat{p} = r$. Furthermore, the risk premium ξ is zero in the situation considered. Finally, due to the assumed tax policy we have again, for disposable income in the household sector, the term $Y_p = Y + r^* W - \bar{G}$. Private wealth W_p is given by $W - \bar{W}_g^a$ in the situation, being considered.

The real portfolio demands of the private sector are again given by:

$$M^d/\bar{p} = m^d(Y, i), \quad m_Y^d > 0, m_i^d < 0, \tag{12.32}$$

$$sB_2^{pd}/\bar{p} = f^d(\xi, W_p) = f^d(\bar{i}^* + \epsilon(s) - i, W_p), \quad f_\xi^d > 0, 0 < f_{W_p}^d < 1, \tag{12.33}$$

$$B_1^{pd} = W_p - f^d(\bar{i}^* + \epsilon(s) - i, W_p) - m^d(Y, i). \tag{12.34}$$

and they are met by the central bank through open market operations in domestic and foreign bonds.

We define the real exchange rate by $\sigma = (sp^*)/p$, i.e., the amount of domestic goods that are exchanged for one unit of the foreign good. This rate reduces to $1/p$ as a result of the above normalization assumptions. Households directly buy investment goods for their firms and use the normal rate of profit in order to judge their performance, which is a given magnitude because of the above assumptions (normal output times the profit share). We therefore consider only one real rate, the rate r, in the following formulation of the consumption decisions (for domestic and foreign goods) and the investment decisions of the household sector:

$$C_1 = C_1(Y_p, W_p, r, \sigma): \quad \text{consumption demand for the domestic good}$$

$$C_2 = C_2(Y_p, W_p, r, \sigma): \quad \text{consumption demand for the foreign good}$$

$$C = C_1(Y_p, W_p, r, \sigma) + C_2(Y_p, W_p, r, \sigma)/\sigma : \text{total consumption}$$

$$I = i(Y, r): \text{investment demand, for domestic goods solely}$$

On this basis the goods market equilibrium or the IS curve of the model is given by:

$$C(Y_p, W_p, r, \sigma) + i(Y, r) + \bar{G} + NX(\cdot) = Y$$

where net exports are based on a standard export function and import demand as determined by C_2. Imports can be suppressed in this equation by reformulating it as

$$Y = C_1(Y + rW - \bar{G}, W - \bar{W}_g^a, r, \sigma) + i(Y, r) + \bar{G} + X(\bar{Y}^*, \sigma), \quad \sigma = 1/p, r = \bar{i}^* - \hat{p}.$$

We have assumed here that exports X, as usual, depend on foreign output and the real exchange rate.

The dynamic equations of the model are the following (the growth of the capital stock is neglected by assumption):

$$\hat{w} = \beta_w(Y - 1) + \gamma\hat{p} + (1 - \gamma)\widehat{sp}^* \tag{12.35}$$

$$\dot{W} = rW + X(\bar{Y}^*, \sigma) - C_2(Y + rW - \bar{G}, W - \bar{W}_g^a, r, \sigma)/\sigma \tag{12.36}$$

The second law of motion is the usual representation of the balance of payments in real terms, whereas the first one is a standard money wage Phillips curve in which cost-pressure items are represented as a weighted average of actual domestic and import price inflation. On the basis of constant markup pricing, this equation is usually transformed into a reduced-form price Phillips curve which, on the basis of our assumptions, then reads:

$$\hat{p} = \frac{1}{1-\gamma}\beta_w(Y-1) \tag{12.37}$$

$$\dot{W} = (\bar{i}^* - \hat{p})W + X(\bar{Y}^*, 1/p) - C_2(Y + (\bar{i}^* - \hat{p})W - \bar{G}, W - \bar{W}_g^a, \bar{i}^* - \hat{p}, 1/p)/p \tag{12.38}$$

We also show here a reduced-form expression for the second law of motion into which the first law has to be inserted in two places in order to arrive at a system of differential equations which, on its right-hand side only, depends on Y, p, W.

The temporary equilibrium output Y in turn depends only on the two state variables p, W by means of the following goods market equilibrium condition:

$$Y = C_1(Y + (\bar{i}^* - \frac{1}{1-\gamma}\beta_w(Y-1))W - \bar{G}, W - \bar{W}_g^a, \bar{i}^* - \frac{1}{1-\gamma}\beta_w(Y-1), p)$$

$$+ i(Y, \bar{i}^* - \frac{1}{1-\gamma}\beta_w(Y-1)) + \bar{G} + X(\bar{Y}^*, p). \tag{12.39}$$

We assume for the time being that the parameters of this equilibrium condition are such that the conventional dependency of IS equilibrium output on the price level results in $\partial Y/\partial p < 0$. With respect to aggregate domestic wealth it is obvious that $\partial Y/\partial W > 0$ holds true.

The resulting dynamic system in the state variables p, W is, by and large, of the same type as the one considered in Rødseth (2000, Ch. 6.6) and can be treated in the same way.

We note that we have to add the law of motion for $K : \dot{K} = i(Y, \bar{i}^* - (1/(1-\gamma)\beta_w(Y-1))$ for a complete treatment of the dynamics of this example of a small open economy. Since, however, the analysis without such capacity effects of investment is already complicated enough we do not go into such an extended dynamic analysis here. Furthermore, we may also return to an endogenous treatment of the variable W_g^a which would increase the complexity of the analysis even further, despite the simple framework that is still chosen here (where portfolio choice does not matter for the analysis of the dynamics of the real part of the model):

$$\hat{p} = \beta_w(Y-1)/(1-\gamma),$$

$$\dot{W}_g^a = (\bar{i}^* - \hat{p})W_g^a + \bar{i}^* m^d(Y, \bar{i}^*) + \bar{T} - \bar{G},$$

$$\dot{W} = (\bar{i}^* - \hat{p})W + X(\bar{Y}^*, 1/p)$$

$$- C_2(Y + (\bar{i}^* - \hat{p})(W - W_g^a) - \bar{i}^* m^d(Y, \bar{i}^*) - \bar{T}, W - W_g^a, \bar{i}^* - \hat{p}, 1/p)/p.$$

This extension would again allow for the discussion of the occurrence of twin deficits and other situations of domestic and foreign debt or surpluses.

For reasons of simplicity, however, we return to the situation where aggregate government wealth (basically the government deficit) stays constant in time, and investigate now the steady-state solution and the dynamics surrounding it of the following system:

$$\hat{p} = \frac{1}{1-\gamma} \beta_w (Y(p, W) - 1)$$

$$\dot{W} = (\bar{i}^* - \hat{p})W + X(\bar{Y}^*, 1/p) - C_2(Y(p, W) + (\bar{i}^* - \hat{p})W - \bar{G}, W - \bar{W}_g^a,$$

$$(\bar{i}^* - \hat{p}), 1/p)/p,$$

where the properties of the IS equilibrium are characterized by the standard partial derivatives discussed above.

With respect to the steady-state solution of this dynamical system we assume that the government pursues – in addition to its tax policy – a constant government expenditure policy that is aimed at fixing the steady-state value of exports at the level $\bar{X}$. This implies that the steady-state value of the price level, p_o, is to be determined from $\bar{X} = X(\bar{Y}^*, 1/p_o)$. Assuming that this equation has a (uniquely determined) positive solution for p_o we then can obtain the steady state value of W from the labor market equilibrium equation $1 = \bar{Y} = Y(p_o, W_o)$. The solution of this equation may be positive or negative and is again uniquely determined, since the right-hand side of this equation is strictly increasing in W_o. The level of government expenditure G that allows for this solution procedure, finally, is given by

$$0 = \bar{i}^* W_o + \bar{X} - C_2(\bar{Y} + \bar{i}^* W_o - G, W_o - \bar{W}_g^a, \bar{i}^*, 1/p_o)/p_o.$$

In this equation, the expenditure level is adjusted such that net imports are equal to the foreign interest income of domestic residents; i.e., an excess of imports over exports is needed in the case of positive foreign bond holdings in the domestic economy in the steady state. Note that the above is also based on the assumption that $i(\bar{Y}, \bar{i}^*) = 0$ holds in the steady state, since there must be a stationary capital stock in the steady state of the model.

We have a straightforward sign structure in the partial derivatives of the first law of motion, due to our simplifying assumption on the goods-market equilibrium equation $Y = Y(p, W)$. They guarantee that price level increases reduce economic activity and thus provide a check on further inflationary tendencies, thus inducing economic activity to increase with dollar-denominated wealth due to its effects on consumption. The second law of motion is, however, much more difficult to handle. Its partial derivative with respect to W is much more involved than the one in the preceding chapter and is given by (since $\hat{p}_o = 0$):

$$\frac{\partial \dot{W}}{\partial W} = \bar{i}^*(1 - \sigma_o C_{2Y_p}) - \sigma_o C_{2Y_p} \frac{\partial Y}{\partial W} - \sigma_o C_{2W_p} + \hat{p}_W[(\sigma_o C_{2Y_p} - 1)W_o + \sigma_o C_{2r}]$$

where we have denoted by $\hat{p}_W$ the partial derivative of the first law of motion with respect to W. We now have considerably more terms in the feedback of foreign debt on its time rate of change than was the case in Ch. 11 for the extremely open economy. These additional terms seem to provide more support for a negative feedback chain compared to this earlier chapter (if the assumptions on $Y(p, W)$ hold true), where we simply found that this partial feedback mechanism became positive (destabilizing) when wealth effects in consumption were sufficiently weak.

The remaining partial derivative for local stability analysis is given by

$$\frac{\partial \dot{W}}{\partial p} = ((\sigma_o C_{2Y_p} - 1)W_o + \sigma_o C_{2r})\hat{p}_p - \sigma_o C_{2Y_p} \frac{\partial Y}{\partial p} + (C_2 + \sigma_o C_{2\sigma} - X_\sigma)/p^2).$$

The first two expressions in this equation are positive in sign whereas the last term in brackets – the quantitative reaction of net imports to price level changes via the real exchange rate channel – is generally assumed to be negative ($\sigma = (s\bar{p}^*)/p = 1/p$). For the Jacobian J we thus, in sum, get as sign structure:

$$ J = \begin{pmatrix} \frac{\partial \hat{p}}{\partial p}p & \frac{\partial \hat{p}}{\partial W}p \\ \frac{\partial \dot{W}}{\partial p} & \frac{\partial \dot{W}}{\partial W} \end{pmatrix} = \begin{pmatrix} - & + \\ \pm & \pm \end{pmatrix}. $$

The easiest case for a stability result is

$$ J = \begin{pmatrix} \frac{\partial \hat{p}}{\partial p} & \frac{\partial \hat{p}}{\partial W} \\ \frac{\partial \dot{W}}{\partial p} & \frac{\partial \dot{W}}{\partial W} \end{pmatrix} = \begin{pmatrix} - & + \\ - & - \end{pmatrix}, $$

i.e., the case where interest effects do not dominate the capital account adjustment process and where the normal reaction of the trade balance (based on the so-called Marshall–Learner conditions) dominates the income, wealth and interest rate effects generated by the general form of a consumption function used in this and the preceding chapter. The steady state is in this case obviously locally asymptotically stable (since trace $J < 0$, det $J > 0$). Graphically, we get in this situation the phase diagram shown Figure 12.2.

In view of this figure we must, however, keep in mind the very restrictive assumptions we made with respect to the IS curve and its replacement by the evolution of the state variables of the dynamics, the reaction of the balance of payments and the dynamics of the capital account, and also the reaction of foreign bond accumulation with respect to price level changes. It is therefore by no means clear how dominant the case of stable price level

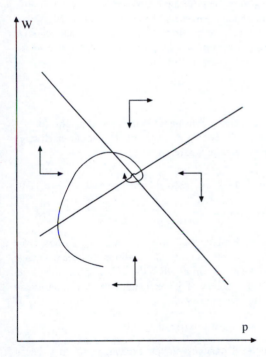

Figure 12.2 Stable inflation and capital account dynamics.

and capital account dynamics is in the set of all possible stability scenarios which the model allows for. In the case of divergence, the question is again what mechanisms in the private sector may then keep the dynamics bounded, or what policy actions are needed to ensure this.

The derived dynamical implications are, by and large, of the type considered in Rødseth (2000, Ch. 6.6), though our consumption and investment functions differ to some extent from the ones used by Rødseth. Note that Rødseth is here using the negative of W in order to characterize the international credit or debt position of the domestic economy. Rødseth also looks into a variety of further issues in his analysis of a Mundell–Fleming regime with an interest and an exchange rate peg. The reader is referred to this analysis for further aspects of this monetary and exchange rate regime.

12.6 Overshooting exchange rate dynamics

As a second case study, we now consider a regime of perfectly flexible exchange rates and given money supply. This implies that the supply of foreign bonds at each moment in time is just given by the stock of these bonds held in the household sector, since domestic bonds are assumed to be nontradables. The supply of financial assets is thus fixed at each moment of time and can only change in time via the flows induced in the capital account. The central bank may use open market operations in domestic bonds to change the composition of these bonds and money in the households' portfolio, but does not issue money otherwise (in particular to buy foreign bonds from domestic residents).

In our reformulation of the Dornbusch overshooting exchange rate dynamics within the framework of an MFT model we also assume for simplicity – just as in the original Dornbusch (1976) approach – that transactions demand in the money demand function is based on full employment output $\bar{Y} = 1$; i.e., we get from the LM curve of our Tobinian portfolio approach the result that the domestic rate of interest is solely dependent on the price level (positively) and on money supply (negatively), i.e.:

$$i = \frac{\ln p - \ln \bar{M}}{\alpha}$$

in the case of the Cagan money demand function considered in the preceding chapter.

For full asset markets equilibrium we need only consider the market for additional foreign bonds which, in the considered exchange rate regime, reads:

$$\frac{sF_p}{p} = f^d(\bar{i}^* + \epsilon(s) - i, \frac{M + B + sF_p}{p}) = f^d(r^{*e} - r, \frac{M + B + sF_p}{p}),$$

$$r^{*e} = \bar{i}^* + \epsilon(s) - \hat{p}, r = i - \hat{p},$$

with $F_p, M + B, p$ given magnitudes in each moment of time. Since $0 < f_2^d < 1$ holds true in a Tobinian portfolio model, we get from this equilibrium condition that the exchange rate s depends negatively on i, F_p and positively on p (when the effect of the price level on the nominal interest rate is ignored). The theory of the exchange rate of the considered Mundell–Fleming regime can thus be represented as follows:

$$s = s(i(p, M), p, F_p), \quad s_1 < 0, s_2 > 0, s_3 < 0, \quad i_1 > 0, i_2 < 0.$$

Note that the overall effect of price level changes on the exchange rate may be an ambiguous one.

Next we consider the IS equilibrium curve of the presently considered situation:

$$Y = C_1(Y + r^{*e}W - \bar{G}, W - \bar{W}_g^a, r, r^{*e}, \sigma) + \frac{I}{K}(Y, r, r^{*e})\bar{K} + \bar{G} + X(\bar{Y}^*, \sigma),$$

with $\sigma = s/p, \bar{p}^* = 1$. One has to use our regressive expectations regime, the dependence of the nominal rate of interest and the real exchange rate on the price level and the functional dependence of the nominal exchange rate on i, p derived above in order to derive conclusions on how the equilibrium output level depends on the price level p. The outcome is ambiguous, but points, to a certain degree, to a (conventional) negative overall dependence of Y on p. We shall assume that this holds true in our following discussion of overshooting exchange rates, since the opposite case would imply a destabilizing feedback of the price level on its rate of change via the Phillips curve mechanism. The dependence of Y on W is obviously a positive one, though we will have ambiguity in the movement of W later on.

We have by now determined the statically endogenous variables of the considered MFT regime i, s, Y by the three equilibrium relationships that now characterize the model. The state variables of the model are again p, W (while the movement of the capital stock is still neglected). The laws of motion for these variables are now given by:

$$\hat{p} = \beta_w(Y - 1)/(1 - \gamma),$$

$$\dot{W} = r^*W + X(\bar{Y}^*, \sigma) - \sigma C_2(Y + r^{*e}W - \bar{G}, W - \bar{W}_g^a, r, r^{*e}, \sigma),$$

where $r^* = \bar{i}^* + \hat{s} - \hat{p}$ and $r^{*e} = \bar{i}^* + \epsilon(s) - \hat{p}$ and $r = i - \hat{p}$. The law of motion for W is now a very complicated one, since the static relationships have to be inserted into it in various places. We will therefore not discuss its (in)stability implications in the following, but just assume that this variable is placed into its new long-run equilibrium position after a shock and kept constant there. We therefore only study the adjustment of the price level p after an open market operation of the central bank (which leaves $M + B$ unchanged). We note, however, that this implies a jump in the variable $W = (sF)/p$ that is neglected in our following analysis of such shocks.

In the construction of a steady-state reference solution we proceed as follows. We assume again that the government pursues an export target $\bar{X}$ by means of its expenditure policy $\bar{G}$, besides the tax policy that keeps W_g^a at a constant level $\bar{W}_g^a$. The steady-state real exchange rate σ_o is then uniquely determined by the equation $\bar{X} = X(\bar{Y}^*, \sigma)$. On this basis we can use the equilibrium condition on the market for foreign bonds to determine the steady-state level of W, since this equilibrium condition can be rewritten as

$$f^d(\xi, W - W_g^a) = W - \sigma_o\bar{F}_c \quad \text{or} \quad 0 = W - \sigma_o\bar{F}_c - f^d(\xi, W - W_g^a) = g(\xi, W),$$

since money supply, and thus F_c, is held constant by the central bank. Since $\epsilon(s_o)$ and ξ_o should be zero in the steady state (to be further justified below), the above equation can be assumed to have a uniquely determined positive solution if the function f^d is chosen appropriately. We note that we only consider positive values of W_o here, since we assume that households and the central bank hold such assets and since firms do not finance their investment expenditures abroad. This situation will change in the models to be considered in the next two chapters.

From the Phillips curve we get next that $Y_o = \bar{Y}$ must hold in the steady-state ($\hat{p}_o = 0$). Furthermore, the regressive expectations scheme is built such that $\epsilon(s_o) = 0$ holds for the steady-state value s_o of the nominal exchange rate (which still remains to be determined). We therefore have $r_o = i_o, r_o^* = r^{*e} = \bar{i}^*$ in the steady-state and postulate that

$I/K(\bar{Y},\bar{i}^*,\bar{i}^*) = 0$ holds for the investment function used in this MFT model. We assume on this basis, in addition, that the government chooses the level of $\bar{G}$ and thus $\bar{X}$ such that $i_o = i_o^*$ is enforced by the IS equation in the steady state:[19]

$$\bar{Y} = C_1(\bar{Y} + \bar{i}W_o - \bar{G}, W_o - \bar{W}_g^a, i_o, \bar{i}^*, \sigma_o) + \frac{I}{K}(\bar{Y}, i_o, \bar{i}^*)\bar{K} + \bar{G} + \bar{X}.$$

On this basis we can then get the steady-state value of the price level p_o from the LM curve $p_o = \bar{M}/m^d(\bar{Y},\bar{i}^*)$ and thus also the steady-state value of the exchange rate $s_o = p_o\sigma_o$.

We thus have quite a different "causality" in the determination of the steady state where fiscal policy has to provide the necessary anchor for a meaningful steady-state solution, whereas in the short run we have that IS–LM–FF curves determine the variables Y, i, s in this order, while the Phillips curve and the balance of payments determine the dynamics of the price level and of domestically held foreign bonds (in real terms). Note that the dynamics of the capital stock still remains excluded from consideration here. Note also that we will simplify in the following even further, since we shall also exclude the complicated adjustment process for $W = sF/p$ from consideration and instead assume that this magnitude will immediately jump to its new steady-state value after any shock and will be kept frozen there. The aim of the following simplified presentation, instead, will be to reconsider the Dornbusch (1976) model of overshooting exchange rates in the context of a Tobinian portfolio model of the financial sector and somewhat advanced formulations of consumption and investment behavior.

Let us now consider an open market operation of the central bank, $dM = -dB$, that increases the money holdings of private agents by reducing their holdings of domestic bonds (which therefore keeps $M + B$ and F_c constant). Our way of constructing a steady state for the dynamics being considered immediately implies that all real magnitudes remain the same (in particular W_o) and that we have, as sole steady-state changes, the following ones:

$$dM/M = dp_o/p_o = ds_o/s_o \quad (\sigma_o = \text{const}, i_o = \bar{i}^*)$$

The long-run reaction of the dynamics is therefore, as in the original Dornbusch (1976) model, a very straightforward one, strict neutrality of money and the relative form of the PPP, i.e., there is no change in the real exchange rate caused by the monetary expansion that is undertaken.

In the short run, prices are fixed and the burden of adjustment in the money market falls entirely on the nominal rate of interest i which is decreased below $\bar{i}^*$ through the monetary expansion. Since the new steady-state value s_o' of the nominal exchange rate is above the old level now, and since the assumed regressive expectations mechanism is completely rational in this respect, we would find that $\epsilon(s_o'/s)$, ϵ' became positive (generating the expectation of depreciation) if the short-run exchange rate remained unchanged. Since we ignore – as described above – adjustments in the value of W, we must however have that the current exchange rate depreciates beyond s_o' in order to imply the expectation of an appreciation of

---

19 In principle, the government here enforces two things in the steady state of the dynamics, namely that the domestic interest rate must then be at the international level, and that the level of exports is such that goods market equilibrium is then assured with, by assumption a zero level of net investment on the investment function. The real exchange rate is then a consequence of the level of $\bar{X}$ needed for goods market equilibrium.

the currency such that $\xi = \hat{i}^* + \epsilon(s_o'/s) - i = 0$ can remain unchanged (due to the unchanged value of W_o,[20] since the adjustment process of W is here ignored).[21] We thus get that i decreases and s increases under the assumed monetary expansion and expect that goods market equilibrium output increases through these two influences, since $\bar{i}^* + \epsilon = i$ has decreased and σ has increased (the price level still being fixed at p_o). Again, an ambiguous reaction may be possible, but we assume here – as before – that goods markets behave normally in this respect.

In the short run, the nominal exchange rate therefore overshoots its new long-run level as in the original Dornbusch model. Due to the increase in the output level beyond its normal level we have now, for the medium run, that the price level starts rising

$$\hat{p} = \beta_w(Y-1)/(1-\gamma) \quad \text{with} \quad Y = Y(p, W_o), \ \partial Y \partial p < 0$$

according to what has been shown above. The dynamics therefore converges back to its steady-state position with output levels falling back to their normal levels, prices rising to their new steady-state value p_o', the exchange rate appreciating back to its risen steady-state value s_o' and the nominal rate of interest rising again to the unchanged international level $\bar{i}^*$. All this takes place in a somewhat simplified portfolio approach to the financial markets (in the place of the UIP condition under rational expectations) and without any complications arising from possibly adverse adjustments through the balance of payments. It is therefore to be expected that a treatment of the full model along the lines of the preceding chapter (there for the extremely open economy) will reveal a variety of more complicated situations and, in the worst case, an unstable dynamics for which the actions of households or the government have to be found that bound their trajectories to economically meaningful domains. The present discussion is therefore only the beginning of a detailed discussion of the Dornbusch mechanism in a fully-fledged MFT model with inflation and balance of payments dynamics.

The dynamic adjustment processes just discussed are summarized in Figure 12.3. We have the simple LMFF curve describing full portfolio equilibrium by way of

$$f^d(\bar{i}^* + \epsilon(s) - i(p), W_o - \bar{W}_g^a) = W_o - \sigma_o \bar{F}_c,$$

where all revaluation effects of assets have been ignored, where transactions balances are still based on normal output and where, most importantly, the dynamics of the state variable W is set aside. The true LMFF curve is, of course, shifting with the changes in W, σ and the output level Y. We have, furthermore, the curve along which the price level is stationary, and which is also not as simple as that shown in this graph (where $\partial Y/\partial s, \partial Y/\partial p < 0$ is assumed) but may be quite complicated due to the assumed consumption and investment behavior.

If the old steady state A is disturbed by an expansionary monetary shock that shifts the old LMFF curve (not shown) into the new position (shown) we have as immediate response (SR) that the exchange rate adjusts (to A') such that full portfolio equilibrium is restored. In the medium run (MR) we then have rising price levels, rising interest rates and falling exchange rates until the new steady-state position (LR) is reached at point B.

20 and also $\bar{W}_g^a, \sigma_o \bar{F}_c$.

21 The argument must be more detailed if the short-run reaction in the value of W is taken into account, but would then of course demand a thorough discussion of the conditions under which dynamics drives this variable back to its steady-state level.

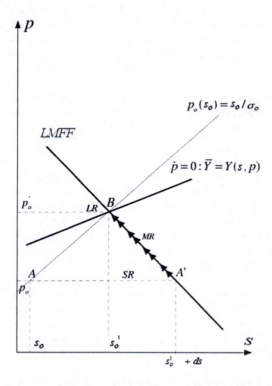

Figure 12.3 The Dornbusch overshooting exchange rate dynamics.

We note that the variables W, W_g^a may be subject to jumps in a regime with flexible exchange rates, but are then following their laws of motion if no further shocks occur (in the case of W) and then remain fixed at their respective new level (in the case of W_g^a). Furthermore, we may also return to an endogenous treatment of the variable W_g^a by making use of lump sum taxation $\bar{T}$ again. This would increase the complexity of the analysis even further:

$$\hat{p} = \beta_w(Y-1)/(1-\gamma),$$

$$\dot{W}_g^a = (\bar{i}^* + \hat{s} - \hat{p})W_g^a + (\bar{i}^* + \hat{s} - i)\frac{M+B}{p} + im^d(Y,i) + \bar{T} - \bar{G},$$

$$\dot{W} = (\bar{i}^* + \hat{s} - \hat{p})W + X(\bar{Y}^*, s\bar{p}^*/p) - (s\bar{p}^*/p)C_2(Y + (\bar{i}^* + \epsilon(s)) - \hat{p})(W - W_g^a)$$

$$- im^d(Y,i) - (\bar{i}^* + \epsilon(s) - i)\frac{M+B}{p} - \bar{T}, W - W_g^a, i - \hat{p}, \bar{i}^* + \epsilon(s) - \hat{p}, s\bar{p}^*/p).$$

This extension would again allow for the discussion of the occurrence of twin deficits and other situations of domestic and foreign debt or surpluses. Note however that the system has become a very complicated one, where the statically endogenous variables i, s have to be obtained from the portfolio part of the model – in interaction with the IS curve of the model which determines equilibrium output Y – and where the growth rate of s has then to be calculated on this basis. This is not at all an easy task and makes an analysis of the model nearly untractable. In view of this, ways have to found that model the dynamics of the exchange rate directly, so that a differentiation of the portfolio equilibrium equations can be avoided.

12.7 Conclusions

In this chapter we added Keynesian demand constraints, a net export function, and now also an investment function to the description of aggregate goods demand. The major change here, however, was the move away from perfect asset substitution and the assumption of imperfect substitutability of financial assets in the place of the UIP condition as used in the previous chapter. This imperfectness is here coupled with the assumption that domestic bonds are nontradables. The amount of foreign bonds held domestically can only be changed to the extent that there is a surplus or a deficit in the current account and not via exchanges of domestic bonds against foreign ones (or vice versa). This will be pursued further in Ch. 15 of this book. We assumed regressive expectations instead of rational expectations, which has two effects: this assumption avoids the questionable jump variable technique of the rational expectations school, and it allows for maximum stability of the dynamics being considered, since only fundamentalist and, in principle, converging expectations revisions are allowed for.

In the goods market, equilibrium conditions are based on aggregate demand functions. We assumed in addition a Tobinian portfolio structure in the financial part of the economy. Due to our use of a standard open-economy money–wage Phillips curve, this real cycle – considered in the second part of the chapter – is considered to be driven by the labor market, which goes significantly beyond the standard Mundell–Fleming model.

12.8 References

ASADA, T., C. CHIARELLA, P. FLASCHEL and R. FRANKE (2003): *Open Economy Macrodynamics. An Integrated Disequilibrium Approach*. Heidelberg: Springer.

DORNBUSCH, R. (1976): Expectations and exchange rate dynamics. *Journal of Political Economy*, 84, 1161–1175.

RØDSETH, A. (2000): *Open Economy Macroeconomics*. Cambridge, UK: Cambridge University Press.

13 Financial crisis, currency crisis and large output loss

13.1 Introduction

With the end of the Bretton Woods system in the 1970s and the financial market liberalization in the 1980s and 1990s, the international economy has experienced several financial crises in certain countries or regions entailing, in most cases, declining economic activity and large output losses. This has occurred regardless of whether the exchange rates were pegged or flexible. There appear to be destabilizing mechanisms at work from which even a flexible exchange rate regime cannot escape. In this chapter we review some of the stylized facts that appear to be common to such financial crises, and develop a Mundell–Fleming–Tobin-type model based on Rødseth (2000, Chapter 6) that takes up Krugman's (1999a,b, 2001) largely graphical suggestions in order to study such real and financial crises generated by large exchange rate swings.

With respect to exchange rate shocks due to currency runs triggering financial and real crises, there are three views, in fact three generations of models, that have been presented in the literature. A first view maintains that news on macroeconomic fundamentals (such as differences in economic growth rates, productivity differences and differences in price levels, in short-term interest rates as well as in monetary policy actions) may cause currency runs. The second view maintains that speculative forces drive exchange rates where there can be self-fulfilling expectations at work, destabilizing exchange rates without deterioration of fundamentals. Third, following the theory of imperfect capital markets, it has recently been maintained that the dynamics of self-fulfilling expectations depend on some fundamentals, for example, the strength and weakness of the balance sheets of economic units such as households, firms, banks and governments. From the latter point of view we can properly study the connection between the deterioration of fundamentals, exchange rate volatility, financial instability and declining economic activity. Although recently diverse micro- as well as macroeconomic theories have been proposed to explain currency runs, financial crises and recessions, we think that those types of models are particularly relevant that show how currency crises may entail destabilizing mechanisms leading, possibly through nonlinearities and multiple equilibria, to large output losses.

Such a model type can be found in Miller and Stiglitz (1999), who base their model on the work by Kiyotaki and Moore (1995), and diverse papers by Krugman (1999a,b, 2001). For a detailed survey of the literature on exchange rate volatility, financial crisis and large output loss, see Semmler (2006, Chapter 12). The work by Krugman is related closest to this chapter. However, it contains somewhat different motivations of Krugman's graphical analysis as to how the destabilizing mechanism, triggered through the currency crises, actually takes its course. Our model is narrower than the framework discussed in Krugman and thus concentrates on a few but essential elements of the currency crises. This is because many behavioral equations of the Mundell–Fleming–Tobin-type model employed remain stable despite large currency depreciation, implied large declines in investment and large output losses.

Whereas the above theories, building on imperfect capital markets, point to the perils of too fast a liberalization of financial markets and to an important role of the government's bank supervisions and guarantees, Burnside et al. (1999) view government guarantees as the cause of currency runs and financial crises. These authors argue that the lack of private hedging of exchange rate risk by firms and banks led, for example, to the financial crisis in Asia. Other authors, following the bank run model by Diamond and Dybvig (1983) (see, for example, Chang and Velasco (1999)), argue that financial crises occur if there is a lack of short-run liquidity. Further surveys of financial crisis models and discussion of policy issues can be found in Edwards (1999) and Rogoff (1999), who discuss the role of the IMF as lender of last resort. Our model will mainly employ some ideas of Miller and Stiglitz (1999) by using a modeling framework suggested by the work of Krugman (1999a,b, 2001).

The remainder of the chapter is organized as follows. Section 13.2 introduces some stylized facts. Section 13.3 presents the basic model. Section 13.4 then adds the budget restrictions and considers the accounting relationships that characterize the model in order to provide a clear picture of the scope of the model. Section 13.5 studies the dynamics under flexible exchange rates and Section 13.6 under the breakdown of a fixed exchange rate system. Section 13.7 concludes the chapter. In an appendix, we present the details of the Mundell–Fleming–Tobin model type employed in Rødseth (2000, Chapter 6) for the study of a variety of exchange rate regimes and their comparative static properties. This is a model type that we have modified and simplified in the main body of this chapter in our presentation of Krugman's (1999a,b, 2001) currency crisis dynamics.

13.2 Stylized facts

In recent times there have been major episodes of international financial crises in certain regions or countries, entailing a large output loss. The balance sheets of firms, households, banks and governments were central in this context. Weak balance sheets of those economic units mean that liabilities are not covered by assets. In particular, heavy external debt denominated in foreign currency, for example dollars, can cause a sudden reversal of capital flows and a currency crisis.

Credit risk and a sudden reversal of capital flows are often built up by a preceding increase in foreign debt. The deterioration of balance sheets of households, firms and banks has often come about by a preceding lending boom, increased risk-taking and an asset price boom. Subsequently a currency crisis is likely to occur, entailing a rise in the interest rate, a stock market crash; a banking crisis and large output loss.

Yet financial and exchange rate volatility do not always lead to an interest rate increase and a stock market crash. It is thus not necessary that a financial instability will be propagated. The major issue is in fact what the assets of the economic units represent. If economic units borrow against future income streams they may have to use net worth as collateral. The wealth of the economic units (or of a country) is represents the discounted future income streams. Sufficient net wealth makes the agents solvent, otherwise they are threatened by insolvency, which is equivalent to saying that the liabilities outweigh the assets. The question is only what good proxies to measure insolvency are, i.e., what sustainable debt is.[1] But, of course, exchange rate volatility and currency crises are relevant factors as well and thus the question arises what the causes of large exchange rate shocks are.

There are typical stylized facts to be observed before and after the financial crises, which have been studied in numerous papers (see for example Mishkin 1998, Milesi-Ferreti and Razen, 1996, 1998, Kamin, 1999). The empirical literature on financial crisis episodes may allow us to summarize the following stylized facts:

- there is a deterioration of balance sheets of economic units (households, firms, banks, the government and the country);
- before the crisis, the ratio of current account deficit to GDP rises;
- preceding the currency crisis, the ratio of external debt to reserve rises, but after the crisis the current account recovers;
- there is a sudden reversal of capital flows and unexpected depreciation of the currency;
- the foreign debt denominated in foreign currency of the economic agents suddenly rises, due to a drastic depreciation of the currency;
- domestic interest rates jump up, partly initiated by the central bank's policy;
- subsequently, stock prices fall;
- a banking crisis occurs, with large loan losses by banks and subsequent contraction of credit (sometimes moderated by a bail-out of failing banks by the government);
- the financial crisis entails a large output loss due to declines in large-scale investment and bankruptcies of firms and financial institutions.

Recent financial crises, such as the Asian crisis of 1997–98, were indeed triggered by a sudden reversal of capital flows and an unexpected strong depreciation of the

---

1 For debt dynamics in a macro model, see Semmler (2006).

currency. Next, we will build up a model which attempts to explain some of the stylized facts, in which we will stress in particular the impact of large currency depreciations on the breakdown of investment decisions and the resulting large output loss. This can occur despite significant improvements in the trade balance. We will use a standard portfolio approach to describe the financial sector of the economy and concentrate on the balance sheets of firms, their investment behavior and the multiplier dynamics that derives from it in order to show how ongoing reallocation of assets into foreign bonds can imply a currency crisis, a breakdown of investment and a large output loss.

13.3 The basic model

Krugman (2001, p. 83) states that "a fully fledged model of balance-sheet driven crisis is necessarily fairly complex". This chapter however shows that Krugman's ideas can indeed be represented in a coherent way, even on the textbook level, if his type of investment function is assumed and if imperfect substitution between financial assets is modeled as in Tobin. We build on a simplified and modified version of the Mundell–Fleming–Tobin model developed by Rødseth (2000, 6.2). We aim at a fully fledged modeling of the balance-sheet-driven crisis considered in Krugman (1999a,b, 2001). With respect to consumption and investment behavior, the model contains only the necessary variables to make Krugman's point and thus does not use wealth and interest rate effects in consumption and investment behavior. Instead, we make use of the following simple representation of consumption, investment and goods market equilibrium:

$$Y = C(Y - \delta\overline{K} - \overline{T}) + I(s) + \delta\overline{K} + \overline{G} + NX(Y, \overline{Y}^*, s). \tag{13.1}$$

We assume behind this equation given price levels $\overline{p}, \overline{p}^*$ at home and abroad, given foreign output $\overline{Y}^*$ and given world interest rate $\overline{i}^*$, as is often done in Mundell–Fleming models of small open economies. We normalize the price levels to "one" for reasons of simplicity, which allows us to identify quantities and value terms in national accounting. We finally assume as usual that $C' + NX_Y < 1, \quad NX_s > 0$ and, as already said, we neglect the influence of the domestic rate of interest on consumption and investment. Since we presume that there is no inflation at home and abroad, we also do not need to consider real interest and real exchange rates in this model type. The assumed type of investment behavior is described in detail below. Note finally that the above equation implicitly assumes that all investment demand concerns domestic goods. This is done in order to get strong multiplier effects on the economy in the case of strong currency depreciation.

Private households consume and save out of their disposable income $Y - \delta\overline{K} - \overline{T}$. We assume that capital stock $\overline{K}$ is given, as is the rate of depreciation δ, and $\overline{T}$ is an assumed lump-sum tax.[2] Feedbacks from the flow of savings into the

---

2 Lump-sum taxes are here calculated net of interest; see Rødseth (2000, Ch. 6) for a similar assumption.

asset holdings of households are still ignored, but could be added as in Rødseth (2000, 6.6) via the government budget constraint, which would however add further laws of motion to the model (see the next section for the discussion of the flow conditions that characterize asset markets as time evolves). Here, however, we only consider explicitly the stock constraint of private households and their portfolio demand functions, as first proposed in Tobin (1969) and as modeled in Rødseth (2000) on various levels of generality:[3]

$$W_p = M_0 + B_0 + sF_{p0} \tag{13.2}$$

$$M = m(Y, i) \tag{13.3}$$

$$sF_p = f(\xi, W_p), \quad \xi = \bar{i}^* + \varepsilon - i \tag{13.4}$$

$$B = W_p - m(Y, i) - f(\xi, W_p). \tag{13.5}$$

Note again that we have normalized the price level to be equal to 1. We here consider the reallocation of money holdings, M_o, fixed-price domestic bond holdings, B_o, and foreign fixed-price bond holdings of domestic households, F_{po}, between money M, dollar-dominated (private) foreign bonds F_p and domestic bonds B (the prices of these bonds are also assumed to be equal to one in terms of their currency, again for reasons of simplicity).

We do not yet consider any specific exchange rate regime of the Mundell–Fleming type and thus do not yet state in detail which of the quantities M, ψ, B, F_p, F_c are to be considered as exogenously determined. Note that ψ is here the foreign bond holdings of the central bank. We may already indicate here that, under the assumption that domestic bonds are not or cannot be traded internationally, a fixed exchange rate regime will imply that $F_p + F_c$ can be considered as fixed, whereas in a flexible exchange rate regime we get that F_p can be considered as fixed, since the CB then need not intervene in the foreign exchange market. Equation (13.2) provides the definition of private wealth currently held in the household sector, with the nominal exchange rate s. Money demand equal to money supply is considered next, as in the usual LM approach. Demand for dollar-denominated bonds sF_p, expressed in domestic currency, is assumed to depend on private wealth W_p and the risk premium ξ, which is defined by the difference between foreign and domestic interest rates augmented by capital gains or losses ε, with ε as the expected rate of depreciation or appreciation. We assume $f_\xi > 0$ and $F_{W_p} \in (0, 1)$ and, of course, $M_Y > 0, m_i < 0$. Demand for domestic bonds B is then determined residually by the Walras law of stocks. With respect to expected

---

3 We present the portfolio model using the gross substitute assumption in the way that asset demands always depend positively on their own rate of return and negatively on the other rates. We therefore define the risk premium on foreign bonds as the negative of the one considered in Rødseth (2000) in order to get a positive dependence of the demand for foreign bonds on the risk premium in place of the negative one in his book, which, however, is but a change in the conventions used.

depreciation ε we assume

$$\varepsilon = \varepsilon(s), \quad \varepsilon' \leq 0, \quad \varepsilon(s_o) = 0 \quad \text{for the steady-state value of } s, \qquad (13.6)$$

which is a general formulation of regressive expectations; see Rødseth (2000, Ch. 1.4) for details.[4] Note here already, however, that we assume that economic agents have perfect knowledge of the relevant steady-state value of s of the model (denoted by s^f) and that they are therefore forward looking in their behavior. It is thus expected that the actual exchange rate will adjust with possibly varying speed to this steady-state value. Such an expectational scheme may also be characterized as asymptotically rational behavior and represents a very fundamental and tranquil type of expected exchange rate adjustments. Expectations are therefore not central to the explanation of the currency crises considered in this chapter.

As the above portfolio demand approach is formulated, we have substitution between money and domestic bonds on the one hand and between domestic and foreign bonds on the other hand, the first determined in reference to the nominal rate of interest i and the second in reference to the risk premium ξ between domestic and foreign bonds. Furthermore, all domestic money and bonds are held by domestic residents. There is thus no international trade in domestic bonds. There is nothing extraordinary involved in our description of the sector of private households, which is characterized by a simple consumption and savings function and a standard portfolio approach to imperfect capital mobility.

The sector of firms, here so far represented only by its net investment function $I(s)$, is however quite different from what is usually used to characterize investment behavior. Investment is here made dependent solely on the nominal exchange rate s. This dependence is represented in Figure 13.1.

We assume here that investment depends negatively on the exchange rate s, and strongly so in an intermediate range of this exchange rate. The story behind this assumption is that depreciation worsens the balance sheet of firms (see the next section), due to the fact that their past investment decisions were financed by foreign bonds (firm bonds denominated in foreign – dollar – currency). Depreciation thus increases the debt of firms when measured in domestic currency and thus lowers the credit rating and the creditworthiness of the firms and their ability to finance current investment. Investment is therefore reduced when depreciation of the domestic currency occurs and, by the assumption made below, in the middle range considered for the exchange rate the investment is reduced to such a degree that it dominates the positive (normal) reaction of net exports NX with respect to exchange rate changes:

$$-I'(s) > NX_s > 0.$$

---

4 A specific formulation would be $\varepsilon = \beta_\varepsilon(s^f/s - 1)$, where s^f denotes the steady-state value the economy is converging to.

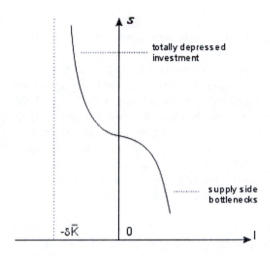

Figure 13.1 A Krugman (2001) type of investment function.

In this range we therefore get for the aggregate demand function

$$Y^d(Y,s): \qquad Y_Y^d \in (0,1) \text{ and } Y_s^d < 0.$$

The latter partial derivative represents a striking difference to the usual assumptions on aggregate demand in models of the Mundell–Fleming type. For very high and very low exchange rates we assume, however, that investment is not very sensitive to further exchange rate changes for two reasons: on the one hand, there are supply bottlenecks for very high investment demand and, on the other hand, there are some investment projects that must and can be continued – despite severe credit rationing of firms – even for very high levels of the exchange rate. For extreme values of the exchange rate we therefore have the usual positive dependence of goods market equilibrium on the level of the exchange rate.

We have already stated that the implications of the government deficit with respect to changes in the supply of money and domestic bonds are still ignored in the current short-term analysis of a small open economy. With respect to the central bank, we assume that it can change not only the supply of money and domestic bond holdings instantaneously through standard open market operations, but also the amount of the dollar-denominated bonds if it desires to do so. Following Rødseth (2000, Ch. 6) we assume, however, that the following constraint must hold true:

$$F_p + F_c = \overline{F}^*,$$

with F_c the foreign bond holdings of the central bank and $\overline{F}^*$ the total amount of dollar-denominated bonds held in the domestic economy (treated separately from the credit given to firms). This assumption can be justified by considering regimes where money can be exchanged against foreign currency only in the domestic economy (through the monetary authority) and by assuming that domestic bonds cannot be traded internationally, which may be a realistic assumption for the type of economy here considered. This closes the short-run equilibrium description of the considered small open economy. Note again that we even get a fixed F_p value if the monetary authority need not intervene in the foreign exchange market.

Finally, we note again that the above feature of investment behavior has been chosen so that in its middle range the investment function is characterized as very elastic with respect to the exchange rate s. For very high and very low exchange rates, however, investment becomes very inelastic in this regard. If the currency is strong (low s), investment runs into a bottleneck and is limited by supply-side conditions, be they actual or only perceived ones. If the currency is very weak, net investment is reduced to its floor level (which may even be negative). In sum, we have an investment behavior formally similar to the one considered in the Kaldor (1940) trade cycle model, but here based on net worth effects resulting from exchange rate changes, instead of an influence of economic activity Y on the net investment of firms.

As in Kaldor (1940) (see also Blanchard and Fischer (1989, p. 532)), we consider the following goods market adjustment process off the IS or goods market equilibrium curve (as simplification of a more general goods market adjustment process where also inventories are adjusted by firms):

$$\dot{Y} = \beta_y(Y^d - Y) = \beta_y(C(Y - \delta\overline{K} - \overline{T}) + I(s) + \delta\overline{K} + \overline{G} + NX(Y, \bar{Y}^*, s) - Y).$$

This dynamic multiplier process is a stable one for any given level of s, since $Y_Y^d - 1 < 0$ was assumed to hold true.

Next, we derive two equilibrium curves, for the goods and asset market equilibrium respectively, situated in the Y, s phase space and surrounded by the multiplier dynamics just introduced. First we consider the IS curve, defined by eq. (13.1), and get from the implicit function theorem for the shape of this curve, with Y the dependent and s the independent variable:

$$Y'(s) = -\frac{I' + NX_s}{C' + NX_Y - 1} \gtreqless 0,$$

due to the sign of the numerator, while the denominator is unambiguously negative. In the mid-range of s-values, discussed above, we thus have $Y'(s) < 0$ and thus a backward-bending IS curve, since I' dominates NX_s in this range, while we have a positive slope for this curve outside of this range, since $|I'|$ then becomes close to zero.

For the IS curve we thus get a scenario as shown in Figure 13.2, where we have also added the output adjustment of firms when economic activity departs from the IS curve. This shows that the IS curve is a global attractor with respect

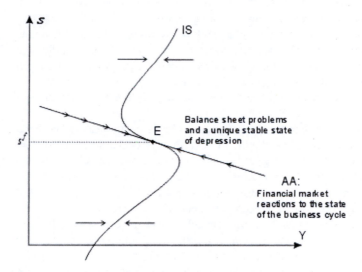

Figure 13.2 IS equilibrium and output adjustment along the AA curve in the case of an output and asset market determined exchange rate).

to output adjustment whenever the economy is displaced from it by a shock. Note also that the IS curve should become very steep for very large and very small values of the exchange rate s, since investment and net exports may then be very insensitive to further exchange rate changes. Note also that this curve should cut the horizontal axis at a positive value of output Y, since $\dot{Y}$ is positive at $Y = 0$, by assumption.

Let us next consider the asset market equilibrium as described by eqs (13.2)–(13.6). From eq. (13.3) we get in the usual way, for any given M, a positive dependence of i on Y and a negative dependence with respect to M, as is generally the case in such simple LM approaches to the money market:

$$i(Y,M), \ i_Y > 0, \ i_M < 0$$

Inserting this reduced-form equation and eq. (13.6) into (13.4) gives rise to:[5]

$$sF_p = f(\bar{i}^* + \varepsilon(s) - i(Y,M), \ M_0 + B_0 + sF_{p0}), \quad M \quad \text{given.}$$

This condensed representation of full asset markets equilibrium will give rise (for flexible exchange rates and thus a given F_p) to a strictly negatively

---

5 Note that the use made of this equation and the F restriction in this paper assumes that domestic bonds are non-tradables, which implies that the tradable amount of foreign bonds is fixed to the domestic holdings of such bonds in each moment of time. In the case of a flexible exchange rate this amount even reduces to F_p due to the non-intervention of the domestic central bank in this case.

sloped equilibrium curve AA (representing the influence of the business cycle on exchange rate determination). This curve cuts the vertical axis by assumption and for reasons of simplicity, will always be drawn as a straight line in the following.[6] Under the Walras law of stocks we thus have a well-defined single curve for the characterization of equilibrium in the financial markets of the economy for any given level of money supply M.[7] Summarizing, we thus have in the present modeling framework a new and extended type of IS–LM diagram, where LM equilibrium is combined with an FF equilibrium for \$-denominated bonds to provide a strictly decreasing function in the Y, s phase space in place of the usual output–interest phase space, the AA asset market equilibrium curve. Furthermore, the IS or goods market equilibrium curve is now situated in the same phase space where its usually assumed strictly positive slope is valid only for very high and very low values of the exchange rate s. We thus have to deal with new slopes of IS–LM curves in a newly defined economic phase space in the following.

13.4 Budget restrictions and national accounting

In this section we consider explicitly the dynamic adjustment of foreign reserves (or bonds) in the domestic economy (as well as flows into domestic money and bond holdings) that occur due to the investment decisions of firms, the saving decisions of households, the decisions of the government and of the central bank, taking also into account the net exports of our model economy. We want to show that all the foreign account flows balance each other in the balance of payments (under certain consistency assumptions on new domestic money and bond supply) so that there is no need – beyond what happens in the stock markets – for the central bank to intervene in order for the foreign exchange market to be in equilibrium. We will in particular describe here the changes in foreign bond holdings of households and the central bank, and the change in the foreign debt of firms.

First of all, we now assume explicitly – as is usually the case – that all income generated by firms is transferred into the household sector, however, formally deducting depreciation in order to arrive at net magnitudes. Since we allow for negative net investment, the amount representing depreciation need not be kept back by and invested within firms. We thus assume here that there is a positive floor to gross investment I^g and that enough foreign credit is available in order to finance at least this minimum amount of investment projects, not scrapped

---

6 Though it may only approach the horizontal axis for exchange rates approaching zero.
7 This distinguishes our approach to the *AA* curve from the one suggested in Krugman (2001), where a "leaning against the wind" strategy seems to be part of the *AA* curve. Leaning against the wind in our model means shifting the AA curve to the left by means of restrictive monetary policy (reduced money supply). This is indeed also stated in Krugman and Obstfeld (2003) where, however, the interest rate parity condition is used for the derivation of the AA curve in place of our explicit (imperfect substitute) portfolio representation of the asset markets.

within a currency crisis. This gives rise to the following budget equations of firms:[8]

$$Y - \delta\bar{K} - s\bar{i}^*F_f = wL^d + \Pi_p, \quad I = s\dot{F}_f,$$

i.e., firms have to pay interest on their foreign debt and transfer all remaining proceeds into the households sector as wages wL^d and profits Π_p. Their investments I (if positive) thus have to be financed completely by new foreign debt, since we assume that investment goods are completely purchased on the international goods markets. They thus represent foreign goods, here however – in the investment demand function – already measured in terms of the domestic currency. This means that the quantity demanded on the world market must depend on the exchange rate with an elasticity that is smaller than -1 in order to give rise to an investment schedule in the domestic currency with the assumed property $I'(s) < 0$. This investment behavior may be due to credit constraints, but also simply due to the fact that such investment is not profitable at the currently prevailing exchange rate.

For the household sector we next get as flow budget constraint, in view of what has been stated for firms:

$$Y - \delta\bar{K} - s\bar{i}^*F_f + s\bar{i}^*F_p - \bar{T} - C = \dot{M} + \dot{B} + s\dot{F}_p.$$

Note that lump-sum taxes are here calculated net of domestic interest payments by the government, similar to the procedures applied in Rødseth (2000, Ch. 6). The government budget constraint thus here simply reads:

$$\bar{G} - \bar{T} = \dot{M} + \dot{B}, \qquad \bar{T} = T - iB.$$

We assume with respect to central bank behavior that all interest income on government bonds that are held by the central bank (due to past open market operations) is transferred back to the government sector and thus does not appear in the government budget constraint as a separate item. We therefore represent explicitly only privately held government bonds in this paper, as is usually done in the literature. The above budget equation of households says that household savings, on its left-hand side, is spent on new money and new domestic bonds as they are supplied by the government; the remainder goes into new foreign bonds. This in fact represents a flow consistency assumption that guarantees that the balance of payments – showing here planned magnitudes solely – will always be balanced in the present framework. Note again that all prices (goods and assets) – up to the exchange rate – are set equal to one in the present form of the model.

---

8 In the case of negative net investment we thus get that firms are paying back part of their foreign debt.

With respect to central bank behavior we finally assume that its (remaining) income (equal to its savings) is spent on the acquisition of foreign reserves in the form of foreign bonds; i.e., we have

$$\bar{si}^{*}F_c = s\dot{F}_c.$$

Aggregating all (dis-)savings (of households, government and the central bank) gives the equation

$$Y - \delta\bar{K} - C - \bar{G} + \bar{si}^{*}(F_p + F_c) - \bar{si}^{*}F_f = s(\dot{F}_p + \dot{F}_c),$$

which in turn implies, due to the assumed goods market equilibrium condition:[9]

$$CA + I = NX + \bar{si}^{*}(F_p + F_c) - \bar{si}^{*}F_f + I = s(\dot{F}_p + \dot{F}_c) = S = S_p + S_g + S_c.$$

Inserting the foreign bonds that finance firms' investment then gives rise to the equality between the current account deficit (or surplus) and the surplus (or deficit) in the capital account, shown in the equation:

$$NX + \bar{si}^{*}(F_p + F_c) - \bar{si}^{*}F_f = s(\dot{F}_p + \dot{F}_c) - s\dot{F}_f.$$

We thus have that the balance of payments is – under the assumption that households absorb the new money and the new domestic bonds shown in the government budget constraint – always balanced. All flows that need foreign currency thus will get this foreign currency and the stock markets are – as assumed – always in equilibrium. Net exports and net interest payments on foreign bonds are always equal in sum to net capital export or net foreign bond import, with households and the central bank as creditors and firms as debtors in the interest and foreign bond flows that are considered. Note that although we have this balance in the balance of payments we have nevertheless included the possibility of credit rationing of firms, subsumed in the assumed shape of the investment function; i.e., investment and its financing do not reflect demand-side aspects solely. The investment function is therefore based to some extent on factual outcomes.

We note again that domestic money can only be exchanged against foreign currency in the domestic economy. Combined with the assumption that domestic bonds are not traded internationally, this is sufficient to provide the constraint $F_p = F_{po}$ for asset reallocations in the case of a flexible exchange rate. In the case of a fixed exchange rate system, this gives an endogenous F_p determination, served by the domestic central bank. These two alternatives will find application in the next two sections of this chapter. Note that the case of an exchange rate that is fixed by the domestic central bank exhibits the inequality $F_p \le F_{po} + F_c$

---

9 This states that the current account surplus *CA* (or deficit) plus net investment must be equal to aggregate savings.

as constraint on the reallocation of foreign bonds between households and the central bank. This therefore characterizes the range in which the central bank may be capable of fixing the domestic exchange rate.

Note finally that the balance sheet effect for firms, here indebted in foreign bonds solely, with no retained earnings and with no equity financing, reads simply:[10]

The balance sheet of firms (current values)

Tangible assets	Liabilities
pK	sF_f
	Net worth (measuring creditworthiness)

The actual change in this balance sheet – through (dis-)investment – is here simply represented by the assumption

$$I(s) = s\dot{F}_f(s), \quad I'(s) < 0, \quad \text{i.e.,} \quad \frac{d\dot{F}_f}{\dot{F}_f} \Big/ \frac{ds}{s} < -1,$$

which is not explained in detail as far as the credit rationing process or voluntary investment reduction underlying this investment schedule are concerned.

Firms, run by domestic households, thus combine labor L^d and capital K, financed solely by foreign financial capital, to produce the output Y and the accounting net worth $pK - sF_f$. Portfolio markets determine the interest rate i and the exchange rate s (if flexible) for any given output level. The goods markets determine the output level Y of firms for any given exchange rate separately in a fixed exchange rate system (where asset markets determine i, F_p) and jointly with the asset markets in the case of a flexible exchange rate. Financial flows caused by the savings and investment decisions of the considered sectors of the economy do not matter in this interaction, but have been considered here in addition for reasons of consistency. Financial crisis in the proper sense of the word is here only present in the assumed investment behavior and its financing condition, up to the consideration of the capital flight parameter α later on, since consumption behavior and asset demands remain stable otherwise (or are not explicitly considered here with respect to critical behavioral nonlinearities). There is also no explicit consideration of bankruptcies here.

In the remaining part of this section we finally summarize our model economy from the perspective of national accounting, based on the budget restrictions just discussed. Due to these restrictions, and to the assumption that the type of financing

---

10 This balance sheet is thus based on the historical (current) value of the capital stock and does not take into account any discounted cash flows here in its formulation of the net worth of firms (equities are also not yet present in the model; their value may be measured by such discounted cash flows). We thus ignore any interest rate effect on the presented measure of the net worth of firms, on the basis of which credit rationing will then be decided.

of the government deficit (the inflow of new money and domestic bonds) is always accepted by the private sector of the economy, we will find again that the balance of payments, representing the real and financial flows planned by the various sectors, is always balanced and thus of no importance for the determination of the exchange rate. This rate is in fact determined solely by a stock or portfolio approach , on the basis of the stocks the economy inherited from the past (disregarding the given foreign debt or credit to firms here).

We start with some notational issues that provide notation not used so far in this chapter:

FD_f:	Financial deficit of firms
FD_g:	Financial deficit of the government
$-FD_p$:	Financial surplus of the private sector
$-FD_c$:	Financial surplus of the central bank
I^g:	Gross investment ($I^g = I + \delta \bar{K}$)
Im, Ex:	Imports and exports of commodities

Firms

Production account		Change of wealth account		Flow of funds account	
Debits	Credits	Debits	Credits	Debits	Credits
δK		I^g	δK	FD_f	$s\dot{F}_f$
$s\bar{i}^* F_f$	I^g		FD_f		
wL^d	G				
Π_p	C				
$s\,Im$	Ex				

Households

Income account		Change of wealth account		Flow of funds account	
Debits	Credits	Debits	Credits	Debits	Credits
T	wL^d	FS_p	S_p	$\dot{M}$	FS_p
C	iB			$\dot{B}$	
S_p	$s\bar{i}^* F_p$			$s\dot{F}_p$	
	Π_p				

The government

We assume again that the given domestic and the foreign price levels are both set equal to 1 by appropriate normalization so that we have to use the nominal

Income account		Change of wealth account		Flow of funds account	
Debits	Credits	Debits	Credits	Debits	Credits
G	$\bar{T} = T - iB$		S_g	FD_g	$\dot{M}$
S_g			FD_g		$\dot{B}$

exchange rate only to express everything in terms of the domestic commodity. We have five sectors in the economy: households, firms, the government, the central bank and the world economy or the foreign account. We distinguish four accounts for the first four sectors: production, income, wealth accumulation and financial account. Our model is based on the assumptions that households and the fiscal authority have no production account and firms no income account (all profits are transferred to the household sector). Of course, all accounts only show items that exist in the model of this paper and thus do exclude many factual items of the system of national accounts.

Note, furthermore, that imports are explicitly represented here in terms of the foreign commodity, whereas their consumption by households, firms and the government is left implicit and expressed in terms of the domestic commodity solely. We here follow the usual practice to summarize the role of imports in the net export function, which therefore represents the influence of the exchange rate on domestic consumption and investment. We stress again that taxes in our model are calculated net of interest paid to the household sector: $\bar{T} = T - iB$, while the interest received by the central bank on government bonds is transferred back into the government sector. Taxes are thus endogenous in the present model, but held constant after interest payments have been deducted. Interest on foreign bonds received by the central bank is counted as income in this sector and used for the further accumulation of foreign bonds by the CB. Note also that money financing of the government deficit is assumed to take place via corresponding open market operations of the central bank which are, however, not represented in this sector but simply stated as final outcome in the government sector.

The central bank

Income account		Change of wealth account		Flow of funds account	
Debits	Credits	Debits	Credits	Debits	Credits
S_c	$s\bar{i}^*F_c$	FS_c	S_c	$s\dot{F}_c$	FS_c

There is, finally, the balance of payments which records the items that concern the current account and the capital account, the latter also including the reserve changes of the central bank. As mentioned above, the balance of payments is always balanced due to our treatment of the budget equations of the four sectors of the economy and thus does not represent a further restriction – besides the stock portfolio equilibrium equations – to the working of the economy.

	Balance of payments	
Debits		*Credits*
	Trade account:	
Imports		Exports
$s\,Im$		Ex
	Interest income account:	
Interest payments to the foreign economy		Interest payments from the foreign economy
$s\bar{i}^* F_f$		$s\bar{i}^* F_p + s\bar{i}^* F_c$
	Capital account:	
$s\dot{F}_p$		$s\dot{F}_f$
	Official reserve transactions of the CB:	
$s\dot{F}_c$		

This concludes our presentation of the flow conditions that characterize the small open economy under consideration. We stress, in view of the above, that the situation considered here is still a fairly ordered one in the case of a crisis. Capital accumulation has been financed by foreign credit throughout and all interest payments are always met at the world rate of interest. However, new credit will become rationed as expressed by the investment function if the balance sheets of firms worsen through depreciation. This credit rationing being given, the crisis considered in this chapter is then a purely macroeconomic one: a Keynesian effective demand depression with large loss in domestic output and income due to large reduction in investment demand, but still with flow consistency, in particular in the balance of payments. The crisis scenario we investigate in this chapter is thus still a partial one with credit-rationed firms and a capital flight parameter (to be introduced below), but otherwise stable portfolio demand equations, a stable expectations scheme, stable behavioral equations on the goods market and given wages and prices.

13.5 Dynamics under flexible exchange rates

We consider here exclusively the case of flexible exchange rates and thus the case where the central bank in general does not need to intervene in the market for foreign exchange or to conduct trade in foreign bonds. The equilibrium in the foreign exchange market can therefore be described by

$$F_{p0} = F_p = \quad \text{const in time,}$$

i.e., the amount of \$-denominated bonds that can be traded in this market is simply given by the amount of such bonds already held by private households. That is so because we continue to assume that domestic bonds cannot be traded internationally and that M (or i) is kept fixed by open market operations (concerning domestic bonds) by the monetary authority. The case of a flexible exchange rate will be used later on to describe the consequences of a breakdown of a fixed exchange rate regime.

Since there is no change in the supply of foreign currency resulting from changes in the reserves F_c of the central bank, we can now determine an asset market equilibrium curve $s(Y)$ from the reduced-form asset market representation provided at the end of the preceding section, which, for any given output level, determines the exchange rate s that clears the asset markets, the interest rate i being determined by $i = i(Y, M)$, the LM curve of the model. According to the implicit function theorem the slope of this curve is given by

$$s'(Y) = -\frac{-f_\xi i_Y}{-F_{p0} + f_\xi \varepsilon' + f_{W_p} F_{p0}}.$$

We have $(f_{W_p} - 1)F_{p0} < 0$ and $f_\xi \varepsilon' \leq 0$, since $f_{W_p} < 1$ and $\varepsilon' \leq 0$ has been assumed. Furthermore, the numerator of the fraction shown is always positive which, in sum, gives that $s'(Y) < 0$ holds; i.e., the asset markets equilibrium curve AA is always negatively sloped, as shown in Figure 13.2 (there as a straight line). We note that the AA curve is the steeper the higher capital mobility as measured by f_ξ becomes, the lower the interest rate elasticity of money demand and the more dominant the demand for dollar bonds is in the portfolio of asset holders (and also the more sluggishly regressively formed expectations are adjusting).

Next, we investigate the implications of a steep AA curve that under otherwise normal conditions gives rise to a situation as shown in Figure 13.3, now exhibiting three IS–AA equilibria. As this figure immediately reveals, however, only two of those are stable when exchange rates are flexible and when output adjusts sluggishly through the dynamic multiplier process. Below E_2, at a point on the AA curve (which is always binding if the exchange rate is perfectly flexible), we have expanding output according to the IS curve and thus convergence to E_1, while the opposite holds true for points above E_2 on the AA curve. We stress that AA equilibrium must here prevail by assumption (when s is treated as a statically endogenous variable), while the economy may temporarily be off the IS curve. As shown, this implies that E_1 and E_3 are attractors, whereas E_2 is a repeller in the considered graphical illustration of our small open economy.

Assume now that – for some reason – the AA curve shifts to the right to AA′ (see again Figure 13.3) so that only the upper stationary equilibrium remains in existence. Assume further that the economy was initially at E_1. Since output Y cannot react instantaneously, the economy must jump to the new asset market equilibrium E_1' and will thus undergo an instantaneous process of strong currency depreciation. Yet, despite such strong depreciation, the economy will not expand its activity level thereafter via the exchange rate effect on net exports, but will

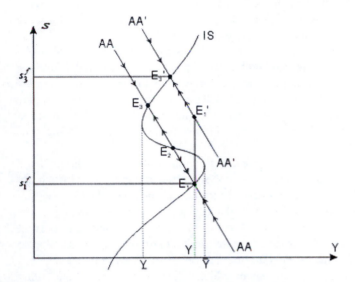

Figure 13.3 Dynamic multiplier analysis under perfectly flexible exchange rates (and thus permanent AA equilibrium): a fold catastrophe.

instead start to contract until the new stationary equilibrium E_3' has been reached, a process accompanied by further depreciation of the currency, as Figure 13.3 shows.

The effects of the considered shift in the asset market equilibrium curve are therefore a sudden first and then a continuous further depreciation of the currency, a radical first and then a continuous improvement in the trade balance (due to rising s and falling Y), a strong first and then a continuous decrease in domestic investment near to its floor and, as a result of this dominant change in aggregate demand, declining economic activity and declining domestic interest rates.

The question now is what the reasons for such a rightward shift in the AA curve (to AA$'$) can be. To provide the grounds for one possible explanation we expand the asset demand curve f as follows:

$$sF_p = f(\bar{i}^* + \varepsilon(s) - i(Y, M), W_p, \alpha), \quad f_\alpha > 0.$$

We use the new parameter α to express the risk of investing in domestic bonds, from the international perspective of domestic asset holders. Since a devaluation of the domestic currency worsens the international position of asset holders, we assume here that dollars represent the preferred currency and that dollar bonds are thus the preferred assets in the household sector. If there is a potential threat of depreciation of the domestic currency, asset holders may gradually decide (as expressed by an increase of the parameter α) to reallocate their asset holdings into dollar-denominated bonds. This process may be considered as capital flight from the domestic currency into the foreign one. An increasing parameter α, expressing increasing \$-liquidity preference,[11] therefore induces reallocation attempts into foreign bonds. Even though they cannot take place here since $F_{po} = F_p$ is fixed in a regime of flexible exchange rates, these attempts nevertheless move E_1 since an increasing parameter α shifts the AA curve to the right. This may even be the case to the extent that this lower equilibrium completely disappears and gives way to the sole equilibrium E_3' shown in Figure 13.3. An increasing parameter α thus indeed produces currency depreciations (but also output expansions as long as the lower equilibrium E_1 remains in existence) and may thus induce further increases in the shift parameter.

What can be done by the central bank to stop this tendency towards small and (if E_1 gets lost) even large depreciations of the domestic currency? One possibility is to increase the domestic rate of interest to counteract such capital flight – by way of a contractionary monetary policy. Reducing money balances through internal open market operations shifts the AA curve to the left and thus may prevent the AA curves – under the assumed capital flight conditions – from shifting so much to the right that the lower equilibrium E_1 gets lost. There is then only some depreciation (if E_1 remains in existence), which still expands output (if α is strong enough to overcome the contractionary impact of the restrictive monetary policy), yet which nevertheless moves the economy closer to the output level where the strong currency equilibrium E_1 (the normal equilibrium, in Krugman's (2001) words) may disappear. This leaning against the wind strategy thus may be of help if α increases, at least to some extent or for some time.

Note again that output expands if α is dominating the monetary strategy, but not to such an extent that the lower equilibrium E_1 gets lost. If, however, the economy gets trapped in E_3', the monetary authority can nevertheless attempt to bring the economy back to the lower, stable part of the IS curve. Contractionary monetary policy moves the economy in the direction towards E_3, and, if continued, thereafter eventually to a situation where the upper equilibrium gets lost. Exchange rate appreciation will then lead the economy vertically down until the asset market equilibrium curve is reached again. From there on we have continuously rising exchange rate and rising output until a new stationary point of type E_1 is reached. It is, however, a questionable assumption that the capital flight parameter α stays in place[12] in the early phase of such economic contraction (caused by restrictive monetary policy), even though this policy tends to increase the domestic nominal rate of interest (which in turn is counteracted, but not fully offset, by the output contraction it leads to).

Note that monetary policy can be made more direct if the interest rate is directly set by the monetary authority, while M is then adjusted to money

---

11 This is to be contrasted with f_ξ, which measures capital mobility for a given state of \$-liquidity preference.

12 In particular, if the rapid depreciation (accompanied by restrictive monetary policy) leads to a significant degree of bankruptcy of firms.

demand $M(Y,i)$ through appropriate technical instruments of the central bank. The expression $i(Y,M)$ in the asset market equilibrium equation is then replaced by an exogenously given i, which is called an interest rate peg. This obviously changes the qualitative results so far discussed considerably, since the AA curve then becomes horizontal with only one unique intersection with the IS curve under all circumstances.[13] Note also that an extended investment function of type

$$\dot{K} = I = I(s(Y), K), \quad I_K < 0, \quad Y^d(Y, K)$$

would now introduce the Kaldor (1940) trade cycle analysis into the present framework.

Note finally that, for given α and an equilibrium position E_1, expansionary monetary policy may lead to a contraction if the economy, via the AA curve, is shifted thereby so much to the right that the equilibrium E_1 gets lost. As long as the economy is on the lower branch, lowering i leads to mild depreciation and to goods market improvements, since the NX effect there dominates the investment effect. Yet, beyond $\overline{Y}$ we reach the region where depreciation accelerates and output contracts (since investment then dominates NX) until stationarity is reached again in a situation where output and investment are at very low levels in a stable state of depression.

In order to investigate exchange rate dynamics in more detail and in less perfect situations, we consider now the excess demand function X on the market for foreign bonds, which is given by:[14]

$$X(s) = f(\overrightarrow{i^*} + \varepsilon(s) - i(Y, M), \, M_o + B_o + sF_{po}) - sF_{po}.$$

The slope of this function is given by

$$f_\xi \varepsilon'(s) + f_{W_p} F_{po} - F_{po} < 0 \quad (f_{W_p} < 1).$$

Excess demand for foreign bonds basically means excess supply of domestic bonds and thus domestic demand for foreign currency. It is therefore natural to assume that

$$\hat{s} = \beta_s X(s)/(sF_{po}) \quad \text{or, slightly modified:} \quad \dot{s} = \beta_s X(s)$$

describes (here in a linear fashion) the reaction of the exchange rate with respect to such excess demand, when capital mobility is high and thus dominating exchange

---

13 The AA curve is again negatively sloped in the case of a Taylor rule which uses the output gap on its right-hand side where, therefore, the interest rate responds again to the state of the business cycle. This implies that it may be wise in certain situations to avoid automatic interest rate movements and thus the possibility of multiple and, in particular, bad equilibrium selections.

14 With $i(Y, M)$ given or simply $i = \overline{i}$ set by the monetary authority.

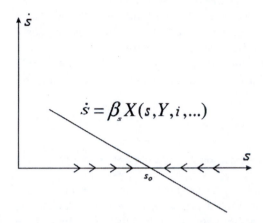

Figure 13.4 The market for foreign bonds and exchange rate adjustments.

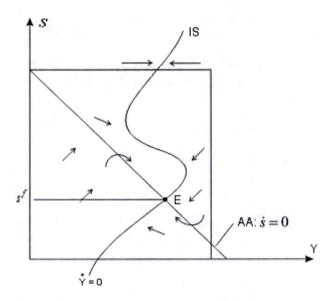

Figure 13.5 The Krugman dynamics extended to the whole Y, s phase space.

rate dynamics. This implies a stable adjustment process of the exchange rate to its equilibrium value s_o – so far only considered – as shown in Figure 13.4.

Using this additional law of motion, the dynamics along the asset market equilibrium curve AA can in fact now be extended to the whole Y, s phase space, as shown in Figure 13.5 (where we have returned for the moment to the consideration of a single stationary point E_1). Note that the AA line is now crossed horizontally in these extended and thus modified dynamics and is not characterized by the motion shown along the AA line as in Figure 13.3.

This latter motion in fact solely characterizes the limit case of infinitely fast exchange rate dynamics, $\beta_s = \infty$, which instantaneously places the exchange rate s on the AA curve, along which output still has to adjust. It thus represents a different dynamical system, as compared to the somewhat sluggish adjustment of the exchange rate that is now considered (the case $\beta_s = \infty$ is approached in a continuous fashion if β_s is approaching ∞; see the thick arrows in Figure 13.5). Note furthermore that the positive orthant is an invariant set of the dynamics under consideration here, which cannot be left since the change in output (in the exchange rate) is always positive sufficiently close to the axis $Y = 0$ $(s = 0)$.[15]

We conjecture, with respect to Figure 13.5, that the sole equilibrium, shown there, is globally asymptotically stable in the positive orthant of $\Re^2$, but do not prove this here (via an appropriate application of Olech's theorem on global asymptotic stability; see Flaschel (1984) in this regard). In fact the dynamics cannot leave the box shown in the figure, but the occurrence of semi-stable limit cycles is not yet excluded thereby unless the adjustment speed of the exchange rate is close to ∞, whereby the dynamics are then close to those of the limit case we considered beforehand. Returning to the situation of Figure 13.3 with its multiple equilibria – embedded now into the dynamics just considered, see Figure 13.6 – this then of course implies again two locally asymptotically stable equilibria and one unstable equilibrium under the new dynamics, as can easily be shown by

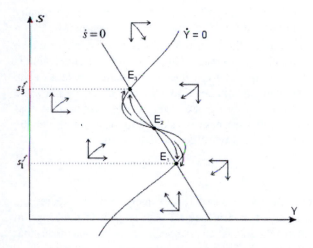

Figure 13.6 The extended dynamics in the Y, s phase space with three equilibria (two stable ones and one saddle).

---

15 The latter always holds if the nonlinearity of the AA curve for small values of the exchange rate s is taken into account, since excess demand on the foreign exchange market must then become positive.

calculating trace and determinant of the corresponding Jacobians. The process thus exhibits the equilibria E_1 and E_3 as (sole) stable equilibria under the now interacting dynamics of output Y and the exchange rate s.

Note also that Figure 13.6 suggests that the dynamics around E_2 is of saddlepoint type, with unstable arms leading to E_1 and E_3 respectively. It is even more difficult to determine the basins of attractions of the two attracting equilibria and to determine what may happen elsewhere in the phase space. Numerical investigations must here be used in addition to determine these basins explicitly. In the following we shall, however, simply assume that the dynamics is generally convergent to either of the two equilibria E_1 and E_3 after all shocks or disturbances. We justify this again with the limit case $\beta_s = \infty$ where global convergence along the AA curve to either one or the other equilibrium is obvious (with the exception of the situation where the economy sits exactly in the unstable equilibrium E_2 between the two others).

We observe finally that – in the case of flexible exchange rates, of course – the assumption of regressive expectations has to be interpreted and applied with care. If the economy converges to either E_1 or E_3 we know that the exchange rate will become stationary again, while the assumed type of regressive expectations $\varepsilon = \varepsilon(s)$, in particular with $\varepsilon'(s) < 0$, would imply that the expected rate of depreciation ε can only be zero in at most one of the three considered equilibria. This however is implausible in an environment where rates of exchange settle down at stationary values. This situation can be remedied as follows.

Assume that the shock shown in Figure 13.3 has hit the economy, eventually leading it to the point E_3'. Imbedded into the new AA$'$ curve shown here is a second shock, namely a revision of the long-run reference value s^f, to which regressive expectations are implicitly referring. This long-run reference value is here supposed to be always determined from the AA$'$ situation, where in the defining equation we have set ε identically equal to zero. It is therefore the value of the exchange rate where stationarity can be assured. We assume here that expectations formation immediately switches to this new long-run value when the α shock has occurred, for example by way of the explicit formula

$$\varepsilon(s) = \beta_\varepsilon(s^f/s - 1),$$

with s^f now the relevant long-run value of the exchange rate s. Regressive expectations are therefore always forward looking with respect to the long-run situation and thus change their schedule when an α shock occurs. This means that the AA$'$ curve is subject to changes, the first caused by the parameter α (from which s^f can then be determined) and the second due to the shift in the ε schedule by means of s^f, which makes the AA$'$ curve steeper and guarantees that at E_3' we arrive at s^f and $\varepsilon = 0$.

Remark: There is another possibility to discuss the change in the long-run exchange rate that regressive expectations are necessarily referring to.

Assume that s_o is the stationary value which the economy is currently approaching. Assume furthermore – again for concreteness – that $\varepsilon(s)$ is given by $\varepsilon(s) = \beta_\varepsilon(s^f/s - 1)$ with $s^f \neq s_o$, but sufficiently close to s_o. Assume finally, as an additional law of motion

$$\dot{s}^f = \beta_{sf}(s - s^f).$$

This adaptive mechanism says that the point of reference in the regressive expectations mechanism is a weighted average (with exponentially declining weights) of past observations of actual exchange rates and thus moving with the occurrence of new observations of actual exchange rates. Extending in this way the 2D dynamics (so far investigated) to a 3D dynamical system implies for its stationary points (which are stable in the above 2D subdynamics) that they are also stable in the extended 3D system for all adjustment speeds of the reference point s^f chosen sufficiently small. This follows easily from an application of the Routh–Hurwitz conditions for local asymptotic stability to the resulting 3D Jacobian. The added minors all have the correct sign (as can be shown by appropriate row operations) and the determinant of the 3D system is dominated by the product of trace and the 2D principal minors, if β_{s_1} is chosen sufficiently small.

We conclude that the considered equilibria E_1 and E_3 preserve the stability properties if the regressive expectations mechanism is assumed to take account only slowly of the new stationary value to which the actual exchange rate is converging. This, however, is only a local argument. Furthermore, the alternative, i.e., partially forward-looking regressive expectations (on s^f), is known from the literature on Dornbusch-type models and gives the asset market equilibrium curve a refined underpinning that is not without interest. Finally, we will see in the next section that currency crises may happen in such conditions, though exchange rate expectations are still of a very fundamental and tranquil type.

We next consider the relevant situation this paper is aiming at, the case of a fixed exchange rate system, where $\varepsilon(s) = 0$ can be assumed to be zero and where the amount of depreciation that takes place in the event of a currency crisis is not foreseen by the economic agents. The discussed dynamics of s can then, therefore, even be considered with $\varepsilon(s) \equiv 0$ and be viewed as being only implicitly present until the currency crisis in fact occurs (and modifies the expectations mechanism as discussed above).

13.6 Currency crisis in a fixed exchange rate regime

Flexible exchange rates do not represent the only exchange rate regime to which this model of large exchange rate swings and real crises can be applied. We now turn to the fixed exchange rate case in order to see – for a normal situation of a seemingly fairly strong currency and high economic activity – how the discussed tendency to capital flight may gradually give rise to situations where the economy becomes trapped in a depressed stationary equilibrium of type E_3. It exhibits there a weak currency and low economic activity but a significant reversal of net exports from a trade deficit to a trade surplus, despite the crisis state into which the economy has jumped and then continually made more severe in the direction of large output loss after the initial depreciation shock. In the fixed exchange rate regime we consider again the cases of fixed money supply. Now, however, the quantity F_p, foreign bond demand realized by households, can depart from the level households already own and can indeed rise beyond this level and be realized until the foreign reserves F_c of the CB become exhausted.

In order to investigate the possibility of an exchange rate crisis for the fixed exchange rate regime by means of the modeling framework of this paper, let us first introduce as reference curve a balanced trade line in its relationship to the IS or goods-market equilibrium curve of Figure 13.3. Obviously, the equation

$$0 = NX(Y,s), \ NX_Y < 0, \ NX_s > 0$$

defines an upward-sloping curve, representing balanced trade in the Y, s phase space. We have positive net exports on the upper part of the IS curve and negative net exports on its lower part. We assume for this curve that Figure 13.7 holds true. This figure shows that output is completely fixed by the exchange rate in our model when a given exchange rate is assumed. In the situation depicted we have a high level of economic activity, a trade deficit due to a strong currency and, based on this high level of activity, a capital market curve AA that would imply slight currency depreciation and even higher economic activity (with a lower trade deficit in addition) in the case of perfect exchange rate flexibility. Note here that the AA curve is however only implicitly present, that it determines in the background of Figure 13.7 the stock of foreign bonds demanded by the public (excess demand being met out of the stocks held by the central bank) and that this curve is based on the assumption of $\varepsilon = 0$ in the fixed exchange rate case. The equilibrium Y may be called a normal equilibrium, as in Krugman (2001).

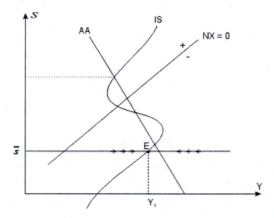

Figure 13.7 Balanced trade line and a normal equilibrium in a fixed exchange rate regime (with "excess demand" for the foreign asset).

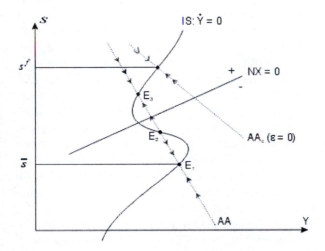

Figure 13.8 Normal real equilibrium, limited intervention range and shadow dynamics in a fixed exchange rate regime.

The dynamics shown in Figure 13.8 (for the case $\beta_s = \infty$ solely) is therefore only a shadow dynamics that would come into existence if the fixing of the exchange rate were abandoned by the central bank. As long as this is not the case, we always have that excess demand for foreign bonds $F_p - F_{po}$ of the private sector, determined by $\bar{s}F_p = f(\bar{i}^* - i(Y, M), M_o + B_o + \bar{s}F_{po}, \alpha)$, is always served by the central bank out of its foreign bond reserves F_c. Current foreign bond reserves are assumed to be sufficiently large to allow for this balancing of the market for foreign currency. This indeed then allows for the fixing of the exchange rate and implies in the course of time – when the capital flight parameter α starts to increase in a continuous fashion – that private households hold more and more foreign bonds in their portfolio without change in the total value of this portfolio, W_p, and thus their nominal wealth position, since the exchange rate is fixed.

We thus assume now that the expression F_p is slowly increasing through the influence (and solely through the influence) of the parameter α, since output is fixed by the given exchange rate. Only the IS curve matters, however, for the domestic equilibrium on the real markets, while the AA curve only determines the position F_p of the stock of foreign bonds currently held in the private sector. Note here again that the expectations mechanism $\varepsilon(s)$ is not present in a system of fixed exchange rates, as long as people do not speculate about an exchange rate crisis in terms of exchange rates, which may nevertheless be approaching through increases in the capital flight parameter α.

Besides the $NX = 0$ curve we show in Figure 13.8 the critical line AA_c where $\alpha = \alpha_c$ has become so large that $\bar{F}^* = F_p$ $(F_c = 0)$ holds, i.e., the central bank no longer has any reserves of the foreign currency. At this critical value of α – or even before this value has been reached – the fixed exchange rate system will break down and will, by assumption, be replaced by the regime of perfectly flexible exchange rates considered in the preceding section. We thus assume now that the ongoing process of a financial capital restructuring of private households – via further increases in the capital flight parameter α – has progressed to such a point that the foreign exchange reserves of the central bank are basically exhausted, as represented by the line AA_c ($\varepsilon = 0$ still). We have already indicated in Figure 13.8 the dynamics that would then come about if the exchange rate were to become flexible and determined by the asset markets of our model. This would, however, then also reestablish the regressive expectations mechanism, based on the now sole equilibrium E_3, and would thus in addition rotate the line AA_c in a clockwise fashion around this equilibrium to the position AA'_c, as explained before and shown in Figure 13.9. In Figure 13.9 we therefore now go on from the potential situation shown in Figure 13.8 to what actually happens if the exchange rate is again the subject of market forces with an adjustment speed $\beta_s = \infty$.

When this situation is reached, the exchange rate – by assumption – becomes completely flexible and the shadow dynamics of Figure 13.8 comes into being, leading the economy in the way described in the preceding section to the bad equilibrium E_3 along the AA'_c curve. The latter is steeper than the intervention limit curve AA_c curve shown, but also runs through the single equilibrium point E_3. In addition, the regressive expectations mechanism about the exchange rate dynamics is thus switched on with a long-run reference value for the exchange rate that is determined through E_3.[16]

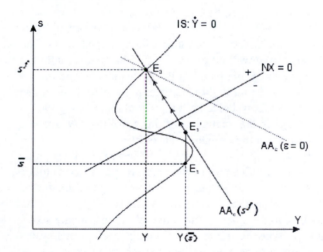

Figure 13.9 Breakdown of the fixed exchange rate regime: currency crisis, investment collapse and large output loss.

16 We thus in fact consider here some sort of asymptotically rational expectations which always know the long-run value of the exchange rate to which the economy will converge. This presumes

The result of such a currency crisis will be (if Figure 13.9 applies) a large initial devaluation of the domestic currency and, based on this a larger and larger loss in output as the currency continues to depreciate towards the value s^f (due to the dominance of the investment crisis). Along this way there will be a radical improvement in the trade balance (too weak, however, to overcome the loss of investment demand). All of this will happen against the background that the domestic central bank has lost nearly all of its currency reserves through the flight from domestic bond demand into foreign bonds. The economy thus tumbles into a real crisis with large output loss, based on a breakdown of investment, only partly counteracted by net exports due to the strong currency depreciation, with a central bank that has become powerless with respect to any further intervention in the foreign exchange market.

Next we consider in addition to the above – again for the case of a fixed exchange rate $\bar{s}$ – a law of motion for the capital flight parameter α that, by assumption, shifts the AA curve to the right if it increases. In the case of fixed exchange rates we have again Figure 13.8 in place of Figure 13.9. It shows as a dotted line the AA curve as an attracting curve which could lead the economy to either E_1 or E_3 if exchange rates were completely flexible (still for $\varepsilon = 0$). Note that we have excess demand for foreign bonds below the AA curve and excess supply above it. We have assumed in Figure 13.9 that flexible exchange rates will come about when AA_c and, immediately thereafter, AA'_c in Figure 13.9 apply in a situation where there is no longer a normal equilibrium point of type E_1.

We have assumed that the demand function f for foreign bonds depends positively on the capital flight parameter α, since an increasing tendency to capital flight means that residents attempt to substitute domestic bonds by foreign ones. Excess demand (calculated before central bank intervention) increasing with α may in fact give rise to a law of motion for α of the following type (presented solely in discrete time here):

$$\alpha_{t+h} = \alpha_t + \beta_\alpha(f(\bar{i}^* - i(Y,M), W_p, \alpha_t) - f(\bar{i}^* - i(Y,M), W_p, \alpha_{t-h})),$$

where $\bar{i}^*, i(Y,M), W_p = M_0 + B_{0,t} + \bar{s}F_{p0,t}$ are all given magnitudes despite the change in the composition of the bond holdings of the public. Note that we have inserted here $\bar{s}F_{p0,t} = f(\bar{i}^* - i(Y,M), W_p, \alpha_{t-h})$ as the result of the past foreign market intervention of the central bank at each point in time, in order to express excess demand by the change in demand that has happened from $t - h$ to t. Demand for foreign bonds and their actual holdings are changing in this manner through time (without any change in total private wealth). An initial increase in this

knowledge of the IS curve and the AA curve for $\varepsilon = 0$, at least for the ranges where investment is very unresponsive to the exchange rate. Under this assumption and the assumption that exchange rate dynamics must come to a rest again, the intersection of these two curves provides the agents with the long-run values of s to be put into their regressive expectations scheme.

demand may therefore set into motion a continuous increase in the parameter α, by way of contagion, as the situation can be interpreted. This may lead to an explosive movement of α if $\bar{s}$ and $\alpha(0)$ are such that there is a positive value for the excess demand function at these initial values.

Assume now again that some shock (for example, coming from a neighboring country) shifts the AA curve to the right to another curve AA$'$. In E_1 we now have excess demand for foreign bonds and thus an increasing α that continues to shift the AA$'$ curve to the right until AA_c is again reached. The normal equilibrium of the economy with a flexible exchange rate shifts during this process towards higher output and exchange rate levels, until it finally disappears. During this process excess demand for foreign bonds may be increasing in an accelerating fashion, so far always met by the central bank. When α continues to increase there may again arise the situation that the reserves of the central bank become exhausted: $F_c = \overline{F}^* - F_p \approx 0$. The fixing of the exchange rate by the central bank will then break down and give rise to the exchange rate adjustments already discussed, leading the economy through a sudden depreciation to point E_1'. Here output will start to decrease and the exchange rate will continue to increase until the new stationary point E_3 is reached. The economy is now trapped in a bad equilibrium E_3 as discussed in Krugman (1999a,b, 2001), but with a significant reversal from trade deficits to a trade surplus.

We stress that this outcome may depend to some extent on the way the above graph has been drawn and therefore only represents the one typical situation when the reserves of the central bank are so large and its intervention lasts so long that the AA_c curve – where it stops its intervention – exhibits only the upper bad equilibrium for the economy with a flexible exchange rate. An alternative situation that may arise in the case of shorter intervention is provided in Figure 13.10, showing overshooting exchange rate depreciation and in fact an increase in economic activity as the currency starts to appreciate after the initial devaluation shock. Still another possibility is indicated in Figure 13.11, where there is again no loss in output, neither large nor small.

Be that as it may, with respect to the likelihood of exchange rate crisis coupled with a dominant collapse in investment behavior and thus large output loss, the return to flexible exchange rates, due to the lack of reserves for a further fixing of the exchange rate, reestablishes the importance of the AA_c curve as a global attractor and the output movement along it – not always to the left if the bad equilibrium applies – until a new stationary point has been reached. Since AA_c is now restricting again the positions of the economy, we return to $X = 0$ and thus possibly also to a stationary value for the capital flight parameter α.

The final consequence of the increasing propensity for capital flight, is in sum, – if Figures 13.10 and 13.11 do not apply – that the exchange rate depreciates radically and that a severe economic depression will be induced, resulting from the balance sheet effect on investment, coupled with a pronounced reversal from a trade deficit to a trade surplus.

A leaning against the wind strategy of the central bank, i.e., an increase in domestic interest rates in order to stop the capital flight, may, due to its shifting

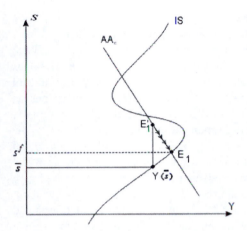

Figure 13.10 No currency crisis and output expansion in the case of a quick return to a flexible exchange rate regime.

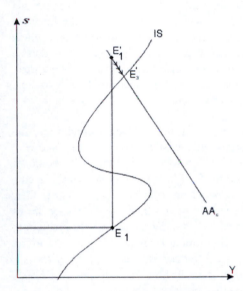

Figure 13.11 Overshooting exchange rate crisis and output improvements due to net export dominance.

the AA′ curves to the left, prevent the breakdown of the exchange rate system for some time, but will eventually fail due to the continuous increase in the parameter α as sketched above. This will then make the subsequent recession even more severe, since sooner or later the AA curve will apply, where $\overline{F}^* = F_p \quad (F_c = 0)$ has been reached.

13.7 Conclusions

We have introduced in this chapter an open economy portfolio model that allows us to study the channels that cause large currency swings and the feedback effects that arise from them. We have demonstrated that large currency swings under flexible exchange rates, as well as slowly progressing and then sudden capital flights under fixed exchange rates, may lead to strong repercussions on the financial market when a large fraction of the domestic debt of firms is denominated in foreign currency. Those repercussions may in turn entail a low level equilibrium and large output losses for the economy. Following a model suggested by Krugman (1999a,b, 2001), we showed rigorously in a dynamic model with multiple equilibria that there are mechanisms at work that can indeed give rise to such phenomena. Our results point to the dangers that may be brought about for a country if financial and capital market liberalization without safety nets and sufficient financial market regulations are pursued too fast, and we have shown that a flexible exchange rate does not exclude such dangers.

We have considered the small and sometimes very large effects of increasing $-liquidity preference in a set-up where the exchange rate was moving – if flexible – countercyclically and where leaning against the wind policies were present via restrictive monetary policy. These policies, which attempt to shift the financial markets equilibrium curve to the left towards reduced output but stronger currency values while trying to neutralize increasing $-liquidity preference, may also be supported by the IMF as lender of last resort. Such efforts may prevent the outbreak of the crisis under consideration, and may be the more appropriate way to cope with the increased vulnerability of small open economies exhibiting a high level of foreign debt.

The model was completely explicit with respect to budget conditions, the accounts of the four sectors of the economy and the balance of payments, showing however in this way the narrow foundations on which this type of crisis model still rests. We have flow consistency and the fulfillment of all plans of the agents of the economy – up to firms which may be rationed for credit or supply in their pursuit of new investment goods. We still have fix-price bonds. Expectations thus solely concern changes in the exchange rate, depreciation or appreciation, and were assumed to be of asymptotically rational (regressive) type. Assuming fix-price bonds means that asset holders can indeed enforce a currency crisis – in a fixed exchange rate system – if they initially hold enough domestic bonds compared to the $-bonds held by the central bank. Speculation on the degree of success of currency attacks are thus easily possible in this framework.

Concerning expectations, one might ask why we did not assume rational expectations (myopic perfect foresight) in this chapter. Presumably this would turn the two equilibria that were stable under regressive expectations into saddlepoint dynamics. Furthermore, the unstable equilibrium in the middle would then become a stable equilibrium, if the dynamic multiplier process is supposed to work with sufficient speed. We would therefore then obtain a situation that is not easily handled by means of the conventional jump variable technique.

One could furthermore then assume that the economy always converges back to the stable equilibrium if displacements from this equilibrium are not too large. Capital flight, however, could again remove the economy from this equilibrium and the economy might then converge along the stable arm of the bad equilibrium to this weak currency situation and thus might repeat what we have done here for regressive expectations. One next step could then be to find the formula for regressive expectations that will place the economy exactly on this stable arm of the saddlepoint dynamics, an exercise that we will not pursue here any further.

Rather than pursuing this type of extension, one might approach goods market behavior with more advanced behavioral functions (as in Rødseth (2000, Ch. 6)) or extend the asset market approach towards flex-price bonds and also add equity issuance of firms. A stock–flow interaction may then be added to the model. Finally, in place of a fixed money supply or its discretionary changes, we could consider interest rate policy rules (Taylor rules) and also a Phillips curve driven price dynamics. The latter could in particular help to elaborate the issue of debt deflation, since firms are already formulated here as being highly indebted and thus also very vulnerable with respect to output price deflation, in particular if wages and foreign interest rates remain at their given magnitudes. Contagion from and to neighboring countries may also become an issue here.

13.8 References

O. BLANCHARD and S. FISCHER (1989): *Lectures on Macroeconomics*. Cambridge, MA.: MIT Press.

BURNSIDE, C., M. EICHENBAUM and S. REBELO (1999): Hedging and financial fragility in fixed exchange rate regimes. *Paper presented at the CEPR Conference on Expectations, Economic Theory and Economic Policy*, Perugia, September.

CHANG, R. and A. VELASCO (1999): Liquidity crises in emerging markets: theory and policy. *NBER working paper* 7272, Cambridge, MA.

DIAMOND, D.W. and P. DYBVIK (1983): Bank runs, deposit insurance, and liquidity. *Journal of Political Economy*, 91:3, 401.

EDWARDS, S. (1999): On crisis prevention: Lessons from Mexico and East Asia. *NBER Working Paper* 7233, Cambridge, MA.

FLASCHEL, P. (1984): Some stability properties of Goodwin's growth cycle. A critical elaboration. *Zeitschrift für Nationalökonomie*, 44, 63–69.

KALDOR, N. (1940): A model of the trade cycle. *Economic Journal*, 50, 78–92.

KAMIN, S.B. (1999): The current international financial crisis: how much is new? *Journal of International Money and Finance*, 18, 501–514.

KIYOTAKI, N. and J. MOORE (1995): Credit cycles. *Journal of Political Economy*, 105, April, 211–248.

KRUGMAN, P. (1999a): Balance sheets, the transfer problem and financial crises. In: P. Isard, A. Razin and A. Rose (eds.): *International Finance and Financial Crisis*. Dordrecht: Kluwer.

KRUGMAN, P. (1999b): Comments on the transfer problem. MIT, mimeo.

KRUGMAN, P. (2001): Crisis: The price of globalization. *Federal Reserve Bank of Kansas City Economic Review*, 75–106.

KRUGMAN, P. and M. OBSTFELD (2003): *International Economics.* New York: Addison-Wesley.

MILESI-FERRETTI, G.M. and A. RAZIN (1996): Current account sustainability: Selected East Asian and Latin American experiences. *NBER working paper* 5791, Cambridge, MA.

MILESI-FERRETTI, G.M. and A. RAZIN (1998): Sharp reduction in current account deficits: An empirical analysis. *NBER working paper* 6310, Cambridge, MA.

MILLER, M. and J. STIGLITZ (1999): Bankruptcy protection against macroeconomic shocks. The World Bank, mimeo.

MISHKIN, F.S. (1998): International capital movement, financial volatility and financial instability. *NBER Working Paper* 6390, Cambridge, MA.

RØDSETH, A. (2000): *Open Economy Macroeconomics.* Cambridge, UK: Cambridge University Press.

ROGOFF, K. (1999): International institutions for reducing global financial instability. *NBER Working Paper* 7265, Cambridge, MA.

SEMMLER, W. (2006): *Asset Prices, Booms and Recessions*, 2nd ed. Heidelberg/New York: Springer.

TOBIN, J. (1969): General equilibrium approach to monetary theory. *Journal of Money, Credit, and Banking*, 1, 15–29.

14 Emerging market economies, currency crises and macroeconomic adjustment

14.1 Introduction

Recent studies on the Asian 1997–98 financial crisis such as the work by Krugman (2000), Mishkin (1998), Miller and Stiglitz (1999), Flaschel and Semmler (2003) and the previous chapter have elaborated on the mechanisms of how a currency crisis can trigger a financial crisis that may lead to a severe economic slowdown. Some authors have claimed that currency hedging could have prevented currency and financial crises. We will also investigate this line of research. Yet, in most recent work on this issue the wage and price levels are usually fixed. Another contribution of this chapter to the currency crisis literature is thus to introduce a currency crisis model with flexible domestic wages and prices in order to model how not only nominal but also (through domestic price level changes) real exchange rate fluctuations affect the dynamics of the macroeconomic activity. In our opinion wage and price dynamics are the missing link to explain what happens in the medium run in a country that has experienced – through a currency and financial crisis – a severe slowdown in its economic activity.

A central feature of the current version of our model is a Krugman (2000)-type investment function which, in particular, reflects the credit market problems that arise for firms after a strong currency devaluation, in a country where credit market frictions exist and where a significant fraction of domestic banks' and firms' debt is denominated in foreign currency.[1] As stated above, the main difference between the model to be presented here and earlier currency crisis models, including Chapter 13 above and Flaschel and Semmler (2003, 2006), is the fact that in this framework, besides the exchange rate, wage and price level changes are also taken into account. This thus allows for richer and more realistic dynamic adjustment mechanisms and, in particular, for a treatment of possible deflationary situations after the occurrence of a currency crisis.

The present chapter is organized as follows: In Sections 14.2–14.4 the model developed in Chapter 13 and by Flaschel and Semmler (2003, 2006) and its

---

1 Such a constellation (exchange rate volatility, imperfect capital markets with credit constraints and liability dollarization) can be found in many emerging market economies. In recent times this constellation could also be found in the transition economies of Eastern Europe.

main implications for output and exchange rate dynamics, and thus for real–financial interaction, will be discussed briefly. Some empirical evidence will also be presented. In Section 14.5 and 14.6, the extended currency crisis model which allows for hedging and wage and price changes respectively is developed. We also investigate the local and global stability implications of the model variants presented. In Section 14.7 the dynamics of the currency and financial crises with a nonlinear Phillips curve will be explored. In the conclusion, Section 14.8, the potentials and limitations of this extended model will be evaluated.

14.2 The basic model

The macroeconomic framework introduced by Flaschel and Semmler (2003) is based on the Mundell–Fleming–Tobin model as formulated and investigated in Rødseth (2000).[2]

The macroeconomic framework employed here is a very simple one. We start with a small open economy where domestic and foreign goods prices are fixed and set, for simplicity, to be equal to one, i.e. $p = 1$, $p^* = 1$. Wage and price fluctuations are thus completely ignored in this basic Krugman-type currency crisis model. Nominal exchange rate variations are thus always equal to real ones. Furthermore, due to the absence of an inflationary environment, it is also presumed that the expected inflation π^e is zero. The analyzed time span is also assumed to be short enough to allow for the assumption of a basically unchanging capital stock K as well as private financial wealth W_p and firms' foreign currency debt F_f, despite the presence of positive or negative net investment and households' savings.

On the assumption that there are no interest or wealth effects on consumption, the aggregate consumption function is assumed to be dependent in a very standard way on national disposable income:

$$C = C(Y^D) = C(Y - \delta \bar{K} - T), \qquad 0 < C_Y < 1. \tag{14.1}$$

The main feature of this currency crisis model is the Krugman (2000) investment function which is based, in a very simple way, on the financial accelerator concept first introduced by Bernanke et al. (1994) as well as on the theory of imperfect credit markets. Focusing especially on the liability dollarization problem, we assume that domestic firms can only finance their investment projects through

2 Note that this type of model does not explain the causes of currency and financial crises by a microfounded, utility-maximizing representative agent approach, but investigates the dynamics of the economic consequences of such crises from a more traditional macroeconomic perspective where, however, all budget equations of the four sectors of the economy are carefully specified. This approach proves useful for investigating the dynamics of currency and financial crises since it can be extended more easily than the rigidly microfounded ones where macroeconomic results are to be derived from an intertemporally optimizing representative household (see also Rødseth (2000, p. 5) in this regard).

loans denominated in foreign currency.[3] Under this assumption, an extremely simple balance sheet of the business sector can be obtained as follows:

Business sector's balance sheet

Assets	Liabilities
pK	sF_f

The net worth of a firm is defined as the difference between its assets and its liabilities (both expressed here in domestic currency).[4] Under the assumption that the observed time span is short enough to exclude the variations of capital stock and debt, the nominal exchange rate is the sole variable that can influence the net worth of the firm. We assume credit market imperfections and more precisely that banks (domestic and foreign) evaluate creditworthiness on the basis of the actual net worth of a domestic firm, or on the dollarized debt-to-capital ratio $\tilde{q} = s\bar{F}_f/\bar{p}\bar{K} = \tilde{q}(s)$.[5] The total of credits awarded, Cr^S, is determined by the banks – under the assumption that firms can only issue foreign currency bonds – and is equal to the change of foreign currency bonds by domestic firms accepted by the credit institutions; i.e., the foreign currency debt of the firms is

$$Cr^S = s\dot{F}_f(\tilde{q}), \quad \frac{\partial Cr^S}{\partial \tilde{q}} < 0 \quad \text{if} \quad \frac{d\dot{F}_f}{\dot{F}_f}\Big/\frac{ds}{s} < -1, \tag{14.2}$$

since $\hat{q} = \hat{s}$. A glance at a firm's balance sheet can clarify why a depreciation of the domestic currency has a negative effect on credit awarded by banks: a rise of the nominal exchange rate leads to an increase in the nominal (and here also the real) value of the firm's liabilities and therefore to a decrease in its net worth.

Under the assumption that investment solely depends on the creditworthiness of the borrowing firms — which in turn depends on the firms' balance sheets — a sharp devaluation can lead to a radical investment contraction and thus to a severe economic slowdown (if investment goods are produced domestically as is assumed to be the case in this model). The aggregate investment function is thus defined as

$$I = \min(I^d, Cr^S), \tag{14.3}$$

which shows clearly that the credit constraint determines the actual investment level, under the assumption that $I^d > Cr^S$ normally holds.

---

3 Here it is irrelevant whether the creditors are foreign or domestic financial institutions. The main point is the currency denomination of the loan, not its origin.

4 See Mishkin (2001, p. 192). Note that no intertemporal considerations are taken into account in this definition, as the firm's net worth is defined solely by means of actual stocks and prices.

5 We assume here $F_f < 0$, indicating a negative foreign currency bond stock held by domestic firms, or, in other words, that firms are indebted.

The relationship between the nominal exchange rate and aggregate credit cannot be considered as a linear one from the global point of view. A possible nonlinearity of the financial accelerator mechanism has already been pointed out by Bernanke et al. (1994, p. 9) as follow: "Financial accelerator effects are stronger, the deeper the economy is in recession." In some of his studies Krugman also referred to the idea that the balance-sheet effect is not always of the same magnitude and that in fact it depends on the actual state of the economy:

> Loosely, the idea is that when the domestic currency is sufficiently strong, most firms are not wealth-constrained, and so the balance sheet effect is weak. When the domestic currency is very weak most of the domestic firms with foreign-currency debt are already bankrupt, so that things can't get any worse, and the pro-competitive effect of depreciation again dominates. So, the perverse region in which depreciation is contractionary is for the intermediate levels of the exchange rate. (Krugman (2000), p. 84)

The shape of the following aggregate investment function represents Krugman's ideas. The elasticity of the investment function now with respect to changes of $\tilde{q}$ is assumed to be state-dependent: for high values of $\tilde{q}$, where the nominal value of the dollarized liabilities of the business sector is significantly higher than the nominal replacement costs of capital, the investment reaction is assumed to be inelastic. In such a situation the firms' balance sheets are in such a bad state that the firms either cannot afford to invest in projects or cannot get any bank loans, so that a further deterioration of their financial situation only has a minimal effect on their investment projects. Therefore, for $s \to \infty$ ($\tilde{q} \to \infty$) the existence of a (still positive) minimal gross investment level or "investment floor" $\underline{I}$ is postulated. Some positive level of gross investment therefore remains, even in the worst scenario that is considered in this chapter, since not all investment projects will be canceled, because of replacement investment and high scrapping costs (see Flaschel and Semmler (2003)).

In the opposite case, where $\tilde{q}$ is low, the firms' dollarized liabilities are low relative to their assets and therefore firms do not face any constraints in the credit markets. In such a benign situation the investment spending is at its maximum. Because of the existence of supply-side bottlenecks, the investment function is assumed to be again very inelastic in such a situation; i.e., for $s \to 0$ ($\tilde{q} \to 0$) aggregate investment is at its maximum level, defined as the "investment ceiling" $\bar{I}$.

For intermediate values of $\tilde{q}$, by contrast, the gross investment function is very elastic with respect to changes in the debt to capital ratio, reflecting the activation of credit constraints.[6] Such an aggregate investment function is shown in Figure 14.1.

---

6 A nonlinear investment function with a similar shape, though in the (Y, K) phase space, was utilized by Varian (1979) – applying some concepts from catastrophe theory –to construct a generalization of Kaldor's 1940 business cycle

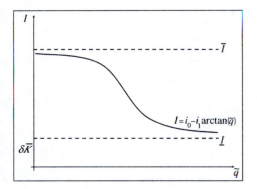

Figure 14.1 An arctan type of investment function.

Even though the above gross investment function is of a very simple nature, it incorporates the financial accelerator concept and, more generally, the basic implications of the theory of imperfect capital markets. The assumption of such a form of investment function leads to the possibility of multiple equilibria and, therefore, to the existence of "normal" and "crisis" steady-states respectively.

The export function also needs some explanation. As in the investment function, we assume in the export function the existence of some kind of "export floor" and "export ceiling". The reason for this assumption may be that there are foreign demand saturation effects and that, even in the case of a very strong real appreciation and a subsequent loss of competitiveness, there might be some domestic products which will still be demanded from abroad, for example because of their uniqueness.

In view of the above type of investment and export behavior, the goods market equilibrium in the small open economy under analysis can be written as

$$Y = C_1(Y - \delta \bar{K} - \bar{T}) + I(s) + \delta \bar{K} + \bar{G} + X(Y^{n*}, s), \tag{14.4}$$

where $\bar{G}$ represents government expenditures (which for simplicity are also assumed to be composed of domestic goods solely). Note that we have removed here from explicit consideration all imported consumption goods C_2 and thus have reduced the representation of aggregate demand to include only domestic consumption goods $C_1 = C - sC_2$. Therefore only exports X have to be considered from now on.

The export function $X(Y^{n*}, s)$ (see Figure 14.2) is furthermore supposed to depend, in a standard way, positively on foreign (normal) output and the nominal exchange rate

$$X_{Y^{n*}} > 0, \qquad X_s > 0.$$

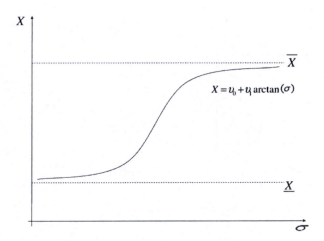

Figure 14.2 An arctan type of export function ($\sigma = s/p$).

The following simple dynamic adjustment process in the goods markets, a traditional type of dynamic multiplier process, is now assumed:

$$\dot{Y} = \beta_y(Y^d - Y) = \beta_y\left[C_1(Y^D) + I(s) + \delta\bar{K} + \bar{G} + X(Y^{n*}, s) - Y\right]. \quad (14.5)$$

Using the implicit function theorem, it follows for the displacement of the IS curve with respect to currency shocks that

$$\left.\frac{\partial Y}{\partial s}\right|_{\dot{Y}=0} = -\frac{I_s + X_s}{C_Y - 1} \gtrless 0.$$

Here follows one of the essential points of this model. The effect of a devaluation of the domestic currency on economic activity depends on the relative strength of the reaction of exports as compared to the reaction of aggregate investment.[7] In the "normal case", where firms are not wealth constrained, the exchange rate effect on investment is supposed to be very weak and thus dominated by the exports effect. Then we have

$$X_s > |I_s| \implies \left|\frac{\partial Y}{\partial s}\right| > 0.$$

In the "fragile case", i.e. in a middle range for the exchange rate, the balance-sheet effect of a devaluation of the domestic currency is assumed to be large, so that it

---

7 The denominator is assumed to be unambiguously negative, so that the sign of the numerator is decisive for the slope of the IS curve.

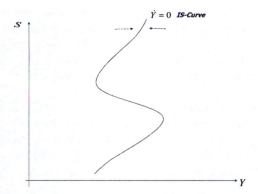

Figure 14.3 The goods market equilibrium curve.

overcomes the positive exports effect:

$$|I_s| > X_s \Longrightarrow \left| \frac{\partial Y}{\partial s} \right| < 0.$$

The resulting $\dot{Y} = 0$ isocline (the IS curve) is outlined in Figure 14.3:

The financial sector is also an important feature of this basic currency crisis model. Following Rødseth (2000), a portfolio approach of Tobin type is chosen, which allows different rates of return on domestic and foreign bonds. The defining financial market equations are:

$$W_p = M_0 + B_{p0} + sF_{p0} \tag{14.6}$$

$$\xi = i - \bar{i}^* - \epsilon \tag{14.7}$$

$$sF_p = f(\xi, W_p, \alpha), \tag{14.8}$$

$$M = m(Y, i), \quad m_Y > 0, \quad m_i < 0 \tag{14.9}$$

$$B_p = W_p - m(Y, i) - f(\xi, W_p) \tag{14.10}$$

$$F_p + F_c + \bar{F}^* = 0 \quad \text{or} \quad F_p + F_c = -\bar{F}^*. \tag{14.11}$$

Equation (14.6) describes the initial financial wealth of the private sector, expressed in domestic currency. Private agents in the small open economy hold domestic money M_0, bonds in domestic currency B_{p0} and bonds in foreign currency F_{p0}. Domestic and foreign-currency bonds are assumed to be imperfect substitutes, which means that the uncovered interest rate parity does not hold. The expected rate of return differential between the two interest-bearing financial assets, with ϵ denoting the expected rate of currency depreciation, is referred to as *risk premium*; see equation (14.7). The risk premium is the extra amount that the investor gets paid over the expected return of a safe asset (in this case the foreign-currency bond) to take the risk of investing in domestic currency (see Rødseth (2000, p. 17)). Because the assumed bond types are traded in different currencies, exchange rate fluctuations must also be taken into account, since they influence the rate of return differential. If the risk premium were zero, then both assets would deliver the same rate of return and thus would be perfect substitutes. In this case perfect capital mobility would exist in the financial markets and the uncovered interest rate parity would hold.[8]

Equation (14.8) stands for the foreign-currency bond market equilibrium. The demand for foreign-currency-denominated bonds is assumed to depend negatively on the risk premium, positively on private financial wealth and positively on the parameter α. This parameter is supposed to represent other foreign exchange market pressures like the propensity for a speculative attack on the domestic currency, political instability, etc.

Equation (14.9) represents the domestic money market equilibrium with the usual reactions of the money demand to changes in interest rates and output. The domestic bond market (equation (14.10)) is then in equilibrium via Walras's law of stocks, if this holds for the bonds denominated in foreign currency.

The last equation, (14.11), describes the equilibrium condition for the foreign exchange market. It states that the aggregate demands of the three sectors – domestic private sector, the monetary authority and foreign sector – sum up to zero (see Rødseth (2000, p. 18)). On the assumption that the supply of foreign-currency bonds from the foreign sector is constant $(-\bar{F}^*)$, the additional amount of foreign-currency bonds available to the private sector (besides its own stocks) is solely controlled by the monetary authorities.[9] The prevailing exchange rate regime thus depends on the disposition of the central bank to supply the private sector with foreign-currency bonds.

The mechanism for expected exchange rate fluctuations is described by the following equation:

$$\varepsilon = \beta_\varepsilon \left(\frac{s_0}{s} - 1 \right), \qquad \varepsilon_s \leq 0. \tag{14.12}$$

It is obvious that we have for the steady-state exchange rate s_0 that $\varepsilon(s_0) = 0$ holds. Note that the exchange rate devaluation expectations can be perceived as purely forward looking and in this respect asymptotically rational, by assuming that economic agents have perfect knowledge of the future steady-state exchange rate level s_0 with respect to which the actual exchange rate is expected to converge in a monotonic fashion after each shock that hits the economy. Flaschel and Semmler

---

8 Even though financial capital markets throughout the world were liberalized during the last decades, it still seems to be a very unrealistic assumption to suppose that international capital mobility is perfect. Significantly high spreads (and thus risk premia) between domestic and international interest rates (for example the US 3-month T-Bill) are observable, especially in emerging market economies.

9 This assumption can be justified by assuming, as in Rødseth (2000), that domestic bonds cannot be traded internationally.

(2003, 2006) therefore call this regressive exchange rate expectation formation mechanism "asymptotically rational".

By inserting the money market equilibrium interest rate (the inverse function of equation (14.9)) in equation (14.8), the financial markets equilibrium or AA curve is derived:

$$sF_p = f\left(i(Y,M_o) - \bar{i}^* - \beta_\varepsilon \left(\frac{s_0}{s} - 1\right), M_o + B_{po} + sF_{po}\right). \qquad (14.13)$$

This equilibrium equation can be interpreted as a representation of the $\dot{s} = 0$ isocline. Under the assumption that the exchange rate does not adjust automatically to foreign exchange market disequilibria, one may postulate as exchange rate dynamics:

$$\dot{s} = \beta_s \left[f\left(i(Y,M) - \bar{i}^* - \beta_\varepsilon \left(\frac{s_0}{s} - 1\right), M + B_p + sF_p, \alpha\right) - sF_p\right]. \qquad (14.14)$$

The slope of the $\dot{s} = 0$ isocline is determined by the implicit function theorem in the following way:

$$\left.\frac{\partial s}{\partial Y}\right|_{\dot{s}=0} = -\frac{f_\xi i_Y}{f_\xi \epsilon_s + (f_{W_p} - 1) F_{po}} < 0.$$

In order to obtain a complete representation of the dynamics of this system, Figure 14.4 shows the IS–AA phase diagram for the case where exchange rate adjustments to disequilibrium situations in the foreign exchange market take place instantaneously. Figure 14.5, shows the phase diagram of the global dynamics for an instantaneously adjusting foreign exchange market.

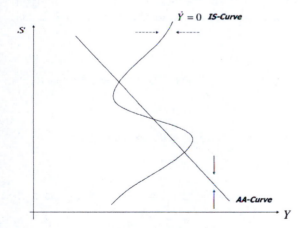

Figure 14.4 The IS–AA global dynamics.

Note that the AA curve becomes binding only if the monetary authorities choose a flexible exchange rate regime. In a pegged exchange rate system, the output level defined by the $\dot{Y} = 0$ isocline at the given exchange rate level fully defines the unique equilibrium of the system. In such a currency system the $\dot{s} = 0$ isocline can be interpreted as a "shadow curve" which represents the exchange rate level that would prevail if the currency were left to float freely. Because the monetary authorities are committed to removing any foreign exchange market disequilibria by buying or selling any amount of foreign currency bonds needed to defend the prevailing exchange rate level, the $\dot{s} = 0$ isocline represents the over-demand or over-supply with which the central bank is confronted. Consequently, the larger the difference between the exchange rate level given by the "shadow curve" and the currency peg level, the higher is the demand for foreign-currency bonds that the domestic central bank has to satisfy, and vice versa.

14.3 Local stability analysis

The Flaschel and Semmler (2003) currency crisis model discussed above consists of the following differential equations:

$$\dot{Y} = \beta_y \left[C(Y - \delta\bar{K} - \bar{T}) + I(s) + \delta\bar{K} + \bar{G} + X(Y^{n*}, s) - Y \right]$$

$$\dot{s} = \beta_s \left[f\left(i(Y, M_o) - \bar{i}^* - \beta_\varepsilon \left(\frac{s_0}{s} - 1 \right), M_o + B_{po} + sF_{po}, \alpha \right) - sF_{po} \right].$$

The Jacobian of this system is

$$J = \begin{bmatrix} \beta_y [C_Y - 1] & \beta_y [I_s + X_s] \\ \beta_s (f_\xi i_Y) & \beta_s (-f_\xi \epsilon_s + (f_{W_p} - 1)F_{p0}) \end{bmatrix}.$$

Because of the nonlinearity of the $\dot{Y} = 0$ isocline three economically meaningful steady states exist in the situation considered, whose local stability properties can be easily calculated:

$$J_{E1} = \begin{bmatrix} - & + \\ - & - \end{bmatrix} \implies \text{tr}(J_{E1}) < 0, \quad \det(J_{E1}) > 0 \implies \text{stable steady-state,}$$

$$J_{E2} = \begin{bmatrix} - & - \\ - & - \end{bmatrix} \implies \text{tr}(J_{E2}) < 0, \quad \det(J_{E2}) < 0 \implies \text{saddle point,}$$

$$J_{E3} = \begin{bmatrix} - & + \\ - & - \end{bmatrix} \implies \text{tr}(J_{E3}) < 0, \quad \det(J_{E3}) > 0 \implies \text{stable steady-state.}$$

The resulting dynamics of this currency crisis model are described by Figure 14.5.

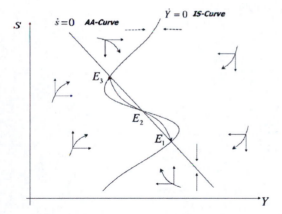

Figure 14.5 The IS-AA dynamics.

Steady state E_1 represents the "normal" steady state, where the economy's output is high as well as the domestic investment activity. In this steady-state, the standard case $|I_s| < X_s$ holds.

Steady state E_2 represents the fragile case with $|I_s| > X_s$: Because a slight deviation of the output level from this steady-state level can lead the economy to a short-run investment boom or to a decline in economic activity, this equilibrium point is unstable.

Steady state E_3 constitutes the "crisis equilibrium". At this equilibrium point investment activity is highly depressed due to the high value of s. Nevertheless, the slope of the $\dot{Y}$ isocline is again positive because of $|I_s| < X_s$, which describes the dominance of exports over (the remaining) investment demand in the situation considered.

14.4 Currency crises in a pegged exchange rate system

In this section the results of the preceding chapter regarding the dynamics of a currency and financial crisis under a fixed exchange rate regime will be recapitulated, and some empirical evidence added, in order to show the effects of such crises on the economic activity of a small open economy with dollarized liabilities, credit constraints and a constant wage and price level. The results presented here will be useful for highlighting the results of the extended 2D model to be discussed below.

Assume the economy is initially at steady-state E_1 in Figure 14.6. The prevailing exchange rate system is a currency peg which is fully backed by the domestic central bank. Now suppose that the demand for foreign-currency bonds increases due to, say, a rise in the "capital flight" parameter α. As long as the central bank is disposed to defend the prevailing currency peg by selling foreign-currency bonds

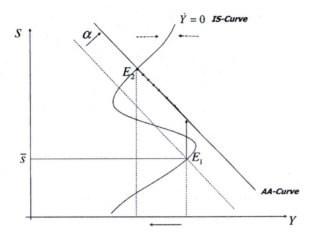

Figure 14.6 The macroeconomic effects of a currency and financial crisis.

or, alternatively, through interest rate increases, there are no real effects on the domestic economic activity.[10]

In the case that the domestic monetary authorities decide to give in to the speculative pressures and to let the exchange rate float, the AA curve becomes the binding curve in the model. The exchange rate then jumps from the initial equilibrium E_1 to the corresponding point on the AA curve (with a still unchanged output level). The sharp devaluation of the domestic currency leads to a severe deterioration of the balance sheet of the business sector and thus to an investment contraction. Because the economic agents consider the exchange rate level at the steady state E_2 as the long-run level, the actual exchange rate depreciates further, reducing investment even further, and thereby aggregate demand and now also domestic output, which follows the large decline in aggregate demand with some time delay until a new goods market equilibrium with a large output loss is reached.

The adjustment process following the currency crisis comes to a rest when the economy arrives at its new equilibrium E_2. Because of the assumption of fixed domestic prices and wages, the economy exhibits no endogenously determined mechanism to return to the initial high output level.[11]

10 Note that this assertion follows from the assumption that interest rates do not directly affect the real side of the economy. This might be a realistic assumption for the short run we are considering here.
11 A fiscal expansion (a right-shift of the IS curve) could bring the economy to a higher output level. Nevertheless, fiscal policy management is much more complicated than monetary policy, and it takes more time to become effective. Furthermore, for many emerging market economies a significant fiscal expansion is not a feasible option because of the large fiscal deficits prevailing in those economies.

Following Krugman (2000), Flaschel and Semmler (2003) and others, forming the core of the twin crisis model presented in the previous section, assumed a negative relationship between the liabilities denominated in foreign currency and the actual investment undertaken by the domestic economy. To check the validity of this assumption, we summarize empirical work by Proaño et al. (2005) in order to investigate empirically the relationship for three countries which suffered the most devastating real effects after their respective currency and financial crises in the 1990s (Mexico, South Korea, Thailand). Following this study we employ a *Vector autoregressive model with exogenous terms* (VARX) (see Lütkepohl (1993, Ch. 10)) of the form:

$$D_t = A_{11}(L)\,D_{t-i} + A_{12}(L)\,Inv_{t-i} + b_1\,X_t + \epsilon_{1t} \tag{14.15}$$

$$Inv_t = A_{21}(L)\,D_{t-i} + A_{22}(L)\,Inv_{t-i} + b_2\,X_t + \epsilon_{2t} \tag{14.16}$$

where D_t represents the domestic currency value of the dollarized liabilities, Inv_t the aggregate domestic investment, X_t a vector of nonstochastic terms as seasonal, impulse and shift dummmies for the exchange rate regime change[12] and ϵ_{1t} and ϵ_{2t} i.i.d. white noise errors. $A_{ii}(L)$ represent scalar lag operators, the length of which is determined by the multivariate versions of the Hannan–Quinn and Schwartz–Bayesian lag order selection criteria. We use quarterly data for the estimations, since time series of higher frequency are not available. The time series of investment, exchange rate and domestic price levels are taken from the International Financial Statistics of the IMF, while the proxy for the dollarized liabilities of the private sector (domestic liabilities to BIS banks) stems from the Joint IMF–OECD–BIS–World Bank External Debt Statistics.[13] The empirical results of these estimations, as well as serial autocorrelation LM tests and multivariate ARCH–LM tests for model adequacy, can be found in Proaño et al. (2005). In the three analyzed countries the VARX estimations deliver a significant and negative coefficient for the effect of dollarized debt on aggregate investment.

Figure 14.7 shows the estimated reaction of the aggregate investment on a 1 percent increase in the domestic currency value of foreign- currency-denominated liabilities. In Mexico and South Korea such a shock produces a fall of around 0.2 percent after four quarters, the reaction in Thailand being somewhat weaker. This reaction might not seem to be particularly significant at first sight, but the fact that during the past currency crises emerging market economies such as Mexico, South Korea, Thailand or Indonesia experienced huge depreciations of their domestic currencies [14] puts these results into perspective.

12 For details of the methodology and data source, see Proaño et al. (2005). Since the breakdown of currency systems can be easily observed in the time series data for all the analyzed countries, the use of a shift and/or an impulse dummy for its representation seems adequate.
13 Corsetti et al. (1998) also use this magnitude as a proxy for foreign currency debt, as well as Aghion et al. (2000) since "these transactions are basically in foreign currency".
14 See Corsetti et al. (1998) for a detailed description of this and other stylized facts on the East Asian 1997–1998 crisis.

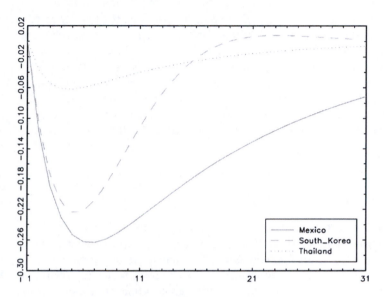

Figure 14.7 VARX impulse response functions.

14.5 Currency crises and hedging

According to Krugman (2000), one of the key ingredients in financial crises is foreign-currency-denominated debt. Given such sort of debt, a sudden currency depreciation – a rising price of foreign exchange – could have serious consequences for the balance sheets of firms. These negative balance sheet effects may cancel out positive effects arising from the trade balance as described by the Marshall–Lerner condition.

The main idea of this section is that some independence of a firm's balance sheet from adverse exchange rate movements can be achieved by corporate risk management[15]. We presume that firms depend on financial markets to hedge their currency exposure. We examine the impact of risk management activities of nonfinancial firms on economic stability by introducing corporate hedging in a Mundell–Fleming–Tobin type model. We here extend the previous model to include hedging. Firms' hedging activity is modeled depending on firm size as well as hedging costs. Referring to the channels mentioned by Krugman (2000), the primary advantage of corporate risk management is the fact that, in general, it is not necessary to officially encourage risk management because it is a natural constituent of business. Furthermore, nowadays, financial derivatives are available in great variety, providing almost perfect hedging possibilities. Hedging currency risk with financial derivatives gives companies

15 For more details of the following model see Röthig et al. (2007).

a protection tool, and might be a key instrument for avoiding "private sector crises" (Goodhart 2000, p. 108).

We implement corporate risk management into a Flaschel and Semmler (2006) type Mundell–Fleming–Tobin model.[16] The decision whether to hedge or not is given exogenously by assuming that only large firms can hedge their currency exposure while small companies depend completely on foreign exchange markets. Alternatively we assume that all firms can hedge and that the hedging decision depends on hedging costs and expected losses due to currency depreciations.

Let us first assume that corporate hedging activity depends solely on firm size. The only hedging instruments available are linear over-the-counter (OTC) currency forward contracts. OTC products are "custom-made" (Neftci 2000, p. 6) and allow therefore for perfect currency hedging. However, the main disadvantage of OTC products is the fact that they are not traded on organized exchanges. The products are not standardized and are therefore generally not available to a large number of customers. Furthermore, OTC derivatives, in general, deliver large amounts of the underlying asset. Smaller amounts of foreign exchange, compatible with specific capital flows of smaller nonfinancial firms, cannot be hedged perfectly with these products. Hence, in addition to restricted access to OTC derivatives, the contract size of OTC products poses a barrier to small firms' hedging activity. In our model, we assume that only large firms have access to OTC derivatives and use these products to hedge their currency exposure perfectly. Small firms do not hedge at all. Empirical evidence supports this approach (see Fender 2000b). Mian (1996, p. 437) investigates corporate hedging policy and concludes:

> I find robust evidence that larger firms are more likely to hedge. This evidence supports the hypothesis that there are economies of scale in hedging and that information and transaction considerations have more influence on hedging activities than the cost of raising capital.

Our model is based on the following assumptions:

1. There are two types of firms: large ones and small ones.
2. Only large firms can hedge their currency exposure, and they hedge it perfectly. Small firms cannot hedge at all. Large firms are completely independent of exchange rate movements, while small firms are subject to adverse developments in foreign exchange markets.
3. There are no hedging costs.
4. Small and large firms are treated on the same basis, except regarding their ability to hedge.
5. Banks and trading partners recognize hedged and unhedged firms by their size.

---

16 For a detailed discussion of the Mundell–Fleming–Tobin model, see Rødseth (2000, Chapter 6).

In our model, hedging activity affects the investment function. The investment function of firm i is given by $I_i(\theta, s)$, where the hedging coefficient θ and the exchange rate s enter in a multiplicative form $(\theta * s)$. The term $\theta * s$ represents the sensitivity of investment to changes in the exchange rate, with hedging coefficient θ:

$$\theta = \begin{cases} 0 & \text{if firm } i \text{ is perfectly hedged (large firm).} \\ 1 & \text{if firm } i \text{ is not hedged (small firm).} \end{cases} \tag{14.17}$$

A perfectly hedged firm's investment function is therefore insensitive to exchange rate movements, whereas unhedged firms are exposed to developments in the foreign exchange markets.

$$I_i = \begin{cases} \bar{I} & \text{if firm } i \text{ is perfectly hedged (large firm).} \\ I(s) & \text{if firm } i \text{ is not hedged (small firm).} \end{cases} \tag{14.18}$$

Figure 14.8 shows a firm's payoff and the investment function in the case without corporate hedging. This investment function is on par with Krugman's (2000) type of investment function in which investment depends negatively on the nominal exchange rate s. The underlying idea is that firms in many developing countries have large amounts of debt denominated in foreign currency. A currency depreciation will worsen these firms' balance sheets, which will decrease their net wealth, leading to an investment contraction. The result of such a development might be a balance-sheet-driven crisis in which sufficiently strong negative balance sheet effects, outweigh positive competitiveness effects, leading to a backward, bending goods market curve (see Krugman 2000, p. 82–84).

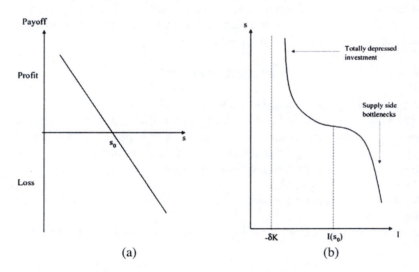

Figure 14.8 Economy consisting of small firms: (a) dependence of the firm's payoffs on s; (b) investment function without hedging.

The payoff function in Figure 14.8 represents any cash flow connected to the liabilities held in foreign currency. In the case of a depreciation of the domestic currency the value of the liabilities increases, resulting in a loss, whereas an appreciation of the domestic currency decreases the value of the liabilities, which can be taken as profit. The payoff function in Figure 14.8 is linear, for simplicity, in order to introduce simple linear hedging techniques to potentiate perfect hedging possibilities.[17] However, the investment function is not linear because of the balance sheet effect connected to the financial accelerator mechanism, as discussed in Bernanke et al. (1994) (see for instance Proaño et al. 2005).

Figure 14.9 corresponds to the first line of equation (14.18), where $I_i = \bar{I}$. The payoff function shows a simple linear currency forward hedging strategy. Here, the central idea is that the forward position generates profits if the spot position generates losses. Profits and losses sum up to zero. If the spot position generates profits as the result of an appreciation, the forward position generates losses, again summing up to zero.[18]

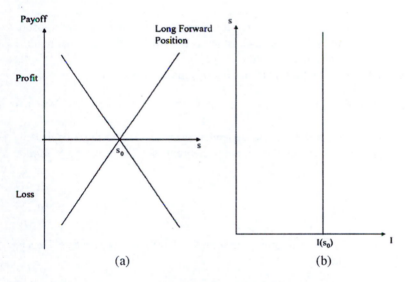

Figure 14.9 Economy consisting of large firms: (a) a single firm's hedged payoffs; (b) investment function with hedging.

17 Perfect hedging possibilities can also be generated using nonlinear instruments such as swaps and options. One could also use structured notes, linking foreign currency risk to credit risk. Another approach is the so-called macro derivatives. These combine risks associated with contract specific variables like exchange rates, interest rates and counterparty default as well as more general variables such as GDP (see Schweimayer 2003). Again, there are many possible hedging strategies but in this context it is appropriate to use simple linear currency forwards. An example of how to conduct currency hedging using forwards and futures is presented in Röthing et al. (2008).
18 For similar graphical representations of linear hedging strategies, see Grannis and Fitzgerald (1989, p. 102) and Gerke and Bank (1998, p. 444).

Since foreign liabilities are perfectly hedged against adverse currency movements, the investment function shown in Figure 14.9 is independent of the exchange rate. Large firms which have access to financial derivatives will hedge their currency exposure and hence, surrender potential gains from an appreciation. Fender (2000a, p. 10) describes the reason as follows: "It is a fundamental insight, that under uncertainty, risk-averse decision-makers will prefer stable income and consumption streams to highly variable ones." Furthermore, trading partners as well as banks recognize a hedged firm just by the fact that this specific firm is a large firm. By knowing this, they can avoid negative balance sheet effects even if the hedge position is an off-balance sheet.

Assuming that there are n firms in the economy, the investment function depends on the average hedging coefficient of the economy

$$\phi = \frac{1}{n} \sum_{i=1}^{n} \theta_i, \quad 0 \leq \phi \leq 1 \tag{14.19}$$

In a perfectly hedged economy, where all n firms hedge their currency exposure perfectly, the investment function is constant: $I(\phi, s) = \bar{I}$. In the case that no firm hedges, the investment function is $I(\phi, s) = I(s)$.

We get the following representation of goods market equilibrium:

$$Y = C(Y - \delta \bar{K} - \bar{T}) + I(\phi, s) + \bar{G} + NX(Y, \bar{Y}^*, s) \tag{14.20}$$

The shape of the IS curve with the dependent variable Y and the independent variable s is given by the implicit function theorem (see Flaschel and Semmler 2006):

$$Y'(s) = -\frac{I_s + NX_s}{C_Y + NX_Y - 1} \tag{14.21}$$

Since $C_Y + NX_Y < 1$ by assumption, the term $C_Y + NX_Y - 1$ is negative. Hence, $Y'(s)$ is upward sloping if

$$NX_s > I_s \tag{14.22}$$

Equation (14.22) holds always true if $\phi = 0$, which means that all firms hedge their currency exposure perfectly. In this case there is no backward-bending IS curve.

The financial markets are fully described by the following equations:[19]

Private wealth: $W_p = M_0 + B_0 + sF_{p0}$ (AA1)

LM curve: $M = m(Y, i), \quad m_Y > 0, m_i < 0$ (AA2)

---

19 See Flaschel and Semmler (2006) and Proaño et al. (2005).

Demand for foreign bonds:	$sF_p = f(\xi, W_p), \quad f_\xi < 0, f_{W_p} \in (0,1)$	(AA3)
Demand for domestic bonds:	$B = W_p - m(Y, i) - f(\xi, W_p)$	(AA4)
Expected depreciation:	$\varepsilon = \beta_\varepsilon(\frac{s_0}{s} - 1), \quad \varepsilon_s \leq 0$	(AA5)
Risk premium:	$\xi = i - \bar{i^*} - \varepsilon$	(AA6)
Foreign exchange market:	$\bar{F^*} = F_p + F_c$	(AA7)

with the domestic interest rate i, the foreign interest rate $\bar{i^*}$, the private foreign bond holdings sF_p, and the central bank's foreign bond holdings F_c. Equation (AA5) presents a typical formulation of regressive expectations as discussed in Rødseth (2000, p. 21), with $\varepsilon_s \leq 0$ and $\varepsilon(s_0) = 0$ for the steady-state exchange rate level s_0. Economic agents have perfect knowledge of the future equilibrium exchange rate and therefore expect the actual exchange rate to adjust to the steady-state value after the occurrence of a shock. Flaschel and Semmler (2006) call these expectations that allow agents to behave forward looking "asymptotically rational".

Solving equation (AA2) for i, inserting the result in equation (AA6) and inserting further equation (AA6) as well as (AA1) in equation (AA3) gives the financial markets equilibrium curve (AA curve):

$$sF_p = f(i(Y, M_0) - \bar{i^*} - \beta_\varepsilon(\frac{s_0}{s} - 1), M_0 + B_0 + sF_{p0}) \tag{14.23}$$

The slope of the AA curve is determined by the implicit function theorem (see for instance Proaño et al. 2005):

$$s'(Y) = -\frac{f_\xi * i_Y}{-f_\xi * \varepsilon_s + (f_{W_p} - 1) * F_{p0}} < 0 \tag{14.24}$$

The AA curve is downward sloping since $f_\xi < 0$, $i_Y > 0$, $\varepsilon_s \leq 0$, $f_{W_p} \in (0,1)$ and $F_{p0} \geq 0$.

We obtain the adjustment process of the goods market equilibrium curve

$$\dot{Y} = \beta_Y[C(Y - \delta\bar{K} - \bar{T}) + I(\phi, s) + \bar{G} + NX(Y, \bar{Y^*}, s) - Y] \tag{14.25}$$

and the following dynamics of the financial markets:

$$\dot{s} = \beta_s[f(i(Y, M_0) - \bar{i^*} - \beta_\varepsilon(\frac{s_0}{s} - 1), M_0 + B_0 + sF_{p0}) - sF_{p0}] \tag{14.26}$$

Figure 14.10 presents IS–AA diagrams for different values of the average hedging coefficient ϕ (cases A, B, C, D). In the following, we discuss the characteristics of these four cases as well as the local stability properties.

- Case A: $\phi = 1$
  In this case no firm is hedged. Consequently there are only small firms that do not have access to hedging tools. Hence this case corresponds to that presented in Krugman (2000) and Flaschel and Semmler (2006). The figure

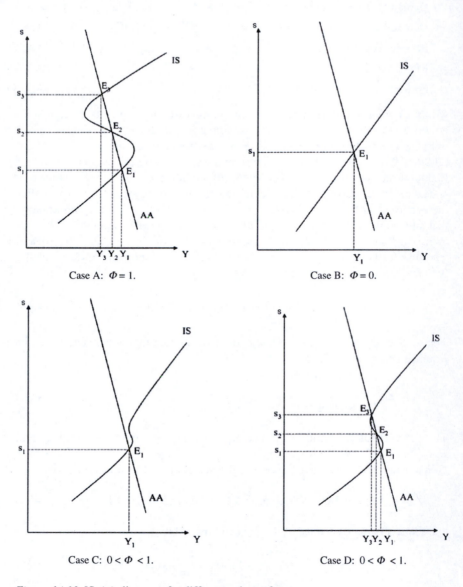

Figure 14.10 IS-AA diagrams for different values of ϕ.

shows multiple equilibria with E_1 representing the "good equilibrium" with high output Y_1 and low exchange rate s_1, white E_3 represents the "crisis equilibrium" with low output Y_3 and high exchange rate s_3.

- Case B: $\phi = 0$

Case B illustrates the situation where all firms are hedged perfectly. With the investment function independent of the exchange rate, net exports remain the only linkage between Y and s. In the case of a perfectly hedged economy there is no backward-bending IS curve and thus there are no multiple equilibria. In this framework a currency crisis cannot occur.

- Cases C and D: $0 < \phi < 1$
  Cases C and D present other possible outcomes, depending on the value of ϕ. With decreasing ϕ the "bad equilibrium" E_3 moves down the AA curve towards higher values of Y and lower values of s. Hence, in the multiple equilibria case (case D), the severity of a currency crisis decreases with growing hedging activity. In case C the hedging activity is sufficient to avoid multiple equilibria. In this case a currency crisis does not occur.

In order to study the stability of the system the Jacobian matrix is derived:

$$ J = \begin{bmatrix} \beta_Y[C_Y + NX_Y - 1] & \beta_Y[I_s + NX_s] \\ \beta_s[f_\xi * i_Y] & \beta_s[-f_\xi * \varepsilon_s + (f_{W_p} - 1) * F_{p0}] \end{bmatrix} $$

Considering $f_\xi < 0, i_Y > 0, f_{W_p} \in [0, 1]$ and $\varepsilon_s \leq 0$, we obtain the following signs:

$$ J = \begin{bmatrix} - & ? \\ - & - \end{bmatrix} $$

Referring to the four cases mentioned above, it depends on the sign of "?" whether a specific equilibrium (E_1, E_2, E_3) is stable or unstable:

- Case A: $\phi = 1$
  $? = \beta_Y[I_s + NX_s]$
  If I_s dominates NX_s (E_2), "?" is negative. The determinant and the trace of the Jacobian are both negative $(\det(J_{E_2}) < 0, \operatorname{tr}(J_{E_2}) < 0)$. Hence, E_2 is a saddle point.[20]
  If NX_s dominates I_s (E_1, E_3), "?" is positive. Hence, $\det(J_{(E_{1,3})}) > 0$ and $\operatorname{tr}(J_{(E_{1,3})}) < 0$, which gives a stable steady state.
- Case B: $\phi = 0$
  Since $I_s = 0$, we get $? = \beta_Y[NX_e] > 0$. We have a single equilibrium (E_1) which is stable since $\det(J_{E_1}) > 0$ and $\operatorname{tr}(J_{E_1}) < 0$.
- Cases C and D: $0 < \phi < 1$
  Case C, the single equilibrium case, is similar to case B. In the equilibrium point (E_1) NX_e dominates I_s, the sign of "?" is positive, $\det(J_{E_1}) > 0$, and $\operatorname{tr}(J_{E_1}) < 0$. The equilibrium E_1 is stable.

The dynamics of the multiple equilibria, case D, is equal to the dynamics of case A. If I_s dominates NX_s (E_2), we get $\det(J_{E_2}) < 0, \operatorname{tr}(J_{E_2}) < 0$. Consequently E_2 is unstable. If NX_s dominates I_s (E_1, E_3), then $\det(J_{(E_{1,3})}) > 0$ and $\operatorname{tr}(J_{(E_{1,3})}) < 0$. Hence, the "good equilibrium" E_1 and the "crisis equilibrium" E_3 are both stable.

---

20 See the "Trace–determinant plane' in Hirsch et al. (2004, p. 63).

For a further elaboration on this type of model, allowing for hedging cost, see Röthig et al. (2007).

The main result of this investigation is that economic stability can be increased by enhancing corporate hedging, either directly by simplifying access to hedging instruments (firm size approach) or indirectly by lowering hedging costs and increasing the awareness of specific risks (hedging costs approach). Under the assumption that firms can limit currency risk by hedging, currency depreciations are more manageable and less likely to result in currency and financial crises. In our model, corporate hedging decreases the backward-bending segment of the goods market curve "that is key to the possibility of crisis" (Krugman 1999, p. 6).

Referring to this result, the main duty of policymakers and corporate officials appears to be the achievement of more transparency and the improvement of information flows. This could be realized by regulating transactions of OTC derivatives, leading to easier access to OTC products and reducing the costs of information and thus the costs of hedging. This does not necessarily mean that the destabilizing influences of rapid currency changes can all be overcome. Destabilizing macroeconomic feedback effects are still possible, but individual firms may, through currency hedging, diversify their currency risk.

14.6 Adding wage and price dynamics

Although our basic currency crisis model is capable of describing some empirically observed features of the last Mexican and East Asian currency and financial crises, as discussed above, it does not take into account another very important dynamics,[21] namely the constant wage and price dynamics. To investigate this issue we revert back to our model without currency hedging. Despite the fact that during a currency and financial crisis price fluctuations probably do not play an important role because of the short time span in which such a twin crisis takes place, they surely are of great importance in the economic recovery process of such

---

21 There are two other main points neglected in the model presented above: The first one is the assumption that the domestic interest rate does not influence domestic economic activity directly. With this assumption, the domestic monetary authorities are not confronted with an exchange-rate policy dilemma during a currency crisis. Theoretically, they are capable of increasing the domestic interest rates indefinitely in order to defend the currency peg without producing any negative effects on the domestic economy. The decision to give in to a speculative attack on the domestic currency here relies more on the level of the foreign exchange reserves that the country has at the time of the currency run, which may of course dissipate during the currency run. The second point is the modeling of exchange rate devaluation expectations and the actual exchange rate fluctuations. Even if the adoption of the "asymptotically rational" devaluation expectations is not completely unrealistic, it implies a very smooth convergence to the long-run steady-state. In the real world there are many more forces at work in the determination of the long-run exchange rate level as well as in the process of adjustment to this level. The fact that the actual exchange rate level is solely determined by disequilibrium situations in the foreign-currency bonds market also seems to leave out important aspects of the real world. These two issues will not be dealt with here, but will be left for further research.

an economy. Real and not only nominal exchange rate fluctuations determine the international competitiveness of the domestic goods and the volume of exports of the economy.

The assumption of constant domestic commodity prices in the context of sharp exchange rate fluctuations is also problematic because the exchange rate can affect the domestic price level through the following channels (see Svensson 1998):

- The exchange rate level affects the domestic currency prices of imported goods, and therefore the CPI inflation rate.
- The exchange rate affects domestic currency prices of intermediate inputs.
- The exchange rate can also influence nominal wage determination through CPI inflation and thus, again, domestic inflation.

Because the exchange rate can influence domestic inflation through so many mechanisms, the assumption of constant domestic prices ignores a variety of effects which can influence the economic development of the small open economy in significant ways.

Given the above shortcomings of the basic model, we will now present an extended version of a currency crisis model. The purpose of this extended model is to show how – besides the exchange rate – domestic price level fluctuations can also influence the macroeconomic performance of a small open economy with dollarized liabilities and credit market constraints. The emphasis of this extended model is not on fiscal imbalances or unsustainable monetary policies (as first- and second-generation currency crisis models), but on the macroeconomic effects of a breakdown of the exchange rate system in conjunction with the fragility of financial markets observed in many emerging market economies.

The core of this extended model still is the balance-sheet state-dependent investment function. Because domestic price fluctuations are now included in addition to the role of the exchange rate, the domestic price level changes now also influence the aggregate investment level of the small open economy (while K, F_f are still kept constant). The inclusion of price fluctuations into the considered dynamics – through a standard Phillips curve mechanism, to be introduced below – coupled with the price-level-dependent investment function indeed brings considerable complexity into the system (in particular in the case of freely floating exchange rates).

As in the model of this and the former chapter, and also as in Krugman (2000), the elasticity of the investment function with respect to changes of $\tilde{q}$ (See section 14.2) is now assumed to be state dependent: for high values of $\tilde{q}$ (p low), where the nominal value of the dollarized liabilities of the business sector is significantly higher than the nominal replacement costs of capital, the investment reaction is assumed to be inelastic. In the opposite case, where $\tilde{q}$ is low (p high), the firms' dollarized liabilities are low relative to their assets and therefore firms do not face any constraints in the credit markets and the investment function is thus assumed to be again very inelastic. The aggregate consumption and export functions remain unchanged, with the only difference that the latter depends now on the real (and not nominal) exchange rate $\sigma = s/p$ (the foreign goods price still set equal to one for simplicity).

The goods market equilibrium can again be expressed as

$$Y = C_1(Y^D) + I(\tilde{q}) + \delta\bar{K} + \bar{G} + X(Y^{n*}, \sigma), \tag{14.27}$$

and the dynamic multiplier is now based on the law of motion

$$\dot{Y} = \beta_y \left[C_1(Y^D) + I(\tilde{q}) + \delta\bar{K} + \bar{G} + X(Y^{n*}, \sigma) - Y \right]. \tag{14.28}$$

On the assumption that a fixed exchange rate system prevails ($\bar{s} = s_0$), the slope of the $\dot{Y} = 0$ isocline is now described, in the extended phase space (Y, p) (for output and the domestic price level), by

$$\left. \frac{\partial Y}{\partial p} \right|_{\dot{Y}=0} = -\frac{I_p + X_p}{C_Y - 1}.$$

It can easily be seen that the slope of the $\dot{Y} = 0$ isocline depends on which of the two opposite effects dominates: the balance-sheet effect $I_p > 0$ or the competitiveness effect $X_p < 0$:

$$I_p > |X_p| \Longrightarrow \left. \frac{\partial Y}{\partial p} \right|_{\dot{Y}=0} > 0$$

and

$$I_p < |X_p| \Longrightarrow \left. \frac{\partial Y}{\partial p} \right|_{\dot{Y}=0} < 0.$$

From the shape of the assumed investment function there results (if its interior part is sufficiently steeper than its counterpart in the export function) that for intermediate values of $\tilde{q}$ the creditworthiness (the balance-sheet) effect is stronger than the "normal" competitiveness effect, changing the slope of the $\dot{Y} = 0$ isocline and therefore opening up the possibility of multiple equilibria in the (Y, p) phase space. The structure of the financial markets is as in the basic approach.

The innovation in this extended currency crisis model is the modeling of domestic price fluctuations through a wage–price Phillips curve. An expectations-augmented, open-economy Phillips curve (on the assumption of a constant productivity production function and mark-up pricing) could be written as

$$\hat{p} = \gamma(Y - Y^n) + \pi_c^e \text{ with } \pi_c^e = (\hat{p}_c)^e \text{ and } p_c = p^\theta (sp^*)^{1-\theta}, \ \theta \in (0, 1). \tag{14.29}$$

We now use p_c for the consumer price level, based on a geometric mean of the domestic and the foreign price level, both expressed in the domestic currency.

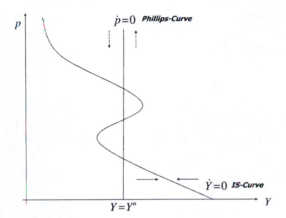

Figure 14.11 Graphical representation of the IS-PC currency crisis model.

Superscript *e* denotes expected variables, implying that marked-up domestic wage inflation is explained in this Phillips curve by the output gap and the expected consumer price inflation rate. This curve can be reduced to

$$\hat{p} = \frac{1}{1-\theta}\gamma(Y - Y^n) \quad \text{or} \quad \dot{p} = (\beta_p(Y - Y^n))p, \tag{14.30}$$

as long as both the exchange rate and the foreign price level are kept fixed and if it is assumed, in addition, that current domestic inflation is perfectly foreseen. More generally, one may simply assume that inflationary expectations are still ignored by this model type in order to save one law of motion and to leave the discussion of destabilizing Mundell-type effects for later extensions of the model (see our discussion of kinked Phillips curves below).

The implied $\dot{p} = 0$ isocline turns out to consist of two parts: for $p > 0$ the isocline is the straight vertical line $Y = Y^n$. Additionally, along the horizontal axis ($p = 0$) $\dot{p} = 0$ also holds. As discussed in the next section, a further – though economically not meaningful – steady-state exists at the intersection of the $\dot{Y} = 0$ isocline and the horizontal axis.

The resulting IS–PC model is represented in Figure 14.11. Note again that financial markets have no explicit representation in this diagram as long as the exchange rate is kept fixed by the central bank.

The extended currency crisis model (under a fixed exchange rate regime) is fully described by the following differential equations:

$$\dot{Y} = \beta_y \left[C_1(Y - \delta\bar{K} - \bar{T}) + I(\tilde{q}) + \delta\bar{K} + \bar{G} + X(Y^{n*}, \sigma) - Y \right],$$
$$\dot{p} = \left[\gamma(Y - Y^n) \right]p.$$

where inflationary expectations are now ignored completely. The Jacobian of this system at the steady-state is given by:

$$J = \begin{bmatrix} \beta_y(C_Y - 1) & \beta_y\left(I'\frac{\partial \tilde{q}}{\partial p} + X_\sigma \frac{\partial \sigma}{\partial p}\right) \\ \gamma p_0 & 0 \end{bmatrix}.$$

Because of the nonlinear shape of the $\dot{Y} = 0$ isocline there exist three possible economically meaningful steady-states,[22] whose local stability properties can easily be calculated:

$$J_{E1} = \begin{bmatrix} - & - \\ + & 0 \end{bmatrix} \Longrightarrow \mathrm{tr}(J_{E1}) < 0, \quad \det(J_{E1}) > 0 \Longrightarrow \text{a stable steady state}$$

$$J_{E2} = \begin{bmatrix} - & + \\ + & 0 \end{bmatrix} \Longrightarrow \mathrm{tr}(J_{E2}) < 0, \quad \det(J_{E2}) < 0 \Longrightarrow \text{a saddle point}$$

$$J_{E3} = \begin{bmatrix} - & - \\ + & 0 \end{bmatrix} \Longrightarrow \mathrm{tr}(J_{E3}) < 0, \quad \det(J_{E3}) > 0 \Longrightarrow \text{a stable steady-state.}$$

The resulting dynamics of our extended currency crisis model (still a fixed exchange rate) are described by Figure 14.12. Steady state E_1 represents the "normal" situation, where the domestic price level is high and therefore (under the assumption of a fixed exchange rate) $\tilde{q}$ is low. In this steady-state the economy's output is at its full employment level, the investment activity is high (due to the low $\tilde{q}$) and the exports are low due to a strong currency – relative to the high domestic price level – and thus low competitiveness.[23] In this steady-state the standard situation $I_p < |X_p|$ holds.

Steady state E_2 represents the fragile case where $I_p > |X_p|$ holds. A slight deviation of the output level from this steady-state level can lead the economy to a short-run investment boom (and to an over-employment situation) or to an economic slowdown or a recession, since this equilibrium point is unstable.

Steady state E_3 constitutes the "crisis equilibrium". At this equilibrium point the investment activity is severely depressed due to the high value of $\tilde{q}$. The economy is at its full-employment level because of the strong production of goods for export, but this is induced by the very low level of domestic prices and thus by the implied

---

22 Due to the nonlinearity of the second law of motion there exists a fourth steady state at the point where the $\dot{Y} = 0$ isocline cuts the horizontal axis. This fourth steady-state is not relevant, however, since it cannot be approached by the trajectories in the present consideration under dynamics.
23 Such a situation could be observed in the years preceding the East Asian crisis (see Corsetti et al. 1998).

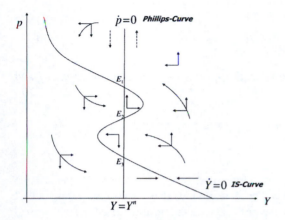

Figure 14.12 Phase-space representation of the IS–PC dynamics with a normal and a bad equilibrium, E_1 and E_3, respectively.

competitiveness of the economy.[24] The reason why this equilibrium might not be the preferable one to be in will be discussed below.

Before discussing the reasons for and the effects of an enforced one-time devaluation of the domestic currency on investment and output, we will first consider the global stability of the system. Global stability analysis of a dynamic model is important because we are considering systems that can be subject to large shocks so that an analysis that is concentrated on the neighborhoods of the two stable steady states is too limited in such an environment. Furthermore – as our subsequent analysis will show – we will always have upper and lower turning points for output as well as the price level if the system is started in a certain bounded domain. There are thus global forces at work that prevent the collapse of economic activity as well as unbounded growth of output. This is partly due to the floors and ceilings we have built into the investment and export function, which also – perhaps more surprisingly – prevent the occurrence of an endless hyperinflation or a deflationary spiral.

We note first of all that the extended currency crisis model allows for nonnegative price levels only (and for zero price levels at best when time goes to infinity). This is due to the fact that the horizontal line is an invariant subset of the dynamics; i.e., trajectories which start in this set must stay in it.

In order to see how the $\dot{Y} = 0$ isocline behaves in the proximity of the horizontal, i.e. for $p \to 0$, $\dot{Y}$ is set equal to zero in equation (14.28) and then solved for Y

---

24 After the East Asian crisis many of the countries that came under attack experienced a reversal in their current account because of the exporting boom that was caused by the sharp devaluation of their currencies (see Corsetti et al. 1998).

(we here assume a linear consumption function for simplicity):

$$Y = \frac{1}{1-c_1}[c_0 + c_1(\delta\bar{K} + \bar{T}) + I(\tilde{q}) + \delta\bar{K} + \bar{G} + X(Y^{n*}, \sigma)]. \tag{14.31}$$

As was assumed in the preceding sections, for $p \to 0$, investment goes to $\underline{I}$ and exports to $\bar{X}$, such that

$$Y^n < \bar{Y} = Y|_{p=0} = \frac{1}{1-c_1}\left[c_0 + c_1(\delta\bar{K} + \bar{T}) + \underline{I} + \bar{G} + \bar{X}\right] > 0$$

comes about.

Because $\underline{I}$ and $\bar{X}$ are finite, it follows that the $\dot{Y} = 0$ isocline must cut the horizontal axis when $p = 0$ is reached. It is obvious that the corresponding output level must lie above the NAIRU level Y^n, i.e., on the right-hand side of the vertical labor market equilibrium curve.

In the same way, the value of Y can be calculated for $p \to \infty$ and it is assumed that

$$Y^n > \underline{Y} = Y|_{p=\infty} = \frac{1}{1-c_1}\left[c_0 + c_1(\delta\bar{K} + \bar{T}) + \bar{I} + \bar{G} + \underline{X}\right] > 0$$

holds true.

The fact that the $\dot{Y} = 0$ isocline converges to a strictly positive value of Y for $p \to \infty$ implies that the vertical axis cannot be reached by the dynamics when started in the positive orthant of the phase space. There are thus always lower turning points for output, as well as for the price level, due to the shape of the $\dot{Y} = 0$ isocline and the underlying assumptions on floors and ceilings in the investment and export functions. The upper turning point of the output dynamics also follows from the same assumptions since the vertical line that starts in the intersection of this isocline with the horizontal axis limits all possible output dynamics. Our choice of investment and export functions thus constrains the dynamics in a vertical strip in the positive orthant, but does not yet exclude the occurrence of hyperinflation as the only possibility for an unlimited explosive spiral.

A further simple assumption, however, suffices here to also exclude the occurrence of hyperinflation from the model. This assumption again concerns the floors and ceilings in the investment and export functions and reads

$$Y^n > C_1(Y^n) + \bar{I} + \bar{G} + \underline{X}.$$

This assumption states that aggregate demand falls below the NAIRU level at least when the price level approaches infinity; i.e.; the ceiling in investment is not so large as to overcome the floor in exports if the real exchange rate approaches zero. Any trajectory to the right of the NAIRU level must therefore experience an upper turning point in the evolution of its price level.

In sum, we therefore obtain the situation shown in Figure 14.13 where we have drawn an invariant domain (that cannot be left by the dynamics) that basically contains the two basins of attraction of the two stable steady states together with besides the stable separatrices of the unstable steady state. We thus conjecture, but cannot prove here, that there are no closed orbits in the considered part of the phase space, i.e., in particular, there are no stable persistent oscillations possible. This then justifies that both the normal and the crisis equilibrium points are taken into consideration as the relevant attractors from the global point of view.

Figure 14.13 conjectures – on the basis of what is stated in Hirsch and Smale (1994, p. 249) – how the two stable arms of the saddle point E_2 will look. It suggests very straightforward domains of the two basins of attraction of the two stable steady-states E_1, E_3. We thus have multiple equilibria in a 2D phase space with a very clear-cut structure of the dynamics in the economically meaningful part of the phase space.

In contrast to our basic model, discussed in Sections 14.2-14.4, where we could have large output loss in the crisis equilibrium, this extended model may raise the question to what extent the lower equilibrium represents a bad equilibrium. We have full employment in the sense of the NAIRU theory, coupled with high exports, but very low investment activity. The growth rate of the capital stock is thus very depressed or even negative. This, of course, is bad for the future evolution of the economy with respect to income and employment growth. Furthermore, if economic activity is moving towards the lower equilibrium, the evolution may be subject to long periods of deflation, in particular if there are downward rigidities in money wage adjustments (a nonlinear Phillips curve), which we will consider briefly below. The dangers of deflation are not fully included in the present model, and thus do not call for particular attention from the monetary authority.

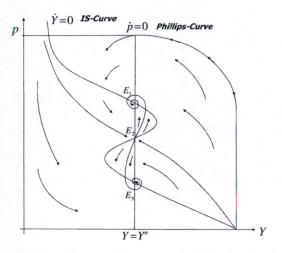

Figure 14.13 The global dynamics with their two basins of attraction.

14.7 The dynamics of a currency crisis in our extended model

Next, we discuss a situation where the economy experiences a financial crisis, after a one-time devaluation of the domestic currency as a result of a speculative attack, and can eventually shift from a "normal" equilibrium with high investment and low exports to a "crisis" equilibrium with depressed investment activity and high exports. This is due to the inclusion of domestic price level adjustments, and is obtained by employing a standard Phillips curve. Assuming again a constant exchange rate after the devaluation, the model dynamics will be sketched in the $p-Y$ space instead of the $s-Y$ space as in the Flaschel and Semmler (2003, 2006) model.

Assume that the economy is initially situated at its upper full employment level. A significant flight into foreign currency can take place in the model through an increase of the α parameter in the foreign currency bond demand. As long as the monetary authorities can defend the old currency peg, the flight into foreign currency does not have any effects apart from a reduction of the foreign exchange reserves of the central bank.[25] Now suppose that the central bank gives in foreign market pressure after a while, because of the dangerous reduction in foreign reserves. It lowers the exchange rate in order to release the pressure from the foreign exchange market; see eq. (14.7) in this regard. It carries out a one-time devaluation (for simplicity we assume that the new exchange rate is then considered by the economic agents as "sustainable"). The effect of the currency devaluation on the $\dot{Y} = 0$ isocline, i.e. the direction of the shift of the isocline, depends on the strength of the balance-sheet and competitiveness effects. To understand this point, consider the original model of Sections 14.2–14.4 where prices were held constant: there too the output reaction to the exchange rate change depended on the strength of the exchange rate effect on investment and exports.

The direction of the shift of the $\dot{Y} = 0$ isocline in the extended 2D model (in the $p-Y$ space) is analogous to the exchange rate effect on output in the original model (in the $s-Y$ space): If $I_s > |X_s|$ holds, the nominal devaluation of the domestic currency will shift the $\dot{Y} = 0$ isocline to the left, and vice versa.

The resulting dynamics of the system after a severe nominal currency devaluation in the first situation are sketched in Figure 14.14.

Directly after the currency crash, the banks take into account the sharp deterioration of the balance sheets of the business sector resulting from the strong devaluation of the domestic currency. As a measure to hedge themselves against "bad creditors", they implement credit constraints and cut the volume of loans granted. The industrial sector, now in a dramatic financial situation, must cancel the majority of the investment projects either voluntarily or due to the credit constraints, thus reducing aggregate demand and therefore inducing unemployment.

---

25 Because a constant money supply is assumed, a full sterilization of money base changes by the central bank is also implicitly assumed.

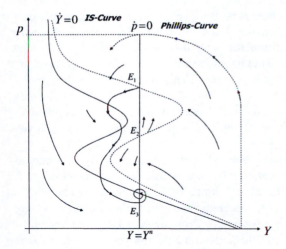

Figure 14.14 The consequences of a breakdown of the currency peg.

Because of this, prices begin to react and start to fall, as a result of the Phillips curve together with the change in economic activity.

We consider now, as an example, the case where the IS curve – with the exception of the zero price level situation – unambiguously shifts to the left as a result of the currency devaluation. The steady state E_3 is assumed, due to the size of the shift of the IS curve, to be the only economically meaningful steady state. Falling prices are then at first accompanied by falling output levels. They lead to a further real depreciation, in addition to the initially caused nominal exchange rate shock. This in turn results in further gains in competitiveness on the international goods market. Sooner or later, the increased foreign demand for domestic goods leads to such an increase in exports that aggregate demand starts rising again, at which point the IS curve is crossed from above by the initiated temporary deflationary process. There could now be a deflationary spiral, since output cannot rise by so much that the NAIRU level is reached again. Instead, output will start falling once again – when the IS curve is crossed again on the way down to the bad equilibrium – which, still further down, leads again to increasing output and then either to monotonic adjustment to the steady-state E_3 or to dampened cycles around it (shown in Figure 14.13). We thus, in sum, observe a deflationary process with fluctuating economic activity below the NAIRU output level until the economy is back to normal output levels with smaller cycles around them.

Falling prices have negative as well as positive effects on aggregate demand: the latter because of an export increase and the former because they reduce the nominal value of the firms' capital, deteriorating even more their financial situation. We thus have initially, therefore, counteracting forces operating simultaneously with a stronger investment effect, and again after a while (implying decreasing output levels), while in between improvements in the trade balance can be so strong that economic activity is then rising, though still always less than normal and thus accompanied by further deflationary pressure. The graphical analysis here shows that the economy will fluctuate around a somewhat persistent underemployment situation (with still falling prices) until the competitiveness effect finally dominates (maybe because the investment level has come close to its "floor" level) and the economy returns to its "full"-employment level. This must happen by assumption since it was assumed that the intersection of the IS curve with the horizontal axis lies to the left of the NAIRU output level. Deflation must therefore come to an end and – maybe also with temporarily increasing price levels – finally approach the steady-state price level at E_3.

Note that the crucial mechanism in this dynamics that allows the economy to return to the full-employment situation is the variation of the domestic price level. Because in the basic model sketched in Sections 14.2–14.4 prices are assumed to be constant, one cannot consider the (medium-run) possibility for the economy to return to a "full"-employment situation. In the basic model, the country which has suffered from a currency and financial crisis is "thrown back" to a lower steady-state output level where it remains because the model dose not produce any endogenous mechanism that would allow the economy to recover from the twin crisis. In this extended version, where we allow prices to be sufficiently flexible, the economic performance of the economy can improve sufficiently through a real depreciation of domestic goods, leading it back to the full-employment level if the ceilings and floors in the investment and the export function are chosen appropriately.

Yet, Keynes (1936, Ch. 2) already had recognized that an economy-wide wage deflation with a simultaneous deflation in money wages is rarely observed. Taking downward money wage rigidity into account, the wage–price Phillips curve can be modified as follows:

$$\hat{p} = \max\left\{\gamma(Y - Y^n), 0\right\}. \tag{14.32}$$

This modified Phillips curve implies that in under-employment situations prices do not fall but instead remain constant. Price changes can only take place in over-employment situations, where the price level is assumed to rise as before. Adding such a kink in money wage behavior modifies the considered dynamics as shown in Figure 14.15.

The empirical observation of downwardly rigid wages has important consequences for the dynamics of the extended model. Assume the country finds itself in the same situation as discussed above. After a run on the foreign currency the monetary authorities are forced to devaluate, so that – under the assumption that $I_s > |X_s|$ holds – aggregate demand declines and the $\dot{Y} = 0$ isocline shifts again to the left. Because, in the entire economic domain to the left of the $\dot{p} = 0$ isocline, we have that $\hat{p} = 0$ holds true, the $\dot{Y} = 0$ isocline is in this domain an attracting curve representing stable depressions. All points on the $\dot{Y} = 0$ isocline to the left of the $\dot{p} = 0$ isocline are thus now equilibrium points. For each of these steady states, there is no longer a mechanism that allows the economy to return to its

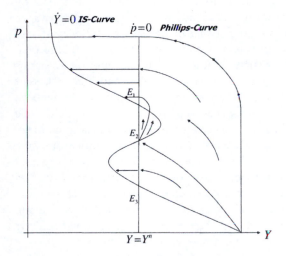

Figure 14.15 The consequences of downward money wage rigidity.

"full"-employment level. The "crisis" equilibrium in the basic model of Sections 14.2–14.4, derived from Flaschel and Semmler (2003), is now just one of these under-employment equilibria.

One may argue, therefore, that the assumed wage rigidity is bad for the working of the economy. However, at present deflation is still too tranquil a process to allow for any other conclusion. Advocates of downward wage flexibility should therefore not yet interpret the present framework as an developed argument that supports their view. Adding real rate-of-interest effects (Mundell effects) to the formulation of aggregate demand, or adding a Fisher debt effect to investment behavior, can easily remove the lower turning point in deflation dynamics from the model. This would therefore imply an economic breakdown, in case the kink in the money wage Phillips curve was not there. The kinked wage Phillips curve prevents or at least delays deflationary processes from working their way. Though stable depressions may be considered a big problem, the remedy to allow for a significant degree of wage flexibility would, in such situations, not revive the economy but make things only worse, in particular in situations where a liquidity trap has become established.

In the present form of the model the kink in wage behavior implies, however, that a stable depression becomes established to the left of the good equilibrium E_1 with no effect on the price level, as was already considered in Flaschel and Semmler (2003).

14.8 Conclusions

Based on the previous chapter, and or the work of Flaschel and Semmler (2003, 2006), where wages and prices were presumed to be fixed, this chapter has studied basic financial crisis mechanisms that are triggered by exchange rate shocks by including hedging and price movements via a Phillips curve to represent the wage–price dynamics. We argue in this chapter that models where currency shocks trigger a financial crisis and a severe economic slowdown need to take into account some specification of the Phillips curve in order to study medium-run scenarios where inflation or deflationary pressures may arise and where the effectiveness of monetary policy is to be considered. The wage and price dynamics have not been made an issue in the work of the third-generation currency crisis models, since research so far has mainly focused on the mechanisms that transmit large currency shocks to the financial sector and to real economic activity. The empirical literature on this issue has primarily focused on the trends preceding financial crisis episodes (such as the deterioration of balance sheets, deterioration of current accounts, and an increasing external debt to reserve ratio) and on the mechanisms of the crisis scenario (such as a sudden reversal of capital flows, unexpected exchange rate depreciation, domestic interest rate jumps, stock price fall, credit and banking crises, and large-scale bankruptcies of firms and financial institutions).

Yet, in order to evaluate what monetary policy can do effectively, it is essential that the medium-run mechanisms and scenarios are explored in models where exchange rates, Phillips curve, and thus the wage–price dynamics, are interacting as well. As we have shown in this chapter, multiple equilibria models appear to be a useful device here too to study various scenarios of the medium run after a financial crisis has been triggered by large exchange rate shocks. Such scenarios might bring with them, as we suggested, depressed investment activities, liquidity traps and debt deflation on the one hand, and periods with high inflationary pressure on the other hand. Yet, we note here that a study of the effectiveness of monetary policy would have to be undertaken more thoroughly, for example if we assume that it follows a Taylor rule to control inflation and output. This is left here for future research.

14.9 References

BERNANKE, B.S., M. GERTLER and GILCHRIST, S. (1994): The financial accelerator and the flight to quality. *NBER Working Paper*, 4789.

BLANCHARD, O. and S. FISHER (1989): *Lectures on Macroeconomics*. Cambridge, MA.: MIT Press.

CORSETTI, G., P. PESENTI and N. ROUBINI (1998): What caused the Asian currency and financial crisis? Part I: A macroeconomic overview. *NBER Working Paper*, 6833.

FENDER, I. (2000a): Corporate hedging: The impact of financial derivatives on the bond credit channel of monetary policy. *BIS Working Paper*, 94.

FENDER, I. (2000b): The impact of risk management on monetary policy transmission: Some empirical evidence. *BIS Working Paper*, 95.

FLASCHEL, P. and W. SEMMLER (2003): Currency crisis, financial crisis and large output loss. *University of Bielefeld Center for Empirical Macroeconomics Working Paper*, 52.

FLASCHEL, P. and W. SEMMLER (2006): Currency crisis, financial crisis and large output loss. In: Chiarella, C., P. Flaschel, R. Franke and W. Semmler (eds): *Quantitative and Empirical Analysis of Nonlinear Dynamic Macromodels*. Amsterdam: Elsevier.

GERKE, W. and M. BANK (1998): *Finanzierung: Grundlagen für die Investitions- und Finanzentscheidungen in Unternehmen.* Stuttgart: Kohlhammer.

GOODHART, C. (2000): Commentary: Crises: the price of globalization? In: *Global Economic Integration: Opportunities and Challenges.* Federal Reserve Bank of Kansas City, 107–110.

GRANNIS, S. and S. FITZGERALD (1989): Dynamic hedging and the use of derivatives. In: Stoakes, C. (ed.): *Managing Global Portfolios.* London: Euromoney Publications.

HIRSCH, M. and S. SMALE (1994): *Differential Equations, Dynamical Systems and Linear Algebra.* New York: Academic Press.

KEYNES, J.M. (1936): *The General Theory of Employment, Interest and Money.* New York: MacMillan.

KRUGMAN, P. (2000): Crises: the price of globalization? In: *Global Economic Integration: Opportunities and Challenges.* Federal Reserve Bank of Kansas City, 75–105.

LÜTKEPOHL, H. (1993): *Introduction to Multiple Time Series Analysis.* 2nd edition. Heidelberg: Springer.

MIAN, S.L. (1996): Evidence on corporate hedging policy. *Journal of Financial and Quantitative Analysis,* 31, 414–439.

MILLER, M. and J. STIGLITZ (1999): Bankruptcy protection against macroeconomic shocks: the case for a "super Chapter 11". http://www.warwick.ac.uk/fac/soc/CSGR/glob-fin/milrstig.pdf.

MISHKIN, F.S. (1998): International capital movements, financial volatility and financial instability. *NBER Working Paper,* 6390.

MISHKIN, F.S. (2001): *The Economics of Money, Banking and Financial Markets.* 6th edition. New York: Addison Wesley Longman.

NEFTCI, S. (2000): *An Introduction to the Mathematics of Financial Derivatives.* 2nd edition. San Diego: Academic Press.

PROAÑO, C., P. FLASCHEL and W. SEMMLER (2005): Currency and financial crises in emerging market economies in the medium run. *Journal of Economic Asymmetries,* 2, 105–130.

RØDSETH, A. (2000): *Open Economy Macroeconomics.* Cambridge, UK: Cambridge University Press.

RÖTHIG, A., W. SEMMLER and P. FLASCHEL (2007): Hedging, speculation, and investment in balance-sheet triggered currency crises. *Australian Economic Papers,* 46:3, 224–23.

SCHWEIMAYER, G. (2003): *Risikomanagement mit Makroderivaten auf Basis zeit-diskreter stochastischer Prozesse.* Aachen: Shaker Verlag.

SVENSSON, L.E. (1998): Open-economy inflation targeting. *NBER Working Paper,* 6545.

TAYLOR, J.B. (2000): Using monetary policy rules in emerging market economies. www.standford.edu/johntayl/.

VARIAN, H.T. (1979): Catastrophe theory and the business cycle. *Economic Inquiry,* 17:1, 14–28.

15 Outlook

International capital flows in the MFT approach

15.1 Introduction

In this chapter we make a decisive (though mathematically still small) step forward in the treatment of the portfolio part of the Mundell–Fleming–Tobin model. In the original formulation of the model in Chapter 12 we assumed, on the one hand, a stock portfolio approach and thus were forced to consider that only part of the flow savings (in fact total savings minus investment) could appear in the capital account of the balance of payments. Using stock asset demand functions excludes, from a formal point of view, the possibility that portfolio readjustments appear in the capital (flow) account. On the other hand, complementing the situation just considered, we assumed that domestic bonds were not traded internationally, which meant – for example, in a regime of flexible exchange rates – that asset holders could not get more dollar-denominated bonds than were already in their (aggregate) possession, and – in a regime of fixed exchange rates – that the total supply of such bonds was limited by the stocks held in the household sector and by the central bank. Portfolio choices were thus limited to the amounts of domestic and foreign bonds (and money) already in existence in the domestic economy, which in this sense was a closed economy (though domestic holdings of foreign bonds changed due to current account deficits or surpluses).

There is therefore an urgent need to overcome these limitations and to allow for international capital flows to appear in the balance of payments that are not limited by the savings behavior of the domestic economy. This implies that domestic bond demand and supply (of both types of bonds) must be reformulated in terms of flows and that the same must be done for foreign demand (or supply) of domestic bonds and foreign supply (or demand) of foreign bonds. We thus have now not only an export function on the market for goods (the goods demand of foreigners), but also their demand and corresponding supply schedules on the international bond markets where domestic and foreign bonds are traded against each other. This enhances the degree of openness of the economy under consideration and allows us to consider the situations of capital flight investigated in Chapters 13 and 14 in more detail than was possible there. In Section 15.2 of this chapter we will enlarge the MFT model in the way discussed above. Section 15.3 will then consider the implications of such an approach to international capital flows for the small economy case.

15.2 Integrating international capital flows into the MFT approach

We use $*$ to denote magnitudes characterizing the foreign economy and the indexes p, g, c to denote private sector, government sector and central bank magnitudes of the domestic economy.

We start again from the budget equations of the three relevant sectors: households, the government and the central bank. With respect to firms, we again assume that all of their income is transferred to the household sector and that households give them credit to finance their investment expenditures (by and large the same as direct investment by the household sector). Note also, with respect to the following, that the central bank may hold government bonds and may change these holdings by way of an open market policy $dB_c = dM$, but that this does not influence the budget equations shown, since all interest income from these bond holdings is transferred back to the government sector which therefore only has to pay interest on the bonds B held by the private sector or abroad. The domestic bond holdings of the central bank can therefore be neglected in the following. In contrast to Chapter 12, we now only consider open market operations as described above and no longer an $\dot{M}$ policy of the central bank, and thus we assume the bank holds a fixed reserve of foreign bonds the interest income of which is transferred to the government sector.

15.2.1 Budget restrictions

The savings decision of households, the government budget constraint and the portfolio adjustment of the private sector now read as follows:

$$p(Y - \bar{T}) + iB_p + s\bar{i}^* F_p \equiv pC + pI + \dot{B} + s\dot{F}_{p1} \quad \text{PBR} \tag{15.1}$$

$$p\bar{T} + s\bar{i}^* F_c + \dot{B} \equiv p\bar{G} + iB \quad \text{GBR} \tag{15.2}$$

$$s\dot{F}_{p2} = \dot{B}^* \quad \text{international capital flows.} \tag{15.3}$$

Note that these equations assume that the allocation of households' savings are based on their consumption and investment decisions and on the assumption that they in fact absorb the new bond issue of the government (which is a restrictive consistency condition). The change implied by their savings in their holdings of foreign bonds is then determined residually. We therefore consider their savings decision as only one step towards their portfolio choice decision. In a next step, they then decide how to reallocate their holdings of domestic and foreign bonds on the international capital markets by either selling or buying domestic bonds on these markets (with behavioral equations, to be introduced below). Their full portfolio adjustment is therefore characterized by

$$s\dot{F}_p - \dot{B}_p = s(\dot{F}_{p1} + \dot{F}_{p2}) + \dot{B} - \dot{B}^*, \quad M/p = m^d(Y, i).$$

In this extension of the standard MFT model, we make these assumptions in order to separate the savings decision of households clearly from their portfolio decision, which may give rise to significant international capital flows in interaction with the behavior of foreign asset holders. Savings and portfolio arrangements are now formulated in terms of flows, while the cash management decision of households (between money and fix-price domestic bonds) is modeled in the traditional way by way of an LM curve which is mirrored by an equivalent stock condition on the market for domestic bonds. In the case of an open market operation of the central bank ($dM = -dB$) it is assumed that this occurrence precedes all other ones and that portfolio adjustments are then performed in the light of this change.

We get as implications for the evolution of domestic and foreign bonds held by the domestic economy ($F = F_p + F_c$):

$$\dot{B}_p = \dot{B} - \dot{B}^* = iB + p(\bar{G} - \bar{T}) - \bar{si}^* F_c - \dot{B}^*$$

$$s\dot{F}_p - \dot{B}^* = s(\dot{F}_{p1} + \dot{F}_{p2}) - \dot{B}^* = p(Y - C - \bar{G} - I) + \bar{si}^* F - iB^*,$$

which (on the basis of a goods market equilibrium condition) is simply the statement that the balance of payments is balanced under the assumed budget equations, since output minus domestic absorption is just net export *NX* and since the other two items in the balance of payments are representing net capital export *NCX* and net interest rate flows.

Considering the same situation from the viewpoint of savings, we can write:

$$pS_p = p(Y - \bar{T}) + iB_p + \bar{si}^* F_p - pC = pI + \dot{B} + s\dot{F}_{p1}$$

$$pS_g = p\bar{T} + \bar{si}^* F_c - iB - p\bar{G} = -\dot{B},$$

which gives for the total savings *pS* of the economy:

$$pS = pY + \bar{si}^* F - iB^* - pC - p\bar{G} = pI + s\dot{F}_{p1} = pI + s\dot{F}_p - \dot{B}^*.$$

This is again a formulation of the fact that the balance of payments must be balanced in the considered situation without any further adjustment processes, solely based on the assumption that the issue of government bonds $\dot{B}$ is in fact accepted by the household sector as it is implicitly made in the above formulation of the budget equations of our economy.

15.2.2 Real disposable income and wealth accounting (actual magnitudes)

In analogy with the Hicksian definition of private disposable income, we now define and rearrange this concept for the aggregate government sector (including the foreign interest income of the central bank). We show on this basis in particular that the aggregate wealth of this sector W_g^a is in its time rate of change – as in the case of the private sector – determined by deducting from its disposable income the consumption of this sector. This then also provides us with a law of motion for real aggregate wealth of the government sector, in addition to the one we have already determined for the total wealth of the economy. These two laws describe on the one hand the evolution of surpluses or deficits in the government sector and the evolution of current account surpluses or deficits, and thus in particular allow the joint treatment of the issue of twin deficits in an open economy with a government sector. On the other hand, capital accumulation and economic growth cannot yet be included .

The government sector

The following calculations concern the sources of income and consider as disposable income that which, when consumed, just preserves the current level of wealth of the considered sector, here the government sector. Thus,

$$
\begin{aligned}
Y_g^a :={}& \bar{T} - \frac{iB}{p} + \frac{s\bar{i}^* F_c}{p} + \hat{p}\frac{M+B}{p} + (\hat{s}-\hat{p})\frac{sF_c}{p} \\
={}& \bar{T} - (i-\hat{p})\frac{M+B}{p} + i\frac{M}{p} + (\bar{i}^* + \hat{s} - \hat{p})\frac{sF_c}{p} \\
={}& \bar{T} + i\frac{M}{p} - (i-\bar{i}^* - \hat{s})\frac{M+B}{p} + (\bar{i}^* + \hat{s} - \hat{p})\frac{-(M+B)+sF_c}{p} \\
={}& \bar{T} + i\frac{M}{p} + \xi\frac{M+B}{p} + r^* W_g^a, \quad \xi = \bar{i}^* + \hat{s} - i, \quad \text{with}
\end{aligned}
$$

$$
W_g^a := \frac{-(M+B)+sF_c}{p} = -\frac{(M+B)}{p} + \frac{sF_c}{p} = W_g + W_c.
$$

This implies

$$
\begin{aligned}
\dot{W}_g^a ={}& \frac{-(\dot{M}+\dot{B})+\dot{s}F_c+s\dot{F}_c}{p} - \frac{\dot{p}}{p}\frac{-(M+B)+sF_c}{p} \\
={}& \frac{-(p\bar{G}+iB-p\bar{T}-\bar{i}^* sF_c)+\hat{s}sF_c}{p} - \hat{p}\frac{-(M+B)+sF_c}{p} \\
={}& \bar{T} - i\frac{B}{p} + \hat{p}\frac{M+B}{p} + (\bar{i}^* + \hat{s} - \hat{p})\frac{sF_c}{p} - \bar{G},
\end{aligned}
$$

which finally gives

$$\dot{W}_g^a = Y_g^a - \bar{G}$$

$$= r^* W_g^a + i\frac{M}{p} + \xi\frac{M+B}{p} + \bar{T} - \bar{G}.$$

The evolution of domestic wealth and domestic bonds held abroad

Since this debt position is currently not assumed as constant, we repeat next the equations for the evolution of total wealth W of the economy in this case and then consider again private disposable income Y_p and private wealth W_p in their interaction with the evolution of aggregate government debt. Note that we assume goods market equilibrium $Y - C - I - G = NX$ in the following derivations ($F = F_p + F_c$).

$$W = \frac{sF}{p} = W_p + W_g + W_c + W^*,$$

$$W_p = \frac{M + B_p + sF_p}{p}, \ W_g = \frac{-M - B}{p}, \ W_c = \frac{sF_c}{p}, \ W^* = \frac{B^*}{p}$$

$$\hat{W} = \hat{s} + \hat{F} - \hat{p}, \quad \text{i.e.}$$

$$\dot{W} = \hat{s}W + \frac{s\dot{F}_p}{p} - \hat{p}W$$

$$= \hat{s}W + \frac{p(Y - C - \bar{G} - I) + s\bar{i}^*F - iB^* + \dot{B}^*}{p} - \hat{p}W$$

$$= (\hat{s} - \hat{p})W + \bar{i}^*\frac{sF}{p} + Y - C - \bar{G} - I - iW^* + \frac{\dot{B}^*}{p}$$

$$= (\bar{i}^* + \hat{s} - \hat{p})W + Y - C - \bar{G} - I - iW^* + \frac{\dot{B}^*}{p}$$

$$= r^*W + Y - C - \bar{G} - I - iW^* + \frac{\dot{B}^*}{p}$$

$$\dot{W}^* = \frac{\dot{B}^*}{p} - \hat{p}W^*$$

Private wealth and income

We have for the definition of private wealth and disposable income:

$$W_p = \frac{M + B_p + sF_p}{p} = W - W_g^a - W^*$$

$$Y_p = Y - \bar{T} + (\bar{i}^* + \hat{s} - \hat{p})\frac{sF_p}{p} + (i - \hat{p})\frac{B}{p} - \hat{p}\frac{M}{p}$$

$$= Y - \bar{T} + (\bar{i}^* + \hat{s} - \hat{p})W_p - (\bar{i}^* + \hat{s} - \hat{p})\frac{M+B}{p} + (i - \hat{p})\frac{B}{p} - \hat{p}\frac{M}{p}$$

$$= Y - \bar{T} + r^*W_p - (\bar{i}^* + \hat{s} - i)\frac{M+B}{p} - i\frac{M}{p}$$

$$= Y - \bar{T} + r^*(W - W_g^a - W^*) - \xi\frac{M+B}{p} - i\frac{M}{p}.$$

From the results on the disposable income of households and the government we finally also get:

$$Y_p = Y - Y_g^a + r^*(W - W^*) \quad \text{or} \quad Y_p + Y_g^a = Y + r^*(W - W^*)$$

as a relationship between total disposable income, domestic product and real interest on domestically held foreign bonds minus foreign holdings of domestic bonds.

15.2.3 The four laws of motion of the MFT economy with international capital flows

Foreign inflation set equal to zero and fixed policy parameters: $\bar{\pi}^* = 0, \bar{M}, \bar{T}, \bar{G},$:

1. $\dot{W} = r^*W + Y - C(Y_p, W - W_g^a - W^*, r, r^*, \sigma) - i(Y, r, r^*) - \bar{G} - iW^*$
    $\quad + \dot{B}^*/p$

2. $\dot{W}_g^a = r^*W_g^a + \xi\frac{M+B}{p} + i\frac{M}{p} + \bar{T} - \bar{G}$

3. $\dot{W}^* = \dot{B}^*/p - \hat{p}W^*$

to be coupled with the law of motion for the price level p:

4. $\hat{p} = \beta_w(Y - 1)/(1 - \gamma) + \hat{s} + \bar{\pi}^*.$

Note that the above laws of motion still assume myopic perfect foresight with respect to the exchange rate and inflation dynamics and thus do not yet distinguish between expected rates of return and actual rates. The former will be used in the behavioral relationships later on, while the latter apply to the actual laws of motion for the considered wealth variables. The distinction between actual and perceived rates of return will become important when exchange rate dynamics is considered later (in our representation of the Dornbusch model in a Tobinian approach to financial markets). Note also that we have extended the consumption and investment function of Rødseth (2000, Ch. 6) slightly, since we intend to distinguish between the consumption of the domestic and the foreign commodity later on and thus have to include explicitly the real exchange rate into the consumption function.

15.2.4 The dynamics of the private sector

We assume now again that taxes are varied endogenously such that government debt, as measured by W_g^a, stays constant in time. In this case the above dynamical system is reduced to the following form:

$$\dot{W} = r^*W + Y - C(Y_p, W_p, r, r^*, \sigma) - i(Y, r, r^*) - \bar{G} - iW^* + \dot{B}^*/p \quad (15.4)$$

$$\dot{W}^* = \dot{B}^*/p - \hat{p}W^* \quad (15.5)$$

$$\hat{p} = \beta_w(Y-1)/(1-\gamma) + \hat{s} + \bar{\pi}^* \quad (15.6)$$

based on the following further definitions and further relationships:

$$r = i - \hat{p} \quad (15.7)$$

$$r^* = \bar{i}^* + \hat{s} - \hat{p} \quad [\text{expected rate} \quad r^{*e} = \bar{i}^* + \epsilon(s) - \hat{p}] \quad (15.8)$$

$$Y_p = Y + r^{*e}(W - W^*) - \bar{G} \quad (15.9)$$

$$W_p = W - \bar{W}_g^a - W^* \quad (15.10)$$

$$\sigma = s/p \quad [\bar{p}^* = 1] \quad (15.11)$$

This dynamical system is to be supplemented by the temporary equilibrium relationships:

$$Y = C_1(Y_p, W_p, r, r^{*e}, \sigma) + i(Y, r, r^{*e}) + \bar{G} + X(\bar{Y}^*, \sigma) \quad (15.12)$$

$$M/p = m^d(Y, i), \quad m^d = kY \exp(-\alpha(\bar{i}^* - i)) \quad \text{for example} \quad (15.13)$$

$$s\dot{F}_{p2}/p = f^d(\xi, W_p) = -f^{d*}(\xi^*, W^*) = \dot{B}^*/p \quad (15.14)$$

with $\xi = \bar{i}^* - \epsilon(s) - i$, $\xi^* = \bar{i}^* - \epsilon^*(s) - i$. The new relationship in these equations is the equation describing equilibrium on the international capital market for domestic against foreign bonds:

$$f^d(\bar{i}^* - \epsilon(s) - i, W - \bar{W}_g^a - W^*) = -f^{d*}(\bar{i}^* - \epsilon^*(s) - i, W^*).$$

It exhibits on its left-hand side the demand of domestic residents for foreign bonds (if positive, otherwise the supply of such bonds) measured in terms of domestic goods. On its right-hand side, $\bar{i}^* - \epsilon^*(s) - i$, it provides the demand of foreigners for domestic bonds (if positive, otherwise the supply of such bonds) also measured in terms of domestic goods. This equilibrium equation describes the capital flows in the capital account that are not caused by the savings decisions within the domestic economy. In the case where $f^{d*}(\cdot, \cdot) = f^d(\bar{i}^* - \epsilon(s) - i, W^*)$ holds (where therefore domestic and foreign asset holders have the same demand schedule), we assume that this implies $f^{d*}(i^* - \epsilon^*(s) - i, W^*) = f^d(i^* - \epsilon^*(s) - i, W_p) = 0$. This is so because both parties are then expecting the same risk premium and should therefore either both be demanders or both be suppliers of foreign bonds, causing a reaction of the exchange rate that reduces the resulting excess demand (or supply) to zero.

15.2.5 Steady-state considerations

The first thing to be noted here is that the regressive expectations mechanisms must fulfill some consistency requirement in order to allow for a meaningful consideration of the steady-state, namely $\epsilon(s_o) = \epsilon^*(s_o) = 0$ for the steady-state value of the exchange rate. Furthermore, we make use of the law of motion for the capital stock in the following steady-state consideration and assume $\hat{K} = I/K = i(Y/K, r, r^{*e}) = 0$ as side condition for these considerations. From the Phillips curve we get $\hat{p} = 0$, $Y_o = \bar{Y}$ and thus $r_o^* = r_o^{*e} = \bar{i}^*$ and $r_o = i_o$ as well as $\xi_o = \bar{i}^* - i = \xi_o^*$.

Next, the conditions $\dot{W}^*, B^* = 0$ imply $f^{d*}(\xi^*, W^*) = 0$. We assume here as a simplified form for the function $f^{d*}(\xi^*, W^*) = f^{d*}(\xi^*)W^*$ a multiplicative expression with $f^{d*}(0, W^*) = 0$. The disappearance of international capital flows in the steady-state therefore implies that $i_o = \bar{i}^*$ must hold true in the steady-state. From the LM curve we then get, in the case of the regime of a given money supply, $p_o = \bar{M}/m^d(\bar{Y}, \bar{i}^*)$. International capital market equilibrium $f^d(0, W - W^* - \bar{W}_g^a) = -f^{d*} = 0$ furthermore implies a steady-state value for $W - W^*$ which, when inserted into the IS curve together with the other steady-state values already determined, implies a steady-state value for the real exchange rate $\sigma = s/p$ and thus also a steady-state value for the nominal exchange rate s.

Since we already had $\dot{B}^* = 0$ we finally get from the established equation for total savings that $\dot{F}_p$ must be zero as well, i.e., $\dot{W}$ will be guaranteed automatically. This however means that there is zero root hysteresis in the levels of both W and W^* since only their difference is uniquely determined in the steady-state. The steady-state value of the capital stock K is, finally, uniquely determined through the condition $0 = i(\bar{Y}/K, \bar{i}^*, \bar{i}^*)$.

15.2.6 A digression

The assumed behavior of domestic agents on the international capital markets for domestic and foreign bonds can be related to the stock portfolio approach of Chapter 12 as follows. We assume that money market equilibrium is already ensured and consider the function $f^d(\xi, W_p)$ as defined in Chapter 2, i.e. as real stock demand for foreign bonds sF_p^d/p. The stock demand for domestic bonds is then characterized residually by $W_p - M/p - f^d(\xi, W_p)$. We now assume, however, that there are adjustment costs with respect to these desired stock changes and that therefore only a portion δ is currently realized as flow demand, giving rise to

$$\frac{s\dot{F}^d_{p2}}{p} = \delta(f^d(\xi, W_p) - f_p), f_p = sF_p/p, \qquad \frac{s\dot{B}^d_{p2}}{p} = \delta([W_p - \frac{M}{p} - f^d(\xi, W_p)] - \frac{B_p}{p}).$$

It is immediately obvious that these induced flows add up to zero and thus transform the initial form of a Walras law of stocks into a Walras law of flows on the asset markets. We stress again that the flow of savings is considered separately from these reallocations in the portfolio of the private agents (which are to be associated with the index 1 in place of the index 2 used above). This brief sketch that transforms stock into flow demands suggests that we should use f_p in addition to W_p in the above presentation of the general MFT model when stock-related capital flows are considered (and in fact W^* in the demand function of foreigners for domestic bonds). For simplicity, however, we use only the aggregate W_p in the flow demand function and characterize this function by the same symbolic expression as the stock demand function.

15.2.7 Summing up

Summarizing the above MFT extension towards the integration of international capital flows, we can state that the model first assumes that cash management comes first and is always characterized by stock money market equilibrium $M/p = m^d(Y, i)$ $[B/p = B^d/p]$. Against this background, domestic agents then plan to reallocate their interest-bearing assets according to the behavioral relationship $f^d(\xi, W_p)$. The flow of savings (with $\dot{M} = 0$ by assumption) is then added to these portfolio changes as far as financial assets are concerned (with additional foreign bonds being determined by $s\dot{F}_{p1} = pNX + s\bar{i}^*F_p$). This verbal ordering of stock and flow interactions is meant to avoid any confusion between international capital flows and the allocation of savings. In the model, the goods, the money and the international capital market are of course considered simultaneously and – for example – used to determine the variables Y, i, s (in the case of flexible exchange rates and a given money supply in the economy).

The money market is here, of course, still of the traditional LM curve type still and can thus be represented graphically in the usual way. Such a graphical representation of the international bond markets is provided in Figure 15.1. There we consider a regime of flexible exchange rates that are to be determined from the interaction of demand and supply on the international capital markets.

Figure 15.1 shows the level of the exchange rate s_o where the domestic demand curve for foreign bonds (the supply curve for domestic bonds) and the foreign demand curve for domestic bonds (the supply curve for foreign bonds) intersect and where therefore capital flow equilibrium is established. The equilibrium exchange rate now also depends on foreign characteristics, in contrast to the case considered in Chapter 12, were domestic bonds were considered as nontraded goods and where therefore the supply of such bonds (in the case of a flexible

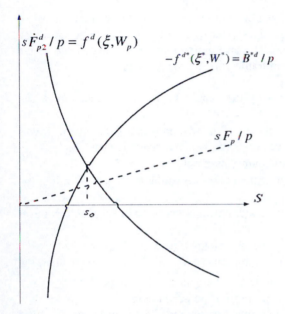

$$s\dot{F}^d_{p2}/p = f^d(\xi, W_p)$$

$$-f^{d*}(\xi^*, W^*) = \dot{B}^{*d}/p$$

$$s\,F_p/p$$

S

s_o

Figure 15.1 Equilibrium on international capital markets.

exchange rate regime) was just given by F_p. In this case the equilibrium in the domestic market for foreign bonds would be determined by the intersection of the f^d curve with the straight line shown in Figure 15.1 and would thus be independent from foreign asset demands – definitely a situation that is too simple to characterize today's international financial system. Note that the $-f^{d*}$ curve is a supply curve of foreign bonds, while in the form f^{d*} it would represent a demand curve for foreign bonds. In the case where it is identical in Figure 15.1 to the f^d curve shown, the intersection of the f^d, f^{d*} must lie on the horizontal axis, i.e. the equilibrium exchange rate then implies that there is no international capital flow.

15.3 Real–financial disequilibrium dynamics: Some basic results

15.3.1 *Regime I: Inflation and international capital flows with interest and exchange rate pegs*

We are now considering the dynamic implications of a particular regime among the ones we have discussed in Chapter 12. We here follow Rødseth (2000, Ch. 6.6) and choose a case where in fact the asset markets are sent into the background of the model, a case which therefore solely studies the interactions of the IS curve with a conventional type of Phillips curve and the dynamics of the balance of payments. The conventional type of IS–PC analysis (without an LM curve) is therefore augmented here by the change in foreign assets from the excess of domestic savings over domestic investment (plus the portfolio reallocations on the international capital markets). The assumptions we employ in order to derive this special case from our general framework are the following:

1. $i = \bar{i}^*$: An interest rate peg by the central bank (via an accommodating monetary policy).
2. $s = \bar{s} = 1$: A fixed exchange rate via an endogenous supply of dollar-denominated bonds by the central bank (which is never exhausted).
3. Given $\bar{Y}^*, \bar{p}^*(\bar{i}^*)$: The small country assumption.
4. $\bar{W}_g^a$: A tax policy of the government that keeps the aggregate wealth of the government fixed.
5. $G_2, I_2 = 0$: Only consumption goods are import commodities, which are never rationed.
6. $\bar{\omega}$: The real wage is fixed by a conventional type of markup pricing.
7. $\bar{r}_f^n$: The normal (capacity utilization) rate of return of firms is fixed (since the real wage is a given magnitude) and set equal to $\bar{i}^*$ for simplicity.
8. $Y^p = \bar{y}^p K, N^d = Y/\bar{x}$: Fixed proportions in production.
9. $\bar{K}$: The capacity effect of investment is ignored. Potential output $\bar{Y}^p = 1$ is therefore a given magnitude.
10. $\bar{Y} = \bar{x}\bar{N} = 1$: A given level of the full employment output.
11. No resale market for used capital goods.

On the basis of the above assumptions we get that the real rates of interest are equalized for the domestic economy: $r^* = i^* + \hat{s} - \hat{p} = i - \hat{p} = r$. Furthermore, the risk premium ξ is zero in the situation considered. Finally, due to the assumed tax policy, we have again for the disposable income in the household sector the term $Y_p = Y + r^*(W - W^*) - \bar{G}$. Private wealth W_p is given by $W - \bar{W}_g^a - W^*$ in the situation under consideration.

The stock demand for money and the excess flow demand for foreign bonds by the private sector (including foreigners) are given by:

$$M^d = pm^d(Y, i) \tag{15.15}$$

$$-s\dot{F}_c/p = f^d(0, W - \bar{W}_g^a - W^*) + f^{d*}(0, W^*), \tag{15.16}$$

and are to be satisfied by an accommodating monetary policy and out of the stocks of foreign bonds held by the central bank.

The real exchange rate $\sigma = (sp^*)/p$, i.e., the amount of domestic goods that are exchanged for one unit of the foreign good, reduces to $1/p$ as a result of the above normalization assumptions. Households directly buy investment goods for their firms and use the normal rate of profit in order to judge their performance, which is a given magnitude because of the above assumptions (normal output times the profit share). We therefore consider only one real rate, r, in the following formulation of the consumption decisions (for domestic and foreign goods) and the investment decisions of the household sector:

$C_1 = C_1(Y_p, W_p, r, \sigma)$: consumption demand for the domestic good

$C_2 = C_2(Y_p, W_p, r, \sigma)$: consumption demand for the foreign good

$C = C_1(Y_p, W_p, r, \sigma) + C_2(Y_p, W_p, r, \sigma)/\sigma$: total consumption

$I = i(Y, r)$: investment demand, for domestic goods only.

On this basis the goods market equilibrium or the IS curve of the model is given by:

$$C(Y_p, W_p, r, \sigma) + i(Y, r) + \bar{G} + NX(\cdot) = Y,$$

where net exports are based on a standard export function and import demand is determined by C_2. Imports can be suppressed in this equation by reformulating it as follows:

$$Y = C_1(Y + r(W - W^*) - \bar{G}, W - W^* - \bar{W}_g^a, r, \sigma) + i(Y, r) + \bar{G} + X(\bar{Y}^*, \sigma),$$

$$r = \bar{i}^* - \hat{p}.$$

We have here assumed that exports X depend as usual on foreign output and the real exchange rate.

The dynamic equations of the model are the following (the growth of the capital stock is neglected by assumption):

$$\hat{p} = \beta_w(Y - 1)/(1 - \gamma) \quad [\hat{w} = \beta_w(Y - 1) + \gamma\hat{p} + (1 - \gamma)\widehat{sp}^*] \tag{15.17}$$

$$\dot{W} = rW + Y - C(Y + r(W - W^*) - \bar{G}, W - W^* - \bar{W}_g^a, r, 1/p)$$

$$- i(Y, r) - \bar{G} - \bar{i}^* W^* + \dot{B}^*/p \tag{15.18}$$

$$\dot{W}^* = \dot{B}^*/p - \hat{p}W^*. \tag{15.19}$$

The second and third laws of motion are our new representation of the balance of payments in real terms, while the first one above is a standard money wage Phillips curve where cost-pressure items are represented as a weighted average of actual domestic and import price inflation. On the basic of constant markup pricing, this equation is usually transformed into a reduced-form price Phillips curve which, on the basis of our assumptions, then reads:

$$\hat{p} = \frac{1}{1 - \gamma}\beta_w(Y - 1) \tag{15.20}$$

$$d(W - W^*)/dt = r(W - W^*) + Y - C(Y + r(W - W^*) - \bar{G}, W - W^*$$

$$- \bar{W}_g^a, r, 1/p) - i(Y, r) - \bar{G} \tag{15.21}$$

We also show here a single reduced-form expression for second and third laws of motion into which the first law has to be inserted in two places in order to arrive at a system of differential equations which, on their right-hand side, depend only on $Y, p, W - W^*$. Note also that the position of the IS curve depends only on the difference $W - W^*$ between real domestic holdings of foreign bonds and foreign holdings of domestic bonds, since the temporary equilibrium output Y depends only on the two state variables $p, W - W^*$ in accordance with the following goods market equilibrium condition:

$$Y = C_1(Y + (\bar{i}^* - \frac{1}{1-\gamma}\beta_w(Y-1))(W - W^*) - \bar{G}, W - W^* - \bar{W}_g^a, \bar{i}^* - \frac{1}{1-\gamma}$$

$$\beta_w(Y-1), p) + i(Y, \bar{i}^* - \frac{1}{1-\gamma}\beta_w(Y-1)) + \bar{G} + X(\bar{Y}^*, p) \qquad (15.22)$$

We assume for the time being that the parameters of this equilibrium condition are such that they result in the conventional dependency of IS equilibrium output on the price level: $\partial Y / \partial p < 0$. With respect to the wealth term $W - W^*$, it is obvious that $\partial Y / \partial (W - W^*) > 0$ holds true.

The resulting dynamical system in the state variables $p, W - W^*$ is by and large of the same type as the one considered in Chapter 12 and can be treated in the same way.

We note that we have to add the law of motion for $K : \dot{K} = i(Y, \bar{i}^* - (1/1-\gamma)\beta_w(Y-1))$, for a complete treatment of the dynamics of this example of a small open economy. Since however the analysis without such capacity effects of investment is already complicated enough, we do not go into such an extended dynamic analysis here. Furthermore, we may also return to an endogenous treatment of the variable W_g^a which would increase the complexity of the analysis even further, despite the simple framework that is still chosen here (where portfolio choice does not matter for the analysis of the dynamics of the real part of the model). Such an extension would again allow for the discussion of the occurrence of twin deficits and other situations of domestic and foreign debt or surpluses.

For reasons of simplicity, however, we return here to the above situation where aggregate government wealth (basically the government deficit) stays constant in time, and investigate now the steady-state solution and the dynamics surrounding it:

$$\hat{p} = \frac{1}{1-\gamma}\beta_w(Y(p, W - W^*) - 1)$$

$$d(W - W^*)/dt = r(W - W^*) + X(\bar{Y}, 1/p) - \sigma C_2(Y + r(W - W^*) - \bar{G}, W$$

$$-W^* - \bar{W}_g^a, r, 1/p),$$

where the properties of the IS equilibrium are characterized by the standard partial derivatives discussed above.

With respect to the steady-state solution of this dynamical system we assume that the government pursues – in addition to its tax policy – a constant government expenditure policy that is aimed at fixing the steady-state value of exports at the level $\bar{X}$. This implies that the steady-state value of the price level, p_o, is to be determined from $\bar{X} = X(\bar{Y}^*, 1/p_o)$. Assuming that this equation has a (uniquely determined) positive solution for p_o, we can then obtain the steady-state value of $W - W^*$ from the labor market equilibrium equation $1 = \bar{Y} = Y(p_o, (W - W^*)_o)$. The solution of this equation may be positive or negative and is again uniquely determined, since the right-hand side of this equation is strictly increasing in $(W - W^*)_o$. The level of government expenditure G that allows for this solution procedure, finally, is then given by

$$0 = r(W - W^*)X(\bar{Y}, 1/p) - \sigma C_2(Y + r(W - W^*) - G, W - W^* - \bar{W}_g^a, r, 1/p)$$

In this equation, the expenditure level is adjusted such that net imports are equal to the foreign interest income of domestic residents; i.e., an excess of imports over exports is needed in the case of positive foreign bond holdings in the domestic economy in the steady-state. Note that the above is also based on the assumption that $i(\bar{Y}, \bar{i}^*) = 0$ holds in the steady-state, since there must be a stationary capital stock in the steady-state of the model.

We now use Ω for the variable $W - W^*$ in order to describe briefly the stability properties of the MFT model with international capital flows. We have a straightforward sign structure in the partial derivatives of the first law of motion due to our simplifying assumptions on the goods-market equilibrium equation $Y = Y(p, \Omega)$, which guarantee that price level increases reduce economic activity and thus provide a check to further inflationary tendencies. Furthermore, they induce economic activity to increase with Ω due to its effects on consumption . The second law of motion is, however, much more difficult to handle. Its partial derivative with respect to Ω is as involved as the corresponding one in Chapter 12 and is given by (since $\hat{p}_o = 0$):

$$\frac{\partial \dot{\Omega}}{\partial \Omega} = \bar{i}^*(1 - \sigma_o C_{2Y_p}) - \sigma_o C_{2Y_p}\frac{\partial Y}{\partial \Omega} - \sigma_o C_{2W_p} + \hat{p}_\Omega[(\sigma_o C_{2Y_p} - 1)\Omega_o + \sigma_o C_{2r}]$$

where we have denoted by $\hat{p}_\Omega$ the partial derivative of the first law of motion with respect to Ω. We have now considerably more terms in the feedback of foreign debt on its time rate of change than was the case in Chapter 11 for the extremely open economy. These additional terms seem to provide more support for a negative feedback chain than in this earlier chapter (if the assumptions on $Y(p, \Omega)$ hold true), where we simply had that this partial feedback mechanism became positive (destabilizing) when wealth effects in consumption were sufficiently weak.

The remaining partial derivative for local stability analysis is given by

$$\frac{\partial \dot{\Omega}}{\partial p} = ((\sigma_o C_{2Y_p} - 1)\Omega_o + \sigma_o C_{2r})\hat{p}_p - \sigma_o C_{2Y_p}\frac{\partial Y}{\partial p} + (C_2 + \sigma_o C_{2\sigma} - X_\sigma)/p^2).$$

The first two expressions in this equation are positive in sign while the last term in brackets – the quantitative reaction of net imports to price level changes via the real exchange rate channel – is generally assumed to be negative ($\sigma = (s\bar{p}^*)/p = 1/p$). For the Jacobian J we thus, in sum, get as sign structure:

$$J = \begin{pmatrix} \frac{\partial \hat{p}}{\partial p}p & \frac{\partial \hat{p}}{\partial \Omega}p \\ \frac{\partial \dot{\Omega}}{\partial p} & \frac{\partial \dot{\Omega}}{\partial \Omega} \end{pmatrix} = \begin{pmatrix} - & + \\ \pm & \pm \end{pmatrix}.$$

The easiest case for a stability result

$$J = \begin{pmatrix} \frac{\partial \hat{p}}{\partial p} & \frac{\partial \hat{p}}{\partial \Omega} \\ \frac{\partial \dot{\Omega}}{\partial p} & \frac{\partial \dot{\Omega}}{\partial \Omega} \end{pmatrix} = \begin{pmatrix} - & + \\ - & - \end{pmatrix},$$

is the case where interest effects do not dominate the capital account adjustment process and where the normal reaction of the trade balance (based on the so-called Marshall–Lerner conditions) dominates the income, wealth and interest rate effects generated by the general form of a consumption function used in this and the preceding chapter. The steady-state is in this case obviously locally asymptotically stable (since trace $J < 0$, det $J > 0$). Graphically, we get in this situation the phase diagram shown in Figure 15.2.

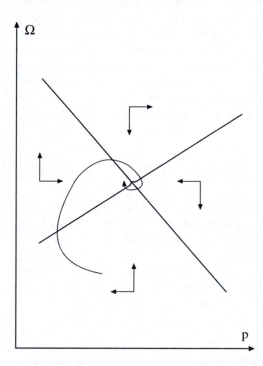

Figure 15.2 An example of stable inflation and capital account dynamics.

In view of this figure we must, however, keep in mind the very restrictive assumptions we made with respect to the IS curve and its deplacement by the evolution of the state variables of the dynamics, the reaction of the balance of payments and the dynamics of the capital account, and also the reaction of foreign bond accumulation with respect to price level changes. It is therefore by no means clear how dominant the case of stable price level and capital account dynamics will be in the set of all possible stability scenarios the model allows for. In the case of divergence the question is, again, which mechanisms in the private sector may then keep the dynamics bounded or which policy actions will be needed to ensure this.

The derived dynamical implications are, by and large, of the type considered in Rødseth (2000, Ch. 6.6), though our consumption and investment functions differ to some extent from the ones used by Rødseth. Note that Rødseth is using the negative of W in order to characterize the international credit or debt position of the domestic economy. Rødseth (2000, Ch. 6.6) also considers a variety of further issues for his analysis of a Mundell–Fleming regime with an interest and an exchange rate peg. The reader is referred to this analysis for further aspects of this monetary and exchange rate regime.

Given the above dynamical system, we can recover the dynamics of the two wealth variables $W.W^*$ as follow:

$$\dot{W}^* = f^{d*}(0, W^*) - \hat{p}(Y(p, \Omega))W^*$$

$$W = \Omega + W^*,$$

which completes the stability result described above.

The worst case scenario for instability will now be described.

15.3.2 Regime II: Overshooting exchange rates and inflation dynamics

As a second case study we now consider a regime of perfectly flexible exchange rates and flexible interest rates; i.e., we now consider the opposite case of a given money supply and a central bank that allows international capital markets to determine the exchange through the supply and demand of foreign and domestic bonds. The IS–LM–FX schedules now in general determine output Y, the domestic rate of interest i and the exchange rate s simultaneously. We simplify this equilibrium portion of the model again by assuming that money demand depends on normal output $\bar{Y}$ instead of actual output. This implies that the interest rate i depends only on the state variable p of the dynamics. Furthermore, inserting this dependency into the equilibrium condition for the international capital market then implies a dependency of the exchange rate s on the state variable of the dynamics that is independent of the characteristics of goods market equilibrium. This equilibrium condition can then be solved for output Y in a third step in order to obtain the comparative statics of the IS curve with respect to the three state variables p, W, W^*. The central bank may use open market operations in domestic bonds to change the composition of these bonds and money in the households' portfolio, but does not issue money otherwise (in particular, to buy foreign bonds from domestic residents).

In the following reformulation of the Dornbusch overshooting exchange rate dynamics within the framework of an MFT model with international capital flows we assume again for simplicity – just as in the original Dornbusch (1976) approach – that transactions demand in the money demand function is based on full employment output $\bar{Y} = 1$; i.e., we get from the LM curve of our Tobinian portfolio approach the result that the domestic rate of interest is solely dependent on the price level (positively) and on money supply (negatively), i.e.:

$$i = \frac{\ln p + \ln \bar{M} + \ln k}{\alpha}$$

in the case of the Cagan money demand function of the preceding chapters.

For full asset markets equilibrium we then only have to add the market for foreign bonds, which reads, in the considered exchange rate regime:

$$s\dot{F}_{p2}/p = f^d(\bar{i}^* - \epsilon(s) - i, W - W^* - \bar{W}_g^a) = -f^{d*}(\bar{i}^* - \epsilon^*(s) - i, W^*) = \dot{B}^*/p.$$

It is easy to see with respect to Figure 15.1 that a decrease in i shifts both curves in this figure to the right, which implies that the exchange rate will increase in such a case. Furthermore, it is also easy to see that an increase in W will also increase the exchange rate and an increase in W^* will decrease it. Finally, an increase in money supply $\bar{M}$ (which increases the steady-state value of the exchange rate – the point of reference for the assumed regressive expectations mechanism in the foreign exchange market – by the same percentage) thus increases the current exchange rate beyond this level and therefore leads to overshooting exchange rate reactions.

Next we consider the IS equilibrium curve of the situation under present consideration:

$$Y = C_1(Y + (\bar{i}^* + \epsilon(s) - \hat{p}(Y))(W - W^*) - \bar{G}, W - W^* - \bar{W}_g^a, \bar{i}^* + \epsilon(s) - \hat{p}(Y),$$

$$i - \hat{p}(Y), s/p) + i(Y, \bar{i}^* + \epsilon(s) - \hat{p}(Y), i - \hat{p}(Y)) + \bar{G} + X(\bar{Y}^*, s/p). \quad (15.23)$$

We assume for the time being that the parameters of this equilibrium condition are such that they result in the conventional dependency of IS equilibrium output on the price level: $\partial Y/\partial p < 0$. With respect to the wealth terms W, W^*; it is obvious that $\partial Y/\partial(W) > 0$ and $\partial Y/\partial(W^*) > 0$ hold true. One of course has to use our regressive expectations regime, the dependence of the nominal rate of interest and the real exchange rate on the price level, and the functional dependence of the nominal exchange rate on W, W^* derived above in order to draw conclusions on how the equilibrium output level depends on the price level p. The outcome is ambiguous, but pointing to a certain degree to a (conventional) negative overall dependence of Y on p. We shall assume that this holds true in our following discussion of overshooting exchange rates, since the opposite case would imply a destabilizing feedback of the price level on its rate of change via the Phillips curve mechanism.

We have by now determined successively the statically endogenous variables of the considered MFT regime i, s, Y by the three equilibrium relationships that now characterize the model. The state variables of the model are now p, W, W^* (while the movement of the capital stock is still neglected). The laws of motion for these variables are now given by:

$$\dot{W} = r^*W + Y - C(Y_p, W_p, r, r^*, \sigma) - \psi(Y, r, r^*) - \bar{G} - iW^* + \dot{B}^*/p \quad (15.24)$$

$$\dot{W}^* = \dot{B}^*/p - \hat{p}W^* \quad (15.25)$$

$$\hat{p} = \beta_w(Y-1)/(1-\gamma) + \epsilon(s) + \bar{\pi}^*, \quad \bar{\pi}^* = 0, \quad (15.26)$$

based on the following further definitions and relationships:

$$r = i - \hat{p} \quad (15.27)$$

$$r^* = \bar{i}^* + \hat{s} - \hat{p} \quad [\text{expected rate} \quad r^{*e} = \bar{i}^* + \epsilon(s) - \hat{p}] \quad (15.28)$$

$$Y_p = Y + r^{*e}(W - W^*) - \bar{G} \quad (15.29)$$

$$W_p = W - \bar{W}_g^a - W^* \quad (15.30)$$

$$\sigma = s/p \quad [\bar{p}^* = 1]. \quad (15.31)$$

The law of motion for W is now a very complicated one, since the static relationships have to be inserted into it in various places. We will therefore not discuss its (in)stability implications in the following, but just assume that this variable is placed into its new long-run equilibrium position after a shock and kept constant there. The same is also applied to the state variable W^*. We therefore study only the adjustment of the price level p after an open market operation of the central bank (which leaves $M+B$ unchanged). We note however that this implies a jump in the variable $W = (sF)/p$ that is neglected in our following analysis of such shocks.

In the construction of a steady-state reference solution we proceed as follows. We again assume that the government pursues an export target $\bar{X}$ by means of its expenditure policy $\bar{G}$, besides the tax policy that keeps W_g^a at a constant level $\bar{W}_g^a$. The steady-state real exchange rate σ_o is then uniquely determined by the equation $\bar{X} = X(\bar{Y}^*, \sigma)$. On this basis we can use the equilibrium condition on the market for foreign bonds to determine the steady-state level of W, given W^*. Since $\epsilon(s_o)$ and ξ_o should be zero in the steady-state (to be further justified below), the above can be assumed to have a uniquely determined positive solution if the functions f^d, f^{d*} are chosen appropriately. We note that we consider only positive values of W_o here for the time being, since we assume that households and the central bank hold such assets and since firms do not finance their investment expenditures abroad.

In accordance with the Phillips curve we get next that $Y_o = \bar{Y}$ must hold in the steady-state ($\hat{p}_o = 0$). Furthermore, the regressive expectations scheme is built such that $\epsilon(s_o) = 0$ holds for the steady-state value s_o of the nominal exchange rate (which still remains to be determined). We thus have $r_o = i_o, r_o^* = r^{*e} = \bar{i}^*$ in the steady-state and postulate that $\psi(\bar{Y}, \bar{i}^*) = 0$ holds for the investment function used in this MFT model. We assume on this basis, in addition, that the government chooses the level of $\bar{G}$ and thus $\bar{X}$ such that $i_o = i_o^*$ is enforced by the IS equation in the steady-state:[1]

$$\bar{Y} = C_1 + I + \bar{G} + \bar{X}.$$

On this basis we can then get the steady-state value of the price level p_o from the LM curve $p_o = \bar{M}/m^d(\bar{Y}, \bar{i}^*)$ and thus also the steady-state value of the exchange rate $s_o = p_o \sigma_o$.

We thus have quite a different "causality" in the determination of the steady-state where fiscal policy has to provide the necessary anchor for a meaningful steady-state solution, whereas in the short run we have that IS–LM–FX curves determine the variables Y, i, s in principle, in this order, while the Phillips curve and the balance of payments determine the dynamics of the price level and of domestically held foreign bonds as well as domestic bonds held by foreigners (in real terms). Note that the dynamics of the capital stock still remains excluded from consideration here. Note also that we will simplify even further in the following, since we shall also exclude the complicated adjustment process for $W = sF/p$ and W^* from consideration and instead assume that these magnitudes will immediately jump to their new steady-state values after any shock and will be kept frozen there. The aim of the following simplified presentation will instead be to reconsider the Dornbusch (1976) model of overshooting exchange rates in the context of an extended Tobinian portfolio model of the financial sector and somewhat advanced formulations of consumption and investment behavior.

Let us now consider an open market operation of the central bank $dM = -dB$, that increases the money holdings of private agents by reducing their holdings of domestic bonds (which therefore keeps $M + B$ and F_c constant). Our way of constructing a steady-state for the dynamics under consideration immediately implies that all real magnitudes remain the same (in particular W_o) and that we have, as sole steady-state changes, the following ones:

$$dM/M = dp_o/p_o = ds_o/s_o \quad (\sigma_o = \text{const}, i_o = \bar{i}^*).$$

---

1 In principle, the government here enforces two things in the steady-state of the dynamics, namely that the domestic interest rate must then be at the international level and that the level of exports is such that goods market equilibrium is then assured with a zero level of net investment, by assumption, on the investment function. The real exchange rate is then a consequence of the level of $\bar{X}$ needed for goods market equilibrium.

The long-run reaction of the dynamics is therefore, as in the original Dornbusch (1976) model, a very straightforward one: strict neutrality of money and the relative form of the PPP, i.e., there is no change in the real exchange rate caused by the monetary expansion that is undertaken.

In the short run, prices are fixed and the burden of adjustment in the money market falls entirely on the nominal rate of interest i which is decreased below $\bar{i}^*$ through the monetary expansion. Since the new steady-state value s'_o of the nominal exchange rate is above the old level now, and since the assumed regressive expectations mechanism is completely rational in this respect, we would find that $\epsilon(s'_o/s), \epsilon'$ would become positive (generating the expectation of depreciation) if the short-run exchange rate remained unchanged. Since we ignore – as described above – adjustments in the value of W, we must however have that the current exchange rate depreciates beyond s'_o in order to imply the expectation of an appreciation of the currency such that $\xi = \hat{i}^* + \epsilon(s'_o/s) - i = 0$ can remain unchanged (due to the unchanged value of W_o,[2] since the adjustment process of W is ignored here).[3] We thus get that i decreases and s increases under the assumed monetary expansion and expect that goods market equilibrium output increases through these two influences, since $\bar{i}^* + \epsilon = i$ has decreased and σ has been increased (the price level still being fixed at p_o). Again, ambiguous reaction may be possible, but we assume here – as before – that goods markets behave normally in this respect.

The nominal exchange rate therefore overshoots in the short run its new long-run level as in the original Dornbusch model. Resulting from the increase in the output level beyond its normal level we have now for the medium run that the price level starts rising according to

$$\hat{p} = \beta_w (Y-1)/(1-\gamma) \quad \text{with} \quad Y = Y(p, W_o), \; \partial Y \partial p < 0$$

and according to what has been shown above. The dynamics therefore converges back to its steady-state position with output levels falling back to their normal levels, prices rising to their new steady-state value p'_o, the exchange rate appreciating back to its risen steady-state value s'_o and the nominal rate of interest rising again to the unchanged international level $\bar{i}^*$. All this takes place in a somewhat simplified portfolio approach to the financial markets (in the place of the UIP condition under rational expectations) and without any complications arising from possibly even adverse adjustments through the balance of payments. It is therefore to be expected that a treatment of the full model along the lines of the preceding chapter (in that case for the extremely open economy) will reveal a variety of more complicated situations and, in the worst case, an unstable

---

2 And also $\bar{W}^a_g, \sigma_o F_c$.

3 The argument must be more detailed if the short-run reaction of the value of W is taken into account, but would then of course demand a thorough discussion of the conditions under which the dynamics drives this variable back to its steady-state level.

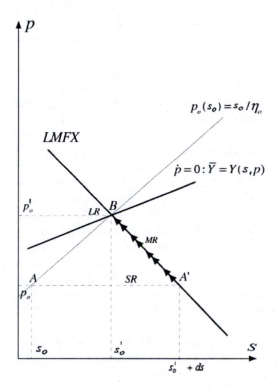

Figure 15.3 The Dornbusch overshooting exchange rate dynamics.

dynamics for which actions of households or the government then have to be found that bound their trajectories to economically meaningful domains. The present discussion is therefore only the beginning of a detailed discussion of the Dornbusch mechanism in a fully-fledged MFT model with inflation, balance of payments dynamics and international capital flows.

The dynamic adjustment processes just discussed are summarized in Figure 15.3. We have again the LMFX curve describing full portfolio equilibrium by way of

$$f^d(\bar{i}^* - \epsilon(s) - i(p), W - W^* - \bar{W}_g^a) = -f^{d*}(\bar{i}^* - \epsilon^*(s) - i(p), W^*),$$

where all revaluation effects of assets have been ignored, where transactions balances are still based on normal output and where, most importantly, the dynamics of the state variables W, W^* are set aside. The true LMFX curve is of course shifting with the changes in W, W^*, σ and the output level Y. We have, furthermore, the curve along which the price level is stationary and which is also not as simple as shown in this graph (where it is assumed that $\partial Y/\partial s, \partial Y/\partial p < 0$), but may be quite complicated due to the assumed consumption and investment behavior.

If the old steady-state A is disturbed by an expansionary monetary shock that shifts the old LMFX curve (not shown) into the new position (shown), we have as immediate response (SR) that the exchange rate adjusts (to A') such that full portfolio equilibrium is restored. In the medium run (MR) we then have rising price levels, rising interest rates and falling exchange rates until the new steady-state position (LR) is reached at point B.

We note that the variables W, W_g^a may be subject to jumps in a regime with flexible exchange rates, but are then following their laws of motion if no further shocks occur (in the case of W) or the variables remain fixed at their new level (in the case of W_g^a). Furthermore, we may also return to an endogenous treatment of the variable W_g^a by making use of lump sum taxation $\bar{T}$. This would increase the complexity of the analysis even further. Such an extension would again allow for discussion of the occurrence of twin deficits and other situations of domestic and foreign debt or surpluses. Note however that the system has become very complicated now, where the statically endogenous variables i, s have to be obtained from the portfolio part of the model – in interaction with the IS curve of the model which determines equilibrium output Y – and where the growth rate of s then has to be calculated on this basis. This is not at all an easy task and makes an analysis of the model nearly untractable. In view of this, ways have to be found that model the dynamics of the exchange rate directly, so that a differentiation of the portfolio equilibrium equations can be avoided.

15.4 Capital flight, global players and the emergence of currency crises

15.4.1 *Regime I: Interest and exchange rate peg.*

Foreigners (and domestic residents) sell domestic bonds against foreign ones on a larger scale and thereby rapidly exhaust the amount of foreign bonds held by the central bank, according to the law of motion

$$-s\dot{F}_c/p = f^d(0, W - \bar{W}_g^a - W^*, f_p) + f^{d*}(0, W^*)$$

based on the following portfolio situation

$$\frac{s\dot{F}_{p2}^d}{p} = \delta(f^d(\xi, W_p) - f_p), f_p = sF_p/p, \quad \frac{s\dot{B}_{p2}^d}{p} = \delta([W_p - \frac{M}{p} - f^d(\xi, W_p)] - \frac{B_p}{p}).$$

The fixed exchange rate regime breaks down and the international capital market then returns to the regime of flexible exchange rates, given by

$$s\dot{F}_{p2}/p = f^d(\bar{i}^* - \epsilon(s) - \bar{i}, W - W^* - \bar{W}_g^a, f_p) = -f^{d*}(\bar{i}^* - \epsilon^*(s) - \bar{i}, W^*) = \dot{B}^*/p,$$

possibly accompanied by a "leaning against the wind" interest rate policy that increases the domestic rate $\bar{i}$ above the international rate in order to attract capital inflows. Nevertheless the domestic currency will depreciate significantly and induce a balance sheet crisis à la Krugman, as considered in Chapters 13 and 14.

The situation described gets even worse and is approached much faster if there are global players who can borrow, with only small capital investment, a larger amount of domestic bonds, exchange them at the given currency peg into foreign bonds, then contribute to produce the exchange rate crisis and pay back their credit with only part of their foreign bond holdings, the rest being their capital gains. A speculative expectation scheme is here needed.

15.4.2 Regime II: Flexible exchange rates and given money supply

The Krugman balance sheet effect is of course also in action in a capital flight situation in a flexible exchange rate regime, and global players can also attempt to make capital gains in such situations.

15.5 Conclusions

As some kind of research outlook, in this chapter we have made a step toward a more extensive treatment of the portfolio part of the Mundell–Fleming–Tobin model. In the original formulation of the model in Chapter 12 we had assumed a stock portfolio approach and thus were forced to consider that only part of the flow savings (in fact total savings minus investment) could appear in the capital account of the balance of payments. Using stock asset demand functions excludes, from a formal point of view, the possibility that portfolio readjustments appear in the capital (flow) account. On the other hand, we assumed that domestic bonds were not traded internationally, which means – for example in a regime of flexible exchange rates – that asset holders could not get more dollar-denominated bonds than they already held in the aggregate. In a regime of fixed exchange rates, this means that the total supply of such bonds was limited by the stocks held in the household sector and by the central bank. Portfolio choices were thus limited to the amounts of domestic and foreign bonds (and money) already in existence in the domestic economy, which in this sense was a closed economy (though demands for domestic holdings of foreign bonds due to current account deficits are allowed for).

There is therefore an urgent need to overcome these limitations and to allow for international capital flows to appear in the balance of payments that are not limited by the savings behavior of the domestic economy. This requires that domestic bond demand and supply (of both types of bonds) must be determined in terms of flows and that the same must hold for foreign demand (or supply) of domestic bonds and foreign supply (or demand) of foreign bonds. We thus have now not only an export function on the market for goods (the goods demand of foreigners), but also their demand and corresponding supply schedules on the international bond markets where domestic and foreign bonds are traded against each other. This enhances the degree of openness of the economy being considered and allows us to consider more appropriately capital flights, as investigated in Chapters 13 and 14. In Section 15.2 of this chapter we enlarged the MFT model in the way discussed above, whereas Section 15.3 considered the implications of such an approach to international capital flows for small economies. Overall, this chapter prepared some preliminary steps toward the stock-flow integration in an open economy. Future research work should concentrate more on the issues raised in this chapter.

15.6 References

ASADA, T., C. CHIARELLA P. FLASCHEL and R. FRANKE (2003): *Open Economy Macrodynamics. An Integrated Disequilibrium Approach.* Heidelberg: Springer.

DORNBUSCH, R. (1976): Expectations and exchange rate dynamics. *Journal of Political Economy*, 84, 1161–1175.

FLASCHEL, P. (2006): Instability problems and policy issues in perfectly open economies. In: T. Asada and T. Ishikawa (eds): *The Economics of Time and Space*. Tokyo: Springer.

FLASCHEL, P., G. GONG, C. PROAÑO and W. SEMMLER (2006): Twin deficits and inflation dynamics in a Mundell–Fleming–Tobin framework. *CEM Working Paper,* 143, Bielefeld University.

GANDOLFO, G. (2001): *International Finance and Open-Economy Macroeconomics.* New York: Springer.

RØDSETH, A. (2000): *Open Economy Macroeconomics.* Cambridge, UK: Cambridge University Press.

Mathematical appendix
Some useful theorems

A1 The concepts of local stability and global stability in a system of differential equations

Let $\dot{x} \equiv dx/dt = f(x)$, $x \in R^n$ be a system of n-dimensional differential equations that has an equilibrium point x^* such that $f(x^*) = 0$, where t is interpreted as "time". The equilibrium point of this system is said to be *locally asymptotically stable* if every trajectory starting sufficiently near the equilibrium point converges to it as $t \to +\infty$. If stability is independent of the distance of the initial state from the equilibrium point, the equilibrium point is said to be *globally asymptotically stable*, or *asymptotically stable in the large*; see Gandolfo (1996, p. 333).

A2 Theorems that are useful for the stability analysis of a system of linear differential equations or the local stability analysis of a system of nonlinear differential equations

Theorem A.1 (Local stability/instability theorem; see Gandolfo (1996, pp. 360–362))

Let $\dot{x}_i = f_i(x)$, $x = [x_1, x_2, \cdots, x_n] \in R^n \mid (i = 1, 2, \cdots, n)$ be an n-dimensional system of differential equations that has an equilibrium point $x^* = [x_1^*, x_2^*, \cdots, x_n^*]$ such that $f(x^*) = 0$. Suppose that the functions f_i have continuous first-order partial derivatives, and consider the Jacobian matrix evaluated at the equilibrium point x^*

$$J = \begin{bmatrix} f_{11} & f_{12} & \cdots & f_{1n} \\ f_{21} & f_{22} & \cdots & f_{2n} \\ \vdots & \vdots & \ddots & \vdots \\ f_{n1} & f_{n2} & \cdots & f_{nn} \end{bmatrix},$$

where $f_{ij} = \partial f_i / \partial x_j$ $(i, j = 1, 2, \cdots, n)$ are evaluated at the equilibrium point.

(i) *The equilibrium point of this system is locally asymptotically stable if all the roots of the characteristic equation $|\lambda I - J| = 0$ have negative real parts.*

(ii) *The equilibrium point of this system is unstable if at least one root of the characteristic equation $|\lambda I - J| = 0$ has a positive real part.*

(iii) *The stability of the equilibrium point cannot be determined from the properties of the Jacobian matrix if all the roots of the characteristic equation $|\lambda I - J| = 0$ have non-positive real parts but at least one root has zero real part.*

Theorem A.2 (see Murata (1977, pp. 14–16))

Let A be an $(n \times n)$ matrix such that

$$A = \begin{bmatrix} a_{11} & a_{12} & \cdots & a_{1n} \\ a_{21} & a_{22} & \cdots & a_{2n} \\ \vdots & \vdots & \ddots & \vdots \\ a_{n1} & a_{n2} & \cdots & a_{nn} \end{bmatrix}.$$

(i) *We can express the characteristic equation $|\lambda I - A| = 0$ as*

$$|\lambda I - A| = \lambda^n + a_1 \lambda^{n-1} + a_2 \lambda^{n-2} + \cdots + a_r \lambda^{n-r} + \cdots + a_{n-1} \lambda + a_n = 0,$$
$$(A.1)$$

where

$$a_1 = -(\text{trace} A) = -\sum_{i=1}^{n} a_{ii}, \quad a_2 = (-1)^2 \sum_{i<j} \begin{vmatrix} a_{ii} & a_{ij} \\ a_{ji} & a_{jj} \end{vmatrix}, \cdots,$$

$$a_r = (-1)^r \sum_{i<j<\cdots<k} \underbrace{\begin{vmatrix} a_{ii} & a_{ij} & \cdots & a_{ik} \\ a_{ji} & a_{jj} & \cdots & a_{jk} \\ \vdots & \vdots & \ddots & \vdots \\ a_{ki} & a_{kj} & \cdots & a_{kk} \end{vmatrix}}_{(r)}, \cdots, \quad a_n = (-1)^n \det A.$$

(ii) *Let λ_i ($i = 1, 2, \cdots, n$) be the roots of the characteristic equation (A.1). Then, we have*

$$\text{trace} J = \sum_{i=1}^{n} a_{ii} = \sum_{i=1}^{n} \lambda_i, \quad \det A = \prod_{i=1}^{n} \lambda_i.$$

Theorem A.3 (Routh–Hurwitz conditions for stable roots in an n-dimensional system; See Murata (1977, p. 92), Gandolfo (1996, pp. 221–222))[1]

---

1 See also Gantmacher (1954) for many details that can be associated with this theorem and Brock and Malliaris (1989) for a compact representation of these conditions.

All of the roots of the characteristic equation (A.1) have negative real parts if and only if the following set of inequalities is satisfied:

$$\Delta_1 = a_1 > 0, \quad \Delta_2 = \begin{vmatrix} a_1 & a_3 \\ 1 & a_2 \end{vmatrix} > 0, \quad \Delta_3 = \begin{vmatrix} a_1 & a_3 & a_5 \\ 1 & a_2 & a_4 \\ 0 & a_1 & a_3 \end{vmatrix} > 0, \cdots,$$

$$\Delta_n = \begin{vmatrix} a_1 & a_3 & a_5 & a_7 & \cdots & 0 \\ 1 & a_2 & a_4 & a_6 & \cdots & 0 \\ 0 & a_1 & a_3 & a_5 & \cdots & 0 \\ 0 & 1 & a_2 & a_4 & \cdots & 0 \\ 0 & 0 & a_1 & a_3 & \cdots & 0 \\ \vdots & \vdots & \vdots & \vdots & \ddots & \vdots \\ 0 & 0 & 0 & 0 & \cdots & a_n \end{vmatrix} > 0.$$

The following theorems A.4–A.6 are corollaries of theorem A.3.

Theorem A.4 (Routh–Hurwitz conditions for a two-dimensional system)

All of the roots of the characteristic equation

$$\lambda^2 + a_1\lambda + a_2 = 0$$

have negative real parts if and only if the set of inequalities

$$a_1 > 0, \quad a_2 > 0$$

is satisfied.

Theorem A.5 (Routh–Hurwitz conditions for a three-dimensional system)

All of the roots of the characteristic equation

$$\lambda^3 + a_1\lambda^2 + a_2\lambda + a_3 = 0$$

have negative real parts if and only if the set of inequalities

$$a_1 > 0, \quad a_3 > 0, \quad a_1a_2 - a_3 > 0 \qquad\qquad\qquad (A.2)$$

is satisfied.

Remark on theorem A.5:
The inequality $a_2 > 0$ is always satisfied if the set of inequalities (A.2) is satisfied.

Theorem A.6 (Routh–Hurwitz conditions for a four-dimensional system)

All roots of the characteristic equation

$$\lambda^4 + a_1\lambda^3 + a_2\lambda^2 + a_3\lambda + a_4 = 0$$

have negative real parts if and only if the set of inequalities

$$a_1 > 0, \quad a_3 > 0, \quad a_4 > 0, \quad \Phi \equiv a_1 a_2 a_3 - a_1^2 a_4 - a_3^2 > 0 \qquad \text{(A.3)}$$

is satisfied.

Remark on theorem A.6:
The inequality $a_2 > 0$ is always satisfied if the set of inequalities (A.3) is satisfied.

A3 Theorems that are useful for the global stability analysis of a system of nonlinear differential equations

Theorem A.7 (Liapunov's theorem; see Gandolfo (1996, p. 410))

Let $\dot{x} = f(x), x = [x_1, x_2, \cdots, x_n] \in R^n$ be an n-dimensional system of differential equations that has the unique equilibrium point $x^* = [x_1^*, x_2^*, \cdots, x_n^*]$ such that $f(x^*) = 0$. Suppose that there exists a scalar function $V = V(x - x^*)$ with continuous first derivatives and with the following properties (1)–(5):

(1) $V \geqq 0$,
(2) $V = 0$ if and only if $x_i - x_i^* = 0$ for all $i \in \{1, 2, \cdots n\}$,
(3) $V \rightarrow +\infty$ as $\|x - x^*\| \rightarrow +\infty$,
(4) $\dot{V} = \sum\limits_{i=1}^{n} \dfrac{\partial V}{\partial(x_i - x_i^*)}\dot{x}_i \leqq 0$,
(5) $\dot{V} = 0$ if and only if $x_i - x_i = 0$ for all $i \in \{1, 2, \cdots, n\}$.*

Then, the equilibrium point x^* of the above system is globally asymptotically stable.

Remark on theorem A.7:
The function $V = V(x - x^*)$ is called the "Liapunov function".

Theorem A.8 (Olech's theorem; see Olech (1963), Gandolfo (1996, pp. 354–355))

Let $\dot{x}_i = f_i(x_1, x_2)$ $(i = 1, 2)$ be a two-dimensional system of differential equations that has the unique equilibrium point (x_1^*, x_2^*) such that $f_i(x_1^*, x_2^*) = 0$ $(i = 1, 2)$. Suppose that the functions f_i have continuous first-order partial derivatives.

Furthermore, suppose that the following properties (1)–(3) are satisfied:

(1) $\frac{\partial f_1}{\partial x_1} + \frac{\partial f_2}{\partial x_2} < 0$ everywhere,

(2) $(\frac{\partial f_1}{\partial x_1})(\frac{\partial f_2}{\partial x_2}) - (\frac{\partial f_1}{\partial x_2})(\frac{\partial f_2}{\partial x_1}) > 0$ everywhere,

(3) $(\frac{\partial f_1}{\partial x_1})(\frac{\partial f_2}{\partial x_2}) \neq 0$ everywhere, or alternatively, $(\frac{\partial f_1}{\partial x_2})(\frac{\partial f_2}{\partial x_1}) \neq 0$ everywhere.

Then, the equilibrium point of the above system is globally asymptotically stable.

A4   Theorems that are useful to establish the existence of closed orbits in a system of nonlinear differential equations

Theorem A.9 (Poincaré–Bendixson theorem; see Hirsch and Smale (1974, ch. 11))

Let $\dot{x}_i = f_i(x_1, x_2)$ $(i = 1, 2)$ be a two-dimensional system of differential equations with the functions f_i continuous. A nonempty compact limit set of the trajectory of this system, which contains no equilibrium point, is a closed orbit.

Theorem A.10 (Hopf bifurcation theorem for an *n*-dimensional system; see Guckenheimer and Holmes (1983, pp. 151–152), Lorenz (1993, p. 96) and Gandolfo (1996, p. 477))[2]

Let $\dot{x} = f(x; \varepsilon), x \in R^n$, $\varepsilon \in R$ be an n-dimensional system of differential equations depending upon a parameter ε. Suppose that the following conditions (1)–(3) are satisfied:

(1)   The system has a smooth curve of equilibria given by $f(x^*(\varepsilon); \varepsilon) = 0$,
(2)   The characteristic equation $|\lambda I - Df(x^*(\varepsilon_0); \varepsilon_0)| = 0$ has a pair of pure imaginary roots $\lambda(\varepsilon_0), \bar{\lambda}(\varepsilon_0)$ and no other roots with zero real parts, where $Df(x^*(\varepsilon_0); \varepsilon_0)$ is the Jacobian matrix of the above system at $(x^*(\varepsilon_0), \varepsilon_0)$ with the parameter value ε_0,
(3) $\frac{d\{Re\lambda(\varepsilon)\}}{d\varepsilon}\Big|_{\varepsilon=\varepsilon_0} \neq 0$, where $Re\lambda(\varepsilon)$ is the real part of $\lambda(\varepsilon)$.

Then, there exists a continuous function $\varepsilon(\gamma)$ with $\varepsilon(0) = \varepsilon_0$, and for all sufficiently small values of $\gamma \neq 0$ there exists a continuous family of non-constant periodic solutions $x(t, \gamma)$ for the above dynamical system, which collapses to the equilibrium point $x^*(\varepsilon_0)$ as $\gamma \to 0$. The period of the cycle is close to $2\pi/Im\lambda(\varepsilon_0)$, where $Im\lambda(\varepsilon_0)$ is the imaginary part of $\lambda(\varepsilon_0)$.

2 See also Strogatz (1994) and Wiggins (1990) in this regard.

Remark on theorem A.10:

We can replace condition (3) in theorem A.10 by the following weaker condition (3a) (see Alexander and York (1978)).

(3a) For all ε which are near but not equal to ε_0, no characteristic root has zero real part.

The following theorem by Liu (1994) provides a convenient criterion for the occurrence of the so called "simple" Hopf bifurcation in an n-dimensional system. The simple Hopf bifurcation is defined as the Hopf bifurcation in which all the characteristic roots *except* a pair of purely imaginary ones have negative real parts.

Theorem A.11 (Liu's theorem; see Liu (1994))

Consider the following characteristic equation with $n \geq 3$:

$$\lambda^n + a_1\lambda^{n-1} + a_2\lambda_{n-2} + \cdots + a_{n-1}\lambda + a_n = 0$$

This characteristic equation has a pair of pure imaginary roots and $(n-2)$ roots with negative real parts if and only if the following set of conditions is satisfied:

$$\Delta_i > 0 \text{ for all } i \in \{1, 2, \cdots, n-2\}, \quad \Delta_{n-1} = 0, \quad a_n > 0,$$

where $\Delta_i (i = 1, 2, \cdots, n-1)$ are Routh–Hurwitz terms defined as

$$\Delta_1 = a_1, \quad \Delta_2 = \begin{vmatrix} a_1 & a_3 \\ 1 & a_2 \end{vmatrix}, \quad \Delta_3 = \begin{vmatrix} a_1 & a_3 & a_5 \\ 1 & a_2 & a_4 \\ 0 & a_1 & a_3 \end{vmatrix}, \cdots,$$

$$\Delta_{n-1} = \begin{vmatrix} a_1 & a_3 & a_5 & a_7 & \cdots & 0 & 0 \\ 1 & a_2 & a_4 & a_6 & \cdots & 0 & 0 \\ 0 & a_1 & a_3 & a_5 & \cdots & 0 & 0 \\ 0 & 1 & a_2 & a_4 & \cdots & 0 & 0 \\ 0 & 0 & a_1 & a_3 & \cdots & 0 & 0 \\ \vdots & \vdots & \vdots & \vdots & \ddots & \vdots & \vdots \\ 0 & 0 & 0 & 0 & \cdots & a_n & 0 \\ 0 & 0 & 0 & 0 & \cdots & a_{n-1} & 0 \\ 0 & 0 & 0 & 0 & \cdots & a_{n-2} & a_n \\ 0 & 0 & 0 & 0 & \cdots & a_{n-3} & a_{n-1} \end{vmatrix}.$$

The following theorems, A.12–A.14, provide us with some convenient criteria for two-dimensional, three-dimensional and four-dimensional Hopf bifurcations respectively. It is worth noting that these criteria provide us with useful information on the "non-simple" as well as the "simple" Hopf bifurcations.

Theorem A.12

The characteristic equation

$$\lambda^2 + a_1\lambda + a_2 = 0,$$

has a pair of pure imaginary roots if and only if the set of conditions

$$a_1 = 0, \quad a_2 > 0$$

is satisfied. In this case, we have the explicit solution $\lambda = \pm i\sqrt{a_2}$, where $i = \sqrt{-1}$.

Proof. Obvious because we have the solution $\lambda = (-a_1 \pm \sqrt{a_1^2 - 4a_2})/2$.

Theorem A.13 (see Asada (1995), Asada and Semmler (1995))

The characteristic equation

$$\lambda^3 + a_1\lambda^2 + a_2\lambda + a_3 = 0$$

has a pair of pure imaginary roots if and only if the set of conditions

$$a_2 > 0, \quad a_1 a_2 - a_3 = 0,$$

is satisfied. In this case, we have the explicit solution $\lambda = -a_1, \pm i\sqrt{a_2}$, where $i = \sqrt{-1}$.

Theorem A.14 (see Yoshida and Asada (2001), Asada and Yoshida (2003))

Consider the characteristic equation

$$\lambda^4 + a_1\lambda^3 + a_2\lambda^2 + a_3\lambda + a_4 = 0. \tag{A.4}$$

(i) *The characteristic equation (A.4) has a pair of pure imaginary roots and two roots with non-zero real parts if and only if either of the following set of conditions (A) or (B) is satisfied:*

(A) $a_1 a_3 > 0, \quad a_4 \neq 0, \quad \Phi \equiv a_1 a_2 a_3 - a_1^2 a_4 - a_3^2 = 0.$
(B) $a_1 = a_3 = 0, \quad a_4 < 0.$

(ii) *The characteristic equation (A.4) has a pair of pure imaginary roots and two roots with negative real parts if and only if the following set of conditions (C) is satisfied:*

(C) $a_1 > 0, \quad a_3 > 0, \quad a_4 > 0, \quad \Phi \equiv a_1 a_2 a_3 - a_1^2 a_4 - a_3^2 = 0.$

Remark on theorem A.14:
(1) The condition $\Phi = 0$ is always satisfied if the set of conditions (B) is satisfied.

(2) The inequality $a_2 > 0$ is always satisfied if the set of conditions (C) is satisfied.

(3) We can derive theorem A.14 (ii) from theorem A.11 as a special case with $n = 4$, although we cannot derive theorem A.14 (i) from theorem A.11.

A5 References

Alexander, J.C. and J.A. York (1978). Global bifurcation of periodic orbits. *American Journal of Mathematics*, 100, 263–292.

Asada, T. (1995). Kaldorian dynamics in an open economy. *Journal of Economics*, 2, 1–16.

Asada, T. and W. Semmler (1995). Growth and finance: An intertemporal model. *Journal of Macroeconomics*, 17, 623–649.

Asada, T. and H. Yoshida (2003). Coefficient criterion for four-dimensional Hopf-bifurcations: A complete mathematical characterization and applications to economic dynamics. *Chaos, Solitons & Fractals*, 18(3), 421–423.

Brock, W.A. and A.G. Malliaris (1989). *Differential Equations, Stability and Chaos in Dynamic Economics*. Amsterdam: North Holland.

Gandolfo, G. (1996). *Economic Dynamics* (Third Edition). Berlin: Springer.

Gantmacher, F.R. (1954). *Theory of Matrices*. New York: Interscience Publishers.

Guckenheimer, J. and P. Holmes (1983). *Nonlinear Oscillations, Dynamical Systems, and Bifurcations of Vector Fields*. Heidelberg: Springer.

Hirsch, M.W. and S. Smale (1974). *Differential Equations, Dynamical Systems, and Linear Algebra*. New York: Academic Press.

Liu, W.M. (1994). Criterion of Hopf bifurcations without using eigenvalues. *Journal of Mathematical Analysis and Applications*, 1982, 250–256.

Lorenz, H.-W. (1993). *Nonlinear dynamical economics and chaotic motion* 2nd ed. Heidelberg: Springer.

Murata, Y. (1977). *Mathematics for Stability and Optimization of Economic Systems*. New York: Academic Press.

Olech, A.M. (1963). On the global stability of an autonomous system in the plane. In: P. Lasalle and P. Díaz (eds.): *Contributions to Differential Equations*, 1, 389–400.

Strogatz, S.H. (1994). *Nonlinear Dynamics and Chaos*. New York: Addison-Wesley.

Wiggins, S. (1990). *Introduction to applied nonlinear dynamical systems and chaos*. Heidelberg: Springer.

Yoshida, H. and Asada, T. (2007). Dynamic analysis of policy lag in a Keynes–Goodwin model: Stability, instability, cycles and chaos. *Journal of Economic Behavior & Organization*, 62(3), 441–469.

Index